Chemistry

for the IB Diploma

Steve Owen

with
Caroline Ahmed
Chris Martin
Roger Woodward

Cambridge University Press's missior   learning, knowledge and research worldwide.

Our IB Diploma resources aim to:

- encourage learners to explore concepts, ideas and topics that have local and global significance
- help students develop a positive attitude to learning in preparation for higher education
- assist students in approaching complex questions, applying critical-thinking skills and forming reasoned answers.

D1340787

CAMBRIDGE
UNIVERSITY PRESS

236166

CAMBRIDGE UNIVERSITY PRESS
Cambridge, New York, Melbourne, Madrid, Cape Town,
Singapore, São Paulo, Delhi, Mexico City

Cambridge University Press
The Edinburgh Building, Cambridge CB2 8RU, UK

www.cambridge.org
Information on this title: www.cambridge.org/9780521182942

© Cambridge University Press 2011

This publication is in copyright. Subject to statutory exception
and to the provisions of relevant collective licensing agreements,
no reproduction of any part may take place without the written
permission of Cambridge University Press.

First published 2011
3rd printing 2013

Printed in the United Kingdom by Latimer Trend

A catalogue record for this publication is available from the British Library

ISBN 978-0-521-18294-2 Paperback with CD-ROM for Windows and Mac

Cambridge University Press has no responsibility for the persistence or
accuracy of URLs for external or third-party internet websites referred to in
this publication, and does not guarantee that any content on such websites is,
or will remain, accurate or appropriate.

This material has been developed independently by the publisher and the
content is in no way connected with nor endorsed by the International
Baccalaureate Organization.

The publisher would like to thank the following teachers for reviewing
the content:
Aidan Hayes, King's College School, London
Ronald F. Owens, Kinston High School, North Carolina

Edge Hill University
Learning Services

Barcode 236166

Contents

Acknowledgements

The author and publishers are grateful for the permissions granted to reproduce photos.

Cover, p. 172 Charles D. Winters/SPL; p. 57*t* Pasquale Sorrentino/SPL; p. 57*b* Martin Dohrn/SPL; p. 138 Photoshot Holdings Ltd/Alamy; p. 160 Tony Craddock/SPL; p. 242*t* Doug Steley C/Alamy; p. 242*b* Tom Wood/Alamy; p. 299 Emilio Segre Visual Archives/American Institute of Physics/SPL; p. 312 Grant Heilman Photography; p. 318*t* Maximilian Stock Ltd/SPL; p. 318*b* Michael McCoy/SPL; p. 319*l* Simon Fraser/SPL; p. 319*r* Mark Leach/Alamy; pp. 320, 436, 443 Martyn F. Chillmaid/SPL; p. 406*l* catnap/Alamy; p. 406*r* David

Nunuk/SPL; p. 412 Jorgen Udvang/Alamy; p. 432, 442 Cordelia Molloy/SPL; p. 445 67photo/Alamy; p. 473 Stephen Giardina/Alamy; p. 480*t* mediacolor's/Alamy; p. 408*b* Michael Dwyer/Alamy

Photos on the CD-ROM
Option A p. 25*l* Maura Fermariello/SPL; p. 25*r* Simon Fraser/SPL; p. 30 Martyn F. Chillmaid; Option B p. 44 Martin Shields/SPL; Option D p. 22 Bo Veisland MI&I/SPL; Option E p. 18 Robert Brook/SPL

SPL = Science Photo Library
t = top, *b* = bottom, *l* = left, *r* = right

Introduction

This book is designed as a complete guide to the IB Chemistry courses at both SL and HL. The book contains all the material required for the main part of the SL and HL courses and the CD-ROM contains the full text of the book in PDF format as well as the Options material (required for Paper 3). Also included on the CD-ROM are a comprehensive guide to Internal Assessment (writing up practical work) and a revision checklist.

Chemistry is about understanding and not just recalling facts, and the emphasis throughout the book and CD-ROM is on explaining the concepts involved in the course. At this level Chemistry should make sense and, hopefully, as you work your way through each chapter you will feel confident that you have fully grasped all the material.

Each chapter is divided into sections which include assessment statements as starting and reference points. Short-answer questions appear throughout the text so you can check your progress and make sure that you have fully understood what has been discussed. There are also links to interactive questions on the CD-ROM, which you can use to further test yourself, as well as animations and simulations that will help you gain a deeper understanding of the concepts. You can link straight through to these features by clicking on the CD icons in the PDF version of the book.

Examination style questions appear at the end of each chapter; these could be used either when you have finished studying a chapter or towards the end of the course when you are preparing for the exams. Overall in the book and the CD-ROM there are well over 1000 questions, so there should be plenty of opportunities to practise all aspects of the course. Answers to all questions are given on the CD-ROM.

How to use this book

Sections that cover material from the Higher Level syllabus only are marked with an 'HL' bar:

HL

As you read this book you will see that certain features are shown in different coloured boxes.

At the start of each section you will find a list of learning objectives, detailing what you will be expected to know after studying the section. The learning objectives are derived from the assessment statements in the syllabus.

Learning objectives

- Understand what is meant by hybridisation
- Predict the hybridisation of an atom in a molecule

Ions are charged particles, which are formed when atoms lose or gain electrons.

Throughout the text, key fact boxes (left) inform you of key definitions and other facts that you should memorise, while info bars (right) give additional information on various subjects related to the text.

Again, a consideration of the formal charges on each atom would regard this structure as less likely.

Theory of Knowledge (TOK) boxes are also found throughout the book. These provide food for thought and support the TOK you will studying in your IB Diploma programme.

 There are various theories of acids and bases. We have encountered the Brønsted–Lowry and Lewis theories.

As you read, you will also see 'test yourself' questions at various points in the text, usually at the end of a section. These will allow you to keep a check on your progress as you work through each chapter.

Test yourself

1 Give the number of protons, neutrons and electrons in the following atoms:

$^{238}_{92}U$ $^{75}_{33}As$ $^{81}_{35}Br$

2 Give the number of protons, neutrons and electrons in the following ions:

$^{40}_{20}Ca^{2+}$ $^{127}_{53}I^-$ $^{140}_{58}Ce^{3+}$

3 If you consider the most common isotopes of elements as given in a basic periodic table, how many elements have more protons than neutrons in an atom?

Throughout the text there are boxes that give information about the applications of chemistry, historical references, internationalism or interesting facts related to the topic under consideration.

It was originally thought that all acids contain oxygen, and the names of this element in English, german (Sauerstoff) and several other languages reflect this mistaken assumption.

The CD symbol indicates extra features that are included on the CD accompanying this book. These include animations, extra sets of questions, simulations and so forth.

 Self-test 1

Moles 1

1.1 Relative masses

Quantitative chemistry

Most chemical reactions involve two or more substances reacting with each other. Chemical substances react with each other in certain ratios, and stoichiometry is the study of the ratios in which chemical substances combine. In order to know the exact quantity of each substance that is required to react we need to know the number of atoms, molecules or ions present in a specific amount of that substance. However, the mass of an individual atom or molecule is so small, and the number of particles that make up even a very small mass is so large, that a more convenient method of working out and discussing reacting quantities had to be developed.

Relative atomic mass (A_r)

The mass of a hydrogen atom is approximately 1.7×10^{-24} g. Such small numbers are not convenient to use in everyday life, so we use scales of **relative** mass. These compare the masses of atoms and molecules, etc. to the mass of an atom of **carbon-12**, which is assigned a mass of exactly **12.00**. As these quantities are **relative**, they have **no units**.

The A_r of silver is 107.87. A naturally occurring sample of silver contains the isotopes ^{107}Ag and ^{109}Ag. The 107 isotope is slightly more abundant than the 109 isotope. Taking into account the amount of each isotope present in a sample (the weighted mean), it is found that, on average, the mass of a silver atom is 107.87 times the mass of $\frac{1}{12}$ of a carbon-12 atom. No silver atoms actually exist with the mass of 107.87; this is just the average relative atomic mass of silver.

Relative molecular mass (M_r)

The M_r is the sum of the relative atomic masses for the individual atoms making up a molecule.

Examples

The relative molecular mass of methane (CH_4) is:

$$12.01 (A_r \text{ of C}) + 4 \times 1.01 (A_r \text{ of H}) = 16.05$$

The relative molecular mass of ethanoic acid (CH_3COOH) is:

$$12.01 + 3 \times 1.01 + 12.01 + 2 \times 16.00 + 1.01 = 60.06$$

If the compound is made up of **ions**, and therefore does not contain discrete molecules, we should really talk about relative **formula** mass. However, relative molecular mass is usually used to refer to the mass of the formula unit of an ionic compound as well.

Learning objectives

- Define **relative atomic mass** and **relative molecular mass**

The relative atomic mass (A_r) of an element is the average mass of the naturally occurring isotopes of the element relative to the mass of $\frac{1}{12}$ of an atom of carbon-12.

The A_r of C is not 12.00, because carbon contains isotopes other than carbon-12 (see page **56**).

The relative molecular mass (M_r) of a compound is the mass of a molecule of that compound relative to the mass of $\frac{1}{12}$ of an atom of carbon-12.

If the compound contains ions, the **relative formula mass** is the mass of the formula unit relative to the mass of $\frac{1}{12}$ of an atom of carbon-12.

Test yourself

1 Work out the relative molecular masses of the following compounds:

SO_2 NH_3 C_2H_5OH $MgCl_2$ $Ca(NO_3)_2$ $CH_3(CH_2)_5CH_3$

PCl_5 $Mg_3(PO_4)_2$ $Na_2S_2O_3$ $CH_3CH_2CH_2COOCH_2CH_3$

Learning objectives

- Understand what is meant by one mole of a substance
- Calculate the mass of one mole of a substance
- Calculate the number of moles present in a specified mass of a substance
- Work out the number of particles in a specified mass and the mass of a molecule

---

The molar mass (M) of a substance is its A_r or M_r in g. The units of molar mass are $g\,mol^{-1}$. For example, the A_r of Si is 28.09, and the molar mass of Si is $28.09\,g\,mol^{-1}$. This means that 28.09 g of Si contains 6.02×10^{23} Si atoms.

Note: when calculating the number of moles present in a mass of substance, the mass must be in grams.

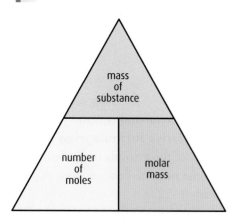

1.2 The mole and Avogadro's constant

Moles

A mole is the amount of substance that contains the same number of particles (atoms, ions, molecules, etc.) as there are carbon atoms in 12 g of carbon-12. This number is called **Avogadro's constant** and has the value $6.02 \times 10^{23}\,mol^{-1}$. It is sometimes given the symbol L (or N_A).

> Avogadro's constant (L) = $6.02 \times 10^{23}\,mol^{-1}$

Thus 12.00 g of carbon-12 contains 6.02×10^{23} carbon atoms.

You can have a mole of absolutely anything. We usually consider a mole of atoms (6.02×10^{23} atoms) or a mole of molecules (6.02×10^{23} molecules), but we could also have, for instance, a mole of ping-pong balls (6.02×10^{23} ping-pong balls).

The A_r of oxygen is 16.00, which means that, on average, each O atom is $\frac{16}{12}$ times as heavy as a carbon-12 atom. Therefore 16 g of O atoms must contain the same number of atoms as 12 g of carbon-12, i.e. 1 mole, or 6.02×10^{23} atoms. Similarly, a magnesium atom is on average $\frac{24.31}{12}$ times as heavy as a carbon-12 atom and, therefore 24.31 g of Mg atoms contains 6.02×10^{23} Mg atoms.

The number of moles present in a certain mass of substance can be worked out using the following equation:

$$\text{no. moles } (n) = \frac{\text{mass of substance}}{\text{molar mass}}$$

This triangle is a useful shortcut for working out all the quantities involved in the equation. If any one of the sections of the triangle is covered up, the relationship between the other two quantities to give the covered quantity is revealed. For example, if mass of substance is covered, we are left with number of moles multiplied by molar mass:

$$\text{mass of substance} = \text{number of moles} \times \text{molar mass}$$

If molar mass is covered, we are left with mass of substance divided by number of moles:

$$\text{molar mass} = \frac{\text{mass of substance}}{\text{no. moles}}$$

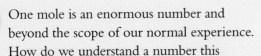

One mole is an enormous number and beyond the scope of our normal experience. How do we understand a number this large? One way is to describe the number in terms of things we are familiar with from everyday life. For instance, one mole of ping-pong balls would cover the surface of the Earth to about 800 times the height of Mount Everest! We know what a ping-pong ball looks like and we may have a rough idea of the height of Mount Everest, so perhaps this description gives us a context in which we can understand 6.02×10^{23}. Another description often used is in terms of a mole of computer paper: one mole of computer printer paper sheets, if stacked one on top of each other, would stretch over 6000 light years (1 light year is the distance that light travels in 1 year) – this is over twice the thickness of our galaxy! Is this description better or worse than the previous one? It certainly sounds more impressive, but does it suffer from the fact that we have no real concept of the size of our galaxy? Can you think of any other ways of describing this number in terms of things you are familiar with from everyday life?

This is an example of a wider idea that we tend to understand things that are beyond our normal experience by reference to things with which we are more familiar.

Worked examples

Calculate the number of moles of Mg atoms in 10.0 g of Mg.

$$\text{no. moles } (n) = \frac{\text{mass of substance}}{\text{molar mass}}$$

Note: the unit for moles is mol.

$$n = \frac{10.0}{24.31} = 0.411 \text{ mol}$$

10.0 g of Mg is 0.411 mol.

The answer is given to three significant figures, as the mass of substance is given to three significant figures.

Calculate the mass of 0.3800 mol CH_3COOH.

$$\text{mass of substance} = \text{number of moles} \times \text{molar mass}$$

$$\text{mass of substance} = 0.3800 \times 60.06 = 22.82 \text{ g}$$

The mass of 0.3800 mol CH_3COOH is 22.82 g.

The answer is given to four significant figures, as the number of moles and the molar mass are given to four significant figures.

2 Copy and complete the table. The first one has been done for you.

Compound	Molar mass / g mol⁻¹	Mass / g	Number of moles / mol
H_2O	18.02	9.01	0.500
CO_2		5.00	
H_2S			0.100
NH_3			3.50
Q		1.00	0.0350
Z		0.0578	1.12×10^{-3}
$Mg(NO_3)_2$		1.75	
C_3H_7OH		2500	
Fe_2O_3			5.68×10^{-5}

Application 1

The mass of a molecule

The mass of one mole of water is 18.02 g. This contains 6.02×10^{23} molecules of water. The mass of one molecule of water can therefore be worked out by dividing the mass of one mole (18.02 g) by the number of molecules it contains (6.02×10^{23}):

$$\text{mass of one molecule} = \frac{18.02}{6.02 \times 10^{23}} = 2.99 \times 10^{-23}\,\text{g}$$

$$\text{mass of one molecule} = \frac{\text{molar mass}}{\text{Avogadro's constant}}$$

Examiner's tip
Remember – the mass of a molecule is a very small number. Do not confuse the mass of a single molecule with the mass of one mole of a substance, which is a number greater than 1.

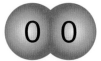
oxygen

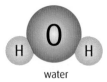
water

The number of particles

When we write 1 mol O_2, it means one mole of O_2 molecules: that is, 6.02×10^{23} O_2 molecules. Each O_2 molecule contains two oxygen atoms; therefore, one mole of O_2 molecules contains $2 \times 6.02 \times 10^{23}$ $= 1.204 \times 10^{24}$ atoms. That is, one mole of O_2 **molecules** is made up of two moles of oxygen **atoms**.

When we talk about 0.1 mol H_2O, we mean 0.1 mol H_2O **molecule**s; i.e. $0.1 \times 6.02 \times 10^{23}$ H_2O molecules; i.e. 6.02×10^{22} H_2O molecules. Each H_2O molecule contains two H atoms and one O atom. The total number of H atoms in 0.1 mol H_2O is $2 \times 6.02 \times 10^{22}$; i.e. 1.204×10^{23} H atoms; i.e. 0.2 mol H atoms.

Each H_2O molecule contains three atoms. Therefore, the total number of atoms in 0.1 mol H_2O is $3 \times 6.02 \times 10^{22}$; i.e. 1.806×10^{23} atoms; i.e. 0.3 mol of atoms.

If we look at Table **1.1** we can see the connection between the number of moles of molecules and the number of moles of a particular atom in that molecule. Figure **1.1** illustrates the relationship between number of particles, number of moles and Avogadro's constant.

Compound	Moles of molecules	Moles of O atoms
H_2O	0.1	0.1
SO_2	0.1	0.2
SO_3	0.1	0.3
H_3PO_4	0.1	0.4
O_3	0.5	1.5
CH_3COOH	0.2	0.4

Table 1.1 The relationship between the number of moles of molecules and the number of moles of particular atoms.

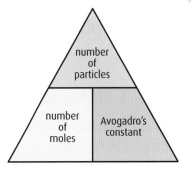

Figure 1.1 The relationship between the number of moles and the number of particles.

If we multiply the number of moles of molecules by the number of a particular type of atom in a molecule (i.e. by the subscript of the atom), we get the number of moles of that type of atom. Thus, in $0.25\,mol\ H_2SO_4$ there are 4×0.25 (i.e. $1.0\,mol$) O atoms.

Examiner's tip
You must be clear which type of particle you are considering. Do you have one mole of atoms, molecules or ions?

Self-test 3

Test yourself

3 Work out the mass of a molecule of each of the following:
 a H_2O
 b NH_3
 c CO_2

4 Work out the total number of hydrogen atoms in each of the following:
 a $1.00\,mol\ H_2$
 b $0.200\,mol\ CH_4$
 c $0.0500\,mol\ NH_3$

5 Calculate the total number of atoms in each of the following:
 a $0.0100\,mol\ NH_3$
 b $0.200\,mol\ C_2H_6$
 c $0.0400\,mol\ C_2H_5OH$

6 Calculate the number of moles of oxygen atoms in each of the following:
 a $0.2\,mol\ H_2SO_4$
 b $0.1\,mol\ Cl_2O_7$
 c $0.03\,mol\ XeO_4$

1.3 Empirical and molecular formulas

Percentage composition of a compound

The percentage by mass of each element present in a compound can be worked out using the following formula.

$$\text{\% by mass of an element} = \frac{\text{no. atoms of the element} \times \text{relative atomic mass}}{\text{relative molecular mass}}$$

Learning objectives

- Determine the percentage composition by mass of a substance
- Understand what is meant by empirical and molecular formulas
- Calculate empirical and molecular formulas

Worked examples

Find the percentage by mass of each element present in $C_6H_5NO_2$.

The relative molecular mass of $C_6H_5NO_2$ is 123.12.

Percentage of carbon: the relative atomic mass of carbon is 12.01, and there are six carbon atoms present, so the total mass of the carbon atoms is 6×12.01, i.e. 72.06.

$$\% \text{ carbon} = \frac{72.06}{123.12} \times 100 = 58.53\% \qquad \% \text{ nitrogen} = \frac{14.01}{123.12} \times 100 = 11.38\%$$

$$\% \text{ hydrogen} = \frac{5 \times 1.01}{123.12} \times 100 = 4.10\% \qquad \% \text{ oxygen} = \frac{2 \times 16.00}{123.12} \times 100 = 25.99\%$$

Calculate the mass of O present in 2.20 g of CO_2.

The relative molecular mass of CO_2 is 44.01. Of this, the amount contributed by the two oxygen atoms is $2 \times 16.00 = 32.00$

So the fraction of the mass of this compound that is contributed by oxygen is $\dfrac{32.00}{44.01}$

Therefore, in 2.20 g of CO_2, the amount of oxygen is $\dfrac{32.00}{44.01} \times 2.20 = 1.60$ g

What mass of HNO_3 contains 2.00 g of oxygen?

The relative molecular mass of HNO_3 is 63.02. Each molecule contains three oxygen atoms with a total mass of 3×16.00, i.e. 48.00.

The oxygen and the HNO_3 are in the ratio 48.00:63.02.

Therefore the mass of HNO_3 containing 2.00 g of oxygen is:

$$\frac{63.02}{48.00} \times 2.00 = 2.63 \text{ g}$$

Alternative method

The percentage of O in HNO_3 is $\dfrac{3 \times 16.00}{63.02} \times 100 = 76.2\%$

so 76.2% of this sample is oxygen and has a mass of 2.00 g.
We need, therefore, to find the mass of 100%, which is given by

$$\frac{100}{76.2} \times 2.00 = 2.63 \text{ g}$$

Note: in order to obtain this answer more figures were carried through on the calculator.

7 Calculate the percentage by mass of oxygen in each of the following compounds:
  a C_2H_5OH
  b CH_3CH_2COOH
  c Cl_2O_7

8 Calculate the mass of oxygen in each of the following samples:
  a 6.00 g of C_3H_7OH
  b 5.00 g of SO_2
  c 10.0 g of P_4O_{10}

9 For each of the following compounds work out the mass of substance that will contain 1.00 g of oxygen.
  a CH_3OH
  b SO_3
  c P_4O_6

Empirical and molecular formulas

> Empirical formula: the simplest whole number ratio of the elements present in a compound.

> Molecular formula: the total number of atoms of each element present in a molecule of the compound. (The molecular formula is a multiple of the empirical formula.)

The molecular formula is a whole number multiple of the empirical formula. Therefore, if the empirical formula of a compound is CH_2, the molecular formula is $(CH_2)_n$ i.e. C_2H_4 or C_3H_6 or C_4H_8, etc.

Worked examples

If the formulas of two compounds are
a $C_4H_{10}O_2$ **b** Re_3Cl_9
what are the empirical formulas?

a We need to find the simplest ratio of the elements present and therefore need to find the highest number that divides exactly into the subscript of each element. In this case, each subscript can be divided by 2, and so the empirical formula is C_2H_5O.
b In this case each subscript is divisible by 3, and so the empirical formula is $ReCl_3$.

The empirical formula of benzene is CH. Given that the molar mass is 78.12 g mol^{-1}, work out the molecular formula.

The mass of the empirical formula unit (CH) is $12.01 + 1.01 = 13.02$. The number of times that the empirical formula unit occurs in the actual molecule (n) is given by:

$$n = \frac{\text{relative molecular mass}}{\text{empirical formula mass}} = \frac{78.12}{13.02} = 6$$

Therefore the molecular formula is $(CH)_6$, which is more commonly written as C_6H_6.

Chemical analysis of a substance can provide the composition by mass of the compound. The empirical formula can then be calculated from these data. In order to work out the molecular formula, the relative molecular mass of the compound is also required.

Worked examples

A compound has the following composition by mass: C, 0.681 g; H, 0.137 g; O, 0.181 g.

a Calculate the empirical formula of the compound.

b If the relative molecular mass of the compound is 88.17, calculate the molecular formula.

a This is most easily done by laying everything out in a table.

	C	H	O
mass / g	0.681	0.137	0.181
divide by relative atomic mass to give number of moles	0.681 / 12.01	0.137 / 1.01	0.181 / 16.00
no. moles / mol	0.0567	0.136	0.0113
divide by smallest to get ratio	0.0567 / 0.0113	0.136 / 0.0113	0.0113 / 0.0113
ratio	5	12	1

Therefore the empirical formula is $C_5H_{12}O$.

b The empirical formula mass of the compound is 88.17. This is the same as the relative molecular mass, and thus the molecular formula is the same as the empirical formula ($C_5H_{12}O$).

If a fluoride of uranium contains 67.62% uranium by mass, what is its empirical formula?

A uranium fluoride contains only uranium and fluorine.

% fluorine = 100.00 − 67.62 = 32.38%

It makes no difference here that the percentage composition is given instead of the mass of each element present, as the percentage is the same as the mass present in 100 g.

	U	F
percentage	67.62	32.38
mass in 100 g / g	67.62	32.38
divide by relative atomic mass to give number of moles	67.62/238.03	32.38/19.00
no. moles	0.2841	1.704
divide by smallest to get ratio	0.2841/0.2841	1.704/0.2841
ratio	1	6

There are therefore six fluorine atoms for every uranium atom, and the empirical formula is UF_6.

The experimental set-up shown in Figure **1.2** can be used to determine the empirical formula of copper oxide. The following experimental results were obtained.

Mass of empty dish / g	24.58
Mass of dish + copper oxide / g	30.12
Mass of dish + copper at end of experiment / g	29.00

Calculate the empirical formula of the copper oxide and write an equation for the reaction.

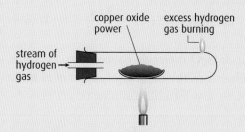

Figure 1.2 Hydrogen gas is passed over the heated copper oxide until all the copper oxide is reduced to copper.

mass of copper oxide at start = $30.12 - 24.58 = 5.54\,g$
mass of copper at end = $29.00 - 24.58 = 4.42\,g$

The difference in mass is due to the oxygen from the copper oxide combining with the hydrogen.

mass of oxygen in copper oxide = $5.54 - 4.42 = 1.12\,g$

From now on, the question is a straightforward empirical formula question:

no. moles of copper = $\dfrac{4.42}{63.55} = 0.0696\,mol$

no. moles of oxygen = $\dfrac{1.12}{16.00} = 0.0700\,mol$

If each number of moles is divided by the smaller number (0.0696):

Cu   **O**

$\dfrac{0.0696}{0.0696} = 1$ $\dfrac{0.0700}{0.0696} = 1.01$

the ratio of copper to oxygen is thus 1:1, and the empirical formula is CuO.

The equation for the reaction is: $CuO + H_2 \rightarrow Cu + H_2O$

Composition by mass from combustion data

Worked examples

An organic compound, **A**, contains only carbon and hydrogen. When 2.50 g of **A** burns in excess oxygen, 8.08 g of carbon dioxide and 2.64 g of water are formed. Calculate the empirical formula.

The equation for the reaction is of the form: $C_xH_y + (x + \tfrac{y}{4})O_2 \rightarrow xCO_2 + \tfrac{y}{2}H_2O$

All the C in the CO_2 comes from the hydrocarbon **A**.

no. moles of CO_2 = $\dfrac{8.08}{44.01} = 0.184\,mol$

Each CO_2 molecule contains one C atom. Therefore the number of moles of C in 2.50 g of the hydrocarbon is 0.184 mol.

All the H in the water comes from the hydrocarbon **A**.

$$\text{no. moles of } H_2O = \frac{2.64}{18.02} = 0.147 \text{ mol}$$

Each H_2O molecule contains two H atoms, so the number of moles of H in 2.64 g of H_2O is $2 \times 0.147 = 0.293$ mol. Therefore, the number of moles of H in 2.50 g of the hydrocarbon is 0.293 mol. The empirical formula and molecular formula can now be calculated.

	C	H
no. moles	0.184	0.293
divide by smaller	0.184/0.184	0.293/0.184
ratio	1.00	1.60

The empirical formula must be a ratio of whole numbers, and this can be obtained by multiplying each number by 5. Therefore the empirical formula is C_5H_8.

An organic compound, **B**, contains only carbon, hydrogen and oxygen. When 1.46 g of **B** burns in excess oxygen, 2.79 g of carbon dioxide and 1.71 g of water are formed.
a What is the empirical formula of **B**?
b If the relative molecular mass is 92.16, what is the molecular formula of **B**?

a The difficulty here is that the mass of oxygen in **B** cannot be worked out in the same way as the previous example, as some of the oxygen in the CO_2 and H_2O comes from the O in **B** (the rest comes from the oxygen in which it is burnt).

$$\text{mass of C in 2.79 g of } CO_2 = \frac{12.01}{44.01} \times 2.79 = 0.76 \text{ g}$$

$$\text{mass of H in 1.71 g of } H_2O = \frac{2.02}{18.02} \times 1.71 = 0.19 \text{ g}$$

mass of O in 1.46 g of **B** is $(1.46 - 0.76 - 0.19) = 0.51$ g

The empirical formula can now be calculated.

	C	H	O
mass / g	0.76	0.19	0.51
moles / mol	0.063	0.19	0.032
ratio	2	6	1

Therefore the empirical formula is C_2H_6O.

b The empirical formula mass is 46.08.

$$\frac{92.16}{46.08} = 2$$

Therefore, the molecular formula is $(C_2H_6O)_2$, i.e. $C_4H_{12}O_2$.

10 Which of the following represent empirical formulas?

C_2H_4 CO_2 CH   HO C_3H_8
C_4H_{10} H_2O H_2O_2 N_2H_4 PCl_5
CH_3COOH $C_6H_5CH_3$

11 Copy the table below and complete it with the molecular formulas of the compounds, given the empirical formulas and relative molecular masses.

Empirical formula	Relative molecular mass	Molecular formula
HO	34.02	
ClO_3	166.90	
CH_2	84.18	
BNH_2	80.52	

12 Analysis of a sample of an organic compound produced the following composition:

C: 0.399 g   **H: 0.101 g**

a Calculate the empirical formula.

b Given that the relative molecular mass is 30.08, determine the molecular formula.

13 If an oxide of chlorine contains 81.6% chlorine, calculate its empirical formula.

14 A compound contains 76.0% iodine and 24.0% oxygen. Calculate the empirical formula of the compound.

15 A compound, **X**, contains 64.8% carbon and 13.6% hydrogen. If the only other element present is oxygen and a single molecule of the compound contains four carbon atoms, calculate the molecular formula of **X**.

16 When 5.60 g of an iron oxide is heated with carbon, 3.92 g of iron is produced. Calculate the empirical formula of the iron oxide.

17 When 1.76 g of a hydrocarbon, **Q**, is burnt in excess oxygen, 5.27 g of carbon dioxide and 2.88 g of water are produced. What is the empirical formula of **Q**?

18 When 2.38 g of a hydrocarbon, **Z**, is burnt in excess oxygen, 7.21 g of carbon dioxide is produced. What is the empirical formula of **Z**?

19 When 4.76 g of an organic compound, **D**, which contains only carbon, hydrogen and oxygen, is burnt in excess oxygen, 10.46 g of carbon dioxide and 5.71 g of water are produced. What is the empirical formula of **D**?

1.4 Chemical equations

Balancing equations

If a reaction involves 5.00 g of one substance reacting with 10.00 g of another substance in a closed container (nothing can be added or escape), then at the end of the reaction there will still be exactly 15.00 g of substance present. This 15.00 g may be made up of one or more products and some reactants that have not fully reacted, but the key point is that there will no more and no less than 15.00 g present.

A chemical reaction involves atoms joining together in different ways and electrons redistributing themselves between the atoms, but it is not possible for the reaction to involve atoms or electrons being created or destroyed.

Learning objectives

- Understand how to balance chemical equations
- Understand how to use state symbols in chemical equations

Mass is conserved in a chemical reaction.

When a chemical reaction is represented by a chemical equation, there must be exactly the same number and type of atoms on either side of the equation, representing the same number of atoms before and after the reaction.

$$C_3H_8 + 5O_2 \rightarrow 3CO_2 + 4H_2O$$

	reactants		products	
atoms	C	3	C	3
	H	8	H	8
	O	10	O	10

Only whole numbers (coefficients) may be added in order to balance a chemical equation.

This equation is balanced.

The chemical formula for water is H_2O, and this formula cannot be changed in any way when balancing an equation. If, for instance, the formula is changed to H_2O_2, then it represents a completely different chemical substance: hydrogen peroxide.

State symbols are often used to indicate the physical state of an element or compound. These may be written as either subscripts after the chemical formula or in normal type.

(s) = solid
(l) = liquid
(g) = gas
(aq) = aqueous (dissolved in water)

Worked examples

Balance the following equation

   ... $N_2(g) + ... H_2(g) \rightarrow ... NH_3(g)$

and work out the sum of the coefficients in this equation.

At the moment there are two N atoms and two H atoms on the left-hand side of the equation but one N atom and three H atoms on the right-hand side. It is not possible for two N atoms to react with two H atoms to produce one N atom and three H atoms; therefore, this equation is not balanced.

It can be balanced in two stages, as follows:

   ... $N_2 + ... H_2 \rightarrow 2NH_3$

atoms	2 N	2 N
	2 H	6 H

   ... $N_2 + 3H_2 \rightarrow 2NH_3$

atoms	2 N	2 N
	6 H	6 H

This equation is now balanced, as there is the same number of each type of atom on both sides of the equation.

The sum of the coefficients in this equation is $1 + 3 + 2 = 6$. The coefficient of N_2 is 1, although we do not usually write this in an equation.

Balance the following equation:

$$\ldots\ C_4H_{10}(g) + \ldots\ O_2(g) \rightarrow \ldots\ CO_2(g) + \ldots\ H_2O(l)$$

Compounds are balanced first, then elements. The oxygen here does not depend on any other element.

$$\ldots\ C_4H_{10}(g) + \ldots\ O_2(g) \rightarrow 4CO_2(g) + 5H_2O(l)$$

There were two oxygen atoms on the left-hand side of the equation, and 2 needs to be multiplied by 6.5 to give 13, the number of oxygen atoms on the other side.

$$\ldots\ C_4H_{10}(g) + 6.5O_2(g) \rightarrow 4CO_2(g) + 5H_2O(l)$$

The equation is balanced as shown, but it looks much neater if balanced with whole numbers. To achieve this, all the coefficients are multiplied by 2 to get rid of the .5.

$$2C_4H_{10}(g) + 13O_2(g) \rightarrow 8CO_2(g) + 10H_2O(l)$$

Self-test 6

Test yourself

20 Balance the following equations:

a $NO + O_2 \rightarrow NO_2$

b $C_3H_8 + O_2 \rightarrow CO_2 + H_2O$

c $CaCO_3 + HCl \rightarrow CaCl_2 + CO_2 + H_2O$

d $C_2H_5OH + O_2 \rightarrow CO_2 + H_2O$

e $WO_3 + H_2 \rightarrow W + H_2O$

f $H_2O_2 \rightarrow O_2 + H_2O$

g $CrO_3 \rightarrow Cr_2O_3 + O_2$

h $Al_4C_3 + H_2O \rightarrow CH_4 + Al_2O_3$

i $HI + H_2SO_4 \rightarrow H_2S + H_2O + I_2$

j $PH_3 + O_2 \rightarrow P_4O_{10} + H_2O$

Conservation of charge

Charge – that is, the number of electrons (and protons) – must also balance in a chemical equation. Ionic equations will be considered further in another chapter, but for the moment here is an example of an ionic equation that is not balanced, although there is the same number of atoms on both sides.

$$Cr_2O_7{}^{2-} + Fe^{2+} + 14H^+ \rightarrow 2Cr^{3+} + 7H_2O + Fe^{3+}$$

The total charge on the left-hand side of this equation is 14+, whereas the total charge on the right-hand side is 9+, so the equation is not balanced (there is a different number of electrons at the end of the reaction from at the beginning). The balanced ionic equation for this reaction is:

$$Cr_2O_7{}^{2-} + 6Fe^{2+} + 14H^+ \rightarrow 2Cr^{3+} + 7H_2O + 6Fe^{3+}$$

We will consider how to balance these equations on pages **381–386**.

Conservation of mass

The fact that mass is conserved in a chemical reaction can sometimes be used to work out the mass of product formed. For example, if 55.85 g of iron reacts **exactly and completely** with 32.06 g of sulfur, 87.91 g of iron sulfide is formed:

$$Fe(s) + S(s) \rightarrow FeS(s)$$

Worked example

Consider the combustion of butane:

$$2C_4H_{10}(g) + 13O_2(g) \rightarrow 8CO_2(g) + 10H_2O(l)$$

10.00 g of butane reacts exactly with 35.78 g of oxygen to produce 30.28 g of carbon dioxide. What mass of water was produced?

The masses given represent an exact chemical reaction, so we assume that all the reactants are converted to products.

The total mass of the reactants = $10.00 + 35.78 = 45.78$ g.

The total mass of the products must also be 45.78 g.

Therefore the mass of water = $45.78 - 30.28 = 15.50$ g.

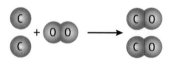

Figure 1.3 Two carbon atoms combine with one oxygen molecule to form two molecules of carbon monoxide.

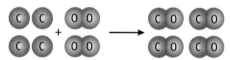

Figure 1.4 Four carbon atoms combine with two oxygen molecules to form four molecules of carbon monoxide.

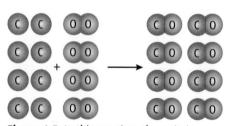

Figure 1.5 In this reaction, the ratio in which the species combine is fixed. So here we have eight carbon atoms combining with four oxygen molecules to form eight molecules of carbon monoxide.

The meaning of chemical equations

Consider the following chemical equation:

$$2C + O_2 \rightarrow 2CO$$

This is shown diagrammatically in Figure **1.3**.

In this reaction, two C atoms combine with one O_2 molecule to form two molecules of CO.

Look at Figure **1.4**. If we started with four C atoms: four C atoms react with two O_2 molecules to form four molecules of CO.

The ratio in which the species combine is fixed in this equation. The number of molecules of oxygen is always half the number of C atoms, and the number of CO molecules produced is the same as the number of C atoms (see Figure **1.5**).

Thus, if we imagine a very large number of C atoms, e.g. 6.02×10^{23}, we know that in this reaction they will combine with half as many molecules of O_2, i.e. 3.01×10^{23} molecules. The number of molecules of CO produced will be the same as the number of C atoms, i.e. 6.02×10^{23} molecules of CO. However, 6.02×10^{23} is one mole, so we can also interpret the equation as one mole of C atoms reacting with half a mole of O_2 molecules to form one mole of CO molecules, or:

$$C + \tfrac{1}{2}O_2 \rightarrow CO \quad \text{i.e.} \quad 2C + O_2 \rightarrow 2CO$$

This equation tells us that **2** mol C atoms react with **1** mol O_2 molecules to form **2** mol CO molecules.

1.5 Calculations involving moles and masses

Learning objectives

- Solve problems involving masses of substances
- Calculate the theoretical and percentage yield in a reaction
- Understand the term **limiting reactant** and solve problems involving this

Using moles

Very often we wish to work out the mass of one reactant that reacts exactly with a certain mass of another reactant – or how much product is formed when certain masses of reactants react. This can be done by calculating the numbers of each molecule or atom present in a particular mass or, much more simply, by using the mole concept.

As we have seen, one mole of any substance always contains the same number of particles, so if we know the number of moles present in a certain mass of reactant we also know the number of particles and can therefore work out what mass of another reactant it reacts with and how much product is formed.

There are three main steps to doing a moles calculation.
1 Work out the number of moles of anything you can.
2 Use the chemical (stoichiometric) equation to work out the number of moles of the quantity you require.
3 Convert moles to the required quantity – volume, mass, etc.

Questions involving masses of substances

Worked examples

Consider the reaction of sodium with oxygen:

$$4Na(s) + O_2(g) \rightarrow 2Na_2O(s)$$

a How much sodium reacts exactly with 3.20 g of oxygen?
b What mass of Na_2O is produced?

a Step 1 – the mass of oxygen is given, so the number of moles of oxygen can be worked out (you could use the triangle shown here).

$$\text{no. moles of oxygen} = \frac{3.20}{32.00} = 0.100 \, \text{mol}$$

Note: the mass of oxygen was given to three significant figures, so all subsequent answers are also given to three significant figures.

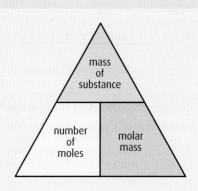

Step 2 – the coefficients in the chemical (stoichiometric) equation tell us that **1 mol O_2** reacts with **4 mol Na**. Therefore 0.100 mol O_2 reacts with 4×0.100 mol Na, i.e. 0.400 mol Na.

Step 3 – convert number of moles to the required quantity: mass in this case.

mass of Na $= 0.400 \times 22.99 = 9.20$ g

> Note: the mass of Na is worked out by multiplying the mass of one mole by the number of moles – the number of moles is **not** multiplied by the mass of 4Na – the four was already taken into account when 0.100 mol was multiplied by 4 to give the number of moles of Na.

b From the coefficients in the equation we know that 1 mol O_2 reacts with 4 mol Na to produce 2 mol Na_2O. Therefore 0.100 mol O_2 reacts with 0.400 mol Na to give 2×0.100 mol Na_2O, i.e. 0.200 mol Na_2O.

molar mass of $Na_2O = 61.98$ g mol^{-1}
mass of $Na_2O = 0.200 \times 61.98 = 12.4$ g

> Alternatively, the mass of Na_2O can be worked out using the idea of conservation of mass, i.e. the mass of Na_2O = mass of O_2 + mass of Na.

Examiner's tip
Masses may also be given in kilograms or tonnes.

1 kg = 1000 g

1 tonne = 1×10^6 g

Before working out the number of moles, you must convert the mass to grams. To convert kilograms to grams, multiply by 1000; to convert tonnes to grams, multiply the mass by 1×10^6.

Consider the following equation.

$$2NH_3 + 3CuO \rightarrow N_2 + 3H_2O + 3Cu$$

If 2.56 g of ammonia (NH_3) is reacted with excess CuO, calculate the mass of Cu produced.

> CuO is in excess: i.e. more than enough is present to react with all the NH_3. This means that we do not need to worry about the number of moles of CuO.

Step 1 – the number of moles of ammonia can be calculated:

$$\frac{2.56}{17.04} = 0.150 \text{ mol of ammonia}$$

Step 2 – two moles of NH_3 produce three moles of Cu, so 0.150 mol NH_3 produces $0.150 \times \frac{3}{2}$ mol Cu, i.e. 0.225 mol Cu.

> The number of moles of Cu is therefore 1.5 times the number of moles of NH_3.

Step 3 – the mass of 1 mol Cu = 63.55 g. The mass of CuO that reacts $= 0.225 \times 63.55 = 14.3$ g.

Formula for solving moles questions involving masses

An alternative way of doing these questions is to use a formula.

$$\frac{m_1}{n_1M_1} = \frac{m_2}{n_2M_2}$$

where

m_1 = mass of first substance

n_1 = coefficient of first substance

M_1 = molar mass of first substance

Worked example

The following equation represents the combustion of butane:

$$2C_4H_{10}(g) + 13O_2(g) \rightarrow 8CO_2(g) + 10H_2O(l)$$

If 10.00 g of butane is used, calculate:

a the mass of oxygen required for the exact reaction

b the mass of carbon dioxide produced.

a We will call butane substance 1 and oxygen substance 2 (this is arbitrary).

$m_1 = 10.00\,\text{g}$ $m_2 = ?$

$n_1 = 2$ $n_2 = 13$

$M_1 = 58.14\,\text{g mol}^{-1}$ $M_2 = 32.00\,\text{g mol}^{-1}$

$$\frac{m_1}{n_1M_1} = \frac{m_2}{n_2M_2}$$

$$\frac{10.00}{2 \times 58.14} = \frac{m_2}{13 \times 32.00}$$

The equation can be rearranged:

$$m_2 = \frac{10.00 \times 13 \times 32.00}{2 \times 58.14} \quad \text{i.e. } m_2 = 35.78\,\text{g}$$

Therefore the mass of oxygen required for the exact reaction is 35.78 g.

b We will call butane substance 1 and carbon dioxide substance 2.

$m_1 = 10.00\,\text{g}$ $m_2 = ?$

$n_1 = 2$ $n_2 = 8$

$M_1 = 58.14\,\text{g mol}^{-1}$ $M_2 = 44.01\,\text{g mol}^{-1}$

$$\frac{10.00}{2 \times 58.14} = \frac{m_2}{8 \times 44.01}$$

The equation can be rearranged:

$$m_2 = \frac{10.00 \times 8 \times 44.01}{2 \times 58.14} \quad \text{i.e. } m_2 = 30.28\,\text{g}$$

Therefore 30.28 g of carbon dioxide is produced.

21 a How many moles of hydrogen gas are produced when 0.4 moles of sodium react with excess water?

$$2Na + 2H_2O \rightarrow 2NaOH + H_2$$

b How many moles of O_2 react with 0.01 mol C_3H_8?

$$C_3H_8 + 5O_2 \rightarrow 3CO_2 + 4H_2O$$

c How many moles of H_2S are formed when 0.02 mol of HCl react with excess Sb_2S_3?

$$Sb_2S_3 + 6HCl \rightarrow 2SbCl_3 + 3H_2S$$

d How many moles of oxygen are formed when 0.6 mol of $KClO_3$ react?

$$2KClO_3(s) \rightarrow 2KCl(s) + 3O_2(g)$$

e How many moles of iron are formed when 0.9 mol CO react with excess iron oxide?

$$Fe_2O_3 + 3CO \rightarrow 2Fe + 3CO_2$$

f How many moles of hydrogen would be required to make 2.4×10^{-3} mol NH_3?

$$N_2 + 3H_2 \rightarrow 2NH_3$$

22 a Calculate the mass of arsenic(III) chloride produced when 0.150 g of arsenic reacts with excess chlorine according to the equation:

$$2As + 3Cl_2 \rightarrow 2AsCl_3$$

b What mass of sulfur is produced when 5.78 g iron(III) sulfide is reacted with excess oxygen?

$$2Fe_2S_3 + 3O_2 \rightarrow 2Fe_2O_3 + 6S$$

c Calculate the mass of iodine that must be reacted with excess phosphorus to produce 5.00 g of phosphorus(III) iodide according to the equation below.

$$2P + 3I_2 \rightarrow 2PI_3$$

d Consider the reaction shown below. What mass of SCl_2 must be reacted with excess NaF to produce 2.25 g of NaCl?

$$3SCl_2 + 4NaF \rightarrow S_2Cl_2 + SF_4 + 4NaCl$$

The fact that a theory can explain experimental observations does not necessarily make it correct. The explanations presented in this book fit in with experimental observations, but this does not mean that they are 'true' – they just represent our interpretation of the data at this stage in time. Each generation of scientists believes that they are presenting a true description of reality, but is it possible for more than one explanation to fit the facts? You, or indeed I, may not be able to think of a better explanation to fit a lot of the experimental observations in modern science, but that does not mean that there isn't one. Consider the following trivial example.

Experimentally, when 100 kg of calcium carbonate is heated, 44 kg of carbon dioxide is obtained. The following calculation can be carried out to explain this.

The equation for the reaction is:

$$CaCO_3 \rightarrow CaO + CO_2$$

$$\text{no. moles of calcium carbonate} = \frac{100}{(20 + 6 + (3 \times 8))}$$

$$= 2 \text{ moles}$$

Two moles of calcium carbonate produces two moles of carbon dioxide.

The mass of two moles of carbon dioxide is $2 \times (6 + (2 \times 8)) = 44$ kg.

Hopefully you can see some mistakes in this calculation, but the result is what we got experimentally. It is also interesting to note that if, in your IB examination, you had just written down the final answer, you would probably have got full marks!

Calculating the yield of a chemical reaction

In any commercial process it is very important to know the yield of a chemical reaction. For instance, if a particular process for the preparation of a drug involves four separate steps and the yield of each step is 95%, it is probably quite a promising synthetic route to the drug. If, however, the yield of each step is only 60%, it is likely that the company would seek a more efficient synthetic process.

The yield of a chemical reaction is usually quoted as a percentage, as that gives more information than just quoting the yield of the product as a mass. Consider the preparation of 1,2-dibromoethane:

$$C_2H_4(g) + Br_2(l) \rightarrow C_2H_4Br_2(l)$$

10.00 g of ethene will react exactly with 56.95 g of bromine.

The **theoretical yield** for this reaction is 66.95 g – this is the maximum possible yield that can be obtained. The **actual yield** of 1,2-dibromoethane may be 50.00 g.

$$\% \text{ yield} = \frac{50.00}{66.95} \times 100 = 74.68\%$$

> The yield of a chemical reaction is the amount of product obtained.

> $$\% \text{ yield} = \frac{\text{actual yield}}{\text{theoretical yield}} \times 100$$

Worked example

$$\underset{\text{ethanol}}{C_2H_5OH(l)} + \underset{\text{ethanoic acid}}{CH_3COOH(l)} \rightarrow \underset{\text{ethyl ethanoate}}{CH_3COOC_2H_5(l)} + \underset{\text{water}}{H_2O(l)}$$

If the yield of ethyl ethanoate obtained when 20.00 g of ethanol is reacted with excess ethanoic acid is 30.27 g, calculate the percentage yield.

The first step is to calculate the maximum possible yield, i.e. the theoretical yield:

molar mass of ethanol = $46.08 \, \text{g mol}^{-1}$

no. moles of ethanol = $\dfrac{20.00}{46.08} = 0.4340 \, \text{mol}$

> Ethanoic acid is in excess, i.e. more than enough is present to react with all the ethanol. This means that we do not need to worry about the number of moles of ethanoic acid.

The chemical equation tells us that 1 mol ethanol produces 1 mol ethyl ethanoate. Therefore, 0.4340 mol ethanol produces 0.4340 mol ethyl ethanoate.

The molar mass of ethyl ethanoate = $88.12 \, \text{g mol}^{-1}$.

The mass of ethyl ethanoate produced = $0.4340 \times 88.12 = 38.24 \, \text{g}$.

Thus, the theoretical yield is 38.24 g, and the actual yield is 30.27 g.

$$\% \text{ yield} = \frac{30.27}{38.24} \times 100 = 79.15\%$$

Therefore the percentage yield of ethyl ethanoate is 79.15%.

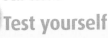
23 Calculate the percentage yield in each of the following reactions.

a When 2.50 g of SO_2 is heated with excess oxygen, 2.50 g of SO_3 is obtained.

$$2SO_2 + O_2 \rightarrow 2SO_3$$

b When 10.0 g of arsenic is heated in excess oxygen, 12.5 g of As_4O_6 is produced.

$$4As + 3O_2 \rightarrow As_4O_6$$

c When 1.20 g ethene reacts with excess bromine, 5.23 g of 1,2-dibromoethane is produced.

$$C_2H_4 + Br_2 \rightarrow CH_2BrCH_2Br$$

Limiting reactant

Very often we do not use exact quantities in a chemical reaction, but rather we use an excess of one or more reactants. One reactant is therefore used up before the others and is called the **limiting reactant**. When the limiting reactant is completely used up, the reaction stops.

Figure **1.6** illustrates the idea of a limiting reactant and shows how the products of the reaction depend on which reactant is limiting.

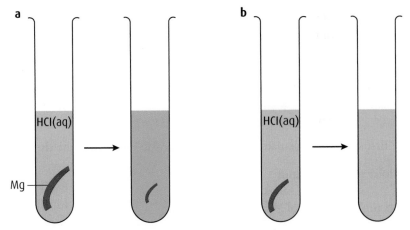

Figure 1.6 The reaction between magnesium and hydrochloric acid. In each test tube a small amount of universal indicator has been added. (**a**) In this test tube, the magnesium is in excess and the reaction finishes when the hydrochloric acid runs out. There is still magnesium left over at the end, and the solution is no longer acidic. (**b**) In this test tube, the hydrochloric acid is in excess. The magnesium is the limiting reactant, and the reaction stops when the magnesium has been used up. The solution is still acidic at the end.

Worked examples

Consider the reaction between magnesium and nitrogen:

$$3Mg(s) + N_2(g) \rightarrow Mg_3N_2(s)$$

10.00 g of magnesium is reacted with 5.00 g of nitrogen. Which is the limiting reactant?

$$\text{no. moles of Mg} = \frac{10.00}{24.31} = 0.4114 \, \text{mol} \qquad \text{no. moles of N}_2 = \frac{5.00}{28.02} = 0.178 \, \text{mol}$$

The equation tells us that 3 mol Mg reacts with 1 mol N_2. So 0.4114 mol Mg reacts with 0.4114 mol N_2 divided by 3, i.e. 0.1371 mol N_2.

Therefore, for an exact reaction, 0.1371 mol of N_2 are required to react with 0.4114 mol Mg. However, 0.178 mol of N_2 are used, which is more than enough to react. This means that N_2 is in excess, as there is more than enough to react with all the Mg present. Magnesium is therefore the limiting reactant.

This can also be seen from working with the number of moles of N_2: 0.178 mol N_2 was used in this reaction. This number of moles of N_2 would require 3×0.178 mol Mg for an exact reaction, i.e. 0.534 mol Mg. However, only 0.4114 mol Mg are present; therefore, the Mg will run out before all the N_2 has reacted.

> Alternatively: divide the number of moles of each reactant by its coefficient in the stoichiometric equation, and the smallest number indicates the limiting reactant.

Consider the reaction between sulfur and fluorine: $S(s) + 3F_2(g) \rightarrow SF_6(g)$

10.00 g of sulfur reacts with 10.00 g of fluorine.

a Which is the limiting reactant?
b What mass of sulfur(VI) fluoride is formed?
c What mass of the reactant in excess is left at the end?

a $\quad \text{no. moles of S} = \dfrac{10.00}{32.06} = 0.3119 \, \text{mol} \qquad \text{no. moles of F}_2 = \dfrac{10.00}{38.00} = 0.2632 \, \text{mol}$

The coefficient of S in the equation is 1 and that of F_2 is 3. 0.3119/1 = 0.3119 and 0.2632/3 = 0.087 73, therefore S is in excess and F_2 is the limiting reactant.

Alternatively, we can reason from the chemical equation, 0.2632 mol F_2 should react with 0.087 73 mol S (i.e. 0.2632 mol S divided by 3). There is more than 0.087 73 mol S present, so S is present in excess and F_2 is the limiting reactant.

For the rest of the question we must work with the limiting reactant.

b When the limiting reactant is used up completely, the reaction stops. This means that the amount of product formed is determined by the amount of the limiting reactant we started with.

From the chemical equation, 0.2632 mol F_2 produces 0.087 73 mol SF_6 (i.e. 0.2632 mol SF_6 divided by 3).

molar mass of SF_6 = 146.06 g mol^{-1}

mass of SF_6 formed = $0.087\,73 \times 146.06 = 12.81$ g

c From the chemical equation, 0.2632 mol F_2 reacts with 0.087 73 mol S (i.e. 0.2632 mol S divided by 3). Originally there were 0.3119 mol S present; therefore the number of moles of sulfur left at the end of the reaction is $0.3119 - 0.087\,73 = 0.2242$.

The mass of sulfur left at the end of the reaction is $0.2242 \times 32.06 = 7.188$ g.

Examiner's tip

To do a moles question you need to know the mass of just one of the reactants. If you are given the masses of more than one reactant, you must consider that one of these reactants will be the limiting reactant and use this one for all subsequent calculations.

For the reaction

$$4Fe_2Cr_2O_4 + 8Na_2CO_3 + 7O_2 \rightarrow 8Na_2CrO_4 + 2Fe_2O_3 + 8CO_2$$

there is 100.0 g of each reactant available. Which is the limiting reactant?

This question could be done by working out the number of moles of each reactant and then comparing them, but there is a shortcut: to work out the masses of each substance if molar quantities reacted:

	$4Fe_2Cr_2O_4$	+	$8Na_2CO_3$	+	$7O_2$	$\rightarrow 8Na_2CrO_4 + 2Fe_2O_3 + 8CO_2$
mass / g =	4×279.70		8×105.99		7×32.00	
mass / g =	1118.80		847.92		224.00	

These are the masses that are required for the exact reaction. As the greatest mass required is that of $Fe_2Cr_2O_4$, if the same mass of each substance is taken, the $Fe_2Cr_2O_4$ will run out first and must be the limiting reactant.

Self-test 9

Test yourself

24 What is the limiting reactant in each of the following reactions?

  a 0.1 mol Sb_4O_6 reacts with 0.5 mol H_2SO_4
$$Sb_4O_6 + 6H_2SO_4 \rightarrow 2Sb_2(SO_4)_3 + 6H_2O$$
  b 0.20 mol $AsCl_3$ reacts with 0.25 mol H_2O
$$4AsCl_3 + 6H_2O \rightarrow As_4O_6 + 12HCl$$
  c 0.25 mol Cu react with 0.50 mol dilute HNO_3 according to the equation:
$$3Cu + 8HNO_3$$
$$\rightarrow 3Cu(NO_3)_2 + 4H_2O + 2NO$$
  d 0.10 mol NaCl reacts with 0.15 mol MnO_2 and 0.20 mol H_2SO_4
$$2NaCl + MnO_2 + 2H_2SO_4$$
$$\rightarrow Na_2SO_4 + MnSO_4 + 2H_2O + Cl_2$$

25 Boron can be prepared by reacting B_2O_3 with magnesium at high temperatures:
$$B_2O_3 + 3Mg \rightarrow 2B + 3MgO$$
What mass of B is obtained if 0.75 g B_2O_3 is reacted with 0.50 g Mg?

26 Iron(III) oxide reacts with carbon to produce iron:
$$Fe_2O_3 + 3C \rightarrow 2Fe + 3CO$$
What mass of Fe is obtained if 10.0 tonnes of Fe_2O_3 is reacted with 1.00 tonne of C?

1.6 Calculations involving volumes of gases

Learning objectives

- Understand Avogadro's law and use it to calculate reacting volumes of gases
- Use the molar volume of a gas in calculations at standard temperature and pressure
- Understand the relationships between pressure, volume and temperature for an ideal gas
- Solve problems using the equation
  $$\frac{P_1 V_1}{T_1} = \frac{P_2 V_2}{T_2}$$
- Solve problems using the ideal gas equation

An ideal gas is a concept invented by scientists to approximate (model) the behaviour of real gases. Under normal conditions (around 1 atm pressure and 0 °C) real gases such as H_2 behave fairly much like ideal gases, and the approximations used here work very well.

Two postulates we use when defining an ideal gas are to say that the molecules themselves have no volume (they are point masses) and that no forces exist between them (except when they collide). This means that the volume occupied by a gas **at a certain temperature and pressure** depends only on the **number of particles present** and not on the nature of the gas.

In other words, at a certain temperature and pressure, the volume of a gas is proportional to the number of moles present.

volume $\propto$ no. moles

Using volumes of gases

> **Avogadro's law**: equal volumes of ideal gases measured at the same temperature and pressure contain the same number of molecules.

In other words $100 \, cm^3$ of H_2 contains the same number of molecules at 25 °C and 1 atm pressure as $100 \, cm^3$ of NH_3, if we assume that they both behave as ideal gases. Under the same conditions, $50 \, cm^3$ of CO_2 would contain half as many molecules.

This means that volumes can be used directly (instead of moles) in equations involving gases:

$$H_2(g) + Cl_2(g) \rightarrow 2HCl(g)$$

The above equation tells us that one mole of H_2 reacts with one mole of Cl_2 to give two moles of HCl. Or one volume of H_2 reacts with one volume of Cl_2 to give two volumes of HCl; i.e. $50 \, cm^3$ of H_2 reacts with $50 \, cm^3$ of Cl_2 to give $100 \, cm^3$ of HCl.

The ideal gas concept is an approximation, which is used to model the behaviour of real gases. Why do we learn about ideal gases when they do not exist? What implications does the ideal gas concept have on the limits of knowledge gained from this course?

Worked examples

In both of these worked examples, assume that all gases behave as ideal gases and that all measurements are made under the same conditions of temperature and pressure.

Consider the following reaction for the synthesis of methanol:

$$CO(g) + 2H_2(g) \rightarrow CH_3OH(g)$$

a What volume of H_2 reacts exactly with $2.50\,dm^3$ of CO?
b What volume of CH_3OH is produced?

a From the equation we know that $1\,mol$ CO reacts with $2\,mol$ H_2. Therefore one volume of CO reacts with two volumes of H_2: $2.50\,dm^3$ of CO reacts with 2×2.50, i.e. $5.00\,dm^3$, of H_2.
b One volume of CO produces one volume of CH_3OH. Therefore the volume of CH_3OH produced is $2.50\,dm^3$.

If $100\,cm^3$ of oxygen reacts with $30\,cm^3$ of methane in the following reaction, how much oxygen will be left at the end of the reaction?

$$CH_4(g) + 2O_2(g) \rightarrow CO_2(g) + 2H_2O(l)$$

From the equation we know that $1\,mol$ CH_4 reacts with $2\,mol$ O_2. Therefore one volume of CH_4 reacts with two volumes of O_2, i.e. $30\,cm^3$ of CH_4 reacts with 2×30, i.e. $60\,cm^3$ of O_2.

The original volume of O_2 was $100\,cm^3$; therefore, if $60\,cm^3$ reacted, the volume of oxygen gas left over at the end of the reaction would be $100 - 60 = 40\,cm^3$.

STP = standard temperature and pressure = 273 K, 1 atm $(1.01 \times 10^5\,Pa)$

Converting volumes of gases to number of moles

As the volume occupied by an ideal gas is dependent only on the number of particles present (assuming pressure and temperature are constant) and not on the nature of the particles, the volume occupied by one mole of any ideal gas under a certain set of conditions will always be the same. The volume occupied by one mole of a gas under certain conditions is called the **molar volume**.

> molar volume of an ideal gas at STP = $22.4\,dm^3\,mol^{-1}$ or $2.24 \times 10^{-2}\,m^3\,mol^{-1}$

This means that under the same set of conditions the volume occupied by one mole of NH_3 is the same as the volume occupied by one mole of CO_2 and one mole of H_2, and this volume is $22.4\,dm^3$ at STP.

The relationship between the number of moles of a gas and its volume is:

$$no.\ moles = \frac{volume}{molar\ volume}$$

This is summarised in Figure **1.7**.

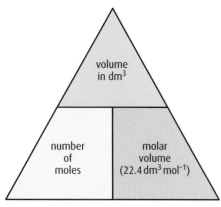

Figure 1.7 The relationship between the number of moles of a gas and its volume.

The absolute, or **Kelvin**, scale of temperature starts at absolute zero, which is the lowest temperature possible. It is the temperature at which everything would be in its lowest energy state. Absolute zero corresponds to 0 K or −273.15 °C (usually taken as −273 °C) and is also the temperature at which the volume of an ideal gas would be zero. It is not possible to actually reach absolute zero, but scientists have managed to get very close – about 1 nanokelvin!

> **1 °C is the same as 1 K, and so 0 °C is equivalent to 273 K**

To convert °C to K add 273:
e.g. 25 °C is equivalent to 25 + 273, i.e. 298 K
To convert K to °C subtract 273:
e.g. 350 K is equivalent to 350 − 273, i.e. 77 °C

Volumes of gases are often given in dm^3 (litres) and so it is important to know how to convert between cm^3 and dm^3.

As 1 dm^3 (1 litre) is equivalent to 1000 cm^3 (1 cm^3 is the same as 1 ml), to convert cm^3 to dm^3 we divide by 1000 (to go from **1000 cm^3** to **1 dm^3**). The conversion is shown in Figure **1.8**.

In different countries around the world different scales of temperature are used: e.g. the Celsius and Fahrenheit scales. The Celsius and Fahrenheit scales are both artificial scales, but the Kelvin scale is an absolute scale. What is the advantage to scientists of using an absolute scale? Why has the absolute scale of temperature not been adopted in everyday life?

The Kelvin scale of temperature is named in honour of William Thompson, Lord Kelvin (1824–1907), a Scottish mathematican and physicist, who first suggested the idea of an absolute scale of temperature. Despite making many important contributions to the advancement of science, Kelvin had doubts about the existence of atoms, believed that the Earth could not be older than 100 million years and is often quoted as saying that 'heavier-than-air flying machines are impossible'.

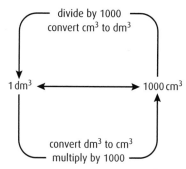

Figure 1.8 Converting between cm^3 and dm^3.

Worked examples

a Calculate the number of moles in 250 cm^3 of O_2 at STP.
b Calculate the volume of 0.135 mol of CO_2 at STP.

a no. moles $= \dfrac{\text{volume in } dm^3}{22.4}$

$250 \, cm^3 = \dfrac{250}{1000} \, dm^3 = 0.250 \, dm^3$

no. moles $= \dfrac{0.250}{22.4} = 0.0112 \, mol$

b volume = no. moles $\times 22.4 = 0.135 \times 22.4 = 3.02 \, dm^3$

Calculate the volume of carbon dioxide (collected at STP) produced when 10.01 g of calcium carbonate decomposes according to the equation:

$$CaCO_3(s) \rightarrow CaO(s) + CO_2(g)$$

Step 1 – work out the number of moles of calcium carbonate:

$$\text{no. moles of calcium carbonate} = \frac{10.01}{100.09} = 0.1000 \, \text{mol}$$

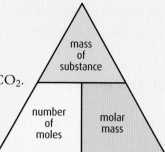

Step 2 – the chemical equation tells us that 1 mol $CaCO_3$ decomposes to give 1 mol CO_2.

Therefore 0.1000 mol $CaCO_3$ decomposes to give 0.1000 mol CO_2.

Step 3 – convert the number of moles to volume.

1 mol of CO_2 occupies 22.4 dm^3 at STP

volume of CO_2 = no. moles × volume of 1 mole (22.4 dm^3)

volume of CO_2 = 0.1000 × 22.4 = 2.24 dm^3

Therefore the volume of CO_2 produced is 2.24 dm^3.

Potassium chlorate(V) decomposes when heated:

$$2KClO_3(s) \rightarrow 2KCl(s) + 3O_2(g)$$

What mass of potassium chlorate(V) decomposes to produce 100.0 cm^3 of oxygen gas measured at STP?

Step 1 – work out the number of moles of O_2. The volume of O_2 must first be converted to dm^3:

$$\text{volume of } O_2 \text{ in dm}^3 = \frac{100.0}{1000} = 0.1000 \, \text{dm}^3$$

$$\text{no. moles of } O_2 = \frac{0.1000}{22.4} = 4.464 \times 10^{-3} \, \text{mol}$$

Step 2 – the chemical equation tells us that 3 mol O_2 are produced from 2 mol $KClO_3$. Therefore the number of moles of $KClO_3$ is two-thirds of the number of moles of O_2:

$$\tfrac{2}{3} \times 4.464 \times 10^{-3} = 2.976 \times 10^{-3} \, \text{mol}$$

Step 3 – convert the number of moles of $KClO_3$ to mass.

molar mass of $KClO_3$ = 122.55 g mol^{-1}

mass of $KClO_3$ = 122.55 × 2.976 × 10^{-3} = 0.3647 g

Therefore the mass of $KClO_3$ required is 0.3647 g.

Formula for solving moles questions involving volumes of gases

An alternative way of doing these questions is to use a formula.

$$\frac{m_1}{n_1 M_1} = \frac{V_2}{n_2 M_v}$$

Note – this is very similar to the equation that was used earlier with masses.

where:

m_1 = mass of first substance (in g)

n_1 = coefficient of first substance

M_1 = molar mass of first substance

V_2 = volume (in dm^3) of second substance if it is a **gas**

n_2 = coefficient of second substance

M_v = molar volume of a gas = 22.4 dm^3 at STP

This equation can be used if the mass of one substance is given and the volume of another substance is required, or vice versa.

If a volume is given and a volume is required, then an alternative form of this equation is:

$$\frac{V_1}{n_1} = \frac{V_2}{n_2}$$

There is no need to convert units of volume to dm^3 with this equation – V_2 will have the same units as V_1.

where:

V_1 = volume of first substance if it is a **gas**

V_2 = volume of second substance

However, with questions involving just gases it is usually easier to work them out using Avogadro's law, as already described.

Worked example

Consider the following equation:

$$2As_2S_3 + 9O_2 \rightarrow 2As_2O_3 + 6SO_2$$

What volume of SO_2 is obtained (measured at STP) when 1.000 kg of As_2S_3 is heated in oxygen?

Let As_2S_3 be substance 1 and SO_2 be substance 2:

m_1 = 1.000 kg = 1000 g

n_1 = 2

M_1 = 246.02 g mol^{-1}

V_2 = ?

n_2 = 6

M_v = 22.4 dm^3 at STP

Mass in g must be used.

$$\frac{1000}{2 \times 246.02} = \frac{V_2}{6 \times 22.4}$$

Rearranging the equation: $V_2 = \dfrac{1000 \times 6 \times 22.4}{2 \times 246.02} = 273$ dm^3

Therefore the volume of SO_2 produced is 273 dm^3.

27 *Assume that all gases behave as ideal gases and that all measurements are made under the same conditions of temperature and pressure.*

   a Calculate the volume of CO_2 produced when $100\,cm^3$ of ethene burns in excess oxygen according to the equation:

$$C_2H_4(g) + 3O_2(g) \rightarrow 2CO_2(g) + 2H_2O(l)$$

   b Calculate the volume of NO produced when $2.0\,dm^3$ of oxygen is reacted with excess ammonia according to the equation:

$$4NH_3(g) + 5O_2(g) \rightarrow 4NO(g) + 6H_2O(g)$$

28 Determine the number of moles present in each of the following at standard temperature and pressure:

   a $0.240\,dm^3$ of O_2 d $400.0\,cm^3$ of N_2
   b $2.00\,dm^3$ of CH_4 e $250.0\,cm^3$ of CO_2
   c $0.100\,dm^3$ of SO_2

29 Work out the volume of each of the following at standard temperature and pressure:

   a $0.100\,mol\ C_3H_8$ d $0.8500\,mol\ NH_3$
   b $100.0\,mol\ SO_3$ e $0.600\,mol\ O_2$
   c $0.270\,mol\ N_2$

30 Sodium nitrate(V) decomposes according to the equation:

$$2NaNO_3(s) \rightarrow 2NaNO_2(s) + O_2(g)$$

   Calculate the volume (in cm^3) of oxygen produced (measured at STP) when $0.820\,g$ of sodium nitrate(V) decomposes.

31 Tin reacts with nitric acid according to the equation:

$$Sn(s) + 4HNO_3(aq)$$
$$\rightarrow SnO_2(s) + 4NO_2(g) + 2H_2O(l)$$

   If $2.50\,g$ of tin are reacted with excess nitric acid what volume of NO_2 (in cm^3) is produced at STP?

32 Calculate the mass of sodium carbonate that must be reacted with excess hydrochloric acid to produce $100.0\,cm^3$ of CO_2 at STP.

$$Na_2CO_3(s) + 2HCl(aq)$$
$$\rightarrow 2NaCl(aq) + CO_2(g) + H_2O(l)$$

33 *Assume that all gases behave as ideal gases and that all measurements are made under the same conditions of temperature and pressure.*

   a Oxygen (O_2) can be converted to ozone (O_3) by passing it through a silent electric discharge.

$$3O_2(g) \rightarrow 2O_3(g)$$

   If $300\,cm^3$ of oxygen is used and 10% of the oxygen is converted to ozone, calculate the total volume of gas present at the end of the experiment.

   b Hydrogen reacts with chlorine according to the equation:

$$H_2(g) + Cl_2(g) \rightarrow 2HCl(g)$$

   What is the total volume of gas present in the container at the end of the experiment if $100\,cm^3$ of hydrogen is reacted with $200\,cm^3$ of chlorine?

'Macroscopic' means 'on a large scale'. The opposite is 'microscopic'. Microscopic properties of a gas are the properties of the particles that make up the gas.

Macroscopic properties of ideal gases

So far all the questions we have dealt with have involved working out volumes of gases at STP. In order to work out volumes of gases under other conditions, we must understand a little about the properties of gases.

The relationship between pressure and volume (Boyle's law)

> At a constant temperature, the volume of a fixed mass of an ideal gas is inversely proportional to its pressure.

This means that if the pressure of a gas is doubled at constant temperature, then the volume will be halved, and vice versa. This relationship is illustrated in Figure **1.9**.

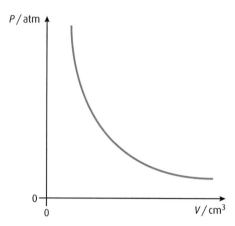

Figure 1.9 The relationship between pressure and volume of a fixed mass of an ideal gas at constant temperature

$$P \propto \frac{1}{V}$$

The relationship can also be written as:

$$P = \frac{k}{V}$$

where k is a constant.
This can be rearranged to give

$$PV = k$$

This means that the product of the pressure and volume of an ideal gas at a particular temperature is a constant and does not change as the pressure and the volume change.

Other graphs can also be drawn to illustrate this relationship (see Figures **1.10** and **1.11**).

As pressure is proportional to $\frac{1}{\text{volume}}$, a graph of pressure against $\frac{1}{\text{volume}}$ would be a straight-line graph that would pass through the origin (although this graph will never actually pass through the origin – the gas would have to have infinite volume at zero pressure). This is shown in Figure **1.10**.

As $PV = k$, where k is a constant, a graph of PV against pressure (or volume) will be a straight, horizontal line. This is shown in Figure **1.11**.

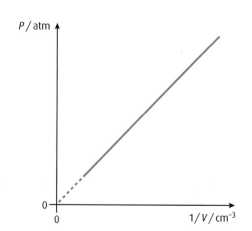

Figure 1.10 The relationship between the pressure and $\frac{1}{\text{volume}}$ of a fixed mass of an ideal gas at constant temperature.

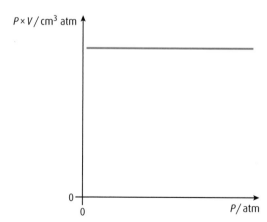

Figure 1.11 The relationship between PV and P for a fixed mass of an ideal gas at constant temperature.

> The volume of a fixed mass of an ideal gas at constant pressure is directly proportional to its temperature in kelvin.

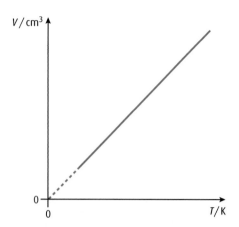

Figure 1.12 The relationship between the volume and temperature (in kelvin) of a fixed mass of an ideal gas at constant pressure.

> An ideal gas can never liquefy, as there are no forces between the molecules.

The relationship between volume and temperature (Charles' law)

If the temperature is in kelvin, the following relationship exists between the volume and the temperature:

$$V \propto T$$

Therefore, if the temperature in **kelvin** is doubled and the pressure remains constant, the volume of the gas is doubled, and vice versa. This means that if an ideal gas has a volume of $200\,cm^3$ at $120\,K$, it will have a volume of $400\,cm^3$ at $240\,K$ if the pressure remains constant. This is illustrated in Figure **1.12**.

This relationship does not work for temperatures in °C (Figure **1.13**). For instance, if the volume of an ideal gas at $25\,°C$ is $500\,cm^3$, the volume it will occupy at $50\,°C$ will be about $560\,cm^3$.

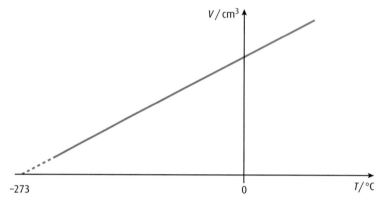

Figure 1.13 The relationship between the volume and temperature (in °C) of a fixed mass of an ideal gas at constant pressure. As can be seen from this graph, the temperature at which the volume of an ideal gas is zero will be −273 °C. This temperature is **absolute zero**.

> This is a **linear** relationship but **not** a **proportional** one, as the graph does not pass through the origin.

The relationship between pressure and temperature

> For a fixed mass of an ideal gas at constant volume, the pressure is directly proportional to its absolute temperature.

Therefore, if the temperature (in **kelvin**) of a fixed volume of an ideal gas is doubled, the pressure will also double (Figure **1.14**).

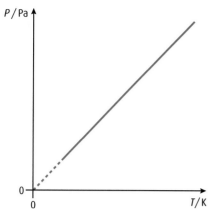

Figure 1.14 The relationship between the pressure and temperature (in kelvin) of a fixed mass of an ideal gas at constant volume.

$P \propto T$

An ideal gas is one that obeys all of the above laws exactly.

The overall gas law equation

The three relationships you have seen can be combined to produce the following equation:

Note: any units may be used for P and V, as long as they are consistent between both sides of the equation.

$$\frac{P_1 V_1}{T_1} = \frac{P_2 V_2}{T_2}$$

Temperature must be in K.

Worked examples

If the volume of an ideal gas collected at $0\,°C$ and 1.00 atmosphere pressure $(1.01 \times 10^5\,Pa)$, i.e. at STP, is $50.0\,cm^3$, what would be the volume at $60\,°C$ and $1.08 \times 10^5\,Pa$?

$P_1 = 1.01 \times 10^5\,Pa$ $P_2 = 1.08 \times 10^5\,Pa$
$V_1 = 50.0\,cm^3$ $V_2 = ?$ The units of P_1 and P_2 are consistent with each other.

$T_1 = 0\,°C = 273\,K$ $T_2 = 60\,°C = 60 + 273\,K = 333\,K$

Temperature must be in K.

$$\frac{P_1 V_1}{T_1} = \frac{P_2 V_2}{T_2}$$

$$\frac{1.01 \times 10^5 \times 50.0}{273} = \frac{1.08 \times 10^5 \times V_2}{333}$$

Rearranging the equation:

$$V_2 = \frac{1.01 \times 10^5 \times 50.0 \times 333}{273 \times 1.08 \times 10^5} = 57.0\,cm^3$$

The units of V_2 are the same as those of V_1.

Therefore, the volume occupied by the gas at $60\,°C$ and $1.08 \times 10^5\,Pa$ is $57.0\,cm^3$.

What temperature (in °C) is required to cause an ideal gas to occupy $1.34\,dm^3$ at a pressure of $2.05\,atm$ if it occupies $756\,cm^3$ at STP?

$P_1 = 2.05$ atm $P_2 = 1.00$ atm

$V_1 = 1.34$ $V_2 = 756\,cm^3$, i.e. $\dfrac{756}{1000}\,dm^3$, i.e. $0.756\,dm^3$

$T_1 = ?$ $T_2 = 273\,K$

> The units of P_1 are the same as those of P_2.

$$\frac{2.05 \times 1.34}{T_1} = \frac{1.00 \times 0.756}{273}$$

> The units of V_1 and V_2 must be made consistent with each other. We could have also changed V_1 to cm^3.

Rearranging the equation:

$$2.05 \times 1.34 \times 273 = 1.00 \times 0.756 \times T_1$$

$$T_1 = \frac{2.05 \times 1.34 \times 273}{1.00 \times 0.756} = 992\,K$$

This must now be converted to °C by subtracting 273.

Temperature $= 992 - 273 = 719\,°C$

Therefore, the temperature must be $719\,°C$ for the gas to occupy a volume of $1.34\,dm^3$.

R is the **gas constant** (ideal gas constant).

n = no. moles

A consistent set of units must be used.

Examiner's tip
A set of units that is equivalent to this uses volume in dm^3 and pressure in kPa – if you use these units you can avoid the problem of converting volumes into m^3.

The ideal gas equation

If the relationships between P, V and T are combined with Avogadro's law, the ideal gas equation is obtained:

$$PV = nRT$$

Although the gas constant R is a universal constant, it can be quoted with various units, and its value depends on these units. The SI units for the gas constant are $J\,K^{-1}\,mol^{-1}$, and this requires the following set of units:

$R = 8.31\,J\,K^{-1}\,mol^{-1}$
Pressure: $N\,m^{-2}$ or Pa
Volume: m^3
Temperature: K

$1\,000\,000\,cm^3 \Leftrightarrow 1\,m^3$
$1000\,dm^3 \Leftrightarrow 1\,m^3$
To convert m^3 to cm^3 multiply by $1\,000\,000$.
To convert cm^3 to m^3 divide by $1\,000\,000$.
To convert m^3 to dm^3 multiply by 1000.
To convert dm^3 to m^3 divide by 1000.

Worked examples

An ideal gas occupies $590 \, cm^3$ at $120 \, °C$ and $2.00 \, atm$. What amount of gas (in moles) is present?

If we use the value of $8.31 \, J \, K^{-1} \, mol^{-1}$ for the gas constant, all values must be converted to the appropriate set of units:

$P = 2.00 \, atm = 1.01 \times 10^5 \times 2 \, Pa = 2.02 \times 10^5 \, Pa$

$V = 590 \, cm^3 = \dfrac{590}{1\,000\,000} \, m^3 = 5.90 \times 10^{-4} \, m^3$

$n = ?$

$R = 8.31 \, J \, K^{-1} \, mol^{-1}$

$T = 120 \, °C = 120 + 273 \, K = 393 \, K$

> To convert atm to Pa, multiply the pressure in atm by 1.01×10^5 (1 atm in Pa).

$PV = nRT$

$2.02 \times 10^5 \times 5.90 \times 10^{-4} = n \times 8.31 \times 393$

Rearranging the equation:

$n = \dfrac{2.02 \times 10^5 \times 5.90 \times 10^{-4}}{8.31 \times 393} = 0.0365 \, mol$

Therefore the number of moles is $0.0365 \, mol$.

> An alternative value of the gas constant and set of units can be used:
>
> **$R = 82.05 \, cm^3 \, atm \, K^{-1} \, mol^{-1}$**
> **Pressure: atm**
> **Volume: cm^3**
> **Temperature: K**
>
> The above example would have been much more straightforward with these units and value for the gas constant, but only $8.31 \, J \, K^{-1} \, mol^{-1}$ is given in the IBO Chemistry Data booklet.

A gas has a density of $1.25 \, g \, dm^{-3}$ at $0 \, °C$ and $1.01 \times 10^5 \, Pa$. Calculate its molar mass.

$density = \dfrac{mass}{volume}$

As we know the density, we know the mass of $1 \, dm^3$ of the gas. If we can find the number of moles in $1 \, dm^3$, we can work out the molar mass.

$P = 1.01 \times 10^5 \, Pa$

$V = 1.00 \, dm^3 = \dfrac{1.00}{1000} \, m^3 = 1.00 \times 10^{-3} \, m^3$

$n = ?$

$R = 8.31 \, J \, K^{-1} \, mol^{-1}$

$T = 0 \, °C = 273 \, K$

Using $PV = nRT$

$$n = \frac{1.01 \times 10^5 \times 1.00 \times 10^{-3}}{8.31 \times 273} = 0.0445\,\text{mol}$$

This number of moles has a mass of 1.25 g.

$$\text{molar mass} = \frac{\text{mass}}{\text{no. moles}}$$

$$\text{molar mass} = \frac{1.25}{0.0445} = 28.1\,\text{g mol}^{-1}$$

What is the molar volume of an ideal gas at 18 °C and 1.01×10^5 Pa? (Give your answer in $\text{m}^3\,\text{mol}^{-1}$ and $\text{dm}^3\,\text{mol}^{-1}$.)

The molar volume of a gas is the volume occupied by one mole of the gas. We are familiar with the value for the molar volume of a gas at STP, which is $22.4\,\text{dm}^3\,\text{mol}^{-1}$.

$P = 1.01 \times 10^5$ Pa $\qquad\qquad V = ?$

$n = 1.00 \qquad\qquad R = 8.31\,\text{J K}^{-1}\,\text{mol}^{-1}$

$T = 18\,°\text{C} = 18 + 273\,\text{K} = 291\,\text{K}$

Using $PV = nRT$:

$$V = \frac{1.00 \times 8.31 \times 291}{1.01 \times 10^5} = 0.0239\,\text{m}^3$$

Therefore the molar volume is $0.0239\,\text{m}^3\,\text{mol}^{-1}$ at 18 °C and 1.01×10^5 Pa. This must be multiplied by 1000 to convert to dm^3: $23.9\,\text{dm}^3\,\text{mol}^{-1}$.

When sodium nitrate(V) (often just called sodium nitrate) is heated, it decomposes to give sodium nitrate(III) (also called sodium nitrite) and oxygen gas. When a certain mass of sodium nitrate(V) is heated, 241 cm³ of oxygen is obtained, measured at 0.973 atm and 22 °C. Calculate the mass of sodium nitrate(III) formed.

$$2\text{NaNO}_3(s) \rightarrow 2\text{NaNO}_2(s) + \text{O}_2(g)$$

One way of approaching the problem is to use the equation:

$$\frac{P_1 V_1}{T_1} = \frac{P_2 V_2}{T_2}$$

to correct the volume of oxygen given off to STP and then work out the number of moles of oxygen gas using the molar volume of a gas at STP ($22.4\,\text{dm}^3\,\text{mol}^{-1}$).

Another, probably easier, way is to use $PV = nRT$ to work out the number of moles of oxygen:

$P = 0.973\,atm = 1.01 \times 10^5 \times 0.973\,Pa = 9.83 \times 10^4\,Pa$

$V = 241\,cm^3 = \dfrac{241}{1\,000\,000}\,m^3 = 2.41 \times 10^{-4}\,m^3$

$n = ?$

$R = 8.31\,J\,K^{-1}\,mol^{-1}$

$T = 22\,°C = 295\,K$

Using $PV = nRT$:

$$n = \frac{9.83 \times 10^4 \times 2.41 \times 10^{-4}}{8.31 \times 295} = 9.66 \times 10^{-3}\,mol$$

This gives the number of moles of O_2.

From the chemical equation, the number of moles of O_2 is half the number of moles of $NaNO_2$. Therefore, the number of moles of $NaNO_2$ is $9.66 \times 10^{-3} \times 2 = 1.93 \times 10^{-2}\,mol$.

The molar mass of $NaNO_2$ is $69.00\,g\,mol^{-1}$, therefore the mass of $NaNO_2$ is $69.00 \times 1.93 \times 10^{-2} = 1.33\,g$.

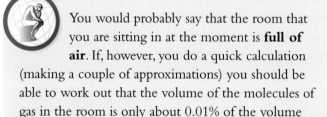

You would probably say that the room that you are sitting in at the moment is **full of air**. If, however, you do a quick calculation (making a couple of approximations) you should be able to work out that the volume of the molecules of gas in the room is only about 0.01% of the volume of the room – scientific reality is very different from our everyday reality. (There is actually a very small probability that all these molecules could at any one time all end up in the same corner of the room – our survival depends on the fact that this probability is very small!)

Self-test 11

Test yourself

In all questions, take the value of the ideal gas constant as $8.31\,J\,K^{-1}\,mol^{-1}$.

34 If a certain mass of an ideal gas occupies $20.0\,cm^3$ at $0\,°C$ and $1.01 \times 10^5\,Pa$, what volume would it occupy at $38\,°C$ and $1.06 \times 10^5\,Pa$?

35 A certain mass of an ideal gas occupies $250.0\,cm^3$ at $20\,°C$ and $9.89 \times 10^4\,Pa$. At what temperature (in $°C$) will it occupy $400.0\,cm^3$ if the pressure remains the same?

36 How many moles of an ideal gas are present in a container if it occupies a volume of $1.50\,dm^3$ at a pressure of $1.10 \times 10^5\,Pa$ and a temperature of $30\,°C$?

37 Calculate the molar mass of an ideal gas if $0.586\,g$ of the gas occupies a volume of $282\,cm^3$ at a pressure of $1.02 \times 10^5\,Pa$ and a temperature of $-18\,°C$.

38 What is the molar volume of an ideal gas at $1.10 \times 10^5\,Pa$ and $100\,°C$?

39 Copper nitrate decomposes when heated according to the equation:

$2Cu(NO_3)_2(s) \rightarrow 2CuO(s) + 4NO_2(g) + O_2(g)$

If $1.80\,g$ of copper nitrate is heated and the gases collected at a temperature of $22\,°C$ and $105\,kPa$:

a what volume (in dm^3) of oxygen is collected?

b what is the total volume of gas collected in cm^3?

40 When a certain mass of Mn_2O_7 decomposed, it produced $127.8\,cm^3$ of oxygen measured at $18\,°C$ and $1.00 \times 10^5\,Pa$. What mass of Mn_2O_7 decomposed?

$2Mn_2O_7(aq) \rightarrow 4MnO_2(s) + 3O_2(g)$

Learning objectives

- Understand what is meant by **solute**, **solvent** and **concentration**
- Solve problems involving solutions

Solutions in water are given the symbol (**aq**) in chemical equations.
aq = aqueous

Reported values for the concentration of gold in seawater vary greatly. A value of about 2×10^{-11} g dm^{-3} or 1×10^{-13} mol dm^{-3} is probably a reasonable estimate. The volume of water in the oceans is estimated as about 1.3×10^{21} dm^3, so there is an awful lot of gold in the oceans. Many people (including Nobel Prize-winning scientist Fritz Haber) have tried to come up with ways to extract the gold. The problem is that the concentrations are so low.

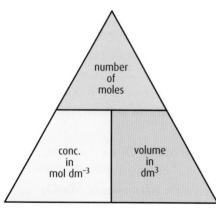

Figure 1.15 The relationship between concentration (conc.), number of moles and volume of solution.

1.7 Calculations involving solutions

Solutions

Solute: a substance that is dissolved in another substance.
Solvent: a substance that dissolves another substance (the solute). The solvent should be present in excess of the solute.
Solution: the substance that is formed when a solute dissolves in a solvent.

Thus, when a sodium chloride solution is prepared, sodium chloride solid (the solute) is dissolved in water (the solvent).

Note: when a solute is dissolved in a certain volume of water, say 100.0 cm^3, the total volume of the solution is not simply 100.0 cm^3, i.e. the sum of the volumes occupied by the solute and the volume of the solvent. The total volume of solution produced will be dependent on the forces of attraction between the solute particles and the solvent particles compared with the forces of attraction in the original solvent. This is why concentration is defined in terms of the volume of the solution rather than the volume of the solvent.

The **concentration** of a solution is the amount of solute dissolved in a unit volume of **solution**. The volume that is usually taken is 1 dm^3. The amount of solute may be expressed in g or mol; therefore the units of concentration are g dm^{-3} or mol dm^{-3}.

Concentrations are sometimes written with the unit **M**, which means mol dm^{-3} but is described as 'molar'. Thus 2 M would refer to a '2 molar solution', i.e. a solution of concentration 2 mol dm^{-3}.

The relationship between concentration, number of moles and volume of solution is:

$$\text{concentration (mol dm}^{-3}) = \frac{\text{no. moles (mol)}}{\text{volume (dm}^3)}$$

This is summarised in Figure **1.15**.

If the concentration is expressed in g dm^{-3}, the relationship is:

$$\text{concentration (g dm}^{-3}) = \frac{\text{mass (g)}}{\text{volume (dm}^3)}$$

Worked examples

If 10.00 g of NaOH is dissolved in water and the volume is made up to 200.0 cm³, calculate the concentration in $mol\,dm^{-3}$ and $g\,dm^{-3}$.

Concentration ($g\,dm^{-3}$)

$$\text{concentration in } g\,dm^{-3} = \frac{\text{mass}}{\text{volume in } dm^3}$$

$$\text{volume in } dm^3 = \frac{200.0}{1000} = 0.2000\,dm^3$$

$$\text{concentration} = \frac{10.00}{0.2000} = 50.00\,g\,dm^{-3}$$

Concentration ($mol\,dm^{-3}$)

molar mass of NaOH $= 40.00\,g\,mol^{-1}$

$$\text{no. moles} = \frac{10.00}{40.00} = 0.2500\,mol$$

$$\text{concentration } (mol\,dm^{-3}) = \frac{\text{no. moles}}{\text{volume in } dm^3}$$

$$\text{concentration} = \frac{0.2500}{0.2000} = 1.250\,mol\,dm^{-3}$$

Alternatively, once we had the concentration in $g\,dm^{-3}$ we could simply divide by the molar mass to get the concentration in $mol\,dm^{-3}$:

$$\text{concentration } (mol\,dm^{-3}) = \frac{50.00}{40.00} = 1.250\,mol\,dm^{-3}$$

Calculate the number of moles of HCl present in 50.0 cm³ of 2.00 $mol\,dm^{-3}$ hydrochloric acid.

$$\text{no. moles} = \text{concentration} \times \text{volume in } dm^3$$

$$\text{no. moles} = 2.00 \times \frac{50}{1000} = 0.100\,mol$$

Therefore the number of moles is 0.100 mol.

Working out the concentration of ions

When ionic substances (see page **89**) dissolve in water, the substance breaks apart into its constituent ions. So, for instance, when copper chloride ($CuCl_2$) dissolves in water, it splits apart into Cu^{2+} and Cl^- ions:

$$CuCl_2(aq) \rightarrow Cu^{2+}(aq) + 2Cl^-(aq)$$

Therefore when 0.100 mol $CuCl_2$ dissolves in water, 2×0.100 mol, i.e. 0.200 mol, Cl^- ions are produced. The concentration of the chloride ions is twice the concentration of the $CuCl_2$.

Worked example

Calculate the number of moles of chloride ions present in $50.0\,\text{cm}^3$ of a $0.0500\,\text{mol}\,\text{dm}^{-3}$ solution of iron(III) chloride ($FeCl_3$) and the total concentration of all the ions present.

no. moles $=$ concentration $\times$ volume in dm^3

$$\text{no. moles of } FeCl_3 = \frac{50.0}{1000} \times 0.0500 = 2.50 \times 10^{-3}\,\text{mol } FeCl_3$$

$$FeCl_3(aq) \rightarrow Fe^{3+}(aq) + 3Cl^-(aq)$$

Therefore dissolving $2.50 \times 10^{-3}\,\text{mol } FeCl_3$ produces $3 \times 2.50 \times 10^{-3}\,\text{mol } Cl^-(aq)$, i.e. $7.50 \times 10^{-3}\,\text{mol } Cl^-(aq)$.

Therefore the number of moles of chloride ions present is $7.50 \times 10^{-3}\,\text{mol}$.

When one $FeCl_3$ unit dissolves in water, four ions are produced ($Fe^{3+} + 3Cl^-$)

Therefore the total concentration of the ions present is four times the concentration of the $FeCl_3$, i.e. $4 \times 0.0500\,\text{mol}\,\text{dm}^{-3}$

Therefore the total concentration of ions present is $0.200\,\text{mol}\,\text{dm}^{-3}$.

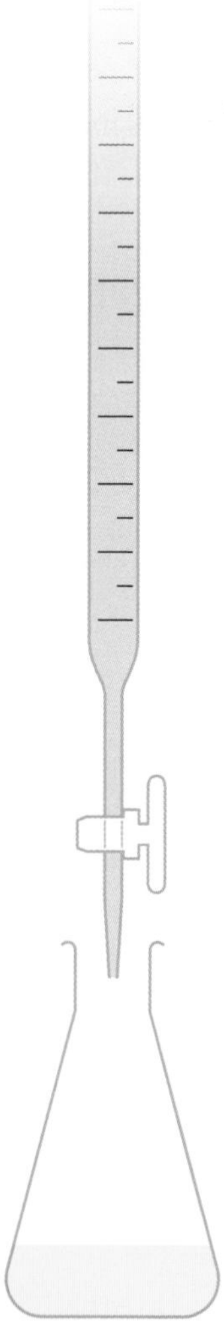

Titrations

Titrations

Titration is a technique for finding out the volumes of solutions that react exactly with each other. One solution is added from a burette to another solution in a conical flask (Figure **1.16**). An indicator is usually required to determine the end point of the titration.

Worked example

Sulfuric acid is titrated against $25.00\,\text{cm}^3$ of $0.2000\,\text{mol}\,\text{dm}^{-3}$ sodium hydroxide solution; $23.20\,\text{cm}^3$ of sulfuric acid is required for neutralisation. Calculate the concentration of the sulfuric acid.

$$2NaOH(aq) + H_2SO_4(aq) \rightarrow Na_2SO_4(aq) + 2H_2O(l)$$

Step 1 – work out the number of moles of sodium hydroxide.

no. moles $=$ concentration $\times$ volume in dm^3

$$\text{no. moles} = 0.2000 \times \frac{25.00}{1000} = 5.000 \times 10^{-3}\,\text{mol}$$

Step 2 – the chemical equation tells us that $2\,\text{mol}$ NaOH react with $1\,\text{mol}$ H_2SO_4. Therefore $5.000 \times 10^{-3}\,\text{mol}$ NaOH react with $\dfrac{5.000 \times 10^{-3}}{2}\,\text{mol}$ H_2SO_4, i.e. $2.500 \times 10^{-3}\,\text{mol}$ H_2SO_4. This is the number of moles of H_2SO_4 in $23.20\,\text{cm}^3$ of sulfuric acid.

Figure 1.16 Titration set up.

Step 3 – convert number of moles to concentration:

$$\text{concentration (mol dm}^{-3}) = \frac{\text{no. moles}}{\text{volume in dm}^3}$$

$$23.20\,\text{cm}^3 = \frac{23.20}{1000}\,\text{dm}^3 = 0.023\,20\,\text{dm}^3$$

$$\text{concentration} = \frac{2.500 \times 10^{-3}}{0.023\,20} = 0.1078\,\text{mol dm}^{-3}$$

Therefore the concentration of the H_2SO_4 is $0.1078\,\text{mol dm}^{-3}$.

Equation for solving moles questions involving solutions

The following equation may be used as an alternative method for solving problems:

$$\frac{c_1 v_1}{n_1} = \frac{c_2 v_2}{n_2}$$

Note: there is no need to convert the volume to dm^3 when this equation is used.

where:
  c_1 = concentration of first substance
  v_1 = volume of first substance
  n_1 = coefficient of first substance
  c_2 = concentration of second substance
  v_2 = volume of second substance
  n_2 = coefficient of second substance

Worked example

For neutralisation, $25.00\,\text{cm}^3$ of phosphoric(V) acid (H_3PO_4) requires $28.70\,\text{cm}^3$ of NaOH of concentration $0.1500\,\text{mol dm}^{-3}$. What is the concentration of the phosphoric(V) acid?

$$H_3PO_4(aq) + 3NaOH(aq) \rightarrow Na_3PO_4(aq) + 3H_2O(l)$$

Let H_3PO_4 be substance 1 and NaOH be substance 2.

$c_1 = ?$ $c_2 = 0.1500\,\text{mol dm}^{-3}$
$v_1 = 25.00\,\text{cm}^3$ $v_2 = 28.70\,\text{cm}^3$
$n_1 = 1$ $n_2 = 3$

$$\frac{c_1 v_1}{n_1} = \frac{c_2 v_2}{n_2}$$

$$\frac{c_1 \times 25.00}{1} = \frac{0.1500 \times 28.70}{3}$$

Rearranging the equation: $c_1 = \dfrac{1 \times 0.1500 \times 28.70}{3 \times 25.00} = 0.057\,40\,\text{mol dm}^{-3}$

Therefore the concentration of H_3PO_4 is $0.057\,40\,\text{mol dm}^{-3}$.

Combined equation for solving moles questions

This equation may be used to solve moles questions involving any combination of concentration, mass and volume of gas:

Note: volume must be converted to dm³ when this combined equation is used.

$$\frac{c_1 v_1}{n_1} = \frac{m_2}{n_2 M_2} = \frac{V_3}{n_3 M_v}$$

where:

c_1 = concentration of first substance (mol dm^{-3})
v_1 = volume of first substance **in dm^3**
n_1 = coefficient of first substance

m_2 = mass of second substance
n_2 = coefficient of second substance
M_2 = molar mass of second substance

V_3 = volume (**in dm^3**) of third substance if it is a **gas**
n_3 = coefficient of third substance
M_v = molar volume of a gas = 22.4 dm^3 at STP

Worked example

Acidified potassium manganate(VII) oxidises hydrogen peroxide to produce oxygen:

$$2KMnO_4(aq) + 3H_2SO_4(aq) + 5H_2O_2(aq) \rightarrow 2MnSO_4(aq) + 8H_2O(l) + K_2SO_4(aq) + 5O_2(g)$$

If 45.00 cm^3 of 0.020 00 mol dm^{-3} KMnO$_4$ is reacted with excess H$_2$O$_2$ and H$_2$SO$_4$, calculate the volume of O$_2$ produced (at STP).

We can use the combined equation:

$$\frac{c_1 v_1}{n_1} = \frac{V_2}{n_2 M_v}$$

Let KMnO$_4$ be substance 1 and O$_2$ be substance 2.

$c_1 = 0.020\,00$ mol dm^{-3}

$v_1 = 45.00$ cm$^3 = \dfrac{45.00}{1000}$ dm$^3 = 0.045\,00$ dm^3

As we are using a combined equation, the volume must be converted to dm^3.

$n_1 = 2 \qquad V_2 = ? \qquad n_2 = 5 \qquad M_v = 22.4$ dm^3 mol^{-1} at STP

$$\frac{0.020\,00 \times 0.045\,00}{2} = \frac{V_2}{5 \times 22.4}$$

Rearranging the equation:

$$V_2 = \frac{0.020\,00 \times 0.045\,00 \times 5 \times 22.4}{2} = 0.050\,40 \text{ dm}^3$$

Therefore the volume of oxygen produced is 0.050 40 dm^3 or 50.40 cm^3.

41 a What mass of sodium sulfate (Na_2SO_4) must be used to make up $250\,cm^3$ of a $0.100\,mol\,dm^{-3}$ solution?

  b What is the concentration of sodium ions in the solution in **a**?

42 Work out the numbers of moles present in the following solutions:

  a $20.0\,cm^3$ of $0.220\,mol\,dm^{-3}$ $NaOH(aq)$

  b $27.8\,cm^3$ of $0.0840\,mol\,dm^{-3}$ $HCl(aq)$

  c $540\,cm^3$ of $0.0200\,mol\,dm^{-3}$ $KMnO_4(aq)$

43 If $29.70\,cm^3$ of sulfuric acid of concentration $0.2000\,mol\,dm^{-3}$ is required for neutralisation of $25.00\,cm^3$ of potassium hydroxide solution, calculate the concentration of the potassium hydroxide solution.

  $2KOH(aq) + H_2SO_4(aq) \rightarrow K_2SO_4(aq) + 2H_2O(l)$

44 Calcium carbonate is reacted with $50.0\,cm^3$ of $0.500\,mol\,dm^{-3}$ hydrochloric acid.

  $CaCO_3(s) + 2HCl(aq)$
  $\rightarrow CaCl_2(aq) + CO_2(g) + H_2O(l)$

  a What mass of calcium carbonate is required for an exact reaction?

  b What volume of CO_2, measured at STP, will be produced?

45 What volume (in cm^3) of $0.0100\,mol\,dm^{-3}$ barium chloride must be reacted with excess sodium sulfate to produce $0.100\,g$ of barium sulfate?

  $BaCl_2(aq) + Na_2SO_4(aq)$
  $\rightarrow BaSO_4(s) + 2NaCl(aq)$

46 If $0.100\,g$ of magnesium is reacted with $25.00\,cm^3$ of $0.200\,mol\,dm^{-3}$ hydrochloric acid, calculate the volume of hydrogen gas produced at STP.

  $Mg(s) + 2HCl(aq) \rightarrow MgCl_2(aq) + H_2(g)$

Water of crystallisation

Some substances crystallise with water as an integral part of the crystal lattice. Examples are $CuSO_4.5H_2O$ and $MgCl_2.6H_2O$. The water is necessary for the formation of the crystals and is called **water of crystallisation**. Substances that contain water of crystallisation are described as **hydrated**, whereas those that have lost their water of crystallisation are described as **anhydrous**. Thus, we talk about 'hydrated copper sulfate' ($CuSO_4.5H_2O$) and 'anhydrous copper sulfate' ($CuSO_4$). Hydrated copper sulfate can be obtained as large blue crystals, but anhydrous copper sulfate is white and powdery.

In the case of hydrated copper sulfate, the water can be removed by heating:

$$CuSO_4.5H_2O \xrightarrow{\text{heat}} CuSO_4 + 5H_2O$$

However, this is not always the case. When hydrated magnesium chloride is heated, magnesium oxide is formed:

$$MgCl_2.6H_2O \xrightarrow{\text{heat}} MgO + 2HCl + 5H_2O$$

Worked examples

When 2.56 g hydrated magnesium sulfate ($MgSO_4.xH_2O$) is heated, 1.25 g of anhydrous magnesium sulfate ($MgSO_4$) is formed. Determine the value of x in the formula.

mass of water given off = 2.56 − 1.25, i.e. 1.31 g

mass of $MgSO_4$ = 1.25 g

This is now basically just an empirical formula question, and we need to find the ratio between the number of moles of $MgSO_4$ and H_2O.

molar mass of H_2O = 18.02 g mol^{-1} | molar mass of $MgSO_4$ = 120.37 g mol^{-1}

no. moles of $H_2O = \dfrac{1.31}{18.02} = 0.0727$ mol | no. moles of $MgSO_4 = \dfrac{1.25}{120.37} = 0.0104$ mol

Divide by smaller number to get the ratio:

$$\frac{0.0727}{0.0104} = 7$$

Therefore, the value of x is 7, and the formula of hydrated magnesium sulfate is $MgSO_4.7H_2O$.

a If 10.00 g of hydrated copper sulfate ($CuSO_4.5H_2O$) is dissolved in water and made up to a volume of 250.0 cm^3, what is the concentration of the solution?
b What mass of anhydrous copper sulfate would be required to make 250.0 cm^3 of solution with the same concentration as in **a**?

a molar mass of $CuSO_4.5H_2O$ = 249.71 g mol^{-1}

no. moles $CuSO_4.5H_2O = \dfrac{10.00}{249.71} = 0.040\,05$ mol

$$\text{concentration} = \frac{\text{no. moles}}{\text{volume in dm}^3} = \frac{0.040\,05}{0.2500} = 0.1602 \text{ mol dm}^{-3}$$

> When a hydrated salt is dissolved in water, the water of crystallisation just becomes part of the solvent, and the solution is the same as if the anhydrous salt were dissolved in water.

Therefore, dissolving 10.00 g of hydrated copper sulfate in water and making up the solution to 250.0 cm^3 produces a copper sulfate solution of concentration 0.1602 mol dm^{-3}.

b The number of moles of $CuSO_4$ present in 250.0 cm^3 solution will be exactly the same as above, i.e. 0.040 05 mol, as the concentration is the same.

> 0.040 05 mol $CuSO_4.5H_2O$ contains 0.040 05 mol $CuSO_4$

molar mass of $CuSO_4$ = 159.61 g mol^{-1}

mass of $CuSO_4$ = molar mass × no. moles = 159.61 × 0.040 05 = 6.392 g

Therefore the mass of anhydrous copper sulfate required to make 250 cm^3 of a solution of concentration 0.1602 mol dm^{-3} is 6.392 g, as opposed to 10.00 g of hydrated copper sulfate. The two solutions will be identical.

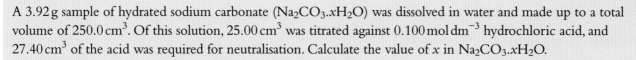

A 3.92 g sample of hydrated sodium carbonate ($Na_2CO_3.xH_2O$) was dissolved in water and made up to a total volume of $250.0\,cm^3$. Of this solution, $25.00\,cm^3$ was titrated against $0.100\,mol\,dm^{-3}$ hydrochloric acid, and $27.40\,cm^3$ of the acid was required for neutralisation. Calculate the value of x in $Na_2CO_3.xH_2O$.

$$Na_2CO_3(aq) + 2HCl(aq) \rightarrow 2NaCl(aq) + CO_2(g) + H_2O(l)$$

Step 1 – work out the number of moles of HCl:

no. moles = concentration × volume in dm^3

$$\text{no. moles} = 0.100 \times \frac{27.40}{1000} = 2.74 \times 10^{-3}\,mol$$

Step 2 – the chemical equation tells us that 2 mol HCl react with 1 mol Na_2CO_3. Therefore 2.74×10^{-3} mol HCl react with $\dfrac{2.74 \times 10^{-3}}{2} = 1.37 \times 10^{-3}$ mol Na_2CO_3. This is the number of moles of Na_2CO_3 in $25.00\,cm^3$.

The original mass of $Na_2CO_3.xH_2O$ was dissolved in a total volume of $250.0\,cm^3$. Therefore the number of moles of Na_2CO_3 in $250.0\,cm^3$ of solution is $1.37 \times 10^{-3} \times 10$, i.e. 1.37×10^{-2} mol.

Step 3 – convert number of moles to mass.

molar mass of $Na_2CO_3 = 105.99\,g\,mol^{-1}$

mass of 1.37×10^{-2} mol Na_2CO_3 = no. moles × molar mass

mass of $Na_2CO_3 = 1.37 \times 10^{-2} \times 105.99 = 1.45\,g$

The total mass of $Na_2CO_3.xH_2O = 3.92\,g$. The mass of this that is due to the water of crystallisation $= 3.92 - 1.45 = 2.47\,g$.

$$\text{no. moles of water of crystallisation} = \frac{\text{mass}}{\text{molar mass}} = \frac{2.74}{18.02} = 0.137\,mol$$

The ratio of the number of moles of water of crystallisation : moles of sodium carbonate can be worked out by dividing the number of moles of water by the number of moles of sodium carbonate:

$$\text{ratio} = \frac{0.137}{1.37 \times 10^{-2}} = 10$$

Therefore the value of x is 10, and the formula for the hydrated sodium carbonate is $Na_2CO_3.10H_2O$.

If sodium sulfate(IV) (sodium sulfite) is boiled with excess sulfur, sodium thiosulfate is obtained:

$$Na_2SO_3(aq) + S(s) \rightarrow Na_2S_2O_3(aq)$$

The mixture is filtered to remove excess sulfur and allowed to crystallise to obtain hydrated sodium thiosulfate ($Na_2S_2O_3.5H_2O$). If $100.0\,cm^3$ of $0.5000\,mol\,dm^{-3}$ sodium sulfate(IV) is used, what is the maximum mass of hydrated sodium thiosulfate crystals that can be formed?

Step 1 – work out the number of moles of Na_2SO_3:

no. moles = concentration × volume in dm^3

no. moles = $0.5000 \times \dfrac{100.0}{1000} = 0.05000\,mol$

Step 2 – the chemical equation tells us that 1 mol Na_2SO_3 produces 1 mol $Na_2S_2O_3$. Therefore 0.05000 mol Na_2SO_3 produces 0.05000 mol $Na_2S_2O_3$.

Step 3 – convert number of moles to mass.

0.05000 mol $Na_2S_2O_3$ crystallises to give 0.05000 mol $Na_2S_2O_3.5H_2O$

molar mass of $Na_2S_2O_3.5H_2O = 248.20\,g\,mol^{-1}$

mass of $Na_2S_2O_3.5H_2O$ = no. moles × molar mass

mass of $Na_2S_2O_3.5H_2O = 0.05000 \times 248.20 = 12.41\,g$

Therefore 12.41 g of $Na_2S_2O_3.5H_2O$ could be obtained.

Back titration

This is a technique by which a known excess of a particular reagent, A, is added to a substance, X, so that they react, and then the excess A is titrated against another reagent to work out how much A reacted with the substance and therefore how many moles of X were present. This is useful when X is an impure substance.

Worked example

Limestone is impure calcium carbonate ($CaCO_3$): 2.00 g of limestone is put into a beaker and 60.00 cm^3 of 3.000 mol dm^{-3} hydrochloric acid is added. They are left to react and then the impurities are filtered off and the solution is made up to a total volume of 100.0 cm^3. Of this solution, 25.00 cm^3 requires 35.50 cm^3 of 1.000 mol dm^{-3} sodium hydroxide for neutralisation. Work out the percentage $CaCO_3$ in the limestone (assume that none of the impurities reacts with hydrochloric acid).

Let us consider the first part of the question: **2.00 g of limestone is put into a beaker and 60.00 cm^3 of 3.000 mol dm^{-3} hydrochloric acid is added:**

$CaCO_3 + 2HCl \rightarrow CaCl_2 + CO_2 + H_2O$

As the limestone is impure, we cannot work out the number of moles of $CaCO_3$ present, but we have enough information to work out the number of moles of HCl:

no. moles of HCl = concentration × volume in dm^3

no. moles of HCl = $3.000 \times \dfrac{60.00}{1000} = 0.1800\,mol$

If the limestone were pure $CaCO_3$, the number of moles present in 2.00 g would be 0.0200 mol, which would react with 0.0400 mol HCl.

This is excess HCl, and when the limestone is reacted with it there will be HCl left over.

The second part of the question is: **They are left to react and then . . . the solution is made up to a total volume of $100.0\,cm^3$.**

This $100.0\,cm^3$ of solution now contains the HCl left over after it has reacted with the $CaCO_3$.

In order to work out the number of moles of HCl that did not react, we must consider the third part of the question: **Of this solution, $25.00\,cm^3$ requires $35.50\,cm^3$ of $1.000\,mol\,dm^{-3}$ sodium hydroxide for neutralisation:**

no. moles of sodium hydroxide = concentration × volume in dm^3

no. moles of sodium hydroxide $= 1.000 \times \dfrac{35.50}{1000} = 0.035\,50\,mol$

This reacts with HCl according to the equation:

$$NaOH + HCl \rightarrow NaCl + H_2O$$

Therefore $0.035\,50\,mol\,NaOH$ reacts with $0.035\,50\,mol\,HCl$. This means that $25.00\,cm^3$ of the HCl solution contained $0.035\,50\,mol\,HCl$. Therefore in $100.0\,cm^3$ of this solution there were $4 \times 0.035\,50$, i.e. $0.1420\,mol$, of HCl. This is the number of moles of HCl left over after it has reacted with the $CaCO_3$.

As $0.1800\,mol\,HCl$ was originally added to the limestone, the amount that reacted with the $CaCO_3$ was $0.1800 - 0.1420$, i.e. $0.0380\,mol$.

$$CaCO_3 + 2HCl \rightarrow CaCl_2 + CO_2 + H_2O$$

$0.0380\,mol\,HCl$ reacts with $\dfrac{0.0380}{2}$, i.e. 0.0190, mol $CaCO_3$

molar mass of $CaCO_3 = 100.09\,g\,mol^{-1}$

mass of $CaCO_3$ = no. moles × molar mass $= 100.09 \times 0.0190 = 1.90\,g$

% $CaCO_3$ in the limestone $= \dfrac{1.90}{2.00} \times 100 = 95.0\%$

Linked reactions

Sometimes the product of one reaction becomes the reactant in a second reaction. A common example of this is the determination of the concentration of copper ions in solution using sodium thiosulfate.

Worked examples

A $25.0\,cm^3$ sample of a solution of copper(II) nitrate is added to $10.0\,cm^3$ of $1\,mol\,dm^{-3}$ potassium iodide. The iodine produced is titrated against $0.0200\,mol\,dm^{-3}$ sodium thiosulfate solution using starch indicator near the end point. $22.50\,cm^3$ of the sodium thiosulfate solution was required for the titration. Calculate the concentration of the copper(II) nitrate solution.

The initial reaction of copper ions with iodide ions is:

$$2Cu^{2+}(aq) + 4I^-(aq) \rightarrow 2CuI(s) + I_2(aq) \quad \textbf{(reaction 1)}$$

A large excess of iodide ions is added to make sure that all the copper ions react. A precipitate of copper(I) iodide is formed as well as the iodine. If we can determine the number of moles of iodine produced in the solution, we can also find the number of moles of copper ions.

The number of moles of iodine is determined by titration with sodium thiosulfate solution:

$$2S_2O_3^{2-}(aq) + I_2(aq) \rightarrow 2I^-(aq) + S_4O_6^{2-}(aq) \quad \textbf{(reaction 2)}$$
thiosulfate ion   tetrathionate ion

The number of moles of thiosulfate in $22.50\,cm^3$ of $0.0200\,mol\,dm^{-3}$ solution:

$$\text{no. moles} = \text{volume in } dm^3 \times \text{concentration} = \frac{22.50}{1000} \times 0.0200 = 4.50 \times 10^{-4}\,mol\,S_2O_3^{2-}$$

From equation **2** we can see that $2\,mol\,S_2O_3^{2-}$ react with $1\,mol\,I_2$. Therefore $4.50 \times 10^{-4}\,mol\,S_2O_3^{2-}$ react with $\dfrac{4.50 \times 10^{-4}}{2}\,mol\,I_2$, i.e. $2.25 \times 10^{-4}\,mol\,I_2$. This is therefore the amount of iodine produced in reaction **1**.

From equation **1**, $2\,mol\,Cu^{2+}$ produce $1\,mol\,I_2$, so the number of moles of Cu^{2+} is twice the number of moles of I_2. Therefore the number of moles of Cu^{2+} is $2 \times 2.25 \times 10^{-4}$, i.e. $4.50 \times 10^{-4}\,mol$.

From equation **1**, $2\,mol\,Cu^{2+}$ react to form $1\,mol\,I_2$. In equation **2**, $1\,mol\,I_2$ reacts with $2\,mol\,S_2O_3^{2-}$. Therefore, overall, $1\,mol\,Cu^{2+}$ is equivalent to $1\,mol\,S_2O_3^{2-}$.

The volume of the solution containing copper ions was $25.0\,cm^3$, and this allows us to work out the concentration:

$$\text{concentration} = \frac{\text{no. moles}}{\text{volume in } dm^3} = \frac{4.50 \times 10^{-4}}{0.0250} = 0.0180\,mol\,dm^{-3}$$

Therefore the concentration of the copper(II) nitrate solution was $0.0180\,mol\,dm^{-3}$.

Once we realise the relationship between the Cu^{2+} in equation **1** and the $S_2O_3^{2-}$ in equation **2**, the question becomes much simpler. A quicker approach to the question is as follows:

$$2Cu^{2+}(aq) + 4I^-(aq) \rightarrow 2CuI(s) + I_2(aq) \quad \textbf{(reaction 1)}$$

$$2S_2O_3^{2-}(aq) + I_2(aq) \rightarrow 2I^-(aq) + S_4O_6^{2-}(aq) \quad \textbf{(reaction 2)}$$

As it is the I_2 that links both the equations, and the coefficient of I_2 is the same in both equations, we can use the coefficients of Cu^{2+} and $S_2O_3^{2-}$ directly.

Let Cu^{2+} be substance 1 and $S_2O_3^{2-}$ be substance 2.

$c_1 = ?$ $c_2 = 0.0200\,mol\,dm^{-3}$

$v_1 = 25.00\,cm^3$ $v_2 = 22.50\,cm^3$

$n_1 = 2$ $n_2 = 2$

$$\frac{c_1 v_1}{n_1} = \frac{c_2 v_2}{n_2}$$

$$c_1 \times \frac{25.00}{2} = \frac{0.0200 \times 22.50}{2}$$

Rearranging the equation:

$$c_1 = \frac{0.0200 \times 22.50}{25.00} = 0.0180\,\text{mol}\,\text{dm}^{-3} \text{ as above}$$

If the coefficients of I_2 were different in the two equations, we would not simply be able to take the coefficients of Cu^{2+} and $S_2O_3^{2-}$ directly. This is considered in the next worked example.

Hydrogen bromide can be formed from red phosphorus by the following reactions:

$2P + 3Br_2 \rightarrow 2PBr_3$ (**reaction 1**)

$PBr_3 + 3H_2O \rightarrow H_3PO_3 + 3HBr$ (**reaction 2**)

Calculate the volume of HBr (measured at STP) produced when 0.500 g of phosphorus is reacted. Assume all other reagents are in excess.

The phosphorus(III) bromide formed in the first reaction reacts further with water in the second reaction to form HBr. In the first equation 2 mol P produce 2 mol PBr_3; however, in the second equation 1 mol PBr_3 reacts further to produce 3 mol HBr.

If we multiply the second equation by 2 so that the coefficient of PBr_3 matches between the equations, we can immediately see the relationship between the coefficients of P and HBr:

$2P + 3Br_2 \rightarrow 2PBr_3$ (**reaction 1**)

$2PBr_3 + 6H_2O \rightarrow 2H_3PO_3 + 6HBr$ (**reaction 2**)   2 mol P produce 6 mol HBr.

$$\frac{m_1}{n_1 M_1} = \frac{V_2}{n_2 M_v}$$

Let P be substance 1 and HBr substance 2.

$m_1 = 0.500\,\text{g}$ $V_2 = ?$

$n_1 = 2$ $n_2 = 6$

$M_1 = 30.97\,\text{g}\,\text{mol}^{-1}$ $M_v = 22.4\,\text{dm}^3$ at STP

$$\frac{0.500}{2 \times 30.97} = \frac{V_2}{6 \times 22.4}$$

Rearranging the equation:

$$V_2 = \frac{0.500 \times 6 \times 22.4}{2 \times 30.97}$$ The volume is in dm^3 because the molar volume was in $\text{dm}^3\,\text{mol}^{-1}$.

$$V_2 = 1.08\,\text{dm}^3$$

Therefore the volume of HBr produced is $1.08\,\text{dm}^3$.

More examples of question types

Some questions can look very difficult at first sight, but a good place to start is to work out the number of moles of whatever you can and see where you can go from there.

Worked examples

A solution of a chloride of formula MCl_x (concentration $0.0170\,\text{mol}\,\text{dm}^{-3}$) reacts with silver nitrate solution to precipitate silver chloride; $25.0\,\text{cm}^3$ of $0.0110\,\text{mol}\,\text{dm}^{-3}$ silver nitrate solution reacts with $5.40\,\text{cm}^3$ of the chloride solution.

a Calculate the number of moles of silver nitrate.
b Calculate the number of moles of the chloride.
c Calculate the formula of the chloride.

a no. moles = concentration × volume in dm^3

$$\text{no. moles of AgNO}_3 = \frac{25.0}{1000} \times 0.0110 = 2.75 \times 10^{-4}\,\text{mol}$$

b $\text{no. moles of MCl}_x = \dfrac{5.40}{1000} \times 0.0170 = 9.18 \times 10^{-5}\,\text{mol}$

c The general equation for the reaction here is:

$$MCl_x(aq) + xAgNO_3(aq) \rightarrow xAgCl(s) + M(NO_3)_x(aq)$$

The silver ions in the solution react with the chloride ions to precipitate silver chloride. The ratio of the number of moles of $AgNO_3$ to the number of moles of MCl_x will give us the value of x.

$$\frac{\text{no. moles of AgNO}_3}{\text{no. moles of MCl}_x} = \frac{2.75 \times 10^{-4}}{9.18 \times 10^{-5}} = 3$$

Therefore the value of x is 3, and the formula of the chloride is MCl_3.

One of the stages in the extraction of arsenic, antimony and bismuth from their ores involves the roasting of the sulfide in oxygen.

$$2M_2S_3 + 9O_2 \rightarrow 2M_2O_3 + 6SO_2$$

A certain mass of the sulfide reacted with $180.0\,\text{cm}^3$ of oxygen gas, measured at $15\,°C$ and $1.00\,\text{atm}$ pressure to produce $0.335\,\text{g}$ of M_2O_3. Determine the identity of the element M.

The first stage is to convert the volume of oxygen to a volume at STP. As the pressure is already $1.00\,\text{atm}$, this is most easily done using:

$$\frac{P_1V_1}{T_1} = \frac{P_2V_2}{T_2}$$

$P_1 = 1.00\,\text{atm}$ $P_2 = 1.00\,\text{atm}$
$V_1 = 180.0\,\text{cm}^3$ $V_2 = ?$
$T_1 = 15\,°C = 288\,K$ $T_2 = 0\,°C = 273\,K$

As the initial and final pressures are the same, the equation simplifies to:

$$\frac{V_1}{T_1} = \frac{V_2}{T_2}$$

$$\frac{180.0}{288} = \frac{V_2}{273}$$

$$V_2 = \frac{180.0 \times 273}{288} = 171\,\text{cm}^3$$

This value should be quoted to three significant figures, as the least number of significant figures in the equation was three; however, more significant figures will be carried through on the calculator.

Therefore, at STP the volume of oxygen would have been $171\,\text{cm}^3$, i.e. $0.171\,\text{dm}^3$.

The number of moles of oxygen can now be worked out:

$$\text{no. moles} = \frac{\text{volume in dm}^3}{22.4}$$

The number of moles of oxygen could have also been worked out directly by using $PV = nRT$.

$$\text{no. moles of oxygen} = \frac{0.171}{22.4} = 7.63 \times 10^{-3}\,\text{mol}$$

Now that we have the number of moles of oxygen, we can use the chemical equation to work out the number of moles of M_2O_3.

From the chemical equation, $9\,\text{mol}\ O_2$ react to form $2\,\text{mol}\ M_2O_3$. Therefore, the number of moles of M_2O_3 is two-ninths of the number of moles of O_2.

$$\text{no. moles of } M_2O_3 = \tfrac{2}{9} \times 7.62 \times 10^{-3} = 1.69 \times 10^{-3}\,\text{mol}$$

Now that we have the number of moles and the mass of M_2O_3, we can work out the molar mass:

$$\text{molar mass} = \frac{\text{mass}}{\text{no. moles}} = \frac{0.335}{1.69 \times 10^{-3}} = 198\,\text{g mol}^{-1}$$

The formula of the compound is M_2O_3, and the molar mass is $198\,\text{g mol}^{-1}$. The relative atomic mass of M can be worked out by taking away three times the relative atomic mass of O and then dividing the answer by 2.

$$\text{mass of } M_2 = 198 - (3 \times 16) = 150$$

$$\text{relative atomic mass of M} = \frac{150}{2} = 75$$

This value is closest to the relative atomic mass of arsenic, 74.92; therefore the element M is arsenic.

Exam-style questions

1 What is the total number of atoms in 1.80 g of water (H_2O)?

    A 6.02×10^{22} **B** 6.02×10^{23} **C** 1.80×10^{23} **D** 1.80×10^{24}

2 88 kg of CO_2 contains

    A 2.0 mol   **B** 2000 mol   **C** 0.50 mol   **D** 3872 mol

3 What is the sum of the coefficients when the following equation is balanced with the smallest possible whole numbers?

    $CuFeS_2 + O_2 \rightarrow Cu_2S + SO_2 + FeO$

    A 7   **B** 8   **C** 11   **D** 12

4 Iron(III) oxide reacts with carbon monoxide according to the equation:

    $Fe_2O_3 + 3CO \rightarrow 2Fe + 3CO_2$

    How many moles of iron are produced when 180 mol of carbon monoxide react with excess iron(III) oxide?

    A 120 mol   **B** 180 mol   **C** 270 mol   **D** 360 mol

5 Propene undergoes complete combustion to produce carbon dioxide and water

    $2C_3H_6(g) + 9O_2(g) \rightarrow 6CO_2(g) + 6H_2O(l)$

    What volume of CO_2 is produced when 360 cm^3 of propene reacts with 360 cm^3 of oxygen at 273 K and 1 atm pressure?

    A 120 cm^3 **B** 240 cm^3 **C** 540 cm^3 **D** 1080 cm^3

6 What mass of $Na_2S_2O_3.5H_2O$ must be used to make up 200 cm^3 of a 0.100 mol dm^{-3} solution?

    A 3.16 g   **B** 4.96 g   **C** 24.8 g   **D** 31.6 g

7 20.00 cm^3 of potassium hydroxide (KOH) is exactly neutralised by 26.80 cm^3 of 0.100 mol dm^{-3} sulfuric acid (H_2SO_4). The concentration of the potassium hydroxide is:

    A 0.0670 mol dm^{-3} **C** 0.268 mol dm^{-3}

    B 0.134 mol dm^{-3} **D** 1.34 mol dm^{-3}

8 Barium chloride solution reacts with sodium sulfate solution according to the equation

$$BaCl_2(aq) + Na_2SO_4(aq) \rightarrow BaSO_4(s) + 2NaCl(aq)$$

When excess barium chloride solution is reacted with $25.00\,cm^3$ of sodium sulfate solution, $0.2334\,g$ of $BaSO_4$ (molar mass $233.4\,g\,mol^{-1}$) is precipitated.

The concentration of sodium ions in the sodium sulfate solution was:

A $0.080\,00\,mol\,dm^{-3}$ **C** $0.001\,000\,mol\,dm^{-3}$

B $0.040\,00\,mol\,dm^{-3}$ **D** $0.002\,000\,mol\,dm^{-3}$

9 When potassium chlorate(V) (molar mass $122.6\,g\,mol^{-1}$) is heated, oxygen gas (molar mass $32.0\,g\,mol^{-1}$) is produced:

$$2KClO_3(s) \rightarrow 2KCl(s) + 3O_2(g)$$

When $1.226\,g$ of potassium chlorate(V) is heated, $0.320\,g$ of oxygen gas is obtained. The percentage yield of oxygen is:

A 100%   **B** 66.7%   **C** 26.1%   **D** 17.4%

10 Elemental analysis of a nitrogen oxide shows that it contains $2.8\,g$ of nitrogen and $8.0\,g$ of oxygen. The empirical formula of this oxide is:

A NO   **B** NO_2 **C** N_2O_3 **D** N_2O_5

11 Nitrogen can be prepared in the laboratory by the following reaction:

$$2NH_3(g) + 3CuO(s) \rightarrow N_2(g) + 3H_2O(l) + 3Cu(s)$$

If $224\,cm^3$ of ammonia, when reacted with excess copper oxide, produces $84\,cm^3$ of nitrogen, calculate the percentage yield of nitrogen. All gas volumes are measured at STP. **[3]**

12 Manganese may be extracted from its ore, hausmannite, by heating with aluminium.

$$3Mn_3O_4 + 8Al \rightarrow 4Al_2O_3 + 9Mn$$

a $100.0\,kg$ of Mn_3O_4 is heated with $100.0\,kg$ of aluminium. Work out the maximum mass of manganese that can be obtained from this reaction. **[4]**

b 1.23 tonnes of ore are processed and $200.0\,kg$ of manganese obtained. Calculate the percentage by mass of Mn_3O_4 in the ore. **[3]**

13 A hydrocarbon contains 88.8% C. $0.201\,g$ of the hydrocarbon occupied a volume of $98.3\,cm^3$ at $320\,K$ and $1.00 \times 10^5\,Pa$.

a Determine the empirical formula of the hydrocarbon. **[3]**

b Determine the molecular formula of the hydrocarbon. **[3]**

14 Limestone is impure calcium carbonate. A 1.20 g sample of limestone is added to excess dilute hydrochloric acid and the gas collected; 258 cm^3 of carbon dioxide was collected at a temperature of 27 °C and a pressure of 1.10×10^5 Pa.

$$CaCO_3(s) + 2HCl(aq) \rightarrow CaCl_2(aq) + CO_2(g) + H_2O(l)$$

   a Calculate the number of moles of gas collected. [3]

   b Calculate the percentage purity of the limestone (assume that none of the impurities in the limestone react with hydrochloric acid to produce gaseous products) [3]

15 25.0 cm^3 of 0.100 mol dm^{-3} copper(II) nitrate solution is added to 15.0 cm^3 of 0.500 mol dm^{-3} potassium iodide. The ionic equation for the reaction that occurs is:

$$2Cu^{2+}(aq) + 4I^-(aq) \rightarrow 2CuI(s) + I_2(aq)$$

   a Determine which reactant is present in excess. [3]

   b Determine the mass of iodine produced. [3]

16 0.0810 g of a group 2 metal iodide, MI$_2$, was dissolved in water and made up to a total volume of 25.00 cm^3. Excess lead(II) nitrate solution (Pb(NO$_3$)$_2$(aq)) was added to the MI$_2$ solution to form a precipitate of lead(II) iodide (PbI$_2$). The precipitate was dried and weighed and it was found that 0.1270 g of precipitate was obtained.

   a Determine the number of moles of lead iodide formed. [2]

   b Write an equation for the reaction that occurs. [1]

   c Determine the number of moles of MI$_2$ that reacted. [1]

   d Determine the identity of the metal, M. [3]

17 0.4000 g of hydrated copper sulfate (CuSO$_4$.xH$_2$O) is dissolved in water and made up to a total volume of 100.0 cm^3 with distilled water. 10.00 cm^3 of this solution is reacted with excess barium chloride (BaCl$_2$) solution. The mass of barium sulfate formed was 3.739×10^{-2} g.

   a Calculate the number of moles of barium sulfate formed. [2]

   b Write an equation for the reaction between copper sulfate solution and barium chloride solution. [1]

   c Calculate the number of moles of copper sulfate that reacted with the barium chloride. [1]

   d Calculate the number of moles of CuSO$_4$ in 0.4000 g of hydrated copper sulfate. [1]

   e Determine the value of x. [3]

Summary

$$\frac{P_1V_1}{T_1} = \frac{P_2V_2}{T_2}$$

molar volume of an ideal gas at STP
= 22.4 dm^3 mol^{-1}

for ideal gases: $pV = nRT$ (T in kelvin)

$$\text{number of moles} = \frac{\text{volume}}{\text{molar volume}}$$

$$\frac{c_1V_1}{n_1} = \frac{c_2V_2}{n_2}$$

Avogadro's law: equal volumes of ideal gases at the same temperature and pressure contain the same number of molecules.

$$\text{concentration (mol dm}^{-3}) = \frac{\text{number of moles (mol)}}{\text{volume (dm}^3)}$$

Use the limiting reactant to determine the amount of products in a reaction.

To find the limiting reactant in a reaction, divide the number of moles of each reactant by its coefficient. The lowest number indicates the limiting reactant.

MOLES

$$\text{percentage yield} = \frac{\text{actual yield}}{\text{theoretical yield}} \times 100$$

Moles calculations
1 Work out the number of moles of anything you can.
2 Use the chemical equation to work out the number of moles of the quantity you require.
3 Convert moles to the required quantity – volume, mass etc.

1 mole is the amount of substance which contains the same number of particles as there are carbon atoms in 12 g of ^{12}C.

Avogadro's constant (L)
= 6.02 × 10^{23} mol^{-1}

$$\text{number of moles} = \frac{\text{mass of substance}}{\text{molar mass}}$$

$$\text{mass of 1 molecule} = \frac{\text{molar mass}}{\text{Avogadro's constant}}$$

molar mass = M_r in g mol^{-1}

Relative atomic mass (A_r): average mass of the naturally occurring isotopes of the element relative to $\frac{1}{12}$ mass of a ^{12}C atom.

Empirical formula: simplest whole number ratio of the elements present in a compound.

Relative molecular mass (M_r): sum of all A_r values in a molecule.

Molecular formula: total number of atoms of each element present in a molecule of the compound.

$$\text{\% by mass of an element in a compound} = \frac{\text{number of atoms in the element} \times A_r}{M_r}$$

2 Atomic structure

Learning objectives

- Understand that an atom is made up of protons, neutrons and electrons
- Define **mass number**, **atomic number** and **isotope**
- Work out the numbers of protons, neutrons and electrons in atoms and ions
- Discuss the properties of isotopes
- Discuss some uses of radioisotopes

An **atom** is the smallest part of an element that can still be recognised as the element.

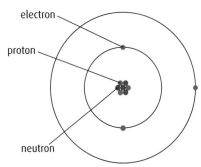

Figure 2.1 A simple representation of a lithium atom (not to scale).

Particle	Relative mass	Relative charge
proton	1	+1
neutron	1	0
electron	5×10^{-4}	−1

Table 2.1 The properties of protons, neutrons and electrons.

Protons and neutrons are made up of other particles: quarks.

2.1 Atoms

Atomic theory

There are approximately 92 elements, plus several more that have been made artificially by nuclear reactions, and probably a few more that have yet to be discovered. As far as we know, there are no more naturally occurring elements: these are the only elements that make up our universe.

An **element** is a substance containing just one type of atom (although see isotopes below). Examples of elements are hydrogen, chlorine, magnesium and iron.

Chemistry is the study of how atoms of the various elements are joined together to make everything we see around us. It is amazing when one imagines that the entire universe can be constructed through combinations of these different elements. With just 92 different building blocks (and in most cases many fewer than this), objects as different as a table, a fish and a piece of rock can be made. It is even more amazing when one realises that these atoms are made up of three subatomic ('smaller than an atom') particles, and so the whole universe is made up of combinations of just three things: protons, neutrons and electrons.

Atoms

In the simplest picture of the atom the electrons orbit around the central nucleus (Figure **2.1**). The nucleus is made up of protons and neutrons (except for a hydrogen atom, which has no neutrons).

The actual mass of a proton is 1.67×10^{-27} kg and the charge on a proton is $+1.6 \times 10^{-19}$ C. Relative masses and charges, shown in Table **2.1**, are used to compare the masses of one particle with another more easily. Because the values are relative, there are **no units**.

From these values it can be seen that virtually all the mass of the atom is concentrated in the nucleus. However, most of the volume of the atom is due to the electrons: the nucleus is very small compared with the total size of the atom.

The diameter of an atom is approximately 1×10^{-10} m and that of a nucleus between about 1×10^{-14} and 1×10^{-15} m, meaning that a nucleus is about 10 000 to 100 000 times smaller than an atom. So, if the nucleus were the size of the full stop at the end of this sentence, the atom would be between 3 and 30 m across.

None of these particles can be observed directly. These particles were originally 'discovered' by the interpretation of experimental data. Do we know or believe in the existence of these particles? If we looked at a science textbook 200 years ago there would be no mention of protons, electrons and neutrons. If we could look at a chemistry textbook 200 years in the future will there be any mention of them? Are these particles a true representation of reality, or a device invented by scientists to make sense of experimental data and provide an explanation of the world around them?

Democritus and his teacher Leucippus, fifth-century BC Greek philosophers, are often credited with first suggesting the idea of the atom as the smallest indivisible particle of which all matter is made.

John Dalton (1766–1844) is generally regarded as the founder of modern atomic theory.

The atomic number **defines an element**: it is unique to that particular element. For example, the element with atomic number 12 is magnesium and that with atomic number 79 is gold. This means that we could use the atomic number of the element instead of its name. However, the name is usually simpler and more commonly employed in everyday speech.

The **overall charge on an atom is zero** and therefore:

Atomic number (Z): the number of protons in the nucleus of an atom.

no. of protons in an atom = no. of electrons

The atomic number is, however, defined in terms of protons, as electrons may be lost or gained when ions are formed in chemical reactions.

The electron was discovered in 1897 by J. J. Thompson at the University of Cambridge, UK.

Mass number (A): the number of protons plus neutrons in the nucleus of an atom.

Therefore:

no. of neutrons in an atom = mass number – atomic number

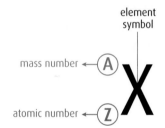

Figure 2.2 Where to place the mass number (A) and atomic number (Z) in the full symbol of an element.

The full symbol of an element includes the atomic number and the mass number (see Figure **2.2**). For example, sodium has an atomic number of 11 and a mass number of 23. The nucleus of sodium contains 11 protons and 12 neutrons ($23 - 11$). Surrounding the nucleus are 11 electrons. The symbol for sodium is $^{23}_{11}\text{Na}$.

Self-test 1

Ions

Ions are charged particles that are formed when an atom loses or gains (an) electron(s).

A **positive** ion is formed when an atom **loses** (an) **electron**(s) so that the ion has more protons(+) than electrons(−) (Figure **2.3**). A **negative** ion is formed when an atom **gains** (an) **electron**(s) so that the ion has more electrons(−) than protons(+).

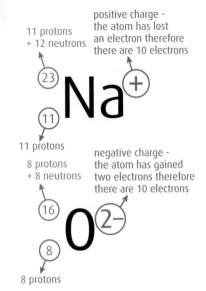

11 protons
+ 12 neutrons

positive charge -
the atom has lost
an electron therefore
there are 10 electrons

(23) Na (+)
(11)

11 protons

8 protons
+ 8 neutrons

negative charge -
the atom has gained
two electrons therefore
there are 10 electrons

(16) O (2−)
(8)

8 protons

Figure 2.3 The number of subatomic particles in the Na⁺ and O²⁻ ions.

The isotopes of hydrogen are sometimes given different names and symbols; hydrogen–1 is called protium; hydrogen–2 is deuterium (D); and hydrogen–3 is tritium (T).

Isotopes

The mass number of chlorine is given in many periodic tables as 35.5. It is not possible to have half a neutron: the mass number that is given is an average, taking into account the presence of isotopes.

Isotopes are different atoms of the same element with different mass numbers: i.e. different numbers of neutrons in the nucleus.

The two isotopes of chlorine are ^{35}Cl (chlorine-35) and ^{37}Cl (chlorine-37). Most naturally occurring samples of elements are composed of a mixture of isotopes, but usually one isotope is far more abundant than the others and the mass number for the most common isotope is quoted.

The numbers of protons, neutrons and electrons in some isotopes are shown in Table **2.2**.

Isotopes have the same chemical properties (they react in exactly the same way) but different physical properties (e.g. different melting points and boiling points).

Isotopes react in the same way because they have the **same numbers of electrons**, and chemical reactions depend only on the number and arrangement of electrons and not on the composition of the nucleus. For example, both protium and deuterium would react in the same way with nitrogen:

$$N_2 + 3H_2 \rightleftharpoons 2NH_3 \qquad N_2 + 3D_2 \rightleftharpoons 2ND_3$$

Isotopes have different physical properties because the different masses mean that they move at different speeds. For example, the boiling point of ^{1}H$_2$ is −253 °C, whereas that of ^{2}H$_2$ is −250 °C. Heavy water (D$_2$O) has a melting point of 3.8 °C and a boiling point of 101.4 °C.

Radioisotopes

Radioisotopes are radioactive isotopes of an element. Radioactivity occurs as a result of processes happening in the nucleus of an atom.

Radioisotopes are potentially extremely **dangerous**, and their use is closely controlled. If people are exposed to too-high doses of radioactivity, serious disease and death can result.

There are three types of radioactivity:
α-emission: α particles (helium nuclei) are emitted from the nucleus of an atom.
β-emission: high-energy electrons are emitted from the nucleus of an atom as a neutron is converted to a proton and an electron.
γ-emission: electromagnetic waves (γ-rays) are emitted from the nucleus of an atom.

Isotope	Protons	Neutrons	Electrons
$^{1}_{1}$H	1	0	1
$^{2}_{1}$H	1	1	1
$^{3}_{1}$H	1	2	1
$^{12}_{6}$C	6	6	6
$^{13}_{6}$C	6	7	6
$^{14}_{6}$C	6	8	6
$^{35}_{17}$Cl	17	18	17
$^{37}_{17}$Cl	17	20	17

Table 2.2 The numbers of subatomic particles in some common isotopes.

^{14}C: radiocarbon dating

The percentage of ^{14}C in the atmosphere is constant, at $1.2 \times 10^{-10}\%$. While an animal or plant is alive, it exchanges CO_2 with the atmosphere, so it contains a steady amount of $1.2 \times 10^{-10}\%$ ^{14}C. When the plant or animal dies it no longer exchanges ^{14}C with the atmosphere, and as the ^{14}C decays (with a half-life of 5730 years), the amount of ^{14}C the organism contains decreases. If the ^{14}C content of the dead material is calculated by either measuring the activity or using a mass spectrometer, the age of the sample can be worked out (Figure **2.4**). This technique works only for substances that were once living; for example, it can be used to date a piece of wood but not a piece of rock.

^{60}Co: radiotherapy

^{60}Co is an artificially produced isotope. It is a γ emitter and is used in the treatment of cancer (Figure **2.5**). An external source of the radiation is used, and the γ-rays destroy cancerous cells.

^{131}I and ^{125}I: medical tracers

^{131}I and ^{125}I are artificial isotopes. Iodine is concentrated in the thyroid gland, and when the patient is given a capsule containing a radioactive isotope of iodine it is possible to generate images of the thyroid gland. Information can thus be gained about the activity of the gland, depending on how much radioiodine is taken up by the various parts of the gland. ^{125}I is used in radioimmunoassay – various substances (e.g. proteins such as insulin) can be 'tagged' with ^{125}I atoms and the take up of these by cells measured by measuring the radiation of a sample.

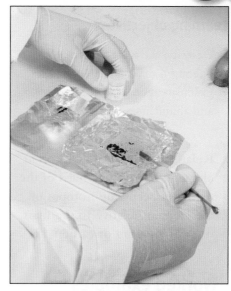

Figure 2.4 A scientist preparing fragments of papyrus scrolls for radiocarbon dating.

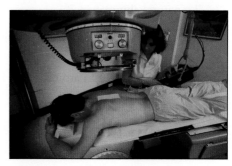

Figure 2.5 A patient undergoing radiotherapy.

Test yourself

1 Give the number of protons, neutrons and electrons in the following atoms:

$^{238}_{92}$U $\quad$ $^{75}_{33}$As $\quad$ $^{81}_{35}$Br

2 Give the number of protons, neutrons and electrons in the following ions:

$^{40}_{20}$Ca^{2+} $\quad$ $^{127}_{53}$I^{-} $\quad$ $^{140}_{58}$Ce^{3+}

3 If you consider the most common isotopes of elements as given in a basic periodic table, how many elements have more protons than neutrons in an atom?

4 The following table shows the number of protons, electrons and neutrons in a series of atoms and ions.

Symbol	Protons	Neutrons	Electrons
D	27	30	25
X	43	54	42
Q	35	44	35
L	27	32	26
M	35	46	36
Z	54	78	54

a Which symbols represent isotopes?
b Which symbols represent positive ions?

Learning objectives

- Describe the stages in the operation of a mass spectrometer
- Calculate relative atomic masses and abundances of isotopes

Relative atomic mass (A_r) of an element: the average mass of the naturally occurring isotopes of the element relative to the mass of $\frac{1}{12}$ of an atom of carbon-12.

The relative atomic mass scale

Because of the different isotopes present, it is most convenient to quote an average mass for an atom; this is the **relative atomic mass, A_r.** $\frac{1}{12}$ of the mass of a carbon-12 atom is defined as having a mass of 1.00 and all masses are quoted relative to this. Thus, the relative atomic mass of oxygen is 16.00, and this means that the average mass of an oxygen atom is 16.00 times the mass of $\frac{1}{12}$ of a carbon-12 atom.

How to calculate relative atomic mass

Worked examples

Lithium has two naturally occurring isotopes:

^{6}Li: natural abundance 7% ^{7}Li: natural abundance 93%

Calculate the relative atomic mass of lithium.

Imagine we have 100 Li atoms: 7 will have mass 6 and 93 will have mass 7.

The average mass of these atoms is:

$$\frac{(7 \times 6) + (93 \times 7)}{100} = 6.93$$

Therefore the A_r of Li is 6.93.

Iridium has a relative atomic mass of 192.22 and consists of Ir-191 and Ir-193 isotopes. Calculate the percentage composition of a naturally occurring sample of iridium.

Again, we will assume that we have 100 atoms and that x of these will have a mass of 191. This means that there will be $(100 - x)$ atoms that have a mass of 193.

The total mass of these 100 atoms will be: $191x + 193(100 - x)$

The average mass of the 100 atoms will be: $\dfrac{191x + 193(100 - x)}{100}$

Therefore we can write the equation: $\dfrac{191x + 193(100 - x)}{100} = 192.22$

$$191x + 193(100 - x) = 19\,222$$

$$191x + 19\,300 - 193x = 19\,222$$

$$-2x = 19\,222 - 19\,300$$

$$-2x = -78$$

Therefore $x = 39$.

This means that the naturally occurring sample of iridium contains 39% Ir-191 and 61% Ir-193.

Alternatively:

$$\frac{A_r - \text{mass number of lighter isotope}}{\text{difference in mass number of two isotopes}} \times 100 = \% \text{ of heavier isotope}$$

In the example here: $\dfrac{(192.22 - 191)}{(193 - 191)} \times 100 = 61\%$

The mass spectrometer

Animation 1

A mass spectrometer can be used to determine the proportion of each isotope present in a sample of an element. Figure **2.6** shows a representation of a basic mass spectrometer.

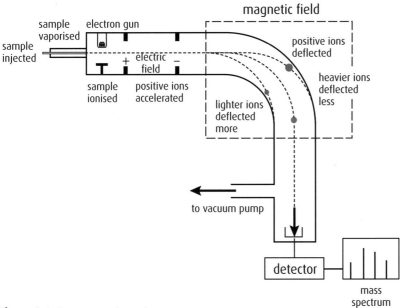

Figure 2.6 A mass spectrometer.

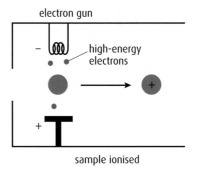

Figure 2.7 Ionisation in a mass spectrometer.

How a mass spectrometer works

1 Vaporisation
The sample is injected and vaporised to produce gaseous atoms/molecules.

2 Ionisation
Atoms/molecules are bombarded with high-energy electrons to produce positive ions (Figure **2.7**):

$$M(g) + e^- \rightarrow M^+(g) + 2e^-$$

The high-energy electrons knock other electrons out of the atoms.

3 Acceleration
The positive ions are accelerated in an electric field (Figure **2.8**).

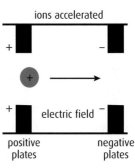

Figure 2.8 Acceleration of positive ions in a mass spectrometer.

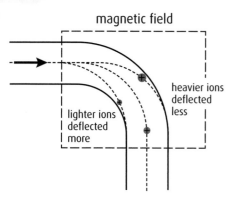

Figure 2.9 Deflection of positive ions in a mass spectrometer.

Note: a particle will only undergo deflection in a magnetic field if it is charged – uncharged particles are not deflected.

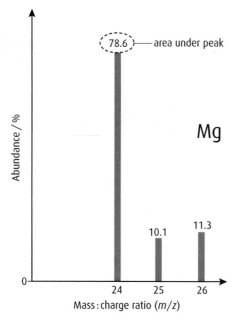

Figure 2.10 The mass spectrum of magnesium.

The smaller the mass : charge ratio, the more the ion is deflected for a certain magnetic field in a mass spectrometer.

4 Deflection

The positive ions are deflected in a magnetic field (Figure **2.9**).

Note: particles are deflected according to their **mass : charge** (*m/z*) **ratio**; i.e. lighter ions and particles of greater charge are deflected more.

A greater magnetic field is required to cause sufficient deflection of ions with higher mass : charge ratio so that they hit the detector.

Usually the particles have only a single positive charge on them and are therefore sorted according to mass.

5 Detection

For one particular magnetic field, particles of only one *m/z* pass through the spectrometer. These hit the detector and produce a signal in the form of an electric current, which is proportional to the number of ions hitting the detector. The magnetic field is varied to scan the whole range of *m/z* values.

The mass spectrum of an element and relative atomic mass

In the mass spectrum of an element, we get **one peak for each of the individual isotopes**. The height of each peak (or, more properly, the area under each peak) is proportional to the number of atoms of this isotope present in the sample. The mass spectrum of magnesium is shown in Figure **2.10**.

The relative atomic mass can be calculated as:

$$A_r = \frac{(78.6 \times 24) + (10.1 \times 25) + (11.3 \times 26)}{100} = 24.3$$

Mass : charge ratio

Sometimes it happens that more than one electron is knocked out of an atom when it is bombarded with high-energy electrons, so that a 2+ ion is produced:

$$M(g) + e^- \rightarrow M^{2+}(g) + 3e^-$$

This ion will be deflected twice as much as M^+ because it has double the charge (there is very little difference in mass as a result of the loss of an extra electron). A $^{24}Mg^{2+}$ ion will therefore produce a peak at an *m/z* value of 12 (i.e. $\frac{24}{2}$) (see Figure **2.11**). Thus, considering the ions $^{24}Al^+$ (*m/z* = 24), $^{40}Ca^{2+}$ (*m/z* = 20) and $^{48}Ti^{3+}$ (*m/z* = 16), as Ti^{3+} has the smallest mass : charge ratio, it will be deflected most at the same magnetic field in a mass spectrometer.

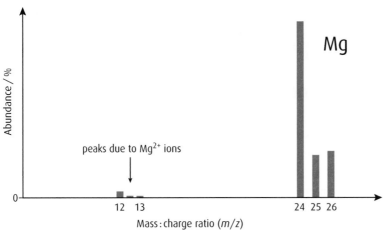

Figure 2.11 The mass spectrum of magnesium, showing the deflection of Mg^{2+} ions.

Test yourself

5 Chromium has four naturally occurring isotopes, and their masses and natural abundances are shown in the table below.

Isotope	Natural abundance (%)
^{50}Cr	4.35
^{52}Cr	83.79
^{53}Cr	9.50
^{54}Cr	2.36

Calculate the relative atomic mass of chromium to two decimal places.

6 Silicon has three naturally occurring isotopes and their details are given in the table below.

Isotope	Natural abundance (%)
^{28}Si	92.2
^{29}Si	4.7
^{30}Si	3.1

Calculate the relative atomic mass of silicon to two decimal places.

7 a Indium has two naturally occurring isotopes: indium-113 and indium-115. The relative atomic mass of indium is 114.82. Calculate the natural abundance of each isotope.

 b Gallium has two naturally occurring isotopes: gallium-69 and gallium-71. The relative atomic mass of gallium is 69.723. Calculate the natural abundance of each isotope.

8 Arrange the following ions in terms of how much they will be deflected in a mass spectrometer (the one that will be deflected most first):

$^{84}_{23}Kr^{2+}$ $^{81}_{35}Br^+$ $^{120}_{50}Sn^{2+}$ $^{23}_{11}Na^+$

Learning objectives

- Work out the electronic arrangement for atoms with up to 20 electrons
- Describe the electromagnetic spectrum
- Describe the emission spectrum of hydrogen
- Explain how emission spectra arise

The main energy level number is called the **principal quantum number** and is given the symbol n. The maximum number of electrons in each shell is given by $2n^2$.

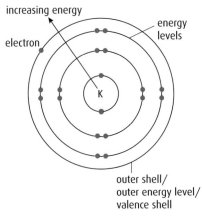

Figure 2.12 The electron arrangement of potassium.

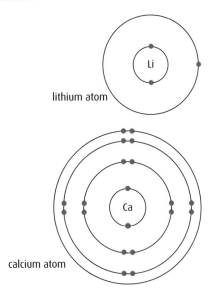

2.3 Electron arrangements and atomic emission spectra

The arrangement of electrons in atoms

At the simplest level of explanation, the electrons in an atom are arranged in **energy levels** (**shells**) about the nucleus. The electron arrangement of potassium can be represented as shown in **Figure 2.12** and is written as 2,8,8,1 or 2.8.8.1.

The lowest energy level, called the first energy level or first shell (sometimes also called the K shell), is the one closest to the nucleus. The shells increase in energy as they get further from the nucleus. The maximum number of electrons in each main energy level is:

main energy level number	1	2	3	4	5
maximum number of electrons	2	8	18	32	50

> The general rule for filling these energy levels is that the electrons fill them from the lowest energy to the highest (from the nucleus out). The first two energy levels must be completely filled before an electron goes into the next energy level. The third main energy level is, however, only filled to 8 before electrons are put into the fourth main energy level. This scheme works up to elements with atomic number 20.

Electron configurations of the first 20 elements

Let's look at two examples.

Lithium

The atomic number of lithium is 3; therefore the lithium atom contains three electrons. The first two electrons go into the lowest energy level (closest to the nucleus). This energy level is then full, so the next electron goes into the second energy level. The electron arrangement for lithium is thus 2,1. We say that lithium has one outer shell electron, or one electron in the **valence** (outer) shell.

Calcium

The atomic number of calcium is 20; therefore the calcium atom contains 20 electrons. The first two electrons go into the first energy level. The next eight go in to the second energy level. The next eight electrons go into the third energy level. The third energy level can actually hold up to 18 electrons, but the remaining 10 electrons go in only after two electrons go into the fourth energy level (for an explanation of why this happens, see page **69**). The electronic configuration of calcium is thus 2,8,8,2. Calcium has two outer shell electrons – two electrons in the valence shell.

9 What are the electronic configurations of the following atoms?

    C   Si   Cl

The electromagnetic spectrum

Light is a form of energy. Visible light is just one part of the electromagnetic spectrum:

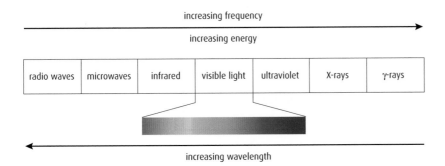

The various forms of electromagnetic radiation are usually regarded as waves that travel at the speed of light in a vacuum $(3.0 \times 10^8 \, \text{m s}^{-1})$ but vary in their frequency/energy/wavelength.

Although electromagnetic radiation is usually described as a wave, it can also display the properties of a particle, and we sometimes talk about particles of electromagnetic radiation, or **photons**.

$$\text{frequency} \propto \frac{1}{\text{wavelength}}$$

$$\text{frequency} \propto \text{energy}$$

Extension

This is known as wave–particle duality.
The energy (E) of a photon is related to its wavelength and frequency:

$$E = \frac{hc}{\lambda} \qquad E = hf$$

λ is the wavelength of the light (in m)
c is the speed of light $(3.0 \times 10^8 \, \text{m s}^{-1})$
f is the frequency of the light (in Hz or s^{-1})
h is Planck's constant $(6.63 \times 10^{-34} \, \text{J s})$

Would our interpretation of the world around us be different if our eyes could detect light in other regions of the electromagnetic spectrum?

White light is visible light made up of all the colours of the spectrum. In order of increasing energy, the colours of the spectrum are:
red < orange < yellow < green < blue < indigo < violet.

Are there really seven colours in the visible spectrum?

Evidence for energy levels in atoms

The hydrogen atom spectrum

Observing the spectrum

When hydrogen gas at low pressure is subjected to a very high voltage, the gas glows reddish pink (Figure **2.13**). The glowing gas can be looked at through a **spectroscope**, which contains a diffraction grating and separates the various wavelengths of light emitted from the gas. As light is emitted by the gas, this is called an **emission spectrum**.

> Gas-discharge lamps are used in, among others, neon signs and sodium vapour lamps, which are used to provide street lighting.

Figure 2.13 Observing the emission spectrum of hydrogen.

In the visible region, the spectrum consists of a series of sharp, bright, lines on a dark background (Figure **2.14**).

> The lines get closer together at higher frequency/energy.

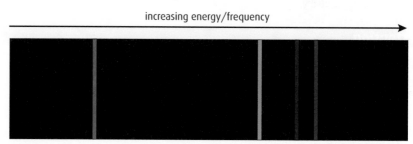
increasing energy/frequency

Figure 2.13 A representation of the atomic emission spectrum of hydrogen.

> Each element has its own unique emission spectrum, and this can be used to identify the element.

This is a **line spectrum**, as opposed to a **continuous spectrum**, which consists of all colours merging into each other:

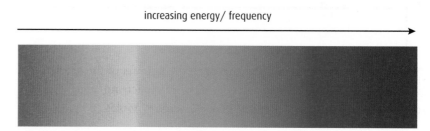
increasing energy/ frequency

> Line spectrum – only certain frequencies/wavelengths of light present.
> Continuous spectrum – **all** frequencies/wavelengths of light present.

How an emission spectrum arises

Passage of the electric discharge causes an electron to be **promoted to a higher energy level** (shell):

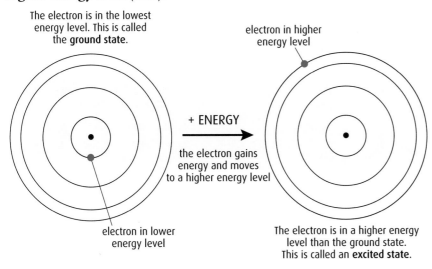

The electron is in the lowest energy level. This is called the **ground state**.

electron in lower energy level

+ ENERGY

the electron gains energy and moves to a higher energy level

electron in higher energy level

The electron is in a higher energy level than the ground state. This is called an **excited state**.

The electron is unstable in this higher level and will **fall to a lower energy level** (Figure **2.15**). As it returns from a level at energy E_2 to E_1, the extra energy $(E_2 - E_1)$ is given out in the form of a **photon of light**. This gives a line in the spectrum. The energy levels can also be shown like this:

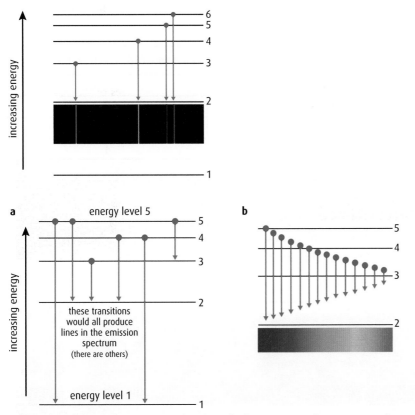

increasing energy

a energy level 5

these transitions would all produce lines in the emission spectrum (there are others)

energy level 1

b

Figure 2.16 (**a**) Electrons in energy levels: only the transitions between two discrete energy levels are possible, and a line spectrum is produced. (**b**) If the electrons in an atom could have any energy, all transitions would be possible. This would result in a continuous spectrum.

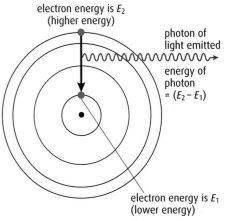

electron energy is E_2 (higher energy)

photon of light emitted

energy of photon = $(E_2 - E_1)$

electron energy is E_1 (lower energy)

Figure 2.15 When an electron falls from a higher to a lower energy level on an atom, a photon of light is emitted.

Because light is given out, this type of spectrum is an **emission spectrum**.

Each line in the spectrum thus comes from the transition of an **electron from a higher energy level to a lower one**.

The fact that a line spectrum is produced provides evidence for electrons being in energy levels (shells): i.e. electrons in an atom are allowed to have only certain amounts of energy (Figure **2.16**).

Infrared and ultraviolet radiation can be detected only with the aid of technology – we cannot interact with them directly. Does this have implications as to how we view the knowledge gained from atomic spectra in these regions?

Note: all transitions to level 1 occur in the ultraviolet region (higher energy); therefore we can deduce that the energy difference between level 1 and any other level is bigger than that between level 2 and any other level.

Note: all the transitions that occur in the visible region of the spectrum (the ones that we can see) involve the electron falling down to level 2 (the Balmer series).

Application 1

Extension

The lines in the hydrogen atom spectra fit a mathematical equation very well. Follow the link to generate the lines in the spectra, plot spectra and find out what this equation is.

Different series of lines

Figure **2.17** shows a representation of the emission spectrum of hydrogen across the infrared, visible and ultraviolet regions. The series in each region consists of a set of lines that get closer together at higher frequency. Each series is named after its discoverer.

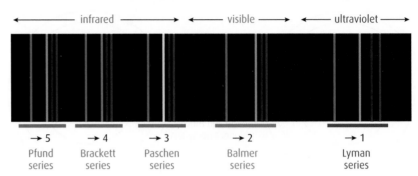

Figure 2.17 A representation of the emission spectrum of hydrogen. The colours and lines in the spectrum in the infrared and ultraviolet regions are just for illustrative purposes.

> The various series of lines occur when the electron falls back down to different energy levels.

For example, the Balmer series arises when an electron falls back down to energy level 2:

Name of series	Area of spectrum	Level to which electron falls back
Lyman	ultraviolet	1
Balmer	visible	2
Paschen	infrared	3
Brackett	infrared	4
Pfund	Infrared	5

Convergence

The lines in the emission spectrum get closer together at higher frequency/energy (Figure **2.18**).

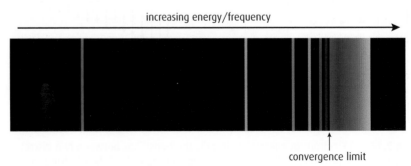

Figure 2.18 A representation of the Lyman series of hydrogen in the ultraviolet region of the electromagnetic spectrum.

Eventually, at the **convergence limit**, the lines merge to form a **continuum**. Beyond this point **the electron can have any energy** and so must be **free from the influence of the nucleus**, i.e. the electron is no longer in the atom (Figure **2.19**).

Extension

The convergence limit is not usually observed, but the frequency can be worked out by plotting a graph of the difference in frequency of successive lines against their frequency and extrapolating the graph to give the frequency when the difference in frequency between successive lines is zero.

Ionisation energy and the convergence limit

Knowing the frequency of the light at the convergence limit can allow us to work out the **ionisation energy**, i.e. the energy for the process:

$$M(g) \rightarrow M^+(g) + e^-$$

> The ionisation energy is the minimum amount of energy required to remove an electron from a gaseous atom.

The ionisation energy for hydrogen represents the minimum energy for the removal of an electron (from level 1 to ∞) (Figure **2.20**), whereas the frequency of the convergence limit in the Lyman series represents the amount of energy given out when an electron falls from outside the atom to level 1 (∞ to 1). These are therefore the same amount of energy.

Note: the ionisation energy of hydrogen can be obtained only from a study of the series of lines when the electron falls back to its ground state (normal) energy level: the Lyman series.

The spectrum of a hydrogen atom is relatively simple, because hydrogen contains only one electron. Ions such as He^+ and Li^{2+}, which also contain one electron, would have spectra similar to hydrogen (although not exactly the same, as the number of protons in the nucleus influences the electron energy levels). For atoms with more electrons, the spectra are much more complex and cannot be explained simply on the basis of main energy levels.

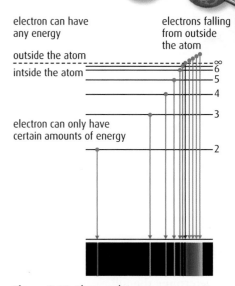

electron can have any energy

electrons falling from outside the atom

outside the atom

intside the atom

electron can only have certain amounts of energy

Figure 2.19 The purple arrow represents the transition giving rise to the convergence limit in the Lyman series for hydrogen.

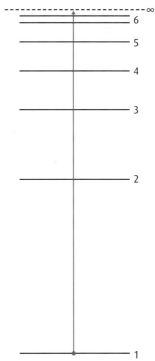

Figure 2.20 The ionisation process in a hydrogen atom.

Test yourself

10 Arrange the following in order of:

   a increasing energy

   b decreasing wavelength

   ultraviolet radiation   infrared radiation

   microwaves   orange light   green light

11 Describe how a line in the Lyman series of the hydrogen atom spectrum arises.

12 Draw an energy level diagram showing the first four energy levels in a hydrogen atom and mark with an arrow on this diagram one electronic transition that would give rise to:

   a a line in the ultraviolet region of the spectrum

   b a line in the visible region of the spectrum

   c a line in the infrared region of the spectrum

Learning objectives

- Determine the full electronic configuration of an atom with up to 54 electrons
- Understand what is meant by an orbital and a subshell (sub energy level)

HL 2.4 Electronic configurations

A more advanced treatment of the electronic structure of atoms

The emission spectra of atoms with more than one electron and other evidence, such as ionisation energy data (see below), suggest that the simple treatment of considering that electrons in atoms occupy only main energy levels is a useful first approximation but can be expanded upon.

Sub energy levels and orbitals

Each main energy level in an atom is made up of sub energy levels (subshells). The first main energy level consists solely of the 1s sub-level, the second main energy level is split into the 2s sub-level and the 2p sub-level. The sub-levels in each main energy level up to 5 are shown in Table **2.3**.

Main energy level	Sub-levels				Number of electrons in each sub-level			
					s	p	d	f
1	1s				2			
2	2s	2p			2	6		
3	3s	3p	3d		2	6	10	
4	4s	4p	4d	4f	2	6	10	14
5	5s	5p	5d	5f	2	6	10	14

Table 2.3 The sub-levels in each main energy level up to level 5.

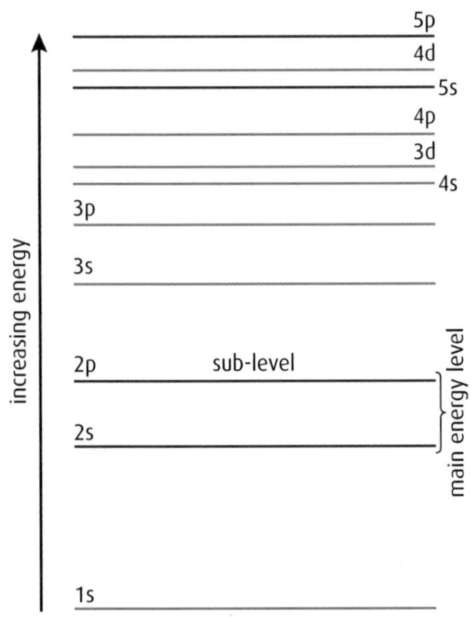

Within any main energy level (shell) the ordering of the sub-levels (subshells) is always s < p < d < f, but there are sometimes reversals of orders between sub-levels in different energy levels. The relative energies of the subshells are shown in Figure **2.21**.

The Aufbau (building-up) principle (part 1)

The Aufbau principle is simply the name given to the process of working out the electronic configuration of an atom.

(diagram, left column)

increasing energy →

5p
4d
5s
4p
3d
4s
3p
3s

2p   sub-level

2s

1s

main energy level

Figure 2.21 The ordering of the energy levels and sub-levels within an atom. The sub-levels within a main energy level are shown in the same colour.

Electrons fill sub-levels from the lowest energy level upwards – this gives the lowest possible (potential) energy.

Thus the full electronic configuration of sodium (11 electrons) can be built up as follows:
- The first two electrons go into the 1s sub-level → $1s^2$: this sub-level is now full.
- The next two electrons go into the 2s sub-level → $2s^2$: this sub-level is now full.
- The next six electrons go into the 2p sub-level → $2p^6$: this sub-level is now full.
- The last electron goes into the 3s sub level → $3s^1$: the full electronic configuration of sodium is thus $1s^2 2s^2 2p^6 3s^1$. This can also be abbreviated to $[Ne]3s^1$, where the electronic configuration of the previous noble gas is assumed and everything after that is given in full.

The full electronic configuration of iron (26 electrons) is: $1s^2 2s^2 2p^6 3s^2 3p^6 4s^2 3d^6$. Note that, because the 4s sub-level is lower in energy than the 3d sub-level it is filled first. In other words, two electrons go into the fourth main energy level before the third main energy level is filled. This can also be written as $[Ar]4s^2 3d^6$.

This is sometimes written as $[Ar]3d^6 4s^2$ to keep the sub-levels in order of the main energy levels.

The full electronic configuration of tin (50 electrons) is: $1s^2 2s^2 2p^6 3s^2 3p^6 4s^2 3d^{10} 4p^6 5s^2 4d^{10} 5p^2$. Or, in abbreviated form: $[Kr]5s^2 4d^{10} 5p^2$.

The order in which the sub-levels are filled can be remembered most easily from the periodic table (Figure **2.21**).

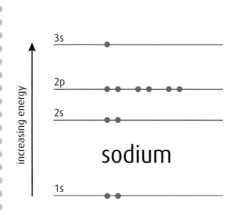

sodium

$[1s^2\ 2s^2\ 2p^6]\ 3s^1$
from neon

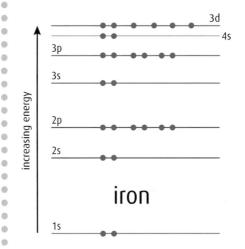

iron

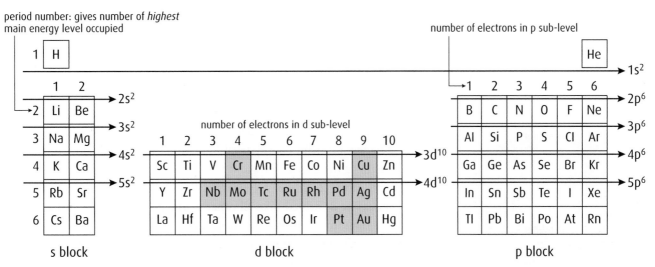

period number: gives number of *highest* main energy level occupied

number of electrons in p sub-level

Figure 2.22 The 'p block' is so named because the highest occupied sub-level is a p sub-level. The period number indicates the highest occupied p sub-level, and the position within the p block gives the number of electrons in the p sub-level. Some exceptions to the general rules for filling sub-levels are highlighted in pink. He has the configuration $1s^2$ and has no p electrons, despite the fact that it is usually put in the p block.

Note: all atoms in the same group (vertical column) in the periodic table have the same outer shell electronic configuration. For example, all the elements in group 6 (like Se) have the outer shell electronic configuration ns^2np^4.
n is the period number.

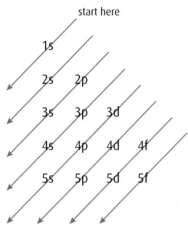

Figure 2.23 Draw out the sub-levels in each main energy level. Starting at 1s, follow the arrows to give the ordering of the sub-levels.

An orbital can contain a maximum of two electrons.

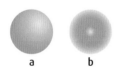

Figure 2.24 (**a**) The shape of a 1s orbital; (**b**) the electron density in a 1s orbital.

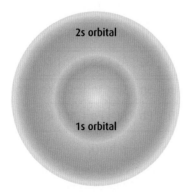

Figure 2.25 A cross section of the electron density of the 1s and 2s orbitals together.

HL

For example, Selenium (Se) is in period 4 and 4 along in the p block; therefore the last part of the electronic configuration is $4p^4$. The full electronic configuration can be worked out from following the arrows:

H→He	$1s^2$				
Li→Be	$2s^2$			B→Ne	$2p^6$
Na→Mg	$3s^2$			Al→Ar	$3p^6$
K→Ca	$4s^2$	Sc→Zn	$3d^{10}$	Ga→Se	$4p^4$

(remember to go down 1 in the d block)

Therefore the electronic configuration is: $1s^22s^22p^63s^23p^64s^23d^{10}4p^4$.

Figure **2.23** shows an alternative way of remembering the order in which sub-levels are filled.

Test yourself

13 Give the full electronic configurations of the following atoms:
    a N   **b** Ar   **c** V
    d Sr   **e** Te

Orbitals

Electrons in atoms occupy atomic orbitals.

> An orbital is a region of space in which there is a high probability of finding an electron. It represents a discrete energy level.

There are four different types of atomic orbital: **s**   **p**   **d**   **f**

The first shell (maximum number of electrons 2) consists of a 1s orbital and this makes up the entire 1s sub-level. This is spherical in shape (Figure **2.24a**).

The 1s orbital is centred on the nucleus (Figure **2.24b**). The electron is moving all the time and the intensity of the colour here represents the probability of finding the electron at a certain distance from the nucleus. The darker the colour the greater the probability of the electron being at that point. This represents the electron density.

The electron can be found anywhere in this region of space (except the nucleus – at the centre of the orbital) but it is most likely to be found at a certain distance from the nucleus.

The second main energy level (maximum number of electrons 8) is made up of the 2s sub-level and the 2p sub-level. The 2s sub-level just consists of the 2s orbital, whereas the 2p sub-level is made up of three 2p orbitals. The 2s orbital (like all other s orbitals) is spherical in shape and bigger than the 1s orbital (Figure **2.25**).

p orbitals have a 'dumb-bell' shape (Figure **2.26**). Three p orbitals make up the 2p sub-level. These point at 90° to each other and are named appropriately as p_x, p_y, p_z (Figure **2.27**). The p_x orbital points along the x axis. The three 2p orbitals all have the same energy – they are described as **degenerate**.

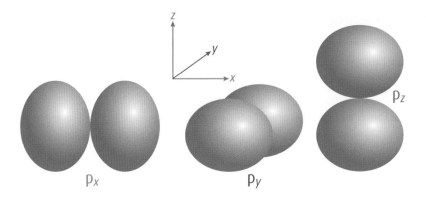

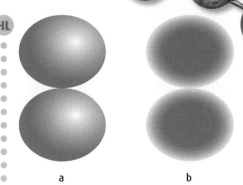

a   b

Figure 2.26 (**a**) The shape of a 2p orbital; (**b**) the electron density in a 2p orbital.

Figure 2.27 The three p orbitals that make up a p sub-level point at 90° to each other.

Figure **2.28** shows the orbitals that make up the 2s and 2p sub-levels in the second main energy level.

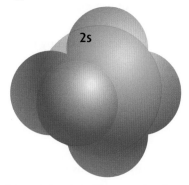

Figure 2.28 The 2s and 2p sub-levels in the second main energy level.

Figure 2.29 One of the five d orbitals in the 3d sub-level.

The third shell (maximum 18 electrons) consists of the 3s, 3p and 3d sub-levels. The 3s sub-level is just the 3s orbital; the 3p sub-level consists of three 3p orbitals; and the 3d sub-level is made up of **five 3d orbitals**. One of the five 3d orbitals is shown in Figure **2.29**.

The fourth shell (maximum 32 electrons) consists of one 4s, three 4p, five 4d and **seven 4f orbitals**. The seven 4f orbitals make up the 4f sub-level. One of the f orbitals is shown in Figure **2.30**.

Figure 2.30 One of the f orbitals in the 4f sub-level.

> Within any sub-shell all the orbitals have the same energy (they are **degenerate**), e.g. the three 2p orbitals are degenerate and the five 3d orbitals are degenerate.

The number of orbitals in each energy level is shown in Table **2.4**.

Main energy level (shell)	s	p	d	f
1	1			
2	1	3		
3	1	3	5	
4	1	3	5	7
5	1	3	5	7

Table 2.4 The number of orbitals in each energy level.

The diagrams of atomic orbitals that we have seen here are derived from mathematical functions that are solutions to the Schrödinger equation. Exact solutions of the Schrödinger equation are only possible for a system involving one electron, i.e. the hydrogen atom. It is not possible to derive exact mathematical solutions for more complex atoms. What implications does this have for the limit of scientific knowledge? When we describe more complex atoms in terms of orbitals, we are actually just extending the results from the hydrogen atom and gaining an approximate view of the properties of electrons in atoms.

Electrons can be regarded as either spinning in one direction (clockwise),

or in the opposite direction (anticlockwise).

Examiner's tip
These diagrams are sometimes described as 'electrons in boxes'.

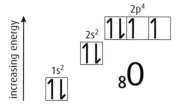

Figure 2.31 The electronic configuration of oxygen.

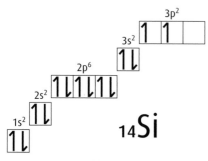

Figure 2.32 The electronic configuration of silicon.

HL Putting electrons into orbitals – the Aufbau principle (part 2)

As well as moving around in space within an orbital, electrons also have another property called **spin**.

There are two rules that must be considered before electrons are put into orbitals.

1 **The Pauli exclusion principle:** the maximum number of electrons in an orbital is two. If there are two electrons in an orbital, they must have opposite spin.

2 **Hund's rule:** electrons fill orbitals of the same energy (degenerate orbitals) so as to give the maximum number of electrons with the same spin.

Here we can see the way three electrons occupy the orbitals of the 2p sub-level:

By contrast, these higher-energy situations do not occur:

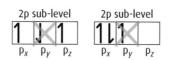

Figures **2.31** and **2.32** show the full electronic configuration of oxygen and silicon atoms, respectively.

There are a small number of exceptions to the rules for filling sub-levels: i.e. electronic configurations that are not quite as expected. Two of these exceptions are **chromium** and **copper**, which, instead of having electronic configurations of the form $[Ar]3d^n4s^2$ have only one electron in the 4s sub-level.

$$_{24}Cr: [Ar]3d^54s^1 \qquad _{29}Cu: [Ar]3d^{10}4s^1$$

The reasons for this are complex and beyond the level of the syllabus, but in general, having the maximum number of electron spins the same within a set of degenerate orbitals gives a lower-energy (more stable) situation.

Test yourself

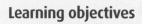

14 Draw out the full electronic configurations of the following atoms, showing electrons in boxes:

   a C   **b** P   **c** Cr

2.5 Ionisation energy

Ionisation energy and evidence for energy levels and sub-levels

The **first** ionisation energy for an element is the energy for the process:

$$M(g) \rightarrow M^+(g) + e^-$$

> The full definition is **the energy required to remove one electron from each atom in one mole of gaseous atoms under standard conditions**, but see later.

The **second** ionisation energy is:

$$M^+(g) \rightarrow M^{2+}(g) + e^-$$

The ***n*th** ionisation energy is:

$$M^{(n-1)+}(g) \rightarrow M^{n+}(g) + e^-$$

For potassium, the highest energy electron is the $4s^1$, and this is the first to be removed:

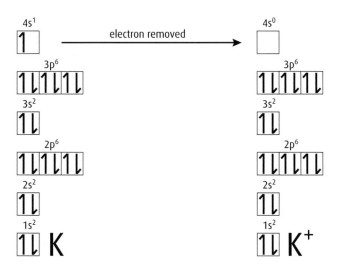

Learning objectives

- Interpret and explain graphs of successive ionisation energies
- Explain the variation in ionisation energy across a period and down a group

> The highest energy electrons are removed first.

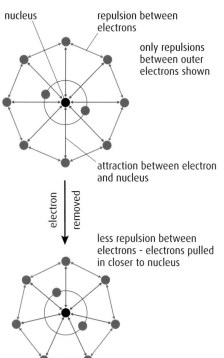

Figure 2.33 When an electron is removed from an atom, the remaining electrons are drawn closer to the nucleus due to reduced repulsion.

HL **The second ionisation energy is always higher than the first**, and this can be explained in two ways:

1 Once an electron has been removed from an atom, a positive ion is created. A positive ion attracts a negatively charged electron more strongly than a neutral atom does. More energy is therefore required to remove the electron from a positive ion.
2 Once an electron has been removed from an atom, there is less repulsion between the remaining electrons. They are therefore pulled in closer to the nucleus (Figure 2.33). If they are closer to the nucleus, they are more strongly attracted and more difficult to remove.

Successive ionisation energies of potassium

This graph shows the energy required to remove each electron in turn from a gaseous potassium atom.

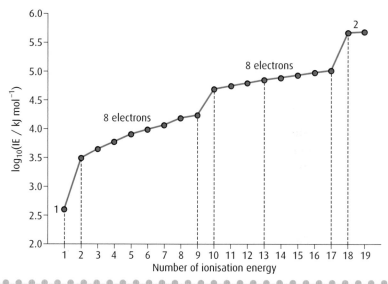

A log scale is being used here to allow all the data to be plotted on one graph, but although on one level this has made the data easier to interpret and supported the explanations that have been given, it has also distorted the data. The difference between the first and second ionisation energies of potassium is about 2600 kJ mol^{-1}, but the difference between the 18th and 19th ionisations energies is over 30 000 kJ mol^{-1}! How can the way data are presented be used by scientists to support their theories? Can you find examples where the scale on a graph has been chosen to exaggerate a particular trend – is scientific knowledge objective or is it a matter of interpretation and presentation? The arguments for and against human-made climate change are a classic example of where the interpretation and presentation of data are key in influencing public opinion.

Plotting the log$_{10}$ of these numbers reduces the range. The first ionisation energy of potassium is 418 kJ mol^{-1}, whereas the 19th is 475 000 kJ mol^{-1}. It would be very difficult to plot these values on a single graph.

The simple electronic configuration of potassium is 2,8,8,1, and this can be deduced directly from the graph above. The large jumps in the graph occur between main energy levels (shells).

The outermost electron in potassium is furthest from the nucleus and therefore least strongly attracted by the nucleus. This electron is thus easiest to remove. It is also **shielded** (**screened**) from the full attractive force of the nucleus by the other 18 electrons in the atom (Figure **2.34**).

Complete shells of electrons between the nucleus and a particular electron reduce the attractive force of the nucleus for that electron. There are three full shells of electrons between the outermost electron and the nucleus, and if this shielding were perfect the **effective nuclear charge** felt by the outer electron would be +1 (19+ in nucleus, 18 shielding electrons). This shielding is not perfect, however, and the effective nuclear charge felt by the outermost electron is higher than +1.

An alternative view of shielding is that the outer electron is attracted by the nucleus but repelled by the inner electrons.

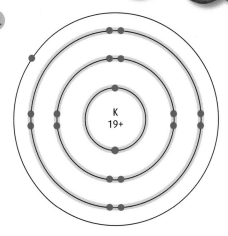

Figure 2.34 The outer electron in a potassium ion is shielded from the full attractive force of the nucleus by the inner shells of electrons (shaded in blue).

Extension

In electrostatics a sphere of charge behaves like a point charge at its centre; therefore relative to the outer electron, spheres of charge inside (the electron shells) behave as if their charge is at the nucleus. The charge felt by the outer electron is thus **19+ + 18− = 1+** acting at the nucleus.

The electrons do not form perfect spheres of charge, and the movement of the outer electron is not simply in an orbit around the nucleus as shown, and this is why the effective nuclear charge felt by the outer electron in potassium is greater than 1. There are various ways of estimating or calculating the effective nuclear charge for a particular electron in an atom (e.g. Slater's rules). Calculations suggest that the effective nuclear charge felt by the outer electron in potassium is about 3.5+.

Once the first electron has been removed, the next electron is considerably more difficult to remove (there is a large jump between first and second ionisation energies). This is consistent with the electron being removed from a **new main energy level** (**shell**). This electron is closer to the nucleus and therefore more strongly attracted. It is also shielded by fewer electrons (the ten electrons in the inner main energy levels), as electrons in the same shell do not shield each other very well (they do not get between the electron and the nucleus).

The ionisation energy now rises steadily as the electrons are removed successively from the same main energy level. There is no significant change in shielding, but as the positive charge on the ion increases it becomes more difficult to remove a negatively charged electron (less electron–electron repulsion, so the electrons are pulled in closer to the nucleus).

There is another large jump in ionisation energies between the ninth and the tenth, as the ninth electron is the last to be removed from the third main energy level but the tenth is the first to be removed from the second level. The tenth electron is significantly closer to the nucleus and is less shielded than the ninth electron to be removed.

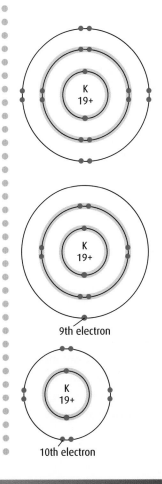

9th electron

10th electron

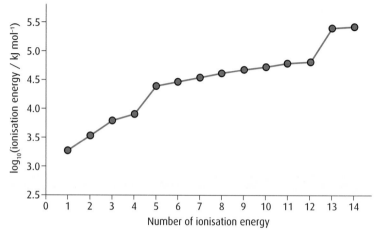

HL Graphs of successive ionisation energy give us information about how many electrons are in a particular energy level. Consider the graph for silicon shown in Figure **2.35**. There is a large jump in the ionisation energy graph between the fourth and the fifth ionisation energies, which suggests that these electrons are removed from different main energy levels. It can therefore be deduced that silicon has four electrons in its outer main energy level (shell) and is in group 4 of the periodic table.

Figure 2.35 The successive ionisation energies of silicon.

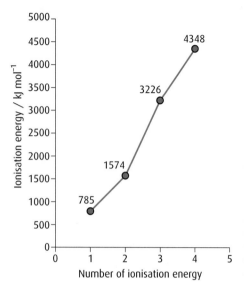

Figure 2.36 The first four ionisation energies of silicon.

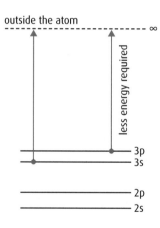

Figure 2.37 More energy is required to remove an electron from the 3s sub-level of silicon than from the 3p sub-level.

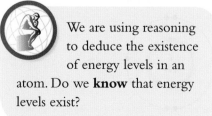 We are using reasoning to deduce the existence of energy levels in an atom. Do we **know** that energy levels exist?

Application 2

If a graph of ionisation energy (rather than $\log_{10}$ ionisation energy) is plotted for the removal of the first few electrons from a silicon atom, more features can be seen on the graph (Figure **2.36**). It can be seen that there is a larger jump in the ionisation energy between the second and third ionisation energies.

The full electronic configuration for silicon is $1s^2 2s^2 2p^6 3s^2 3p^2$. The first two electrons are removed from the 3p sub-level (subshell), whereas the third electron is removed from the 3s sub-level (Figure **2.37**). The 3p sub-level is higher in energy than the 3s sub-level, and therefore less energy is required to remove the electron. This provides evidence for the existence of sub energy levels (subshells) in an atom.

Test yourself

15 The table shows the successive ionisation of some elements. Deduce which group in the periodic table each element is in.

| | Ionisation energy / kJ mol^{-1} | | |
Number of ionisation energy	Element X	Element Z	Element Q
1	1085	736	1400
2	2349	1448	2851
3	4612	7719	4570
4	6212	10522	7462
5	37765	13606	9429
6	47195	17964	53174

Variation in ionisation energy across a period HL

The first ionisation energies for the elements in period 2, from Li to Ne, are plotted in Figure **2.38**.

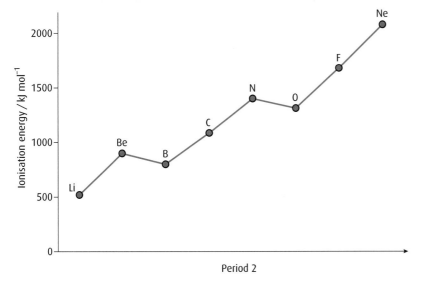

Figure 2.38 The first ionisation energies for the period 2 elements.

The nuclear charge increases from Li (3+) to Ne (10+) as protons are added to the nucleus (Figure **2.39**). The electrons are all removed from the same main energy level and, as electrons in the same energy level do not shield each other very well, there is no big change in shielding. Therefore the force on the outer electrons increases from left to right across the period, and the outer electron is more difficult to remove for neon. The neon atom is also smaller than the lithium atom, and so the outer electron is closer to the nucleus and more strongly held.

This can also be explained in terms of the effective nuclear charge felt by the outer electron in neon being higher.

There are two exceptions to the general increase in ionisation energy across a period.

The first exception is that boron has a lower first ionisation energy than beryllium.

Despite the fact that B has a higher nuclear charge (more protons in the nucleus) than Be, the ionisation energy is lower. The electronic configurations of Be and B are:

Be $1s^2 2s^2$ B $1s^2 2s^2 2p^1$

The general trend is that ionisation energy increases from left to right across a period.

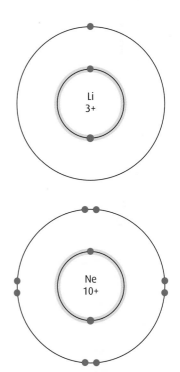

Figure 2.39 Ne has more protons in the nucleus, but the amount of shielding from inner electrons is roughly the same as in Li.

Extension

An alternative, more in-depth explanation is that the 2p electron in B is shielded to a certain extent by the 2s electrons, and this increase in shielding from Be to B offsets the lowering in energy of the 2p sub-level that occurs as the nuclear charge increases. 2s electrons shield the 2p electrons, as there is a significant probability of the 2s electron existing closer to the nucleus, and therefore getting between the 2p electron and the nucleus.

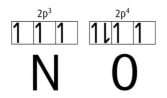

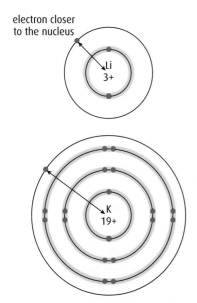

Figure 2.41 In a larger atom the outer electron is further from the nucleus and therefore less attracted by it. The first ionisation energy will be lower.

> Down a group in the periodic table the ionisation energy **decreases**.

The major difference is that the electron to be removed from the boron atom is in a 2p sub-level, whereas it is in a 2s sub-level in beryllium. The 2p sub-level in B is higher in energy than the 2s sub-level in Be, and therefore less energy is required to remove an electron from B.

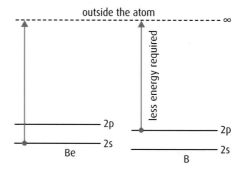

> **The second exception is that the first ionisation energy of oxygen is lower than that of nitrogen.**

The electronic configurations for nitrogen and oxygen are:

$$N \ 1s^2 2s^2 2p^3 \qquad O \ 1s^2 2s^2 2p^4$$

The major difference is that oxygen has two electrons paired up in the same p orbital, but nitrogen does not. An electron in the same p orbital as another electron is easier to remove than one in an orbital by itself because of the repulsion from the other electron.

> When two electrons are in the same p orbital they are closer together than if there is one in each p orbital. If the electrons are closer together, they repel each other more strongly. If there is greater repulsion, an electron is easier to remove.

Variation in ionisation energy down a group

The variation in first ionisation energy down a group can be seen in Figure **2.40**. First ionisation energy decreases because the size of the atoms increases so that the outer electron is further from the nucleus and therefore less strongly attracted by the nucleus (Figure **2.41**).

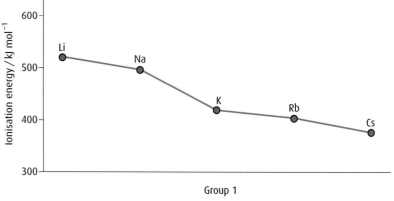

Figure 2.40 Variation in first ionisation energy down group 1.

Although the nuclear charge increases down a group, this is largely balanced out by an increase in shielding down the group, as there are more electron energy levels (shells). It is thus increase in size that causes the decrease in ionisation energy down the group.

The force between two charges $\propto \dfrac{1}{r^2}$, where r is the distance between the charges.

HL

Application 3

Extension

As with many situations in chemistry, things are not always as simple as they appear at first glance. Look carefully at the trends in ionisation energy down group 3 and group 4. See if you can come up with an explanation for these trends.

The transition metals

The transition metals will be considered in more detail in another chapter, but they are mentioned here for completeness. These elements represent a slight departure from the 'last in, first out' rule for ionisation energy. Although the sub-levels are filled in the order 4s then 3d, **the 4s electrons are always removed before the 3d electrons**.

The full electronic configuration for an iron atom is $1s^2 2s^2 2p^6 3s^2 3p^6 4s^2 3d^6$. The electronic configuration for Fe^{2+} is $1s^2 2s^2 2p^6 3s^2 3p^6 3d^6$. The electronic configuration for Fe^{3+} is $1s^2 2s^2 2p^6 3s^2 3p^6 3d^5$.

Self-tests 5 & 6

Test yourself

16 Work out the full electronic configurations of the following ions:
    a Ca^{2+} **b** Cr^{3+} **c** Co^{2+} **d** Cs^+

Extension

When removing electrons we should not really think about in which order they were put into the atom but consider the stability of the final ion. The electronic arrangement of the final ion will be that which generates the ion of lowest energy. s electrons are generally better at shielding other electrons than are d electrons; thus, by removing the 4s electrons, the shielding of the remaining 3d electrons is reduced, and these are lowered in energy. If the 3d electrons are removed, there is no real energy advantage in terms of reduced shielding; therefore it is less favourable to remove the 3d electrons. Overall, what this all amounts to is that, **in the ion, the 3d sub-level is lower in energy than the 4s orbital**.

Exam-style questions

1 Which of the following contains 50 neutrons?

    A $^{50}_{23}V$ **B** $^{89}_{39}Y^+$ **C** $^{91}_{40}Zr^+$ **D** $^{86}_{37}Rb^-$

2 Which of the following will be deflected least in a mass spectrometer?

    A $^{142}_{60}Nd^+$ **B** $^{238}_{92}U^{2+}$ **C** $^{102}_{44}Ru^+$ **D** $^{127}_{53}I^+$

3 Which of the following has more electrons than neutrons?

    A $^{9}_{4}Be^{2+}$ **B** $^{31}_{15}P^{3-}$ **C** $^{79}_{35}Br^-$ **D** $^{40}_{20}Ca^{2+}$

4 Rhenium has two naturally occurring isotopes, ^{185}Re and ^{187}Re. The relative atomic mass of rhenium is 186.2. What are the natural abundances of these isotopes?

    A 40% ^{185}Re and 60% ^{187}Re

    B 60% ^{185}Re and 40% ^{187}Re

    C 12% ^{185}Re and 88% ^{187}Re

    D 88% ^{185}Re and 12% ^{187}Re

5 Which of the following electronic transitions in the hydrogen atom will be of highest energy?

    A $n = 8 \rightarrow n = 4$ **C** $n = 9 \rightarrow n = 3$

    B $n = 7 \rightarrow n = 2$ **D** $n = 6 \rightarrow n = 2$

HL 6 Within any main energy level the correct sequence, when the sub energy levels (subshells) are arranged in order of increasing energy, is:

    A s   p   f   d   **C** s   p   d   f

    B d   s   f   p   **D** s   d   p   f

7 Which of the following contains ten electrons in d orbitals and 18 electrons in p orbitals?

    A Cs   **B** Cu   **C** Rb   **D** Cd

8 Which of the following does **not** have three unpaired electrons?

    A P   **B** V   **C** Mn^{3+} **D** Ni^{3+}

9 In which of the following does the second element have a lower first ionisation energy than the first?

    A Si   C

    B Na   Mg

    C Be   B

    D Ar   Ne

10 The first four ionisation energies of an element are shown in the table below.

Ionisation energy	kJ mol⁻¹
1st	418
2nd	3046
3rd	4403
4th	5866

In which group in the periodic table is this element?

        A group 1   **B** group 2   **C** group 3   **D** group 4

11 a Define the terms **atomic number** and **isotopes** of an element. [3]

   b State the number of protons, neutrons and electrons in an atom of $^{57}_{26}$Fe. [2]

   c A sample of iron from a meteorite is analysed in a mass spectrometer.
     i State the order in which the stages occur in the operation of a mass spectrometer. [2]
     ii Explain what happens at each stage in the operation of a mass spectrometer. [5]
     iii The following results were obtained from the analysis of the iron:

Isotope	Abundance / %
^{54}Fe	5.80
^{56}Fe	91.16
^{57}Fe	3.04

     Calculate the relative atomic mass of this sample, giving your answer to two decimal places. [2]

12 a Describe the difference between a **continuous spectrum** and a **line spectrum**. [2]

   b Sketch a diagram of the emission spectrum of hydrogen in the visible region, showing clearly the relative energies of any lines. [2]

   c Explain how a line in the visible emission spectrum of hydrogen arises. [3]

13 a Write the full electronic configuration of an atom of rubidium. [1]

   b State and explain how the first ionisation energy of rubidium compares with that of potassium. [3]

   c Write an equation showing the second ionisation of rubidium. [2]

   d Explain why the second ionisation of rubidium is substantially higher than the first ionisation energy. [3]

   e State and explain how the first ionisation energy of strontium compares with that of rubidium. [3]

14 a Write the full electronic configuration of the O^{2-} ion. [1]

   b Give the formula of an atom and an ion that are isoelectronic with the O^{2-} ion. [2]

   c Explain why the first ionisation energy of oxygen is lower than that of nitrogen. [2]

   d Sketch a graph showing the variation of **second** ionisation energy for the elements in period 2 of the periodic table from lithium to neon. [3]

Summary

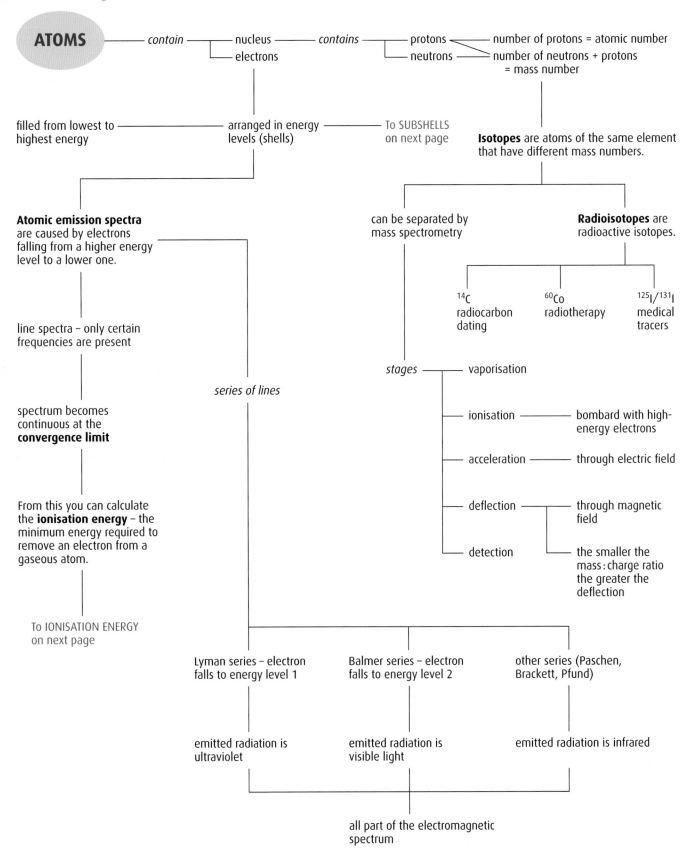

ATOMS — *contain* — nucleus — *contains* — protons — number of protons = atomic number

electrons — neutrons — number of neutrons + protons = mass number

filled from lowest to highest energy — arranged in energy levels (shells) — To SUBSHELLS on next page

Isotopes are atoms of the same element that have different mass numbers.

Atomic emission spectra are caused by electrons falling from a higher energy level to a lower one.

can be separated by mass spectrometry

Radioisotopes are radioactive isotopes.

^{14}C radiocarbon dating

^{60}Co radiotherapy

^{125}I/^{131}I medical tracers

line spectra – only certain frequencies are present

stages — vaporisation

ionisation — bombard with high-energy electrons

acceleration — through electric field

series of lines

spectrum becomes continuous at the **convergence limit**

deflection — through magnetic field

detection — the smaller the mass : charge ratio the greater the deflection

From this you can calculate the **ionisation energy** – the minimum energy required to remove an electron from a gaseous atom.

To IONISATION ENERGY on next page

Lyman series – electron falls to energy level 1

Balmer series – electron falls to energy level 2

other series (Paschen, Brackett, Pfund)

emitted radiation is ultraviolet

emitted radiation is visible light

emitted radiation is infrared

all part of the electromagnetic spectrum

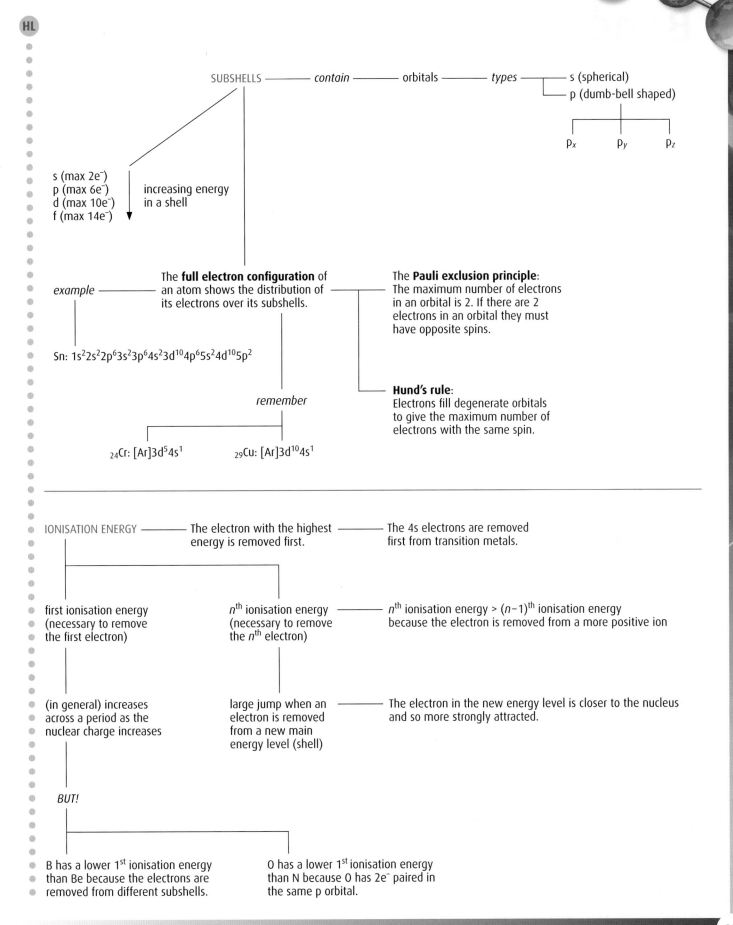

SUBSHELLS —— *contain* —— orbitals —— *types* —┬— s (spherical)
└— p (dumb-bell shaped)

p_x p_y p_z

s (max 2e⁻)
p (max 6e⁻)   increasing energy
d (max 10e⁻)   in a shell
f (max 14e⁻)

example —— The **full electron configuration** of an atom shows the distribution of its electrons over its subshells.

The **Pauli exclusion principle**: The maximum number of electrons in an orbital is 2. If there are 2 electrons in an orbital they must have opposite spins.

Sn: $1s^2 2s^2 2p^6 3s^2 3p^6 4s^2 3d^{10} 4p^6 5s^2 4d^{10} 5p^2$

Hund's rule: Electrons fill degenerate orbitals to give the maximum number of electrons with the same spin.

remember

$_{24}$Cr: [Ar]$3d^5 4s^1$ $_{29}$Cu: [Ar]$3d^{10} 4s^1$

IONISATION ENERGY —— The electron with the highest energy is removed first. —— The 4s electrons are removed first from transition metals.

first ionisation energy (necessary to remove the first electron)

n^{th} ionisation energy (necessary to remove the nth electron) —— n^{th} ionisation energy > $(n-1)^{th}$ ionisation energy because the electron is removed from a more positive ion

(in general) increases across a period as the nuclear charge increases

large jump when an electron is removed from a new main energy level (shell) —— The electron in the new energy level is closer to the nucleus and so more strongly attracted.

BUT!

B has a lower 1st ionisation energy than Be because the electrons are removed from different subshells.

O has a lower 1st ionisation energy than N because O has 2e⁻ paired in the same p orbital.

3 Bonding

Learning objectives

- Recognise the formulas of ionic and covalent compounds
- Understand how ions are formed and recall the formulas of some common ions
- Work out the formulas of ionic compounds from the charges on the ions
- Describe the structure of sodium chloride as an example of an ionic lattice
- Explain the physical properties of ionic compounds in terms of structure and bonding

Ionic compound: **metal** and **non-metal**
Covalent compound: two or more **non-metals**

Ionic bonding is the electrostatic attraction between oppositely charged ions.

Ions are charged particles, which are formed when atoms lose or gain electrons.

Electrostatic attraction: positive charges attract negative charges and vice versa.

Isoelectronic: same number of electrons.

3.1 Ionic bonding

Bonding

Compounds may be divided into two main classes according to the bonding in them: that is, they are either **ionic** or **covalent** compounds. The type of bonding present can usually be deduced by looking at the formula of a compound. Covalent compounds are those between two or more non-metallic elements, whereas ionic compounds are usually between a metallic element and a non-metallic one. For example, NaCl is an ionic compound, but CH_4 is a covalent one.

There are some compounds for which the distinction is not so clear. For instance, ammonium chloride does not contain any metallic elements but has ionic bonding between the ammonium ion (NH_4^+) and the chloride ion (Cl^-). In addition to this, within the NH_4^+ ion there is covalent bonding.

Generally, as a rough rule of thumb, elements that are close together in the periodic table form covalent compounds but elements that are far apart in the periodic table form ionic compounds. Thus elements from groups 1 and 7 combine to form ionic compounds (CsF being the most ionic) but elements from groups 4, 5, 6 and 7 combine to form covalent compounds. This is discussed in terms of electronegativity on page **120**.

Ionic bonding

Positive ions are usually formed by metallic elements by the loss of (an) electron(s). For example, magnesium loses the two electrons in its highest energy level (outer shell) to form a 2+ ion:

$$Mg \rightarrow Mg^{2+} + 2e^-$$

Negative ions are usually formed by non-metallic elements by the gain of (an) electron(s). For example, oxygen gains two electrons to fill up its outer shell (highest occupied energy level):

$$O + 2e^- \rightarrow O^{2-}$$

At the simplest level, when elements in the main groups of the periodic table (groups 1, 2, 3 (to a certain extent), 5, 6 and 7) form ions, electrons are gained or lost to generate the electronic configuration of the nearest **noble gas**. That is, electrons are gained or lost to generate an ion that is isoelectronic with the nearest noble gas.

Another way of saying this is that electrons are lost or gained to generate a full outer shell of electrons. Although this is true for the first 20 elements, it is not generally true after that because of the existence of transition metals (and d orbitals).

The fact that it is **not generally true** can be seen by looking at **transition metal ions**.

> The transition metals can form more than one ion. For instance, iron can form iron(II) – Fe^{2+} – and iron(III) – Fe^{3+}.

The Fe^{2+} ion has 24 electrons, and the Fe^{3+} ion has 23 electrons, so neither is isoelectronic with a noble gas.

The 4s electrons are lost first when a transition metal atom forms an ion; therefore the electronic configurations of Fe^{2+} and Fe^{3+} are:

Fe^{2+} $1s^2 2s^2 2p^6 3s^2 3p^6 3d^6$
Fe^{3+} $1s^2 2s^2 2p^6 3s^2 3p^6 3d^5$

The number of electrons lost by elements in groups 1 to 3 when they form ions is given by the group number. For instance, magnesium, in **group 2** of the periodic table, has two outer shell electrons, and therefore forms a **2+** ion (Figure **3.1**).

HL

These do not have noble gas electronic configurations.

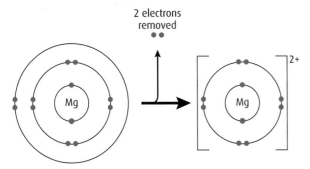

2 electrons removed

Figure 3.1 The Mg^{2+} ion is **isoelectronic** with the noble gas atom neon.

Note: metal atoms do not 'want' to form ions with noble gas electronic configurations; for instance, it takes the input of over $2000\,kJ\,mol^{-1}$ of energy to remove two electrons from a magnesium atom to form the Mg^{2+} ion.

The number of electrons gained by elements in groups 5 to 7 when they form ions is given by eight minus the group number. For instance oxygen, in **group 6** of the periodic table, has six outer shell electrons and therefore gains $(8-6) = 2$ electrons to form a **2−** ion (Figure **3.2**).

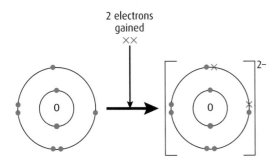

2 electrons gained

Figure 3.2 The O^{2-} ion is **isoelectronic** with the noble gas atom neon.

When an ionic compound is formed, **electrons are transferred** from one atom to another to form positive and negative ions. Electrons cannot be created or destroyed; therefore, the **total number of electrons lost must always equal the total number gained**. You can see this in the formation of magnesium oxide (MgO):

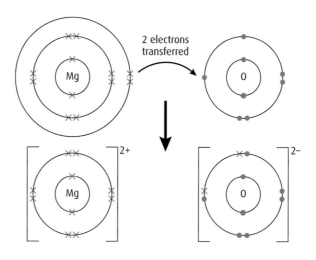

In the formation of magnesium fluoride, one Mg atom must combine with two F atoms, as Mg loses two electrons when it forms an ion but each F atom can gain only one electron. The formula of magnesium fluoride is thus MgF_2 (Figure **3.3**).

The formulas of ions

The formulas of commonly encountered positive ions are given in Table **3.1** and of some negative ions in Table **3.2**.

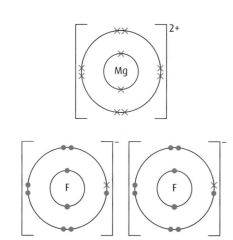

Figure 3.3 The ions in magnesium fluoride.

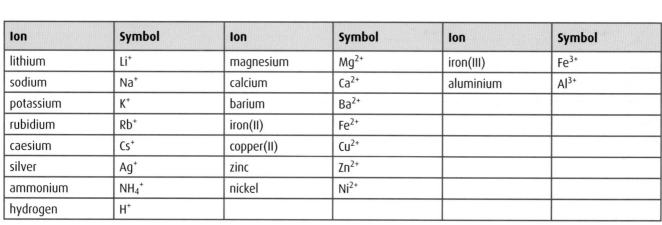

Ion	Symbol	Ion	Symbol	Ion	Symbol
lithium	Li^+	magnesium	Mg^{2+}	iron(III)	Fe^{3+}
sodium	Na^+	calcium	Ca^{2+}	aluminium	Al^{3+}
potassium	K^+	barium	Ba^{2+}		
rubidium	Rb^+	iron(II)	Fe^{2+}		
caesium	Cs^+	copper(II)	Cu^{2+}		
silver	Ag^+	zinc	Zn^{2+}		
ammonium	NH_4^+	nickel	Ni^{2+}		
hydrogen	H^+				

Table 3.1 Positive ions.

Ion	Symbol	Ion	Symbol	Ion	Symbol
fluoride	F^-	oxide	O^{2-}	nitride	N^{3-}
chloride	Cl^-	sulfide	S^{2-}	phosphate	PO_4^{3-}
bromide	Br^-	carbonate	CO_3^{2-}		
iodide	I^-	sulfate	SO_4^{2-}		
hydroxide	OH^-				
hydrogencarbonate	HCO_3^-				
nitrate	NO_3^-				

Table 3.2 Negative ions.

Working out the formulas of ionic compounds

To work out the formula of aluminium fluoride, we need to consider the number of electrons lost by aluminium and gained by fluorine. Aluminium is in group 3 of the periodic table and so forms a 3+ ion by the loss of three electrons, whereas fluorine, in group 7, gains one electron to generate a full outer shell and a 1− ion. The three electrons transferred from the Al must be gained by three separate F atoms; therefore the formula of aluminium fluoride is AlF_3.

Another way to look at this is to consider that the overall charge on the compound is zero, so the 3+ charge on the Al^{3+} ion must be cancelled out by $3 \times 1-$ charge on $3F^-$ ions, i.e. $Al^{3+}(F^-)_3$.

Similarly, the formula of magnesium hydroxide is $Mg(OH)_2$, where the 2+ charge on the Mg^{2+} ion is cancelled out by the $2 \times 1-$ charge on two OH^- ions, i.e. $Mg^{2+}(OH^-)_2$.

A shortcut to working out formulas is to switch over the charges on the ions to generate the formula. For example:

$$Al^{3+} \diagdown\!\!\!\!\diagup O^{2-} \longrightarrow Al_2O_3$$

Transition metals ions can form more than one ion, and so the oxidation number of the ion is usually given with the name. For example, iron can form iron(II) sulfate or iron(III) sulfate. The Roman numeral in brackets indicates the oxidation number of the ion, which is the same as the charge on the ion. Iron(III) sulfate, therefore, contains the Fe^{3+} ion and has the formula $Fe_2(SO_4)_3$. Iron(II) sulfate contains the Fe^{2+} ion and has the formula $FeSO_4$.

The ionic bond and ionic crystals

An ionic bond is an **electrostatic** attraction between oppositely charged ions.

Examiner's tip
The formulas and charges of ions such as sulfate and nitrate must be learnt, but the formulas of ions formed by elements in groups 1, 2, 3, 5, 6 and 7 can be worked out.

The brackets around the OH are essential as, otherwise the formula would read $MgOH_2$, and would indicate the presence of only one O atom.

Rubies and sapphires are mainly aluminium oxide.

These are all **giant structures** – there are no individual molecules of sodium chloride. Instead, the bonding extends fairly uniformly throughout the whole structure.

A crystal of sodium chloride consists of a giant lattice of Na⁺ and Cl⁻ ions (Figure **3.4**). All the Na⁺ ions in the crystal attract all the Cl⁻ ions, and vice versa, and it is this attraction between oppositely charged ions that holds the crystal together. These electrostatic forces are strong; therefore it is difficult to break apart the lattice structure.

It is often better to avoid the term 'ionic bond' and rather talk about 'ionic bonding' as a whole – the dotted lines in the diagrams of the lattice structures are **not** ionic bonds, they are simply there to give a better idea of the shape. Ionic bonding (electrostatic attractions between oppositely charged ions) extends throughout the whole structure in all directions – there are no individual ionic bonds.

a

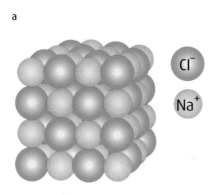

b

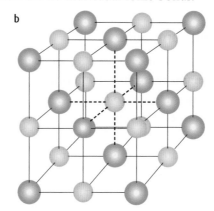

c

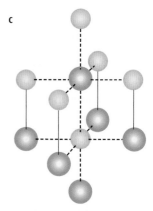

Figure 3.4 (**a**) A space-filling diagram of the NaCl lattice. The lattice keeps on going in three dimensions – only a tiny part of the structure is shown. (**b**) An expanded view of the NaCl lattice. (**c**) Each Na⁺ ion is surrounded by six Cl⁻ ions in an octahedral array, and vice versa.

Extension

This is only one possible lattice for ionic crystals. The type of lattice adopted depends on the formula of the crystal and the ratio of the radii of the positive and negative ions.

Examples of physical properties are melting point, solubility, electrical conductivity, etc. Chemical properties are how a substance reacts.

Extension

Coulomb's law – the force between two charges – is given by:

$$F = \frac{1}{4\pi\varepsilon_o} \times \frac{q_1 q_2}{r^2}$$

where q_1 and q_2 are charges, r is the distance between the charges and ε_o is the permittivity of free space.

Physical properties of ionic compounds

Melting points and boiling points

Ionic compounds have high melting points and boiling points. For instance, sodium chloride has a melting point of 801 °C and a boiling point of over 1400 °C, while magnesium oxide has a melting point of over 2800 °C and a boiling point of about 3600 °C.

The high melting and boiling points of ionic solids are due to the strong electrostatic forces between the oppositely charged ions. When the ionic solid is melted, the electrostatic forces throughout the giant lattice must be broken, and because these are so strong a lot of energy is required.

Magnesium oxide has a much higher melting point than sodium chloride, because the electrostatic attractions between the 2+ and 2− ions in the magnesium oxide lattice are much stronger than between the 1+ and 1− ions in sodium chloride. A higher temperature is required to provide sufficient energy to separate the ions in magnesium oxide. The force between ions is proportional to the product of the charges (all other things being equal).

Volatility

Ionic solids have low volatility ('volatility' refers to how readily a substance evaporates). The volatility of ionic substances is low, because the electrostatic forces between the ions are strong.

Electrical conductivity in ionic solids

Ionic solids do not conduct electricity when solid. In the solid state, the ions are held tightly in position in the lattice structure so that they are not free to move around (other than vibrate).

When the ionic substance is melted the ions are able to move freely throughout the liquid. Positive ions are then able to move towards a negative electrode and negative ions towards a positive electrode, thus allowing the conduction of electricity.

Solubility in water

Ionic substances are often soluble in water. Water is a polar solvent, and energy is released when the ions are hydrated by being surrounded by water molecules (see Figure **3.5**). This energy pays back the energy required to break apart the ionic lattice.

Electrical conductivity in ionic solutions

Aqueous solutions (solutions dissolved in water) of ionic substances conduct electricity. This is because the **ions** are free to move around (Figure **3.6**).

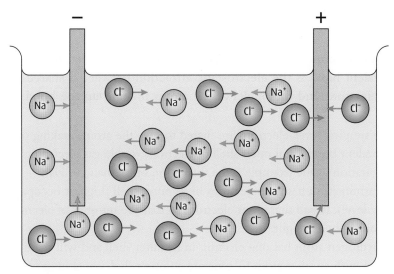

Figure 3.6 Ions move towards the oppositely charged electrode.

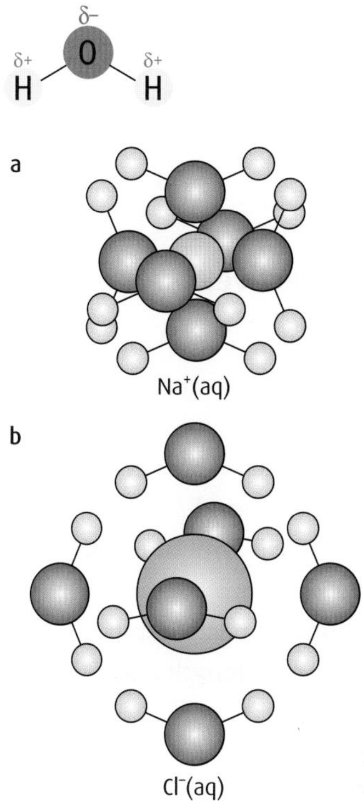

Figure 3.5 Hydrated sodium (**a**) and chloride (**b**) ions.

Solubility in non-polar solvents

Ionic solids are not usually soluble in non-polar solvents such as hexane. This is because a great deal of energy is required to break apart the ionic lattice, and this is not paid back by the energy released when the non-polar solvent forms interactions with the ions (van der Waals' forces). This will be considered in more detail on pages **132–133**.

Hardness

Although ionic solids are hard, due to the strong forces between the ions, they are also brittle. This is because a slight displacement of one layer relative to another results in repulsive forces between the ions and the crystal breaks apart (Figure **3.7**). This will be compared with the malleability of metals in the section on metallic bonding (see page **138**).

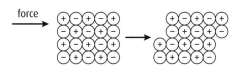

Figure 3.7 When a force is applied to an ionic solid, layers can shift relative to each other. If similarly charged ions line up, the crystal will break apart.

Test yourself

1 State whether the following compounds have ionic or covalent bonding.

   LiF   **CF₄**   **CaO**   **NH₃**   **PCl₃**   **CuCl₂**

2 Write the formulas of the following compounds.

a magnesium oxide	**b** barium sulfate	**c** calcium hydroxide
d sodium oxide	**e** strontium sulfide	**f** aluminium oxide
g lithium nitride	**h** magnesium phosphate	**i** magnesium fluoride
j potassium sulfate	**k** ammonium carbonate	**l** silver sulfide
m silver nitrate	**n** ammonium chloride	**o** copper nitrate
p rubidium carbonate		

Learning objectives

- Understand that a covalent bond is formed when electrons are shared
- Understand what is meant by a dative covalent bond
- Work out Lewis structures for molecules and ions
- Understand the relationship between bond strength and bond length

3.2 Covalent molecular substances

Covalent bonding

> Covalent bonding occurs when atoms share electrons, and a covalent bond is the electrostatic attraction between a shared pair of electrons and the nuclei of the atoms making up the bond.

At the simplest level, electrons are shared to give the atoms making up the covalent bond a full outer shell of electrons (noble gas electronic configuration). One example is the formation of methane (CH_4).

A carbon atom has four electrons in its outer shell (highest occupied energy level). It will share four electrons so that the number of electrons in its outer shell is eight.

A hydrogen atom has one electron in its outer shell and will share one electron with another atom to generate an outer shell containing two electrons: i.e. a full outer shell (the same number of electrons as helium).

carbon atom

hydrogen atom

In methane the shared electrons are in the outer shell of both atoms making up the bond, and so each atom has a full outer shell of electrons (Figure **3.8**).

Two alternative ways of representing the covalent bonding in methane are shown in Figure **3.9**. These are Lewis structures. Lewis structures will be discussed below.

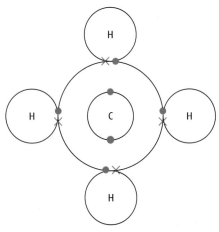

Figure 3.8 The covalent bonding in CH_4.

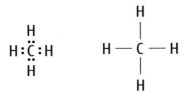

Figure 3.9 Two different types of Lewis structure for methane. In the second one, the line between the atoms represents a shared pair of electrons: that is, a covalent bond.

Consider the bonding in water (H_2O): an oxygen atom has six electrons in its outer shell and so will share two electrons to generate a full outer shell (eight electrons) or an octet of electrons.

The covalent bonding in water is shown in Figure **3.10**.

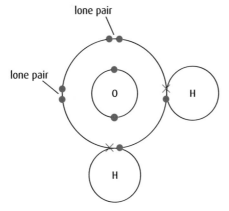

Figure 3.10 Covalent bonding in water. All atoms have full outer shells of electrons.

The pairs of electrons in the outer shell of oxygen that are not involved in the covalent bonds are called lone pairs of electrons. There are two lone pairs in the outer shell of the oxygen atom in a molecule of water. Alternative representations of the covalent bonding in water are shown in Figure **3.11**.

Multiple bonds

It is possible for more than one pair of electrons to be shared between two atoms. A double bond results from the sharing of two pairs of electrons, and a triple bond arises when three pairs of electrons are shared. For example, the covalent bonding in an oxygen molecule, O_2, is shown in Figure **3.12**.

Four electrons – that is, two pairs – are shared, and therefore there is a double bond between oxygen atoms.

The covalent bonding in the nitrogen molecule, N_2, is shown in Figure **3.13**. A nitrogen atom shares three electrons to generate a full outer shell; therefore, six electrons are shared when two nitrogen atoms combine to form N_2.

Three shared pairs of electrons between two atoms indicates a triple bond. More examples of molecules with multiple bonding are shown in Figure **3.14** (overleaf).

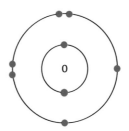

A lone pair is a pair of electrons in the outer shell of an atom, which is not involved in covalent bonding.

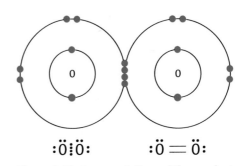

Figure 3.11 Lewis structures for water.

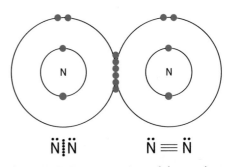

Figure 3.12 Representations of the covalent bonding in O_2.

Figure 3.13 Representations of the covalent bonding in N_2.

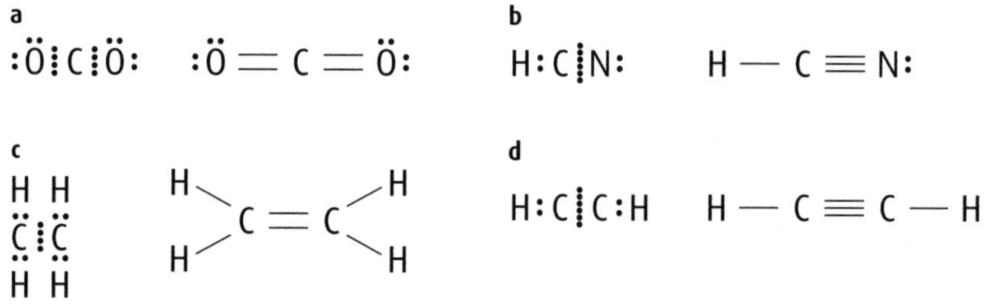

a

$:\ddot{O}:C:\ddot{O}:$ $:\ddot{O} = C = \ddot{O}:$

b

$H:C \vdots N:$ $H - C \equiv N:$

c

H H
$\ddot{C} \vdots \ddot{C}$
H H

$\begin{matrix} H \\ \diagdown \\ \end{matrix} C = C \begin{matrix} H \\ \diagup \end{matrix}$ with H below

d

$H:C \vdots C:H$ $H - C \equiv C - H$

Figure 3.14 Covalent bonding in (**a**) CO_2, (**b**) HCN, (**c**) C_2H_4 (ethene) and (**d**) C_2H_2 (ethyne).

In the cases above, with the exception of H, all atoms have eight electrons in their outer shell. This is called an **octet**, and the atom is said to have **attained an octet** or **completed its octet**. In most covalent molecules, each atom will have an octet in its outer shell.

However, it is not always the case that formation of a covalent bond results in a noble gas electronic configuration and eight electrons in the outer shell. In BF_3 (Figure **3.15**), boron has only six electrons in its outer shell. This is because a boron atom has only three electrons in its outer shell and can therefore share a maximum of three electrons. A sulfur atom has six electrons in its outer shell, and it can share all of these when it forms covalent bonds in SF_6 (Figure **3.16**). The S atom has 12 electrons in its outer shell, and we talk about sulfur having **expanded its octet**, as it has more than eight electrons in its outer shell. Only elements in period 3 or higher can expand their octet.

Examiner's tip
Expansion of the octet is very rarely encountered at Standard Level.

Figure 3.15 Covalent bonding in BF_3.

Figure 3.16 Covalent bonding in SF_6.

What holds the atoms together in a covalent bond?

A covalent bond is the electrostatic interaction between the positively charged nuclei of both atoms and the shared pair of electrons.

The electrons are negatively charged and, as the shared electrons are attracted to the nuclei (positively charged) of both atoms simultaneously, this holds the atoms together (Figure **3.17**).

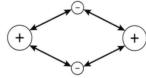

Figure 3.17 The positively charged nuclei attract the negatively charged electrons in the bond.

As can be seen from Table **3.3**, triple bonds are stronger than double bonds, which are stronger than a single bond. This is because the attraction of the two nuclei for three electron pairs (six electrons) in a triple bond is greater than the attraction for two electron pairs (four electrons) in a double bond, which is greater than the attraction for one electron pair (two electrons) in a single bond (Figure **3.18**).

Strength
single bonds
double bonds
triple bonds
increasing strength

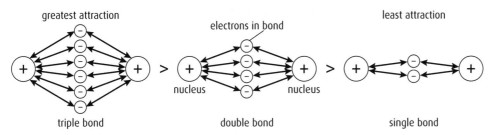

Figure 3.18 The more electrons make up a covalent bond, the greater the attraction between the electrons and the nuclei, and therefore the stronger the bond.

It should also be noted that triple bonds are shorter than double bonds, which are shorter than single bonds. This is, again, due to greater attraction between the bonding electrons and the nuclei when there are more electrons in the bond.

In general, when we are comparing just single bonds, the longer the bond the weaker it is. Data for two groups in the periodic table are shown in Table **3.4**.

Bond	Length / nm	Bond energy / kJ mol⁻¹
C–C	0.154	348
C=C	0.134	612
C≡C	0.120	837
C–O	0.143	360
C=O	0.122	743

Table 3.3 The relationship between number of bonds and bond length/strength.

Group 4			Group 7		
Bond	Length / nm	Energy / kJ mol⁻¹	Bond	Length / nm	Energy / kJ mol⁻¹
C–C	0.154	348	Cl–Cl	0.199	242
Si–Si	0.235	226	Br–Br	0.228	193
Ge–Ge	0.241	188	I–I	0.267	151

Table 3.4 The relationship between length of bonds and bond strength.

Length
single bonds
double bonds
triple bonds
↓ decreasing length

If we consider the data for group 4, it can be seen that the single bond between the elements gets weaker as the bond gets longer. This is because, as the atoms get bigger, the electron pair in the covalent bond is further away from the nuclei of the atoms making up the bond. If the electron pair is further away from the nuclei it is less strongly attracted and the covalent bond is weaker (Figure **3.19**). A similar trend can be seen down group 7.

The trends should only really be compared down a group, as elements in the same group have the same number of outer shell electrons, and therefore any effects due to effective nuclear charge or shielding are most similar. In general, comparisons such as this are most useful and valid when similar molecules, bonds or compounds are considered.

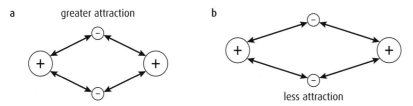

Figure 3.19 The bond in (**a**) is a shorter bond in which the bonding electrons are closer to the nuclei than in (**b**).

Dative covalent bonds (coordinate link)

> A dative covalent bond (USA: coordinate covalent bond) is a type of covalent bond in which **both electrons come from the same atom**.

Once a dative covalent bond has been formed, it is identical to an 'ordinary' covalent bond. For example, **NH_4^+** can be formed when H^+ becomes bonded to NH_3:

$$NH_3 + H^+ \rightarrow NH_4^+$$

H^+ does not have any electrons with which to form a covalent bond, but NH_3 has a lone pair of electrons, which can be used to form a covalent bond (Figure **3.20**).

A dative covalent bond is sometimes shown as an arrow (Figure **3.21a**). Once it has been formed, a dative bond is, however, the same as any other covalent bond. The ammonium ion can be represented as shown in Figure **3.21b**, in which no distinction is made between the individual bonds.

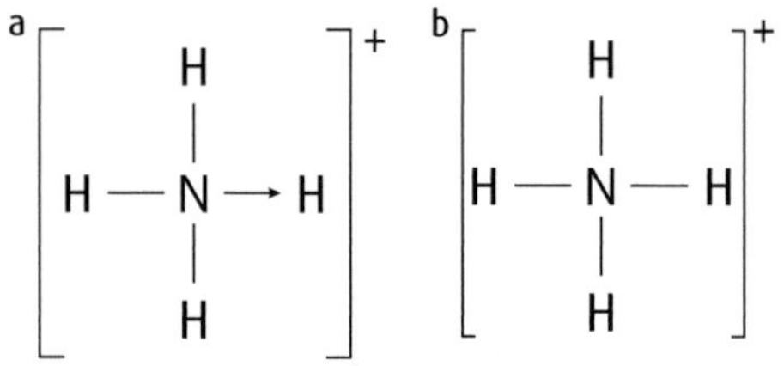

H_3O^+ is formed when a lone pair of electrons is donated from the O in H_2O to the H^+:

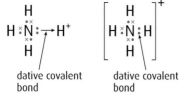

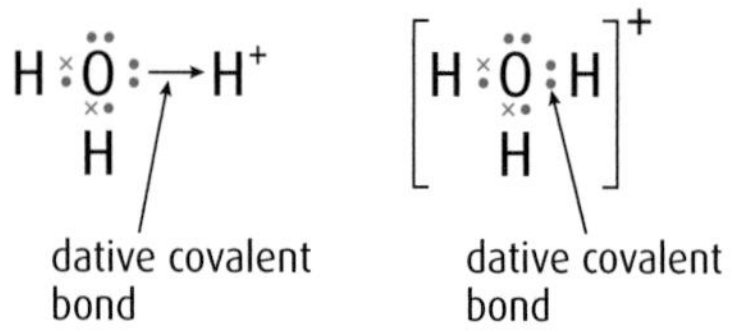

Figure 3.20 Dative covalent bonding in NH_4^+.

Figure 3.21 The ammonium ion, **(a)** with the dative bond shown and **(b)** with no distinction between the types of bonds.

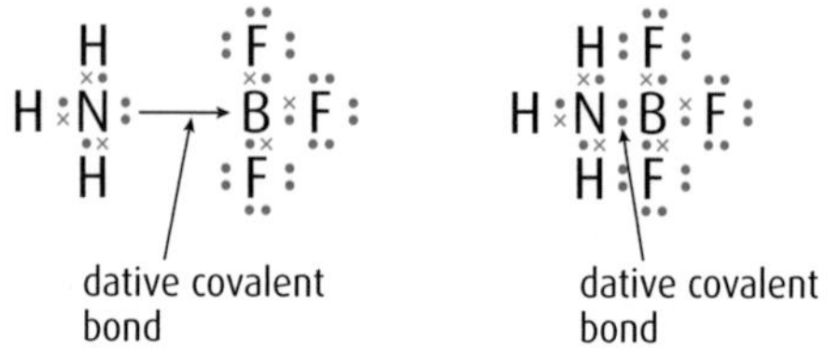

This is an example of a Lewis acid–base reaction (see page **314**).

NH_3 and BF_3 can combine to form an **adduct** (two molecules bonded together):

In BF_3 there are only six electrons in the outer shell of the boron; therefore there is space for the boron to accept a pair of electrons.

CO

Normally carbon shares four electrons to form four covalent bonds, and oxygen shares two to form two covalent bonds. If a carbon atom combines with an oxygen atom with the formation of two covalent bonds, we get the structure shown in Figure **3.22**. However, in this structure, although the oxygen atom has a full outer shell (octet), the carbon atom only has six electrons in its outer shell.

Both atoms can attain an octet if the oxygen atom donates a pair of electrons to carbon in the formation of a dative covalent bond. There is thus a triple bond between the two atoms, made up of two 'ordinary' covalent bonds and one dative covalent bond (Figure **3.23**). Both atoms have a lone pair of electrons.

Figure 3.22 The structure of carbon monoxide if two 'ordinary' covalent bonds were formed.

Figure 3.23 The structure of carbon monoxide if two 'ordinary' covalent bonds and one dative covalent bond were formed.

Other ways of representing the bonding in carbon monoxide are shown in Figure **3.24**.

$:C \equiv O:$ or $: C \equiv O:$ or $|C \equiv O|$

Figure 3.24 Other ways of showing the bonding in carbon monoxide.

Dative covalent bonds are important in the bonding in transition metal complexes.

Covalent bonds in terms of orbitals

A covalent bond is formed when **two atomic orbitals, each containing one electron, overlap.** The atomic orbitals combine to form a molecular orbital in which both electrons are paired up (Figures **3.25** and **3.26**). These electrons belong to both atoms simultaneously.

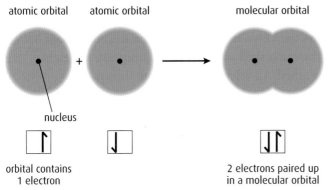

Figure 3.25 The overlap of two s orbitals to form a covalent bond.

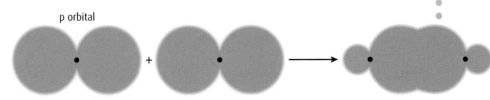

Figure 3.26 The overlap of two p orbitals to form a covalent bond.

Lewis (electron dot) structures

Lewis structures are diagrams showing **all the valence (outer shell) electrons** in a molecule (or ion). Examples of Lewis structures are shown in Figure **3.27**. Electrons may be shown individually as dots or crosses, or a line may be used to represent a pair of electrons, as in the Lewis structure of CO.

Dots and crosses can be used in Lewis structures to indicate where the electrons originally came from.

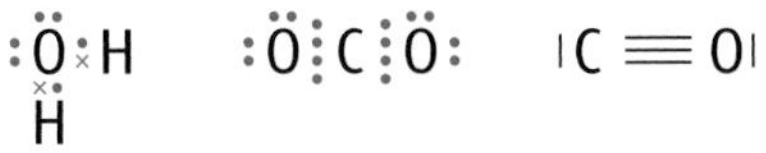

$:\ddot{O}\,^\times_\times H$ $:\ddot{O}:C:\ddot{O}:$ $|C \equiv O|$
$\quad H$

Figure 3.27 Lewis structures for H_2O, CO_2 and CO, showing all outer shell electrons.

Rules for working out Lewis structures:

1 Make sure that the **outer** atoms have eight electrons in their outer shell (except, of course hydrogen, which should have two). This is done by using single bonds, double bonds, triple bonds and + or − charges.

Note: the **outer atom** is usually the more electronegative atom (except when H is also present in the molecule).

2 If the central atom is from **period 2** it should have **no more than eight electrons** in its outer shell. It should generally (but not always) have a noble gas electronic configuration.

3 If the central atom is from **period 3** it may have **up to 18 electrons** in its outer shell.

Let us consider a few examples and go through the steps for drawing the Lewis structures.

NF₃

The central atom is nitrogen and the three outer atoms are F. F has seven electrons in its outer shell and therefore only needs to form one single bond to have a full outer shell.

Therefore, in order for each F atom to have eight electrons in its outer shell, three single bonds between the nitrogen and the fluorine must be formed.

Figure **3.28** shows the Lewis structure for NF₃. Each outer atom has eight electrons in the outer shell and the central atom also has eight electrons in its outer shell. All valence electrons are shown.

Figure 3.28 The Lewis structure for NF₃.

CO₃²⁻

C is the central atom and the Os are the outer atoms. O has six electrons in its outer shell and therefore needs two more electrons for a full octet. O can attain a full outer shell by forming a double bond or by forming a single bond and gaining another electron as a negative charge:

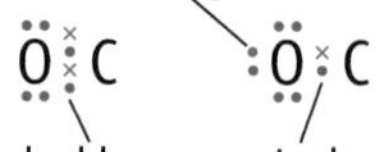

double bond / single bond (negative charge)

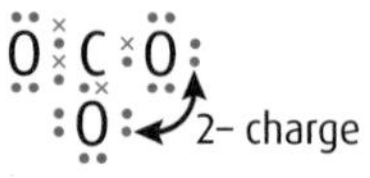

As the C atom has only four electrons in its outer shell, it does not have enough electrons to form three double bonds with the oxygens, but it does have enough electrons to form one double bond and two single bonds.

The **overall charge on the ion must be included** and square brackets used around the ion. The Lewis structure for CO₃²⁻ is thus shown in Figure **3.29**.

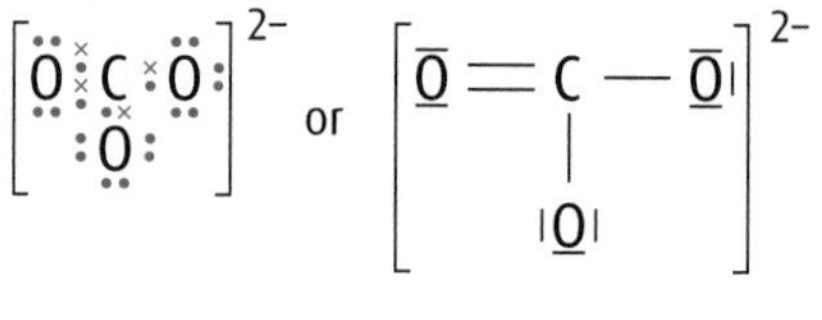

Figure 3.29 The Lewis structure for CO₃²⁻.

As a final check, you should make sure that the central atom has no more than eight electrons in its outer shell, as it is from period 2.

SO₂

Two different Lewis structures are possible for SO₂.

Approach 1

S expands its octet. Each oxygen can achieve an octet by forming a double bond.

The electron for the negative charge will come from sodium, calcium, etc. – the CO₃²⁻ ion cannot be formed in isolation, a metal atom must lose an electron at the same time to form the 2− charge.

Examiner's tip
You must remember to show lone pairs. A very common mistake is to forget to show the lone pairs on the outer atoms.

Examiner's tip
Expansion of the octet is very rarely encountered at Standard Level.

A sulfur atom has six electrons in its outer shell and so, when it forms two double bonds it will have ten electrons in its outer shell and is said to have expanded its octet. This is possible for elements in period 3 and below in the periodic table. The maximum number of electrons in the third shell (the outer shell in sulfur) is 18.

Elements in period 3 have d orbitals available for bonding.

Approach 2

S does not expand its octet. In some educational systems, Lewis structures are drawn as far as possible with all atoms having a maximum of eight electrons in their outer shell: that is, no expansion of the octet. Sulfur can, therefore, form a maximum of two normal covalent bonds. If these are both formed to the same oxygen atom, we get the structure shown here:

$$\ddot{O} \vdots S \vdots \quad \ddot{O}$$

However, in this structure there is no bond between the sulfur and the right-hand O atom. Of course, it is fairly obvious the structure can be completed by a dative bond between the sulfur and the oxygen, so that all atoms have eight electrons in their outer shell:

$$\ddot{O} \vdots S \vdots \ddot{O}$$

The Lewis structure can also be represented as in Figure **3.30**.

SO_4^{2-}

Approach 1

Each oxygen could complete its octet by forming a double bond to sulfur. Double bonds to two of the oxygen atoms give them full outer shells, but sulfur cannot form four double bonds as it does not have enough electrons (eight electrons are needed for the formation of four double bonds). There are therefore two single bonds to the other two oxygen atoms. The octet on each oxygen is completed by using the two electrons from the 2− charge. Two representations of the Lewis structure are shown in Figure **3.31**.

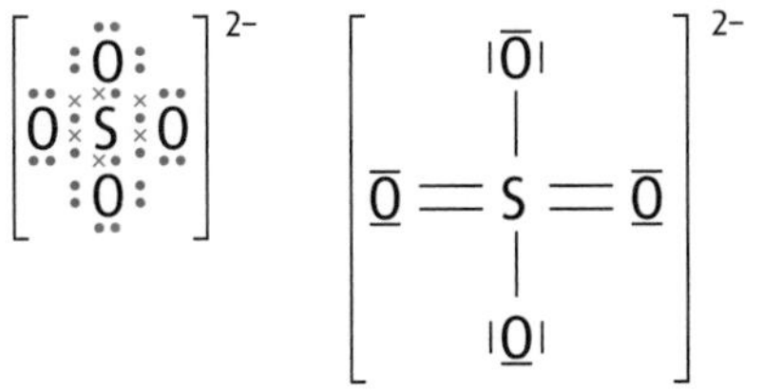

$$\left[\begin{array}{c} :\ddot{O}: \\ \ddot{O} \vdots S \vdots \ddot{O} \\ :\ddot{O}: \end{array} \right]^{2-} \quad \left[\begin{array}{c} |\overline{O}| \\ | \\ \overline{O} = S = \overline{O} \\ | \\ |\overline{O}| \end{array} \right]^{2-}$$

Figure 3.31 Two representations of the Lewis structure for SO_4^{2-}.

Approach 2

Here four single bonds are formed, two of which are dative covalent bonds (Figure **3.32**). Each atom (not just the oxygens) has eight electrons in its outer shell.

Both approaches to working out Lewis structures are valid, although more detailed considerations involving working out the formal charge on each atom would suggest that the structure with two double bonds is a better representation of the bonding in the molecule. The short S–O distance in SO_2 would also suggest that double bonds are present between atoms.

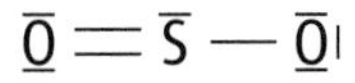

$$\overline{O} = \overline{S} - \overline{O}|$$

Figure 3.30 A Lewis structure for SO_2.

$$\left[\begin{array}{c} :\ddot{O}: \\ :\ddot{O} \vdots S \vdots \ddot{O}: \\ :\ddot{O}: \end{array} \right]^{2-}$$

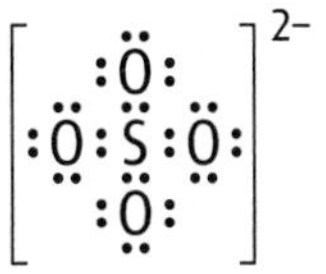

Figure 3.32 An alternative Lewis structure for SO_4^{2-}.

Again, a consideration of the formal charges on each atom would regard this structure as less likely.

Alternative method for working out Lewis structures

This approach is useful for working out the Lewis structures of molecules/ions just containing period 2 atoms.

1 Add up the total number of valence electrons of all the atoms in the molecule/ion.
2 Divide by two to get the total number of valence electron **pairs**.
3 Each pair of electrons is represented by a line.
4 Arrange the lines (electron pairs) so that all the atoms are joined together by at least single bonds and the outer atoms have full outer shells, i.e. are connected to four lines.
5 Rearrange the lines (electron pairs) so that every period 2 atom has four pairs of electrons. The outer atoms already have four pairs, so this should normally only involve moving lone pairs so that they become bonding pairs of electrons.

NO_3^-

total no. electrons = 5   +   3×6   +   1   = 24e⁻
              N   3×O   negative charge

There are therefore $\dfrac{24}{2}$ = 12 pairs of electrons, shown here by 12 lines.

| | | | | | | | | | | | |

Three must be now used to join all the atoms together:

```
        O
        |
   O — N — O
```

This leaves nine lines (electron pairs) that will be distributed as lone pairs of electrons on the O atoms (as O is the outer atom) to give each an **octet**.

```
       |Ō|
        |
  |Ō — N — Ō|
```

Now each O is 'attached to four lines' (has four pairs of electrons in its outer shell) and all the electrons have been used. The nitrogen, however, has only three pairs of electrons in its outer shell, and one of the lines needs to be moved from being a lone pair on the O to make a double bond between the N and an O. This does not change the number of electrons in the outer shell of the O but will increase the number of electrons in the outer shell of the N to eight.

The final Lewis structure for the NO_3^- ion is shown in Figure **3.33**.

This is a purely mechanical technique for working out the Lewis structure and does not really involve any understanding of the bonding in the ion. The Lewis structure showing the electrons as dots and crosses is probably clearer (Figure **3.34**).

Figure 3.33 The final Lewis structure for NO_3^-.

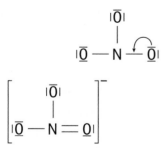

Figure 3.34 The Lewis structure of NO_3^- with the electrons shown individually.

NO₂⁻

total no. electrons = 5 + 2×6 + 1 = 18e⁻

N   2×O   negative charge

There are therefore $\dfrac{18}{2}$ = 9 pairs of electrons

| | | | | | | | |

The atoms are joined together using two lines:

O — N — O

More lines are added to the outer atoms to give them each an octet:

I$\overline{\text{O}}$ — N — $\overline{\text{O}}$I

So far, only eight lines (electron pairs) have been used and the last line must be put as a lone pair on the N. It cannot be put anywhere else, as the Os already have four electron pairs each.

I$\overline{\text{O}}$ — $\underline{\text{N}}$ — $\overline{\text{O}}$I

N only has three electron pairs and so a lone pair is moved from an O to form a double bond:

I$\overline{\text{O}}$ — $\underline{\text{N}}$ ⌒ $\overline{\text{O}}$I

This results in the Lewis structure for NO₂⁻ shown in Figure **3.35**.

It is important to note that the Lewis structure could be drawn the other way round and that this is entirely equivalent (Figure **3.36**).

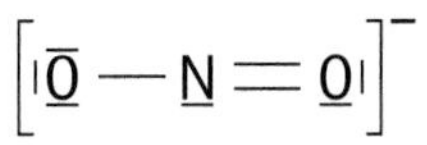

O₃

Ozone is isoelectronic with NO₂⁻ and has the same Lewis structure:

I$\overline{\text{O}}$ — $\underline{\text{O}}$ = OI

NO₂⁺ and CO₂

NO₂⁺ and CO₂ are isoelectronic with each other and have the same Lewis structures (Figures **3.37** and **3.38**).

This technique for drawing Lewis structures is useful for molecules/ions involving just period 2 elements, but it also works for compounds involving period 3 elements (and below) if approach 2 (the idea that the atoms do not expand their octet) is adopted.

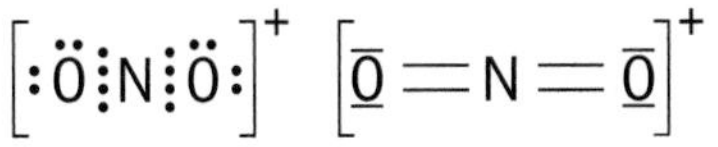

Examiner's tip
NO₂ has been asked about in examinations. It has an odd number of electrons and therefore an unpaired electron. The Lewis structure can be shown with an N=O double bond and an N → O dative bond. The unpaired electron would then be on the N.

$$\left[\text{I}\overline{\text{O}} - \underline{\text{N}} = \text{OI}\right]^{-}$$

Figure 3.35 The final Lewis structure for NO₂⁻.

$$\left[\text{I}\overline{\text{O}} = \underline{\text{N}} - \overline{\text{O}}\text{I}\right]^{-}$$

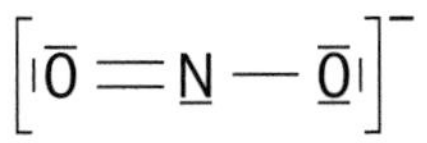

Figure 3.36 An alternative Lewis structure for NO₂⁻.

$$\left[:\ddot{\text{O}}:\text{N}:\ddot{\text{O}}:\right]^{+} \quad \left[\overline{\text{O}} = \text{N} = \underline{\text{O}}\right]^{+}$$

Figure 3.37 The Lewis structures for NO₂⁺.

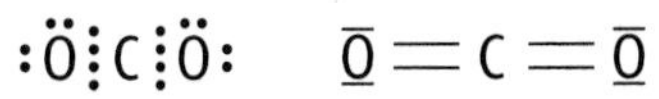

$$:\ddot{\text{O}}:\text{C}:\ddot{\text{O}}: \qquad \overline{\text{O}} = \text{C} = \overline{\text{O}}$$

Figure 3.38 The Lewis structures for CO₂.

Self-test 2

Test yourself

3 Work out Lewis structures for the following:

a H₂S	**b** PCl₃	**c** CCl₄	**d** COF₂
e HCN	**f** CS₂	**g** FNO	**h** N₂H₄
i H₂O₂	**j** PCl₄⁺	**k** NO⁺	**l** OCN⁻

4 Some harder ones – these are likely only to be encountered at Higher Level:

a XeF₄	**b** PCl₆⁻	**c** ClO₄⁻	**d** XeO₄
e BrF₅	**f** POCl₃	**g** ClF₃	**h** N₂O
i SF₄	**j** XeO₆⁴⁻	**k** I₃⁻	**l** N₃⁻

Learning objectives

- Work out the shapes of molecules and ions with up to four negative charge centres
- Predict bond angles in molecules/ions
- **HL** Work out the shapes of molecules and ions with five or six negative charge centres

Or, more precisely, how points can be arranged on the surface of a sphere to be as far away from each other as possible.

Because a double bond is made up of two electron pairs but repels as if it were one electron pair, it is better to talk about the number of **negative charge centres**, where a negative charge centre is either a lone pair, the electron pair that makes up a single bond or the electrons pairs (together) that make up a multiple bond.

Figure 3.39 (**a**) This symbol indicates a bond coming out of a plane. (**b**) This symbol indicates a bond going in to a plane.

3.3 Shapes of molecules

Shapes of molecules: valence shell electron pair repulsion (VSEPR) theory

We can predict the shapes of molecules using the **v**alence **s**hell **e**lectron **p**air **r**epulsion (VSEPR) theory.

> Pairs of electrons in the valence (outer) shell of an atom repel each other and will therefore take up positions in space to minimise these repulsions, i.e. to be as far apart in space as possible.

The pairs of electrons may be either non-bonding pairs (lone pairs) or bonding pairs (pairs of electrons involved in covalent bonds).

Basic shapes

The shape of a molecule, therefore, depends on the number of electron pairs in the outer shell of the central atom. There are five basic shapes (for two to six electron pairs), which are derived from the idea of how a number of things, joined to a central point, can be arranged in space to be as far apart from each other as possible.

However, first of all we will just consider molecules with up to four pairs of electrons around the central atom. The basic shapes and bond angles are shown in Table **3.5**.

No. electron pairs	Shape	Diagram	Bond angle	Example
2	linear	Y — X — Y	180°	$BeCl_2(g)$
3	trigonal planar	Y⟍X⟋Y ∣ Y	120°	BF_3
4	tetrahedral	Y ∣ Y⧸X⟍Y ∣ Y	109.5°	CH_4

Table 3.5 Basic molecule shapes and bond angles.

How to predict the shapes of molecules

1. Draw a Lewis structure for the molecule or ion.
2. Count up the number of electron **pairs** (bonding pairs and lone pairs) in the outer shell of the central atom. **A multiple bond counts as a single electron pair**, because the electrons are constrained to occupy the same region of space.
3. Look at Table **3.5** to get the basic shape (spatial arrangement of the negative charge centres). See Figure **3.39** for how to show 3D shapes.

4 A lone pair is just an electron pair in the outer shell of an atom and, as such, it contributes to the overall shape of the molecule but cannot itself be 'seen'.

5 State the **actual shape** of the molecule.

CH₄

The Lewis structure for CH₄ is shown in Figure **3.40**.

The number of electrons pairs in the outer shell of the central atom (C) is four, i.e. there are four negative charge centres. These four negative charge centres repel each other and take up positions in space to be as far away from each other as possible. The shape that allows four things to be as far away from each other as possible is tetrahedral. Therefore, the four electron pairs (negative charge centres) are arranged tetrahedrally around the C atom. The shape of the methane molecule is tetrahedral and the H–C–H bond angle is 109.5°:

Figure 3.40 The Lewis structure for CH₄.

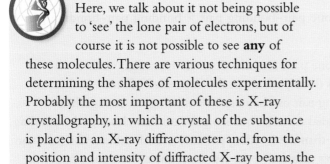

NH₃

The Lewis structure for NH₃ is shown in Figure **3.41**.

Bonding pairs of electrons: 3 (in 3 single bonds)
Non-bonding pairs of electrons: 1 (in 1 lone pair)
Negative charge centres: 4

As these four negative charge centres repel each other and take up positions in space to be as far apart as possible, the electrons pairs are distributed in a tetrahedral arrangement. The basic shape is tetrahedral, but a lone pair is just a pair of electrons in the outer shell of the central atom and, although it repels the other pairs of electrons and influences the shape, it cannot be 'seen'. The shape adopted by the atoms is therefore trigonal pyramidal (a pyramid with a triangular base) (Figure **3.42**).

Figure 3.41 The Lewis structure for NH₃.

Figure 3.42 The shape of the NH₃ molecule is based on a tetrahedron, but the actual shape is trigonal pyramidal.

The H–N–H bond angle here is smaller than in a perfect tetrahedron, because the lone pair repels the bonding pairs of electrons more than they repel each other. This will be considered in more detail below.

Here, we talk about it not being possible to 'see' the lone pair of electrons, but of course it is not possible to see **any** of these molecules. There are various techniques for determining the shapes of molecules experimentally. Probably the most important of these is X-ray crystallography, in which a crystal of the substance is placed in an X-ray diffractometer and, from the position and intensity of diffracted X-ray beams, the shape of the molecules, all angles and bond lengths can be calculated. The lone pairs of electrons cannot be detected by this technique. Do we know or believe the shapes of molecules stated here? Which ways of knowing do we use to interact with this microscopic world? In biology, microscopes are used to 'view' things that are too small to be seen with the naked eye. Is there a difference between the use of a microscope to interact with this invisible world and the use of an X-ray diffractometer? What about the use of electron microscopes?

Figure 3.43 The Lewis structure for CO_2.

CO_2

The Lewis structure for CO_2 is shown in Figure **3.43**.

> Bonding pairs of electrons: 4 (in 2 double bonds)
> Non-bonding pairs of electrons: 0
> Negative charge centres: 2 (as a double bond) counts as one negative charge centre – the 4 electrons that make up the double bond are constrained to occupy the same region of space

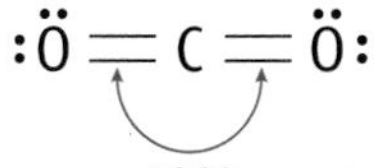

180°

As these two negative charge centres repel each other and take up positions in space to be as far apart as possible, the negative charge centres are distributed in a linear arrangement, and the shape adopted by the atoms is linear.

SO_2

The Lewis structure for SO_2 is shown in Figure **3.44**.

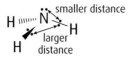

Figure 3.44 The Lewis structure for SO_2.

> Bonding pairs of electrons: 4 (in 2 double bonds)
> Non-bonding pairs of electrons: 1 (1 lone pair on S)
> Negative charge centres: 3 (as a double bond, counts as 1 negative charge centre)

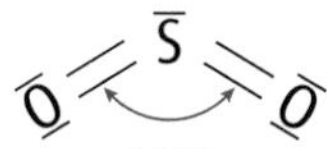

As these three negative charge centres repel each other and take up positions in space to be as far apart as possible, the negative charge centres are distributed in a trigonal planar (flat triangle) arrangement. The lone pair on S is just a pair of electrons in its outer shell and cannot be 'seen'. The shape adopted by the atoms is therefore **bent** (also called 'angular', or 'V-shaped').

Again the bond angle is slightly less than the ideal angle in a trigonal planar structure (120°), and this results from the extra repulsion of a lone pair, so that the bonding pairs are pushed closer together and the bond angle is reduced.

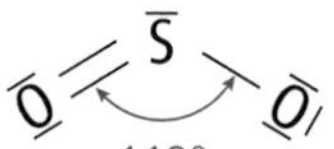

119°

If the Lewis structure had been drawn differently, with S not expanding its octet, this would have made no difference to the predicted shape.

119°

Lone pairs and bond angles

The order of repulsion for pairs of electrons is:

> lone pair–lone pair > lone pair–bonding pair > bonding pair–bonding pair

smaller distance

larger distance

This is because lone pairs are held closer to the central nucleus than are bonding pairs (lone pairs are in the outer shell of the central atom, whereas a bonding pair can be imagined as being, on average, halfway between the bonded atoms). The lone pairs are thus closer to the bonding pairs of electrons than the bonding pairs are to each other and repel them more strongly. This means that the repulsion due to lone pairs causes the bond angles to become smaller.

Consider CH_4, NH_3 and H_2O, each of which has four electron pairs in the outer shell of the central atom (Table **3.6**). The basic shape is the arrangement of the electron pairs in the outer shell of the central atom. The greater the number of lone pairs present, the smaller the H–X–H bond angle. This is due to greater repulsion from lone pairs than from bonding pairs of electrons. Two lone pairs cause greater repulsion than one, so the bond angle gets smaller as the number of lone pairs increases.

Molecule	Lewis structure	Bonding pairs	Lone pairs	Basic shape	Actual shape	H–X–H bond angle
CH_4	H H:C:H H	4	0	tetrahedral	tetrahedral	109.5°
NH_3	H H:N: H	3	1		trigonal pyramidal	107.3°
H_2O	:O:H H	2	2		bent	104.5°

Table 3.6 Structural characteristics of CH_4, NH_3 and H_2O.

Note: both SO_2 and H_2O have bent structures, but the SO_2 structure is based on trigonal planar whereas the H_2O structure is based on tetrahedral. This means that the bond angle is larger in SO_2.

Predicting the shapes of ions

The approach to predicting the shapes of ions is exactly the same as for neutral molecules.

NH_4^+

The Lewis structure for NH_4^+ is shown in Figure **3.45**.

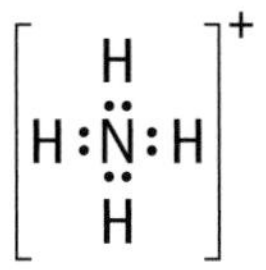

Bonding pairs of electrons: 4
Non-bonding pairs of electrons: 0
Negative charge centres: 4

As these four negative charge centres repel each other and take up positions in space to be as far apart as possible, the electrons pairs are distributed in a tetrahedral arrangement:

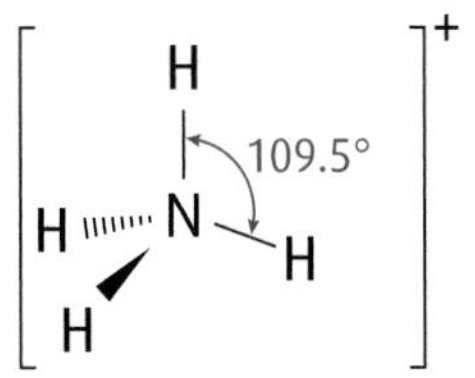

$$\begin{bmatrix} H \\ H\text{......}N\diagdown H \\ \diagup \quad 109.5° \\ H \end{bmatrix}^+$$

Examiner's tip
A general rule of thumb, if you are asked to predict a bond angle in a particular molecule, just take two or three degrees off the basic angle (the bond angle in the basic shape) for each lone pair present on the central atom. For example, a bent molecule based on a trigonal planar structure (one lone pair on the central atom) could have a bond angle of $120 - 3 = 117°$. There is no scientific basis for doing this, but it is useful for answering examination questions.

$$\begin{bmatrix} H \\ H:N:H \\ H \end{bmatrix}^+$$

Figure 3.45 The Lewis structure for NH_4^+.

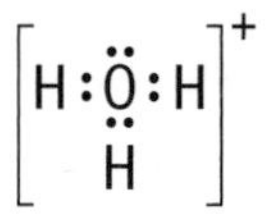

$$\left[\text{H} : \ddot{\text{O}} : \text{H} \atop \qquad \text{H} \right]^{+}$$

Figure 3.46 The Lewis structure for H_3O^+.

$$\left[\text{H} \overset{\ddot{\text{O}}}{\cdots} {\atop \text{H}} \text{H} \right]^{+}$$

No definitive value for the bond angle in H_3O^+ exists. Values have been measured, but they depend on the actual compound.

$$\left[:\ddot{\text{O}} : \text{N} : \ddot{\text{O}} : \right]^{-}$$

Figure 3.46 The Lewis structure for NO_2^-.

$$\left[\text{O} {=} \overset{\ddot{\text{N}}}{} {\diagdown} \text{O} \right]^{-}$$

No definitive value for the bond angle in NO_2^- exists. Values have been measured, but they depend on the actual compound.

$$\begin{array}{cc} \text{H} & \text{H} \\ :\ddot{\text{N}} & : \ddot{\text{N}} : \\ \text{H} & \text{H} \end{array}$$

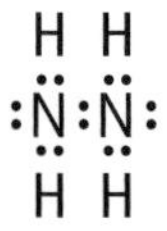

Figure 3.48 The Lewis structure for N_2H_4.

H_3O^+

The Lewis structure for H_3O^+ is shown in Figure **3.46**.

Bonding pairs of electrons: 3
Non-bonding pairs of electrons: 1
Negative charge centres: 4

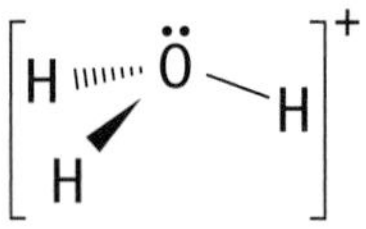

As these four negative charge centres repel each other and take up positions in space to be as far apart as possible, the electron pairs are distributed in a tetrahedral arrangement. One of the electron pairs is a lone pair, so the actual shape of the ion is trigonal pyramidal. This structure is based on tetrahedral (bond angle 109.5°) with one lone pair, so a bond angle of about 107° for the H–O–H bond could be predicted (the molecule is isoelectronic with ammonia).

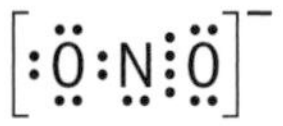

NO_2^-

The Lewis structure for NO_2^- is shown in Figure **3.47**.

Bonding pairs of electrons: 3 (1 single bond and 1 double bond)
Non-bonding pairs of electrons: 1
Negative charge centres: 3 (as a double bond counts as 1 negative charge centre)

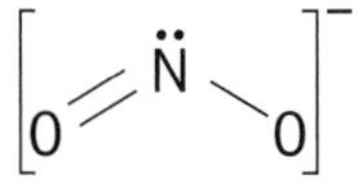

As these three negative charge centres repel each other and take up positions in space to be as far apart as possible, the electrons pairs are distributed in a trigonal planar arrangement. One of the electron pairs is a lone pair, so the actual shape of the ion is bent.

This structure is based on trigonal planar (bond angle 120°) with one lone pair, so a bond angle of about 117° could be predicted.

Molecules with more than one central atom

The approach to predicting the shapes of molecules with more than one central atom is the same as for other molecules, except that each 'central atom' must be considered separately.

N_2H_4

The Lewis structure for N_2H_4 is shown in Figure **3.48**. In this molecule, the two N atoms are 'central atoms', and each one must be considered separately:

Left-hand nitrogen	Right-hand nitrogen
bonding pairs of electrons: 3	bonding pairs of electrons: 3
non-bonding pairs of electrons: 1	non-bonding pairs of electrons: 1
negative charge centres: 4	negative charge centres: 4

It can be seen that the arrangement of electron pairs around each nitrogen is tetrahedral and, with one lone pair on each nitrogen, the shape about each N atom is trigonal pyramidal:

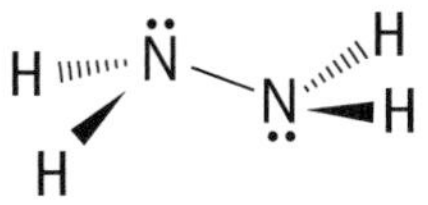

H⟍N̈⟍H
     ⟍N̈⟍H
   H   ⟍H

C_2H_2

The Lewis structure for C_2H_2 is shown in Figure **3.49**. In ethyne, each C is considered separately, but each one is identical. For each C:

Bonding pairs of electrons: 4 (1 single bond and 1 triple bond)
Non-bonding pairs of electrons: 0
Negative charge centres: 2

The triple bond counts as one negative charge centre, so, with two negative charge centres around each C, the shape is linear about each C and therefore linear overall:

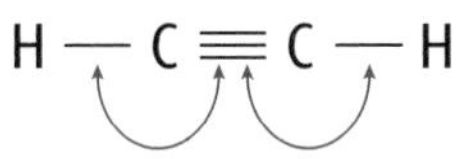

$$H - C \equiv C - H$$
180°   180°

Self-test 3

Test yourself

5 Work out the shapes of the following molecules or ions and predict their bond angles:

a H_2S	b PCl_3	c CF_4	d HCN
e COF_2	f CS_2	g FNO	h PCl_4^+
i OCN^-	j O_3	k C_2F_4	l NO_2^+

Molecules with five or six negative charge centres around the central atom

The basic shapes for five or six negative charge centres are shown in Table **3.7**. The approach to working out the shapes of these molecules and ions is the same as that we have already seen.

No. electron pairs	Shape	Diagram	Bond angle	Example
5	trigonal bipyramid	Y⟍Y|⟍X—Y⟍Y|Y	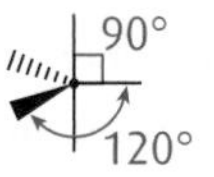 90° 120°	PF_5
6	octahedral	Y|Y⟍X⟍Y⟍Y|Y	 90°	SF_6

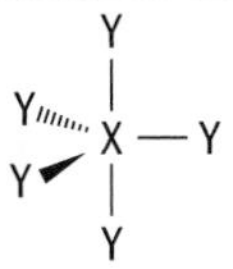

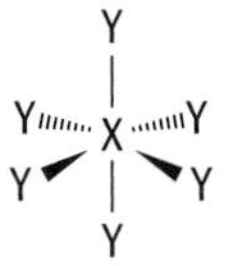

Table 3.7 The basic shapes for molecules with five or six negative charge centres.

HL

VSEPR gives us no information about how the two NH_2 groups are twisted relative to each other, and in the gas phase hydrazine adopts the conformations with the two NH_2 groups staggered relative to each other.

H⟍
H⟍N⟍H
   H

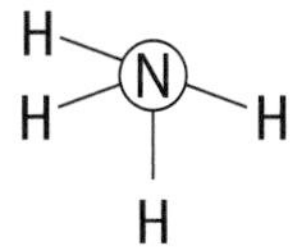

view of a hydrazine molecule looking down the N—N bond

$$H:C \vdots C:H$$

Figure 3.49 The Lewis structure for C_2H_2.

Figure 3.50 The Lewis structure for PF_5.

PF_5

The Lewis structure for PF_5 is shown in Figure **3.50**.

Bonding pairs of electrons: 5
Non-bonding pairs of electrons: 0
Negative charge centres: 5

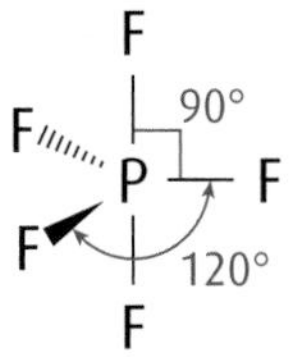

As these five negative charge centres repel each other and take up positions in space to be as far apart as possible, the electrons pairs are therefore distributed in a trigonal bipyramidal arrangement, and the shape adopted by the atoms is also trigonal bipyramidal (two triangular-based pyramids on top of each other). It is not possible to arrange five things on the surface of a sphere so that they are evenly spaced from each other, and there are two different bond angles in a trigonal bipyramid.

The positions around the middle in a trigonal bipyramid are described as equatorial, and the position above and below the central triangle are described as axial:

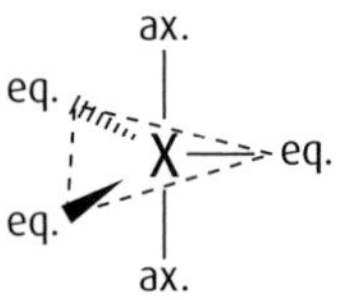

> In a trigonal bipyramid, the axial and equatorial positions are not equivalent. Lone pairs always go in the equatorial position.
>
> It is important to realise that this applies only to trigonal bipyramidal structures.

SF_4

The Lewis structure for SF_4 is shown in Figure **3.51**.

Bonding pairs of electrons: 4
Non-bonding pairs of electrons: 1
Negative charge centres: 5

As these five negative charge centres repel each other and take up positions in space to be as far apart as possible, the electrons pairs are distributed in a trigonal bipyramidal arrangement. One of these electron pairs is a lone pair, and this adopts an equatorial position in the trigonal bipyramid (Figure **3.52**).

The lone pair causes the other bonding pairs to bend away from it, and a better representation of the actual structure is:

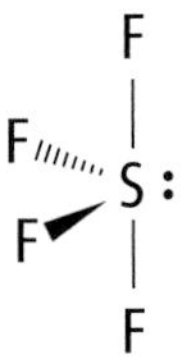

Figure 3.51 The Lewis structure for SF_4.

Figure 3.52 The shape predicted for the SF_4 molecule is a 'see-saw' shape.

This arrangement of the lone pairs always going in the equatorial position is often discussed in terms of the repulsion between the pairs of electrons. The repulsion between electron pairs at 90° to each other is greater than between pairs at 120° to each other. Having the lone pairs (which cause greater repulsion than bonding pairs of electrons) in equatorial positions limits the number of 90° repulsions to two. Having the lone pairs in axial positions would mean that there would be three 90° repulsions, i.e. greater repulsion overall and a less stable molecule.

An alternative explanation is in terms of the hybridisation of the central atom (discussed below). A trigonal bipyramid involves two different hybridisation schemes: sp^2 for the equatorial positions and pd for the axial positions. An s orbital has lower energy than a p or a d orbital, and therefore if a lone pair occupies an sp^2 orbital it is lower in energy than if it is in a pd orbital. As a lone pair exists solely on the central atom, this should be in the orbital with the lowest available energy, i.e. an sp^2 orbital, in the equatorial position.

ClF₃

The Lewis structure for ClF_3 is shown in Figure **3.54**.

Bonding pairs of electrons: 3
Non-bonding pairs of electrons: 2
Negative charge centres: 5
Arrangement of negative charge centres: trigonal bipyramidal

Two of the electron pairs are lone pairs and take up equatorial positions in the trigonal bipyramid. The actual shape adopted by the molecule is often described as 'T-shaped'.

The lone pairs cause the other bonding pairs to bend away from them. A better description of the structure might be 'arrow-shaped':

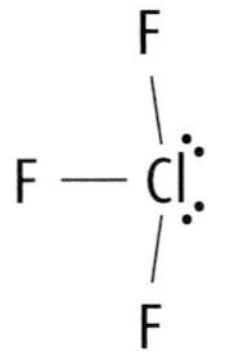

$$F - \overset{F}{\underset{F}{\diagdown}} Cl\!:$$

I₃⁻

I_3^- has three lone pairs and two bonding pairs around the central atom (Figure **3.55**), so the electron pairs are distributed in a trigonal bipyramidal arrangement. The shape is linear, with three lone pairs around the middle of the trigonal bipyramid.

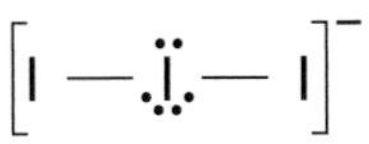

$$\left[I - \overset{..}{\underset{..}{I}} - I \right]^-$$

The actual bond angles in SF_4 are shown in Figure **3.53**. It can be seen that, in this case, the lone pair has a very large influence on the bond angles – more than just a couple of degrees. Care must be exercised here, however – if you wrote down the angle of 102° for the bond angle in your examination, it could be marked incorrect, as it is quite a bit smaller than 120°.

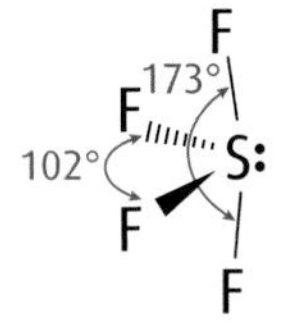

Figure 3.53 The actual bond angles for the SF_4 molecule.

Figure 3.54 The Lewis structure for ClF_3.

$$F - \overset{F}{\underset{F}{\diagdown}} Cl\!:$$

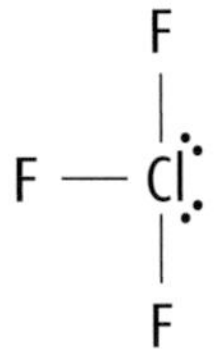

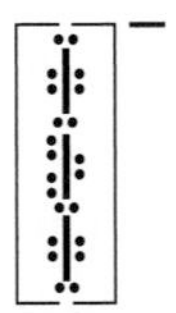

Figure 3.55 The Lewis structure for I_3^-.

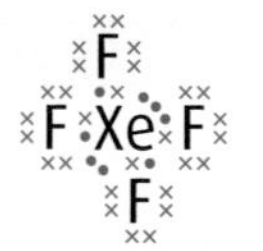

Figure 3.56 The Lewis structure for XeF₄.

XeF₄ can be prepared by heating xenon with excess fluorine at high temperature and pressure in a nickel container. It is a white, crystalline solid at room temperature.

Figure 3.57 The Lewis structure for BrF₅.

Examiner's tip
Two, three and four negative charge centres are required for Higher Level and Standard Level. Higher Level students also require 5 and 6 negative charge centres.

'Basic shape' is the arrangement of the electron pairs around the central atom.

Lone pairs repel bonding pairs of electrons more than the bonding pairs repel each other. Therefore the presence of lone pairs results in a closing up of bond angles.

XeF₄

XeF₄ has four bonding pairs and two lone pairs around the central atom (Figure **3.56**). The arrangement of electron pairs is octahedral, and the two lone pairs take up positions opposite each other to minimise repulsion. The actual shape adopted by the molecule is square planar.

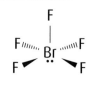

BrF₅

BrF₅ has five bonding pairs and one lone pair around the central atom (Figure **3.57**). The arrangement of the electron pairs is octahedral, and the actual shape of the molecule is square pyramidal.

The lone pair causes the four Fs on the base of the pyramid to bend away from it slightly due to greater repulsion between a lone pair and a bonding pair than between two bonding pairs:

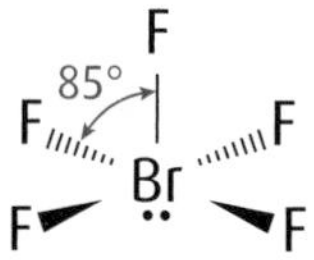

Self-test 4

Test yourself

6 Work out the shapes of the following molecules and ions and predict their bond angles:

a BrF_3 **b** ClF_5 **c** SO_2Cl_2 (S central atom)
d SeF_4 **e** XeF_2 **f** AsF_6^-
g TeF_5^- **h** $F_2ClO_2^-$ (Cl central atom)
i I_3^+ **j** ICl_2^-

VSEPR summary

The shapes taken up by molecules depend on the number of **pairs** of electrons in the outer shell of the central atom. To take account of molecules containing multiple bonds, this is often expressed in terms of negative charge centres, where one multiple bond counts as one negative charge centre.

Pairs of electrons in the outer shell of an atom repel each other. The pairs of electrons may be either bonding pairs or lone pairs. The pairs of electrons take up positions in space to minimise repulsions in a molecule, i.e. to be as far apart from each other as possible. The basic shapes adopted are shown in Table **3.8**.

Lone pairs influence the shapes of molecules but cannot actually be 'seen'. The shapes of some specific molecules are shown in Table **3.8**.

Total negative charge centres	Bonding pairs	Lone pairs	Basic shape	Actual shape	Example
2	2	0	linear	linear	CO_2, NO_2^+, HCN, $BeCl_2$
3	3	0	trigonal planar	trigonal planar	BF_3, SO_3, NO_3^-, CO_3^{2-}
3	2	1	trigonal planar	bent, V-shaped, angular	SO_2, O_3, NO_2^-
4	4	0	tetrahedral	tetrahedral	CCl_4, XeO_4, NH_4^+, BCl_4^-, SO_4^{2-}, PO_4^{3-}
4	3	1	tetrahedral	trigonal pyramidal	NH_3, PCl_3, XeO_3, H_3O^+, ClO_3^-, $SOCl_2$
4	2	2	tetrahedral	bent, V-shaped, angular	H_2O, SCl_2, ClF_2^+, I_3^+
5	5	0	trigonal bipyramidal	trigonal bipyramidal	PF_5, XeO_3F_2
5	4	1	trigonal bipyramidal	'see-saw'	SF_4, XeO_2F_2
5	3	2	trigonal bipyramidal	'T-shaped' (arrow)	BrF_3, $XeOF_2$
5	2	3	trigonal bipyramidal	linear	I_3^-, XeF_2
6	6	0	octahedral	octahedral	SF_6, PF_6^-, XeO_6^{4-}, IO_6^{5-}
6	5	1	octahedral	square pyramidal	SF_5^-, BrF_5, XeF_5^+, $XeOF_4$
6	4	2	octahedral	square planar	XeF_4, SF_4^{2-}

Table 3.8 The basic and actual shapes of some specific molecules.

3.4 Hybridisation

Hybridisation

HL

> Hybridisation is the **mixing** of atomic orbitals to produce a new set of orbitals (the same number as originally) that have characteristics of the original orbitals and are better arranged in space for covalent bonding.

To form a covalent bond, an **orbital containing one electron is required**. These orbitals overlap to form a covalent bond (Figure 3.58). Carbon has the outer shell electronic configuration $2s^2 2p^2$:

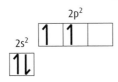

As it has only two unpaired electrons, carbon should form two covalent bonds. However, it is well known that carbon virtually always forms four covalent bonds. One of the electrons in the 2s orbital must then be promoted to the 2p subshell to give four unpaired electrons.

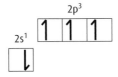

Learning objectives

- Understand what is meant by hybridisation
- Predict the hybridisation of an atom in a molecule

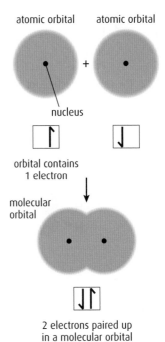

Figure 3.58 A covalent bond formed by two orbitals overlapping.

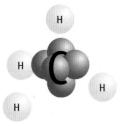

Figure 3.59 The bond angles of CH₄.

Figure 3.60 The p orbitals in CH₄.

Hybridisation produces orbitals that point towards the atoms to which they are bonding, so it produces more effective bonding. Although promotion requires energy, this is more than paid back by the extra energy released when C forms four bonds as opposed to two.

sp³ indicates that one s and three p orbitals have been mixed together.

H H
C∶C
H H

Figure 3.62 The Lewis structure for C₂H₄.

HL This **requires energy**. However, bond formation releases energy and the formation of four bonds instead of two more than pays back the energy needed to promote an electron to a higher subshell.

Carbon now has four unpaired electrons and can form four covalent bonds, but the atomic orbitals do not point in the correct direction for bonding. CH_4 is tetrahedral with bond angles of 109.5° (Figure **3.59**), but the p orbitals are at 90° to each other (Figure **3.60**).

When carbon forms methane, the four atomic orbitals on carbon, **one s** and **three p**, then **mix** to give four **sp³ hybrid orbitals**, which point to the vertices of a tetrahedron. This is the process of **hybridisation** (Figure **3.60**).

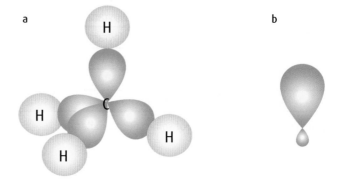

Figure 3.61 (a) Four sp³ hybrid orbitals point towards the vertices of a tetrahedron and are better set up for bonding to the H atoms; **(b)** one sp³ orbital.

The four sp³ hybrid orbitals all have the same energy (they are degenerate):

sp³
| ↑ | ↑ | ↑ | ↑ |

C₂H₄

The Lewis structure for ethene is shown in Figure **3.62**.

The shape about each C atom is trigonal planar, and the molecule is planar overall:

$$ \overset{H}{\underset{H}{\diagdown}} C = C \overset{H}{\underset{H}{\diagup}} $$

Of the three p orbitals on each C atom, one of them is not in the same plane as the H atoms or the other C atom. This p orbital is not involved in hybridisation. Mixing the **two p orbitals and one s orbital all in the same plane** produces **three sp²** orbitals pointing towards the corners of an equilateral triangle:

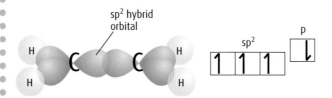

sp² hybrid orbital

sp²
| ↑ | ↑ | ↑ |
p
| ↑↓ |

This leaves one p orbital, containing one electron, perpendicular to the single bond (σ) framework on each C atom:

These p orbitals are involved in formation of the second component of the double bond (π component) (Figure **3.63**).

C₂H₂

The Lewis structure for ethyne is shown in Figure **3.64**.

The linear shape means that one s and one p orbital on each carbon are hybridised to produce two sp hybrid orbitals at 180° to each other. The two p orbitals at 90° to the C–H bonds are not involved in the hybridisation.

Only the p orbitals shown here are involved in hybridisation:

Hybridisation of **one s and one p orbital** produces **two sp** hybrid orbitals pointing away from each other at 180° on each C. This leaves two p orbitals on each C that are not involved in hybridisation:

These p orbitals overlap side-on to produce two π bonds (Figure **3.65**).

The number of hybrid orbitals is always the same as the number of atomic orbitals from which they were produced:

Hybridisation	Orbitals used	No. hybrid orbitals produced	Shape
sp	1 × s, 1 × p	2	linear
sp²	1 × s, 2 × p	3	trigonal planar
sp³	1 × s, 3 × p	4	tetrahedral

The hybridisation scheme adopted in a molecule depends on the shape of the molecule.

Extension

Other hybridisation schemes, involving d orbitals, can be used to rationalise the bonding in 5 and 6 coordinate molecules – for instance, sp³d² for an octahedral shape.

HL

The double bond is made of two different components – a sigma (σ) bond, which results from the head-on overlap of two sp² orbitals, and a pi (π) bond which arises from the side-on overlap of two p orbitals. σ and π bonds will be discussed in more detail below.

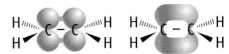

Figure 3.63 The p orbitals overlap side on to form the second component of the double bond.

H:C⋮C:H

Figure 3.64 The Lewis structure for C₂H₂.

Figure 3.65 Bonding in ethyne. The two π bonds are shown in different colours for clarity.

Determining the hybridisation of an atom in a molecule or ion

In order to determine the hybridisation of a particular atom in a molecule/ion, the basic shape, i.e. the arrangement of negative charge centres (electron pairs) on the central atom, must be determined:

Negative charge centres	Basic shape	Hybridisation
2	linear	sp
3	trigonal planar	sp^2
4	tetrahedral	sp^3

BF$_3$

The Lewis structure for BF$_3$ is shown in Figure **3.66**.

There are three negative charge centres, which give rise to a trigonal planar shape, and therefore the B atom is **sp^2** hybridised.

NH$_3$

The Lewis structure for NH$_3$ is shown in Figure **3.67**.

There are four negative charge centres (three bonding pairs of electrons and one lone pair); therefore, the basic shape (arrangement of the negative charge centres) is **tetrahedral** and the hybridisation of the N atom is **sp^3**.

CO$_2$

The Lewis structure for CO$_2$ is shown in Figure **3.68**.

There are two negative charge centres around the C (two double bonds); therefore, the basic shape is linear and the hybridisation of the C atom is **sp**.

O$_3$

The Lewis structure for O$_3$ is shown in Figure **3.69**.

There are three negative charge centres around the central O atom, and therefore the basic shape is trigonal planar and the hybridisation of the central O is **sp^2**.

Table **3.9** shows the hybridisation of the central atom in several molecules and ions.

Negative charge centres	Basic shape	Hybridisation	Examples
2	linear	sp	CO$_2$, HCN, C$_2$H$_2$, NO$_2^+$
3	trigonal planar	sp^2	BF$_3$, SO$_3$, NO$_3^-$, CO$_3^{2-}$, SO$_2$, BF$_3$, NO$_2^-$
4	tetrahedral	sp^3	CCl$_4$, XeO$_4$, NH$_4^+$, BCl$_4^-$, SO$_4^{2-}$, PO$_4^{3-}$ NH$_3$, PCl$_3$, XeO$_3$, H$_3$O$^+$, ClO$_3^-$, SOCl$_2$ H$_2$O, SCl$_2$, ClF$_2^+$

Table 3.9 Hybridisation of the central atom.

Figure 3.66 The Lewis structure for BF$_3$.

Figure 3.67 The Lewis structure for NH$_3$.

Figure 3.68 The Lewis structure for CO$_2$.

Figure 3.69 The Lewis structure for O$_3$.

With organic compounds this can be simplified: when C forms just single bonds, the shape is tetrahedral and the hybridisation is sp^3; when C forms a double bond, the shape is trigonal planar and the hybridisation is sp^2; and when C forms a triple bond, the shape is linear and the hybridisation is sp.

Test yourself ● ● ● ● ● ● ● ● ● ● ● ● ● ●

7 Predict the hybridisation of the central atom in each of the following
  a BCl_3 **b** NCl_3 **c** OCl_2 **d** CCl_4
  e $BeCl_2$ **f** H_2S **g** PCl_4^+ **h** OCN^-
  i SeO_3 **j** FNO

8 What is the hybridisation of the N atoms in each of the following?
  a N_2H_4 **b** N_2H_2

9 What is the hybridization of the C atoms in each of the following?
  a C_2F_4 **b** C_2F_2 **c** C_2F_6 **d** COF_2

Is hybridisation real? There is evidence from ultraviolet photoelectron spectroscopy to suggest that it is not. Why then do we still use this theory? There is a more advanced theory of bonding called molecular orbital theory, but this is much more complicated and does not allow us to draw lines (bonds) between atoms in the same way. Is a more advanced theory always more useful? What are the implications of using something that we know to be nothing more than a mathematical device for making predictions? How can we justify this?

3.5 Sigma and pi bonding

Sigma (σ) and pi (π) bonding

A covalent bond is formed when two atomic orbitals, each containing one electron, overlap. When these orbitals overlap **head on**, the bond formed is a normal single bond and is called a **sigma (σ)** bond:

Learning objectives

- Understand the difference between a sigma and a pi bond
- Predict the number of sigma and pi bonds in molecules

A covalent bond can also be formed when an atomic orbital containing two electrons overlaps with an empty orbital. This is a dative covalent bond.

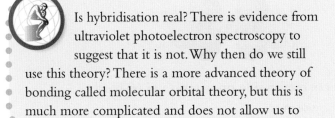

s orbital   s orbital   sigma bond

head-on overlap

H   H   H —— H

sigma bond

Sigma bonds can be formed by the axial overlap of any two orbitals, i.e. two p orbitals, an s orbital and a p orbital, an sp^3 hybrid orbital and an s orbital, a d orbital and a p orbital, and so on:

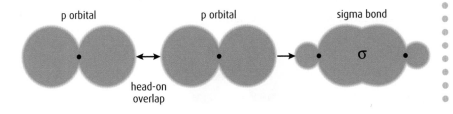

p orbital   p orbital   sigma bond

head-on overlap

Sigma bonds result from the axial (head-on) overlap of atomic orbitals. The electron distribution in a sigma bond lies mostly along the axis joining the two nuclei.

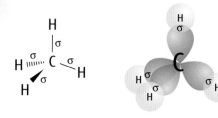

π bond – **sideways** overlap of parallel p orbitals. The electron density in the pi bond lies above and below the internuclear axis.

	Bond energy / kJ mol⁻¹
C–C	348
C=C	612

Table 3.10 Bond energies in single and double bonds.

Extension

Life is never that simple in chemistry – compare the strength of single and double bonds for O–O and N–N bonds.

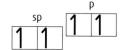

HL ## CH₄

Methane contains only single bonds between carbon atoms. These are σ bonds formed when sp³ hybrid orbitals on the carbon atom overlap head on with the s orbitals of each H atom.

C₂H₄

In forming the single bonds in ethene, each carbon uses three sp² hybrid orbitals and three electrons.

This leaves one p orbital, containing one electron, on each C atom at 90° to the sigma bond framework:

These p orbitals can overlap **side on** to form a **pi (π)** bond:

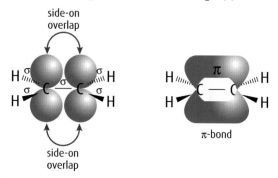

Thus a double bond consists of two components:

$$H \overset{\text{\textbackslash}}{\underset{H}{}} C \overset{\pi}{\underset{\sigma}{=}} C \overset{H}{\underset{H}{}}$$

That these components are indeed different can be seen from the bond energies in Table **3.10**.

A C=C bond is less than twice the strength of a C–C single bond, meaning that the π bond in ethene is not as strong as the C–C σ bond. Side-on overlap (π bond) is not as effective as head-on overlap – there is a more direct attraction between the electron pair and the nuclei in a σ bond.

C₂H₂

The hybridisation of each C in ethyne is sp, which means that there are two p orbitals, each containing one electron on each C.

Each sp hybrid orbital contains one electron; these are used to bond to a hydrogen atom and the other C atom:

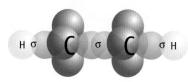

The p orbitals on each C then overlap side on to form two π bonds at 90° to each other:

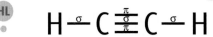

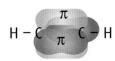

A triple bond thus consists of one σ bond and two π bonds (Figure **3.70**).

Figure 3.70 The triple bond in C_2H_2.

Summary	
single	σ
double	σ + π
triple	σ + 2π

Self-test 6

Test yourself

10 Work out the number of sigma and pi bonds in each of the following:

   a O_2 **b** N_2 **c** BCl_3

   d CO_2 **e** H_2CO **f** HCN

   g N_2F_2 **h** CO   **i** CH_3CHCH_2

   j $SOCl_2$ **k** $HCCCH_3$ **l** H_2SO_4

Extension question

11 There is one isomer of C_3H_4 that contains two C=C double bonds. Determine the shape of this molecule. Is it planar?

3.6 Delocalisation

Delocalisation

> Delocalisation is the sharing of a pair of electrons between three or more atoms.

O_3

The Lewis structure for O_3 is shown in Figure **3.71**. This structure would suggest the molecule would be unsymmetrical, with one O–O distance shorter than the other. Based on O–O and O=O distances in other molecules, we might predict this structure:

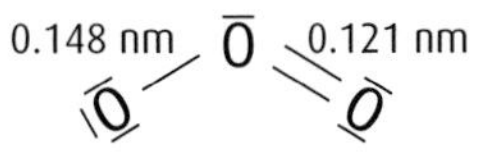

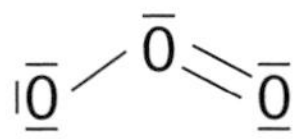

0.148 nm $\overline{O}$ 0.121 nm

However, when the O–O bond lengths in ozone are measured, both are found to be the same at 0.128 nm (i.e. mid-way between the single bond and double bond lengths). This can be explained by the idea of **delocalisation**. If the sigma framework (single bonds) of this molecule is shown (Figure **3.72**), then it can be seen that there is a p orbital on each O atom that is perpendicular to the plane of the molecule.

The p orbital on oxygen 1 can overlap with the p orbital on oxygen 2, which is part of the π bond. In this way, the electron pair of the π bond is spread (delocalised) over all three atoms (Figure **3.73**).

Learning objectives

- Understand what is meant by delocalisation of electrons
- Predict whether electrons will be delocalised in a molecule/ion

$\overline{|O}$ $\diagup$ $\overline{O}$ $\diagdown$ $\underline{O|}$

Figure 3.71 The Lewis structure for O_3.

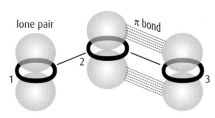

Figure 3.72 The sigma framework and p orbitals for O_3.

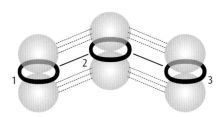

Figure 3.73 O_3 has a delocalised π system.

The bond order of a single bond is 1, a double bond has bond order 2 and a triple bond has bond order 3.

Extension

There are four electrons in the π delocalised system here. To understand why this does not result in two double bonds between the atoms, we have to use a more complex approach to the bonding, called molecular orbital theory. Two of the electrons in the π system occupy a bonding molecular orbital and the other two electrons occupy a molecular orbital that is non-bonding between the atoms.

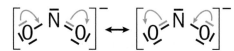

Figure 3.75 The two possible Lewis structures for NO_2^-. The curly arrows indicate movement of a pair of electrons.

These alternative Lewis structures are sometimes called resonance structures. The equal bond lengths are sometimes explained by the idea of a resonance hybrid. The resonance hybrid is a hybrid of these two structures, i.e. a form that is not one structure or the other but somewhere in between. In this case, with equal contributions from both resonance forms, the bond lengths in the resonance hybrid would be expected to be equal.

The delocalised system can be shown using dashed lines between atoms (Figure **3.74**). As the π bond is shared between two O–O bonds rather than just one, we consider that each bond has a half share of it, and we talk about the O–O **bond order** being 1.5. Each O–O bond is thus identical and somewhere between a single bond and a double bond.

Figure 3.74 The dashed lines represent the delocalisation of electrons.

We can recognise molecules or ions that are likely to have a delocalised π system by drawing Lewis structures. If it is possible to draw more than one Lewis structure, where the only difference between them is the position of a double bond and a lone pair (if there is one), then it is likely that this molecule/ion will have a delocalised structure.

NO_2^-

The fact that NO_2^- is a delocalised structure is suggested by the bond lengths in NO_2^-, in which both N–O bond lengths are equal, at 0.118 nm. This can be compared with an N=O bond length of 0.114 nm and an N–O bond length of 0.140 nm. The two possible Lewis structures are shown in Figure **3.75**.

These two structures are basically identical except for the position of the double bond (and a lone pair), and therefore a delocalised structure is predicted. The arrows show the delocalisation of the π bond between the two N–O bonds. The π bond (shown in orange in Figure **3.75**) is shared between two bonds, and the N–O bond order here is 1.5. The delocalised structure of NO_2^- can be represented as shown in Figure **3.76**.

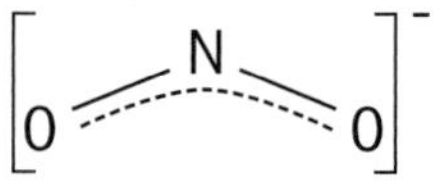

$$\left[O \diagdown \overset{N}{} \diagup O \right]^-$$

Figure 3.76 NO_2^- is isoelectronic with O_3 and therefore adopts a similar structure.

CO_3^{2-}

Three equivalent Lewis structures can be drawn for the carbonate ion (Figure **3.77**). By moving the double bond around, identical Lewis structures are obtained (one can just be rotated into the next).

In the structure of the carbonate ion there are **not** two long bonds and one short one; **all C–O bonds are the same length and between the length of a single bond and a double bond**. This can be explained

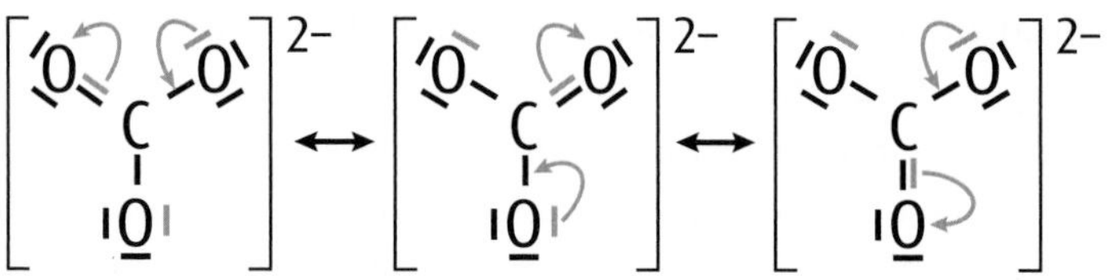

Figure 3.77 The three possible Lewis structures for CO_3^{2-}.

by the ion having a π delocalised system over the whole ion. The π bond (shown in orange in Figure **3.77**) is shared over three C–O bonds; therefore the C–O bond order is $1 + \frac{1}{3}$, i.e. $1\frac{1}{3}$.

There is a p orbital on each atom and these overlap side on to form the π delocalised system. The electrons in this system do not belong to any one atom but are rather delocalised over the whole ion:

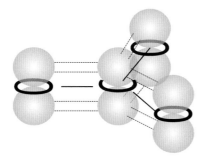

The delocalisation in the carbonate ion can be represented as shown in Figure **3.78**.

NO$_3^-$

NO$_3^-$ is isoelectronic with CO$_3^{2-}$ and therefore has the same structure. The Lewis structures are shown in Figure **3.79**.

Figure 3.79 The various equivalent Lewis structures for NO$_3^-$. The bond in orange is shared between three bonds.

A double bond is shared among three bonds, so each bond is actually of order $1\frac{1}{3}$. The delocalised structure is shown in Figure **3.80**.

All the N–O bond lengths are equal, and are between that of an N–O single bond and that of an N=O double bond. The N–O bond length here is 0.124 nm, which can be compared with the N–O bond length of 0.118 nm in NO$_2^-$. The bond order of the N–O bonds in NO$_2^-$ is 1.5, whereas it is 1.33 in NO$_3^-$, therefore the bond lengths would be expected to be longer in NO$_3^-$.

RCOO$^-$

A carboxylate ion is formed when a carboxylic acid dissociates (page **314**):

$$RCOOH \rightleftharpoons RCOO^- + H^+$$

For example, ethanoic acid:

$$CH_3COOH \rightleftharpoons CH_3COO^- + H^+$$

The Lewis structure is shown in Figure **3.81**. From this, you would expect one C–O bond to be short (double bond) and the other to be long (single

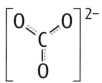

Figure 3.78 Delocalisation in CO$_3^{2-}$.

Examiner's tip
When asked for a Lewis structure of a species such as NO$_3^-$ in the examination you must show a structure with all bonds and lone pairs, i.e. one of the structures shown in Figure **3.78**. You must not show the delocalised structure unless specifically asked for this.

Figure 3.80 Delocalisation in NO$_3^-$.

Figure 3.81 The Lewis structure for RCOO$^-$.

bond). However, **both C–O bond lengths are equal and between the length of a double bond and a single bond.**

Two equivalent Lewis structures for this ion are shown in Figure **3.82**. The delocalised structure is shown in Figure **3.83**.

Let us consider the parent acid, RCOOH, and look at whether delocalisation is possible there. The Lewis structure of the acid is:

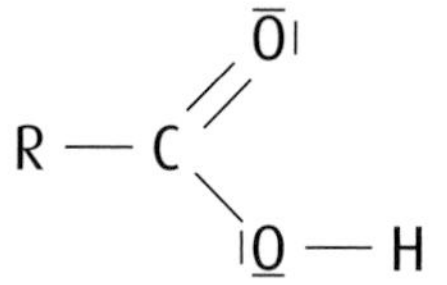

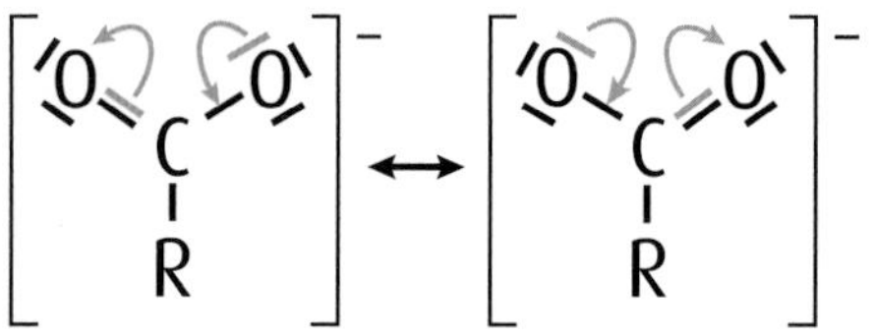

Figure 3.82 Two equivalent Lewis structures for RCOO⁻.

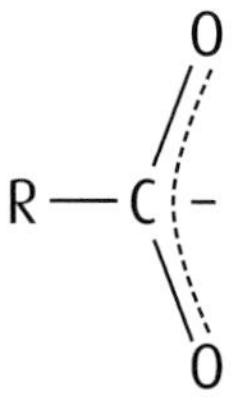

Figure 3.83 The C–O bond order in this ion is 1.5.

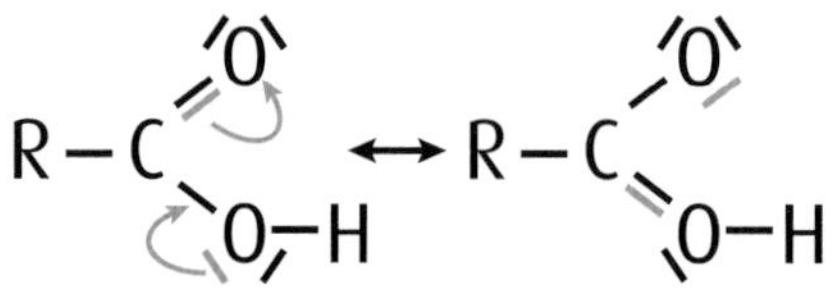

If we try and move the double bond around (Figure **3.84**), it can be seen that these two Lewis structures are different – in the second structure the O now has three bonds, whereas neither O has three bonds in the first structure. The difference between the Lewis structures indicates that there is no delocalisation in this molecule.

Figure 3.84 Delocalisation is not possible in RCOOH.

C₆H₆ (benzene)

A ring structure for benzene with alternating double and single bonds was originally proposed by Friedrich Auguste Kekulé (Figure **3.85**).

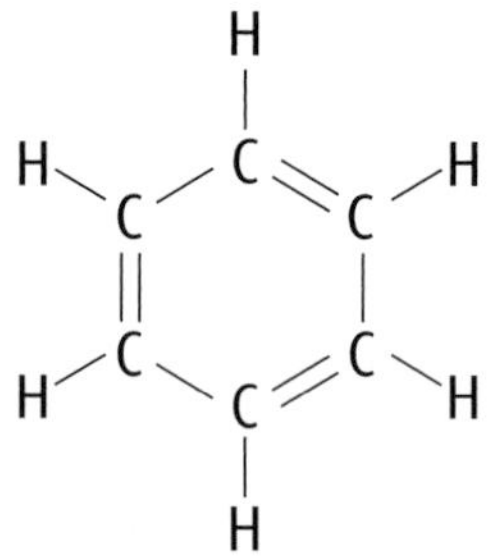

One piece of evidence against this being the best representation of the structure of benzene came when it became possible to measure bond lengths. All the C–C bond lengths in benzene are equal and, at 0.139 nm, are between the C=C bond length of 0.134 nm and the single bond length of 0.154 nm.

This was originally explained by a resonance hybrid with equal contributions from the two structures:

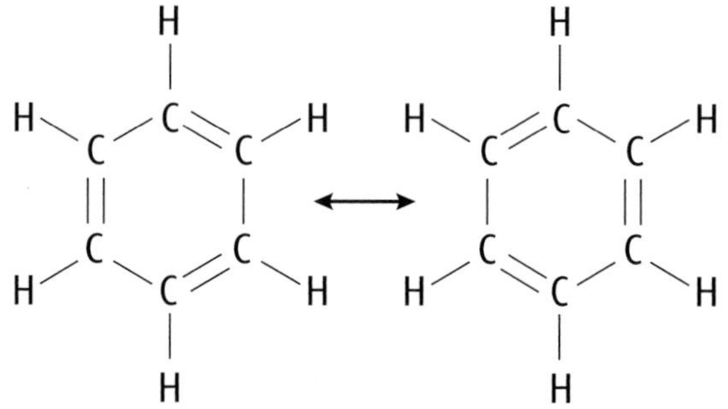

However, it is now much better explained by the idea of delocalisation.

The sigma framework (without the double bonds) and p orbitals on each C atom are shown in Figure **3.86**.

Figure 3.85 The benzene structure with alternating single and double bonds is still known as 'Kekulé benzene'.

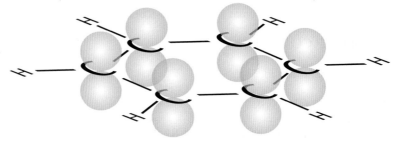

Figure 3.86 The sigma framework for C₆H₆.

It can be seen that, instead of the p orbitals just overlapping side on between adjacent C atoms to give three **π** bonds, delocalisation can occur over the whole structure:

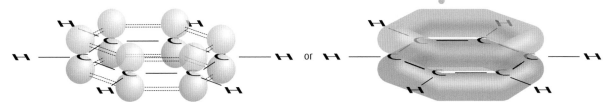

Thus, benzene has a **π** delocalised ring of electrons, which extends all around the ring of carbon atoms. The structure of benzene is usually drawn as a hexagon, with a ring in the middle indicating the **π** delocalised system.

Although experimental evidence falsified Kekulé's theory of the structure of benzene, it continues to be used. At university level, the benzene ring is still usually drawn in the Kekulé form, with alternating double and single bonds. The idea of resonance was developed to account for this disagreement between theory and experiment – an attempt to rescue the theory. Does this example make it even more difficult to distinguish between scientific theories and pseudoscientific ones? Karl Popper used the idea of falsifiability as the mark of a scientific theory and as a way of distinguishing it from a pseudoscientific one. Marxism was regarded by Popper as an example of pseudoscience, because if the theory disagreed with practice, the theory was adapted to account for any discrepancy and so became unfalsifiable.

Test yourself

12 Work out the X–O bond order in each of the following delocalised structures:

   a SO_4^{2-} **b** PO_4^{3-} **c** ClO_4^-

3.7 Polarity

Electronegativity

In a covalent bond between two **different** atoms, the atoms do not attract the electron pair in the bond equally. How strongly the electrons are attracted depends on the **size of the individual atoms and their nuclear charge**.

In the F_2 molecule, the two F atoms attract the electrons in the bond equally and thus the electrons lie symmetrically (Figure **3.87**). This molecule is non-polar.

Learning objectives

- Understand what is meant by electronegativity
- Predict whether a molecule will be polar

Electronegativity is a measure of the attraction of an atom in a molecule for the electron pair in the covalent bond of which it is a part.

a

F   F
+   +

b

:F̈----+----F̈:

electrons symmetrically distributed in covalent bond

Figure 3.87 (a) The electron density in F_2; **(b)** F_2 is a non-polar molecule.

$^{\delta+}H — F^{\delta-}$

However, in HF, F is more electronegative than H and attracts the electrons in the H–F bond more strongly than the H atom does. The electrons in the bond thus lie closer to the F than to the H (Figure **3.88**). H–F is a polar molecule. The unsymmetrical distribution of electron density results in small charges on the atoms. F is δ− because the electrons in the bond lie closer to F, whereas electron density has been pulled away from H, so it is δ+.

electrons lie, on average, closer to F

Figure 3.88 (**a**) The electron density in HF; (**b**) HF is a polar molecule.

δ− indicates a small negative charge.

Pauling electronegativities

There are various scales of electronegativity and it is important to realise that, although they are derived from physical quantities (such as bond energies), the numbers themselves are not physical quantities; they have **no units** and must only be used in a comparative way. The most commonly used scale of electronegativity is that developed by Linus Pauling. The electronegativity values for some elements are shown in Table **3.11**.

Non-metals have higher electronegativities than metals.

Noble gases do not have electronegativity values as they do not form compounds.

Examiner's tip
You do not need to learn these electronegativity values, but you should be aware of trends and recognise very electronegative atoms such as N, Cl, O and F.

H 2.1							
Li 1.0	Be 1.5		B 2.0	C 2.5	N 3.0	O 3.5	F 4.0
Na 0.9	Mg 1.2		Al 1.5	Si 1.8	P 2.1	S 2.5	Cl 3.0
K 0.8	Ca 1.0		Ga 1.6	Ge 1.8	As 2.0	Se 2.4	Br 2.8
Rb 0.8	Sr 1.0		In 1.7	Sn 1.8	Sb 1.9	Te 2.1	I 2.5

Table 3.11 Pauling electronegativities for some elements.

Examiner's tip
To remember the trends in electronegativity, just remember that F is the atom with the highest electronegativity. Electronegativity must then increase across a period to F and decrease down a group from F.

Atoms with similar electronegativities will form covalent bonds. Atoms with widely different electronegativities will form ionic bonds. The difference in electronegativity can be taken as a guide to how ionic or how covalent the bond between two atoms is likely to be.

Electronegativity generally decreases down a group and increases across a period. This will be discussed in more depth in Chapter **4**.

Linus Pauling related the electronegativity difference between two atoms to the ionic character of a bond. He suggested that an electronegativity difference of 1.7 corresponded to 50% ionic character in a bond and reasoned that a greater electronegativity difference than this corresponded to a structure that was more ionic than covalent, whereas if the difference is less than that the bonding is more covalent than ionic. This is a useful idea, but it must be used with great caution. For instance, KI (electronegativity difference 1.7) would come out of this discussion as having 50% ionic and 50% covalent character, and NaI (difference of 1.6) would appear to be mostly covalent, whereas both behave as predominantly ionic compounds. Pauling, in his original discussion of this, was actually referring to diatomic molecules and not to macroscopic compounds.

Examiner's tip
If asked about this, assume that the bonding between two elements is ionic if the difference is more than 1.7, and covalent if the difference is less than 1.7.

Polar molecules

The electronegativity difference between two atoms covalently bonded together results in the electrons lying more towards one atom than the other. We call such a bond **polar**. However, whether an overall molecule is polar also depends on the shape of the molecule.

For a molecule to be polar it must have a **positive end to the molecule and a negative end**. For instance, HCl, NH$_3$ and H$_2$O are all polar (Figure **3.89**). These molecules all have an overall **dipole moment**, and the arrow indicates the direction of the dipole moment.

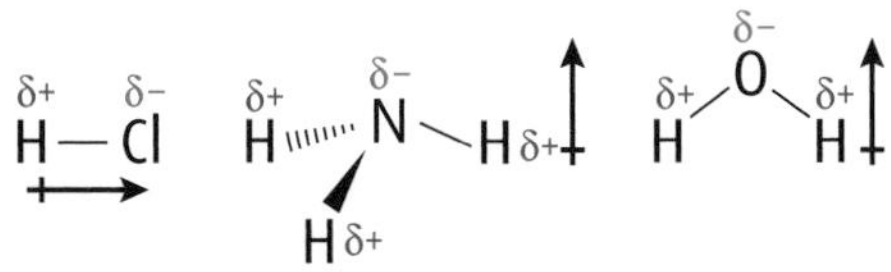

Figure 3.89 These molecules are all polar: one end of the molecule is slightly positive compared with the other end. The arrow indicates the dipole moment.

Although individual bonds may be polar, the overall molecule may be non-polar if, owing to the symmetry of the molecule, the dipole moments of the individual bonds cancel out.

Saying that a molecule has a dipole moment is just another way of saying that it is polar.

CO$_2$ is a non-polar molecule. Each C–O bond is polar, because oxygen is more electronegative than carbon, but overall the dipoles cancel so that there is no overall dipole moment and the molecule is non-polar.

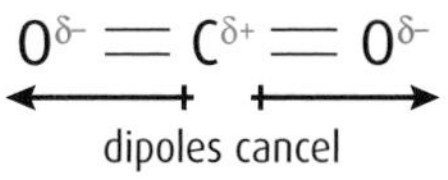

BF$_3$ is also non-polar. Again, each individual bond is polar but the dipoles cancel.

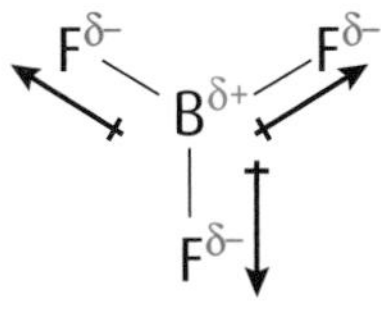

CCl₄ is non-polar, but CHCl₃ is polar (Figure **3.90**).

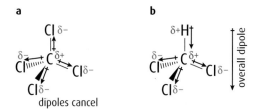

dipoles cancel

Figure 3.90 a CCl₄ is non-polar because the individual dipoles cancel. **b** CHCl₃ is polar because the dipoles do not cancel; there is a positive end to the molecule and a negative end. Although the C in CHCl₃ is shown as δ+, it is not as positive as the H (as C is more electronegative than H); therefore, the C is slightly negative compared with the H, although it is positive overall in the molecule.

Examiner's tip

Examination answer as to why CCl₄ is non-polar: 'although each individual bond is polar due to the difference in electronegativity of the atoms, because of the symmetry of the molecule the dipoles cancel'.

Extension

Dipole moment is the product of the charge and the distance between the charges. The unit is the debye (D).

Some polar and non-polar molecules are shown in Table **3.12**.

Polar	Non-polar
HCl, H₂O, NH₃, SO₂, CHCl₃, CH₂Cl₂, CH₃Cl₃, SCl₂, XeO₃, PCl₃, SOCl₂, POCl₃	CO₂, C₂H₂, C₂Cl₄, BF₃, XeF₂, XeF₄, SF₆, PF₅, XeO₄, SO₃
	These molecules are non-polar, because the symmetry of the molecules causes the individual dipole moments of the bonds to cancel out.

Table 3.12 Some polar and non-polar molecules.

Self-test 7

Test yourself

13 Arrange the following atoms in order of electronegativity (smallest first):

   Cl   O   H   Br   Na

14 Select the polar molecules from the following list. For the polar molecules, draw diagrams showing the dipoles.

HBr	**HCN**	**PH₃**	**SCl₂**	**CF₄**
N₂	**OCl₂**	**O₃**	**BCl₃**	**C₂Cl₂**
H₂S	**CH₂Cl₂**			

HL 15 Sort the following molecules into polar and non-polar molecules. For the polar molecule draw diagrams showing the dipoles.

   XeF₆   XeF₄   SF₄   PCl₅   SF₂
   SF₆   ClF₅   BrF₃   SOCl₂

3.8 Intermolecular forces

Intermolecular forces

Br₂ is a liquid at room temperature. It consists of discrete molecules in which the two Br atoms are joined by a covalent bond (an **intra**molecular force). But if Br₂ is to be a liquid, there must be some forces between molecules holding them in the liquid state (otherwise it would be a gas). These forces are **inter**molecular forces (Figure **3.91**).

There are various types of intermolecular forces. The main type between non-polar atoms/molecules is the **van der Waals' force**. Van der Waals'

Learning objectives

* Understand how intermolecular forces arise
* Understand how physical properties of covalent molecular substances depend on the intermolecular forces
* Predict relative boiling points of substances

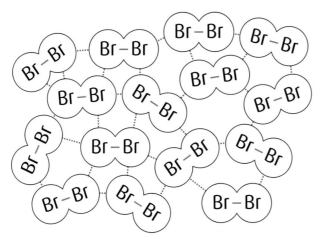

Figure 3.91 Intermolecular and intramolecular forces in liquid bromine. Intramolecular forces are shown in red and intermolecular forces are the dashed lines in blue.

forces are much weaker than covalent bonds. Therefore, when bromine is heated to form a gas, the Br_2 molecules (held together by covalent bonds) remain intact and it is the van der Waals' forces that are broken (Figure **3.92**).

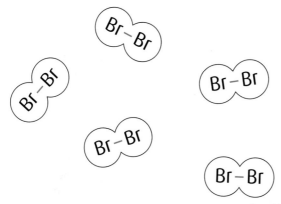

Figure 3.92 Gaseous bromine. Intramolecular forces (covalent bonds) are still present, but intermolecular forces have been broken.

How van der Waals' forces arise

> Van der Waals' forces are temporary (instantaneous) dipole-induced dipole interactions.

Consider liquid argon. The forces between two argon atoms are shown in Figure **3.93**. The electrons in an atom are in constant motion, and at any one time the electrons will not be symmetrically distributed about the nucleus. This results in a temporary (instantaneous) dipole in the atom, which will induce an opposite dipole in a neighbouring atom. These dipoles will attract each other so that there is an attractive force between atoms. Although the dipoles are constantly disappearing and reappearing, the overall force between the argon atoms is always attractive, because a dipole always induces an opposite one.

In general, van der Waals' forces get stronger as the number of electrons in a molecule increases. As the number of electrons increases, the relative

> Intramolecular forces are forces within a molecule.
> Intermolecular forces are forces between molecules.

> Intermolecular forces are much weaker than covalent bonds.

> Van der Waals' forces are also sometimes called London dispersion forces.

> Van der Waals' forces are present between all molecules in solid and liquid states.

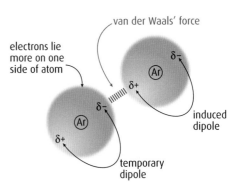

Figure 3.93 The origin of van der Waals' forces.

In general, van der Waals' forces get stronger as the relative molecular mass increases.

molecular mass also increases, and we normally talk about 'an increase in the strength of van der Waals' forces as the relative molecular mass increases'.

A clear correlation between boiling point and relative molecular/atomic mass can be seen down group 7 (blue line) and down group 0 (red line) in Figure **3.94**.

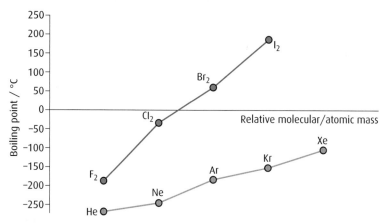

Figure 3.94 Variation in boiling points of elements in groups 7 and 0.

Consider group 7: fluorine (M_r 38.00) is a gas at room temperature, but iodine (M_r 253.80) is a solid. This is because there are more electrons in an iodine molecule, and the atoms making up the molecule are larger. More electrons means that the temporary dipoles will be larger with more electrons moving around. The larger atoms in the molecule means that the outer electrons will be less strongly held, and therefore the induced dipoles will also be larger.

Care must, however, be exercised when using this rule of thumb. If the above data for group 7 and group 0 are plotted together against relative molecular mass (relative atomic mass for group 0), we get the following graph, which does not show a clear correlation:

Comparisons are most useful when comparing similar substances – for instance, the elements within a group or a series of similar compounds.

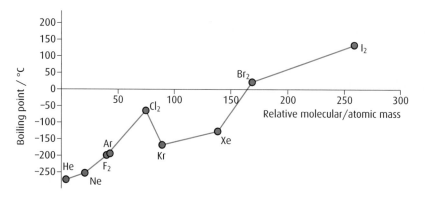

As the length (and so the relative molecular mass) of a hydrocarbon chain increases, so do the boiling points. Thus butane (C_4H_{10}) has a higher boiling point than ethane (C_2H_6) (Figure **3.95**). A higher boiling point means that the van der Waals' forces between molecules are stronger. The forces between the molecules are stronger because there are more atoms, and therefore more electrons, present in butane than in ethane.

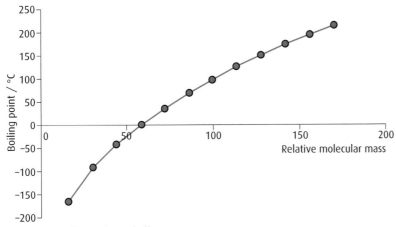

Figure 3.95 Boiling points of alkanes.

Polar molecules

Because of the electronegativity difference between H and Cl, the H–Cl molecule is polar.

van der Waals' forces are present between the molecules in HCl(l) but, owing to the polarity of the molecules, there are also other intermolecular forces present (Figure **3.96**). These are called **permanent dipole– permanent dipole** interactions, or usually just **dipole–dipole attractions**.

The intermolecular forces between molecules, which are polar (permanent dipole–permanent dipole interactions as well as van der Waals' forces) are stronger than between non-polar molecules (only van der Waals' forces), all other things being equal.

In general, all other things being equal, these permanent dipole interactions would be expected to cause melting points and boiling points to be higher for polar molecules.

If we compare propane and ethanal, both have a relative molecular mass of 44 and therefore the strength of van der Waals' forces should be similar. However, ethanal is a polar molecule and has dipole–dipole interactions as well as van der Waals' forces. The intermolecular forces between molecules of ethanal are therefore stronger than between propane molecules and ethanal has a significantly higher boiling point (more energy must be supplied to break the forces between molecules):

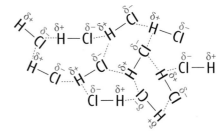

Figure 3.96 Permanent dipole–permanent dipole interactions exist between molecules. These are shown in purple.

All other things being equal: this basically means that we should compare compounds with relative molecular masses as similar as possible.

If molecules with similar relative molecular masses are compared, polar molecules have higher melting and boiling points than non-polar molecules.

Molecule	Lewis structure	M_r	Boiling point / °C
propane	H H H | | | H — C — C — C — H | | | H H H	44	−42
ethanal	H | H — C — C = O | \ H H	44	21

A similar situation is seen when we compare Br_2 with ICl:

Compound	M_r	Boiling point /°C
Br_2	159.80	59
ICl	162.35	100

The relative molecular masses of these two compounds are very similar, and so the strength of the van der Waals' forces are similar. However, ICl is polar (Cl is more electronegative than I), whereas Br_2 is non-polar. The intermolecular forces are stronger in ICl because of the permanent dipole–permanent dipole interactions. Stronger intermolecular forces means that the boiling point of ICl is higher than that of Br_2.

That we simply cannot say that polar molecules have stronger intermolecular forces and higher boiling points than non-polar molecules can be seen if we compare Br_2 with three other interhalogen compounds:

Compound	M_r	Boiling point /°C	Polar/non-polar?
Br_2	159.80	59	non-polar
ClF	54.45	−100	polar
BrF	98.90	20	polar
ClBr	115.35	5	polar

Br_2 is the only molecule here that is non-polar, but it has the highest boiling point as a result of its greatest relative molecular mass and, therefore, strongest van der Waals' forces.

Extension

Explain why BrF has a higher boiling point than ClBr, despite ClBr having the greater relative molecular mass.

This will also be discussed on pages **487–491**.

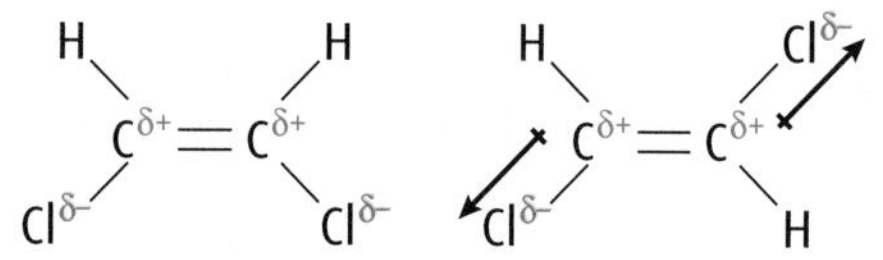

cis-1,2-dichloroethene
polar

trans-1,2-dichloroethene
non-polar

Figure 3.97 *Cis*- and *trans*-1,2-dichloroethene.

(HL) Comparison of *cis*- and *trans*-1,2-dichloroethene

Cis-1,2-dichloroethene and *trans*-1,2-dichloroethene are geometrical isomers – they differ only in the orientation of the Cl atoms about the C=C (Figure **3.97**).

Compound	M_r	Boiling point /°C	Polar/non-polar?
cis-1,2-dichloroethene	96.94	60.5	polar
trans-1,2-dichloroethene	96.94	48.7	non-polar

Both molecules have the same relative molecular mass and are identical, except that one is polar and the other is not. The difference between the boiling points is then solely due to the permanent dipole–dipole interactions in the *cis* form.

Hydrogen bonding

Hydrogen bonding influences many properties of substances – it is responsible for ice floating in water, it is the force between strands of DNA, it helps maintain the 3D structure of proteins, it is the reason that ethanol is soluble in water. It could be argued that hydrogen bonding is the reason why life on Earth exists as we know it!

The origin of hydrogen bonding

Let us compare the boiling points of the hydrides of group 6 elements:

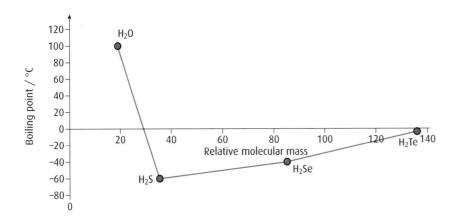

Group 6 hydride	Boiling point / °C
H_2O	100
H_2S	−60
H_2Se	−41
H_2Te	−4

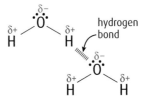

Figure 3.98 A hydrogen bond between two water molecules. The hydrogen bond is the dashed purple line between the lone pair of a δ− oxygen on one molecule and the δ+ hydrogen on the other molecule.

The boiling point increases from H_2S to H_2Te, as would be expected from the increase in the strength of van der Waals' forces as the relative molecular mass increases.

H_2O has, however, a much higher boiling point than would be expected from its relative molecular mass. This suggests that there must be intermolecular forces other than van der Waals' forces between H_2O molecules and that these intermolecular forces are stronger than van der Waals' forces. These extra intermolecular forces between H_2O molecules are called hydrogen bonds. A hydrogen bond between two water molecules is shown in Figure **3.98**.

> It is important to realise that, although hydrogen bonding is the strongest of the intermolecular forces, it is much weaker than covalent bonding.

Hydrogen bonding occurs between molecules when a very electronegative atom (**N, O, F**) is joined to a hydrogen atom in the molecule. The electronegative atom withdraws electron density from the H, polarising the bond such that there is a strong interaction between the δ+ H and the δ− atom (N, O, F) on the other molecule.

The hydrogen bonding between ammonia molecules and hydrogen fluoride molecules is shown in Figure **3.99**.

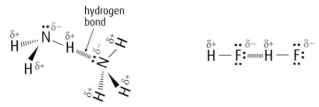

Figure 3.99 Hydrogen bonding between ammonia and hydrogen fluoride molecules.

Extension

There is more to hydrogen bonding than just an electrostatic interaction between dipoles. When H is attached to a very electronegative atom, the electron density is pulled away strongly from the H. There is then an interaction between the electron density of the lone pair on N, O or F in one molecule and the H nucleus in a different molecule. There is thus a directional component to hydrogen bonds. If the interaction were purely dipole–dipole, Cl, with the same electronegativity as N, would also be expected to participate in hydrogen bonding, but it does not. This could be explained by the higher energy and more diffuse lone pair on the Cl not interacting effectively with the H.

> The requirements for H bonding are that the H atom is attached to a very electronegative atom – N, O, F – which possesses at least one lone pair of electrons.

We can work out whether there will be hydrogen bonding between molecules simply by looking at whether the molecule contains N/O/F joined directly to an H atom:

Hydrogen bonding between molecules	No hydrogen bonding between molecules
HF	HCl
H_2O	H_2S
NH_3	PH_3
CH_3CH_2OH	CH_3OCH_3
$CH_3CH_2NH_2$	CH_3CH_2F
Hydrogen bonding between molecules, as there is an H joined directly to an N, O or F atom.	No hydrogen bonding between molecules, as H is not joined to N, O or F.

There is no hydrogen bonding between molecules of CH_3CH_2F, as the H is not joined directly to an F atom:

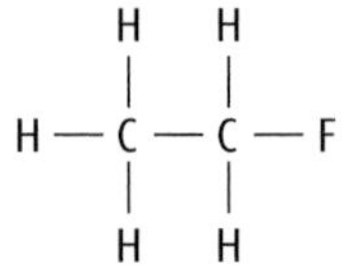

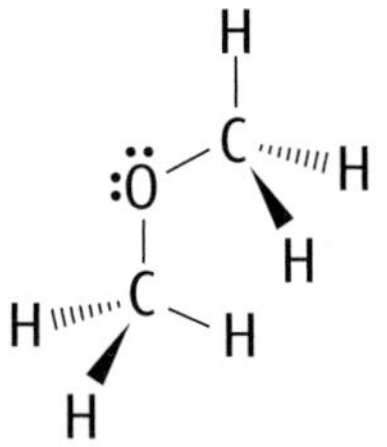

CH_3OCH_3 is an ether with the structure shown in Figure **3.100**. It is a polar molecule, but there is no hydrogen bonding between molecules.

The hydrogen bonding between some molecules of ethanol is shown in Figure **3.101**.

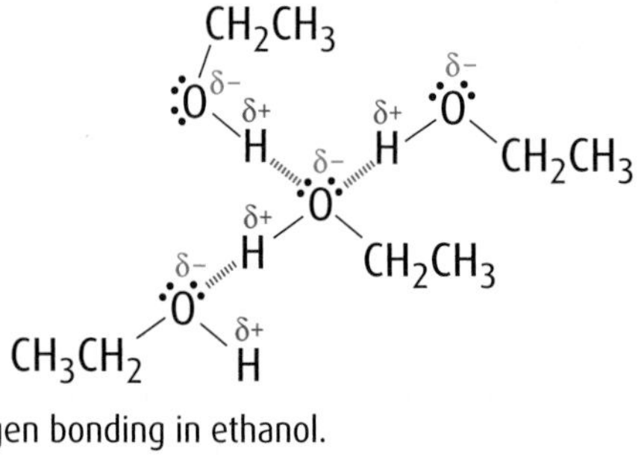

Figure 3.101 Hydrogen bonding in ethanol.

Figure 3.100 The Lewis structure for CH_3OCH_3.

Hydrogen bonding can influence the solubility of substances in water, and often molecules that are able to hydrogen bond are soluble in water – this will be discussed below.

HL Hydrogen bonding can also occur within molecules

Consider the *cis* and *trans* forms of butenedioic acid:

cis-but-2-ene-1,4-dioic acid (maleic acid)	*trans*-but-2-ene-1,4-dioic acid (fumaric acid)
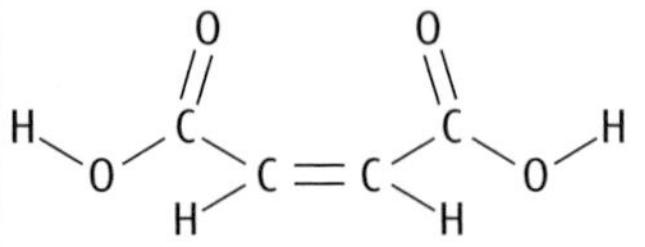	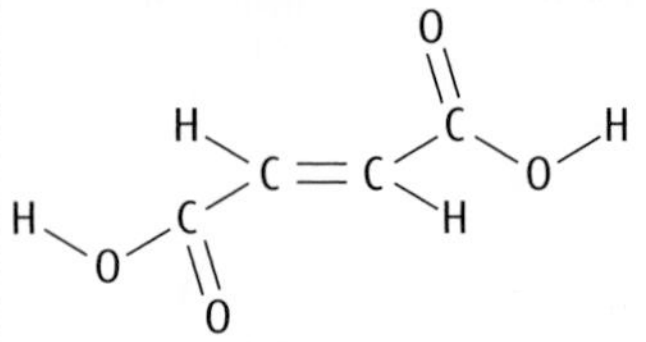
melting point: 130 °C	melting point: 287 °C

The *cis* form has a lower melting point, because as well as intermolecular hydrogen bonding it is also able to participate in intramolecular hydrogen bonding (Figure **3.102**). This means that there is less hydrogen bonding **between** molecules and that the intermolecular forces are weaker than in the *trans* form. The *trans* form participates only in intermolecular hydrogen bonding, as the COOH groups are further away from each other; the intermolecular forces are therefore stronger in the *trans* form.

Figure 3.102 Intramolecular hydrogen bonding in *cis*-but-2-ene-1,4-dioic acid.

Melting and boiling points

> Only intermolecular forces are broken when covalent molecular substances are melted or boiled – covalent bonds are **not** broken.

We have looked at several factors that influence the strength of intermolecular forces and hence the melting and boiling points of covalent substances. Now let us consider all the above points together with some examples.

> The stronger the intermolecular forces, the more energy must be supplied to break them and the higher the boiling point.

> Intermolecular forces increase in strength as:
> van der Waals' forces < permanent dipole–dipole < hydrogen bonding
> WEAKEST ————————————————————→ STRONGEST

If relative molecular masses are approximately equal, then the boiling points usually go in the order shown in Table **3.13**.

> **Relative molecular mass** – generally substances with higher relative molecular masses have higher melting points and boiling points due to stronger van der Waals' forces.

Type of substance		Strongest intermolecular force
substances containing H bonded to O, N, F	decreasing boiling point	hydrogen bonding
polar substances		permanent dipole–dipole
non-polar substances		van der Waals' forces (temporary dipoles)

Table 3.13 Boiling points in substances with different intermolecular forces.

Worked examples

Compare the boiling points of sulfur, chlorine and argon.

Sulfur, chlorine and argon are all non-polar substances, and therefore the strongest intermolecular forces are van der Waals' forces. Any difference between these substances is thus due to the strength of van der Waals' forces, which is affected by relative molecular mass (relative atomic mass for argon). Sulfur forms S_8 molecules with a relative molecular mass of 256.48; Cl_2 has a relative molecular mass of 70.90; and Ar has a relative atomic mass of 39.95. Therefore the boiling point of sulfur would be expected to be highest, as S_8 has a greater relative molecular mass and therefore stronger van der Waals' forces than Cl_2 and Ar. More energy is thus required to break the intermolecular forces in sulfur than to break the intermolecular forces in chlorine and the interatomic forces in Ar. Chlorine would be expected to have a higher boiling point than Ar, again due to the greater mass and the stronger van der Waals' forces.

The actual boiling points for these substances are:

Sulfur: 113 °C   Chlorine: −34 °C   Argon: −186 °C

Compare the boiling points of propane ($CH_3CH_2CH_3$), methoxymethane (CH_3OCH_3) and ethanol (CH_3CH_2OH).

Let us compare the relative molecular masses of these substances:

$CH_3CH_2CH_3$: 44.11 CH_3OCH_3: 46.08 CH_3CH_2OH: 46.08

The relative molecular masses are all very similar, and therefore the strength of the van der Waals' forces are going to be similar.

The next thing we can look at is whether any of the molecules are polar:

$CH_3CH_2CH_3$: non-polar CH_3OCH_3: polar CH_3CH_2OH: polar

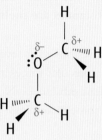

The presence of the very electronegative O atom in CH_3OCH_3 and CH_3CH_2OH means that these substances are polar. $CH_3CH_2CH_3$ is the only non-polar molecule and will have the lowest boiling point, as the only forces between molecules are van der Waals' forces. van der Waals' forces are the weakest of the intermolecular forces.

CH_3OCH_3 and CH_3CH_2OH are both polar and have the same relative molecular mass, but CH_3CH_2OH has the higher boiling point because it has an H joined to an O, and therefore there is hydrogen bonding between molecules.

Hydrogen bonding in CH_3CH_2OH is a stronger intermolecular force than the permanent dipole interactions in CH_3OCH_3; therefore the intermolecular forces are stronger between molecules of CH_3CH_2OH than between molecules of CH_3OCH_3.

The boiling points of these compounds are:

$CH_3CH_2CH_3$: −42 °C CH_3OCH_3: −25 °C CH_3CH_2OH: 78 °C

Self-tests 8 & 9

Test yourself

16 Arrange the following molecules in order of increasing boiling point (lowest first):

  a CH_4 CCl_4 CF_4

  b NH_3 PH_3 AsH_3

  c NH_3 N_2H_4 CH_4

  d CH_3OH CH_3F C_2H_4

  e H_2O H_2S H_2O_2

  f $CH_3CH_2CH_2CH_2OH$ $CH_3CH_2OCH_2CH_3$ $CH_3CH_2CH_2CH_2CH_3$

  g N_2 F_2 HF Ne

17 Arrange the following substances in order of increasing boiling point:

  a $NaCl$ $SiCl_4$ CCl_4 HCl

  b Br_2 HBr $CaBr_2$ PBr_3

  c C_4H_{10} C_3H_7OH C_3H_8 CH_3CH_2COOH C_4H_9OH

Solubility

It is often said, when referring to solubility, that 'like dissolves like'. What this means is that:

> generally a substance will dissolve in a solvent if the intermolecular forces in the solute and solvent are similar.

Whether a substance dissolves depends (in part) on how much energy is needed to break intermolecular forces in the solvent and solute and then how much energy is released, to pay back this energy, when intermolecular forces are formed between solvent and solute molecules in the solution.

HL Solubility is discussed here from the point of view of energy. The influence of entropy on solubility will be considered on page **227**.

Pentane is readily soluble in hexane but insoluble in water

The amount of energy required to break the van der Waals' forces in pure hexane and pure pentane is paid back when van der Waals' forces are formed between the molecules of hexane and pentane (Figure **3.103**). Pentane does not dissolve in water because there is hydrogen bonding between water molecules. If pentane were to dissolve in water there would be van der Waals' forces between water molecules and pentane. The energy released if van der Waals' forces were to form between water molecules and pentane molecules would not pay back the energy required to break the hydrogen bonds between water molecules, as hydrogen bonds are stronger than van der Waals' forces (Figure **3.104**).

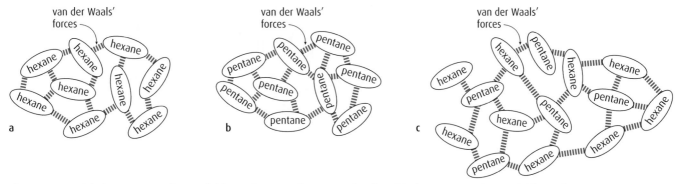

Figure 3.103 (a) There are van der Waals' forces between hexane molecules; **(b)** there are van der Waals' forces between pentane molecules; **(c)** there are van der Waals' forces between hexane and pentane molecules when pentane dissolves in hexane.

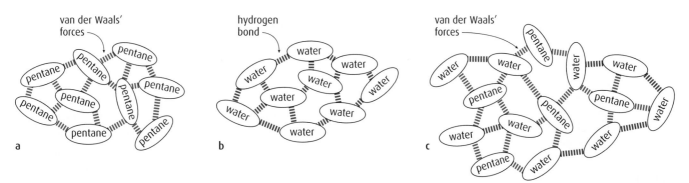

Figure 3.104 (a) There are van der Waals' forces between pentane molecules; **(b)** there are hydrogen bonds between water molecules; **(c)** pentane does not dissolve in water because only van der Waals' forces would be formed between pentane and water molecules.

Substances that are able to participate in hydrogen bonding will generally be soluble in water, as they are able to hydrogen bond to the water.

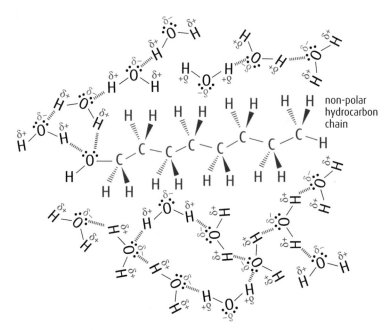

Figure 3.105 Hydrogen bonding between water and ethanol.

Ethanol is soluble in water

Ethanol (C_2H_5OH) is very soluble in water, because ethanol is able to hydrogen bond to the water (Figure **3.105**). The hydrogen bonding between water and ethanol molecules in the solution releases energy and pays back the energy to break the hydrogen bonds in pure water and pure ethanol.

Longer chain alcohols become progressively less soluble in water

Octan-1-ol is insoluble in water. Although there is some hydrogen bonding between the O–H group of the alcohol and the water molecules, the long hydrocarbon chain prevents water molecules on either side from hydrogen bonding to each other (Figure **3.106**). Energy is needed to break the hydrogen bonds between the water molecules, but this is not paid back as only van der Waals' forces form between the water molecules and the hydrocarbon part of the molecule.

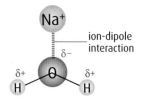

a

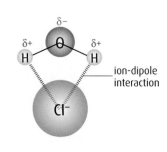

b

Figure 3.107 Ion–dipole interactions (**a**) between water and sodium ions; and (**b**) between water and chloride ions.

Figure 3.106 The hydrocarbon chain in octan-1-ol prevents hydrogen bonding between water molecules on either side.

Dissolving ionic substances

Consider the dissolving of sodium chloride:

$$NaCl(s) \xrightarrow{\text{'+ water'}} NaCl(aq)$$

The aqueous solution contains aqueous ions (Na^+(aq) and Cl^-(aq)). Ion–dipole interactions form between the water and the ions (Figure **3.107**). Energy is required to break the electrostatic forces in the ionic lattice but energy is released when hydrated ions are formed. If the energy released when the hydrated ions are formed is comparable to the energy required to break apart the lattice then the substance is generally soluble.

Ionic substances are not usually soluble in non-polar solvents such as hexane, because the interactions between the ions and the hexane molecules would be weak van der Waals' forces. Sodium chloride is insoluble in hexane because the energy released when a sodium ion or a chloride ion is surrounded by hexane molecules (solvated) is not enough to pay back the energy required to break apart the lattice.

Comparison of the physical properties of ionic and covalent molecular substances

Table **3.14** shows a comparison of the physical properties of ionic and covalent molecular substances.

Ionic	Covalent molecular
usually solids with high melting points	may be solid, liquid or gas at room temperature
strong electrostatic forces in the giant lattice structure must be broken	only intermolecular forces broken when the substances are melted or boiled; intermolecular forces are weaker than the electrostatic forces in an ionic lattice; no covalent bonds are broken when covalent molecular substances are melted or boiled
non-volatile	often volatile
strong electrostatic forces in the lattice	weak intermolecular forces
often soluble in water and usually insoluble in organic solvents	not usually soluble in water but soluble in organic solvents
strong interactions between the ions and the polar water molecules provide the energy to break apart the lattice structure	substances dissolve when intermolecular forces in solvent and solute are similar; molecules that are able to hydrogen bond to water are usually soluble
do not conduct electricity in the solid state but do conduct when molten or in aqueous solution, because of mobile ions	do not conduct electricity in any state
ions not free to move in solid state as held tightly in the lattice structure; ions free to move around when molten or dissolved in water	no ions or free electrons present; some substances, such as HCl, dissolve in water with ionisation – HCl(aq) conducts electricity

Table 3.14 The physical properties of ionic and covalent molecular substances compared.

3.9 Giant covalent substances

Giant covalent (macromolecular) structures

Allotropes of carbon

Allotropes are different forms of the same element. For instance, diamond, graphite and fullerene are all allotropes of carbon. They all contain only carbon atoms, but these atoms are joined together differently in each structure.

Diamond

Diamond has a giant covalent (macromolecular) structure. There are no individual molecules – the whole structure, continuing in three dimensions, represents one giant molecule (Figure **3.108**). Each carbon atom is joined to four others, in a **tetrahedral** array, by covalent bonds.

Learning objectives

- Describe the structures and bonding of giant covalent substances
- Explain the physical properties of giant covalent substances in terms of structure and bonding

Diamond is the hardest naturally occurring substance. It also has the highest thermal conductivity of any substance – more than five times that of copper. Both these properties make it suitable for use on drill bits. Diamond-encrusted drills can be used to drill through rock.

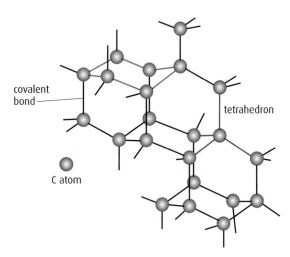

Figure 3.108 Part of the diamond structure, which is based on **puckered** hexagonal rings. One hexagon is highlighted in **red**.

Diamond has a very high melting point and boiling point (about 4000 °C) because **covalent bonds must be broken** when diamond is melted/boiled. Diamond is very hard for the same reason.

Diamond does not conduct electricity, because all the electrons are held strongly in covalent bonds and are therefore not free to move around in the structure.

Diamond is not soluble in water or organic solvents, as the forces between the atoms are too strong. The energy to break these covalent bonds would not be paid back when the C atoms were solvated.

Graphite

Like diamond, graphite has a giant covalent structure. Unlike diamond, however, it has a layer structure (Figure **3.109**). Each C is covalently bonded to three others in a trigonal planar array.

Substances with giant structures are sometimes called network solids.

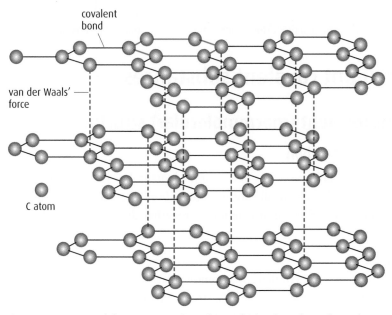

Figure 3.109 Part of the structure of graphite, which is based on **planar** hexagonal rings. One hexagon is highlighted in **red**.

There are covalent bonds between the C atoms within a layer but only van der Waals' forces between the layers (some of these are shown in blue in Figure **3.109**). The presence of weak forces between the layers is usually given as the explanation that graphite is a good lubricant (used in pencils, for example) – not much force is required to separate the layers. However, it has a very high melting/boiling point, because covalent bonds within the layers must be broken when it is melted/boiled.

Because of the strong covalent bonds between atoms, graphite is not soluble in water or non-polar solvents.

Graphite conducts electricity because each C atom forms only three covalent bonds, and the extra electrons not used in these bonds (carbon has four outer shell electrons) are able to move within the layers.

As only three covalent bonds are formed by each carbon atom in the layers, each C atom possesses one p orbital, containing one electron, perpendicular to the plane of the layers. These p orbitals can overlap side on to give a **π delocalised system** extending over the whole layer. Movement of electrons within this system allows conduction of electricity within layers. Graphite is, however, an electrical insulator perpendicular to the plane of the layers.

HL

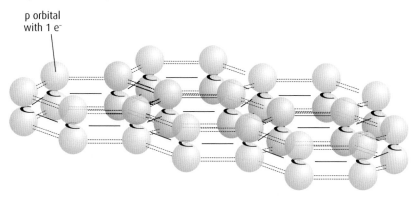

p orbital with 1 e⁻

C₆₀ fullerene (buckminsterfullerene)

The third allotrope of carbon that will be considered here is a molecular rather than a giant structure. It consists of individual C_{60} molecules, with covalent bonds within the molecule and van der Waals' forces between the molecules (Figure **3.110**).

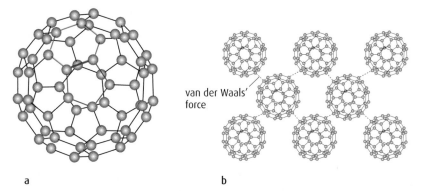

van der Waals' force

a   b

Figure 3.110 **(a)** One molecule of C_{60}. The structure is based on hexagons (in red) and pentagons (in blue); **(b)** van der Waals' forces exist between C_{60} molecules in the solid state.

Extension

The lubricant properties of graphite are usually explained as being due to the weak forces between layers of carbon atoms. However, graphite is a poor lubricant in a vacuum and it is now believed that the lubricant properties come from adsorbed water molecules.

Diamond and graphite are **giant** structures but fullerene is a **molecular** structure. The melting points of diamond and graphite are therefore substantially higher than that of fullerene, as covalent bonds must be broken when diamond and graphite are melted but only intermolecular forces (van der Waals' forces) when fullerene melts (it actually undergoes sublimation at about 530 °C).

C_{60} is insoluble in water but soluble in some organic solvents such as benzene. The energy to break the van der Waals' forces between the C_{60} molecules is paid back by the energy released when van der Waals' forces are formed between the C_{60} molecules and the solvent.

C_{60} does not conduct electricity. Although each C forms three bonds in the C_{60} molecule, so that there is delocalisation of electrons over the molecule, the molecular structure means that electrons are not able to move from one molecule to the next.

Silicon

Silicon has a giant covalent (macromolecular) structure similar to that of diamond. Each Si is joined to four others in a tetrahedral array by covalent bonds.

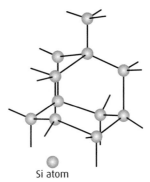

Si atom

Si has high melting and boiling points because a lot of energy must be supplied to break the covalent bonds present.

The melting point of Si (1420 °C) is much lower than that of diamond (about 3800 °C) as Si–Si bonds are longer and therefore weaker than C–C bonds. The C–C bonds are stronger because a C atom is smaller than an Si atom, and therefore the shared electron pair is closer to the nuclei in a C–C bond than in an Si–Si bond.

Silicon dioxide

SiO_2 (quartz) has a giant covalent structure. Each Si is bonded to four oxygen atoms in a tetrahedral array. Each oxygen is bonded to two Si atoms. Due to two lone pairs on each oxygen atom, the basic shape about each Si–O–Si unit is bent (based on tetrahedral).

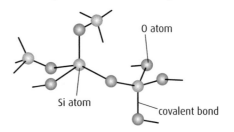

O atom

Si atom

covalent bond

The formula is SiO_2, because each Si has a half share of four oxygen atoms, i.e. $Si(O_{1/2})_4 = SiO_2$. SiO_2 has high melting and boiling points, because covalent bonds between atoms must be broken in order to melt/boil it, and this requires a lot of energy.

Extension

Si is a semiconductor. It conducts electricity but, unlike metallic conductors, the conductivity increases as the temperature increases. Although there are apparently no free electrons in silicon, the conductivity can be explained by **band theory**. The orbitals on adjacent atoms overlap to give a band of orbitals delocalised over the whole structure. The band gap between the valence band (full) and conduction band (empty) in silicon is small enough that electrons can be excited from the valence band to the conduction band at normal temperatures. Electrons in the conduction band means that silicon conducts electricity. In diamond the outer electrons are held more strongly than in silicon, and therefore the band gap between conduction and valence bands is greater, so electrons cannot be excited to the conduction band at normal temperatures and diamond does not conduct electricity.

Quartz is a piezoelectric material and is used in clocks and watches.

3.10 Metallic bonding

The structure of a metal is shown in Figure **3.111**.

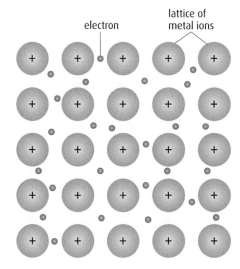

Figure 3.111 A metallic structure. This is a giant structure – there are no individual molecules.

Learning objectives

- Describe the structure of, and bonding in, metals
- Explain some of the properties of metals in terms of structure and bonding

Metals contain a **regular lattice arrangement of positive ions surrounded by a 'sea' of delocalised electrons**.

Metallic elements have relatively low ionisation energies and so form positive ions more easily than do non-metals.

The electrons are described as **delocalised**, because they do not belong to any one metal atom, but rather are able to move throughout the structure. The metallic bond is thus electrostatic in nature, resulting from the attraction between the positive metal ions and the negatively charged delocalised electrons. Each electron is attracted by all the positive ions in the structure; thus the whole lattice is held together.

The melting points of sodium and magnesium are compared below:

Metal	sodium	magnesium
Melting point / °C	98	649

There are several reasons why magnesium has a higher melting point than sodium. The first of these is that magnesium forms a 2+ ion compared with sodium, which forms a 1+ ion. This means that the electrostatic attraction between the ions and the delocalised electrons is stronger in magnesium.

The second reason why magnesium has a higher melting point than sodium, is that there are two delocalised electrons per atom in magnesium; therefore there will be a greater number of electrostatic attractions between the ions and the delocalised electrons.

The third reason is that the Mg^{2+} ion (65 pm) is smaller than the Na^+ ion (98 pm), and therefore the delocalised electrons are closer to the nucleus of the positive ion in magnesium and more strongly attracted.

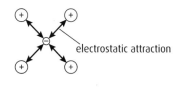

electrostatic attraction

Animation 1

Metallic bonding is the electrostatic attraction between the positive ions in the lattice and the delocalised electrons.

Na   Mg

Some other physical properties of metals are shown in Table **3.15**.

Physical property	Comment
lustrous	shiny, when freshly scratched/cut
good conductors of electricity	e.g. copper is used for electrical wires; conduction decreases as temperature increases
good conductors of heat	although the best conductor is diamond
ductile	may be drawn into wires
malleable	may be hammered into shape – many uses arise from the ability to easily shape metals, e.g. making car bodies

Table 3.15 Some physical properties of metals.

Metals conduct electricity because the delocalised electrons are free to move around.

Metals are **malleable/ductile** because of the **non-directionality** of the bonding. The metal ions in the lattice attract the delocalised electrons in all directions. Thus, when two layers slide over each other, the bonding in the resulting structure is exactly the same as in the original:

Extension

Dislocation movement makes the process of the layers moving over each other easier.

This can be compared with ionic solids, which are brittle, as displacement of one layer relative to the other results in like charges repelling each other:

Self-tests 10 & 11

Metals such as iron have a wide range of uses, such as in construction (bridges, cars, etc). Iron is usually used in the form of steel, an alloy of iron and carbon. The fact that mild steel is malleable makes it ideal for the construction of car bodies (and for crushing them afterwards!).

Test yourself

18 Arrange the following in order of increasing boiling point (lowest first):

   a SO_2 SiO_2 CO_2
   b C(diamond)   Si C_{60}
   c Al   Mg   Na

19 Arrange the following in order of solubility in water (least soluble first):

   a NaCl C_6H_{12} $C_5H_{11}OH$
   b CH_3Cl $CaCl_2$ CH_4

Exam-style questions

1   What is the formula of the compound formed between lithium and nitrogen?

    A LiN_2 **B** LiN_3 **C** Li_3N **D** Li_3N_2

2   Which of the following contains both ionic and covalent bonding?

    A NaCl   **B** NH_4Cl **C** CCl_4 **D** PCl_3

3   What is the shape of NO_2^+?

    A Linear   **C** Trigonal planar
    B Bent   **D** Tetrahedral

4   Which of the following is polar?

    A CO_2 **B** CCl_4 **C** BF_3 **D** PCl_3

5   Which of the following molecules exhibits hydrogen bonding?

    I NH_3 **II** CH_3NH_2 **III** HF   **IV** CH_3F

    A I, II and III only   **C** I and III onlyI
    B V only   **D** III and IV only

6   In which of the following are the molecules arranged in order of increasing boiling point (lowest first)?

    A NH_3 N_2 Br_2
    B H_2O H_2S H_2Se
    C CH_3Cl CH_2Cl_2 $CHCl_3$
    D C_4H_{10} C_3H_8 C_2H_5OH

7   What is the F–B–F bond angle in BF_4^-?

    A 109.5°   **B** 107°   **C** 120°   **D** 90°

8   Which of the following will be the worst conductor of electricity?

    A Mg(s)   **C** $MgCl_2$(l)
    B $SiCl_4$(l)   **D** C(graphite,s)

HL 9   When the compounds C_2H_6, C_2H_4, C_2H_2 and C_6H_6 are arranged in order of increasing C–C bond lengths (shortest first) the correct order is:

    A C_2H_6 C_2H_4 C_2H_2 C_6H_6
    B C_6H_6 C_2H_4 C_2H_2 C_2H_6
    C C_2H_2 C_6H_6 C_2H_4 C_2H_6
    D C_2H_2 C_2H_4 C_6H_6 C_2H_6

10 The number of π bonds and hybridisation of C in a molecule of hydrogen cyanide, HCN are:

	number of π bonds	hybridisation
A	3	sp^2
B	2	sp
C	1	sp^2
D	2	sp^3

11 Which of the following contains delocalised electrons?

A CO_2 **B** O_3 **C** SiO_2 **D** OCl_2

12 In which of the following is the distribution of electron pairs around the central atom octahedral?

A BCl_4^- **B** SF_4 **C** PCl_4^+ **D** XeF_4

13 a Describe the principles of the valence shell electron pair repulsion theory for predicting the shapes of molecules. **[4]**

b Predict the shapes and bond angles of the following molecules: **[4]**
 i PCl_3
 ii CO_2

c Explain why carbon dioxide is a non-polar molecule but sulfur dioxide is polar. **[3]**

d Draw a Lewis structure for carbon monoxide and explain whether it has a shorter or longer C–O bond length than carbon dioxide. **[3]**

14 Explain the following in terms of structure and bonding.

a Sodium oxide has a high melting point, does not conduct electricity when solid but conducts electricity when molten. **[4]**

b Sodium has a lower melting point than magnesium. **[3]**

c Phosphine, PH_3, has a lower boiling point than ammonia, NH_3, and arsine, AsH_3. **[3]**

d Silicon dioxide has a much higher melting point than carbon dioxide. **[3]**

15 a Explain the term 'hybridisation'. **[2]**

b Predict the hybridisation of the carbon atoms in ethene (C_2H_4) and ethyne (C_2H_2). **[2]**

c Explain, by reference to ethene and ethyne, what is meant by the terms 'sigma bond' and 'pi bond'. **[4]**

16 a Use the valence shell electron pair repulsion theory to predict the shapes and bond angles of the following molecules or ions:
 i SO_4^{2-} **ii** XeF_4 **iii** SF_4 **[6]**

b Explain whether XeF_4 is polar or non-polar. **[2]**

c Explain how you would expect the S–O bond length in SO_4^{2-} to compare with that in SO_2. **[2]**

Summary

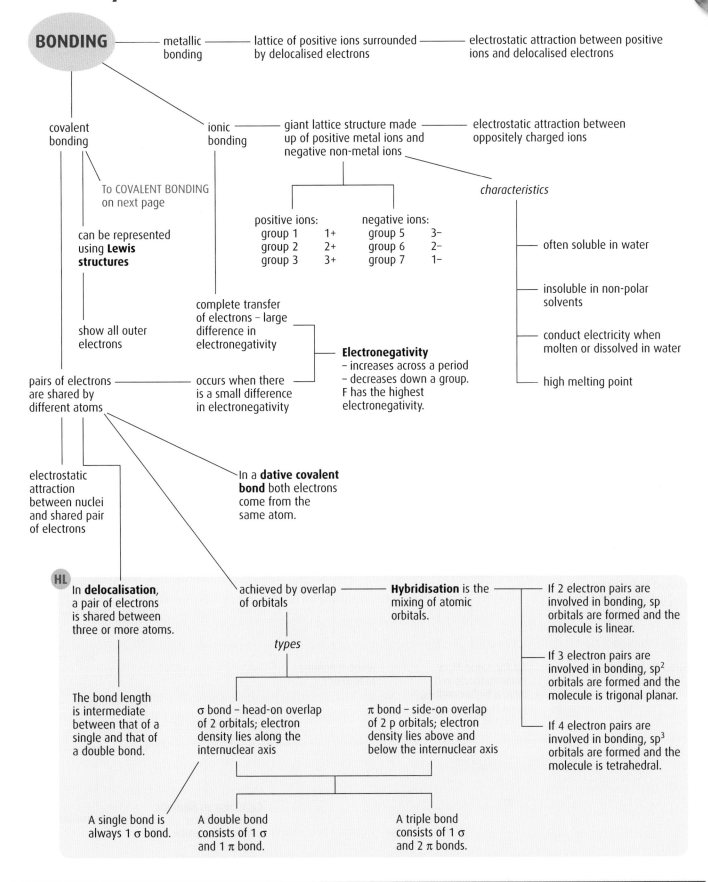

BONDING — metallic bonding — lattice of positive ions surrounded by delocalised electrons — electrostatic attraction between positive ions and delocalised electrons

ionic bonding — giant lattice structure made up of positive metal ions and negative non-metal ions — electrostatic attraction between oppositely charged ions

covalent bonding

To COVALENT BONDING on next page

can be represented using **Lewis structures**

show all outer electrons

characteristics

positive ions:
group 1   1+
group 2   2+
group 3   3+

negative ions:
group 5   3–
group 6   2–
group 7   1–

often soluble in water

insoluble in non-polar solvents

conduct electricity when molten or dissolved in water

high melting point

complete transfer of electrons – large difference in electronegativity

Electronegativity
– increases across a period
– decreases down a group.
F has the highest electronegativity.

pairs of electrons are shared by different atoms

occurs when there is a small difference in electronegativity

electrostatic attraction between nuclei and shared pair of electrons

In a **dative covalent bond** both electrons come from the same atom.

HL

In **delocalisation**, a pair of electrons is shared between three or more atoms.

achieved by overlap of orbitals

Hybridisation is the mixing of atomic orbitals.

If 2 electron pairs are involved in bonding, sp orbitals are formed and the molecule is linear.

If 3 electron pairs are involved in bonding, sp^2 orbitals are formed and the molecule is trigonal planar.

If 4 electron pairs are involved in bonding, sp^3 orbitals are formed and the molecule is tetrahedral.

types

The bond length is intermediate between that of a single and that of a double bond.

σ bond – head-on overlap of 2 orbitals; electron density lies along the internuclear axis

π bond – side-on overlap of 2 p orbitals; electron density lies above and below the internuclear axis

A single bond is always 1 σ bond.

A double bond consists of 1 σ and 1 π bond.

A triple bond consists of 1 σ and 2 π bonds.

Summary – continued

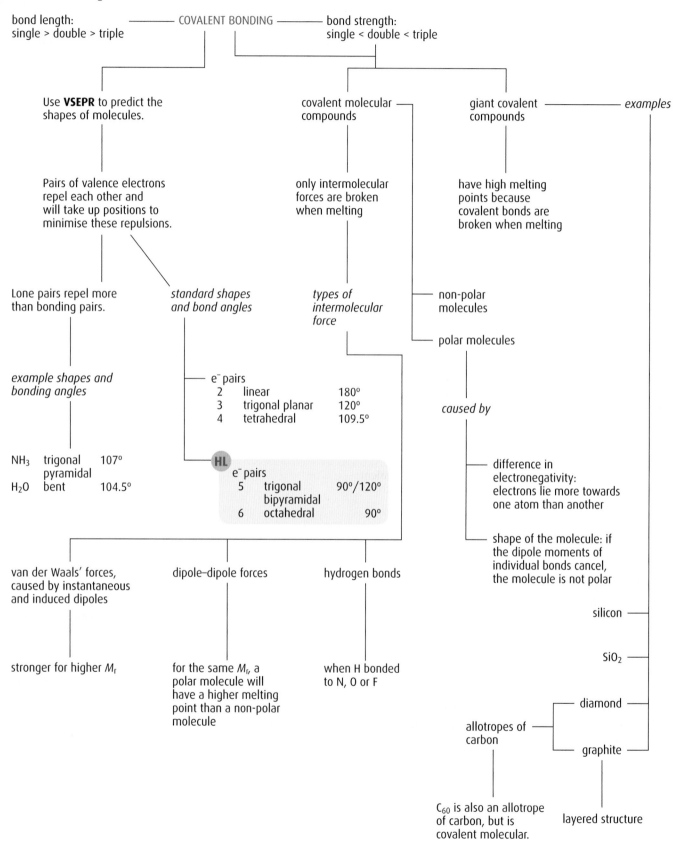

bond length:
single > double > triple

COVALENT BONDING

bond strength:
single < double < triple

Use **VSEPR** to predict the shapes of molecules.

covalent molecular compounds

giant covalent compounds

examples

Pairs of valence electrons repel each other and will take up positions to minimise these repulsions.

only intermolecular forces are broken when melting

have high melting points because covalent bonds are broken when melting

Lone pairs repel more than bonding pairs.

standard shapes and bond angles

types of intermolecular force

non-polar molecules

polar molecules

example shapes and bonding angles

e⁻ pairs

2	linear	180°
3	trigonal planar	120°
4	tetrahedral	109.5°

caused by

| NH₃ | trigonal pyramidal | 107° |
| H₂O | bent | 104.5° |

HL

e⁻ pairs

| 5 | trigonal bipyramidal | 90°/120° |
| 6 | octahedral | 90° |

difference in electronegativity: electrons lie more towards one atom than another

shape of the molecule: if the dipole moments of individual bonds cancel, the molecule is not polar

van der Waals' forces, caused by instantaneous and induced dipoles

dipole–dipole forces

hydrogen bonds

silicon

SiO₂

stronger for higher M_r

for the same M_r, a polar molecule will have a higher melting point than a non-polar molecule

when H bonded to N, O or F

diamond

allotropes of carbon

graphite

C₆₀ is also an allotrope of carbon, but is covalent molecular.

layered structure

The periodic table 4

4.1 The periodic table

> **Learning objectives**
>
> - Understand how the elements in the periodic table are arranged
> - Understand the terms **group** and **period**
> - Understand how the electronic configuration of an element relates to its position in the periodic table

The elements in the periodic table are arranged in order of atomic number, starting with hydrogen, which has atomic number 1. The groups are arranged in the vertical columns in the periodic table and the periods are arranged in the horizontal rows (Figure **4.1**).

Most of the elements in the periodic table are metals – these are shown in yellow in Figure **4.1**. The rest of the elements are non-metals, although some elements, such as Si, Ge and Sb, which are near the dividing line between metals and non-metals, are sometimes classified as semi-metals or metalloids.

period number	1	2											3	4	5	6	7	0
1	H 1																	He 2
2	Li 3	Be 4											B 5	C 6	N 7	O 8	F 9	Ne 10
3	Na 11	Mg 12											Al 13	Si 14	P 15	S 16	Cl 17	Ar 18
4	K 19	Ca 20	Sc 21	Ti 22	V 23	Cr 24	Mn 25	Fe 26	Co 27	Ni 28	Cu 29	Zn 30	Ga 31	Ge 32	As 33	Se 34	Br 35	Kr 36
5	Rb 37	Sr 38	Y 39	Zr 40	Nb 41	Mo 42	Tc 43	Ru 44	Rh 45	Pd 46	Ag 47	Cd 48	In 49	Sn 50	Sb 51	Te 52	I 53	Xe 54
6	Cs 55	Ba 56	La 57	Hf 72	Ta 73	W 74	Re 75	Os 76	Ir 77	Pt 78	Au 79	Hg 80	Tl 81	Pb 82	Bi 83	Po 84	At 85	Rn 86
7	Fr 87	Ra 88	Ac 89															

group number ⟶ 3

Figure 4.1 The periodic table. Hydrogen is sometimes shown, as here, in group 1. It may also be placed in the middle of the periodic table and not in any group.

The symbols of the elements that are solid at room temperature and pressure are shown in black in Figure **4.1**, whereas those that are gases are in blue and liquids are in red.

Some of the groups in the periodic table are given names. Commonly used names are shown in Figure **4.2**. The noble gases are sometimes also called the 'inert gases'.

In the periodic table shown in Figure **4.1** it can be seen that the atomic numbers jump from 57 at La (lanthanum) to 72 at Hf (hafnium). This is because some elements have been omitted. These are the lanthanide elements. The actinide elements, which begin with Ac (actinium), have also been omitted from Figure **4.1**. Figure **4.2** shows a long form of the periodic table, showing these elements as an integral part.

> Hydrogen is the most abundant element in the universe: about 90% of the atoms in the universe are hydrogen. Major uses of hydrogen include making ammonia and hydrogenation of unsaturated vegetable oils, both discussed in later chapters.

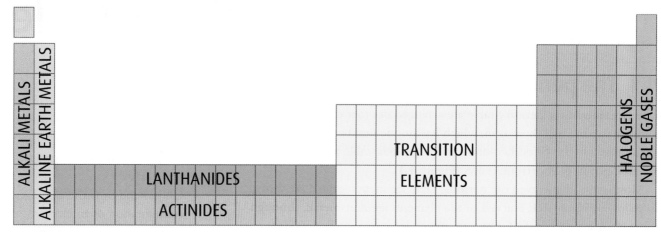

Figure 4.2 The long form of the periodic table, with the names of some of the groups. Hydrogen, though sometimes placed in group 1, does not count as an alkali metal.

The modern periodic table has developed from one originally conceived by Russian chemist Dmitri Mendeleev in 1869. Mendeleev suggested that the elements were arranged in order of atomic weight (what we would now call relative atomic mass) and produced a table in which elements with similar chemical properties were arranged in horizontal groups. Mendeleev took several risks when presenting his data – he suggested that some elements had not been already discovered and left spaces for them in his table. Not only did he leave spaces but he also predicted the properties of these unknown elements – he made his hypotheses falsifiable, which added great weight to his theory. The predictions he made were later found to be extremely accurate – the mark of a good theory is that it should be able to be used to predict results that can be experimentally confirmed or refuted. He also suggested that the atomic weight of some elements were incorrect – he realised that Te belonged in the same group as O, S and Se, but its atomic weight was higher than iodine and so it should be placed after iodine. Instead of then abandoning his theory, he questioned the accuracy of the atomic weight of tellurium and placed it before iodine. This is, of course, the correct place for Te, but Mendeleev's assumption that the atomic weight was lower than that of iodine was not correct.

German Chemist Julius Lothar Meyer was working on the arrangements of elements at the same time as Mendeleev and came to very similar conclusions – why is Mendeleev remembered as the father of the modern periodic table rather than Meyer?

Mendeleev puzzled over the arrangement of elements in the periodic table until he had a dream in which he claims to have seen the arrangement. Kekulé also came up with the ring structure of benzene after a dream. Does it matter how a scientist comes up with a hypothesis? What is the difference between a scientific and a non-scientific hypothesis? Is it the origins of the hypothesis or the fact that it can be tested experimentally (is falsifiable) that makes it scientific?

The periodic table and electronic configurations

The group number of an element indicates the number of electrons in its outer shell (the highest main energy level). Thus, all elements in group 1 have one electron in their outer shell, all elements in group 2 have two electrons in their outer shell, etc. The period number indicates the number of shells (main energy levels) in an atom.

Four elements are named after the small village of Ytterby in Sweden: yttrium, terbium, erbium and ytterbium.

1																	0
H 1	2						number of electrons in **outer** shell →	3	4	5	6	7					He 2
Li 3	Be 4										B 5	C 6	N 7	O 8	F 9	Ne 10
Na 11	Mg 12										Al 13	Si 14	P 15	S 16	Cl 17	Ar 18
K 19	Ca 20	Sc 21	Ti 22	V 23	Cr 24	Mn 25	Fe 26	Co 27	Ni 28	Cu 29	Zn 30	Ga 31	Ge 32	As 33	Se 34	Br 35	Kr 36
Rb 37	Sr 38	Y 39	Zr 40	Nb 41	Mo 42	Tc 43	Ru 44	Rh 45	Pd 46	Ag 47	Cd 48	In 49	Sn 50	Sb 51	Te 52	I 53	Xe 54
Cs 55	Ba 56	La 57	Hf 72	Ta 73	W 74	Re 75	Os 76	Ir 77	Pt 78	Au 79	Hg 80	Tl 81	Pb 82	Bi 83	Po 84	At 85	Rn 86
Fr 87	Ra 88	Ac 89															

number of shells (vertical axis labelled 1–7)

Let us consider P: this is in period 3 and group 5 and thus has three shells of electrons and five electrons in the outer shell. Selenium (Se) is in period 4 and group 6; it therefore has four shells of electrons and six electrons in the outer shell. The noble gases (group 0) have either two (He) or eight electrons in their outer shell.

4.2 Physical properties

Variation of properties down a group and across a period

In the next few sections we will consider how various physical properties vary down a group or across a period in the periodic table.

Electronegativity

In a covalent bond between two different atoms, the atoms do not attract the electron pair in the bond equally. How strongly the electrons are attracted depends on the **size of the individual atoms and their nuclear charge**.

Electronegativity decreases down a group – this is because the size of the atom increases down a group. Consider hydrogen bonded to either F or Cl (Figure **4.3**). The bonding pair of electrons is closer to the F nucleus in HF than it is to the Cl nucleus in HCl. Therefore the electron pair is more strongly attracted to the F nucleus in HF and F has a higher electronegativity than Cl.

Learning objectives

- Define first ionisation energy and electronegativity of an element
- Understand trends in atomic radius, first ionisation energy and electronegativity across a period
- Understand trends in atomic radius, first ionisation energy and electronegativity down group 1 and group 7
- Explain the variation of melting points for elements across period 3 and down group 1 and group 7

Application 1

Electronegativity is a measure of the attraction of an atom in a molecule for the electron pair in the covalent bond of which it is a part.

Chlorine's higher nuclear charge does not make it more electronegative than flourine because the shielding from inner shells (shown with blue shading in Figure **4.3**) increases from F to Cl such that the effective nuclear charge felt by the bonding electrons is approximately the same in each case (+7 in each case, if shielding were perfect).

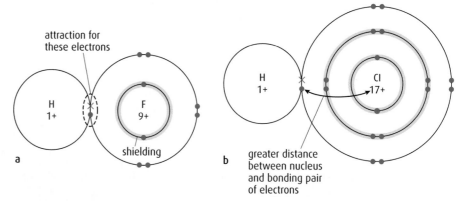

Figure 4.3 Hydrogen bonded to (**a**) fluorine and (**b**) chlorine.

Electronegativity increases across a period – the reason for this is the increase in nuclear charge across the period with no significant change in shielding. The shielding remains approximately constant because atoms in the same period have the same number of inner shells.

Thus, if an N–H bond is compared with an F–H bond (Figure **4.4**), the electrons in the N–H bond are attracted by the seven protons in the nucleus, but the electrons in the F–H bond are attracted by the nine protons in the F nucleus. In both cases the shielding is approximately the same (because of two inner shell electrons).

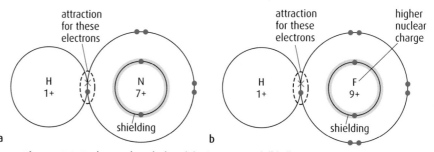

Figure 4.4 Hydrogen bonded to (**a**) nitrogen and (**b**) fluorine.

First ionisation energy

The **first** ionisation energy for an element is the energy required to remove the outermost electron from a gaseous atom: that is, the energy for the following process:

$$M(g) \rightarrow M^+(g) + e^-$$

The full definition of first ionisation energy is: the energy required to remove one electron from each atom in one mole of gaseous atoms under standard conditions.

Variation in first ionisation energy down a group

The decrease in first ionisation energy down a group can be seen in Figure **4.5**. This is because the size of the atom increases so that the outer electron is further from the nucleus and therefore less strongly attracted by the nucleus (Figure **4.6**).

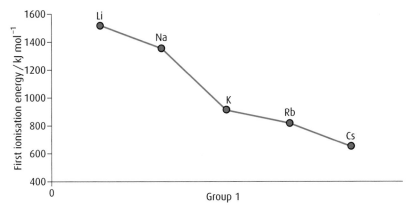

Figure 4.5 First ionisation energy for group 1.

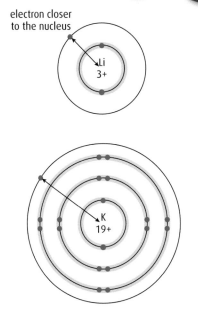

Figure 4.6 Potassium has a lower first ionisation energy than lithium.

> Down any group in the periodic table the first ionisation energy decreases.

Although the nuclear charge also increases down a group, this is largely balanced out by an increase in shielding down the group, as there are more electron energy levels (shells). It is the increase in size that governs the change in first ionisation energy.

Variation in first ionisation energy across a period

> The general trend is that first ionisation energy increases from left to right across a period. This is because of an increase in nuclear charge across the period.

The nuclear charge increases from Na (11+) to Ar (18+) as protons are added to the nucleus. The electrons are all removed from the same main energy level (third shell) and electrons in the same energy level do not shield each other very well. Therefore the force on the outer electrons due to the nucleus increases from left to right across the period and the outer

The increase in first ionisation energy (Figure **4.7**) can also be explained in terms of the effective nuclear charge felt by the outer electron in argon being higher. The effective nuclear charge felt by the outer electron in a sodium atom would be 11 (nuclear charge) − 10 (number of inner shell electrons), i.e. 1+ if shielding were perfect. The effective nuclear charge felt by the outer electrons in an argon atom would be 18 (nuclear charge) − 10 (number of inner shell electrons), i.e. 8+ if shielding were perfect.

There are two exceptions to the general increase in first ionisation energy across a period, and these are discussed on pages **77** and **78**. This is required only by Higher Level students.

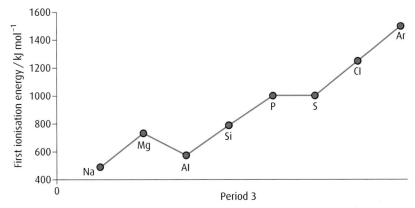

Figure 4.7 The variation in first ionisation energy across period 3 in the periodic table.

electron is more difficult to remove from an argon atom. The argon atom is also smaller than the sodium atom and, therefore, the outer electron is closer to the nucleus and more strongly held.

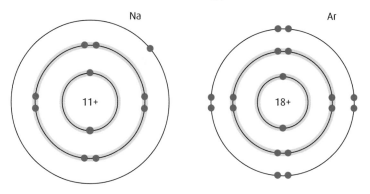

Atomic radius

The atomic radius is basically used to describe the size of an atom. The larger the atomic radius, the larger the atom.

The atomic radius is usually taken to be half the internuclear distance in the element. For example, in a diatomic molecule such as chlorine, where two identical atoms are joined together, the atomic radius would be defined as shown in Figure **4.8**.

> Atomic radius increases down a group.

This is because, as we go down a group in the periodic table the atoms have increasingly more electron shells. For example, potassium has four shells of electrons but lithium has only two:

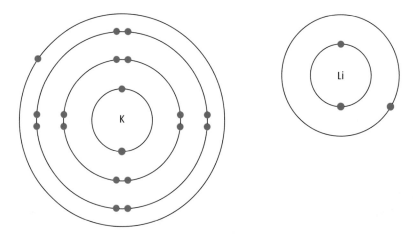

Although the nuclear charge is higher for K, the number of electrons and hence the repulsion between electrons is also greater, and this counteracts any effects due to a greater number of protons in the nucleus.

Figure **4.9** shows the variation of the atomic radius across period 3 in the periodic table.

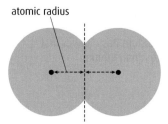

Figure 4.8 The atomic radius of chlorine atoms in a molecule.

Extension

It is possible to define two different atomic radii: the covalent radius and the van der Waals' radius.

> Atomic radius decreases across a period.

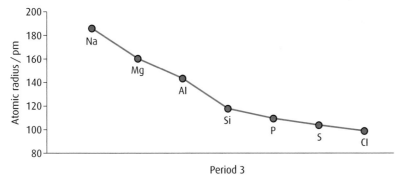

$$1\,\text{pm} = 1 \times 10^{-12}\,\text{m}$$

Figure 4.9 The variation in atomic radius across period 3. No atomic radius is shown for argon, as it does not form covalent bonds and the internuclear distance between atoms bonded together cannot be measured.

Extension

Although it is not possible to measure an atomic radius for Ar, it is possible to measure a value for the van der Waals' radius of this element.

The reason that atomic radius decreases across a period is basically the same reason electronegativity and ionisation energy increase: an increase in nuclear charge across the period but no significant increase in shielding.

Sodium and chlorine have the same number of inner shells of electrons (and hence the amount of shielding is similar); however, chlorine has a nuclear charge of 17+ whereas sodium has a nuclear charge of only 11+. This means that the outer electrons are pulled in more strongly in chlorine than in sodium and the atomic radius is smaller.

Ionic radius

The ionic radius is a measure of the size of an ion.

> In general, the **ionic radii of positive ions are smaller than their atomic radii**, and the **ionic radii of negative ions are greater than their atomic radii**.

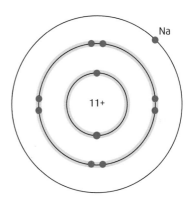

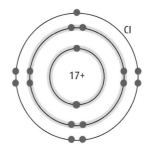

For instance, Figure **4.10** (overleaf) shows a comparison of the atomic and ionic radii (1+ ion) for the alkali metals. Each 1+ ion is smaller than the atom from which it is formed (by loss of an electron).

Na is larger than Na^+ as it has one extra shell of electrons – the electronic configuration of Na is 2, 8, 1, whereas that of Na^+ is 2, 8. Also, they both have the same nuclear charge pulling in the electrons (11+), but there is a greater amount of electron–electron repulsion in Na, as there are 11 electrons compared with only 10 in Na^+. The electron cloud is therefore larger in Na than in Na^+, as there are more electrons repelling for the same nuclear charge pulling the electrons in.

The fact that negative ions are larger than their parent atoms can be seen by comparing the sizes of halogen atoms with their ions (1−) in Figure **4.11** (overleaf). Cl^- is larger than Cl, because it has more electrons for the same nuclear charge and, therefore, greater repulsion between electrons. Cl has 17 electrons and 17 protons in the nucleus. Cl^- also has 17 protons in the nucleus, but it has 18 electrons. The repulsion between 18 electrons is greater than between 17 electrons, so the electron cloud expands as an extra electron is added to a Cl atom to make Cl^-.

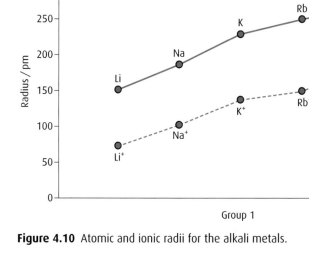

Figure 4.10 Atomic and ionic radii for the alkali metals.

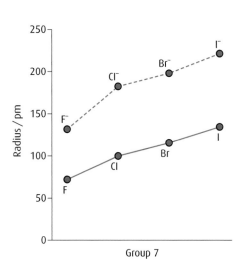

Figure 4.11 A comparison of size between halogens and their ions.

The variation of ionic radius across a period is not a clear-cut trend, as the type of ion changes from one side to the other. Thus positive ions are formed on the left-hand side of the period and negative ions on the right-hand side.

For positive ions there is a decrease in ionic radius as the charge on the ion increases, but for negative ions the size increases as the charge increases (Figure **4.12**).

Let us consider Na^+ and Mg^{2+}: both ions have the same electronic configuration, but Mg^{2+} has one more proton in the nucleus (Figure **4.13**). Because there is the same number of electrons in both ions, the amount of electron–electron repulsion is the same; however, the higher **nuclear** charge in Mg^{2+} means that the electrons are pulled in more strongly and so the ionic radius is smaller.

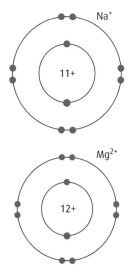

Figure 4.13 Mg^{2+} is smaller than Na^+.

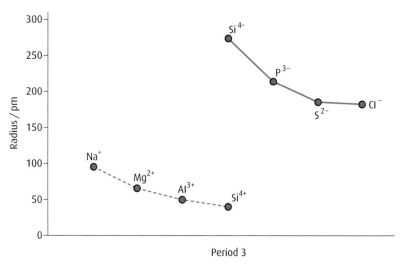

Figure 4.12 Variation of ionic radius of positive and negative ions across period 3.

Now let us consider P^{3-} and S^{2-}: both ions have the same number of electrons. S^{2-} has the higher **nuclear** charge, and therefore, as the amount of electron–electron repulsion is the same in both ions, the electrons are pulled in more strongly in S^{2-} (Figure **4.14**).

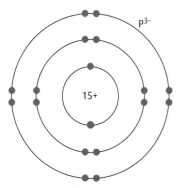
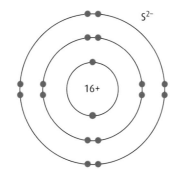

Figure 4.14 S^{2-} is smaller than P^{3-}.

Self-test 1

Test yourself

1 Give the names of the following elements:
  a the element in period 3 and group 4
  b the element in period 5 and group 6
  c the element in the same group as sulfur but in period 6
  d a halogen in period 5
  e an element in the same period as potassium that has five outer shell electrons

2 State whether the following properties increase or decrease across a period:
  a electronegativity
  b atomic radius

3 Arrange the following in order of increasing radius (smallest first):
  a Ba   Mg   Sr   Ca
  b O^{2-} Na^+ F^-
  c Na Na^+ K Al^{3+}
  d S   Cl I^- Cl^- S^{2-}

4 Are the following **true** or **false**?
  a A germanium atom is smaller than a silicon atom, but silicon has a higher first ionisation energy.
  b Selenium has a higher first ionisation energy and electronegativity than sulfur.
  c Antimony has a higher first ionisation energy and electronegativity than tin.
  d Cl^- is bigger than Cl, but Se^{2-} is smaller than Se.
  e Iodine has a higher electronegativity than tellurium but a lower electronegativity than bromine.

Melting point

All the trends we have investigated so far (electronegativity, atomic radius, ionisation energy) have varied in the same way down any group or across any period: that is, ionisation energy always decreases down a group and electronegativity always increases across a period. The variation of melting point of the elements down a group changes from group to group and depends on the type of bonding in the element.

Variation in melting point down group 1

The variation in melting point down group 1 (the alkali metals):

Melting point decreases down group 1.

Melting point decreases down group 1.

Liquid sodium is used as a coolant in some nuclear reactors.

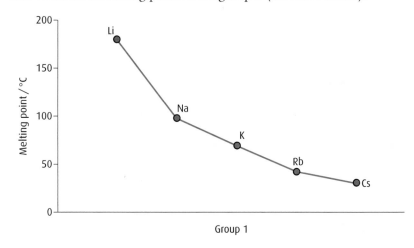

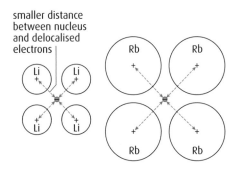

Figure 4.15 The delocalised electrons are attracted more strongly in lithium than in rubidium.

The bonding in all these elements is metallic. The solid is held together by an electrostatic attraction between the positive ions in the lattice and the delocalised electrons (see page **137**).

The attraction for the delocalised electrons is actually due to the nucleus of the positive ion, and therefore as the ion gets larger as we go down the group, the nucleus becomes further from the delocalised electrons and the attraction becomes weaker (Figure **4.15**). This means that less energy is required to break apart the lattice as we go down group 1.

Variation in melting point down group 7

The variation of melting point of halogens down group 7 (the halogens):

Melting point increases down group 7.

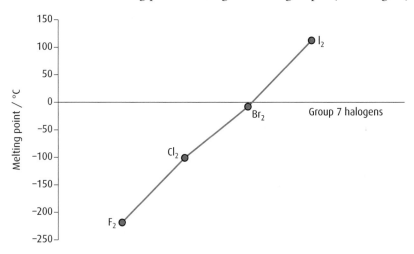

As the relative molecular masses of the X_2 halogen molecules increase, the van der Waals' forces between molecules get stronger. This means that more energy must be supplied to separate the molecules from each other.

Variation of melting point across period 3

In order to understand the variation in melting point across period 3, we must look at how the structure and bonding in the elements changes across the period (see Table **4.1** and Figure **4.16**). The melting point

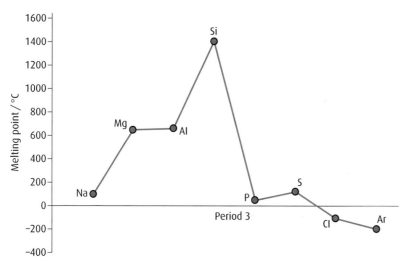

Figure 4.16 Variation in melting point across period 3.

	Na	Mg	Al	Si	P	S	Cl	Ar
Melting point (°C)	98	649	660	1410	44	119	−101	−189
Boiling point (°C)	883	1090	2467	2355	280	445	−34	−186
Structure	metallic			giant covalent	covalent molecular			atomic
Species present	Na⁺ ions	Mg²⁺ ions	Al³⁺ ions	Si atoms	P₄ molecules	S₈ molecules	Cl₂ molecules	Ar atoms

Table 4.1 Variation in melting point across period 3.

increases from sodium to magnesium to aluminium, which all have metallic bonding. There is then a substantial increase to the melting point of silicon, which has a giant covalent (macromolecular) structure. After silicon there is a sharp decrease in melting point as the structure and bonding change from giant covalent to covalent molecular.

The reason the melting point increases from sodium to magnesium to aluminium can be understood by comparing the metallic bonding in sodium and magnesium (Figure **4.17**). There are several reasons why

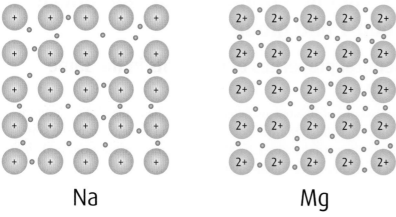

Figure 4.17 Metallic bonding in sodium and magnesium.

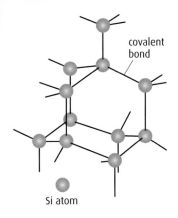

covalent bond

Si atom

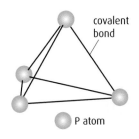

covalent bond

P atom

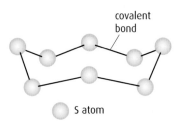

covalent bond

S atom

magnesium has a higher melting point than sodium. The first of these is that magnesium forms a 2+ ion, whereas sodium forms a 1+ ion. This means that the electrostatic attraction between the ions and the delocalised electrons is stronger in magnesium. Also, there are two delocalised electrons per atom in magnesium, so there will be a greater number of electrostatic attractions between the ions and the delocalised electrons. Thirdly, the Mg^{2+} ion (65 pm) is smaller than the Na^+ ion (98 pm), and therefore the delocalised electrons are closer to the nucleus of the positive ion in magnesium and more strongly attracted.

Silicon has a very high melting point because it has a giant covalent structure, and covalent bonds must be broken when it is melted. Covalent bonds are very strong, and a lot of energy is required to break them.

There are various allotropes (structural modifications) of phosphorus. The data given in Table **4.1** are for white phosphorus, which is the most common form of phosphorus. It consists of P_4 tetrahedra with van der Waals' forces between them. These P_4 tetrahedra also exist in the liquid state, and therefore only van der Waals' forces are broken when phosphorus is melted. Van der Waals' forces are weak and little energy is required to break them. The melting point of phosphorus is therefore much lower than that of silicon, because, when phosphorus is melted, only weak van der Waals' forces are broken rather than covalent bonds.

Sulfur, like phosphorus, has a covalent molecular structure, with van der Waals' forces between molecules. A sulfur molecule, however, consists of eight atoms and, as S_8 has a significantly higher relative molecular mass than P_4, the van der Waals' forces are stronger between S_8 molecules than between P_4 molecules. More energy is thus required to break the van der Waals' forces between S_8 molecules than between P_4 molecules, and sulfur has a higher melting point than phosphorus.

Going fom sulfur to argon, the realtive mass of the molecule (atom in the case of argon) decreases. Sulfur exists as S_8 molecules (M_r 256.48), chlorine as Cl_2 molecules (M_r 70.90) and argon as atoms (A_r 39.95). Thus, the decrease in melting point from sulfur to argon can be attributed to a decrease in van der Waals' forces as the mass of the particles decreases.

4.3 Chemical properties of elements in group 1 and group 7

Chemical properties of elements in the same group

The reactions of an atom are determined by the number of electrons in the outer shell (highest main energy level), and as elements in the same group in the periodic table have the same number of electrons in their outer shell, they react in basically the same way.

Learning objectives

- Understand that elements in the same group have similar chemical properties
- Describe some reactions of elements in group 1 and group 7

Reactions of the elements in group 1

The elements in group 1 are all reactive metals that react readily with, among other things, oxygen, water and halogens. The atoms all have one electron in their outer shell, and reactions virtually all involve the loss of this outer shell electron to form the positive ion, M^+. The reactions become more vigorous as we descend through the group, because the ionisation energy decreases as the size of the atom increases. This means that, for example, Cs loses its outer electron to form a positive ion much more easily than Na and will react more vigorously.

Reaction with oxygen

The alkali metals react vigorously with oxygen and all tarnish rapidly in air. The general equation for the reaction is:

$$4M(s) + O_2(g) \rightarrow 2M_2O(s)$$

Reaction with water

The alkali metals react rapidly with water. The general equation for the reaction is:

$$2M(s) + 2H_2O(l) \rightarrow 2MOH(aq) + H_2(g)$$

An alkaline solution is formed. The alkali metal hydroxides are strong bases and ionise completely in aqueous solution (page **319**).

The reaction with water becomes more vigorous as we descend down the group: thus, sodium melts into a ball, fizzes rapidly and moves around on the surface of the water, potassium bursts into flames (lilac) and caesium explodes as soon as it comes into contact with water.

Reactions of the elements in group 7

The atoms of the elements in group 7 all have seven electrons in their outer shell and react either by gaining an electron to form the X^- ion or by forming covalent compounds. The reactivity decreases down the group, and fluorine is the most reactive element known, reacting directly with virtually every other element in the periodic table. The variation in reactivity of the halogens cannot be as easily explained as for the alkali metals. The very high reactivity of fluorine can be explained in terms of an exceptionally weak F–F bond and the strength of bonds it forms to other atoms. The reactivity in terms of the formation of X^- ions can be related to a decrease in electron affinity (energy released when an electron is added to a neutral atom) down the group as the electron is added to a shell further away from the nucleus, but this is only part of the story, and several factors must be considered when explaining the reactivity of the halogens.

The halogens all react with the alkali metals to form salts. The general equation is:

$$2M(s) + X_2(g) \rightarrow 2MX(s)$$

The salts formed are all white/colourless, fairly typical ionic compounds. They contain M^+ and X^- ions. All alkali metal chlorides, bromides and iodides are soluble in water and form colourless, neutral solutions.

M_2O is a basic oxide that will dissolve in water to form an alkaline solution, containing M^+ and OH^- ions.

Li, Na and K are all less dense than water.

Chlorine is produced by the electrolysis of brine (see Option **C**). Worldwide annual production is about 60 million tons. Chlorine and its compounds are involved in the production of about 90% of the most important pharmaceuticals. Its biggest single use is in the production of PVC.

How vigorous the reaction is depends on the particular halogen and alkali metal used; the most vigorous reaction occurs between fluorine and caesium, and the least vigorous reaction between lithium and iodine.

Displacement reactions of halogens

These are reactions between a solution of a halogen and a solution containing halide ions and are discussed in more detail on page **388**. A small amount of a solution of a halogen is added to a small amount of a solution containing a halide ion, and any colour changes are observed (see Table **4.2**). Potassium chloride, bromide and iodide solutions are all colourless. The colours of chlorine, bromine and iodine solutions are shown in Figure **4.18**.

	KCl(aq)	**KBr(aq)**	**KI(aq)**
Cl₂(aq)	no reaction	orange solution	dark red/brown solution
Br₂(aq)	no reaction	no reaction	dark red/brown solution
I₂(aq)	no reaction	no reaction	no reaction

Table 4.2 Results of reactions between halogen solutions and solutions containing halide ions.

The reactions that occur are:

$$Cl_2(aq) + 2KBr(aq) \rightarrow 2KCl(aq) + Br_2(aq)$$
Ionic equation: $Cl_2(aq) + 2Br^-(aq) \rightarrow 2Cl^-(aq) + Br_2(aq)$

$$Cl_2(aq) + 2KI(aq) \rightarrow 2KCl(aq) + I_2(aq)$$
Ionic equation: $Cl_2(aq) + 2I^-(aq) \rightarrow 2Cl^-(aq) + I_2(aq)$

$$Br_2(aq) + 2KI(aq) \rightarrow 2KBr(aq) + I_2(aq)$$
Ionic equation: $Br_2(aq) + 2I^-(aq) \rightarrow 2Br^-(aq) + I_2(aq)$

The more reactive halogen displaces the halide ion of the less reactive halogen from solution. Thus, chlorine displaces bromide ions and iodide ions from solution, and bromine displaces iodide ions from solution.

4.4 Properties of the oxides of period 3 elements

Oxides of period 3 elements

Table **4.3** shows the formulas, structure and bonding of the oxides of period 3 elements.

Sodium oxide, magnesium oxide and aluminium oxide

These all have giant ionic structures. The ions are held in the lattice structure by strong electrostatic forces, and therefore they all have high melting points. MgO and Al_2O_3, which consist of highly charged ions, both have melting points of over 2000 °C. When the solids are melted ionic liquids are formed. The ions are free to move around in the liquids, and they all conduct electricity.

Orange colour, due to the production of bromine.

Red-brown colour, due to the production of iodine.

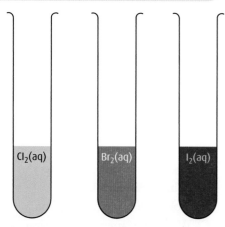

Figure 4.18 Chlorine solution is pale yellow–green, bromine solution is orange, and iodine solution is red–brown.

Learning objectives

- Relate trends in the properties of the oxides of period 3 elements to their structure and bonding
- Describe the reactions of period 3 oxides with water

	Na	Mg	Al	Si	P	S	Cl
Name of oxide	sodium oxide	magnesium oxide	aluminium oxide	silicon(IV) oxide	phosphorus(III) oxide	sulfur(IV) oxide	chlorine(I) oxide
					phosphorus(V) oxide	sulfur(VI) oxide	chlorine(VII) oxide
Formula of oxide	Na_2O	MgO	Al_2O_3	SiO_2	P_4O_6	SO_2	Cl_2O
					P_4O_{10}	SO_3	Cl_2O_7
Physical state at 25 °C	solid				liquid	gas	gas
					solid	liquid	liquid
Bonding in oxide	ionic			covalent			
Structure	giant			simple molecular			
Species present in liquid state	Na^+ and O^{2-} ions	Mg^{2+} and O^{2-} ions	Al^{3+} and O^{2-} ions	Si and O atoms	P_4O_6 molecules	SO_2 molecules	Cl_2O molecules
					P_4O_{10} molecules	SO_3 molecules	Cl_2O_7 molecules
Electrical conductivity when molten	good			none			
	liquid oxides conduct electricity as mobile ions present in liquid state			do not conduct electricity in liquid state as no ions present.			

Table 4.3 Properties of the oxides of the period 3 elements.

Covalent oxides

The structures of the covalent oxides of period 3 elements are shown in Table **4.4**. Substances with van der Waals' forces/dipole–dipole interactions between molecules have low melting points, as these forces are weak and little energy is required to break them.

Notes on the structures

P_4O_6 is a covalent molecular liquid at room temperature that freezes at 24 °C. The structure is based on a tetrahedron of phosphorus atoms with an oxygen atom bridging each edge. There is no direct bonding between the P atoms. P_4O_{10} has a structure that is basically the same as that of P_4O_6 except that there are four additional O atoms doubly bonded to each P atom.

In SO_2, there are three negative charge centres around the S atom, and so the molecule is based on a trigonal planar shape (see Figure **4.19**). As one of the negative charge centres is a lone pair, the shape is bent. O is more electronegative than S, and the molecule is polar. (It is also possible to draw an alternative Lewis structure for SO_2 in which the octet on the S is not expanded – this is discussed on page **97**).

Sulfur(VI) oxide (also called sulfur trioxide) is a colourless liquid at room temperature. The structure of the liquid is complex, and SO_3 molecules trimerise (three molecules join together) to a certain extent to form S_3O_9. The structure of the molecule present in the gaseous state is shown in the diagram in Table **4.4** (page **158**).

Examiner's tip

Only part of this section is required by Standard Level students – if you are studying Standard Level Chemistry, you should understand that the bonding in the oxides changes from ionic to covalent across the period. You should not have to recall the structures of the oxides.

Figure 4.19 The Lewis structure for SO_2.

	Silicon	Phosphorus	Sulfur	Chlorine
Bonding in oxide	giant covalent	covalent molecular	covalent molecular	covalent molecular
Structure	giant	simple molecular		
	Si atom, O atom, covalent bond	O atom, P atom, covalent bond	S atom	Cl_2O, Cl atom
	SiO_2	P_4O_6	SO_2	Cl_2O
	covalent bonds broken when melted – high melting point	van der Waals' forces between molecules – low melting point	dipole–dipole interactions and van der Waals' forces between molecules – low melting point	
Structure		O atom, P atom, covalent bond	S atom	Cl atom
		P_4O_{10}	SO_3	Cl_2O_7
		van der Waals' forces between molecules – low melting point; higher melting point than P_4O_6 due to higher M_r	van der Waals' forces between molecules – low melting point; higher melting point than SO_2 due to higher M_r	dipole–dipole interactions and van der Waals' forces between molecules – low melting point; higher melting point than Cl_2O due to higher M_r

Table 4.4 The structure of covalent oxides of the period 3 elements.

Extension

Although there are four pairs of electrons around the central, bridging O atom in Cl_2O_7, the bond angle is 119°. Can you provide an explanation for this?

Although SO_3 is non-polar and SO_2 is polar, SO_3 has a higher relative molecular mass than SO_2, meaning that the van der Waals' forces between molecules are stronger and that SO_3 has a higher melting point than SO_2.

Cl_2O_7 is a colourless liquid at room temperature. Its structure involves two ClO_4 tetrahedra linked by a bridging oxygen atom.

Reactions of period 3 oxides with water

A summary of the structure and bonding of the period 3 oxides and their reactions with water is shown in Table **4.5**.

In general, metallic oxides are basic and non-metallic oxides are acidic.

	Sodium	Magnesium	Aluminium	Silicon	Phosphorus	Sulfur	Chlorine
Formula of oxide	Na_2O	MgO	Al_2O_3	SiO_2	P_4O_6	SO_2	Cl_2O
					P_4O_{10}	SO_3	Cl_2O_7
Nature of element	metal			non-metal			
Bonding in oxide	ionic			giant covalent	covalent molecular		
Nature of oxide	basic		amphoteric	acidic			
Reaction with water	soluble and reacts	sparingly soluble, some reaction	insoluble		soluble and reacts		
Solution formed	alkaline	slightly alkaline	–		acidic		

Table 4.5 Bonding and reaction with water in the period 3 oxides.

A basic oxide is one that will react with an acid to form a salt and, if soluble in water, will produce an alkaline solution. Sodium oxide reacts with water to form sodium hydroxide, according to the equation:

$$Na_2O(s) + H_2O(l) \rightarrow 2NaOH(aq)$$

Sodium oxide reacts with acids such as sulfuric acid to form salts:

$$Na_2O(s) + H_2SO_4(aq) \rightarrow Na_2SO_4(aq) + H_2O(l)$$

Magnesium oxide, because of the high charges on the ions, is not very soluble in water, but it does react to a small extent to form a solution of magnesium hydroxide, which is alkaline:

$$MgO(s) + H_2O(l) \rightarrow Mg(OH)_2(aq)$$

Aluminium is right on the dividing line between metals and non-metals and forms an amphoteric oxide (some of the properties of a basic oxide and some of an acidic oxide). Aluminium is here exhibiting properties that are between that of a metal (basic oxide) and a non-metal (acidic oxide).

Aluminium oxide does not react with water, but it displays amphoteric behaviour in that it reacts with acids and bases to form salts.

Reaction with acids:

$$Al_2O_3 + 6H^+ \rightarrow 2Al^{3+} + 3H_2O$$

Reaction with alkalis/bases:

$$Al_2O_3 + 2OH^- + 3H_2O \rightarrow 2Al(OH)_4^-$$

The remaining oxides in Table **4.5** are all acidic oxides. An acidic oxide is one that reacts with bases/alkalis to form a salt and, if soluble in water, will produce an acidic solution.

Examiner's tip
The reactions highlighted like this one must be learnt for examinations.

Amphoteric oxide – reacts with both acids and bases.

Phosphoric(V) acid is an ingredient of Coca-Cola®.

P_4O_6 (phosphorus(III) oxide) and P_4O_{10} (phosphorus(V) oxide) form phosphoric(III) and phosphoric(V) acid, respectively, when they react with water:

$$P_4O_6(s) + 6H_2O(l) \rightarrow 4H_3PO_3(aq)$$

$$P_4O_{10}(s) + 6H_2O(l) \rightarrow 4H_3PO_4(aq)$$

SO_2 (sulfur(IV) oxide) and SO_3 (sulfur(VI) oxide) form sulfuric(IV) and sulfuric(VI) acid, respectively, when they react with water:

$$SO_2(g) + H_2O(l) \rightarrow H_2SO_3(aq)$$

$$SO_3(g) + H_2O(l) \rightarrow H_2SO_4(aq)$$

Cl_2O (chlorine(I) oxide) and Cl_2O_7 (chlorine(VII) oxide) form acidic solutions (chloric (I) acid and chloric (VII) acid, respectively) when they react with water:

$$Cl_2O(g) + H_2O(l) \rightarrow 2HClO(aq)$$

$$Cl_2O_7(l) + H_2O(l) \rightarrow 2HClO_4(aq)$$

Self-test 2

Test yourself

5 Write balanced equations for the following reactions:
   a rubidium with water
   b potassium with bromine
   c chlorine solution with potassium bromide solution
   d sodium oxide with water
   e sulfur(VI) oxide with water

6 State the type of structure and bonding in each of the following:
   a SO_2 b SiO_2 c Na_2O d Al_2O_3

7 Arrange the following in order of increasing melting point (lowest first):
   a Cl_2 Na F_2 K
   b Si   Mg Cl_2 Ar   Ne
   c Na_2O P_4O_{10} O_2

8 State whether an acidic or alkaline solution will be formed when each of the following is dissolved in/reacted with water:
   a SO_3
   b MgO
   c Na

Non-metal oxides such as SO_2 are produced in various industrial processes and when coal is burnt. This can be responsible for **acid rain**, which can, among other things, kill fish in lakes and trees in forests.

Nitrogen oxides (NO_x) may be formed in internal combustion engines, and these are involved in the formation of photochemical smog in cities.

Figure 4.20 A photochemical smog over Hong Kong.

4.5 Properties of the chlorides of period 3 elements HL

Learning objectives

- Relate trends in the properties of the chlorides of period 3 elements to their structure and bonding
- Describe the reactions of period 3 chlorides with water

Chlorides of period 3

Table **4.6** shows some data for some of the chlorides of period 3 elements. Sodium and magnesium chloride are both high-melting-point ionic solids. They consist of a giant lattice of positive and negative ions (Figure **4.21**). The oppositely charged ions attract each with strong electrostatic forces, and therefore a lot of energy is required to separate the ions. The bonding in these compounds is considered on pages **84–90**.

When NaCl or $MgCl_2$ are melted, the ions become free to move around, and so the molten salts conduct electricity.

	Na	Mg	Al	Si	P	Cl
Formula of chloride	NaCl	$MgCl_2$	'AlCl₃' = Al_2Cl_6	$SiCl_4$	PCl_3, PCl_5	Cl_2
Bonding in chloride	ionic	ionic	covalent molecular*	covalent molecular	covalent molecular**	covalent molecular
State at 25 °C	solid	solid	solid	liquid	PCl_3 liquid PCl_5 solid	gas
Electrical conductivity of molten chloride	good	good	none	none	none	none
Species present in liquid state	Na^+ and Cl^- ions	Mg^{2+} and Cl^- ions	Al_2Cl_6 molecules	$SiCl_4$ molecules	PCl_3 / PCl_5 molecules	Cl_2 molecules

Table 4.6 Properties of the chlorides of the period 3 elements.

Extension

★ Actually bonding in the solid state is more ionic with six coordinate Al present. Covalent molecular (Al_2Cl_6) is present in liquid and gaseous states.

★★ PCl_5 exists as $[PCl_6]^-[PCl_4]^+$ in the solid state but is covalent molecular in the liquid state.

The bonding in aluminium chloride is complicated, and it undergoes a change in structure and bonding as it changes state. For simplicity, we will assume that the bonding is covalent molecular in all states. The Lewis structure for $AlCl_3$ shows that the Al only has six electrons in its outer shell.

In order to generate an octet, two $AlCl_3$ molecules come together to form a dimer. A dative covalent bond is formed from a lone pair on a Cl atom on one $AlCl_3$ unit to an Al on the other $AlCl_3$ unit.

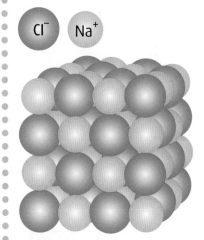

Figure 4.21 The ionic lattice in sodium chloride.

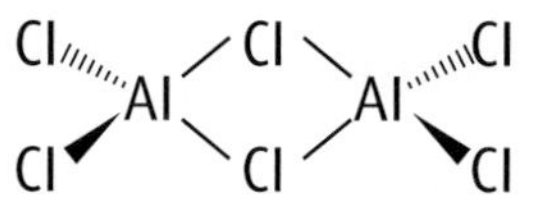

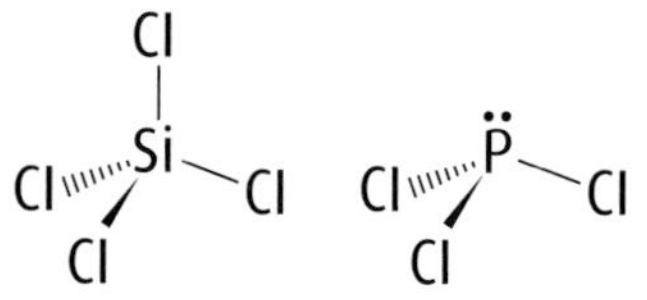

Figure 4.22 (a) The SiCl$_4$ molecule. (b) The PCl$_3$ molecule.

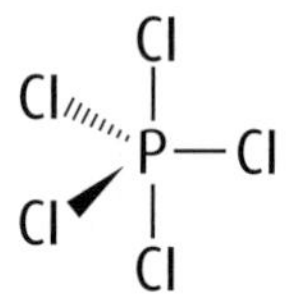

HL With four pairs of electrons around each Al atom, the shape about each Al atom is approximately tetrahedral, and the Al$_2$Cl$_6$ molecule is non-planar.

There are van der Waals' forces between the Al$_2$Cl$_6$ molecules, and as these are relatively weak, little energy is required to break them. This means that Al$_2$Cl$_6$ has a low melting point and boiling point. Because only Al$_2$Cl$_6$ molecules (and no ions) are present in liquid aluminium chloride it does not conduct electricity.

SiCl$_4$ and PCl$_3$ are covalent molecular liquids. They consist of individual SiCl$_4$ or PCl$_3$ molecules. SiCl$_4$ is tetrahedral, whereas PCl$_3$ has a trigonal pyramidal (based on tetrahedral) shape (see Figure **4.22**).

In both cases there are van der Waals' forces between the molecules and, as little energy is required to break these, they have low melting points and boiling points – both are liquids at room temperature. As there are no ions present in liquid silicon chloride or liquid phosphorus(III) chloride, but only SiCl$_4$ or PCl$_3$ molecules, neither substance conducts electricity.

The bonding in PCl$_5$ is a little more complex, as it actually consists of octahedral [PCl$_6$]$^-$ and tetrahedral [PCl$_4$]$^+$ ions in the solid state. This ionic bonding leads to PCl$_5$ being a solid at room temperature (although the electrostatic forces between these large ions are not very strong and the melting point of PCl$_5$ is only 167 °C). When PCl$_5$ melts it forms a covalent molecular liquid containing trigonal bipyramidal molecules. The forces between these molecules are van der Waals' forces. As PCl$_5$ has a higher relative molecular mass than PCl$_3$, the van der Waals' forces between molecules would be expected to be stronger between the PCl$_5$ molecules, leading to PCl$_5$ having a higher boiling point than PCl$_3$.

Only PCl$_5$ molecules are present in the liquid state, and therefore, as no ions are present, liquid PCl$_5$ does not conduct electricity.

Cl$_2$ is a covalent molecular gas consisting of diatomic molecules. There are only weak van der Waals' forces between the molecules in liquid chlorine and, as Cl$_2$ has a relatively low relative molecular mass, these are weak enough to be broken at temperatures below room temperature. This means that Cl$_2$ is a gas at room temperature. There are no ions present in liquid chlorine, and so it does not conduct electricity.

Reactions of period 3 chlorides with water

Table **4.7** summarises the reactions of period 3 chlorides with water.

	Sodium	Magnesium	Aluminium	Silicon	Phosphorus	Chlorine
Formula of chloride	NaCl	MgCl$_2$	'AlCl$_3$' = Al$_2$Cl$_6$	SiCl$_4$	PCl$_3$, PCl$_5$	Cl$_2$
Reaction with water	dissolves, no reaction	dissolves, very slight reaction	fairly vigorous reaction with water; fumes in moist air	vigorous reaction	vigorous reaction	dissolves and reacts slightly
pH (aqueous solution)*	7	6.2	3	1	1	2
Acidity	neutral	slightly acidic	acidic	acidic	acidic	acidic

* pH depends on concentration – these are approximate values for a 0.1 mol dm^{-3} solution.

Table 4.7 Reaction with water in the period 3 chlorides.

Sodium chloride dissolves in water. The ions separate from each other and become hydrated:

$$NaCl(s) \xrightarrow{\text{excess water}} Na^+(aq) + Cl^-(aq)$$

Magnesium chloride also dissolves in water (with the liberation of a great deal of heat), but because of the higher charge density (higher charge : radius ratio) of Mg^{2+} ions compared with Na^+ ions there is some polarisation of water, which causes the release of some H^+ ions from water. This can be represented by the equation:

$$[Mg(H_2O)_6]^{2+}(aq) \rightleftharpoons [Mg(H_2O)_5(OH)]^+(aq) + H^+(aq)$$

The charge on the Mg^{2+} ion is not very high, however, and the position of equilibrium lies mostly to the left.

Anhydrous aluminium chloride fumes in moist air because of the production of hydrogen chloride gas. This reaction can be represented by an equation such as:

$$AlCl_3(s) + 3H_2O(l) \rightleftharpoons Al(OH)_3(s) + 3HCl(g)$$

With excess water, the aluminium chloride dissolves according to the equation:

$$AlCl_3(s) + 6H_2O(l) \rightarrow [Al(H_2O)_6]^{3+}(aq) + 3Cl^-(aq)$$

The acidity of the solution is a result of the ionisation of the aqueous Al^{3+} ion:

$$[Al(H_2O)_6]^{3+}(aq) \rightleftharpoons [Al(H_2O)_5(OH)]^{2+}(aq) + H^+(aq)$$

This occurs to a much greater extent than with Mg^{2+}, as the Al^{3+} ion is smaller and more highly charged than the Mg^{2+} ion and causes greater polarisation of water molecules.

Silicon chloride reacts very vigorously with water, with the production of a great deal of heat and fumes of hydrogen chloride gas. The $SiCl_4$ is hydrolysed completely by water, and the reaction can be represented by an equation such as:

$$SiCl_4(l) + 4H_2O(l) \rightarrow Si(OH)_4(s) + \underset{\text{hydrochloric acid}}{4HCl(aq)}$$

The acidity of the solution is due to the production of HCl in the reaction, which dissolves in the water to produce hydrochloric acid.

Phosphorus(III) chloride reacts very vigorously in water, with the production of heat and fumes of hydrogen chloride gas. Phosphoric(III) acid and hydrochloric acid are formed:

$$PCl_3(l) + 3H_2O(l) \rightarrow \underset{\substack{\text{phosphoric(III)} \\ \text{acid}}}{H_3PO_3(aq)} + \underset{\text{hydrochloric acid}}{3HCl(aq)}$$

This is discussed in more detail on pages **357** and **358**.

Extension

The reaction is actually more complicated than this, and $Si(OH)_4$ undergoes condensation polymerisation to form $SiO_2.xH_2O$.

HL Phosphorus(V) chloride reacts very vigorously with water, with the production of heat and fumes of hydrogen chloride gas. Phosphoric(V) acid and hydrochloric acid are formed:

$$PCl_5(l) + 4H_2O(l) \rightarrow \underset{\substack{\text{phosphoric(V)}\\\text{acid}}}{H_3PO_4(aq)} + \underset{\text{hydrochloric acid}}{5HCl(aq)}$$

Chlorine dissolves in water and reacts to a certain extent. The relevant reactions are:

$$Cl_2(g) \xrightarrow{\text{excess water}} Cl_2(aq)$$

$$Cl_2(aq) + H_2O(l) \rightleftharpoons \underset{\text{hydrochloric acid}}{HCl(aq)} + \underset{\substack{\text{chloric(I)}\\\text{acid}}}{HOCl(aq)}$$

The solution is acidic mainly as a result of the production of hydrochloric acid. Chloric(I) acid is a very weak acid ($pK_a = 7.43$).

Extension

Cl_2 dissolves better in alkaline solution, as the equilibrium is shifted to the right.

Test yourself

9 Arrange the following in order of increasing melting point (lowest first):
   a Cl_2 $SiCl_4$ PCl_5 NaCl
   b PCl_3 $SiCl_4$ $MgCl_2$ $AlCl_3$

10 State whether each of the following is **true** or **false**.
   a Liquid sodium chloride conducts electricity but liquid phosphorus(III) chloride does not.
   b $SiCl_4$ and NaCl both have giant structures.
   c $SiCl_4$ and PCl_5 are both liquids at room temperature and pressure.
   d PCl_3 and PCl_5 both react with water to form H_3PO_4.
   e $MgCl_2$ reacts with water to form a neutral solution, but $SiCl_4$ reacts to form an acidic solution.

Learning objectives

- Describe the characteristic properties of transition metals
- Explain why transition metals have variable oxidation states
- Explain the formation and describe the shape of complex ions
- Explain why transition metal complex ions are coloured
- Describe some uses of transition metals and their compounds as catalysts

Examiner's tip
Remember that Cr and Cu have slightly different electronic configurations.

4.6 The transition elements

The transition elements (d block)

The first row d-block elements are:

Sc	Ti	V	Cr	Mn	Fe	Co	Ni	Cu	Zn
21	22	23	24	25	26	27	28	29	30

There are also two other rows of d-block elements.

They are called **d**-block elements because the subshell being filled across this series is the 3**d** subshell. The electronic configurations range from $[Ar]4s^23d^1$ for scandium to $[Ar]4s^23d^{10}$ for zinc.

Sc	Ti	V	Cr	Mn	Fe	Co	Ni	Cu	Zn
$[Ar]4s^23d^1$	$[Ar]4s^23d^2$	$[Ar]4s^23d^3$	$[Ar]4s^13d^5$	$[Ar]4s^23d^5$	$[Ar]4s^23d^6$	$[Ar]4s^23d^7$	$[Ar]4s^23d^8$	$[Ar]4s^13d^{10}$	$[Ar]4s^23d^{10}$

The **transition elements** can be defined as different from the d-block elements, and the definition we will use here is:

> a transition element is an element that forms at least one stable oxidation state (other than 0) with a partially filled d subshell

HL

These are often called transition **metals** rather than transition elements.

According to this definition, scandium and zinc are not counted as transition elements, as the only ion formed by Sc is the 3+ ion, with electronic configuration $1s^2 2s^2 2p^6 3s^2 3p^6$ (no d electrons), and that formed by Zn is the 2+ ion, with electronic configuration $1s^2 2s^2 2p^6 3s^2 3p^6 3d^{10}$ (**full** d subshell).

Scandium and zinc do not exhibit some of the characteristic properties of transition metals detailed below (e.g. they do not form coloured compounds).

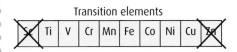

Transition elements

Properties of the transition elements

We have already studied the variation in properties of a set of eight elements across the periodic table when we looked at the properties of period 3 elements. The transition elements also form a set of eight elements across the periodic table, but these are much more similar to each other than the elements across period 3. For instance, they are all metals rather than showing a change from metal to non-metal.

The variation in first ionisation energy and atomic radius of the transition elements and period 3 elements are compared in Figures **4.23** and **4.24**. It can be seen that the variation of ionisation energy and atomic radius across the series of the transition elements is much smaller than across period 3.

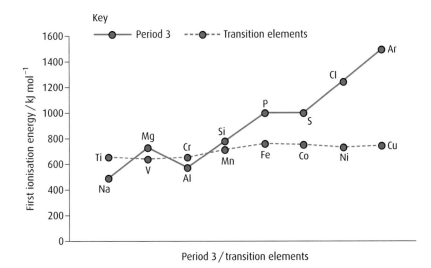

Figure 4.23 A comparison of the variation of first ionisation energy across period 3 with that across the transition metal series.

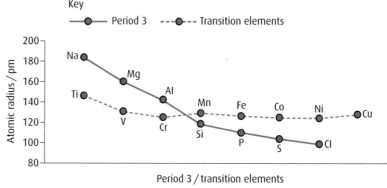

Figure 4.24 A comparison of the variation of atomic radius across period 3 with that across the transition metal series.

Because of their similarity it is possible to draw up a list of characteristic properties of transition elements:

- Transition elements are all typical metals, i.e. they have high melting points and densities.
- Transition elements can exhibit more than one oxidation number in compounds/complexes.
- Transition elements form complex ions.
- Transition elements usually form coloured compounds/complexes.
- Transition elements and their compounds/complexes can act as catalysts in many reactions.

Ionisation of transition elements

Transition elements form positive ions. The electronic configurations of some transition metal ions are shown in Table **4.8**.

Element	Electronic configuration	Ion	Electronic configuration
Cr	$[Ar]4s^13d^5$	Cr^{2+}	$[Ar]3d^4$
		Cr^{3+}	$[Ar]3d^3$
Mn	$[Ar]4s^23d^5$	Mn^{2+}	$[Ar]3d^5$
Fe	$[Ar]4s^23d^6$	Fe^{2+}	$[Ar]3d^6$
		Fe^{3+}	$[Ar]3d^5$
Co	$[Ar]4s^23d^7$	Co^{2+}	$[Ar]3d^7$
Cu	$[Ar]4s^13d^{10}$	Cu^+	$[Ar]3d^{10}$
		Cu^{2+}	$[Ar]3d^9$

Table 4.8 Electronic configurations of transition metals and their ions.

Examiner's tip
The last four properties are most important for examinations.

The 4s electrons are always removed before the 3d electrons when an ion is formed.

Variable oxidation numbers

HL

The positive oxidation numbers (oxidation states) exhibited by the transition elements are shown in Figure **4.25**.

The greatest number of different oxidation numbers and the highest oxidation numbers are found in the middle of the series. From Ti to Mn there is an increase in the total number of electrons in the 4s and 3d subshells, so the maximum oxidation number increases. Mn has the electronic configuration $[Ar]4s^2 3d^5$ and therefore a maximum oxidation state of +7. Fe has eight electrons in the 4s and 3d subshells and would be expected to have a maximum oxidation state of +8, but the ionisation energy increases from left to right across the transition elements series and it becomes more difficult to reach the highest oxidation numbers towards the right-hand side of the series. The chemistry of copper and nickel is, for the same reason, dominated by the lower oxidation numbers.

> **All transition metals show oxidation number +2.** In most cases this is because they have two electrons in the 4s subshell, and removal of these generates an oxidation number of +2.

Ti	V	Cr	Mn	Fe	Co	Ni	Cu
			7				
		6	6	6			
	5	5	5	5			
4	4	4	4	4	4	4	4
3	3	3	3	3	3	3	3
2	2	2	2	2	2	2	2
1	1	1	1	1	1	1	1
0	0	0	0	0	0	0	0

Figure 4.25 Oxidation numbers of transition metals in compounds. Not all oxidation numbers are common.

Why more than one oxidation number?

The 4s and 3d subshells are close in energy, and there are no big jumps in the successive ionisation energies when the 4s and 3d electrons are removed; therefore the number of electrons lost will depend on a variety of factors, such as lattice enthalpy, ionisation energy and hydration enthalpy. Electrons are not removed to generate the nearest noble gas electronic configuration. The graph in Figure **4.26** (overleaf) shows a comparison of the first seven ionisation energies of Mg and Mn. It can be seen that there is a very large jump between the second and third ionisation energies of Mg, but there are no such jumps for Mn.

> Oxidation numbers are discussed further on pages **376–378**.

> Oxidation number and oxidation state are the same thing.

> **Examiner's tip**
> The oxidation numbers highlighted in Figure **4.25** are mentioned specifically on the syllabus – you should remember these.

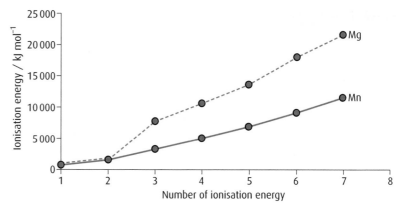

Figure 4.26 Comparison of successive ionisation energies of Mg and Mn.

> A ligand must possess a lone pair of electrons.

> A ligand is a Lewis base.

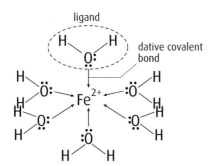

Figure 4.27 A complex ion.

Extension

There is a strong case for considering the bonding in a transition metal complex ion as having a significant ionic component. Crystal field theory and ligand field theory consider the bonding from a more ionic point of view.

Neutral ligands	1– ligands
H_2O	Cl^-
NH_3	CN^-
CO	Br^-

Complex ions

A complex ion consists of a central transition metal ion surrounded by **ligands**.

> **Ligands** are negative ions or neutral molecules that use lone pairs of electrons to bond to a transition metal ion to form a complex ion. Dative covalent bonds (coordinate links) are formed between the ligand and the transition metal ion.

The structure of $[Fe(H_2O)_6]^{2+}$ is shown in Figure **4.27**. H_2O is the ligand in this complex ion. The shape of this complex ion is octahedral and it is called the hexaaquairon(II) ion. Other ways of drawing this complex ion are shown in Figure **4.28**.

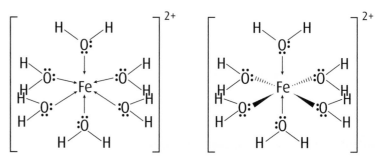

Figure 4.28 Alternative representations of the $[Fe(H_2O)_6]^{2+}$ complex ion.

All transition elements, with the exception of Ti, form an octahedral complex ion with the formula $[M(H_2O)_6]^{2+}$ in solution.

The oxidation number of a transition metal in a complex ion

The oxidation number of a transition metal in a complex ion may be worked out from the charges on the ligands. Ligands may be either neutral or negatively charged.

In $[Fe(H_2O)_6]^{2+}$ all the ligands are neutral. The overall charge on the ion is just due to the Fe, so the oxidation number of Fe must be **+2**.

In **[Ni(CN)₄]²⁻** all the ligands have a 1− charge, so the total charge on all four ligands is 4−. The overall charge on the ion is 2−; therefore, the oxidation state of Ni must be **+2** to cancel out 2− from the 4− charge.

Shapes of complex ions

The shapes of some complex ions are shown in Table **4.9**.

Transition metal complexes do **not** obey valence shell electron pair repulsion (VSEPR) theory rules, so although six coordinate complexes are virtually **always octahedral**, four coordinate complexes may be tetrahedral or square planar.

HL Some scientists believe that the bonding between a transition metal and a ligand is purely ionic. All scientists have the same experimental data available to them − to what extent is scientific knowledge objective and to what extent is it a matter of interpretation and belief?

Complex ion	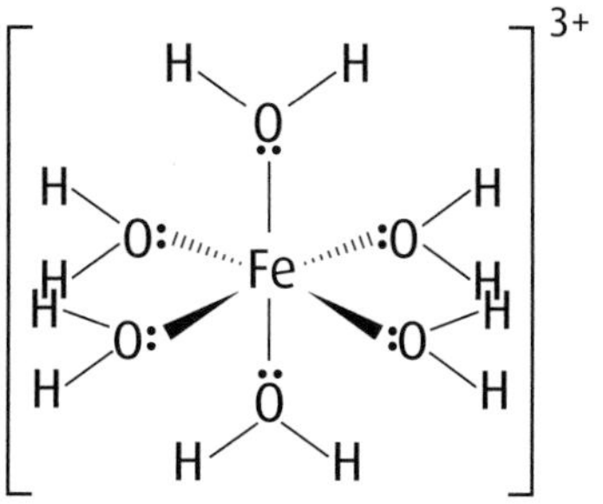	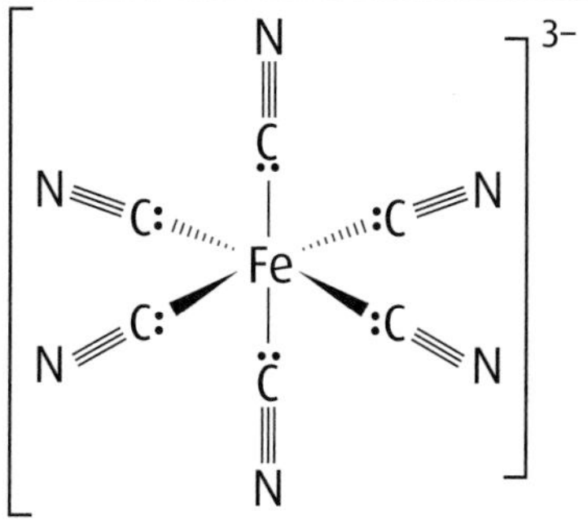
Formula	$[Fe(H_2O)_6]^{3+}$	$[Fe(CN)_6]^{3-}$
Shape	octahedral	octahedral
Oxidation number of metal	+3	+3
Name	hexaaquairon(III) ion	hexacyanoferrate(III) ion
Complex ion	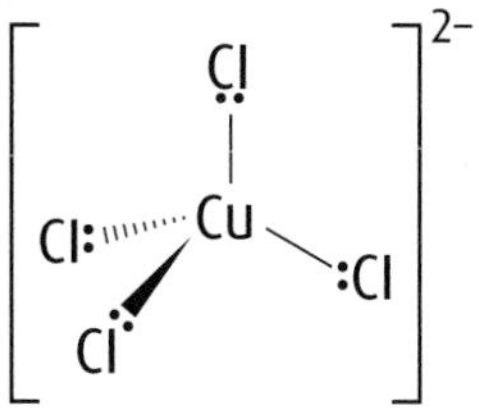	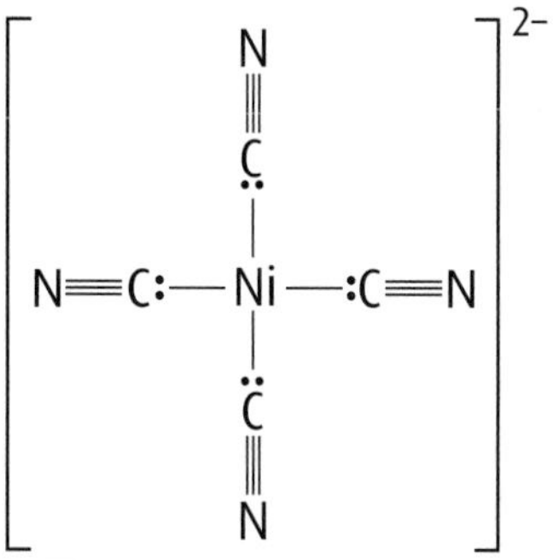
Formula	$[CuCl_4]^{2-}$	$[Ni(CN)_4]^{2-}$
Shape	tetrahedral	square planar
Oxidation number of metal	+2	+2
Name	tetrachlorocuprate(II) ion	tetracyanonickellate(II) ion
Complex ion		
Formula	$[Ag(NH_3)_2]^+$	
Shape	linear	
Oxidation number of metal	+1	
Name	diamminesilver(I) ion	

Table 4.9 The shapes of some complex ions.

Formation of complex ions

Complex ions may undergo substitution reactions in which, for example, H_2O ligands are replaced by other ligands.

Addition of concentrated hydrochloric acid to copper sulfate solution:

$$[Cu(H_2O)_6]^{2+}(aq) + 4Cl^-(aq) \rightleftharpoons [CuCl_4]^{2-}(aq) + 6H_2O(l)$$
pale blue   yellow

> As the HCl is added, the yellow $[CuCl_4]^{2-}$ complex ion is formed. Therefore, as HCl is added the solution changes colour from blue to green (mixture of blue and yellow). According to Le Chatelier's principle, the position of equilibrium shifts to the right as Cl^- is added.

When iron(III) salts are dissolved in water, very little of the pale purple $[Fe(H_2O)_6]^{3+}(aq)$ ion is present. The $[Fe(H_2O)_6]^{3+}(aq)$ ion is unstable in aqueous solution, as the 3+ charge on the metal ion causes the water molecules to be strongly polarised so that the ion dissociates:

$$[Fe(H_2O)_6]^{3+}(aq) \rightleftharpoons [Fe(H_2O)_5(OH)]^{2+}(aq) + H^+$$

The $[Fe(H_2O)_6]^{3+}$ ion can then only be prepared in strongly acidic solution.

If a high concentration of cyanide ions is added to a solution containing the $Fe^{3+}(aq)$ ion, the $[Fe(CN)_6]^{3-}$ ion can be formed. We can represent the reaction as:

$$[Fe(H_2O)_6]^{3+}(aq) + 6CN^-(aq) \rightleftharpoons [Fe(CN)_6]^{3-}(aq) + 6H_2O(l)$$
red/orange

If ammonia solution is added to a solution of silver nitrate, the colourless $[Ag(NH_3)_2]^+$ ion is formed:

$$[Ag(H_2O)_2]^+(aq) + 2NH_3(aq) \rightleftharpoons [Ag(NH_3)_2]^+(aq) + 2H_2O(l)$$

Formation of coloured complexes

The colours of some complex ions are shown in Table **4.10**.

In a gaseous transition metal ion, all the 3d orbitals have the same energy – that is, they are degenerate. However, when the ion is surrounded by ligands in a complex ion, these d orbitals are split into two groups. In an octahedral complex ion there are two orbitals in the upper group and three orbitals in the lower group.

Le Chatelier' principle – a strongly acidic solution means that the concentration of H^+ ions is high and the position of equilibrium is shifted to the left-hand side.

See page **357** – all 3+ ions in solution are acidic.

Complex ion	Colour
$[Cu(H_2O)_6]^{2+}$	blue
$[Cu(NH_3)_4(H_2O)_2]^{2+}$	deep blue/violet
$[Fe(SCN)(H_2O)_5]^{2+}$	blood red
$[Ni(H_2O)_6]^{2+}$	green

Table 4.10 The colours of some complex ions.

Extension

The d orbitals in a complex ion are higher in energy than the d orbitals in an isolated ion.

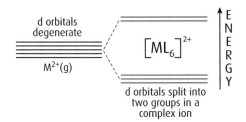

Energy in the form of a certain frequency of visible light can be absorbed to promote an electron from the lower set of orbitals to the higher set:

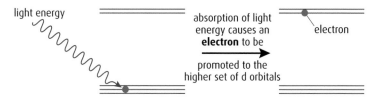

When white light travels through copper sulfate solution, orange light is absorbed, promoting an electron from the lower set of d orbitals to the higher set. This means that the light coming out contains all the colours of the spectrum except orange and so appears blue, the complementary colour to orange.

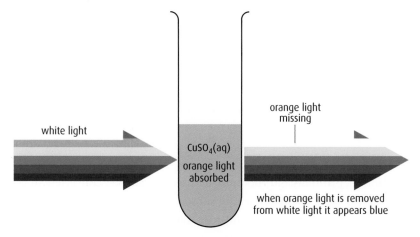

Let us consider the Sc^{3+} ion or the Ti^{4+} ion. These both have no electrons in the 3d subshell and so are colourless, as it is not possible to absorb energy to promote a 3d electron.

The Cu^+ ion and the Zn^{2+} ion both have 10 3d electrons (Figure **4.29**), and as there is no space in the upper set of orbitals it is not possible to promote an electron to the upper set of orbitals. No light in the visible region of the spectrum is absorbed, and these ions are colourless.

What do we mean when we say that a solution of copper sulfate is blue? Is **blueness** a property of copper sulfate solution, or is the blueness in our minds? What colour would copper sulfate solution be in orange light? Or in the dark?

Catalytic ability

The elements and their compounds/complexes can act as catalysts. For example, finely divided iron is the catalyst in the Haber process for the production of ammonia:

$$N_2(g) + 3H_2(g) \rightleftharpoons 2NH_3(g)$$

HL **Extension**

The d orbitals are split in different ways in different-shaped complex ions.

For a substance to appear coloured, certain frequencies of light in the visible region of the spectrum must be absorbed.

Formation of coloured complex ions/compounds requires the presence of a partially filled d subshell.

White light is a mixture of all colours (frequencies) of visible light.

Figure 4.29 A Cu^+ or Zn^{2+} ion has 10 3d electrons.

Extension

$Cr_2O_7^{2-}$ (orange), CrO_4^{2-} (yellow) and MnO_4^- (purple) are all very highly coloured, but they have no d electrons. They are coloured because of a different mechanism from the one described here.

This is discussed further on page **441**.

Vanadium(V) oxide (V_2O_5) has been used as a catalyst for the conversion of sulfur(IV) oxide into sulfur(VI) oxide in the Contact process for production of sulfuric(VI) acid:

$$2SO_2(g) + O_2(g) \rightleftharpoons 2SO_3(g)$$

Manganese(IV) oxide (MnO_2) is a commonly used catalyst in the decomposition of hydrogen peroxide:

$$2H_2O_2(aq) \rightarrow O_2(g) + 2H_2O(l)$$

Finely divided nickel is used in the hydrogenation of alkenes to form alkanes, for example:

$$H_2C=CH_2(g) + H_2(g) \rightarrow H_3C-CH_3(g)$$

Cobalt is a constituent of vitamin B_{12} (cobalamin). The vitamin is not actually an enzyme, but rather a co-factor for enzymes. Most of the reactions catalysed by enzymes associated with vitamin B_{12} are rearrangement reactions of the type:

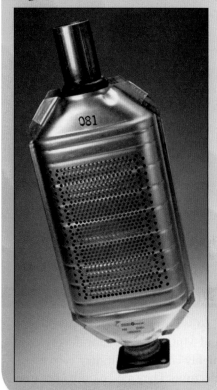

Catalytic converters are important in reducing pollution caused by the burning of fossil fuels in car engines.

Palladium, platinum and rhodium are used in catalytic converters in cars to remove, as far as possible, harmful substances from the exhaust gases. Palladium and rhodium are second-row transition elements, and platinum is a third-row transition element. Reactions such as the following occur in a catalytic converter:

$$2CO + 2NO \rightarrow 2CO_2 + N_2$$

$$2C_8H_{18} + 25O_2 \rightarrow 16CO_2 + 18H_2O$$

$$2CO + O_2 \rightarrow 2CO_2$$

Catalysts are important in the Haber and Contact processes

A catalyst is used to speed up the rate of a reaction. As well as the obvious result of this – that the product is produced more quickly – catalysts are important in industrial processes for other reasons. For example, if a catalyst is used, the reaction may be run at a lower temperature, meaning less fuel must be burnt to provide energy. The key reactions in both the Haber process and the Contact process involve an exothermic reaction, and by using a catalyst, a lower temperature can be used, which improves the yield of the product (a catalyst does not itself affect the yield of a reaction, but using a lower temperature does). A catalyst allows the product to be produced more quickly and at a lower temperature and therefore improves the overall cost effectiveness of these processes.

The Haber and Contact processes are discussed on pages **296–300**.

Some chemistry of transition elements

Here we will look at the chemistry of some transition metal ions that ties together chemistry from several areas of the course.

Iron

The most common oxidation states for iron are +2 and +3. Most iron(II) salts are oxidised slowly by the air to iron(III) salts. This can be seen if we consider the standard electrode potentials (see page **392**) for the relevant reactions:

$$Fe^{3+}(aq) + e^- \rightleftharpoons Fe^{2+}(aq) \qquad E^\ominus = +0.77\,V$$

$$O_2(g) + 4H^+(aq) + 4e^- \rightleftharpoons 2H_2O(l) \qquad E^\ominus = +1.23\,V$$

Oxygen is a strong enough oxidising agent to oxidise Fe^{2+} to Fe^{3+}:

$$4Fe^{2+}(aq) + O_2(g) + 4H^+(aq) \rightarrow 4Fe^{3+}(aq) + 2H_2O(l) \qquad E^\ominus_{cell} = +0.46\,V$$

> The value for the cell potential is positive, which indicates that the reaction is spontaneous. See page **392** for more details.

We have already seen that $Fe^{3+}(aq)$ is acidic because of the hydrolysis reaction:

$$[Fe(H_2O)_6]^{3+}(aq) \rightleftharpoons [Fe(H_2O)_5(OH)]^{2+}(aq) + H^+$$

As the hexa-aqua complex is not present, solutions of iron(III) are yellow and not violet.

Chromium(VI) and chromium(III)

The most important chromium(VI) complexes are the yellow chromate(VI), $[CrO_4]^{2-}$, and the orange dichromate(VI), $[Cr_2O_7]^{2-}$, ions. These two species exist in equilibrium in aqueous solution, the dichromate(VI) ion predominating in acidic solution:

$$\underset{\text{yellow}}{2[CrO_4]^{2-}} + 2H^+ \rightleftharpoons \underset{\text{orange}}{[Cr_2O_7]^{2-}} + H_2O$$

Addition of acid shifts the equilibrium position to the right in order to use up the H^+ that has been added. If alkali is added, it reacts with the H^+ ions, causing the position of equilibrium to shift to the left-hand side to replace the H^+ ions that have been removed as far as possible.

The +6 oxidation state is strongly oxidising, and acidified dichromate(VI) is used as an oxidising agent in organic chemistry, e.g. in the oxidation of primary alcohols to aldehydes and then carboxylic acids:

$$C_2H_5OH + [O] \rightarrow CH_3CHO + H_2O$$

$$CH_3CHO + [O] \rightarrow CH_3COOH$$

> The film *Erin Brockovich* describes the true story of a woman's fight against a major corporation that was releasing carcinogenic chromium(VI) into the drinking water supply of a town in California, USA.

In the process the orange dichromate(VI) ion is reduced to the green Cr^{3+} ion:

$$Cr_2O_7^{2-}(aq) + 14H^+(aq) + 6e^- \rightleftharpoons 2Cr^{3+}(aq) + 7H_2O(l) \quad E^\ominus = +1.33\,V$$

The $[Cr(H_2O)_6]^{3+}$ ion is actually violet. However, this does not exist in aqueous solution, as it is acidic ($pK_a = 4.1$).

$$[Cr(H_2O)_6]^{3+} \rightleftharpoons [Cr(H_2O)_5(OH)]^{2+} + H^+$$

The +3 oxidation state is the most stable and common one for chromium.

Manganese(IV) and manganese(VII)

The +7 oxidation state for manganese is typified by the dark purple manganate(VII) ion (permanganate ion).

The MnO_4^- ion is tetrahedral and strongly oxidising in both acidic and alkaline solution:

$$\underset{\text{purple}}{MnO_4^-(aq)} + 8H^+(aq) + 5e^- \rightleftharpoons \underset{\text{pale pink}}{Mn^{2+}(aq)} + 4H_2O(l) \qquad E^\ominus = +1.51\,V$$

In less strongly acidic or basic medium, manganese(IV) oxide is formed:

$$MnO_4^-(aq) + 4H^+(aq) + 3e^- \rightleftharpoons \underset{\text{black}}{MnO_2(s)} + 2H_2O(l)$$

MnO_2 is the only important compound with Mn in the +4 oxidation state. It is most commonly encountered as the catalyst for decomposition of hydrogen peroxide (see above).

MnO_2 is strongly oxidising and is reduced to Mn^{2+}, which is the most stable oxidation state for Mn:

$$MnO_2(s) + 4HCl(aq) \rightarrow MnCl_2(aq) + Cl_2(g) + 2H_2O(l)$$

Copper

The most stable oxidation state of copper is +2, which is familiar as the pale blue $[Cu(H_2O)_6]^{2+}$ ion in aqueous solutions of copper salts. Copper also, however, forms some copper(I) compounds and complexes.

In aqueous solution the copper(I) ion is unstable and disproportionates according to the equation:

$$2Cu^+(aq) \rightarrow Cu(s) + Cu^{2+}(aq)$$

The favourability of this reaction can be seen from a consideration of the standard electrode potentials for the half reactions:

$$Cu^{2+}(aq) + e^- \rightleftharpoons Cu^+(aq) \qquad\qquad E^\ominus = +0.15\,V$$

$$Cu^+(aq) + e^- \rightleftharpoons Cu(s) \qquad\qquad E^\ominus = +0.52\,V$$

Overall then:

$$2Cu^+(aq) \rightarrow Cu(s) + Cu^{2+}(aq) \qquad\qquad E^\ominus_{cell} = +0.37\,V$$

See Fe^{3+}, above.

It will oxidise alcohols to aldehydes etc. It is a stronger oxidising agent than $Cr_2O_7^{2-}$.

MnO_2 is insoluble in water.

Disproportionation – the same element is oxidised and reduced.

Beryllium–copper alloys are used for springs and contacts in mobile phones.

Copper(I) iodide is formed when potassium iodide solution is added to a solution of copper(II) (e.g. copper(II) sulfate):

$$2Cu^{2+}(aq) + 4I^-(aq) \rightarrow \underset{\text{white precipitate}}{2CuI(s)} + I_2(aq)$$

This reaction is used in the determination of the concentration of a solution of Cu^{2+} ions. Excess potassium iodide is added to a sample of the $Cu^{2+}(aq)$, and the iodine released is titrated against a standard solution of sodium thiosulfate ($Na_2S_2O_3$).

Most copper(I) compounds are white/colourless due to having a full 3d subshell, although an exception is the red copper(I) oxide, Cu_2O.

Self-test 3

Test yourself

11 Give the full electronic configuration of the following ions:
   a Ni^{2+} **b** Co^{3+} **c** V^{3+} **d** Mn^{4+}

12 Give the oxidation state of the transition metal in each of the following complex ions
   a $[Ni(H_2O)_6]^{2+}$ **b** $[Fe(CN)_6]^{4-}$
   c $[MnCl_4]^{2-}$ **d** $[Co(NH_3)_6]^{3+}$
   e $[Co(NH_3)_5Br]^{2+}$ **f** $[Co(NH_3)_4Br_2]^+$
   g $[FeO_4]^{2-}$ **h** $Ni(CO)_4$

13 Which of the following compounds are likely to be coloured?
   TiF_4 VF_5 MnF_3 CoF_2 $CuBr$ $ZnCl_2$

Exam-style questions

1 Which of the following properties decrease in value down group 7?

   A electronegativity and first ionisation energy
   B melting point and electronegativity
   C melting point and atomic radius
   D ionic radius and first ionisation energy

2 Which of the following is a transition element?

   A Te   **B** Sb   **C** Ba   **D** V

3 Which of the following forms an alkaline solution when added to water?

   A SO_3 **B** Na_2O **C** P_4O_{10} **D** SiO_2

4 Which of the following is true for two elements in the same group in the periodic table?

    A they have the same physical properties
    B they have similar chemical properties
    C they have the same electronegativity
    D they have the same number of shells of electrons

5 A non-metallic element, X, forms a gaseous oxide with the formula X_2O that reacts with water to form an acidic solution. The element X is most likely to be:

    A Na   **B** S   **C** Cl   **D** P

HL

6 Which of the following chlorides produces a neutral solution when added to water?

    A $MgCl_2$ **B** NaCl   **C** $SiCl_4$ **D** PCl_3

7 Which of the following chlorides has the highest melting point?

    A $MgCl_2$ **B** $SiCl_4$ **C** PCl_5 **D** PCl_3

8 What is the oxidation state of chromium in $K_3[Cr(CN)_6]$?

    A +6   **B** −6   **C** +3   **D** −3

9 Which of the following complex ions would be expected to be colourless?

    A $[Ni(H_2O)_6]^{2+}$ **C** $[Cu(H_2O)_6]^{2+}$
    B $[Zn(H_2O)_6]^{2+}$ **D** $[Co(H_2O)_6]^{2+}$

10 Which of the following is **not** a characteristic property of transition metals?

    A they form complex ions
    B they have full d subshells
    C they exhibit more than one oxidation state in compounds
    D they form coloured compounds

11 **a** The atomic and ionic radii of some elements are given in the table:

Element	Atomic radius / pm	Ionic radius / pm
Na	186	98
Al	143	45
Cl	99	181
K	231	133

  i Explain why the atomic radius of aluminium is smaller than that of sodium. [2]

  ii Explain why the ionic radius of aluminium is smaller than its atomic radius but the atomic radius of chlorine is larger than its atomic radius. [4]

  iii Explain why the ionic radius of potassium is smaller than that of chlorine. [2]

b Explain the following in terms of structure and bonding:

  i Sodium has a higher melting point than potassium. [3]

  ii Silicon has a higher melting point than chlorine. [3]

c State the formula of phosphorus(V) oxide and write an equation for its reaction with water. [2]

HL 12 **a** Explain the following in terms of structure and bonding:

  i Sodium chloride has a higher melting point than silicon tetrachloride. [3]

  ii Sodium chloride conducts electricity when molten but silicon tetrachloride does not. [2]

b Draw a diagram showing the bonding in aluminium chloride and write an equation to show its reaction with water. [3]

c What is the oxidation state of iron in the complex ion $[FeCl_6]^{4-}$? [1]

d **i** Explain why the complex ion $[Cu(H_2O)_6]^{2+}$ is coloured. [3]

  ii When concentrated hydrochloric acid is added to an aqueous solution of copper sulfate, the colour of the solution changes from blue to green. Write an equation for the reaction that occurs and describe the shape of the complex ion formed. [2]

e Give an example of a reaction, including an equation, in which a named first-row transition element acts as a catalyst. [2]

Summary

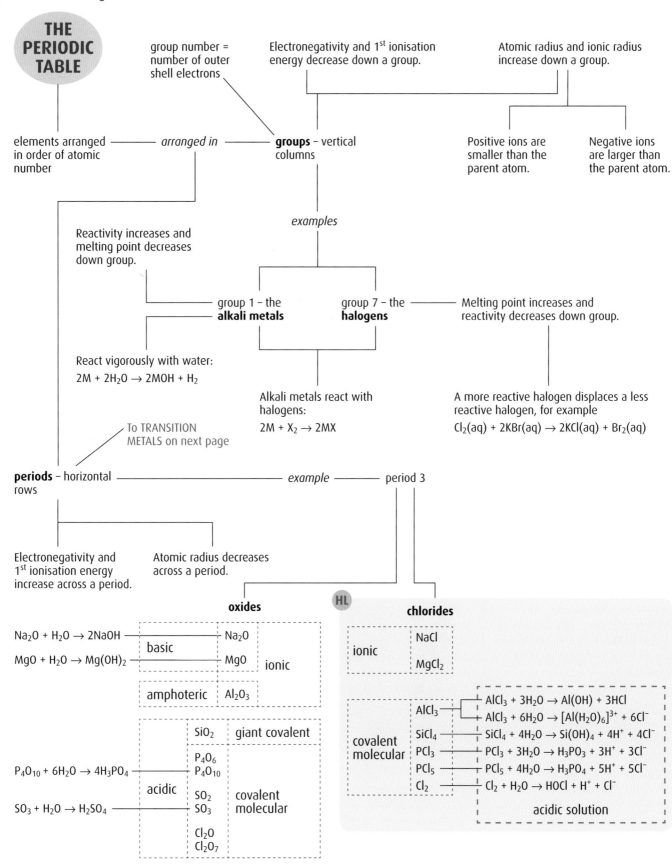

THE PERIODIC TABLE

group number = number of outer shell electrons

Electronegativity and 1st ionisation energy decrease down a group.

Atomic radius and ionic radius increase down a group.

elements arranged in order of atomic number —— *arranged in* —— **groups** – vertical columns

Positive ions are smaller than the parent atom.

Negative ions are larger than the parent atom.

Reactivity increases and melting point decreases down group.

examples

group 1 – the **alkali metals**

group 7 – the **halogens**

Melting point increases and reactivity decreases down group.

React vigorously with water:
$2M + 2H_2O \rightarrow 2MOH + H_2$

To TRANSITION METALS on next page

Alkali metals react with halogens:
$2M + X_2 \rightarrow 2MX$

A more reactive halogen displaces a less reactive halogen, for example
$Cl_2(aq) + 2KBr(aq) \rightarrow 2KCl(aq) + Br_2(aq)$

periods – horizontal rows —— *example* —— period 3

Electronegativity and 1st ionisation energy increase across a period.

Atomic radius decreases across a period.

oxides

HL

chlorides

$Na_2O + H_2O \rightarrow 2NaOH$ —— Na₂O

basic

$MgO + H_2O \rightarrow Mg(OH)_2$ —— MgO

ionic

amphoteric | Al₂O₃

| | SiO₂ | giant covalent |

$P_4O_{10} + 6H_2O \rightarrow 4H_3PO_4$ —— | P₄O₆ |
| | P₄O₁₀ |

acidic | SO₂ |
| SO₃ | covalent molecular |

$SO_3 + H_2O \rightarrow H_2SO_4$ —— SO₃

| Cl₂O |
| Cl₂O₇ |

ionic | NaCl |
| MgCl₂ |

covalent molecular

AlCl₃ —— $AlCl_3 + 3H_2O \rightarrow Al(OH) + 3HCl$
—— $AlCl_3 + 6H_2O \rightarrow [Al(H_2O)_6]^{3+} + 6Cl^-$

SiCl₄ —— $SiCl_4 + 4H_2O \rightarrow Si(OH)_4 + 4H^+ + 4Cl^-$

PCl₃ —— $PCl_3 + 3H_2O \rightarrow H_3PO_3 + 3H^+ + 3Cl^-$

PCl₅ —— $PCl_5 + 4H_2O \rightarrow H_3PO_4 + 5H^+ + 5Cl^-$

Cl₂ —— $Cl_2 + H_2O \rightarrow HOCl + H^+ + Cl^-$

acidic solution

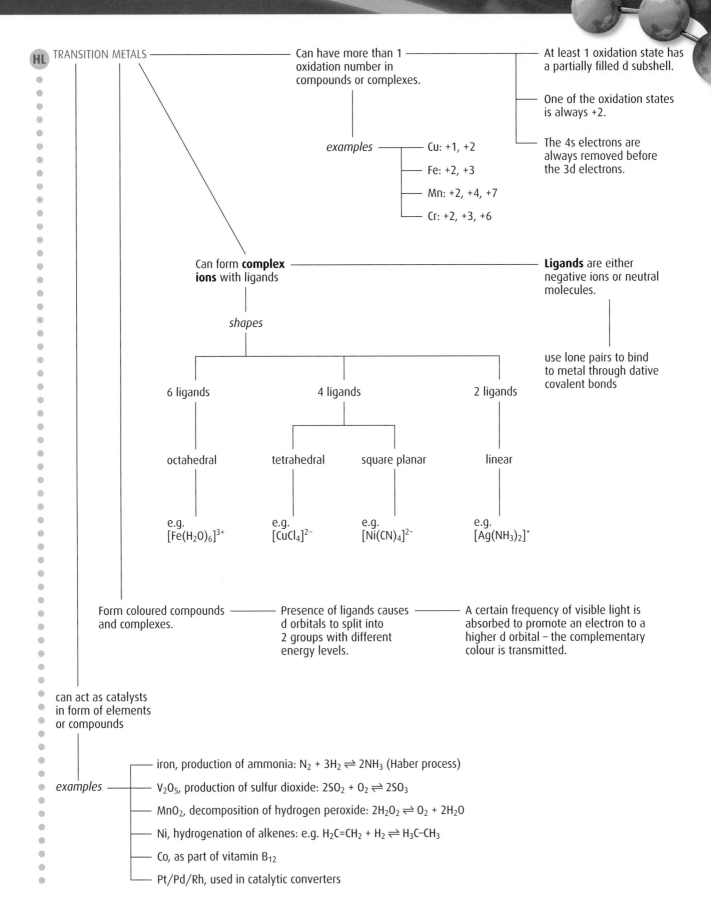

HL TRANSITION METALS —— Can have more than 1 oxidation number in compounds or complexes.

At least 1 oxidation state has a partially filled d subshell.

One of the oxidation states is always +2.

The 4s electrons are always removed before the 3d electrons.

examples
- Cu: +1, +2
- Fe: +2, +3
- Mn: +2, +4, +7
- Cr: +2, +3, +6

Can form **complex ions** with ligands

Ligands are either negative ions or neutral molecules.

use lone pairs to bind to metal through dative covalent bonds

shapes

6 ligands	4 ligands		2 ligands
octahedral	tetrahedral	square planar	linear
e.g. $[Fe(H_2O)_6]^{3+}$	e.g. $[CuCl_4]^{2-}$	e.g. $[Ni(CN)_4]^{2-}$	e.g. $[Ag(NH_3)_2]^+$

Form coloured compounds and complexes. —— Presence of ligands causes d orbitals to split into 2 groups with different energy levels. —— A certain frequency of visible light is absorbed to promote an electron to a higher d orbital – the complementary colour is transmitted.

can act as catalysts in form of elements or compounds

examples
- iron, production of ammonia: $N_2 + 3H_2 \rightleftharpoons 2NH_3$ (Haber process)
- V_2O_5, production of sulfur dioxide: $2SO_2 + O_2 \rightleftharpoons 2SO_3$
- MnO_2, decomposition of hydrogen peroxide: $2H_2O_2 \rightleftharpoons O_2 + 2H_2O$
- Ni, hydrogenation of alkenes: e.g. $H_2C=CH_2 + H_2 \rightleftharpoons H_3C-CH_3$
- Co, as part of vitamin B_{12}
- Pt/Pd/Rh, used in catalytic converters

5 Energetics

Learning objectives

- Explain what is meant by **exothermic** and **endothermic** reactions
- Draw enthalpy level diagrams for exothermic and endothermic reactions
- Understand what is meant by **stability**

5.1 Exothermic and endothermic reactions

Chemical reactions may be classified as either exothermic or endothermic. An exothermic reaction gives out heat to the surroundings (Figure **5.1**). An endothermic reaction takes in heat from the surroundings (Figure **5.2**).

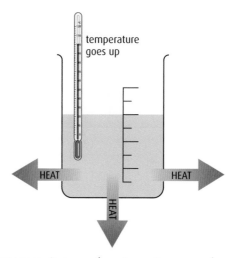

Figure 5.1 The heat energy in an exothermic reaction comes from the decrease in internal energy (the total energy of all the particles) of the system (e.g. by making chemical bonds).

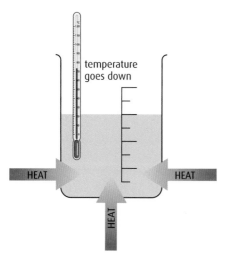

Figure 5.2 The heat energy in an endothermic reaction is converted to internal energy (e.g. by breaking chemical bonds).

To be more precise, the enthalpy change is the heat energy exchanged with the surroundings at **constant pressure**.

Δ means a change in a quantity.

> Exothermic reactions: chemical reactions that result in the release of heat to the surroundings – the reaction vessel gets **hotter**.

> Endothermic reactions: heat is taken in from the surroundings – the reaction vessel gets **colder**.

We talk about the **enthalpy change** of a system. The enthalpy change is basically the amount of heat energy taken in/given out in a chemical reaction. Enthalpy is given the symbol H and enthalpy change is ΔH.

Note: it is **not possible to measure the enthalpy (H) of a system** (related to the total energy of all the particles making up a substance), only the enthalpy change (ΔH) when the system moves from an initial state to some final state.

> ΔH for an **exothermic** reaction is **negative**.
> ΔH for an **endothermic** reaction is **positive**.

Exothermic reactions

Consider a reaction such as methane burning in oxygen:

$$CH_4(g) + 2O_2(g) \rightarrow CO_2(g) + 2H_2O(l) \qquad \Delta H = -890\,\text{kJ mol}^{-1}$$

This reaction is **exo**thermic, as heat is given out to the surroundings.

Figure **5.3** shows the enthalpy change for an exothermic reaction such as the combustion of methane. No scale is shown on the vertical axis, as we cannot measure the initial enthalpy or final enthalpy of the system. We can, however, measure the enthalpy change of a reaction as the amount of heat given out, and this is shown by the red arrow. The reaction is exothermic, and the enthalpy of the products is less than that of the reactants. The negative sign for the enthalpy change indicates a decrease in enthalpy.

We more normally use an enthalpy level diagram to show the enthalpy change of a reaction (Figure **5.4**).

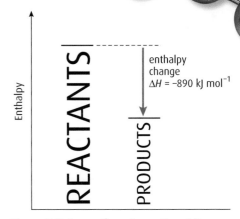

Figure 5.3 An exothermic reaction: ΔH negative.

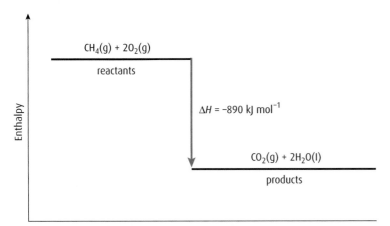

Figure 5.4 An enthalpy level diagram for the combustion of methane.

In an exothermic reaction the products are at a lower energy (enthalpy) level than the reactants, and we say that the products are more **stable** than the reactants.

Endothermic reactions

An example of an endothermic reaction is that between nitrogen and oxygen to form nitrogen(II) oxide (nitric oxide):

$$N_2(g) + O_2(g) \rightarrow 2NO(g) \qquad \Delta H = +181\,\text{kJ mol}^{-1}$$

Heat energy must be put into the system, as the products have greater energy than the reactants. The sign of ΔH is positive, indicating the increase in enthalpy in an endothermic reaction.

The enthalpy level diagram for this reaction is shown in Figure **5.5**. The products have greater energy (enthalpy) and are less stable than the reactants.

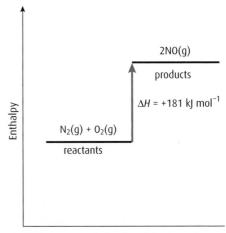

Figure 5.5 An enthalpy level diagram for an endothermic reaction.

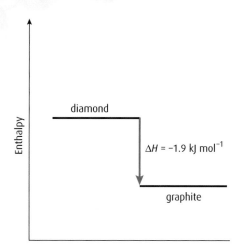

Figure 5.6 An enthalpy level diagram for the reaction in which diamond is turned into graphite.

Stability

If a reaction is exothermic it involves a decrease in the enthalpy of the system and we will often talk about the products being more **stable** than the reactants.

$$C_{diamond} \rightarrow C_{graphite} \qquad \Delta H = -1.9\,kJ\,mol^{-1}$$

Graphite is at a lower enthalpy level than diamond and is therefore $1.9\,kJ\,mol^{-1}$ more stable than diamond (Figure **5.6**).

Methane and oxygen are unstable with respect to the combustion products, carbon dioxide and water:

$$CH_4(g) + 2O_2(g) \rightarrow CO_2(g) + 2H_2O(l) \qquad \Delta H = -890\,kJ\,mol^{-1}$$

It is important to make the distinction between **thermodynamic stability** and **kinetic stability**. Although graphite is thermodynamically more stable than diamond (at a lower energy level) and carbon dioxide and water are thermodynamically stable with respect to methane and oxygen, in both cases, under normal conditions, the reactants are kinetically stable with respect to the products. This means that the reaction of diamond to become graphite is very, very slow under normal conditions!

If a little bit of energy, in the form of a spark, is provided to the methane–oxygen mixture, the reaction proceeds very quickly. This suggests that there is some energy barrier that must be overcome before reaction can occur. This energy barrier is called the **activation energy** (Figure **5.7**).

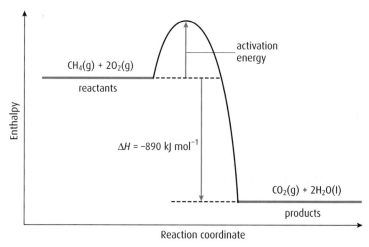

Figure 5.7 An enthalpy level diagram for an exothermic reaction showing the activation energy.

The activation energy is the minimum energy that colliding particles must have before collision results in a chemical reaction – this will be considered in more detail on pages **246–251**.

In general, all other things being equal, the higher the activation energy, the slower the reaction. Thus, although the products may be more stable than the reactants, it is still perfectly possible to have a bottle of the reactants on the shelf in the chemical store cupboard, and to keep them there for several years, as long as the activation energy is sufficiently high that the reaction does not occur at a measurable rate under normal conditions.

There is no connection between these two ideas. A chemical reaction could be extremely exothermic and proceed very slowly, whereas in another, very fast, reaction the products may be only slightly more stable than the reactants.

> How exo- or endothermic a reaction is does not tell us anything about how quickly a reaction occurs. For example:
>
> $$CCl_4(l) + 2H_2O(l) \rightarrow CO_2(g) + 4HCl(g) \qquad \Delta H = -52\,kJ\,mol^{-1}$$
>
> $$SiCl_4(l) + 2H_2O(l) \rightarrow SiO_2(s) + 4HCl(g) \qquad \Delta H = -16\,kJ\,mol^{-1}$$
>
> The lower reaction occurs rapidly; the upper one immeasurably slowly.

The enthalpy level diagram for an endothermic reaction is shown in Figure **5.8**. It is a fairly good rule of thumb that exothermic reactions tend to occur spontaneously, whereas endothermic reactions do not. This is often explained using the analogy that 'water always flows downhill', i.e. a system will always move to lower energy by giving out energy to the surroundings.

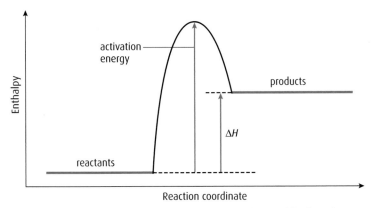

Figure 5.8 In an endothermic reaction, the products are less stable than the reactants.

However, endothermic reactions do occur, and they are perhaps much more common than we realise; ice melting at room temperature, salt dissolving in water, and water evaporating are all endothermic processes that seem to occur fairly readily.

This suggests that perhaps enthalpy change is not the fundamental process that drives a chemical reaction. Another thermodynamic function that is more fundamental in determining whether a reaction occurs spontaneously will be considered in Section **5.8** (Higher Level only).

5.2 Calculation of enthalpy changes from experimental data

Measuring enthalpy changes

In this section we will consider how to measure enthalpy changes of combustion reactions. In order to understand how this works, we will first consider specific heat capacity.

Learning objectives

- Understand the principle of experimental methods for determining enthalpy changes
- Work out enthalpy changes from experimental data

Specific heat capacity has units of $J\,g^{-1}\,K^{-1}$ or $J\,g^{-1}\,{}°C^{-1}$. Units that are also encountered are $kJ\,kg^{-1}\,K^{-1}$ or $J\,kg^{-1}\,K^{-1}$.

1 K is the same as 1 °C when temperature changes are being considered.

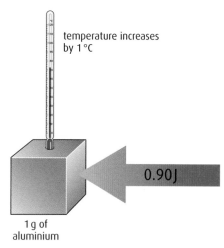

temperature increases by 1 °C

0.90 J

1 g of aluminium

Figure 5.9 The specific heat capacity of aluminium is $0.90\,J\,g^{-1}\,{}°C^{-1}$.

ΔT is the change in temperature.

Specific heat capacity

In chemistry we usually take the definition of specific heat capacity (c) to be:

> the energy required to raise the temperature of 1 g of substance by 1 K (1 °C). It can also be defined as the energy to raise the temperature of 1 kg of substance by 1 K.

The specific heat capacity of aluminium is $0.90\,J\,g^{-1}\,{}°C^{-1}$. Therefore, if 0.90 J of heat energy is put into 1 g of aluminium, the temperature is raised by 1 °C (Figure **5.9**).

If 1.80 J of heat energy were put into this block of aluminium, the temperature would go up by 2 °C. If the 1 g block of aluminium were replaced by a 2 g block of aluminium, then 1.80 J would be required to raise the temperature by 1 °C, as 0.90 J is required to raise the temperature of each 1 g by 1 °C. The amount of heat energy required is therefore proportional to the mass and the temperature change. An equation can thus be derived for how much heat energy (q) must be supplied to raise the temperature of mass m by $\Delta T\,°C$:

$$q = mc\Delta T$$

The specific heat capacity indicates how much energy is required to heat up a substance, and therefore substances with higher specific heat capacities are more difficult to heat up than substances with lower specific heat capacities. For example, the specific heat capacity of iron is roughly half that of aluminium; therefore if the same amount of heat energy is supplied to 10 g of each metal, the temperature of the iron will go up by twice the amount.

The specific heat capacity also applies when a substance cools; so, for instance, when 1 g of aluminium cools from 21 °C to 20 °C, 0.90 J of energy is given out. This can be used to calculate the specific heat capacity of an unknown metal.

Worked example

40.0 g of an unknown metal is heated to 91.3 °C and then plunged into 100.0 g of water at 21.3 °C. The water and the metal reach a common temperature of 28.4 °C. Given that the specific heat capacity of water is $4.18\,J\,g^{-1}\,{}°C^{-1}$, calculate the specific heat capacity of the metal.

The amount of heat energy supplied to the water is given by: $q_1 = mc\Delta T$

so: $q_1 = 100.0 \times 4.18 \times (28.4 - 21.3) = 2970\,J$

The energy given out when the metal block cools is given by:

$$q_2 = 40.0 \times c \times (91.3 - 28.4) = 2516c$$

where c is the specific heat capacity of the metal. The heat energy supplied to heat the water comes from the cooling of the block of metal, so $q_1 = q_2$

Therefore: $2970 = 2516c$

and $c = 1.18\,\mathrm{J\,g^{-1}\,^{\circ}C^{-1}}$

Measuring the enthalpy change of combustion reactions

The basic technique is that the heat given out in a combustion reaction is used to heat another substance of known specific heat capacity, such as water. The equation $q = mc\Delta T$ can be used to calculate the amount of heat given out.

The experimental set-up shown in Figure **5.10** could be used to determine the enthalpy change when 1 mole of a liquid substance is burnt. The mass and temperature change of the water must be measured, as well as the mass change of the alcohol.

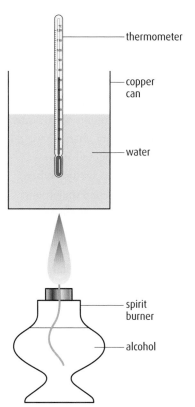

Figure 5.10 An experiment to work out the enthalpy change when 1 mole of an alcohol is burnt.

Worked example

Use the following experimental data to determine the enthalpy change when 1 mole of ethanol (C_2H_5OH) is burnt:

Mass of water = 150.00 g
Initial temperature of water = 19.5 °C
Maximum temperature of water = 45.7 °C
Initial mass of spirit burner = 121.67 g
Final mass of spirit burner = 120.62 g

The temperature change of the water = $45.7 - 19.5 = 26.2\,^{\circ}C$

The amount of heat energy supplied to the water is given by:

$$q = mc\Delta T$$

$$q = 150.00 \times 4.18 \times 26.2 = 16\,400\,\mathrm{J}$$

This amount of heat energy is supplied by the burning of the ethanol.

mass of ethanol burnt = $121.67 - 120.62 = 1.05\,\mathrm{g}$

The number of moles of ethanol burnt is given by:

$$\text{no. moles} = \frac{\text{mass}}{\text{molar mass}}$$

Note – the mass of water and **not** the mass of ethanol is used here – it is the water that is being heated.

The specific heat capacity of water is $4.18\,\mathrm{J\,g^{-1}\,^{\circ}C^{-1}}$.

The molar mass of ethanol is $46.08\,\mathrm{g\,mol^{-1}}$. Therefore:

$$\text{no. moles ethanol burnt} = \frac{1.05}{46.08} = 0.0228\,\mathrm{mol}$$

When $0.0228\,\mathrm{mol}$ ethanol are burnt, $16\,400\,\mathrm{J}$ of heat energy are produced. Therefore the amount of energy released when 1 mole is burnt is given by:

$$\text{energy} = \frac{16\,400}{0.0228} = 721\,000\,\mathrm{J\,mol^{-1}}$$

The enthalpy change when 1 mole of ethanol is burnt is therefore:

$$\Delta H = -721\,\mathrm{kJ\,mol^{-1}}$$

More than three significant figures were carried through on the calculator to give this final answer.

The value of the enthalpy change is negative because the combustion reaction is exothermic.

When we carry out experiments to measure enthalpy changes we often get unexpected values. What criteria do we use when carrying out these experiments to decide whether there are flaws in the experiment or flaws in the theory? This is an example of a more general problem, and it is sometimes too easy to dismiss an 'anomalous' result as being due to systematic errors in the experiment. The opposite also occasionally happens, and a new theory is put forward from an experiment that is possibly flawed – **cold fusion** is an example of this (originally announced by Pons and Fleischmann in 1989).

The accepted literature value for the enthalpy change of combustion of ethanol is $-1371\,\mathrm{kJ\,mol^{-1}}$, so it can be seen that this experiment does not give a very accurate answer. There are several major flaws (systematic errors) in the experimental set-up. The most major problem is that of **heat loss to the surroundings**. Of the heat energy released when the ethanol burns, only some of it goes into heating the water – the rest goes into heating the copper can and the surrounding air. The experiment could have been improved by determining the specific heat capacity of the can and taking this into account when doing the calculation, insulating the can so that less heat is lost through the can to the surroundings, using some sort of draught shields to reduce convection currents around the experiment, etc.

Another major problem with the experiment is **incomplete combustion of the ethanol**. When ethanol undergoes complete combustion the equation for the reaction is:

$$C_2H_5OH + 3O_2 \rightarrow 2CO_2 + 3H_2O$$

However, if there is not a sufficient supply of oxygen to the flame, some of the ethanol can burn to produce carbon monoxide and soot (carbon) as well as water. This is called incomplete combustion and gives out less heat than complete combustion. Incomplete combustion causes the flame to be yellow/orange rather than blue because of the presence of soot particles, and the soot can also be seen on the bottom of the copper can.

Other, more minor, problems with the experiment include evaporation of the water and alcohol.

More accurate values for the enthalpy change of a combustion reaction require the use of a **bomb calorimeter**. This is a heavily insulated piece of apparatus in which the substance is ignited electronically in a plentiful supply of oxygen.

Test yourself

You may assume that the specific heat capacity of water is 4.18 J g^{-1}°C^{-1}.

1 Work out the specific heat capacities of each metal from the data given:

   a Gold – the temperature of 2.00 g of gold is raised by 11.7 °C when 3.00 J of energy is supplied.

   b Silver – the temperature of 100.0 g of silver is raised by 2.12 °C when 50.0 J of energy is supplied.

2 a When 1.20 g of hexane (C$_6$H$_{14}$) is burnt, the temperature of 250.0 g of water is raised by 56.0 °C. Calculate the enthalpy change when 1 mole of hexane is burnt.

   b When 2.00 kg of octane (C$_8$H$_{18}$) is burnt, the temperature of 500 kg of water is raised by 46.0 °C. Calculate the enthalpy change when 1 mole of octane is burnt.

3 Use the following experimental data to determine the enthalpy change when 1 mole of propan-1-ol is burnt:

   Mass of water = 200.00 g
   Initial temperature of water = 18.2 °C
   Maximum temperature of water = 38.6 °C
   Initial mass of spirit burner = 185.51 g
   Final mass of spirit burner = 184.56 g

4 The actual value for the enthalpy change when 1 mole of propan-1-ol is burnt is −2010 kJ mol^{-1}. Account for any differences between this value and the one calculated from the experimental data in question 3.

Enthalpy changes in solution

A general method for measuring enthalpy changes involving solutions in the laboratory is to measure out known amounts of reagents, record their initial temperatures, mix together the reagents in a polystyrene cup and record the maximum/minimum temperature observed. The specific heat capacity of the final solution is assumed to be the same as water. Before we look at some examples of how to do this, we must consider a couple of definitions.

Enthalpy change of neutralisation (ΔH$_n$) is the enthalpy change when 1 mole of H$_2$O molecules are formed when an acid (H$^+$) reacts with an alkali (OH$^-$) under standard conditions:

$$H^+(aq) + OH^-(aq) \rightarrow H_2O(l)$$

The enthalpy change of neutralisation is always **exothermic**.

Enthalpy change of solution (ΔH$_{sol}$) is the enthalpy change when 1 mol of solute is dissolved in excess solvent to form a solution of 'infinite dilution' under standard conditions, e.g.:

$$NH_4NO_3(s) \xrightarrow{\text{excess } H_2O} NH_4^+(aq) + NO_3^-(aq)$$

$$\Delta H_{sol} = +25.7 \text{ kJ mol}^{-1}$$

'Infinite dilution' means that any further dilution of the solution produces no further enthalpy change, i.e. the solute particles are assumed not to interact with each other in the solution.

The enthalpy change of solution may be exothermic or endothermic.

Worked examples

Consider the following experiment: $100.0\,cm^3$ of $1.00\,mol\,dm^{-3}$ potassium hydroxide solution was measured out and poured into a polystyrene cup and the temperature of the potassium hydroxide solution was taken; then $120.0\,cm^3$ of $1.00\,mol\,dm^{-3}$ hydrochloric acid was measured out and the initial temperature was taken. The hydrochloric acid was in excess to make sure that all the potassium hydroxide reacted. The hydrochloric acid was then poured into the polystyrene cup and the mixture stirred rapidly. The maximum temperature was recorded.

The results of this experiment:

Initial temperature of potassium hydroxide
solution = 19.7 °C

Initial temperature of hydrochloric acid = 19.7 °C

Maximum temperature reached = 25.9 °C

Temperature change of the mixture = 6.2 °C

Total volume of the reaction mixture = $220.0\,cm^3$

We will assume that the density of the mixture is the same as that of water, and so $220.0\,cm^3$ of solution has a mass of $220.0\,g$.

> Assumption: the density of the potassium hydroxide and hydrochloric acid
> solutions are the same as water, so $1\,cm^3$ of solution has a mass of $1\,g$.

We can work out how much heat (q) has been released in this reaction by looking at the temperature change of the mixture.

$$q = mc\Delta T = 220 \times 4.18 \times 6.2 = 5700\,J$$

> Assumption: the specific heat capacity of the mixture is the same as that of water.
> This is a fairly reasonable assumption, as the reaction mixture is mostly water.

To work out the enthalpy change of neutralisation, we need to know how many moles of water have been formed. The equation for the reaction is:

$$KOH + HCl \rightarrow KCl + H_2O$$

no. moles KOH = concentration × volume in dm^3

$$\text{no. moles KOH} = 1.00 \times \frac{100}{1000} = 0.100\,mol$$

$$\text{no. moles HCl} = 1.00 \times \frac{120}{1000} = 0.120\,mol$$

The HCl is in excess and the number of moles of water produced is $0.100\,mol$. Therefore $5700\,J$ of energy is released when $0.100\,mol$ of water is formed.

The definition of enthalpy change of neutralisation is the enthalpy change when 1 mole of water is produced. Therefore, for 1 mole of water formed:

$$\text{heat energy released} = \frac{1}{0.100} \times 5700 = 57\,000\,\text{J}\,\text{mol}^{-1}$$

Therefore, the enthalpy change of neutralisation, $\Delta H_n = -57.0\,\text{kJ}\,\text{mol}^{-1}$.

> This is negative, as the reaction is exothermic.

The accepted literature value for the heat of neutralisation of KOH with HCl is $-57.2\,\text{kJ}\,\text{mol}^{-1}$. Possible errors in this experiment are heat loss to the surroundings and the assumptions that have been made about the specific heat capacities and the density of the solutions.

a 100.0 cm^3 of 1.00 mol dm^{-3} potassium hydroxide solution was reacted with 100.0 cm^3 of 1.00 mol dm^{-3} hydrochloric acid. The temperature rise was 6.82 °C. Calculate the enthalpy change of neutralisation.

b The experiment in part **a** was repeated with 50.0 cm^3 of 1.00 mol dm^{-3} potassium hydroxide solution and 50.0 cm^3 of 1.00 mol dm^{-3} hydrochloric acid. Calculate the temperature change of the reaction mixture.

a We can use the method used in the previous example to calculate the enthalpy change of neutralisation:

$$q = mc\Delta T = 200 \times 4.18 \times 6.82 = 5700\,\text{J}$$

The number of moles of KOH and HCl in this case are the same, both 0.100 mol. Therefore 0.100 mol of water are formed.

$$\text{heat energy released} = \frac{1}{0.100} \times 5700 = 57\,000\,\text{J}\,\text{mol}^{-1}$$

Therefore the enthalpy change of neutralisation, $\Delta H_n = -57.0\,\text{kJ}\,\text{mol}^{-1}$.

b A shortcut can be used to answer this part. The volume of each solution is half that in part **a** but the concentrations are the same. Therefore we can deduce that the number of moles of water formed will be half as much as in part **a**. This means that half as much heat energy will be given out in the neutralisation reaction. However, the total volume of reaction mixture that is being heated is half the original volume; therefore only half as much heat energy will be required to heat it to the same temperature. The temperature change in this experiment is thus the same as in part **a**, i.e. 6.82 °C.

Consider the following experiment: 100.0 cm^3 of water was measured out and poured into a polystyrene cup and the temperature of the water was taken; 5.20 g of ammonium chloride was measured out. The ammonium chloride was added to the water and the solution stirred vigorously until all the ammonium chloride had dissolved. The minimum temperature was recorded.

The results of this experiment:

Initial temperature of water = 18.3 °C
Minimum temperature = 15.1 °C

Temperature change of the mixture = 3.2 °C

We will assume that the density of the solution is the same as that of water, and so 100.0 cm^3 of solution has a mass of 100.0 g. We can work out how much heat has been absorbed in this reaction by looking at the temperature change of the mixture:

$q = mc\Delta T = 100.0 \times 4.18 \times 3.2 = 1340\,J$

Assumption: the specific heat capacity of the solution is the same as that of water.

To work out the enthalpy change of solution, we need to know how many moles of ammonium chloride dissolved.

no. moles NH$_4$Cl = $\dfrac{\text{mass}}{\text{molar mass}}$

molar mass of NH$_4$Cl = 53.50 g mol^{-1}

Therefore, the number of moles of NH$_4$Cl that dissolve = $\dfrac{5.20}{53.50}$ = 0.0972 mol.

Therefore 1340 J of energy is absorbed when 0.0972 mol NH$_4$Cl dissolve.

The definition of enthalpy change of solution is the enthalpy change when 1 mole of substance dissolves. Therefore, for 1 mole of NH$_4$Cl dissolving:

heat energy absorbed = $\dfrac{1}{0.0972} \times 1340 = 13\,800\,J\,mol^{-1}$

This is positive, as the reaction is endothermic.

Therefore the enthalpy change of solution, $\Delta H_{sol} = +13.8\,kJ\,mol^{-1}$.

The accepted value for the enthalpy change of solution of ammonium chloride is 15.2 kJ mol^{-1}. Errors in this experiment include absorption of heat from the surroundings and the assumptions about the specific heat capacity of the solution being the same as that of water. The mass of the ammonium chloride was also not taken into account when working out the heat energy released in the experiment (i.e. it was not included in the mass of the solution). The results from this experiment are greatly improved by vigorous stirring of the solution, as the ammonium chloride does not dissolve instantaneously. If it is allowed to dissolve slowly, there is more time for heat to be absorbed from the surroundings and the temperature drop is not as large as expected. This effect can be reduced by using the technique of the next experiment.

The following experiment may be used to determine the enthalpy change of reaction for:

$Zn(s) + CuSO_4(aq) \rightarrow ZnSO_4(aq) + Cu(s)$

50.0 cm^3 of 0.200 mol dm^{-3} copper(II) sulfate solution was placed in a polystyrene cup. The temperature was recorded every 30 seconds for two minutes. At 2 minutes 30 seconds, 1.20 g of powdered zinc was added. The mixture was stirred vigorously and the temperature recorded every half minute for several minutes. The results obtained were then plotted to give the graph shown in Figure 5.11.

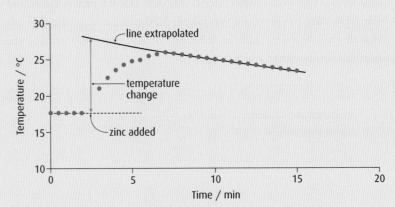

Figure 5.11 Temperature against time for the reaction of zinc with copper sulfate solution.

The problem with this reaction is that it does not occur instantaneously, and so, although heat is being given out in the reaction, at the same time the reaction mixture is also cooling down by losing heat to the surroundings. From the graph it can be seen that there is an initial rise in temperature, where heat being given out by the reaction is the major factor, but after that the reaction mixture cools. By extrapolating the line back from this cooling part of the curve, we can estimate the temperature from which the mixture appears to be cooling. If we look at the value of the temperature on this curve at 2 minutes 30 seconds, the point at which the zinc was added, we should get an estimate of the temperature rise if the reaction had occurred instantaneously. It can be seen that this temperature rise is greater than the temperature rise actually measured in the experiment.

From the graph we estimate the temperature change as 10.3 °C.

The heat given out in the reaction is given by:

> Assumption: the density of copper sulfate solution is the same as that of water.

$$q = mc\Delta T = 50.0 \times 4.18 \times 10.3 = 2150\,J$$

To work out the enthalpy change of reaction, we need to know how many moles of copper sulfate reacted (the zinc was in excess).

$$\text{no. moles of } CuSO_4 = \text{concentration} \times \text{volume in } dm^3$$

$$\text{no. moles of } CuSO_4 = 0.200 \times \frac{50.0}{1000} = 0.010\,mol$$

Therefore 2150 J of energy is released when 0.010 mol of copper sulfate reacts.

For the reaction of 1 mole of copper sulfate:

$$\text{heat energy released} = \frac{1}{0.010} \times 2150 = 215\,000\,J\,mol^{-1}$$

> This is negative, as the reaction is exothermic.

Therefore the enthalpy change of reaction = $-215\,kJ\,mol^{-1}$.

The extrapolation of the line is very much a matter of judgement and could introduce errors into the calculation.

Self-test 2

Test yourself

5 a 200.0 cm³ of 0.150 mol dm⁻³ hydrochloric acid is mixed with 100.0 cm³ of 0.300 mol dm⁻³ sodium hydroxide solution. The temperature rose by 1.36 °C. If both solutions were originally at the same temperature, calculate the enthalpy change of neutralisation.

   b Predict the temperature rise if the experiment in part **a** is repeated using:

   i 400.0 cm³ of 0.150 mol dm⁻³ hydrochloric acid and 200.0 cm³ of 0.300 mol dm⁻³ sodium hydroxide solution

   ii 200.0 cm³ of 0.300 mol dm⁻³ hydrochloric acid and 100.0 cm³ of 0.600 mol dm⁻³ sodium hydroxide solution

   iii 50.0 cm³ of 0.300 mol dm⁻³ hydrochloric acid and 25.0 cm³ of 0.600 mol dm⁻³ sodium hydroxide solution.

6 a When 1.00 g of magnesium chloride is dissolved in 50.0 cm³ of water the temperature goes up from 21.5 °C to 29.1 °C. Calculate the enthalpy change of solution of magnesium chloride.

   b Predict the temperature change when 2.00 g of magnesium chloride is dissolved in 100 cm³ of water.

   c Predict the temperature change when 2.00 g of magnesium chloride is dissolved in 50.0 cm³ of water.

Learning objectives

- Use Hess's law to calculate enthalpy changes

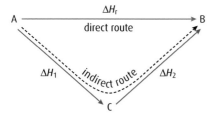

Figure 5.12 An enthalpy cycle.

Extension

This is basically just a question of vectors:

$$\overrightarrow{AB} = \overrightarrow{AC} + \overrightarrow{CB}$$

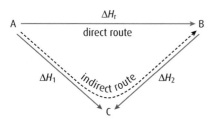

Figure 5.13 If we know the enthalpy change for the conversion B → C rather than C → B, the arrow between B and C is the other way around.

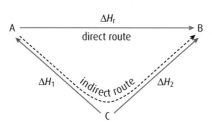

Figure 5.14 If we know the enthalpy change for the conversion C → A rather than A → C, the arrow between A and C is the other way around.

5.3 Hess's law

Hess's law

It is not always possible to design experiments to measure certain enthalpy changes, and so we often have to use data from reactions in which the enthalpy change can be measured to work out the enthalpy change for a particular reaction in which it cannot be measured directly. In order to do this, we use Hess's law.

> The enthalpy change accompanying a chemical reaction is independent of the pathway between the initial and final states.

What this basically means is that, if we consider the conversion of A into B, the enthalpy change for the reaction is the same if we go directly from A to B or indirectly via other reactions and intermediates (Figure **5.12**).

Thus, if we know the value for ΔH_1 (for the conversion of A to C) and ΔH_2 (for the conversion of C to B) we can work out the value of the enthalpy change ΔH_r for the conversion of A into B using this cycle. Hess's law states that the enthalpy change for the direct conversion of A to B is exactly the same as the enthalpy change for the indirect route between A and B. Therefore, in this case:

$$\Delta H_r = \Delta H_1 + \Delta H_2$$

Let us consider a slightly different situation in which the enthalpy changes we know are:

$$A \rightarrow C = \Delta H_1 \qquad B \rightarrow C = \Delta H_2$$

This produces a slightly different cycle, in which the arrow for ΔH_2 is the other way around, because the reaction we know is from B to C (Figure **5.13**). Now, the enthalpy change from A to B is given by: $\Delta H_r = \Delta H_1 - \Delta H_2$. We have $-\Delta H_2$ in this case, as the conversion C → B on the indirect route (A → C → B) goes in the opposite direction to the arrow we have drawn.

Another possible situation is one in which we know:

$$C \rightarrow A = \Delta H_1 \qquad C \rightarrow B = \Delta H_2$$

This is shown in Figure **5.14**. Here the enthalpy change for the direct route is given by: $\Delta H_r = -\Delta H_1 + \Delta H_2$. In going from A → C → B, we go the wrong way along the ΔH_1 arrow (therefore the sign is negative) but the right way along the ΔH_2 arrow (therefore the sign is positive).

Why Hess's law works

The reason Hess's law works can be understood from Figure **5.15**.

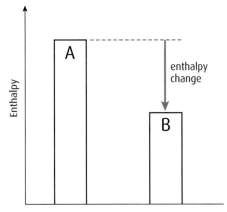

Figure 5.15 Enthalpy is basically a property of a substance under a certain set of conditions. This means that the enthalpy depends on the substance and the conditions. Thus A has a certain amount of enthalpy and B has a certain amount of enthalpy, and these are fixed for a particular set of conditions. The route that is taken between A and B cannot affect the amount of enthalpy A or B have, and therefore the difference in enthalpy between A and B is constant.

Some definitions

Enthalpy changes have different values, depending on the conditions under which they are measured; therefore, to make them transferable, they are all quoted for the same set of conditions, which is called **standard conditions**. If an enthalpy change is not measured under standard conditions, its value is corrected to standard conditions. An enthalpy change under standard conditions is called a **standard enthalpy change** and has the symbol $\Delta H^{\ominus}$, where the symbol $\ominus$ means under standard conditions.

> **Standard enthalpy change of reaction ($\Delta H_r^{\ominus}$)** is the enthalpy change (heat given out or taken in) when molar amounts of reactants as shown in the stoichiometric equation react together under standard conditions to give products.

For example, for the reaction $N_2(g) + 3H_2(g) \rightarrow 2NH_3(g)$, the enthalpy change of reaction is $-92\,kJ\,mol^{-1}$. This means that 92 kJ of heat energy are given out when $1\,mol\,N_2$ reacts with $3\,mol\,N_2$ to form $2\,mol\,NH_3$.

If the equation is written as:

$$\tfrac{1}{2}N_2(g) + \tfrac{3}{2}H_2(g) \rightarrow NH_3(g) \qquad\qquad \Delta H_r^{\ominus} = -46\,kJ\,mol^{-1}$$

then the enthalpy change of reaction is for $0.5\,mol\,N_2$ reacting, and the enthalpy change is half as much.

Working out enthalpy changes

We are not always able to determine enthalpy changes directly from experiments and Hess's law can then be used to work out unknown enthalpy changes from ones that are known.

Extension

Enthalpy is a **state function**.

> **Standard conditions:**
> Pressure = $1.01 \times 10^5\,Pa$
> (1 atmosphere)
> Temperature = $298\,K$ ($25\,°C$)

Extension

For this course we assume that 'standard conditions' refers to a temperature of 298 K. For more advanced work, the temperature should always be stated for a standard enthalpy change. This is often written as $\Delta H_{298}^{\ominus}$ of $\Delta H^{\ominus}(298\,K)$.

Worked examples

Given the following enthalpy changes below, calculate the enthalpy change for the reaction:

$$2CO(g) + O_2(g) \rightarrow 2CO_2(g)$$

$$2C(s) + O_2(g) \rightarrow 2CO(g) \qquad \Delta H^\ominus = -222 \, kJ \, mol^{-1} \qquad \Delta H_1 \qquad \textbf{Reaction 1}$$

$$C(s) + O_2(g) \rightarrow CO_2(g) \qquad \Delta H^\ominus = -394 \, kJ \, mol^{-1} \qquad \Delta H_2 \qquad \textbf{Reaction 2}$$

Three methods will be considered for working out the enthalpy change.

Method A (using a cycle)

The enthalpy changes given are used to construct a cycle. The enthalpy change that we have to find is put at the top of the cycle.

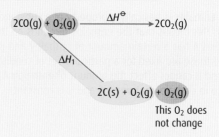

Only the first reaction has been added here. **Reaction 1** is highlighted in yellow and shows the reaction of 2C and 1 O_2 to form 2CO. The other O_2, highlighted in orange, remains unchanged, and there is no enthalpy change for this. This means that the total enthalpy change along the red arrow is ΔH_1.

If **Reaction 2** is now added to complete the cycle, it must be multiplied by 2, as we need to form $2 \, mol \, CO_2$. The enthalpy change must also be multiplied by 2, hence $2\Delta H_2$:

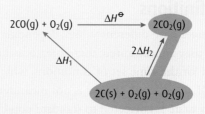

$$2C(s) + 2O_2(g) \rightarrow 2CO_2(g) \qquad 2\Delta H_2$$

Reaction 2 is highlighted in green.

The values can now be put into the cycle:

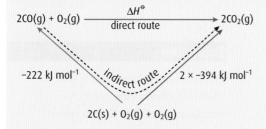

The overall enthalpy change is given by

$$\Delta H^\ominus = -\Delta H_1 + 2\Delta H_2$$

$$\Delta H^\ominus = -(-222) + (2 \times -394) = -566 \, kJ \, mol^{-1}$$

This is worked out from Hess's law: the enthalpy change for the direct route is the same as that for the indirect route. As the direction of the indirect route arrow is opposite to that of the red arrow, the sign of the quantity on the red arrow is reversed.

Method B (manipulating the equations)

In this method we rearrange the equations for the data given to give the equation for the reaction corresponding to the enthalpy change we have to find.

First, **Reaction 1** is reversed to give 2CO on the left-hand side, as in the overall equation:

$$2CO(g) \rightarrow 2C(s) + O_2(g) \qquad \Delta H^{\ominus} = +222\,kJ\,mol^{-1} \qquad \text{sign changed}$$

Now **Reaction 2** is multiplied by 2 to give $2CO_2$ on the right-hand side, as in the overall equation:

$$2C(s) + 2O_2(g) \rightarrow 2CO_2(g) \qquad \Delta H^{\ominus} = -788\,kJ\,mol^{-1} \qquad \text{enthalpy change multiplied by 2}$$

We now have 2CO on the left-hand side and $2CO_2$ on the right-hand side, as in the overall equations. The two equations and their enthalpy changes are now added together and common terms cancelled to produce the overall equation and its enthalpy change:

$$\begin{aligned}
2CO(g) &\rightarrow \cancel{2C}(s) + \cancel{O_2}(g) & \Delta H^{\ominus} &= +222\,kJ\,mol^{-1} \\
\cancel{2C}(s) + \cancel{2}O_2(g) &\rightarrow 2CO_2(g) & \Delta H^{\ominus} &= -788\,kJ\,mol^{-1} \\
\hline
2CO(g) + O_2(g) &\rightarrow 2CO_2(g) & \Delta H^{\ominus} &= -566\,kJ\,mol^{-1}
\end{aligned}$$

Method C (using an enthalpy level diagram)

Figure **5.17** shows an enthalpy level diagram for this reaction.

The total difference in enthalpy between the top and bottom on both sides must be the same, because the diagram starts at a certain enthalpy level (that of $2C + 2O_2$) and ends at a certain level (that of $2CO_2$).

The total enthalpy difference on the left-hand side is $-222 + \Delta H_r$. The total enthalpy difference on the right-hand side is 2×-394, i.e. $-788\,kJ\,mol^{-1}$. The difference in enthalpy on the two sides are equal; therefore $-788 = -222 + \Delta H_r$. Rearranging this we get $\Delta H_r = -566\,kJ\,mol^{-1}$.

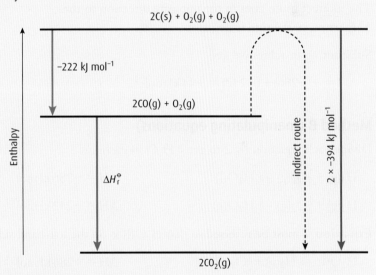

Figure 5.17 Exothermic processes are shown as downward arrows and endothermic processes would be shown as upward arrows.

Using this method for working out the enthalpy change from an enthalpy level diagram can sometimes run into trouble when the arrows of the enthalpy changes do not all go in the same direction on one particular side, and therefore an alternative method for working out the enthalpy change is generally preferred. This uses the same approach as for the cycle, where the enthalpy change for the direct route between reactants and products (shown as $\Delta H_r^{\ominus}$) is equated to the enthalpy change for the indirect route.

Thus we can write:

$$\Delta H_r^{\ominus} = +222 + 2 \times -394 = -566\,kJ\,mol^{-1}$$

The sign of -222 is changed to positive because the indirect route takes us in the opposite direction to this arrow.

Use the enthalpy change data given below to work out the enthalpy change for the process:

$H_2O(l) \rightarrow H_2O(g)$

$2H_2(g) + O_2(g) \rightarrow 2H_2O(l)$	$\Delta H_1 = -572\,kJ\,mol^{-1}$	**Reaction 1**
$2H_2(g) + O_2(g) \rightarrow 2H_2O(g)$	$\Delta H_2 = -484\,kJ\,mol^{-1}$	**Reaction 2**

Method A (enthalpy cycle)

Each enthalpy change given should be divided by 2, as the enthalpy change for the reaction we have to find just involves 1 H_2O:

$$H_2(g) + \tfrac{1}{2}O_2(g) \rightarrow H_2O(l) \qquad \Delta H_3 = -286\,kJ\,mol^{-1}$$

$$H_2(g) + \tfrac{1}{2}O_2(g) \rightarrow H_2O(g) \qquad \Delta H_4 = -242\,kJ\,mol^{-1}$$

A cycle can be constructed.

The enthalpy change for the direct route is the same as that for the indirect route:

$$\Delta H = -\Delta H_3 + \Delta H_4$$

The indirect route goes in the opposite direction to the ΔH_3 arrow, so the sign is negative.

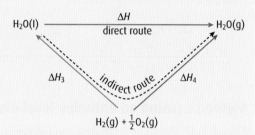

Substituting in values we get:

$$\Delta H = -(-286) + (-242) = +44\,kJ\,mol^{-1}$$

Method B (manipulating equations)

Divide each equation by 2 to get 1 H_2O in each:

$$H_2(g) + \tfrac{1}{2}O_2(g) \rightarrow H_2O(l) \qquad \Delta H = -286\,kJ\,mol^{-1}$$

$$H_2(g) + \tfrac{1}{2}O_2(g) \rightarrow H_2O(g) \qquad \Delta H = -242\,kJ\,mol^{-1}$$

Equation 1 must be reversed so that $H_2O(l)$ is on the left-hand side, as in the overall equation:

$$H_2O(l) \rightarrow H_2(g) + \tfrac{1}{2}O_2(g) \qquad \Delta H = +286\,kJ\,mol^{-1}$$

We now have the correct numbers of H_2O on the correct sides and can add the two equations together:

$$H_2O(l) \rightarrow \cancel{H_2(g)} + \cancel{\tfrac{1}{2}O_2(g)} \qquad \Delta H = +286\,kJ\,mol^{-1}$$
$$\cancel{H_2(g)} + \cancel{\tfrac{1}{2}O_2(g)} \rightarrow H_2O(g) \qquad \Delta H = -242\,kJ\,mol^{-1}$$
$$\overline{H_2O(l) \rightarrow H_2O(g) \qquad \Delta H = +44\,kJ\,mol^{-1}}$$

Method C (enthalpy level diagram)

Each enthalpy change given should be divided by 2 as the enthalpy change for the reaction we have to find just involves 1 H_2O:

$$H_2(g) + \tfrac{1}{2}O_2(g) \rightarrow H_2O(l) \qquad \Delta H_3 = -286\,kJ\,mol^{-1}$$

$$H_2(g) + \tfrac{1}{2}O_2(g) \rightarrow H_2O(g) \qquad \Delta H_4 = -242\,kJ\,mol^{-1}$$

We can construct an enthalpy level diagram:

The enthalpy change for the direct route is the same as that for the indirect route:

$$\Delta H = -\Delta H_3 + \Delta H_4$$

The indirect route goes in the opposite direction to the ΔH_3 arrow, so the sign is negative.

Substituting in values we get:

$$\Delta H = -(-286) + (-242) = +44\,\text{kJ}\,\text{mol}^{-1}$$

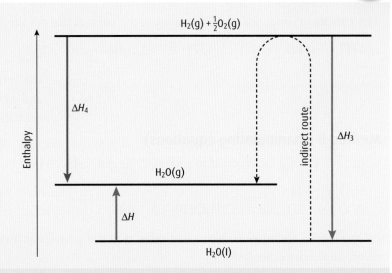

A more complicated enthalpy change calculation can be attempted if we consider the reaction:

$$C_2H_4(g) + H_2O(g) \rightarrow C_2H_5OH(l)$$

Use the following information to work out the enthalpy change for this reaction:

$H_2O(l) \rightarrow H_2O(g)$	$\Delta H_1 = +44\,\text{kJ}\,\text{mol}^{-1}$	**Reaction 1**
$C_2H_5OH(l) + 3O_2(g) \rightarrow 2CO_2(g) + 3H_2O(l)$	$\Delta H_2 = -1371\,\text{kJ}\,\text{mol}^{-1}$	**Reaction 2**
$C_2H_4(g) + 3O_2(g) \rightarrow 2CO_2(g) + 2H_2O(l)$	$\Delta H_3 = -1409\,\text{kJ}\,\text{mol}^{-1}$	**Reaction 3**

Method A (enthalpy cycle)

The following cycle can be constructed:

$$C_2H_4(g) + H_2O(g)\ (+3O_2(g)) \xrightarrow{\ \Delta H^{\ominus}\ } C_2H_5OH(l)\ (+3O_2(g))$$

$\Delta H_3 \searrow$

$2CO_2(g) + 2H_2O(l) + H_2O(g)$

ΔH_2

ΔH_1

$2CO_2(g) + 2H_2O(l) + H_2O(l)$

$3O_2(g)$ has been added to each side of the original equation, but as the same thing has been added to both sides, this does not affect the overall enthalpy change.

This cycle shows the individual enthalpy changes involved. All arrows are drawn in the same direction as the equations given. The values can be substituted into the cycle:

$$C_2H_4(g) + H_2O(g)\ (+3O_2(g)) \xrightarrow[\text{direct route}]{\ \Delta H^{\ominus}\ } C_2H_5OH(l)\ (+3O_2(g))$$

$-1409\,\text{kJ}\,\text{mol}^{-1}$

$2CO_2(g) + 2H_2O(l) + H_2O(g)$

indirect route $-1371\,\text{kJ}\,\text{mol}^{-1}$

$+44\,\text{kJ}\,\text{mol}^{-1}$

$2CO_2(g) + 2H_2O(l) + H_2O(l)$

The arrow for the indirect route goes in the opposite direction to the arrow for the enthalpy changes ΔH_1 and ΔH_2.

The enthalpy change for the direct route is the same as that for the indirect route.

$$\Delta H^{\ominus} = -1409 - (+44) - (-1371) = -82\,\text{kJ}\,\text{mol}^{-1}$$

> The cycle could have been simplified by reversing the enthalpy change ΔH_1 and incorporating ΔH_1 and ΔH_3 into one step, but care must be then taken with the sign of ΔH_1.

Method B (manipulating equations)

Reactions **1** and **2** are reversed to give $H_2O(g)$ and C_2H_5OH on the correct sides:

$H_2O(g) \rightarrow H_2O(l)$	$\Delta H_1 = -44\,\text{kJ}\,\text{mol}^{-1}$
$2CO_2(g) + 3H_2O(l) \rightarrow C_2H_5OH(l) + 3O_2(g)$	$\Delta H_2 = +1371\,\text{kJ}\,\text{mol}^{-1}$

All the species are now on the correct sides, as in the overall equation. These equations are now added and common species cancelled:

$H_2O(g) \rightarrow \cancel{H_2O}(l)$	$\Delta H_1 = -44\,\text{kJ}\,\text{mol}^{-1}$
$2\cancel{CO_2}(g) + 3\cancel{H_2O}(l) \rightarrow C_2H_5OH(l) + 3\cancel{O_2}(g)$	$\Delta H_2 = +1371\,\text{kJ}\,\text{mol}^{-1}$
$C_2H_4(g) + 3\cancel{O_2}(g) \rightarrow 2\cancel{CO_2}(g) + 2\cancel{H_2O}(l)$	$\Delta H_3 = -1409\,\text{kJ}\,\text{mol}^{-1}$
$C_2H_4(g) + H_2O(g) \rightarrow C_2H_5OH(l)$	$\Delta H = -82\,\text{kJ}\,\text{mol}^{-1}$

Method C (enthalpy level diagram)

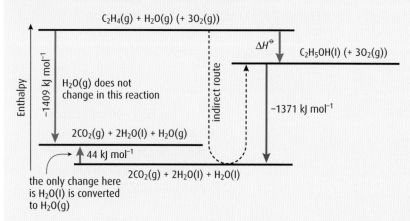

$3O_2$ is added to both sides of the equation, as this is required for the combustion reactions, but this does not change the enthalpy change that we are calculating, as it is exactly the same on both sides.

Because the arrows on the left-hand side go in opposite directions, it is much easier to work out the enthalpy change in terms of the direct and indirect route between reactants and products.

$$\Delta H^{\ominus} = -1409 - 44 + 1371 = -82\,\text{kJ}\,\text{mol}^{-1}$$

> The signs of two of the enthalpy changes were reversed, as the indirect route arrow goes in the opposite direction to those two arrows.

Examiner's tip
Only one of these methods needs to be understood. Find a method that you are happy with and ignore the others!

Test yourself

7 a Use the data below to calculate the enthalpy change for the process:

$C_2H_5OH(l) \rightarrow C_2H_5OH(g)$

$C_2H_5OH(l) + 3O_2(g) \rightarrow 2CO_2(g) + 3H_2O(l)$ $\Delta H = -1371\,kJ\,mol^{-1}$

$C_2H_5OH(g) + 3O_2(g) \rightarrow 2CO_2(g) + 3H_2O(l)$ $\Delta H = -1415\,kJ\,mol^{-1}$

  b Use the data below to calculate the enthalpy change for the process:

$C_6H_6(l) \rightarrow C_6H_6(g)$

$2C_6H_6(l) + 15O_2(g) \rightarrow 12CO_2(g) + 6H_2O(l)$ $\Delta H = -6544\,kJ\,mol^{-1}$

$2C_6H_6(g) + 15O_2(g) \rightarrow 12CO_2(g) + 6H_2O(l)$ $\Delta H = -6606\,kJ\,mol^{-1}$

8 a Use the data below to calculate the enthalpy change for the reaction:

$BrF(g) + 2F_2(g) \rightarrow BrF_5(l)$

$BrF(g) + F_2(g) \rightarrow BrF_3(l)$ $\Delta H = -242\,kJ\,mol^{-1}$

$BrF_3(l) + F_2(g) \rightarrow BrF_5(l)$ $\Delta H = -158\,kJ\,mol^{-1}$

  b Use the data below to calculate the enthalpy change for the reaction:

$ClF_3(g) + F_2(g) \rightarrow ClF_5(g)$

$Cl_2(g) + 3F_2(g) \rightarrow 2ClF_3(g)$ $\Delta H = -328\,kJ\,mol^{-1}$

$Cl_2(g) + 5F_2(g) \rightarrow 2ClF_5(g)$ $\Delta H = -510\,kJ\,mol^{-1}$

9 Use the data below to work out an enthalpy change for the reaction:

$C_2H_2(g) + 2H_2(g) \rightarrow C_2H_6(g)$

$C_2H_2(g) + 2\frac{1}{2}O_2(g) \rightarrow 2CO_2(g) + H_2O(l)$ $\Delta H = -1300\,kJ\,mol^{-1}$

$H_2(g) + \frac{1}{2}O_2(g) \rightarrow H_2O(l)$ $\Delta H = -286\,kJ\,mol^{-1}$

$C_2H_6(g) + 3\frac{1}{2}O_2(g) \rightarrow 2CO_2(g) + 3H_2O(l)$ $\Delta H = -1560\,kJ\,mol^{-1}$

5.4 Bond enthalpies

Enthalpy changes for reactions in the gas phase can be worked out if we know the amount of energy required/released when bonds are broken/made. To be able to do this we must first consider the definition of bond enthalpy (also just called **bond energy**):

> **bond enthalpy** is the enthalpy change when 1 mole of covalent bonds, in a gaseous molecule, are broken under standard conditions.

For example, the H–H bond enthalpy is $436\,kJ\,mol^{-1}$, which can be represented by the equation:

$H_2(g) \rightarrow 2H(g)$ $\Delta H^\ominus = +436\,kJ\,mol^{-1}$

1 mole of H_2 molecules is broken apart to give 2 moles of gaseous hydrogen atoms.

Learning objectives

- Define average bond enthalpy
- Use bond energies to calculate enthalpy changes

The H–Cl bond enthalpy is $431\,\text{kJ}\,\text{mol}^{-1}$, which is represented by:

$$HCl(g) \rightarrow H(g) + Cl(g) \qquad\qquad \Delta H^{\ominus} = +431\,\text{kJ}\,\text{mol}^{-1}$$

$HCl(g) \rightarrow \frac{1}{2}H_2(g) + \frac{1}{2}Cl_2(g)$
does **not** represent the bond
enthalpy of HCl. $\frac{1}{2}H_2(g)$
represents half a mole of H_2
molecules and is not the same
as $H(g)$, which is 1 mole of
gaseous H atoms.

Bond enthalpies can be calculated only for substances in the gaseous state.

If we consider the process:

$$Br_2(l) \rightarrow 2Br(g) \qquad\qquad \Delta H^{\ominus} = +224\,\text{kJ}\,\text{mol}^{-1}$$

This does not represent the bond enthalpy of the Br–Br bond, as this reaction can be broken down into two processes:

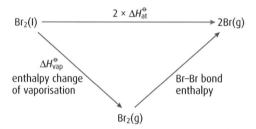

The Br–Br bond enthalpy is $193\,\text{kJ}\,\text{mol}^{-1}$, and the enthalpy change of vaporisation (for formation of 1 mol gaseous molecules) is $31\,\text{kJ}\,\text{mol}^{-1}$.

The process $Br_2(l) \rightarrow 2Br(g)$ is called atomisation, and energy must be supplied to break the van der Waals' forces between the bromine molecules as well as to break the Br–Br bonds. The enthalpy change for this process is twice the enthalpy change of atomisation (ΔH_{at}).

$\Delta H^{\ominus}_{at}$ is the enthalpy change for formation of 1 mole of gaseous atoms.

Energy must be supplied to break apart two atoms in a molecule against the attractive force holding them together. Therefore, the process of breaking bonds must be endothermic, i.e. the enthalpy change is positive.

Energy is released when two atoms come together to form a bond. Therefore, the process of making bonds is exothermic, i.e. the enthalpy change is negative.

Bond breaking requires energy (endothermic): ΔH positive.
Bond making releases energy (exothermic): ΔH negative.

Bond enthalpies are defined in terms of **breaking** bonds and, therefore, have **positive** values.

Some average bond enthalpies are shown in Table **5.1**.

The bond energies given in tables are **average** values. For example, the C–H bond energy is slightly different in ethane (C_2H_6) from that in benzene (C_6H_6), so the value quoted in the tables is an average value, averaged over the values for the C–H bond in many compounds. This can introduce some inaccuracies into calculations involving bond energies. Bond energy calculations are therefore most accurate when they involve only breaking/making a few bonds.

Bond	Bond enthalpy /kJ mol^{-1}	Bond	Bond enthalpy /kJ mol^{-1}	Bond	Bond enthalpy /kJ mol^{-1}	Bond	Bond enthalpy /kJ mol^{-1}
H–H	436	C–H	412	O–O	146	C–O	360
C–C	348	Si–H	318	O=O	496	C=O	743
C=C	612	N–H	388	Si–O	374	C≡O	1070
C≡C	837	P–H	322	F–F	158	C–N	305
Si–Si	226	O–H	463	Cl–Cl	242	C=N	613
N–N	163	S–H	338	Br–Br	193	C≡N	890
N=N	409	F–H	562	I–I	151	C–F	484
N≡N	944	Cl–H	431	N–Cl	200	C–Cl	338
P–P	172	Br–H	366	Si–F	590	C–Br	276
S–S	264	I–H	299	N–F	278	C–I	238

Table 5.1 Average bond enthalpies.

Average bond enthalpy is the average amount of energy required to break 1 mole of covalent bonds, in a gaseous molecule under standard conditions. 'Average' refers to the fact that the bond enthalpy is different in different molecules and therefore the value quoted is the average amount of energy to break a particular bond in a range of molecules.

Extension

Why is bond making exothermic?
When two atoms are a long way apart, the electrical potential energy of the two together is a maximum (consider separating the two atoms from where they are bonded together to where they are an infinite distance apart – work must be done against the force holding them together, so the potential energy increases). As they approach closer together, owing to the attractive force between them, the potential energy decreases and this energy is released as heat. This can be likened to a ball falling to Earth – as the ball and the Earth come together, the potential energy of the system is first of all converted to kinetic energy and then to heat as the two collide.

Using bond enthalpies to work out enthalpy changes for reactions

Example

Consider the reaction between ethene and bromine to produce 1,2–dibromoethane:

$$C_2H_4(g) + Br_2(g) \rightarrow C_2H_4Br_2(g)$$

What is the enthalpy change for this reaction?

If the species are drawn as structural formulas, then all the bonds can be seen clearly:

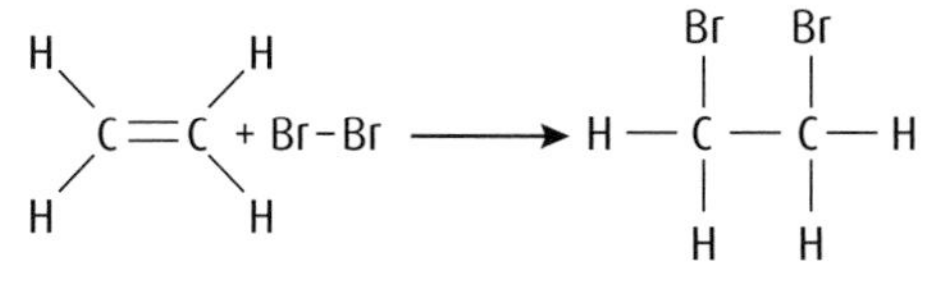

Bromine and 1,2-dibromoethane are both liquids under standard conditions. The equation here is for the reaction in the gas phase, and the enthalpy change will not be the same as for the reaction involving liquid bromine to form $C_2H_4Br_2(l)$.

This is **not** how the reaction occurs, it is just a way of allowing us to work out the enthalpy change.

We imagine the reaction happening with all the bonds in the reactant being broken:

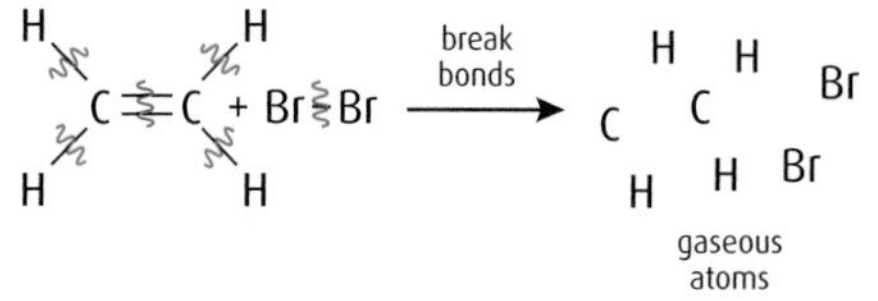

Then new bonds form to make the products:

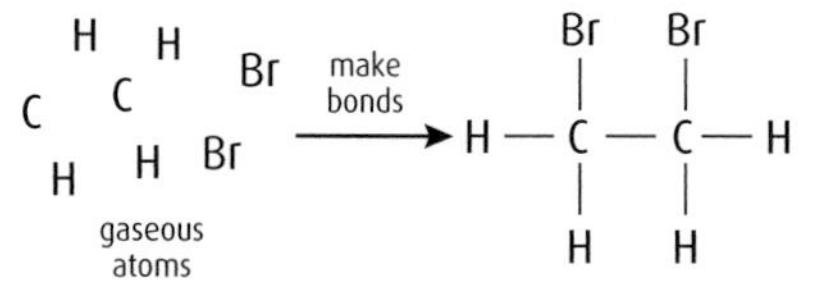

The bond energies can then be added up to work out the enthalpy change:

Bond broken	Bond energy / $kJ\,mol^{-1}$	Number of bonds	Total energy / $kJ\,mol^{-1}$
C–H	412	4	1648
C=C	612	1	612
Br–Br	193	1	193
Total energy to break all bonds			2453

The total enthalpy change when all the bonds are broken is $+2453\,kJ\,mol^{-1}$. This is positive, as breaking bonds is an endothermic process.

Bond made	Bond energy / $kJ\,mol^{-1}$	Number of bonds	Total energy / $kJ\,mol^{-1}$
C–H	412	4	1648
C–C	348	1	348
C–Br	276	2	552
Total energy released when bonds made			2548

The total enthalpy change when all the bonds are made is $-2548\,kJ\,mol^{-1}$. This is negative, as making bonds is an exothermic process.

If we add up these enthalpy changes, we get the overall enthalpy change for the reaction:

$$\Delta H^{\ominus} = 2453 - 2548 = -95\,kJ\,mol^{-1}$$

The overall process is sometimes summarised as:

$$\Delta H_r = \Sigma(\text{bonds broken}) - \Sigma(\text{bonds made})$$

where the bond energies are taken directly from the bond energies table and no signs changed, i.e. all values are put in as positive.

This approach would give:

$$\Delta H^{\ominus} = [(4 \times 412) + (1 \times 612) + (1 \times 193)] - [(4 \times 412) + (1 \times 348) + (2 \times 276)]$$

A shortcut to do this question would be to realise that there are four C–H bonds in ethene and four C–H bonds in 1,2-dibromoethane, and therefore there is no need to make or break these bonds:

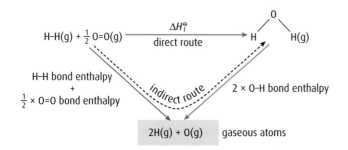

If the enthalpy change for

$$C_2H_4(g) + Br_2(g) \rightarrow C_2H_4Br_2(g)$$

is calculated using enthalpy changes of formation (see Higher Level section on page **207**), the value obtained is $-121\,\text{kJ}\,\text{mol}^{-1}$, which is different from the value of $-95\,\text{kJ}\,\text{mol}^{-1}$ obtained through bond enthalpy calculations. The value obtained from the enthalpy changes of formation is expected to be more reliable, as the enthalpy changes of formation are specific to the particular substances, whereas the bond enthalpies are average values. The C–H bond energies in C_2H_4 and $C_2H_4Br_2$ would not be expected to be the same, and the values used for the C=C and C–C bonds are not necessarily the actual bond energies in these compounds.

Extension

The hybridisation of the C atom can significantly affect the C–H bond enthalpy.

Using a cycle in calculations involving bond enthalpies

Example

Using bond enthalpies given in the table, we can calculate the enthalpy change for the reaction:

$$H_2(g) + \tfrac{1}{2}O_2(g) \rightarrow H_2O(g)$$

A cycle can be drawn:

Bond	Bond enthalpy / kJ mol^{-1}
H–H	436
O=O	496
O–H	463

H–H(g) + $\tfrac{1}{2}$O=O(g) $\xrightarrow[\text{direct route}]{\Delta H_f^{\ominus}}$ H$\overset{O}{\diagdown}$H(g)

H–H bond enthalpy
+
$\tfrac{1}{2}$ × O=O bond enthalpy

indirect route

2 × O–H bond enthalpy

2H(g) + O(g)   gaseous atoms

A reaction in the gas phase will be endothermic if less energy is released when bonds are formed (exothermic) than is required to break bonds (endothermic). This could be the case if stronger/more bonds are broken than are formed.

A reaction in the gas phase will be exothermic if more energy is released when bonds are formed (exothermic) than is required to break bonds (endothermic). This could be the case if stronger/more bonds are made than are broken.

The values can be substituted into the cycle:

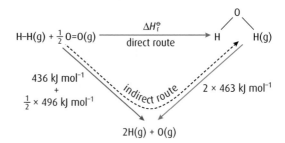

The enthalpy change for the direct route is the same as that for the indirect route. The direction of the arrow for the indirect route is opposite to that of the red arrow, and therefore the sign of this enthalpy change must be reversed.

$$\Delta H_r^\ominus = (436 + \tfrac{1}{2} \times 496) - (2 \times 463) = -242\,\text{kJ}\,\text{mol}^{-1}$$

If we wanted to find the enthalpy change for the formation of liquid water from its elements, i.e. for the process:

$$H_2(g) + \tfrac{1}{2}O_2(g) \rightarrow H_2O(l)$$

we would also have to know the enthalpy change of vaporisation of water, i.e. the enthalpy change for the process:

$$H_2O(l) \rightarrow H_2O(g) \qquad \Delta H_{vap} = +41\,\text{kJ}\,\text{mol}^{-1}$$

This can be incorporated in to the cycle above as:

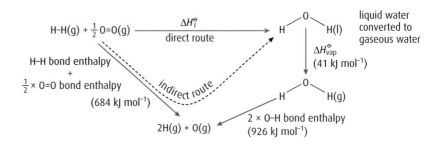

The enthalpy change for the reaction is:

$$\Delta H_r^\ominus = 684 - 926 - 41 = -283\,\text{kJ}\,\text{mol}^{-1}$$

Working out a bond enthalpy from an enthalpy change of reaction

Example

Using the bond enthalpies for the F–F and Br–Br bonds and the enthalpy change of reaction given, we can calculate the mean Br–F bond energy in BrF$_3$:

$$Br_2(g) + 3F_2(g) \rightarrow 2BrF_3(g) \qquad \Delta H^\ominus = -545\,\text{kJ}\,\text{mol}^{-1}$$

This is most easily done using the equation:

$$\Delta H_r = \Sigma(\text{bonds broken}) - \Sigma(\text{bonds made})$$

$$-545 = [193 + (3 \times 158)] - [6 \times \text{Br–F}]$$

Rearranging this we get:

$$6 \times \text{Br–F} = 193 + (3 \times 158) + 545$$

$$6 \times \text{Br–F} = 1212$$

Therefore the Br–F bond enthalpy is $\frac{1212}{6}$, i.e. $202\,\text{kJ}\,\text{mol}^{-1}$.

Using bond enthalpies and enthalpies of atomisation

In order to use bond enthalpies, the substances **must be in the gas phase**. This is because intermolecular forces must also be taken into account in the liquid and solid states. Thus, in order to use bond enthalpies with solids and liquids we must first generate gaseous species. This can either be done as above, using the enthalpy change of vaporisation or, more directly, using the standard enthalpy change of atomisation.

> **Standard enthalpy change of atomisation ($\Delta H_{at}^{\ominus}$)** is the enthalpy change when 1 mole of gaseous atoms is formed from the element under standard conditions.

For example:

$$\tfrac{1}{2}H_2(g) \rightarrow H(g) \qquad \Delta H_{at}^{\ominus} = +218\,\text{kJ}\,\text{mol}^{-1}$$
$$\tfrac{1}{2}Cl_2(g) \rightarrow Cl(g) \qquad \Delta H_{at}^{\ominus} = +121\,\text{kJ}\,\text{mol}^{-1}$$
$$Na(s) \rightarrow Na(g) \qquad \Delta H_{at}^{\ominus} = +109\,\text{kJ}\,\text{mol}^{-1}$$

The use of the enthalpy change of atomisation can most easily be seen with an example.

Example

We can calculate the enthalpy change for the process:

$$3C(s) + 4H_2(g) \rightarrow C_3H_8(g)$$

using the data in the table and the enthalpy change of atomisation of carbon:

$$C(s) \rightarrow C(g) \qquad \Delta H_{at}^{\ominus} = 715\,\text{kJ}\,\text{mol}^{-1}$$

Note: formation of **1 mole of atoms**.

ΔH_{at} is endothermic

The values for the enthalpy changes of atomisation of hydrogen and chlorine are half the bond enthalpy values in Table **5.1** on page **201**. The bond enthalpy for Cl_2 refers to breaking 1 mole of covalent bonds to produce 2 moles of gaseous atoms, whereas the enthalpy change of atomisation for chlorine refers to breaking half a mole of covalent bonds to produce 1 mole of gaseous atoms.

Bond	Bond enthalpy / kJ mol⁻¹
C–H	412
H–H	436
C–C	348

A cycle can be used to work out the overall enthalpy change:

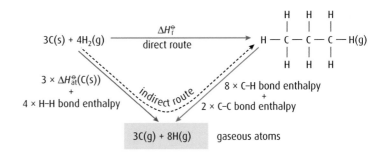

In the left-hand process, represented by the blue arrow, the enthalpy change of atomisation is used to convert carbon into gaseous atoms. The values can be substituted into the cycle:

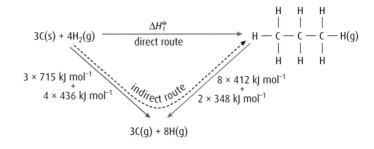

The published value for this enthalpy change is $-104\,\text{kJ}\,\text{mol}^{-1}$; so, in this case, there is fairly good agreement between data worked out using bond enthalpies and in other ways.

The value of the unknown enthalpy change is given by:

$$\Delta H^{\ominus} = ((3 \times 715) + (4 \times 436)) - ((8 \times 412) + (2 \times 348))$$

$$\Delta H^{\ominus} = -103\,\text{kJ}\,\text{mol}^{-1}$$

Self-test 4

Test yourself

10 Use the bond enthalpies in Table **5.1** on page **201** to work out the enthalpy changes for the following reactions:
  a $CH_4(g) + Cl_2(g) \rightarrow CH_3Cl(g) + HCl(g)$
  b $C_2H_2(g) + 2H_2(g) \rightarrow C_2H_6(g)$
  c $CO(g) + Cl_2(g) \rightarrow COCl_2(g)$

11 Calculate the mean Cl–F bond enthalpy, given the following data:
  $Cl_2(g) + 3F_2(g) \rightarrow 2ClF_3(g)$ $\Delta H^{\ominus} = -164\,\text{kJ}\,\text{mol}^{-1}$
  and the Cl–Cl and F–F bond enthalpies in Table **5.1** (page **201**).

  Both ClF_3 and ClF_5 just contain single bonds between Cl and F.

12 Calculate the mean Cl–F bond energy, given the following data:
  $ClF_3(g) + F_2(g) \rightarrow ClF_5(g)$ $\Delta H^{\ominus} = -91\,\text{kJ}\,\text{mol}^{-1}$
  and the F–F bond enthalpy in Table **5.1** (page **201**).

13 Work out the enthalpy change for the following reaction:
  $S(s) + F_2(g) \rightarrow SF_2(g)$

Enthalpy change of atomisation of sulfur / kJ mol⁻¹	223
S–F bond energy / kJ mol⁻¹	327
F–F bond energy / kJ mol⁻¹	158

5.5 Calculating enthalpy changes

HL

Some more definitions

> **Standard enthalpy change of combustion ($\Delta H_c^{\ominus}$)** is the enthalpy change when 1 mole of a substance is completely burnt in oxygen under standard conditions.

The standard enthalpy change of combustion is always negative, as combustion is always an **exothermic** process. For example:

$$CH_4(g) + 2O_2(g) \rightarrow CO_2(g) + 2H_2O(l) \qquad \Delta H_c^{\ominus} = -890\,kJ\,mol^{-1}$$

> **Standard enthalpy change of formation ($\Delta H_f^{\ominus}$)** is the enthalpy change when 1 mole of the substance is formed from its elements in their standard states under standard conditions.

The equation that represents the enthalpy change of formation of methane is:

$$C(s) + 2H_2(g) \rightarrow CH_4(g)$$

Or, for ammonia, the enthalpy change of formation is for the reaction:

$$\tfrac{1}{2}N_2(g) + \tfrac{3}{2}H_2(g) \rightarrow NH_3(g)$$

which shows the formation of **1 mole** of ammonia.

The standard state of nitrogen is $N_2(g)$, whereas that of iodine is $I_2(s)$. These are the states in which these substances exist at 25 °C and 1 atmosphere pressure.

The standard enthalpy change of formation of any element in its standard state is zero because, by definition, no heat energy is taken in or given out when 1 mole of element in its standard state is formed from 1 mole of element in its standard state.

$$I_2(s) \rightarrow I_2(s) \qquad\qquad \Delta H_f^{\ominus} = 0$$

The standard enthalpy change of formation may be exothermic or endothermic, depending on the substance.

In the next sections we will look at how to use given values for enthalpy changes to work out other enthalpy changes.

Using standard enthalpy change of combustion data to calculate enthalpy changes

Given the following enthalpy changes of combustion, we can work out the enthalpy change for the reaction:

$$C_2H_4(g) + H_2(g) \rightarrow C_2H_6(g)$$

Learning objectives

- Calculate enthalpy changes, given standard enthalpy changes of formation or combustion

Examiner's tip
Although this section is Higher Level only, Standard Level students may also find a study of the examples useful practice in solving problems involving enthalpy changes.

The carbon here is graphite, which is the most stable form of carbon.

Standard state is the physical state in which a substance exists under standard conditions. More precisely, it is the state in which the pure substance exists at 1 atm and a specified temperature (assume 298 K).

$\Delta H_f^{\ominus}$ for any element in its standard state is zero.

Note: state symbols must always be included in equations for enthalpy changes, as the enthalpy change will be different depending on the state of a substance. For example, the standard enthalpy change of formation of $I_2(g)$ is not zero.

	$\Delta H_c^{\ominus}$ / kJ mol^{-1}
$C_2H_4(g)$	−1409
$H_2(g)$	−286
$C_2H_6(g)$	−1560

The processes on the left-hand (blue) arrow are the combustion of the reactants to form carbon dioxide and water. The process on the right-hand (red) arrow is the combustion of the product to form exactly the same combustion products as the reactants. $3\frac{1}{2}O_2$ is added to both sides of the original equation, as oxygen is needed for the combustion reactions. However, as the same amount of oxygen is added to both sides, this makes no difference to the overall enthalpy change.

This is worked out from Hess's law: the enthalpy change for the direct route is the same as that for the indirect route. As the direction of the indirect route arrow is opposite to that of the red arrow, the sign of the quantity on the red arrow is reversed.

The reaction(s) for the combustion of the **product(s)** is/are always reversed.

HL We are given enthalpy change of combustion data, so we know the enthalpy changes for the following reactions:

$$C_2H_4(g) + 3O_2(g) \rightarrow 2CO_2(g) + 2H_2O(l) \qquad \Delta H_c^{\ominus} = -1409 \text{ kJ mol}^{-1}$$

$$H_2(g) + \tfrac{1}{2}O_2(g) \rightarrow H_2O(l) \qquad \Delta H_c^{\ominus} = -286 \text{ kJ mol}^{-1}$$

$$C_2H_6(g) + 3\tfrac{1}{2}O_2(g) \rightarrow 2CO_2(g) + 3H_2O(l) \qquad \Delta H_c^{\ominus} = -1560 \text{ kJ mol}^{-1}$$

Four different methods for doing this type of question will be looked at.

Method 1

An enthalpy cycle can be constructed:

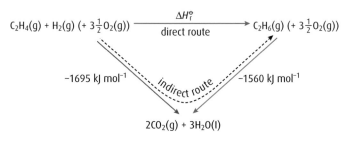

$$\Delta H_c[C_2H_4(g)] + \Delta H_c[H_2(g)] = -1409 - 286 = -1695 \text{ kJ mol}^{-1}$$

The values can be substituted into the cycle:

$$\Delta H_r^{\ominus} = -1695 - (-1560) = -135 \text{ kJ mol}^{-1}$$

The standard enthalpy change for this reaction is −135 kJ mol^{-1}.

Note: at no point is any carbon dioxide or water formed in this reaction. The cycle represents a way of working out the enthalpy change – it does not indicate how the reaction actually occurred.

Method 2

The equations given above must be rearranged to give the overall equations related to the enthalpy change we are trying to find. In order to do this, the third enthalpy change is reversed, so that C_2H_6 appears on the right-hand side, as in the overall reaction.

Substances that are the same on both sides are cancelled out, and that leaves the overall equation. The enthalpy changes are simply added up to give the enthalpy change of reaction.

$$C_2H_4(g) + 3O_2(g) \rightarrow 2CO_2(g) + 2H_2O(l) \quad \Delta H_c^\ominus = -1409 \text{ kJ mol}^{-1}$$

$$H_2(g) + \tfrac{1}{2}O_2(g) \rightarrow H_2O(l) \quad\quad\quad \Delta H_c^\ominus = -286 \text{ kJ mol}^{-1}$$

$$2CO_2(g) + 3H_2O(l) \rightarrow C_2H_6(g) + 3\tfrac{1}{2}O_2(g) \; -\Delta H_c^\ominus = +1560 \text{ kJ mol}^{-1}$$

$$\overline{C_2H_4(g) + H_2(g) \rightarrow C_2H_6(g) \quad\quad\quad \Delta H_r^\ominus = -135 \text{ kJ mol}^{-1}}$$

Let us look at this technique in more detail:

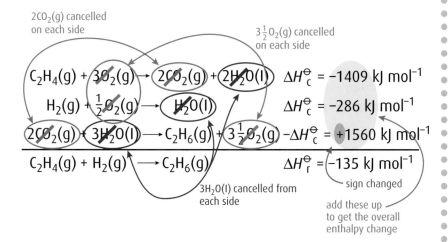

Method 3

In this method we will use an enthalpy level diagram to calculate the enthalpy change:

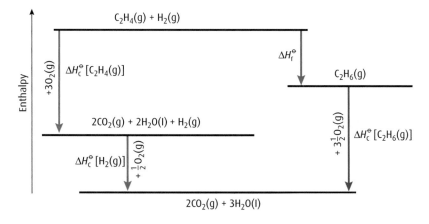

A downward arrow in the diagram represents an exothermic process and an upward arrow represents an endothermic process.

HL The values can be substituted into the diagram:

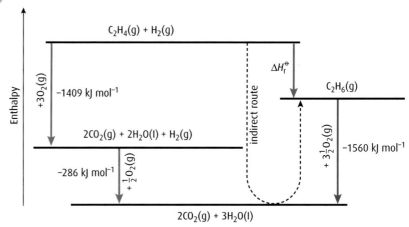

The enthalpy change for the direct route (marked as $\Delta H_r^{\ominus}$) is equal to that for the indirect route. We can therefore write:

$$\Delta H_r^{\ominus} = -1409 - 286 + 1560$$

The sign of the enthalpy change marked in blue is reversed, as the indirect route goes in the opposite direction to this arrow.

Therefore:

$$\Delta H_r^{\ominus} = -135 \, \text{kJ mol}^{-1}$$

Method 4

The last method uses an equation:

$$\Delta H_r = \Sigma \Delta H_c (\text{reactants}) - \Sigma \Delta H_c (\text{products})$$

So:

$$\Delta H_r = [-1409 + (-286)] - [-1560] = -1695 + 1560$$

$$\Delta H_r = -135 \, \text{kJ mol}^{-1}$$

Because the arrows on individual sides all go in the same direction, we could have also equated the total enthalpy change on the left-hand side to that on the right-hand side.

Σ means 'sum of'

Examiner's tip
You only need to use one of the methods to solve problems. Find a method that you are happy with and use that in each case.

Worked example

Given the following enthalpy changes of combustion, work out the enthalpy change of formation of benzoic acid ($C_6H_5COOH(s)$).

	$\Delta H_c^{\ominus} / \text{kJ mol}^{-1}$
C(s)	−394
$H_2(g)$	−286
$C_6H_5COOH(s)$	−3227

The equation for the enthalpy change of formation is:

$$7C(s) + 3H_2(g) + O_2(g) \rightarrow C_6H_5COOH(s)$$

Enthalpy change of formation: formation of 1 mole of substance from its constituent elements in their standard states.

As in the previous example, the data that we have been given are enthalpy changes of combustion, so the methods used will be the same as above.

Method 1 (cycle)

The information given is:

$$C(s) + O_2(g) \rightarrow CO_2(g) \qquad\qquad \Delta H_c^\ominus = -394 \, \text{kJ mol}^{-1}$$

$$H_2(g) + \tfrac{1}{2}O_2(g) \rightarrow H_2O(l) \qquad\qquad \Delta H_c^\ominus = -286 \, \text{kJ mol}^{-1}$$

$$C_6H_5COOH(s) + 7\tfrac{1}{2}O_2(g) \rightarrow 7CO_2(g) + 3H_2O(l) \qquad\qquad \Delta H_c^\ominus = -3227 \, \text{kJ mol}^{-1}$$

This can be used to construct an enthalpy cycle. The quantity we need to find is written along the top, and the arrows from both sides go **down** to the combustion products:

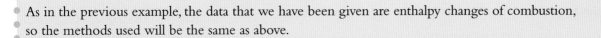

The enthalpy change of combustion of C must be multiplied by 7, as there are 7 moles of C on the left-hand side of the equation. Similarly, the enthalpy change of combustion of H_2 is multiplied by 3.

Total enthalpy change for combustion of reactants:

$$(7 \times -394) + (3 \times -286) = -3616 \, \text{kJ mol}^{-1}$$

The values can be put into the cycle:

There is no enthalpy change of combustion for oxygen, as oxygen does not burn in oxygen! The O_2 on the left-hand side is incorporated into the CO_2 and H_2O of the combustion products.

The indirect route goes in the opposite direction to the red arrow, therefore the sign of this enthalpy change is reversed.

The enthalpy change for the direct route is equal to the enthalpy change for the indirect route:

$$\Delta H_f^\ominus = -3616 - (-3227)$$

Therefore the standard enthalpy change of formation of benzoic acid is $-389 \, \text{kJ mol}^{-1}$.

Method 2 (manipulating equations)

$$C(s) + O_2(g) \rightarrow CO_2(g) \qquad\qquad \Delta H_c^\ominus = -394 \, \text{kJ mol}^{-1} \qquad \textbf{Equation 1}$$

$$H_2(g) + \tfrac{1}{2}O_2(g) \rightarrow H_2O(l) \qquad\qquad \Delta H_c^\ominus = -286 \, \text{kJ mol}^{-1} \qquad \textbf{Equation 2}$$

$$C_6H_5COOH(s) + 7\tfrac{1}{2}O_2(g) \rightarrow 7CO_2(g) + 3H_2O(l) \qquad\qquad \Delta H_c^\ominus = -3227 \, \text{kJ mol}^{-1} \qquad \textbf{Equation 3}$$

These equations have to be rearranged to give the overall equation:

$$7C(s) + 3H_2(g) + O_2(g) \rightarrow C_6H_5COOH(s)$$

Equation 1 must be multiplied by 7 to give $7C(s)$, and **Equation 2** must be multiplied by 3 to give $3H_2(g)$. The enthalpy changes are then also multiplied by these numbers:

$$7C(s) + 7O_2(g) \rightarrow 7CO_2(g) \qquad\qquad \Delta H^\ominus = -2758\,\text{kJ}\,\text{mol}^{-1}$$
$$3H_2(g) + 1\tfrac{1}{2}O_2(g) \rightarrow 3H_2O(l) \qquad\qquad \Delta H^\ominus = -858\,\text{kJ}\,\text{mol}^{-1}$$

Equation 3 must then be reversed so that $C_6H_5COOH(s)$ is on the products side, as in the overall equation:

$$7CO_2(g) + 3H_2O(l) \rightarrow C_6H_5COOH(s) + 7\tfrac{1}{2}O_2(g) \qquad \Delta H^\ominus = +3227\,\text{kJ}\,\text{mol}^{-1}$$

The sign of the enthalpy change for **Equation 3** has changed, as the enthalpy change is now for the reverse reaction.

The equations are now added together and terms that are the same on both sides are cancelled, which should produce the overall equation for the enthalpy change we are trying to find:

$$7C(s) + 7O_2(g) \rightarrow 7CO_2(g) \qquad\qquad \Delta H^\ominus = -2758\,\text{kJ}\,\text{mol}^{-1}$$
$$3H_2(g) + 1\tfrac{1}{2}O_2(g) \rightarrow 3H_2O(l) \qquad\qquad \Delta H^\ominus = -858\,\text{kJ}\,\text{mol}^{-1}$$
$$\underline{7CO_2(g) + 3H_2O(l) \rightarrow C_6H_5COOH(s) + 7\tfrac{1}{2}O_2(g) \qquad \Delta H^\ominus = +3227\,\text{kJ}\,\text{mol}^{-1}}$$
$$7C(s) + 3H_2(g) + O_2(g) \rightarrow C_6H_5COOH(s) \qquad \Delta H^\ominus = -389\,\text{kJ}\,\text{mol}^{-1}$$

> Note: only $7\tfrac{1}{2}O_2(g)$ out of the $8\tfrac{1}{2}O_2(g)$ are cancelled from the left-hand side, as there are only $7\tfrac{1}{2}O_2(g)$ on the right-hand side.

Therefore the standard enthalpy change of formation of $C_6H_5COOH(s)$ is $-389\,\text{kJ}\,\text{mol}^{-1}$.

Method 3 (enthalpy level diagram)

In the enthalpy level diagram showing the overall process and the enthalpy changes of combustion, we have assumed that the enthalpy change of formation of $CH_3COOH(s)$ is exothermic and have drawn the arrow downwards. We have no real way of knowing this before doing the calculations, but it doesn't matter if we have drawn it the wrong way round, as it will still work out correctly in the calculation.

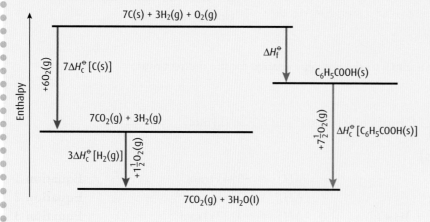

The values for the enthalpy changes are put in:

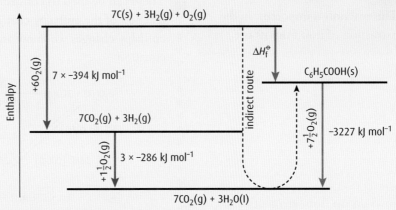

The enthalpy change for the direct route is equated to that for the indirect route:

$$\Delta H_f^\ominus = (7 \times -394) + (3 \times -286) + 3227$$

The sign of the enthalpy change marked in red in the diagram is reversed, as the indirect route goes in the opposite direction to this arrow.

$$\Delta H_f^\ominus = -389 \, \text{kJ mol}^{-1}$$

Method 4 (equation)

$$\Delta H_r = \Sigma \Delta H_c(\text{reactants}) - \Sigma \Delta H_c(\text{products})$$

So:

$$\Delta H_f^\ominus = [(7 \times -394) + (3 \times -286)] - [-3227] = -3616 + 3227$$

$$\Delta H_f^\ominus = -389 \, \text{kJ mol}^{-1}$$

	$\Delta H_c^\ominus / \text{kJ mol}^{-1}$
C(s)	−394
H_2(g)	−286
C_6H_5COOH(s)	−3227

Using enthalpy change of formation data to calculate other enthalpy changes

We will use similar methods to before, but there are some changes, as we have different data (enthalpy change of formation instead of enthalpy change of combustion). The technique we use is determined by the data we are given (not what we are trying to find).

Given the enthalpy changes of formation in the table, calculate the standard enthalpy change for the reaction:

$$Fe_2O_3(s) + 3CO(g) \rightarrow 2Fe(s) + 3CO_2(g)$$

	$\Delta H_f^\ominus / \text{kJ mol}^{-1}$
Fe_2O_3(s)	−822
CO(g)	−111
CO_2(g)	−394

Method 5

We will set up an enthalpy change cycle. The equations of the reactions for which we know the enthalpy changes are:

$$2Fe(s) + \tfrac{3}{2}O_2(g) \rightarrow Fe_2O_3(s) \qquad \Delta H_f^\ominus = -822 \, \text{kJ mol}^{-1}$$

$$C(s) + \tfrac{1}{2}O_2(g) \rightarrow CO(g) \qquad \Delta H_f^\ominus = -111 \, \text{kJ mol}^{-1}$$

$$C(s) + O_2(g) \rightarrow CO_2(g) \qquad \Delta H_f^\ominus = -394 \, \text{kJ mol}^{-1}$$

Enthalpy change of formation: formation of 1 mole of substance from its constituent elements in their standard states.

HL

These can be used to construct a cycle, in which the equation for the reaction of the enthalpy change we want to find is along the top and the enthalpy changes we know are from the elements to the substances in this equation:

This reaction is important in the extraction of iron from its ore.

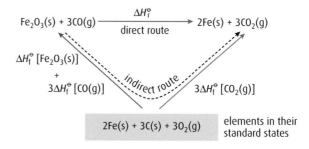

Arrows go **up** from elements.

The total enthalpy change for the formation of the reactants ($Fe_2O_3(s)$ and $3CO(g)$) from their elements is:

$$\Delta H_f^{\ominus}[Fe_2O_3(s)] + 3\Delta H_f^{\ominus}[CO(g)] = -822 + 3 \times (-111) = -1155\,kJ\,mol^{-1}$$

The standard enthalpy change of formation of Fe(s) is 0, as it is an element in its standard state.

The total enthalpy change for the formation of the products ($2Fe(s)$ and $3CO_2(g)$) from their elements is:

$$2\Delta H_f^{\ominus}[Fe(s)] + 3\Delta H_f^{\ominus}[CO_2(g)] = 0 + 3 \times (-394) = -1182\,kJ\,mol^{-1}$$

These values can be added to the cycle:

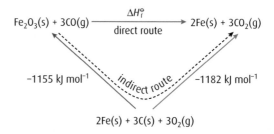

The enthalpy change for the direct route is the same as the enthalpy change for the indirect route. The indirect route goes in the opposite direction to the blue arrow and therefore the sign of this enthalpy change is reversed:

$$\Delta H_r^{\ominus} = -(-1155) + (-1182) = -27\,kJ\,mol^{-1}$$

Therefore the enthalpy change of reaction is $-27\,kJ\,mol^{-1}$.

Method 6

In this method, the equations are rearranged to give the equation for the reaction corresponding to the enthalpy change we have to find.

The equations for the reactions we have been given are:

$2Fe(s) + \frac{3}{2}O_2(g) \rightarrow Fe_2O_3(s) \qquad \Delta H_f^{\ominus} = -822\,kJ\,mol^{-1}$ **Equation 1**

$C(s) + \frac{1}{2}O_2(g) \rightarrow CO(g) \qquad \Delta H_f^{\ominus} = -111\,kJ\,mol^{-1}$ **Equation 2**

$C(s) + O_2(g) \rightarrow CO_2(g) \qquad \Delta H_f^{\ominus} = -394\,kJ\,mol^{-1}$ **Equation 3**

The equation for the reaction we have to find is:

$$Fe_2O_3(s) + 3CO(g) \rightarrow 2Fe(s) + 3CO_2(g)$$

Equations 1 and **2** must be reversed to give Fe_2O_3 and CO on the left-hand (reactants) side:

$$Fe_2O_3(s) \rightarrow 2Fe(s) + \tfrac{3}{2}O_2(g) \qquad\qquad \Delta H^{\ominus} = +822\,kJ\,mol^{-1}$$

$$CO(g) \rightarrow C(s) + \tfrac{1}{2}O_2(g) \qquad\qquad \Delta H^{\ominus} = +111\,kJ\,mol^{-1}$$

Note sign change.

Equations 2 and **3** must be multiplied by 3 to give $3CO$ and $3CO_2$, respectively:

$$3CO(g) \rightarrow 3C(s) + \tfrac{3}{2}O_2(g) \qquad\qquad \Delta H^{\ominus} = +333\,kJ\,mol^{-1}$$

$$3C(s) + 3O_2(g) \rightarrow 3CO_2(g) \qquad\qquad \Delta H^{\ominus} = -1182\,kJ\,mol^{-1}$$

As the equations are multiplied by 3, the enthalpy changes must also be multiplied by 3.

The correct reactants and products are now on each side. The equations are added together and species that are the same are cancelled from each side:

$$Fe_2O_3(s) \rightarrow 2Fe(s) + \cancel{\tfrac{3}{2}O_2(g)} \qquad \Delta H^{\ominus} = +822\,kJ\,mol^{-1}$$
$$3CO(g) \rightarrow \cancel{3C(s)} + \cancel{\tfrac{3}{2}O_2(g)} \qquad \Delta H^{\ominus} = +333\,kJ\,mol^{-1}$$
$$\underline{\cancel{3C(s)} + \cancel{3O_2(g)} \rightarrow 3CO_2(g) \qquad \Delta H^{\ominus} = -1182\,kJ\,mol^{-1}}$$
$$Fe_2O_3(s) + 3CO(g) \rightarrow 2Fe(s) + 3CO_2(g) \qquad \Delta H^{\ominus} = -27\,kJ\,mol^{-1}$$

The equations involving the formation of the reactants are always the ones that are reversed when enthalpy changes of formation have been given.

Therefore the enthalpy change of reaction is $-27\,kJ\,mol^{-1}$.

Method 7

In this method we will draw an enthalpy level diagram:

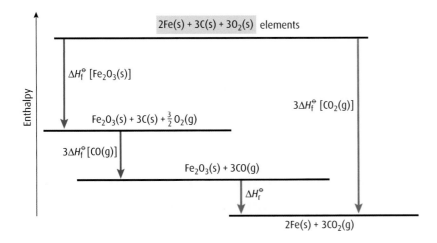

HL The values can then be substituted into the diagram:

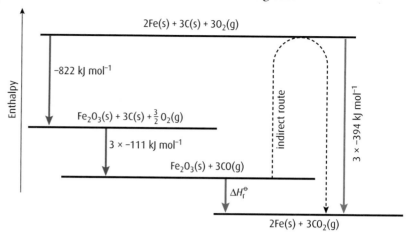

The enthalpy change for the direct route is equated to that for the indirect route:

$$\Delta H_r^{\ominus} = -(3 \times -111) - (-822) + (3 \times -394)$$

$$\Delta H_r^{\ominus} = +333 + 822 - 1182$$

$$\Delta H_r^{\ominus} = -27 \, \text{kJ mol}^{-1}$$

Method 8

In this method we use an equation. In this case, where we have been given standard enthalpy changes of formation, the equation is:

$$\Delta H_r = \Sigma \Delta H_f(\text{products}) - \Sigma \Delta H_f(\text{reactants})$$

Therefore, in this case, for the equation:

$$Fe_2O_3(s) + 3CO(g) \rightarrow 2Fe(s) + 3CO_2(g)$$

$$\Delta H_r^{\ominus} = [(2 \times 0) + (3 \times -394)] - [(-822) + (3 \times -111)]$$

$$\Delta H_r^{\ominus} = (-1182) - (-1155)$$

Therefore the enthalpy change of reaction is $-27 \, \text{kJ mol}^{-1}$.

Determining an enthalpy change of formation from an enthalpy change of reaction

If we are given an enthalpy change of reaction and some enthalpy changes of formation it is possible to work out a missing enthalpy change of formation.

Example

Given that the standard enthalpy change of formation of ethane ($C_2H_6(g)$) is $-85 \, \text{kJ mol}^{-1}$, and given the equation below, work out the enthalpy change of formation of ethyne ($C_2H_2(g)$).

$$C_2H_2(g) + 2H_2(g) \rightarrow C_2H_6(g) \qquad \Delta H^{\ominus} = -311 \, \text{kJ mol}^{-1}$$

The signs of two of the enthalpy changes are reversed, as the direction of the indirect route arrow goes in the opposite direction to these two arrows.

	$\Delta H_f^{\ominus} / \text{kJ mol}^{-1}$
$Fe_2O_3(s)$	−822
$CO(g)$	−111
$CO_2(g)$	−394

This is probably most easily done by using the equation from method 8
above (although the other methods could be used instead):

$$\Delta H_r^\ominus = \Sigma \Delta H_f^\ominus(\text{products}) - \Sigma \Delta H_f^\ominus(\text{reactants})$$

$$-311 = -85 - [\Delta H_f^\ominus(C_2H_2(g)) + 2 \times 0]$$

Rearranging the equation gives:

$$\Delta H_f^\ominus(C_2H_2(g)) = -85 + 311$$

Therefore the standard enthalpy change of formation of ethyne is $+226\,\text{kJ}\,\text{mol}^{-1}$.

Which method to choose

We have looked at eight different methods for working out enthalpy changes. Methods 1, 2, 3 and 4 are entirely equivalent, and when enthalpy change of combustion data are given, any of these four methods may be used. Similarly, when enthalpy change of formation data are given, any one of methods 5, 6, 7 and 8 may be used. **The key point is, however, to choose a method based on the data that are given and not on what has to be found.** For instance, if you are asked to determine an enthalpy change of combustion and have been given enthalpy change of formation data, then you would choose one of methods 5, 6, 7 and 8, as these are the methods to use when enthalpy change of formation data has been **given**.

If you look closely at the methods above, method 1 is very similar to method 5, and method 2 is basically the same as method 6, etc. Once you have understood the basic principles of the methods, there is no need for any artificial distinctions between them.

Self-test 5

Test yourself

14 Write equations for the enthalpy change of formation of the following:
   a HF(g)
   b $CH_3Cl(g)$
   c $H_2O(l)$
   d $C_5H_{11}OH(l)$

15 Calculate the enthalpy change for the following reaction, given the data in the table:

$$C_4H_8(g) + H_2(g) \rightarrow C_4H_{10}(g)$$

	$\Delta H_c^\ominus$ / kJ mol^{-1}
$C_4H_8(g)$	−2717
$C_4H_{10}(g)$	−2877
$H_2(g)$	−286

16 Calculate the enthalpy change of formation of propanone ($CH_3COCH_3(l)$), given the following data:

	$\Delta H_c^\ominus$ / kJ mol^{-1}
$CH_3COCH_3(l)$	−1817
$C(s)$	−394
$H_2(g)$	−286

17 Calculate the enthalpy change for the following reaction, given the enthalpy changes of formation in the table:

$$S_2Cl_2(l) + Cl_2(g) \rightarrow 2SCl_2(g)$$

	$\Delta H_f^\ominus$/kJmol^{-1}
$S_2Cl_2(l)$	−59.4
$SCl_2(g)$	−19.7

18 Calculate the enthalpy change for the following reaction, given the enthalpy changes of formation in the table:

$$4BCl_3(l) + 3SF_4(g)$$
$$\rightarrow 4BF_3(g) + 3SCl_2(g) + 3Cl_2(g)$$

	$\Delta H_f^\ominus$/kJmol^{-1}
$BCl_3(l)$	−427
$SCl_2(g)$	−19.7
$SF_4(g)$	−775
$BF_3(g)$	−1137

19 Calculate the enthalpy change of formation of $NO_2(g)$ from the following data:

$$2Pb(NO_3)_2(s) \rightarrow 4NO_2(g) + 2PbO(s) + O_2(g)$$
$$\Delta H = +602\,\text{kJ mol}^{-1}$$

	$\Delta H_f^\ominus$/kJmol^{-1}
$Pb(NO_3)_2(s)$	−452
$PbO(s)$	−217

HL 5.6 Enthalpy changes for ionic compounds

So far the energy cycles we have drawn have been for covalent substances. In this section we will consider an enthalpy level diagram for ionic substances. Before we look at this diagram we must consider some definitions.

First ionisation energy is the enthalpy change when one electron is removed from each atom in 1 mole of gaseous atoms under standard conditions:

$$M(g) \rightarrow M^+(g) + e^-$$

Second ionisation energy is the enthalpy change for the process:

$$M^+(g) \rightarrow M^{2+}(g) + e^-$$

First electron affinity is the enthalpy change when one electron is added to each atom in 1 mole of gaseous atoms under standard conditions:

$$X(g) + e^- \rightarrow X^-(g)$$

Learning objectives

- Understand how to draw a Born–Haber cycle
- Understand the factors that affect the value of lattice enthalpy

All ionisation energies are **endothermic**

The (g) symbol is essential in these equations.

The first electron affinity is **exothermic** for virtually all elements; it is a favourable process to bring an electron from infinity to where it feels the attractive force of the nucleus in an atom.

Second electron affinity is enthalpy change for the process:

$$X^-(g) + e^- \rightarrow X^{2-}(g)$$

Lattice enthalpy ($\Delta H_{latt}^{\ominus}$) is the enthalpy change when 1 mole of an ionic compound is broken apart into its constituent gaseous ions under standard conditions.

For example, for NaCl:

$$NaCl(s) \rightarrow Na^+(g) + Cl^-(g) \quad \Delta H_{latt}^{\ominus} = +771\,kJ\,mol^{-1}$$

Note, for ammonium nitrate the equation is:

$$NH_4NO_3(s) \rightarrow NH_4^+(g) + NO_3^-(g)$$

Born–Haber cycles

A Born–Haber cycle is an enthalpy level diagram breaking down the formation of an ionic compound into a series of simpler steps. For example, for sodium chloride, we will show the stages in construction of the cycle. The first step we put in is the equation for the enthalpy change of formation:

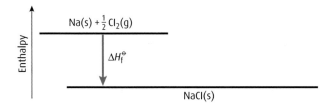

The cycle gives us an alternative route between the elements (Na(s) + $\frac{1}{2}$Cl$_2$(g)) and the ionic compound (NaCl(s)). NaCl(s) can be broken apart into its constituent gaseous ions – this is the lattice enthalpy:

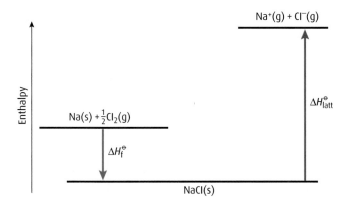

This step gives us an idea of what we are aiming at so, to complete the cycle, Na(s) and $\frac{1}{2}$Cl$_2$(g) must be converted into gaseous ions.

HL

The second electron affinity is always **endothermic**. It is an unfavourable process to add an electron to an ion which is already negatively charged, due to repulsion between the negative charges.

Look carefully to determine whether lattice enthalpy is exothermic or endothermic, as it can be defined in either direction, i.e. as the making or breaking of the lattice. Here it is defined as the breaking of the lattice and is an endothermic process: energy must be supplied to separate the ions against the attractive forces holding them in the lattice.

The enthalpy change of formation for NaCl(s) is exothermic, and the arrow is shown in the downward, negative, direction.

The Born–Haber cycle was developed by two Nobel-prize-winning German scientists: Fritz Haber (1868–1934) and Max Born (1882–1970). Max Born was the grandfather of the singer Olivia Newton-John, star of the film *Grease*.

The arrow for ΔH_{latt} goes upwards, indicating an endothermic process.

The Na(s) is first converted into Na$^+$(g) in two steps:

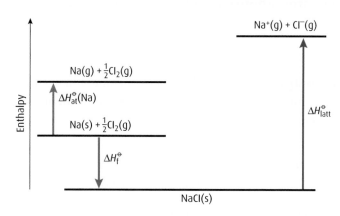

The sodium must be converted to gaseous atoms before it can be ionised, as the definition of ionisation energy is removal of an electron from a gaseous atom.

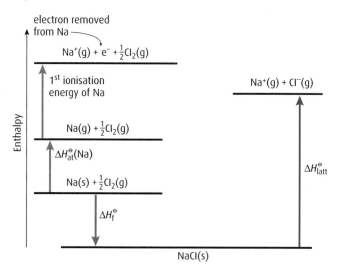

The sodium has been converted into the required species (Na$^+$(g)), and now we must do the same with the chlorine. The first stage is atomisation of chlorine:

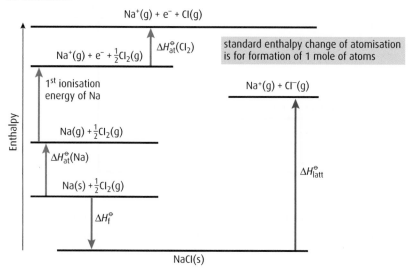

standard enthalpy change of atomisation is for formation of 1 mole of atoms

The cycle can now be connected and completed by adding the electron removed from the sodium atom to the chlorine atom (Figure **5.18**). This process is the first electron affinity of chlorine and is exothermic, therefore the arrow goes downwards.

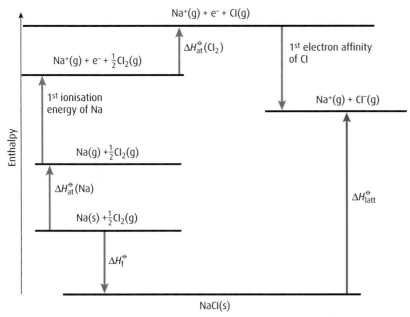

Figure 5.18 The Born–Haber cycle for NaCl. Upward arrows represent endothermic processes, whereas downward arrows represent exothermic processes.

If all the quantities in the cycle except one are known, then application of Hess's law allows the last quantity to be worked out. For example, let us calculate the lattice enthalpy of sodium chloride.

The values can be put into the diagram:

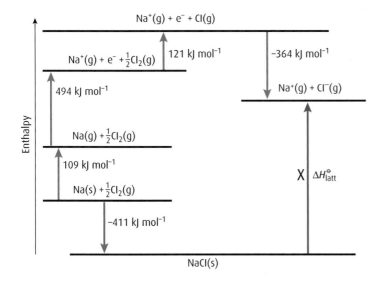

ΔH_{at} (Na(s))	$109 \, kJ \, mol^{-1}$
ΔH_{at} (Cl$_2$(g))	$121 \, kJ \, mol^{-1}$
first ionisation energy (Na)	$494 \, kJ \, mol^{-1}$
first electron affinity (Cl)	$-364 \, kJ \, mol^{-1}$
ΔH_f (NaCl(s))	$-411 \, kJ \, mol^{-1}$

HL Hess's law is used. The enthalpy change for the direct route is the same as that for the indirect route.

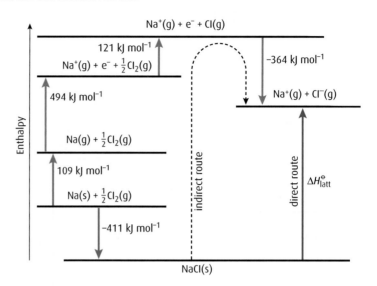

The sign of −411 was reversed as the direction of the indirect route arrow goes against the direction of this arrow.

Therefore:

$$\Delta H^{\ominus}_{\text{latt}} = 411 + 109 + 494 + 121 - 364$$

$$\Delta H^{\ominus}_{\text{latt}} = 771 \, \text{kJ mol}^{-1}$$

Worked example

Draw a Born–Haber cycle for magnesium oxide and use it to work out the second electron affinity of oxygen.

Enthalpy term	Enthalpy change / kJ mol^{-1}
$\Delta H^{\ominus}_{\text{at}} \, [\text{Mg(s)}]$	150
$\Delta H^{\ominus}_{\text{at}} \, [\text{O}_2\text{(g)}]$	248
first ionisation energy (Mg)	736
second ionisation energy (Mg)	1450
first electron affinity (O)	−142
$\Delta H^{\ominus}_{\text{f}} \, (\text{MgO})$	−602
$\Delta H^{\ominus}_{\text{latt}} \, (\text{MgO})$	3889

The Born Haber cycle is shown in Figure **5.18**.

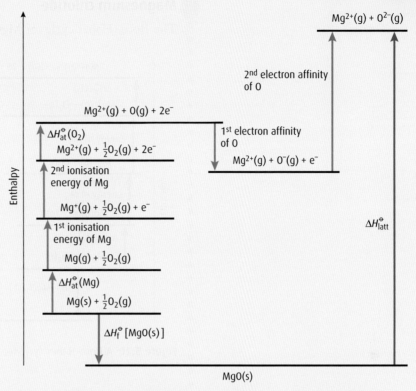

Figure 5.18 A Born–Haber cycle for MgO. The first electron affinity for O(g) is negative, but the second electron affinity is positive.

The second electron affinity of O is worked out most easily by applying Hess's law and looking at the enthalpy change for the direct route and the indirect route (Figure **5.19**).

The signs of the enthalpy changes highlighted in Figure **5.19** are reversed, as the direction of the indirect route was in the opposite direction to the arrows on the diagram. The enthalpy change for the direct route is the same as that for the indirect route: second electron affinity of O = 142 − 248 − 1450 − 736 − 150 − 602 + 3889 = 845 kJ mol^{-}1.

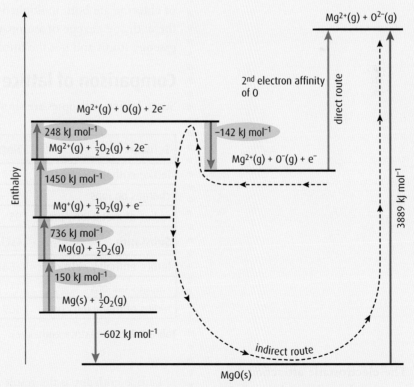

Figure 5.19 The Born–Haber cycle for MgO, showing the enthalpy changes for which the sign must be changed to work out the second electron affinity of oxygen.

HL Magnesium chloride

The Born–Haber cycle for $MgCl_2$ is shown in Figure **5.20**.

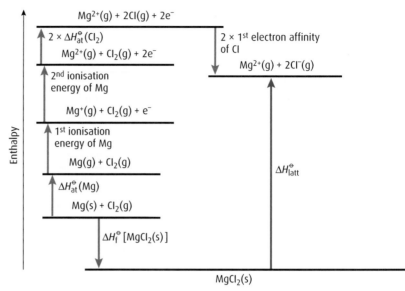

Figure 5.20 A Born–Haber cycle for $MgCl_2$.

The only difference here from the other Born–Haber cycles considered above is that the enthalpy change of atomisation and the electron affinity of chlorine are both multiplied by 2. Remember that the definition of the enthalpy change of atomisation refers to the formation of 1 mole of gaseous atoms and not the breaking of 1 mole of covalent bonds.

Comparison of lattice enthalpies

Some lattice enthalpies are shown in Table **5.2**.

Substance	NaCl		MgCl$_2$		MgO	
lattice enthalpy / kJ mol^{-1}	+771		+2526		+3791	
charges on ions	1+	1−	2+	1−	2+	2−
radius of metal ion / pm	95		65		65	
Substance	CsCl		BaCl$_2$		BaO	
lattice enthalpy / kJ mol^{-1}	+645		+2056		+3054	
charges on ions	1+	1−	2+	1−	2+	2−
radius of metal ion / pm	169		135		135	

Table 5.2 Some lattice enthalpies.

The electrostatic attraction between ions depends on the **charge on the ions** and the **size of the ions** (ionic radii).

Lattice enthalpy is the result of electrostatic attractions between oppositely charged ions in the giant lattice. The greater the electrostatic attraction between the ions, the more energy has to be supplied to break apart the lattice.

The effect of charge

$MgCl_2$ has a higher lattice enthalpy than NaCl (Figure **5.21**).

> The higher the charge on the ions, the more strongly they will attract each other – and therefore the greater the lattice enthalpy.

The force between ions is proportional to the product of the charges, so the force of attraction increases along the series:

$$1+/1- < 1+/2- < 2+/2-$$

The effect of size

CsCl has a smaller lattice enthalpy than NaCl.

Ions act like point charges, i.e. a positive ion such as Na^+ behaves as if its ionic charge all acts at its centre and a negative ion such as Cl^- behaves as if a $1-$ charge exists at its centre. The greater the ionic radii, the greater the distance between the centres of the ions and, therefore, the smaller the attraction between the ions and the smaller the lattice enthalpy (Figure **5.22**).

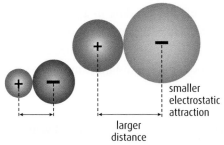

Figure 5.22 Smaller ions have a greater attraction between them.

Thus we can see that $MgCl_2$ has a larger lattice enthalpy than NaCl, not just because the Mg^{2+} ion has a higher charge than the Na^+ ion, but also because the Mg^{2+} ion is smaller.

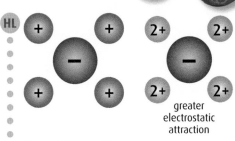

HL

greater electrostatic attraction

Figure 5.21 NaCl contains 1+ and 1– ions, whereas $MgCl_2$ contains 2+ and 1– ions.

> Lattice enthalpy is larger for smaller ions.

Examiner's tip
The greatest lattice enthalpy is obtained for small, highly charged ions. When comparing different compounds, the effect of charge causes a larger change in lattice enthalpy than do size variations.

Worked example

Arrange the following compounds in order of increasing lattice enthalpy:

BaCl₂   **LiF**   **ZnS**

The most important factor in determining the lattice enthalpy is the charge on the ions. ZnS contains 2+ and 2– ions, $BaCl_2$ contains 2+ and 1– ions and LiF contains 1+ and 1– ions. The order of increasing lattice enthalpy is thus:

$$LiF < BaCl_2 < ZnS$$

The attraction between 2+/2– ions in ZnS is greater than that between 2+/1– ions in $BaCl_2$, which is greater than between 1+/1– ions in LiF.

Because the melting point of an ionic substance depends on the force of attraction between ions, a substance with a high lattice enthalpy would also be expected to have a high melting point (Table **5.3**).

Substance	Lattice enthalpy / kJ mol⁻¹	Melting point / °C
NaCl	+771	801
MgO	+3791	2852
KCl	+711	770
CaO	+3401	2614
CsCl	+645	645
BaO	+3054	1918

Table 5.3 The lattice enthalpies and melting points of some substances.

Comparison of theoretical and experimental lattice enthalpy values

Assuming a **totally ionic model** in which the bonding is solely due to the attraction between oppositely charged ions, a **theoretical** value for the lattice enthalpy can be calculated using various equations.

The Born–Haber cycle gives us an **experimental** value for the lattice enthalpy, and by comparing the theoretical and experimental values we can get an idea of how ionic the bonding in a particular compound is. If the values are exactly the same, that would suggest complete ionic bonding; however, if there is a significant difference between the values, then it suggests that the bonding has a significant degree of covalency.

For instance, for NaCl:

Theoretical value / kJ mol⁻¹	Experimental value / kJ mol⁻¹
766	771

If the theoretical and experimental values for silver iodide are compared, it can be seen that there is a much larger difference between the two values, and this indicates a larger degree of covalent character in the bonding. In this case, a purely ionic model for the bonding is not entirely appropriate.

Theoretical value / kJ mol⁻¹	Experimental value / kJ mol⁻¹
736	876

Covalent character in the bonding can result from polarisation of the negative ion by the positive one. A small highly charged cation such as Mg^{2+} is able to polarise neighbouring negative ions. This effect is especially large if the anion is large, such as I^-.

Consider MgI_2: the Mg^{2+} ion polarises the I^- ion, i.e. pulls electron density away from it. There is now shared electron density between the two nuclei (some covalent character in the bonding). The difference between the experimental and theoretical lattice enthalpies for MgI_2 is almost 400 kJ mol^{-1}, and the bonding includes a significant contribution from covalent bonding.

Extension

Equations that can be used to do this are the Born–Landé, Born–Mayer and Kapustinskii equations. These are complicated and involve terms for the structure and the size of the ions and their charge, as well as other terms.

This close agreement between the two values indicates a very high degree of ionic character in NaCl.

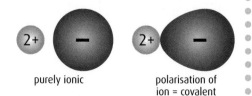

purely ionic   polarisation of ion = covalent character

226

This is an example of using a mathematical model to describe a scientific system.

A mathematical equation/system of equations is developed to approximate as closely as possible the behaviour or properties of a real system. The Born–Landé, Born–Mayer and Kapustinskii equations represent equations with different levels of sophistication, taking different factors into account to predict values for lattice energies.

Scientists use mathematical modelling to try to predict the possible effects of climate change. A model is developed, tested against climate data from the past and, if there is good agreement, used to make predictions about what may happen in the future. Does complete agreement of theoretical values from a mathematical model with experimental values indicate that the model provides a true description of reality?

Self-test 6

Test yourself

20 Use the data in the table to calculate the first electron affinity of Br.

	/kJmol^{-1}
ΔH_{at} [K(s)]	90
ΔH_{at} [Br$_2$(l)]	112
first ionisation energy (K)	418
ΔH_{latt} (KBr)	670
ΔH_f (KBr(s))	−394

21 Use the data in the table to calculate the lattice enthalpy of BaF$_2$.

	/kJmol^{-1}
ΔH_{at} [Ba(s)]	176
ΔH_{at} [F$_2$(g)]	79
first ionisation energy (Ba)	502
second ionisation energy (Ba)	966
first electron affinity (F)	−348
ΔH_f (BaF$_2$(s))	−1201

22 Arrange the following in order of increasing lattice enthalpy (smallest first):

LiF   KCl   CaO
CaS   CaCl$_2$

23 State whether the following enthalpy changes are *always exothermic*, *always endothermic* or *sometimes exothermic and sometimes endothermic*:

   a first ionisation energy
   b second ionisation energy
   c enthalpy change of atomisation
   d enthalpy change of formation
   e first electron affinity
   f second electron affinity

5.7 Entropy

The dissolving of sodium chloride (common salt) in water is an example of an endothermic process that occurs spontaneously at room temperature. The idea of an endothermic reaction occurring spontaneously goes against our experience from everyday life that things do not seem to move spontaneously from a lower to a higher energy state (a book does not jump from a lower shelf to a higher one but will fall to a lower shelf if the shelf it is on breaks). Endothermic processes such as the melting of

Learning objectives

- Understand what is meant by entropy
- Predict the sign of the entropy change for a given reaction
- Work out entropy changes from standard entropy values

Entropy is a measure of the randomness or disorder of a system.

Note: not kJ.

Actual values of entropy can be calculated from experimental data, as opposed to enthalpy, for which only an enthalpy change can be measured.

The Austrian physicist Ludwig Boltzmann (1844–1906) developed a statistical approach to entropy. His famous equation, $S = k \log W$, is inscribed on his gravestone.

ice at room temperature and water evaporating are relatively common, however, and this suggests that it is not just a consideration of the energy changes involved that can be used to predict whether a reaction occurs spontaneously. The examples of endothermic processes mentioned here all have one thing in common: they all involve an increase in **disorder**. In a sodium chloride solution the Na^+ and Cl^- ions are dispersed throughout the solution and are moving around, which is a much more disordered, or random, arrangement than a separate crystal of sodium chloride and a beaker of pure water. Similarly, liquid water is much more disordered than a solid lump of ice, as in the liquid form all the molecules are moving around each other randomly. This property of disorder is called **entropy**, and it is possible to assign values to the entropy of a system and the entropy change for a reaction. An endothermic reaction can only occur if it involves an increase in entropy.

Entropy is given the symbol S. The units of entropy are $J K^{-1} mol^{-1}$.

$S^{\ominus}$ is called the **standard entropy**. It is possible to work out values for standard entropies for substances; for example, the standard entropy of $H_2(g)$ is $131 J K^{-1} mol^{-1}$, and the standard entropy of $NaCl(s)$ is $72.4 J K^{-1} mol^{-1}$.

An entropy change is represented by the symbol $\Delta S^{\ominus}$.

A positive value for $\Delta S^{\ominus}$ indicates an increase in entropy, i.e. an increase in disorder.

For example, ΔS for the process $H_2O(l) \rightarrow H_2O(g)$ is $+119 J K^{-1} mol^{-1}$. The disorder of the system has increased, as the molecules of water in the gas phase are moving around much more.

A negative value for $\Delta S^{\ominus}$ indicates a decrease in entropy, i.e. an decrease in disorder.

For example, ΔS for the process $NH_3(g) + HCl(g) \rightarrow NH_4Cl(s)$ is $-285 J K^{-1} mol^{-1}$. Two molecules of gas being converted into a solid results in a decrease in disorder, i.e. a decrease in entropy.

How to predict the sign of an entropy change

Gases have higher entropy than liquids, which have higher entropy than solids (Figure **5.23**).

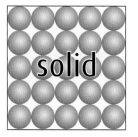
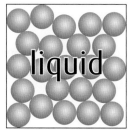
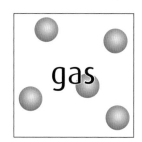

Figure 5.23 In a solid, the particles vibrate about mean positions; in a liquid, the particles move around each other; in a gas, the particles move at high speeds in all directions.

HL

This is an approximate rule of thumb, which is useful when considering the same substance in different states or similar substances. When considering very different substances, it must be used with caution. For instance, $S^\ominus$ for $(NH_4)_2SO_4(s)$ is $220\,J\,K^{-1}\,mol^{-1}$, whereas that for $CCl_4(l)$ is $214\,J\,K^{-1}\,mol^{-1}$ and that for $HCl(g)$ is $187\,J\,K^{-1}\,mol^{-1}$.

Table **5.4** shows the values of standard entropies for elements across period 2 in the periodic table. Lithium to carbon are all solid elements and have low entropy values at 298 K, but nitrogen to neon are all gases and have much higher entropy values.

Element	Li	Be	B	C	N_2	O_2	F_2	Ne
State	solid	solid	solid	solid	gas	gas	gas	gas
$S^\ominus$/$JK^{-1}mol^{-1}$	29	10	6	6	192	205	203	146

Table 5.4 Standard entropies for elements across period 2.

To predict the sign of the entropy change in a reaction, we must consider whether there is an increase or decrease in disorder in the system. As gases have significantly higher entropy than solids and liquids, the most important factor in determining whether a chemical reaction involves an increase or decrease in entropy is whether there is an increase or decrease in the number of moles of **gas** (Table **5.5**).

Increase in number of moles of **gas**: ΔS +ve (**entropy increases**).

Decrease in number of moles of **gas**: ΔS −ve (**entropy decreases**).

Reaction	Entropy	$\Delta S^\ominus$	Explanation
$N_2(g) + 3H_2(g) \rightarrow 2NH_3(g)$	decrease	−	4 moles of gas on the left-hand side converted to 2 moles of gas on the right-hand side; a decrease in the number of moles of gas suggests a decrease in disorder and therefore a decrease in entropy
$CaCO_3(s) \rightarrow CaO(s) + CO_2(g)$	increase	+	1 mole of solid becomes 1 mole of solid and 1 mole of gas; therefore the number of moles of gas increases
$CH_4(g) + 2O_2(g) \rightarrow CO_2(g) + 2H_2O(l)$	decrease	−	3 moles of gas converted to 1 mole of gas
$C_2H_4(g) + H_2(g) \rightarrow C_2H_6(g)$	decrease	−	2 moles of gas converted to 1 mole of gas

Table 5.5 Entropy changes for some reactions.

If the number of moles of gas is the same on both sides of an equation, as in this one:

$$F_2(g) + Cl_2(g) \rightarrow 2ClF(g)$$

the prediction could be made that the entropy change for this reaction would be approximately zero.

HL Calculating an entropy change for a reaction

Values of $\Delta S^{\ominus}$ may be worked out from **standard entropies, $S^{\ominus}$:**

> entropy change
> = total entropy of products − total entropy of reactants
>
> $$\Delta S^{\ominus} = \Sigma S^{\ominus}_{\text{products}} - \Sigma S^{\ominus}_{\text{reactants}}$$

	$S^{\ominus}/\text{JK}^{-1}\text{mol}^{-1}$
N_2	192
H_2	131
NH_3	193

The standard entropy values are multiplied by the appropriate coefficients in the equation.

Example

Calculate the standard entropy change for the following reaction:

$$N_2(g) + 3H_2(g) \rightarrow 2NH_3(g)$$

$$\Delta S^{\ominus} = (2 \times 193) - [192 + (3 \times 131)]$$

$$\Delta S^{\ominus} = -199\,\text{J K}^{-1}\,\text{mol}^{-1}$$

That there is a decrease in entropy corresponds to the prediction made above based on the number of moles of gas.

Self-test 7

Test yourself

24 Work out whether each of the following processes involves an increase or decrease in entropy:
 a $C_2H_2(g) + 2H_2(g) \rightarrow C_2H_6(g)$
 b $2C_2H_6(g) + 7O_2(g) \rightarrow 4CO_2(g) + 6H_2O(l)$
 c $COCl_2(g) \rightarrow CO(g) + Cl_2(g)$
 d $2C(s) + O_2(g) \rightarrow 2CO(g)$

25 Use the entropy values in the table to calculate the standard entropy change in each of the following reactions:
 a $CH_4(g) + 2O_2(g) \rightarrow CO_2(g) + 2H_2O(l)$
 b $2Cu(NO_3)_2(s) \rightarrow 2CuO(s) + 4NO_2(g) + O_2(g)$
 c $4BCl_3(l) + 3SF_4(g) \rightarrow 4BF_3(g) + 3SCl_2(g) + 3Cl_2(g)$

Substance	$S^{\ominus}/\text{JK}^{-1}\text{mol}^{-1}$
$CH_4(g)$	186
$O_2(g)$	103
$CO_2(g)$	214
$H_2O(l)$	70
$Cu(NO_3)_2(s)$	193
$CuO(s)$	43
$NO_2(g)$	240
$BCl_3(l)$	206
$SF_4(g)$	292
$BF_3(g)$	254
$SCl_2(g)$	282
$Cl_2(g)$	83

Learning objectives

- Calculate values of ΔG for a reaction
- Work out whether a reaction is spontaneous from the sign of ΔG
- Predict how the spontaneity of a reaction varies with temperature

5.8 Spontaneity

Spontaneous reaction: one that occurs without any outside influence, i.e. no input of energy.

Predicting whether a reaction will be spontaneous (HL)

If sodium and oxygen are put together in an isolated container (one with no connection to the outside world) at 25 °C, they will react spontaneously to produce sodium oxide:

$$4Na(s) + O_2(g) \rightarrow 2Na_2O(s)$$

This reaction will occur by itself – nothing has to be done to make the reaction occur. This is an example of a spontaneous reaction.

If methane and oxygen are put into an isolated container at 25 °C, they will react together spontaneously to form carbon dioxide and water. This reaction, although it is spontaneous, is not a very fast reaction at room temperature (unless a spark is supplied) and would have to be left for a very long time before a significant amount of carbon dioxide and water could be detected. Similarly, the conversion of diamond to graphite at room temperature is a spontaneous process, but luckily occurs immeasurably slowly!

Whether a reaction will be spontaneous or not under a certain set of conditions can be deduced by looking at how the **entropy of the Universe** changes as the reaction occurs. The second law of thermodynamics states that for a process to occur spontaneously it must result in an increase in the entropy of the Universe.

The Universe may be regarded as being composed of the system (the chemical reaction) and the surroundings (Figure **5.24**).

The entropy change of the Universe is given by:

$$\Delta S_{Universe} = \Delta S_{surroundings} + \Delta S_{system}$$

If the value of $\Delta S_{Universe}$ is positive, the entropy of the Universe increases and the reaction occurs spontaneously.

When heat is given out in a chemical reaction, the surroundings get hotter, the particles move around more, and therefore the entropy of the surroundings increases. The entropy change of the surroundings can thus be related to the enthalpy change of the system. A new equation can be derived from the equation of the entropy change of the Universe given above. The new equation is:

$$\Delta G = \Delta H - T\Delta S$$

ΔG is called the change in **Gibbs free energy**, or just the **free energy change**. Or, under standard conditions, we have $\Delta G^{\ominus}$, which is the **standard free energy change**.

ΔG is related to the entropy change of the Universe, and from the condition that for a reaction to occur spontaneously the entropy of the Universe must increase we can derive the condition:

for a reaction to be spontaneous, ΔG for the reaction must be negative.

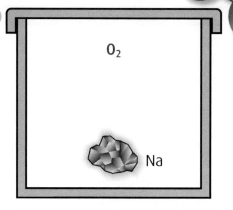

A spontaneous reaction does not have to happen quickly.

The first law of thermodynamics is basically a statement of the principle of conservation of energy: the energy of the Universe remains constant.

Figure 5.24 The Universe!

The units of ΔG are usually $kJ\,mol^{-1}$.

T must be in K.

The subscripts are now omitted, as both ΔH and ΔS refer to the system, i.e. the chemical reaction.

The entropy change of the surroundings depends on the temperature and is given by:

$$\Delta S_{\text{surroundings}} = \frac{-\Delta H_{\text{system}}}{T}$$

($-\Delta H$ because an exothermic reaction (ΔH negative) causes the entropy of the surroundings to increase ($\Delta S_{\text{surroundings}}$ positive))

$$\Delta S_{\text{Universe}} = \Delta S_{\text{surroundings}} + \Delta S_{\text{system}}$$

$$\Delta S_{\text{Universe}} = \frac{-\Delta H_{\text{system}}}{T} + \Delta S_{\text{system}}$$

$$-T\Delta S_{\text{Universe}} = \Delta H_{\text{system}} - T\Delta S_{\text{system}}$$

$-T\Delta S_{\text{Universe}}$ is given the symbol ΔG.

This is under standard conditions, so we use the symbol $\Delta G^{\ominus}$.

Note: temperature must be in kelvin.

Examiner's tip
If you are asked to calculate a **standard** free energy change and no temperature is given, you can assume that the temperature is 298 K.

	$\Delta G_{\text{f}}^{\ominus}/\text{kJ}\,\text{mol}^{-1}$
$SO_2(g)$	−300
$SO_3(g)$	−370

J. Willard Gibbs (1839–1903) was an American mathematician and scientist.

HL Calculating $\Delta G^{\ominus}$

The standard free energy change for a reaction can be calculated in two ways.

Method 1
Using $\Delta G^{\ominus} = \Delta H^{\ominus} - T\Delta S^{\ominus}$ to calculate $\Delta G^{\ominus}$.

Example
We can calculate $\Delta G^{\ominus}$ at 298 K for:

$$C_2H_2(g) + 2H_2(g) \rightarrow C_2H_6(g)$$

given the following information:

$\Delta H^{\ominus} = -313\,\text{J}\,\text{K}^{-1}\,\text{mol}^{-1}$ $\quad\quad$ $\Delta S^{\ominus} = -233\,\text{J}\,\text{K}^{-1}\,\text{mol}^{-1}$

$\Delta H^{\ominus}$ is in kJ but $\Delta S^{\ominus}$ is in J, and in order to combine them they must be converted so they are both in kJ or J. As $\Delta G^{\ominus}$ is usually quoted in kJ, $\Delta S^{\ominus}$ will be converted to kJ. Therefore:

$$\Delta S^{\ominus} = \frac{-233}{1000} = -0.233\,\text{kJ}\,\text{K}^{-1}\,\text{mol}^{-1}$$

$$\Delta G^{\ominus} = -313 - 298 \times (-0.233) = -244\,\text{kJ}\,\text{mol}^{-1}$$

As the value of ΔG is negative, the reaction is spontaneous.

Method 2
Using the standard free energy of formation to calculate $\Delta G^{\ominus}$:

$$\Delta G^{\ominus} = \Sigma\Delta G_{\text{f}}^{\ominus}(\text{products}) - \Sigma\Delta G_{\text{f}}^{\ominus}(\text{reactants})$$

Standard free energy of formation is the free energy change for the formation of 1 mole of substance from its elements in their standard states and under standard conditions.

Example
Given the data in the table, we can calculate the standard free energy change for the reaction:

$$2SO_2(g) + O_2(g) \rightarrow 2SO_3(g)$$

Using the formula for $\Delta G^{\ominus}$ given above:

$$\Delta G^{\ominus} = [2 \times -370] - [(2 \times -300) + 0] = -140\,\text{kJ}\,\text{mol}^{-1}$$

This reaction is spontaneous, as ΔG is negative.

The $\Delta G_{\text{f}}^{\ominus}$ for oxygen is zero, as it is an element in its standard state.

Worked example

Consider the decomposition of $Mg(NO_3)_2(s)$:

$$2Mg(NO_3)_2(s) \rightarrow 2MgO(s) + 4NO_2(g) + O_2(g)$$

Use the following data to work out $\Delta G^{\ominus}$ and thus whether the reaction will be spontaneous at 25 °C.

	$Mg(NO_3)_2(s)$	$MgO(s)$	$NO_2(g)$	$O_2(g)$
$\Delta H_f^{\ominus}$ / kJ mol^{-1}	−790	−602	34	0
$S^{\ominus}$ / J K^{-1} mol^{-1}	164	27	240	205

To calculate the enthalpy change, we have been given ΔH_f and so can use:

$$\Delta H = \Sigma \Delta H_f(\text{products}) - \Sigma \Delta H_f(\text{reactants})$$

$$\Delta H^{\ominus} = [(2 \times -602) + (4 \times 34) + 0] - [(2 \times -790)] = 512\,\text{kJ mol}^{-1}$$

To calculate the entropy change we use:

$$\Delta S = \Sigma S(\text{products}) - \Sigma S(\text{reactants})$$

$$\Delta S^{\ominus} = [(2 \times 27) + (4 \times 240) + 205] - [(2 \times 164)] = 891\,\text{J K}^{-1}\text{mol}^{-1}$$

At 298 K:

$$\Delta G^{\ominus} = \Delta H^{\ominus} - T\Delta S^{\ominus}$$

$$\Delta G^{\ominus} = 512 - 298 \times \frac{891}{1000} = 246\,\text{kJ mol}^{-1}$$

$\Delta S^{\ominus}$ is divided by 1000 to convert to kJ.

Thus, at 298 K the reaction is **not** spontaneous because ΔG is positive.

Because ΔS is positive, as the temperature is increased $T\Delta S$ will become larger until it is eventually bigger than ΔH and the reaction will be spontaneous.

We can estimate the temperature at which this reaction is going to become spontaneous. As the temperature is increased, ΔG will become less and less positive, until it becomes zero, and then it will be negative. Thus, if we work out the temperature at which ΔG becomes zero, the reaction will be spontaneous at any temperature above that.

When $\Delta G = 0$, this means that the reaction has no tendency to proceed in either direction, and so the system is in equilibrium.

Using

$$\Delta G = \Delta H - T\Delta S$$

$$0 = 512 - T \times \frac{891}{1000}$$

This calculation is only approximate, as the values of ΔH and ΔS change with temperature, and we have used $\Delta H^{\ominus}$ and $\Delta S^{\ominus}$, i.e. the values at 298 K.

Rearranging the equation gives:

$$T = 575\,\text{K}$$

This means that this reaction is likely to become spontaneous above 575 K (302 °C).

Actually the situation has been oversimplified here, and reactions that appear to have a positive value of ΔG can occur. Consider the Haber process for the production of ammonia:

$$N_2(g) + 3H_2(g) \rightleftharpoons 2NH_3(g)$$

Equilibrium can be attained from either direction, i.e. starting with either nitrogen and hydrogen or with pure ammonia. The reaction has a positive value of ΔG in one direction and a negative value in the other, but this is for complete conversion of 1 mole of nitrogen and 3 moles of hydrogen to 2 moles of ammonia. However, the equilibrium state has a lower Gibbs free energy than either pure nitrogen and hydrogen or pure ammonia, and therefore the reaction from pure reactants or products to the equilibrium mixture has a negative ΔG value.

HL Non-spontaneous reactions

If a reaction is non-spontaneous it does not mean that it can never happen, it just means that it will not happen without external influence. For instance, in the above worked example we can increase the temperature to make the reaction spontaneous.

Consider the following reaction:

$$2H_2O(l) \rightarrow 2H_2(g) + O_2(g) \qquad \Delta G^{\ominus} = +474\,\text{kJ}\,\text{mol}^{-1}$$

This reaction is not spontaneous at 25 °C, but it can be made to happen at this temperature by the continuous passage of an electric current (electrolysis).

The effect of changing temperature on the spontaneity of a reaction

Consider a reaction for which ΔH is positive and ΔS is positive:

$$\Delta G = \Delta H - T\Delta S$$

In this case, at low temperatures, the reaction is **not** spontaneous, as $T\Delta S$ is smaller than ΔH, so ΔG is positive. As the temperature is raised, $T\Delta S$ becomes larger, and as this is being subtracted from ΔH, ΔG becomes smaller. When $T\Delta S$ is larger than ΔH, ΔG is negative, and the reaction becomes spontaneous. Therefore, as the temperature is increased, this reaction becomes more spontaneous.

Now consider a reaction for which ΔH is positive and ΔS is negative. In this case, at low temperatures, the reaction is **not** spontaneous. However, as ΔS is negative $-T\Delta S$ in the equation is positive, and this means that the value of ΔG will increase as the temperature is increased. The consequence of $-T\Delta S$ being positive is that this reaction will never be spontaneous.

Both the reactions considered here so far have been endothermic reactions and it can be seen that:

> an endothermic reaction can only occur spontaneously if it involves an increase in entropy (and the temperature is sufficiently high).

An exothermic reaction (ΔH negative) will always be spontaneous at some temperature. If the reaction involves an increase in entropy (ΔS positive) then $-T\Delta S$ will be negative. As ΔH is also negative, ΔG will always be negative, and the reaction will always be spontaneous.

If the reaction involves a decrease in entropy (ΔS negative), the reaction will be spontaneous at lower temperatures, when ΔH is more negative than $-T\Delta S$ is positive. It will, however, become less spontaneous as the temperature increases (as $-T\Delta S$ is positive and becomes more positive as the temperature increases). At higher temperatures $-T\Delta S$ will be more positive than ΔH is negative, and therefore ΔG will be positive and the reaction will be non-spontaneous at higher temperatures.

ΔH	ΔS	−TΔS	ΔG	Spontaneous?
−	+	−	negative	at all temperatures
+	+	−	becomes **more** negative as temperature increases	becomes more spontaneous as temperature increases
−	−	+	becomes **less** negative as temperature increases	becomes less spontaneous as temperature increases
+	−	+	positive	never

Reactions for which ΔS is positive become more spontaneous as temperature increases, but reactions for which ΔS is negative become less spontaneous as temperature increases.

Self-test 8 & Application 1

Test yourself

26 Given the data below, calculate $\Delta G^{\ominus}$ for the following reaction at 298 K and state whether it is spontaneous or not:
$$C_2H_4(g) + H_2(g) \rightarrow C_2H_6(g)$$
$$\Delta H^{\ominus} = -137\,kJ\,mol^{-1} \text{ and}$$
$$\Delta S^{\ominus} = -55.3\,J\,K^{-1}\,mol^{-1}$$

27 Given the data below, calculate $\Delta G^{\ominus}$ for the following reaction and state whether it is spontaneous or not at 298 K:
$$C_3H_8(g) + 5O_2(g) \rightarrow 3CO_2(g) + 4H_2O(l)$$
$$\Delta H^{\ominus} = -2219\,kJ\,mol^{-1} \text{ and}$$
$$\Delta S^{\ominus} = -373.3\,J\,K^{-1}\,mol^{-1}$$

28 Calculate $\Delta G^{\ominus}$ for the following reaction, given the $\Delta G_f^{\ominus}$ values in the table:
$$CaCO_3(s) \rightarrow CaO(s) + CO_2(g)$$

Substance	ΔG$_f^{\ominus}$/kJ mol^{-1}
CaCO$_3$(s)	−1129
CaO(s)	−604
CO$_2$(g)	−395

29 Calculate $\Delta G^{\ominus}$ for the following reaction, given the $\Delta G_f^{\ominus}$ values in the table:
$$C_5H_{12}(l) + 8O_2(g) \rightarrow 5CO_2(g) + 6H_2O(l)$$

Substance	ΔG$_f^{\ominus}$/kJ mol^{-1}
C$_5$H$_{12}$(l)	−9.2
H$_2$O(l)	−237.2
CO$_2$(g)	−395

Is the reaction spontaneous at 298 K?

30 Consider the decomposition of $Pb(NO_3)_2(s)$:
$$2Pb(NO_3)_2(s) \rightarrow 2PbO(s) + 4NO_2(g) + O_2(g)$$
$$\Delta H^{\ominus} = +598\,kJ\,mol^{-1} \quad \Delta G^{\ominus} = +333\,kJ\,mol^{-1}$$
a Work out the value for $\Delta S^{\ominus}$ at 298 K.
b Assuming that ΔH and ΔS do not change with temperature, calculate the temperature, in °C, above which this reaction will become spontaneous.

31 For each of the following reactions, predict whether it becomes more or less spontaneous as temperature increases:
a $N_2O_4(g) \rightarrow 2NO_2(g)$
b $N_2(g) + 3H_2(g) \rightarrow 2NH_3(g)$
c $2KNO_3(s) \rightarrow 2KNO_2(s) + O_2(g)$
d $2AgNO_3(s) \rightarrow 2Ag(s) + 2NO_2(s) + O_2(g)$

Exam-style questions

1   The specific heat capacity of a liquid is $4.00\,J\,g^{-1}\,K^{-1}$; $2000\,J$ of heat energy is supplied to $100.0\,g$ of the liquid. By how much would the temperature of the liquid increase?

    A $278\,K$ **B** $5\,K$ **C** $80\,K$ **D** $20\,K$

2   Which of the following is correct about endothermic reactions?

    A   Heat energy is taken in and the temperature increases.
    B   Heat energy is given out and the temperature increases.
    C   Heat energy is taken in and the temperature decreases.
    D   Heat energy is given out and the temperature decreases.

3   Use the following information:

$$2H_2(g) + O_2(g) \rightarrow 2H_2O(l) \qquad \Delta H = -572\,kJ\,mol^{-1}$$
$$2H_2(g) + O_2(g) \rightarrow 2H_2O(g) \qquad \Delta H = -484\,kJ\,mol^{-1}$$

to calculate the enthalpy change for the process:

$$H_2O(g) \rightarrow H_2O(l)$$

    A $-88\,kJ\,mol^{-1}$ **C** $+88\,kJ\,mol^{-1}$
    B $-44\,kJ\,mol^{-1}$ **D** $+44\,kJ\,mol^{-1}$

4   Use the bond enthalpies in the table to calculate the enthalpy change (in $kJ\,mol^{-1}$) for the reaction:

$$CH_4(g) + 2Cl_2(g) \rightarrow CH_2Cl_2(g) + 2HCl(g)$$

Bond	Bond enthalpy / $kJ\,mol^{-1}$
C–H	410
Cl–Cl	240
C–Cl	340
H–Cl	430

    A -720 **B** $+240$ **C** $+620$ **D** -240

HL 5   Which of the following processes is exothermic?

    A $Br_2(l) \rightarrow 2Br(g)$ **C** $CaF_2(s) \rightarrow Ca^{2+}(g) + 2F^-(g)$
    B $Na(g) \rightarrow Na^+(g) + e^-$ **D** $Cl(g) + e^- \rightarrow Cl^-(g)$

6 Use the approximate enthalpy change of combustion values given in the table to calculate the enthalpy change (in $kJ\,mol^{-1}$) for the reaction:

$$C_4H_6(g) + 2H_2(g) \rightarrow C_4H_{10}(g)$$

Substance	$\Delta H_c^{\ominus}\,/\,kJ\,mol^{-1}$
$C_4H_6(g)$	−2595
$C_4H_{10}(g)$	−2875
$H_2(g)$	−285

    A 290   **B** −290   **C** −5   **D** 5

7 Use the enthalpy change of formation values in the table to calculate the enthalpy change for the following reaction:

$$4NH_3(g) + 3O_2(g) \rightarrow 2N_2(g) + 6H_2O(l)$$

Substance	$\Delta H_f^{\ominus}\,/\,kJ\,mol^{-1}$
$NH_3(g)$	−46
$H_2O(l)$	−286

    A $-240\,kJ\,mol^{-1}$ **C** $-1532\,kJ\,mol^{-1}$
    B $-332\,kJ\,mol^{-1}$ **D** $-1900\,kJ\,mol^{-1}$

8 Which of the following reactions has a $\Delta S^{\ominus}$ value that is negative?

    A $2H_2O_2(aq) \rightarrow 2H_2O(l) + O_2(g)$
    B $CaCO_3(s) \rightarrow CaO(s) + CO_2(g)$
    C $CaCO_3(s) + 2HCl(aq) \rightarrow CaCl_2(aq) + CO_2(g) + H_2O(l)$
    D $2C_4H_{10}(g) + 13O_2(g) \rightarrow 8CO_2(g) + 10H_2O(l)$

9 Which of the following will have the largest value of lattice enthalpy?

    A NaCl   **B** MgO   **C** CaO   **D** $MgBr_2$

10 Using the data given below, calculate the value of $\Delta G^{\ominus}$, for the following reaction at 298 K:

$$SO_2(g) + Cl_2(g) \rightarrow SO_2Cl_2(l)$$
$\Delta H^{\ominus} = -97.3\,kJ\,mol^{-1}$ and $\Delta S^{\ominus} = -254.4\,J\,K^{-1}\,mol^{-1}$

    A $-21.5\,kJ\,mol^{-1}$ **C** $-173.1\,kJ\,mol^{-1}$
    B $75\,714\,kJ\,mol^{-1}$ **D** $-97.0\,kJ\,mol^{-1}$

11 a Explain what you understand by the term 'average bond enthalpy'. [2]

b Use the average bond enthalpies given in the table to calculate the enthalpy change for the combustion of ethanol vapour, according to the equation:

$$C_2H_5OH(g) + 3O_2(g) \rightarrow 2CO_2(g) + 3H_2O(g)$$ [3]

Bond	C–H	C–C	C–O	O–H	O=O	C=O
Bond enthalpy / kJ mol^{-1}	412	348	360	463	496	743

c Explain why bond enthalpies could not be used to work out the enthalpy change for the reaction:

$$C_2H_5OH(l) + 3O_2(g) \rightarrow 2CO_2(g) + 3H_2O(l)$$ [2]

d Consider the reaction:

$$N_2O_4(g) \rightarrow 2NO_2(g) \qquad \Delta H^{\ominus} = +57\,kJ\,mol^{-1}$$

Draw an enthalpy level diagram for this reaction and explain whether NO_2 or N_2O_4 is more stable. [3]

HL **12 a** Define 'standard enthalpy change of formation'. [2]

b Write a chemical equation for the standard enthalpy change of formation of propan-1-ol. [2]

c Use the standard enthalpy change of combustion values given in the table to calculate the standard enthalpy change of formation of propan-1-ol. [3]

Substance	$\Delta H_c^{\ominus}$ / kJ mol^{-1}
$CH_3CH_2CH_2OH(l)$	−2010
$C(s)$	−394
$H_2(g)$	−286

d Use the standard entropy values in the table below to calculate the entropy change for the complete combustion of propan-1-ol and justify the sign of the entropy change. [3]

Substance	$S^{\ominus}$ / J K^{-1} mol^{-1}
$CH_3CH_2CH_2OH(l)$	196.6
$CO_2(g)$	214
$H_2O(l)$	69.9
$O_2(g)$	205

e Calculate the standard free energy change, $\Delta G^{\ominus}$, for the complete combustion of propan-1-ol and explain whether the reaction will be spontaneous at 25 °C. [3]

13 Hydrazine, N_2H_4, has been used as a rocket fuel.

   a Draw a Lewis structure for hydrazine. [1]

   b Write a chemical equation to represent the enthalpy change of formation of gaseous hydrazine. [2]

   c Use bond enthalpies from the table to calculate the enthalpy change of formation of gaseous hydrazine. [3]

Bond	N≡N	N=N	N-N	H-H	N-H
Bond enthalpy / kJ mol^{-1}	944	409	163	436	388

   d The equation for the combustion of liquid hydrazine is:

$$N_2H_4(l) + O_2(g) \rightarrow N_2(g) + 2H_2O(l) \quad \Delta H = -622\,kJ\,mol^{-1}$$

     The enthalpy change of formation of $H_2O(l)$ is $-286\,kJ\,mol^{-1}$.

     Use these data to calculate the enthalpy change of formation of liquid hydrazine. [3]

   e Calculate the enthalpy change for the process:

$$N_2H_4(l) \rightarrow N_2H_4(g)$$ [2]

14 **a** Define 'lattice enthalpy'. [2]

   b Write chemical equations to represent the following enthalpy changes: [3]
     i the lattice enthalpy of potassium chloride
     ii the first electron affinity of chlorine
     iii the first ionisation energy of potassium

   c Construct a Born–Haber cycle for the formation of potassium chloride and use it and the values in the table to calculate the lattice enthalpy of potassium chloride. [5]

Process	Enthalpy change / kJ mol^{-1}
ΔH_{at} (K(s))	90
ΔH_{at} (Cl$_2$(g))	121
first ionisation energy (K)	418
first electron affinity (Cl)	−364
ΔH_f (KCl(s))	−436

   d Explain why the value of the lattice enthalpy for calcium chloride is substantially greater than that for potassium chloride. [2]

Summary

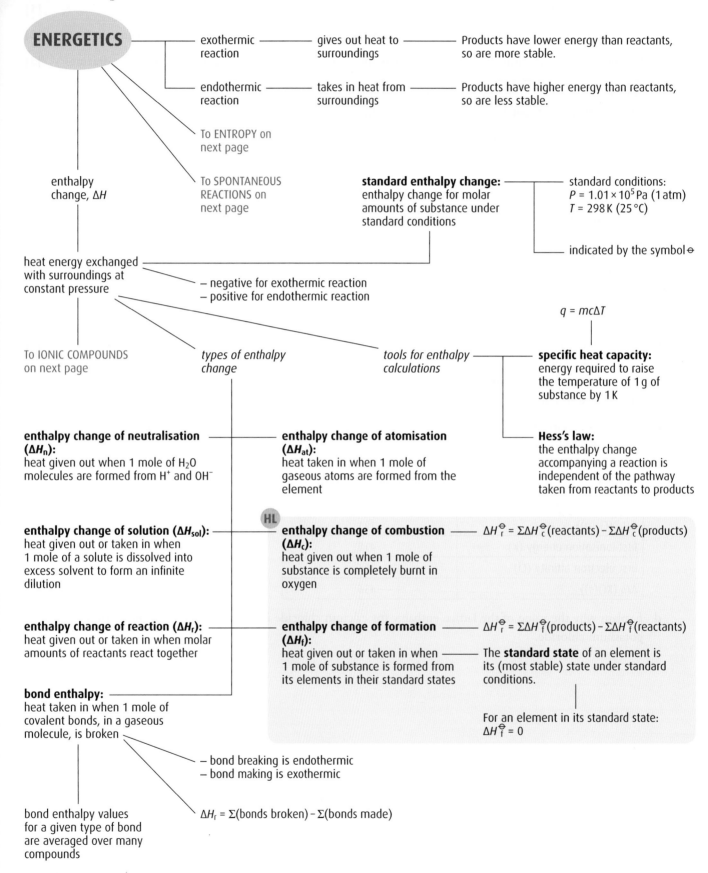

ENERGETICS

exothermic reaction — gives out heat to surroundings — Products have lower energy than reactants, so are more stable.

endothermic reaction — takes in heat from surroundings — Products have higher energy than reactants, so are less stable.

To ENTROPY on next page

To SPONTANEOUS REACTIONS on next page

enthalpy change, ΔH

standard enthalpy change: enthalpy change for molar amounts of substance under standard conditions

standard conditions:
$P = 1.01 \times 10^5$ Pa (1 atm)
$T = 298$ K (25 °C)

indicated by the symbol $\ominus$

heat energy exchanged with surroundings at constant pressure

– negative for exothermic reaction
– positive for endothermic reaction

$q = mc\Delta T$

To IONIC COMPOUNDS on next page

types of enthalpy change

tools for enthalpy calculations

specific heat capacity: energy required to raise the temperature of 1 g of substance by 1 K

enthalpy change of neutralisation (ΔH_n): heat given out when 1 mole of H_2O molecules are formed from H^+ and OH^-

enthalpy change of atomisation (ΔH_{at}): heat taken in when 1 mole of gaseous atoms are formed from the element

Hess's law: the enthalpy change accompanying a reaction is independent of the pathway taken from reactants to products

HL

enthalpy change of solution (ΔH_{sol}): heat given out or taken in when 1 mole of a solute is dissolved into excess solvent to form an infinite dilution

enthalpy change of combustion (ΔH_c): heat given out when 1 mole of substance is completely burnt in oxygen

$\Delta H_r^\ominus = \Sigma \Delta H_c^\ominus(\text{reactants}) - \Sigma \Delta H_c^\ominus(\text{products})$

enthalpy change of reaction (ΔH_r): heat given out or taken in when molar amounts of reactants react together

enthalpy change of formation (ΔH_f): heat given out or taken in when 1 mole of substance is formed from its elements in their standard states

$\Delta H_r^\ominus = \Sigma \Delta H_f^\ominus(\text{products}) - \Sigma \Delta H_f^\ominus(\text{reactants})$

The **standard state** of an element is its (most stable) state under standard conditions.

bond enthalpy: heat taken in when 1 mole of covalent bonds, in a gaseous molecule, is broken

For an element in its standard state:
$\Delta H_f^\ominus = 0$

– bond breaking is endothermic
– bond making is exothermic

bond enthalpy values for a given type of bond are averaged over many compounds

$\Delta H_r = \Sigma(\text{bonds broken}) - \Sigma(\text{bonds made})$

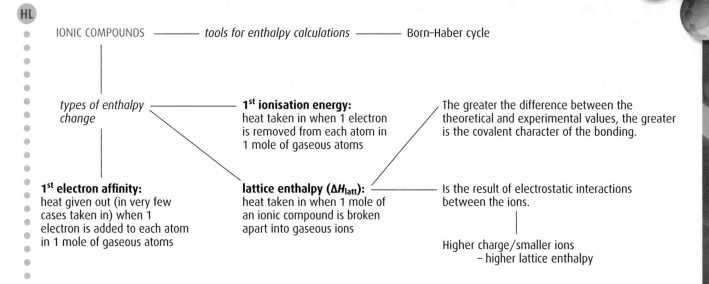

IONIC COMPOUNDS ———— *tools for enthalpy calculations* ———— Born–Haber cycle

types of enthalpy change

1st ionisation energy:
heat taken in when 1 electron is removed from each atom in 1 mole of gaseous atoms

The greater the difference between the theoretical and experimental values, the greater is the covalent character of the bonding.

1st electron affinity:
heat given out (in very few cases taken in) when 1 electron is added to each atom in 1 mole of gaseous atoms

lattice enthalpy (ΔH_{latt}):
heat taken in when 1 mole of an ionic compound is broken apart into gaseous ions

Is the result of electrostatic interactions between the ions.

Higher charge/smaller ions – higher lattice enthalpy

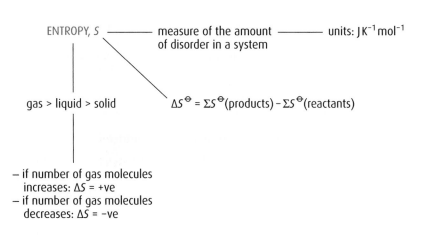

ENTROPY, S ———— measure of the amount of disorder in a system ———— units: $J\,K^{-1}\,mol^{-1}$

gas > liquid > solid

$$\Delta S^{\ominus} = \Sigma S^{\ominus}(\text{products}) - \Sigma S^{\ominus}(\text{reactants})$$

– if number of gas molecules increases: $\Delta S = +ve$
– if number of gas molecules decreases: $\Delta S = -ve$

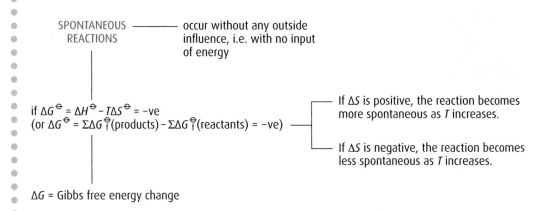

SPONTANEOUS REACTIONS ———— occur without any outside influence, i.e. with no input of energy

if $\Delta G^{\ominus} = \Delta H^{\ominus} - T\Delta S^{\ominus} = -ve$
(or $\Delta G^{\ominus} = \Sigma \Delta G_f^{\ominus}(\text{products}) - \Sigma \Delta G_f^{\ominus}(\text{reactants}) = -ve$)

If ΔS is positive, the reaction becomes more spontaneous as T increases.

If ΔS is negative, the reaction becomes less spontaneous as T increases.

ΔG = Gibbs free energy change

6 Rates of reaction

Learning objectives

- Understand what is meant by and define the rate of a chemical reaction
- Describe experimental methods for measuring the rates of various types of chemical reactions
- Analyse numerical and graphical data from rate experiments

Animations 1 & 2

Figure 6.1 Rusting is a very slow chemical reaction but one that costs economies billions of dollars each year.

Figure 6.2 An explosion is a very fast reaction – gases and a great deal of heat are generated very quickly.

Instead of a measuring cylinder, a gas burette or a gas syringe could also be used.

6.1 Determining the rate of a chemical reaction

What is the rate of a reaction?

When we consider the rate of a chemical reaction what we are looking at is how **fast** the reaction happens. This can be thought of in terms of how quickly the reactants are used up or how quickly the products are produced.

> **Rate of reaction** is the speed at which reactants are used up or products are formed.

Experiments to measure the rate of reaction

Consider the reaction between calcium carbonate and hydrochloric acid:

$$CaCO_3(s) + 2HCl(aq) \rightarrow CaCl_2(aq) + CO_2(g) + H_2O(l)$$

The rate of this reaction can be measured in various ways, two of which will be considered here:

1 measurement of the rate at which CO_2 is produced
2 measurement of the rate at which the mass decreases

Measurement of the rate at which CO_2 is produced

The apparatus is set up as shown in Figure **6.3** without the calcium carbonate. The bung on the conical flask (or Erlenmeyer flask) is removed, the calcium carbonate added, the bung quickly replaced and the timer started. This experiment can be used to generate a graph of volume of carbon dioxide produced against time by noting down the volume on the measuring cylinder every 10 seconds and then plotting the data. Sample data for this experiment are shown on the next page.

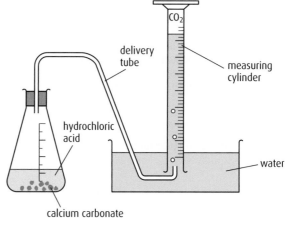

Figure 6.3 An experiment to measure rate of CO_2 production.

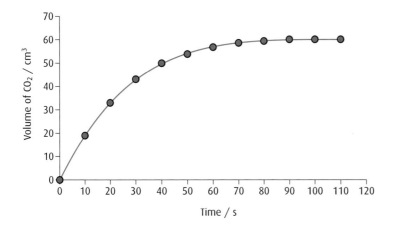

Time / s	Volume of CO_2 / cm^3
0	0.0
10	19.0
20	33.0
30	44.0
40	50.0
50	54.0
60	56.5
70	58.5
80	59.5
90	60.0
100	60.0
110	60.0

The reaction appears to finish at 90 s, as no more gas is produced after that. The average rate of reaction during the first 90 s can then be worked out as:

$$\text{average rate} = \frac{\text{change in volume}}{\text{time}} = \frac{60.0}{90} = 0.67 \, cm^3 \, s^{-1}$$

The rate at any particular time is given by the slope (gradient) of the graph at that time. This can be worked out by drawing a tangent to the curve at that point (Figure **6.4**).

The gradient of the tangent is given by:

$$\text{gradient} = \frac{\text{change in volume}}{\text{time}} = \frac{64}{30} = 2.1 \, cm^3 \, s^{-1}$$

Therefore the initial rate of reaction is $2.1 \, cm^3 \, s^{-1}$.

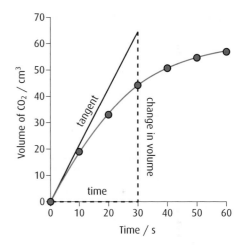

Figure 6.4 The tangent is drawn at the initial point to determine the initial rate.

This means that, initially, the gas is being produced at a rate of $2.1 \, cm^3$ per second.

It can be seen from the form of the graph that the gradient decreases as time goes on, in other words, the rate is fastest at the beginning and gets slower. At 90 s the reaction has stopped, and the gradient of the graph is zero.

Measurement of the rate at which the mass decreases

The rate for this reaction can also be measured by measuring the speed at which the mass decreases. The experimental set-up for this is shown in Figure **6.5**. The mass decreases as carbon dioxide is given off. The data for this experiment are shown overleaf.

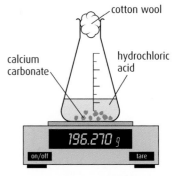

Figure 6.5 The cotton wool allows the gas to escape but stops mass being lost as a result of splashes.

Time / s	Mass / g
0	196.270
10	196.235
20	196.210
30	196.189
40	196.178
50	196.171
60	196.166
70	196.163
80	196.161
90	196.160
100	196.160
110	196.160

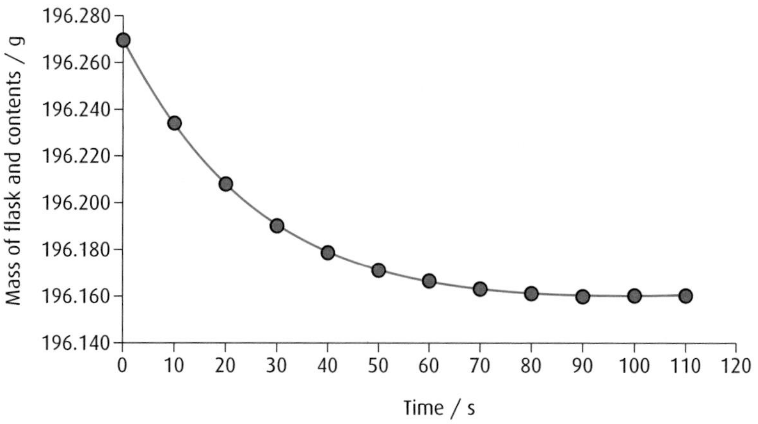

Time / s	Mass lost / g
0	0.000
10	0.035
20	0.060
30	0.081
40	0.092
50	0.099
60	0.104
70	0.107
80	0.109
90	0.110
100	0.110
110	0.110

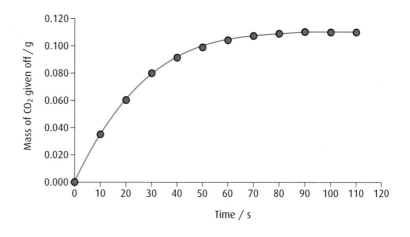

Alternatively, the mass of carbon dioxide lost can be worked out ($196.270 -$ mass at any time), and this can be plotted as shown below.

Rates for other reactions may be worked out by, for example, following changes in colour, pH, temperature, etc. during the reaction.

The average rate of reaction and initial rate of reaction could be worked out from either graph, using the same techniques as above. In this case we get:

$$\text{average rate} = \frac{\text{change in mass}}{\text{time}} = \frac{0.110}{90} = 1.22 \times 10^{-3} \, \text{g s}^{-1}$$

The initial rate is given by drawing a tangent at the initial point and in this case the initial rate is $4.0 \times 10^{-3} \, \text{g s}^{-1}$.

Rate of reaction defined

Although the above reactions were followed by looking at changes in volume and mass, rates are most often considered in terms of changing concentrations. We can thus define the rate of reaction:

> **rate of reaction** is the change in concentration of reactants or products per unit time.

Unit time could be 1 second, 1 minute, etc.

Units for rate of reaction are therefore $mol\,dm^{-3}\,s^{-1}$, $mol\,dm^{-3}\,min^{-1}$, etc.

The average rate over a period of time can be worked out as:

> $$\text{average rate} = \frac{\text{change in concentration}}{\text{time}}$$

For the reaction $A + B \rightarrow C$, the rate at which the reactants are used up is equal to the rate at which the products are produced, i.e. if the rate of reaction with respect to A is $0.12\,mol\,dm^{-3}\,s^{-1}$, the rate of reaction with respect to C will also be $0.12\,mol\,dm^{-3}\,s^{-1}$.

However, for the reaction $A \rightarrow 2D$, the rate at which D is produced will be twice the rate at which A is used up, as 1 mole of A will produce 2 moles of D. Therefore, if the rate of reaction with respect to A is $0.16\,mol\,dm^{-3}\,s^{-1}$, the rate of reaction with respect to D will be $0.32\,mol\,dm^{-3}\,s^{-1}$.

The rate of reaction at any time may be found from a graph of concentration against time by drawing a tangent at the particular time and finding the gradient (slope) of the tangent, in a similar way to that shown for a volume against time graph in Figure **6.4**.

Extension

The rate of reaction may also be defined in terms of calculus notation. Thus, for the reaction:

$$A + B \rightarrow C + D$$

The rate of reaction could be given as $\dfrac{d[C]}{dt}$, where [C] is the concentration of C.

As the concentration of A is decreasing, $\dfrac{-d[A]}{dt}$ is equal to $\dfrac{d[C]}{dt}$ and, for this reaction:

> $$\text{rate} = \frac{-d[A]}{dt} = \frac{-d[B]}{dt} = \frac{d[C]}{dt} = \frac{d[D]}{dt}$$

Learning objectives

- Understand that the average energy of particles in a gas is proportional to its temperature in kelvin
- Define the **activation energy** of a reaction
- Describe and explain the collision theory
- Understand the effect of surface area of solid reactants, temperature, catalysts, concentration and pressure on the rate of reaction
- Sketch the Maxwell–Boltzmann distribution and use it to explain the effect of a change in temperature on the rate of a reaction and how a catalyst speeds up a reaction

Animations 3 & 4

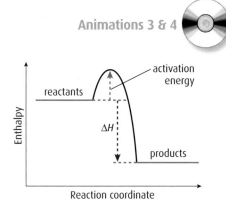

Figure 6.6 An enthalpy diagram, showing the activation energy for an exothermic reaction.

Not every collision with energy greater than the activation energy results in a reaction.

Animation 5

Collision theory

Reaction rates are generally discussed in terms of **collision theory**. This states that, for a reaction to occur, particles must **collide**; however, for these collisions to result in a reaction, two conditions must be fulfilled:

1 the collision must involve more than a certain **minimum amount of energy**
2 molecules must collide with the **correct orientations**

Note: not all collisions result in a reaction.

The collision must involve more than a certain minimum amount of energy

Particles must collide with sufficient energy in order to react. The minimum amount of energy that the colliding particles must possess for a collision to result in a reaction is called the **activation energy (E_a)**. Thus, if two particles with less that the activation energy collide, they will just bounce off each other and no reaction will result; however, if the particles have energy greater than or equal to the activation energy, then, assuming the orientation of the collision is also correct, the particles will react. A collision that results in a reaction is called a **successful** or **effective** collision.

Activation energy (E_a) is the minimum amount of energy that colliding particles must possess for a collision to result in a reaction.

The activation energy for an exothermic reaction is shown on the enthalpy level diagram in Figure **6.6**.

The activation energy is the energy needed to overcome repulsion (internuclear and between electrons), to start breaking bonds, to deform molecules and to allow rearrangement of atoms, electrons, etc.

Molecules must collide with the correct orientations

If molecules do not collide with the correct orientation they will not react:

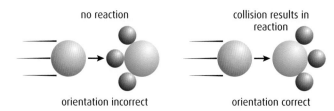

The main factors that affect the rate of a chemical reaction are:

1 concentration of reactants
2 pressure for reactions involving gases
3 surface area of solid reactants
4 temperature
5 catalysis

These will be considered in turn.

The effect of concentration on the reaction rate

With more particles in a certain volume, the particles collide more often (the collision frequency is higher), and therefore there is greater chance of a successful collision (i.e. one that results in a reaction) occurring in a certain time (Figure **6.7**).

The effect of pressure on the reaction rate

The effect of increasing the pressure is essentially the same as that of increasing the concentration of gaseous reactants. As the pressure is increased, the collision frequency increases (Figure **6.8**).

> Only reactions involving gases are significantly affected by changing the pressure.

> **Examiner's tip**
> We are dealing here with how **quickly** the reaction occurs and you must therefore have the idea of **time** in your explanation – it is not correct here to say that 'the particles collide more' you must write something like 'the particles collide **more often/more frequently**' or 'there are more collisions **in a certain time**'.

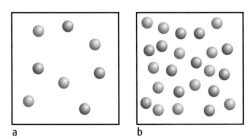

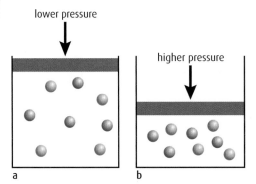

Figure 6.7 (**a**) Lower concentration – the particles are further apart and collide less frequently; (**b**) higher concentration – the particles are closer together and collide more frequently.

Figure 6.8 (**a**) Lower pressure – the particles are further apart and collide less frequently; (**b**) higher pressure – the particles are closer together and collide more frequently.

The effect of surface area of solid reactants

Reaction generally only occurs at the surface of a solid. Making a solid more finely divided increases the surface area and therefore the number of particles exposed at the surface. The effective concentration of the particles of the solid has thus been increased and there is greater chance of a particle of the other reactant colliding with a particle on the surface and reaction occurring (Figure **6.9**).

The relationship between temperature and the energy of particles in a gas

Before we can understand the effect of temperature on the rate of a chemical reaction, we must look at how changing the temperature affects how the particles in a gas move.

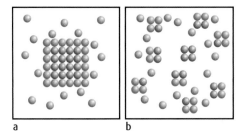

Figure 6.9 (**a**) Low surface area – only the particles coloured green are exposed on the surface and able to collide with the red particles; (**b**) high surface area – particles coloured both green and blue are exposed and are able to collide with the red particles.

For an ideal gas:

> the average kinetic energy of the particles in a gas is proportional to its temperature in kelvin.

Thus, if a sample of oxygen is heated from 300 K to 600 K, the **average** energy of the particles is doubled.

This relationship does **not** depend on the identity of the gas. Thus the average kinetic energy of the particles in a sample of helium at 300 K is the same as the average kinetic energy of the particles in oxygen at 300 K. However, because the mass of an O_2 molecule is eight times the mass of a helium atom, the helium atoms will be travelling substantially faster at the same temperature.

A consequence of this relationship between temperature and kinetic energy is that a large increase in temperature is required for a significant increase in the collision frequency – you will see the importance of this in the next section.

The effect of temperature on the rate of reaction

Increasing the temperature has a major effect on the rate of the reaction. As the temperature increases, the rate of reaction increases exponentially (Figure **6.10**).

It is often said that, as a rough rule of thumb, a rise in temperature of 10 K causes the reaction rate to be **approximately** doubled. (This will be investigated in more detail below.)

As the temperature increases, the molecules have more energy and therefore move faster. This means that the **collision frequency increases, i.e. the particles collide more often**. This is, however, only a **minor effect** and can explain only a small increase in rate (approximately 2% for a 10 K rise in temperature) as the temperature increases. The major cause of the increase in rate as the temperature increases is that, not only do the particles collide more often, but they also **collide harder**, that is, with more energy, so that there is **greater chance that a collision will result in reaction**.

Let us consider a sample of gas: the molecules are constantly colliding with each other and, therefore, do not all have the same speed and hence energy. This is shown in Figure **6.11**, which represents the **Maxwell–Boltzmann** distribution of molecular kinetic energies **at a particular temperature**. It can be seen that there are only a few particles with high energy and only a few with very low energy. Most particles have energy around the average energy.

> The main reason that the rate of reaction increases with temperature is an **increase in the number of particles with energy greater than or equal to the activation energy**.

> At the same temperature lighter particles travel faster than heavier ones.

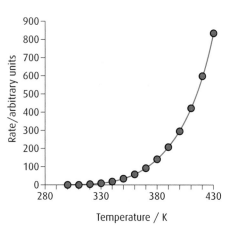

Figure 6.10 The rate of a reaction increases exponentially as the temperature rises.

Features to note on Figure **6.11**:
- it is **not** symmetrical
- no molecules have zero kinetic energy
- at higher energy the line does not reach the energy axis
- the area under the curve represents the total number of particles and will not change as the temperature changes

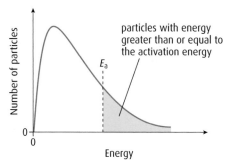

Figure 6.11 The Maxwell–Boltzmann distribution of the energy of the particles in a sample of gas. The shaded area represents the particles that have sufficient energy to react when they collide.

Extension

This graph is actually a histogram, where each bar in the histogram represents the number of molecules in a certain narrow range of kinetic energies.

The vertical axis may also be labelled as 'number of particles with a certain amount of energy' or 'proportion of particles with a certain amount of energy'.

As the temperature is increased, this distribution of energies changes (Figure **6.12**). At higher temperatures the curve is flatter and the maximum has moved to the right. There are thus fewer particles with lower energy and more particles with higher energy. With more particles having energy greater than or equal to the activation energy at the higher temperature, a greater proportion of collisions will be successful, and therefore the rate of reaction will increase. The areas underneath the curves are the same, however, because the number of particles does not change if the temperature is increased.

Application 1

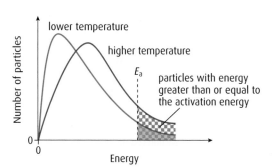

Figure 6.12 The shaded area represents the number of particles with energy greater than or equal to the activation energy at the lower temperature. The checked area represents the number of particles with energy greater than or equal to the activation energy at the higher temperature.

How do we know when we encounter a new reaction that the rate will increase when we increase the temperature? This comes form the idea of inductive reasoning – inductive reasoning is a fundamental tool of scientists, and to a certain extent chemistry would not exist in the form it does without inductive reasoning. Inductive reasoning allows us to generalise from the specific; for instance, if we carry out a series of experiments and each one gives us the result that increasing the temperature increases the rate of reaction, then we postulate a general law that the rate of reaction increases with temperature. How is it possible to do this when we have not studied every single chemical reaction? Indeed a philosopher would say that this is not rational, and there is no logical basis for being able to do this – this is the problem with induction. Common sense, however, would tell us that the rate of reaction for every simple reaction should increase as temperature increases; we rely on the uniformity of nature and we cannot imagine a situation in which it would not be true. But can we know this, or only believe it to be true? Is there a difference between a scientist having faith in induction and religious faith?

Catalysis

Animation 6

> A catalyst is a substance that increases the rate of a chemical reaction without itself being used up in the reaction.

An example of a catalyst is manganese(IV) oxide in the decomposition of hydrogen peroxide solution:

The catalyst is often written above the arrow and does not appear in the chemical equation, as it does not change in the reaction.

$$2H_2O_2(aq) \xrightarrow{\text{MnO}_2} 2H_2O(l) + O_2(g)$$

Without the catalyst the reaction occurs very slowly, but it is very rapid once the catalyst has been added.

> A catalyst acts by allowing the reaction to proceed by **an alternative pathway of lower activation energy**.

Catalysts are important in many industrial processes – see pages **171**, **172**, **298** and **299**.

This is shown on the energy level diagram:

HL

Higher Level only: the mechanism is different for a catalysed reaction (see page **267**).

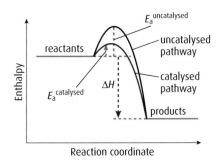

If we look at the Maxwell–Boltzmann distribution we can understand why a lower activation energy results in a faster reaction (Figure **6.13**).

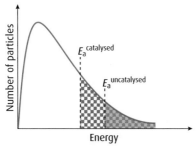

Figure 6.13 The shaded area represents the number of particles with energy greater than or equal to the activation energy for the uncatalysed reaction. The checked area represents the number of particles with energy greater than or equal to the activation energy for the catalysed reaction. A larger number of particles have energy greater than the activation energy; therefore a greater proportion of collisions result in reaction and the reaction rate increases.

Although collision theory is consistent with experimental results, this does not prove that the theory is correct. The mark of a scientific theory, and what distinguishes it from a non-scientific one, is the idea of falsifiability – so far collision theory has been supported by experimental evidence, but if new experimental data are produced that cannot be explained using the collision theory, then the theory will have to be modified or dismissed in favour of a new theory that does explain all the experimental data. Collision theory is the best explanation (at this level) of the experimental data produced so far. Other explanations may be possible, but this interpretation of the results is widely accepted at the moment, and the theory is used to make predictions and explain phenomena.

Self-test 1

Test yourself

1 A series of experiments was carried out to measure the volume of gas produced when magnesium reacts with dilute hydrochloric acid.

In the first experiment, 0.10 g of Mg ribbon was reacted with 30 cm³ of $0.50\,mol\,dm^{-3}$ HCl. The data for this experiment is recorded in the table. The reaction was carried out at 20 °C. The equation for the reaction is:

$$Mg + 2HCl \rightarrow MgCl_2 + H_2$$

a Draw a graph of this data and state and explain in terms of the collision theory how the rate of reaction changes with time.

b Use your graph to calculate the initial rate of the reaction with units.

c Calculate the average rate for the first 120 s.

d The experiment was repeated under the same conditions, except that 0.10 g of powdered Mg was used. On the same set of axes you used in part a sketch the graph that would be obtained. Label this graph **X**.

e The original experiment was repeated, except that 0.05 g of Mg ribbon was used. On the same axes sketch the graph that would be obtained. Label this graph **Y**.

f The original experiment was repeated at 10 °C. On the same axes sketch the graph that would be obtained. Label this graph **Z**.

g Sketch the Maxwell–Boltzmann distribution for the original experiment and the experiment at 10 °C and use this to explain the effect of a change in temperature on the rate of this reaction.

Time / s	Volume of gas / cm³
0	0.0
15	18.6
30	32.3
45	44.3
60	54.8
75	62.7
90	68.4
105	72.6
120	74.9
135	75.4
150	75.6
165	75.6
180	75.6

Catalysts may be heterogeneous or homogeneous. Heterogeneous catalysts are in a different physical state from the reactants, whereas homogeneous catalysts are in the same physical state as the reactants.

Learning objectives

- Explain the terms **rate constant** and **order of reaction**
- Work out the rate expression (rate equation) from numerical data and solve problems related to it
- Sketch and explain graphs of concentration against time and rate against time for zero-, first- and second-order reactions

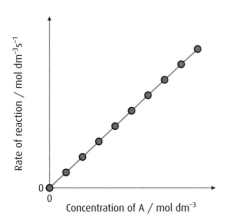

Figure 6.14 Possible concentration–time graph for a reaction A → B.

Note **small _k_ – not capital**.

The rate constant is only a constant for a particular reaction at a particular temperature.

HL 6.3 The rate expression

The rate equation/rate expression

In this section we will consider the quantitative effect of changes in conditions on the rate of reaction.

A rate of reaction is usually affected by a change in concentration of the reactants. Consider the reaction A → B. If a series of experiments is carried out in which the concentration of A is varied and the rate of reaction measured, a graph like the one in Figure **6.14** might be plotted.

From this graph it can be seen that the **rate of reaction is directly proportional to the concentration of A**. For this reaction we can write:

$$\text{rate} \propto [A]$$

where [A] is the concentration of A. And, by adding a constant of proportionality, we can write:

$$\text{rate} = k[A]$$

This equation is called a **rate equation** or **rate expression**. _k_ is called the rate constant.

> The rate expression is an **experimentally determined** equation that relates the rate of reaction to the concentrations of substances in the reaction mixture.

In general, we can write a rate expression (rate equation) for any reaction, e.g. for the reaction:

$$x\text{A} + y\text{B} \rightarrow \text{C} + \text{D}$$

This could be of the form:

> $$\text{rate} = k[A]^m[B]^n$$

> The **rate constant** is a constant of proportionality relating the concentrations in the experimentally determined rate expression to the rate of a chemical reaction.

> The **order of a reaction** with respect to a particular reactant is the **power** of the reactant's concentration in the experimentally determined rate equation.

In the rate expression above, the order with respect to A is *m* and the order with respect to B is *n*. The overall order is *m* + *n*.

If we consider our original rate expression, rate = k[A], again: this reaction is **first order with respect to A** (as the power of [A] is 1) and first order overall.

The rate expression **can be determined only from experimental data** – that is, from a series of experiments in which the effect of changing the concentration of the reactants on the rate of reaction is investigated. The important thing to realise is that there is no connection between the chemical equation for a reaction and the rate expression, i.e. we can **not** simply look at an equation such as 2A + B → C + D and deduce that the order with respect to A is 2 and that with respect to B is 1. The reason for this is that the reaction may not occur in one single step – this will be considered in more detail below.

Experimental determination of the rate expression

Consider the reaction A + B → C. The dependence of the reaction rate on the concentrations of A and B can be determined by conducting the following set of experiments.

Firstly, a series of experiments is carried out using a **fixed amount of B** and changing the concentration of A each time. Each experiment should yield a graph of concentration of A against time. The initial rates may be worked out from these graphs by drawing tangents to the graph at the initial point. From this data the order of the reaction with respect to A may be determined by plotting a graph of initial rate against concentration of A.

The experiments are now repeated using a **fixed amount of A** and varying the concentration of B. This allows the order of reaction with respect to B to be calculated.

When the orders with respect to A and B are known, the rate expression and hence a value for the rate constant, may be worked out.

Determining the order of reaction and the rate expression from experimental data

Example

Consider the data for the reaction 2A → B, given in Table **6.1**.
We want to determine:
1 the order with respect to A
2 the rate expression
3 the value of the rate constant (with units)
4 the rate of reaction when [A] = 1.3 mol dm^{-3}

HL

The **overall order** of reaction is the **sum** of the powers of the concentration terms in the experimentally determined rate equation.

Examiner's tip
Remember that the rate expression can be determined only from experimental data and not from the chemical (stoichiometric) equation.

The initial rate is taken, as this is the only point at which we know the concentration of A and concentration of B, as none has been used up.

Experiment	[A] / mol dm^{-3}	Rate / mol dm^{-3} s^{-1}
1	1.0	0.60
2	2.0	1.2
3	5.0	3.0

Table 6.1 Experimental data for the reaction 2A → B.

1 If we consider experiments 1 and 2, we can see that, as the concentration of A is doubled from $1.0\,\text{mol}\,\text{dm}^{-3}$ to $2.0\,\text{mol}\,\text{dm}^{-3}$, the rate of reaction also doubles from $0.60\,\text{mol}\,\text{dm}^{-3}\,\text{s}^{-1}$ to $1.2\,\text{mol}\,\text{dm}^{-3}\,\text{s}^{-1}$. Thus, the concentration is multiplied by a factor of 2 and the rate goes up by a factor of 2^1. This means that the order with respect to A is 1: in other words, the reaction is first order with respect to A. This can be summarised as:

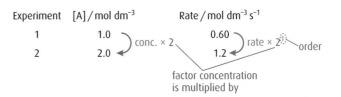

The fact that the order of reaction with respect to A is 1 can be further confirmed by looking at experiments 1 and 3. As the concentration of A is multiplied by a factor of 5, the rate of reaction is multiplied by a factor of 5^1.

2 The reaction is first order with respect to A, so the rate expression is: rate $= k[\text{A}]$.

> As the order with respect to A is 1, the order is omitted from the rate expression.

3 To find the value of k, we substitute the values from any experiment into the rate expression. If this is done with the values from experiment 1, we get:

$$0.60 = k \times 1.0$$

This can be rearranged to give: $k = 0.60$.

k has units, and these can be worked out from the rate expression by substituting in units:

$$\text{rate} = k[\text{A}] \rightarrow \text{mol}\,\text{dm}^{-3}\,\text{s}^{-1} = k \times \text{mol}\,\text{dm}^{-3}$$

$\text{mol}\,\text{dm}^{-3}$ can be cancelled from each side:

$$\cancel{\text{mol}\,\text{dm}^{-3}}\,\text{s}^{-1} = k \times \cancel{\text{mol}\,\text{dm}^{-3}}, \text{ so } \text{s}^{-1} = k$$

Therefore the units of k are s^{-1} in this case, and the rate constant is $0.6\,\text{s}^{-1}$.

4 The rate of reaction when $[\text{A}] = 1.3\,\text{mol}\,\text{dm}^{-3}$ can be worked out by substituting this value into the rate expression with the value of k:

$$\text{rate} = k[\text{A}]$$

$$\text{rate} = 0.60 \times 1.3$$

Therefore the rate of reaction is $0.78\,\text{mol}\,\text{dm}^{-3}\,\text{s}^{-1}$.

This could also have been worked out by realising that the reaction is first order with respect to A, and that $1.3\,\text{mol}\,\text{dm}^{-3}$ is 1.3 times the concentration of A in experiment 1, and therefore the rate of reaction is 1.3^1 times the rate of reaction in experiment 1.

Worked examples

Experiment	[A] / mol dm^{-3}	[B] / mol dm^{-3}	Rate / mol dm^{-3} h^{-1}
1	0.10	0.10	0.50
2	0.30	0.10	4.50
3	0.30	0.20	4.50

Given these data for the reaction: $3A + B \rightarrow C + D$ determine:

a the order with respect to A

b the order with respect to B

c the overall order of the reaction

d the rate expression

e the value of the rate constant (with units)

f the rate of reaction when [A] = 1.60 mol dm^{-3} and [B] = 0.30 mol dm^{-3}

a To find the order with respect to A, we must consider experiments 1 and 2, because the only thing that changes between these two experiments is the concentration of A (the concentration of B remains constant). From experiment 1 to experiment 2, the concentration of A is multiplied by a factor of 3 and the rate goes up by a factor of 9, i.e. 3^2. This means that the order with respect to A is 2, i.e. the reaction is second order with respect to A.

Experiment	[A] / mol dm^{-3}	[B] / mol dm^{-3}	Rate / mol dm^{-3} h^{-1}
		remains constant	
1	0.10	0.10	0.50
2	0.30	0.10	4.50

conc. × 3   rate × 3^2 order

factor concentration is multiplied by

b To find the order with respect to B, we must consider experiments 2 and 3, because the only thing that changes between these two experiments is the concentration of B (the concentration of A remains constant). From experiment 2 to experiment 3, the concentration of B is multiplied by a factor of 2 and the rate does not change, i.e. it is multiplied by a factor of 2^0. This means that the order with respect to B is 0, i.e. the reaction is zero order with respect to B.

> Any number to the power zero is 1.

c The overall order of reaction is the sum of the orders with respect to A and B: $2 + 0$. Therefore the overall order is 2.

d The rate expression is: rate = $k[A]^2[B]^0$, which is usually just written as: rate = $k[A]^2$.

e The value of the rate constant can be calculated by substituting values from any experiment into the rate expression. It doesn't matter which experiment is taken, but values must not be taken from different experiments. If we use the data from experiment 2:

rate = $k[A]^2$

$4.50 = k \times 0.30^2$

$k = 50$

To work out the units for k, the units of concentration and rate must be substituted into the rate expression:

$$\text{mol}\,\text{dm}^{-3}\text{h}^{-1} = k(\text{mol}\,\text{dm}^{-3})^2$$

$\text{mol}\,\text{dm}^{-3}$ can be cancelled from each side:

$$\cancel{\text{mol}\,\text{dm}^{-3}}\,\text{h}^{-1} = k(\text{mol}\,\text{dm}^{-3})^{\cancel{2}}$$

i.e. $\text{h}^{-1} = k\,\text{mol}\,\text{dm}^{-3}$.

> Alternatively, at this stage it can be seen that the units of k must include $\text{mol}^{-1}\,\text{dm}^3$ for the powers of mol and dm to be 0 on both sides.

This can be rearranged to give:

$$\frac{\text{h}^{-1}}{\text{mol}\,\text{dm}^{-3}} = k$$

i.e. $k = \text{mol}^{-1}\,\text{dm}^3\,\text{h}^{-1}$

> When a quantity with a power is brought from the bottom to the top of an expression, the sign of the power changes, i.e. $\frac{1}{x^2}$ is equivalent to x^{-2}.

Therefore the value of the rate constant, k, is $50\,\text{mol}^{-1}\,\text{dm}^3\,\text{h}^{-1}$.

> It is actually best practice to write any positive powers first, so this is better written as $50\,\text{dm}^3\,\text{mol}^{-1}\,\text{h}^{-1}$.

f The rate of reaction when $[A] = 1.60\,\text{mol}\,\text{dm}^{-3}$ and $[B] = 0.30\,\text{mol}\,\text{dm}^{-3}$ can be worked out by substituting these values together with the value of k into the rate expression:

$$\text{rate} = k[A]^2 = 50 \times 1.60^2 = 128\,\text{mol}\,\text{dm}^{-3}\,\text{h}^{-1}.$$

Given these data for the reaction:
$2P + Q \rightarrow R + S$ determine:

a the order with respect to P
b the order with respect to Q
c the overall order of the reaction
d the rate expression
e the value of the rate constant (with units)

Experiment	$[P]/\text{mol}\,\text{dm}^{-3}$	$[Q]/\text{mol}\,\text{dm}^{-3}$	Rate $/\text{mol}\,\text{dm}^{-3}\,\text{s}^{-1}$
1	1.20	2.00	5.00×10^{-3}
2	2.40	2.00	1.00×10^{-2}
3	6.00	8.00	0.100

a To find the order with respect to P, we must consider experiments 1 and 2, because the only thing that changes between these two experiments is the concentration of P (the concentration of Q remains constant). From experiment 1 to experiment 2, the concentration of P is multiplied by a factor of 2 and the rate goes up by a factor of 2, i.e. 2^1. This means that the order with respect to P is 1, i.e. the reaction is first order with respect to P.

b It is a more difficult problem to find the order with respect to Q, as there are no two experiments in which the concentration of P remains constant, and so we cannot easily see how just changing $[Q]$ affects the rate. One way of getting around this is to add another row to the table:

Experiment	$[P]/\text{mol}\,\text{dm}^{-3}$	$[Q]/\text{mol}\,\text{dm}^{-3}$	Rate $/\text{mol}\,\text{dm}^{-3}\,\text{s}^{-1}$
1	1.20	2.00	5.00×10^{-3}
2	2.40	2.00	1.00×10^{-2}
2A			
3	6.00	8.00	0.100

We can fill in the values in this new row by realising that the order with respect to P is 1. If the concentration of P in experiment 2A is five times that in experiment 1, and as [Q] is the same in both experiments, the rate in experiment 2A will be $5 \times 5.00 \times 10^{-3}$ i.e. 2.50×10^{-2} mol dm^{-3} s^{-1}.

Experiment	[P]/mol dm^{-3}	[Q]/mol dm^{-3}	Rate/mol dm^{-3} s^{-1}
1	1.20	2.00	5.00×10^{-3}
2	2.40	2.00	1.00×10^{-2}
2A	**6.00**	**2.00**	**2.50×10^{-2}**
3	6.00	8.00	0.100

The concentration of P has been chosen to be the same as that in experiment 3.

We can now consider experiments 2A and 3 and see the effect of just changing the concentration of Q on the rate of reaction. From experiment 2A to experiment 3, the concentration of Q is multiplied by a factor of 4 and the rate changes by a factor of 4^1. This means that the order with respect to Q is 1.

Another way to approach this, without adding another row to the table, is to just consider experiments 1 and 3.

Experiment	[P]/mol dm^{-3}	[Q]/mol dm^{-3}	Rate/mol dm^{-3} s^{-1}
1	1.20	2.00	5.00×10^{-3}
2	2.40	2.00	1.00×10^{-2}
3	6.00	8.00	0.100

We know that going from experiment 1 to experiment 3 the concentration of P has increased by a factor of 5. As the reaction is first order with respect to P, the cause of this will be to multiply the rate of reaction by a factor of 5^1, i.e. 5. If this were done without any change in the concentration of Q, the rate of reaction would be $5 \times 5.00 \times 10^{-3}$, i.e. 2.50×10^{-2} mol dm^{-3} s^{-1}. However, the rate of reaction in experiment 3 is 0.100, which is four times 2.50×10^{-2}. Thus the effect of multiplying the concentration of Q by 4 is that the rate of reaction is multiplied by 4^1; therefore the order with respect to Q is 1. This approach is, of course, entirely equivalent to adding an extra row to the table.

c The order with respect to P is 1 and the order with respect to Q is 1, so the overall order is $1 + 1$, i.e. 2.

d The rate expression is: rate $= k[P]^1[Q]^1$, which is usually just written as: rate $= k[P][Q]$.

e The value of the rate constant can be calculated by substituting values from any one experiment into the rate expression. If we use the data from experiment 3:

$0.100 = k \times 6.00 \times 8.00$

$0.100 = k \times 48.0$

$k = 2.08 \times 10^{-3}$

To work out the units for k, the units of concentration and rate must be substituted into the rate expression:

$\text{mol dm}^{-3}\text{s}^{-1} = k \times \text{mol dm}^{-3} \times \text{mol dm}^{-3}$

mol dm^{-3} can be cancelled from each side:

$\cancel{\text{mol dm}}^{-3}\text{s}^{-1} = k \times \cancel{\text{mol dm}}^{-3} \times \text{mol dm}^{-3}$

i.e. $\text{s}^{-1} = k \times \text{mol dm}^{-3}$.

This can be rearranged to give:

$$\frac{s^{-1}}{mol\,dm^{-3}} = k$$

$$k = mol^{-1}\,dm^3\,s^{-1}$$

Therefore the value of the rate constant, k, is $2.08 \times 10^{-3}\,mol^{-1}\,dm^3\,s^{-1}$.

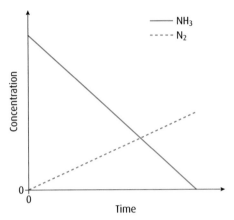

Figure 6.15 Concentration of reactant and product against time for a zero-order reaction.

> **The rate is independent of the concentration.**

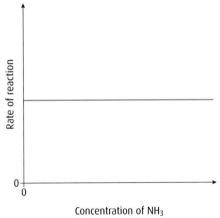

Figure 6.16 Rate against concentration for a zero-order reaction.

Zero-order reactions

Let us consider a zero-order reaction – the decomposition of ammonia on a tungsten surface:

$$2NH_3(g) \rightarrow N_2(g) + 3H_2(g)$$

The concentration of ammonia decreases at a constant rate in this reaction. The constant rate is indicated by the graph of concentration against time being a straight line (Figure **6.15**). A straight line has a constant gradient (slope) and indicates that the rate does not change as the concentration of NH_3 changes.

The concentration of the nitrogen increases at a constant rate, indicated by the straight dashed line in Figure **6.15**.

The two graphs of concentration against time were drawn at the same scale, and it can be seen that the magnitude of the gradient of the line for N_2 is half that for NH_3. This is because in the chemical equation for this reaction the coefficient of NH_3 is 2 but that of N_2 is 1; therefore N_2 is produced at half the rate at which the NH_3 is used up.

Changing the concentration of ammonia has no effect on the rate of the reaction (Figure **6.16**).

The rate expression is: rate = k, which shows that the rate is constant. The units of the rate constant are the same as that of rate, i.e. concentration time^{-1}. A set of units for the rate constant could therefore be $mol\,dm^{-3}\,s^{-1}$.

> The rate equation for this reaction is: rate = k.
> The units of k are conc. time^{-1} (i.e. units could be $mol\,dm^{-3}\,s^{-1}$ or $mol\,dm^{-3}\,h^{-1}$, etc.).

First-order reactions

Let us consider a first-order reaction – the decomposition of hydrogen iodide on a platinum surface:

$$2HI(g) \rightarrow H_2(g) + I_2(g)$$

The rate of this reaction is directly proportional to the concentration of HI, as shown by the straight line through the origin in Figure **6.17**.

The graph in Figure **6.18** shows how the concentration of HI decreases with time. This exhibits an exponential decay and has a constant **half-life**. The time taken for the concentration to drop by half does not depend on concentration in a first-order reaction, e.g. the time taken for the concentration to fall from $0.1\,mol\,dm^{-3}$ to $0.05\,mol\,dm^{-3}$ is the same as the time taken for the concentration to fall from $0.08\,mol\,dm^{-3}$ to $0.04\,mol\,dm^{-3}$.

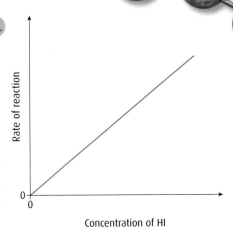

Figure 6.17 Rate against concentration for a first-order reaction.

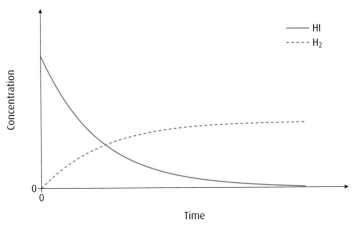

Figure 6.18 Concentration of reactant and product against time for a first-order reaction.

The rate is directly proportional to the concentration.

The dashed line in Figure **6.18** shows the increase in concentration of one of the products (H_2) with time. The rate of production of H_2 is half the rate at which HI is used up, which can be seen from the coefficients in the chemical equation:

$$2HI \rightarrow H_2 + I_2$$

The rate equation for this reaction is: rate = $k[HI]$. The units of k are time^{-1}.

Second-order reactions

Let us consider a second-order reaction – the decomposition of hydrogen iodide without a catalyst:

$$2HI(g) \rightarrow H_2(g) + I_2(g)$$

Figure **6.19** shows how the rate of reaction varies with the concentration of hydrogen iodide.

It can be proved that a reaction is second order (rather than third order, etc.) by plotting a graph of rate against concentration of HI squared (Figure **6.20**, overleaf). As the rate is proportional to $[HI]^2$, this graph is a straight line through the origin.

The half-life is related to the rate constant by the equation

$$\text{rate constant} = \frac{0.693}{(\text{half-life})}$$

The rate of reaction is proportional to concentration squared.

Figure **6.21** (overleaf) shows how the concentration of HI changes with time. This is **not** an exponential relationship and does not have a constant half-life.

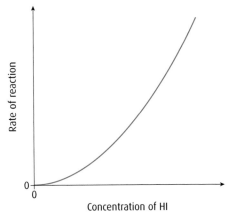

Figure 6.19 Rate against concentration for a second-order reaction.

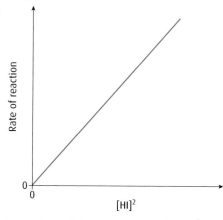

Rate of reaction

$[HI]^2$

Figure 6.20 Rate against concentration^2 for a second-order reaction.

The rate equation for this reaction is: rate = $k[HI]^2$.
The units of the rate constant are: concentration^{-1} time^{-1} (i.e. units could be mol^{-1} dm^3 s^{-1}).

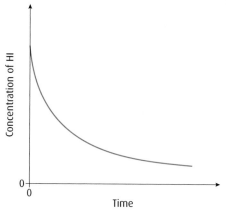

Concentration of HI

Time

Figure 6.21 Concentration of reactant against time for a second-order reaction.

HL The units of the rate constant

It can be seen from the treatment above that the units of the rate constant are related to the overall order of the reaction. This is summarised in Table **6.2**.

Overall order	Units of k	Example of units
0	concentration time^{-1}	mol dm^{-3} s^{-1}
1	time^{-1}	s^{-1}
2	concentration^{-1} time^{-1}	mol^{-1} dm^3 s^{-1}
3	concentration^{-2} time^{-1}	mol^{-2} dm^6 s^{-1}

Table 6.2 The relationship between overall order of the reaction and units of the rate constant.

For a zero-order reaction, the units of k are the same as that of rate. Each time the overall order increases by 1 the units of k are divided by concentration.

Generally the units of k are: concentration$^{(1 - \text{overall order})}$ time^{-1}.

Self-tests 2 & 3

Test yourself

2 Consider the following data for the reaction:
$A + 2B \rightarrow C + D$

Experiment	[A] / mol dm^{-3}	[B] / mol dm^{-3}	Rate / mol dm^{-3} s^{-1}
1	0.200	0.100	0.0200
2	0.400	0.100	0.0400
3	0.400	0.200	0.160

a Deduce the order of reaction with respect to A and with respect to B.
b What is the overall order of reaction?
c Work out a value for the rate constant of this reaction with units.
d What will be the rate of reaction when the concentration of A is 0.100 mol dm^{-3} and that of B is 0.0500 mol dm^{-3}?

3 Consider the following data for the reaction:
$2X + 4Y \rightarrow Q + 2R$

Experiment	[X] / mol dm^{-3}	[Y] / mol dm^{-3}	Rate / mol dm^{-3} s^{-1}
1	1.50×10^{-2}	3.00×10^{-2}	1.78×10^{-3}
2	4.50×10^{-2}	3.00×10^{-2}	5.34×10^{-3}
3	4.50×10^{-2}	1.20×10^{-1}	2.14×10^{-2}

a Write the rate expression for this reaction.
b Calculate a value for the rate constant from this data.
c What are the units of the rate constant?

4 A reaction is zero order with respect to P and second order with respect to Q. What would be the effect of doubling the concentration of P and the concentration of Q on the overall rate of reaction?

5 Consider the following data for the reaction:

$$2D + 3E \rightarrow 2C + B$$

Experiment	[D] / mol dm^{-3}	[E] / mol dm^{-3}	Rate / mol dm^{-3} s^{-1}
1	2.50×10^{-3}	5.00×10^{-3}	4.28×10^{-4}
2	1.00×10^{-2}	5.00×10^{-3}	1.71×10^{-3}
3	4.00×10^{-2}	2.00×10^{-2}	6.84×10^{-3}

a Work out the order of reaction with respect to D.
b Work out the order of reaction with respect to E.
c What is the rate expression for the reaction?
d Work out a value with units for k, the rate constant, for this reaction.
e What is the rate of reaction when the concentration of D is 0.0600 mol dm^{-3} and that of E is 0.0300 mol dm^{-3}?

6.4 The Arrhenius equation

The Arrhenius equation

In a rate expression such as rate = k[A][B], the effect of temperature variation is accounted for by a change in the value of the rate constant.

As the temperature increases, the rate constant increases exponentially.

The **Arrhenius equation** shows the variation of the rate constant with temperature.

A is called the pre-exponential factor, A-factor or frequency factor and contains information related to the **frequency of collisions** and the **orientation of the collisions**. **A is essentially a constant** (it varies only slightly with temperature).

Learning objectives

- Understand that increasing the temperature causes the rate constant to increase
- Work out values of activation energy using the Arrhenius equation

$$k = Ae^{\frac{-E_a}{RT}}$$

$e^{-E_a/RT}$ represents the fraction of collisions that have $E \geq E_a$. However, not all collisions with $E \geq E_a$ result in reaction. The molecules must collide in the correct orientation, and A contains a factor that allows for this.

R is the gas constant, i.e. $8.31\,\mathrm{J\,K^{-1}\,mol^{-1}}$.

T is the temperature in kelvin.

T/K	$k/\mathrm{s^{-1}}$
300	0.00088
350	0.0037
400	0.0108
450	0.0250
500	0.0487
550	0.0842
600	0.133
650	0.195
700	0.272

Table 6.3 Sample experimental values for k for a reaction.

Strictly speaking, what we have worked out is $\ln\!\left(\dfrac{k}{\mathrm{s^{-1}}}\right)$. The natural log of the rate constant divided by its units is worked out to produce a pure number with no units.

Earlier we mentioned the rule of thumb that if the temperature is increased by 10 K the rate of reaction doubles. To investigate to what extent this is true, follow the link to a simulation that uses the Arrhenius equation to calculate the ratio between the rate at two different temperatures.

The Arrhenius equation may also be written in the form:

$$\ln k = \frac{-E_\mathrm{a}}{R} \times \frac{1}{T} + \ln A$$

The Arrhenius equation in this form can be used to work out a value for the activation energy for a reaction. In order to do this the following procedure must be followed.

1 Conduct a series of experiments at a range of temperatures.
2 Calculate a rate constant for each temperature.
3 Plot a graph of $\ln k$ (y-axis) against $\dfrac{1}{T}$ (x-axis), where T is the absolute temperature (in kelvin). This graph should be a straight line. The gradient of the graph is $\dfrac{-E_\mathrm{a}}{R}$, where R is the gas constant.

Let us now consider this in more detail: once we have carried out the series of experiments we could have data such as listed in Table 6.3. $1/T$ and $\ln k$ must now be calculated:

$\dfrac{1}{T}/\mathrm{K^{-1}}$	$\ln k$
0.00333	−7.03
0.00286	−5.60
0.00250	−4.53
0.00222	−3.69
0.00200	−3.02
0.00182	−2.47
0.00167	−2.02
0.00154	−1.63
0.00143	−1.30

A graph of the natural logarithm of the rate constant ($\ln k$) against the inverse of the temperature in kelvin $\left(\dfrac{1}{T}\right)$ produces a straight-line graph (Figure 6.22).

Extension

The Arrhenius equation is an experimental law that is followed approximately by most reactions over a limited temperature range. There are actually a few reactions that get slower as temperature increases, which would correspond to a negative activation energy using this equation.

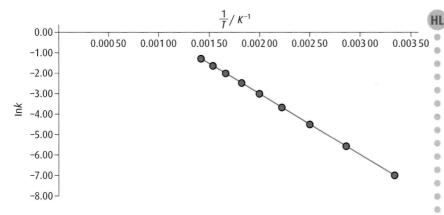

Figure 6.22 $\ln k$ against $\frac{1}{T}$.

We can understand why a straight-line graph is produced by comparing the Arrhenius equation with the equation of a straight line ($y = mx + c$, where m is the gradient and c is the intercept on the y-axis):

$$\underbrace{\ln k}_{y} = \underbrace{\left(\frac{-E_a}{R}\right)}_{m} \times \underbrace{\left(\frac{1}{T}\right)}_{x} + \underbrace{\ln A}_{c}$$

Thus, the Arrhenius equation is the equation of a straight line, where $\ln k$ is y and $\frac{1}{T}$ is x. From this equation we can see that the gradient of this straight line is $\frac{-E_a}{R}$. From the graph in Figure **6.22** we can work out the gradient of the straight line:

$$\text{gradient} = \frac{(-1.3) - (-7.0)}{0.001\,43 - 0.003\,33}$$

i.e. the gradient = $-3000\,\text{K}$.

The gradient of the line is equal to $\frac{-E_a}{R}$, so:

$$\frac{-E_a}{R} = -3000$$

$$E_a = 3000 \times R$$

$$E_a = 3000 \times 8.31 = 24\,900\,\text{J}\,\text{mol}^{-1}$$

i.e. the activation energy = $24.9\,\text{kJ}\,\text{mol}^{-1}$.

The effect of a catalyst on the value of the rate constant

The effect of a catalyst on the rate equation, rate = $k[\text{A}][\text{B}]$, is to **increase the value of the rate constant**.

> The units of the gradient are obtained by dividing the units of $\ln k$ (no units) by the units of $\frac{1}{T}$ (K^{-1}).

> The units of E_a are obtained as follows:
>
> $$E_a = 3000 \times R$$
>
> Substituting units into this equation:
>
> $$E_a = \text{K} \times \text{J}\,\text{K}^{-1}\,\text{mol}^{-1}$$
>
> K cancels with K^{-1}, so the units of E_a are $\text{J}\,\text{mol}^{-1}$.

> E_a is smaller, and as e is raised to a negative power, this makes the value of $e^{-E_a/RT}$ bigger

Note for both these questions that the value of the gas constant is 8.31 J K⁻¹ mol⁻¹.

6 Use the following data to calculate a value for the activation energy for the reaction $P + Q \rightarrow Z$

$\frac{1}{T}$ / K⁻¹	ln$k$
0.002 50	2.27
0.002 22	4.14
0.002 00	5.64
0.001 82	6.86
0.001 67	7.88
0.001 54	8.75
0.001 43	9.49
0.001 33	10.1
0.001 25	10.7

7 Use the following data to calculate a value for the activation energy for the reaction $A + B \rightarrow C$

Temperature / K	k / mol⁻¹ dm³ s⁻¹
400	1.74×10^{-2}
450	3.53×10^{-1}
500	3.92
550	28.1
600	145
650	581
700	1.91×10^{3}
750	5.35×10^{3}
800	1.32×10^{4}

Learning objectives

- Understand what is meant by the mechanism of a reaction and the rate-determining step
- Work out reaction mechanisms from experimental data and relate a given mechanism to the experimental data

$[NO_2]^2$ because there are two NO_2 molecules and doubling the concentration of each will cause the rate to double.

A **reaction mechanism** consists of a series of steps that make up a more complex reaction. Each simple step involves a maximum of **two** molecules colliding.

6.5 Mechanisms of reactions

Reaction mechanisms

In this section we will consider why the rate equation cannot be derived directly from the chemical equation for a reaction. Consider the reaction:

$$2NO_2(g) + F_2(g) \rightarrow 2NO_2F(g)$$

If this reaction were to occur in one single step, all three molecules must collide together at exactly the same time, and we would expect that doubling the concentration of any one of the three reactant molecules would double the chance of a collision and therefore the rate of the reaction. The rate of reaction in this case would therefore depend on $[NO_2]^2$ and $[F_2]$, and the rate expression would be:

$$\text{rate} = k[NO_2]^2[F_2]$$

The rate expression obtained from experiment is, however,

$$\text{rate} = k[NO_2][F_2]$$

The fact that these two expressions are different suggests that the reaction does not occur in just one step in which all three molecules collide and break apart to form the products. This was always going to be unlikely, as the chance of three gas molecules all colliding at exactly the same time is extremely small. This reaction must occur in a series of steps, and it is most likely that each step involves just two molecules colliding. A mechanism that has been proposed for this reaction is:

$$NO_2 + F_2 \rightarrow NO_2F + F \qquad \textbf{Step 1}$$
$$NO_2 + F \rightarrow NO_2F \qquad \textbf{Step 2}$$

The first thing that must be checked with the mechanism is that it agrees with the overall chemical equation. In order to do this, species that are the same on both sides of the equations are cancelled and the two equations are added together:

$$NO_2 + F_2 \rightarrow NO_2F + \cancel{F} \qquad \textbf{Step 1}$$
$$\underline{NO_2 + \cancel{F} \rightarrow NO_2F} \qquad \textbf{Step 2}$$
$$2NO_2 + F_2 \rightarrow 2NO_2F \qquad \textbf{Overall equation}$$

> The mechanism must be consistent with the overall chemical equation.

> F is produced in step 1 and used up again in step 2. F is an intermediate.

Now we need to see whether this mechanism agrees with the experimental rate expression. Each step involves just two species colliding, and therefore we can derive the rate expression for each step directly from the equation:

Step 1:   rate = $k_1[NO_2][F_2]$
Step 2:   rate = $k_2[NO_2][F]$

> k_1 is the rate constant for Step 1.

It can be seen that the rate expression for Step 1 is the same as the experimental rate expression, and so it would seem that this step governs the overall rate of reaction and that the second step has no apparent effect on the rate. Step 1 is called the **rate-determining step** of the mechanism and occurs significantly more slowly than Step 2.

> The slowest step in a reaction mechanism is called the rate-determining step.

$$NO_2 + F_2 \xrightarrow{\text{slow}} NO_2F + F \qquad \textbf{Step 1} \qquad \textbf{rate-determining step}$$
$$NO_2 + F \xrightarrow{\text{fast}} NO_2F \qquad \textbf{Step 2}$$

Step 2 is fast compared with the rate-determining step and has, effectively, no influence on the overall rate of reaction. This means that changing the concentrations of the species present in this step does not affect the rate of the reaction to any great extent, so the concentrations of these species do not occur in the rate equation.

The idea of a rate-determining step can be seen by analogy with a football stadium. The owners of the football club Rapid Kinetics have considered various options for speeding up the process of getting the spectators to their seats. They have broken down the process of getting to the seats into three separate steps:
1 getting to the stadium by road
2 getting into the stadium
3 getting to your seat once you are in the stadium.
It was suggested that the owners of the club could apply to the local council to improve the roads and the traffic flow leading up to the stadium, and someone else suggested that they could install lifts and escalators in the stadium to improve the process of getting around the stadium, but then some bright spark noticed the main problem: that there was only one gate to get into the stadium! Improving the roads around the stadium and installing lots of lifts and escalators, would have very little effect on the rate of the overall process of people getting to their seats because the rate-determining step is getting people through the one turnstile into the stadium. They need to work on improving the rate of the rate-determining step, and it could be expected that doubling the number of gates to get into the stadium would double the speed of the overall process.

Let us consider another mechanism, this time for the reaction:

$$A + 2B \rightarrow C$$

$B + B \rightarrow Q$	**Step 1**	**rate-determining step**
$Q + A \rightarrow C$	**Step 2**	**fast**

Let us first check that the mechanism agrees with the chemical equation:

$B + B \rightarrow \cancel{Q}$	**Step 1**
$\cancel{Q} + A \rightarrow C$	**Step 2**
$\overline{2B + A \rightarrow C}$	**Overall equation**

Step 1 is the rate-determining step, so the concentrations of the reactants involved in this step affect the rate of the overall reaction and occur in the rate expression. Step 2 is a fast step that occurs after the rate-determining step, and therefore the species involved in this step do not affect the rate of reaction or occur in the rate expression. This means that B occurs twice in the rate expression and A not at all. The rate expression consistent with this mechanism is:

rate $= k[\text{B}]^2$

In both examples we have considered, the rate-determining step is the first step. Let us now consider a mechanism in which the rate-determining step is the second step.

For the same overall equation, $A + 2B \rightarrow C$, another possible mechanism could be:

$B + B \rightleftharpoons Q$	**Step 1**	**fast**
$Q + A \rightarrow C$	**Step 2**	**rate-determining step**

This is basically the same as the previous mechanism, except that the second step is the rate-determining step. The species in Step 2 influence the rate of the reaction, and we can write the rate expression as:

rate $= k[\text{Q}][\text{A}]$

However, Q is produced by the reaction between two molecules of B, and we can replace [Q] with $[\text{B}]^2$ in the rate expression. Therefore the rate expression that is consistent with this mechanism would be:

rate $= k[\text{B}]^2[\text{A}]$

Which of the two above mechanisms is more likely to be the actual mechanism for the reaction can be worked out by experimentally determining the rate equation for this reaction.

From the treatment above we can see that:

> the rate equation contains concentrations of **reactants** involved **up to and including** the rate-determining step.

Q is an intermediate.

Extension

Step 1 is an equilibrium reaction. At equlibrium the rate of the forward reaction is the same as the rate of the reverse reaction, i.e.

rate of forward reaction $= k_f[\text{B}]^2$

rate of reverse reaction $= k_r[\text{Q}]$

$k_f[\text{B}]^2 = k_r[\text{Q}]$

which can be rearranged to give:

$$[\text{Q}] = \frac{k_f[\text{B}]^2}{k_r}$$

The concentration of Q is thus proportional to the concentration of B squared.

Intermediates do not appear in the rate equation.

This can be further seen with another possible mechanism for this reaction:

$A + B \rightleftharpoons S$	**Step 1**	**fast**
$S + B \rightarrow C$	**Step 2**	**rate-determining step**

> S is an intermediate.

The reactants involved up to and including the rate-determining step are A once and B twice, so the rate equation would also be:

$$\text{rate} = k[B]^2[A]$$

There is no way simple way of distinguishing between the two above mechanisms experimentally.

A reaction involving a catalyst

$$CH_3COCH_3(aq) + I_2(aq) \rightarrow CH_3COCH_2I(aq) + HI(aq)$$

The reaction is acid (H^+) catalysed.
The experimental rate expression is:

$$\text{rate} = k[CH_3COCH_3][H^+]$$

The rate expression does not include I_2, so this must become involved only after the rate-determining step.
At a simple level the mechanism could be proposed as:

$CH_3COCH_3 + \mathbf{H^+} \rightarrow X$	**rate-determining step**
$X + I_2 \rightarrow CH_3COCH_2I + HI + \mathbf{H^+}$	**fast**

> X is an intermediate.

The **catalyst** is involved in the rate-determining step but is regenerated in the second step, and therefore does not appear in the overall chemical equation.

> H^+ will cancel out when both equations are added together.

S_N1 versus S_N2 mechanisms

In this section, we will consider the kinetics of the reactions that will be studied further on pages **459** and **461**.
Consider the reaction:

$$(CH_3)_3CBr + OH^- \rightarrow (CH_3)_3COH + Br^-$$

This is a nucleophilic substitution reaction of 2-bromo-2-methylpropane. The experimentally determined rate expression for this reaction is:

$$\text{rate} = k[(CH_3)_3CBr]$$

OH^- does not occur in the rate expression and therefore can be involved only in a fast step after the rate-determining step. The mechanism for this reaction has been suggested as:

$(CH_3)_3CBr \rightarrow (CH_3)_3C^+ + Br^-$	**rate-determining step**
$(CH_3)_3C^+ + OH^- \rightarrow (CH_3)_3COH$	**fast**

Molecularity is the number of 'molecules' that react in a particular step (usually the rate-determining step).

HL The reaction is described as an S_N1 mechanism, where S stands for substitution, N for nucleophilic (the attacking species is a nucleophile in this case) and 1 the molecularity of the rate-determining step. In this case, the molecularity is 1 because one molecule reacts in the rate-determining step.

$CH_3CH_2CH_2Br$ (1-bromopropane) also undergoes a nucleophilic substitution reaction:

$$CH_3CH_2CH_2Br + OH^- \rightarrow CH_3CH_2CH_2OH + Br^-$$

This time the rate expression is different:

$$\text{rate} = k[CH_3CH_2CH_2Br][OH^-]$$

With both reactants from the original equation appearing once only in the rate expression, this suggests that this reaction occurs in just one step and the mechanism is simply:

$$CH_3CH_2CH_2Br + OH^- \rightarrow CH_3CH_2CH_2OH + Br^-$$

As there is only one step it is, of course, also the rate-determining step. This reaction mechanism is described as S_N2, where the 2 refers to the molecularity of the only step.

Summary of 'rules' for writing mechanisms

1 The mechanism must agree with the overall stoichiometric equation.
2 A maximum of two particles can react in any one step.
3 All species in the rate equation must appear in the mechanism in or before the rate-determining step.
4 The power of a particular reactant's concentration in the rate equation indicates the number of times it appears in the mechanism up to and including the rate-determing step.

Because a mechanism is consistent with the experimental rate expression does not mean that the mechanism is correct. It can never be proved that a mechanism is correct, only that it is incorrect. A mechanism is accepted as long as it agrees with the experimental data, but if new experimental data are produced that are not consistent with the mechanism, the mechanism is disproved and a new mechanism must be developed that agrees with these and other experimental data.

8 Consider the reaction:

$$2A + 3B \rightarrow 4C + D$$

The rate expression is: rate = $k[B]^2$.

A proposed mechanism for this reaction is:

$A + B \rightarrow 2C + D$	**Step 1**	**slow**
$A + 2B \rightarrow C + D$	**Step 2**	**fast**

Suggest three reasons why this is not a suitable mechanism for this reaction.

9 Consider the reaction:

$$P + 2Q \rightarrow R + S$$

A student has suggested some possible two-step mechanisms for this reaction:

Mechanism 1

$$Q + Q \xrightarrow{\text{slow}} X$$

$$P + X \xrightarrow{\text{slow}} R + S$$

Mechanism 2

$$Q + P \overset{\text{fast}}{\rightleftharpoons} Z + R$$

$$Q + Z \xrightarrow{\text{fast}} S$$

Mechanism 3

$$Q + P \xrightarrow{\text{slow}} Y + S$$

$$Q + Y \xrightarrow{\text{fast}} R$$

Mechanism 4

$$Q + P \xrightarrow{\text{slow}} Y + S$$

$$Q + Z \xrightarrow{\text{fast}} R$$

a Write the rate expression that would be consistent with Mechanism 1.

b Explain why Mechanism 4 cannot be the mechanism for this reaction.

c The experimentally determined rate expression for this reaction is rate = $k[P][Q]$. Which mechanism is consistent with the experimental data?

10 Consider the reaction:

$$2NO + Br_2 \rightarrow 2NOBr$$

The rate expression is rate = $k[NO]^2[Br_2]$. Suggest two different mechanisms that are consistent with this rate expression.

11 Consider the reaction:

$$2X + Y \rightarrow 2Z$$

The rate expression for this reaction is rate = $k[X][Y]$. Suggest a mechanism for this reaction.

Exam-style questions

1 Which of the following best explains why an increase in temperature causes the rate of a reaction to increase?

    A the particles collide more

    B the particles collide more frequently

    C more particles have energy greater than the activation energy

    D the activation energy is lower at higher temperature

2 An experiment was carried out to measure the rate of decomposition of hydrogen peroxide according to the equation:

$$2H_2O_2(aq) \rightarrow 2H_2O(l) + O_2(g)$$

$56.0\,cm^3$ of gas was produced in 30.0 seconds. The average rate of reaction during this time was:

    A $1.87\,cm^3\,s^{-1}$ **C** $0.536\,s\,cm^{-3}$

    B $28.0\,cm^3\,min^{-1}$ **D** $112\,min\,cm^{-3}$

3 Which of the following will **not** increase the rate of the reaction?

$$Mg(s) + 2HCl(aq) \rightarrow MgCl_2(aq) + H_2(g)$$

    A increasing the surface area of the magnesium
    B increasing the volume of hydrochloric acid used
    C increasing the concentration of the hydrochloric acid
    D increasing the temperature

4 In the decomposition of hydrogen peroxide, manganese(IV) oxide is a catalyst. Which of the following best describes the function of a catalyst and its mode of action?

    A it speeds up the reaction by increasing the activation energy
    B it slows down the reaction by decreasing the collision frequency of particles
    C it speeds up the reaction by allowing the reaction to occur by an alternative pathway of lower activation energy
    D it speeds up the reaction by increasing the average energy of the particles

5 In the reaction between 1.00 g marble chips (calcium carbonate) and 25.0 cm³ hydrochloric acid, which of the following sets of conditions should give the fastest rate of reaction?

    A $0.50 \, mol \, dm^{-3}$ HCl(aq) and small marble chips at 20 °C
    B $0.10 \, mol \, dm^{-3}$ HCl(aq) and small marble chips at 30 °C
    C $0.30 \, mol \, dm^{-3}$ HCl(aq) and small marble chips at 70 °C
    D $0.50 \, mol \, dm^{-3}$ HCl(aq) and large marble chips at 30 °C

HL **6** The rate expression for the reaction $CO + NO_2 \rightarrow CO_2 + NO$ is: rate $= k[NO_2]^2$. When the concentration of CO is increased by a factor of 2 and the concentration of NO_2 is increased by a factor of 3, the rate of reaction is increased by a factor of:

    A 3   **B** 6   **C** 9   **D** 18

7 Consider the following experimental data for the reaction:

$$2NO + Br_2 \rightarrow 2NOBr$$

[NO] / mol dm⁻³	[Br₂] / mol dm⁻³	Rate / mol dm⁻³ s⁻¹
0.10	0.10	0.010
0.20	0.10	0.040
0.20	0.30	0.12

The rate expression for this reaction is:

    A rate $= k[NO]^2[Br_2]$ **C** rate $= k[NO_2]^2[Br_2]^3$
    B rate $= k[NO_2] + [Br_2]$ **D** rate $= k[NO_2][Br_2]$

8 The activation energy for a reaction can be calculated from a graph of:

    A $\ln k$ vs T **C** $\ln k$ vs $\frac{1}{T}$
    B $\frac{1}{k}$ vs $\ln T$ **D** $\ln k$ vs $\ln T$

9 Consider the reaction:

$$2NO(g) + O_2(g) \rightarrow 2NO_2(g)$$

Some possible mechanisms for this reactions are:

I	$NO(g) + NO(g) \rightleftharpoons N_2O_2(g)$	fast
	$N_2O_2(g) + O_2(g) \rightarrow 2NO_2(g)$	slow
II	$NO(g) + NO(g) \rightarrow N_2O_2(g)$	slow
	$N_2O_2(g) + O_2(g) \rightarrow 2NO_2(g)$	fast

III	$NO(g) + O_2(g) \rightleftharpoons NO_3(g)$	fast
	$NO_3(g) + NO(g) \rightarrow 2NO_2(g)$	slow
IV	$NO(g) + O_2(g) \rightarrow NO_3(g)$	slow
	$NO_3(g) + NO(g) \rightarrow 2NO_2(g)$	fast

The rate expression for this reaction is: rate $= k[NO]^2[O_2]$. Which of these mechanisms is/are consistent with this rate expression?

| **A** | **I** only | **C** | **II** and **III** only |
| **B** | **I** and **IV** only | **D** | **I** and **III** only |

10 The units of k for a reaction with rate expression: rate $= k[A]^2$ could be:

| **A** | $mol\,dm^{-3}\,s^{-1}$ | **C** | $mol^2\,dm^{-6}\,s^{-1}$ |
| **B** | $mol^{-1}\,dm^3\,h^{-1}$ | **D** | $mol^{-2}\,dm^6\,h^{-1}$ |

11 Explain by reference to the Maxwell–Boltzmann distribution why the rate of a reaction in the gas phase increases as temperature increases. [4]

12 The data in the table refer to the reaction:

$$CaCO_3(s) + 2HCl(aq) \rightarrow CaCl_2(aq) + CO_2(g) + H_2O(l)$$

Time / s	Volume of CO$_2$ produced / cm^3
0	0.0
10	16.0
20	30.0
30	41.0
40	47.0
50	51.0
60	53.5
70	55.5
80	56.5
90	57.0
100	57.0
110	57.0

a Explain, with the aid of a diagram, how these data could be obtained experimentally. [3]

b Plot these data on graph paper and label the line **B**. [2]

c Use the graph that you have plotted in part **b** to state and explain where the rate of reaction is fastest. [2]

d The original data were collected for an experiment using 1.00 g of calcium carbonate and 20.0 cm^3 of 0.300 mol dm^{-3} hydrochloric acid at 20 °C. The experiment was then repeated using exactly the same conditions, except that the temperature of the HCl(aq) was 30 °C.

Sketch, on the same axes as your graph in part **b**, the curve that would be obtained. Label this graph **D**. [2]

e i Calculate the maximum volume of carbon dioxide (in cm^3) that should have been collected in the original experiment if 1.00 mol CO_2 occupies 24.0 dm^3 under these conditions. [3]

ii Explain why the volume of gas collected is less than you predicted in part **i**. [1]

HL 13 The following data refer to the reaction:

$$X + 2Y \rightarrow Z$$

Experiment	Concentration of X / mol dm^{-3}	Concentration of Y / mol dm^{-3}	Rate of reaction / mol dm^{-3} s^{-1}
1	0.500	0.500	3.20×10^{-3}
2	0.250	0.500	1.60×10^{-3}
3	0.250	0.250	8.00×10^{-4}

a Explain what is meant by the term 'order of reaction'. [2]

b Deduce the rate expression for this reaction. [4]

c Calculate the rate constant with units for this reaction. [2]

d What is the rate of reaction when the concentrations of X and Y are both 0.100 mol dm^{-3}? [2]

e State and explain how the value of the rate constant for this reaction will change as the temperature increases. [2]

14 Under certain conditions the decomposition of phosphine, PH_3, is zero order. The equation for the reaction is:

$$4PH_3(g) \rightarrow P_4(g) + 6H_2(g)$$

a Sketch a graph showing how the concentration of phosphine varies with time. [2]

b Sketch a graph showing how the rate of decomposition of phosphine varies as the concentration of phosphine changes. [2]

15 Consider the gas phase reaction between nitrogen(II) oxide and oxygen:

$$2NO(g) + O_2(g) \rightarrow 2NO_2(g) \qquad \Delta H = -113 \text{ kJ mol}^{-1}$$

The rate expression for the reaction is: rate $= k[NO]^2$.

a Explain why the rate expression cannot be derived from the stoichiometric equation. [2]

b Explain what is meant by the rate-determining step in a chemical reaction. [1]

c Suggest a two-step mechanism for this reaction. [3]

d If the total volume of the reaction container is doubled at constant temperature, state and explain the effect on the rate of this reaction. [2]

e Sketch, on the same axes, an enthalpy level diagram for this reaction with and without a catalyst. Clearly label the curves and the activation energy of the catalysed and uncatalysed reaction. [4]

Summary

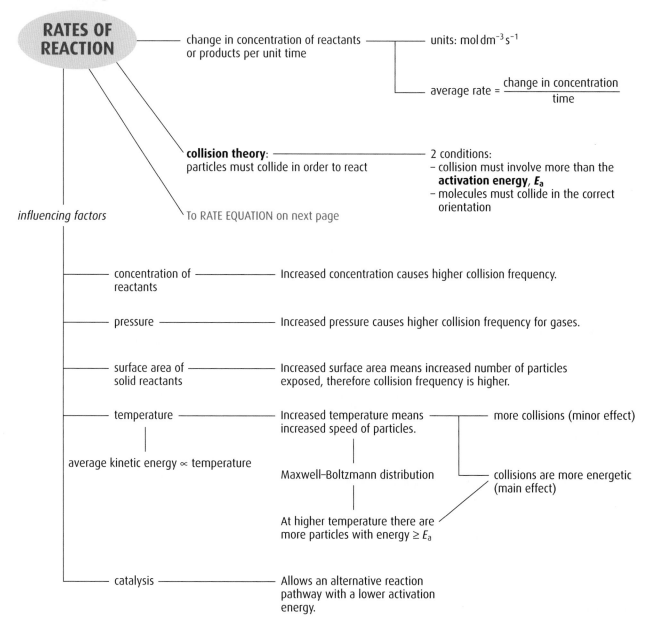

RATES OF REACTION — change in concentration of reactants or products per unit time

units: $mol\,dm^{-3}\,s^{-1}$

average rate = $\dfrac{\text{change in concentration}}{\text{time}}$

collision theory: particles must collide in order to react

2 conditions:
- collision must involve more than the **activation energy, E_a**
- molecules must collide in the correct orientation

To RATE EQUATION on next page

influencing factors

concentration of reactants — Increased concentration causes higher collision frequency.

pressure — Increased pressure causes higher collision frequency for gases.

surface area of solid reactants — Increased surface area means increased number of particles exposed, therefore collision frequency is higher.

temperature — Increased temperature means increased speed of particles.

average kinetic energy ∝ temperature

Maxwell–Boltzmann distribution

At higher temperature there are more particles with energy $\geq E_a$

more collisions (minor effect)

collisions are more energetic (main effect)

catalysis — Allows an alternative reaction pathway with a lower activation energy.

Summary – continued

HL

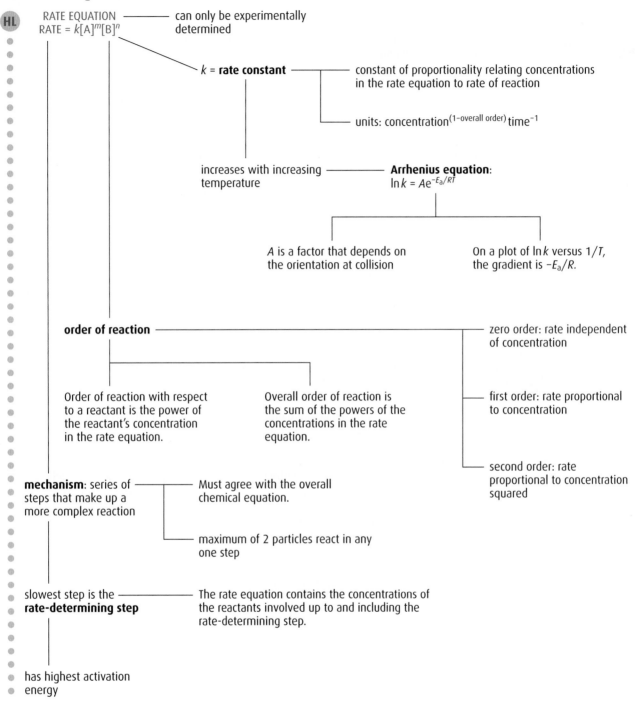

RATE EQUATION — can only be experimentally
RATE = $k[A]^m[B]^n$ determined

k = **rate constant** — constant of proportionality relating concentrations
in the rate equation to rate of reaction

units: concentration$^{(1-\text{overall order})}$ time^{-1}

increases with increasing — **Arrhenius equation:**
temperature $\ln k = Ae^{-E_a/RT}$

A is a factor that depends on
the orientation at collision

On a plot of $\ln k$ versus $1/T$,
the gradient is $-E_a/R$.

order of reaction

zero order: rate independent
of concentration

Order of reaction with respect
to a reactant is the power of
the reactant's concentration
in the rate equation.

Overall order of reaction is
the sum of the powers of the
concentrations in the rate
equation.

first order: rate proportional
to concentration

second order: rate
proportional to concentration
squared

mechanism: series of — Must agree with the overall
steps that make up a chemical equation.
more complex reaction

maximum of 2 particles react in any
one step

slowest step is the — The rate equation contains the concentrations of
rate-determining step the reactants involved up to and including the
rate-determining step.

has highest activation
energy

Equilibrium 7

7.1 Equilibrium

Reversible reactions

As the name suggests, reversible reactions are reactions that can go either way. In a common reversible reaction calcium carbonate, when heated strongly, decomposes to form calcium oxide and carbon dioxide. But calcium oxide also reacts with carbon dioxide to form calcium carbonate:

$$CaCO_3(s) \rightleftharpoons CaO(s) + CO_2(g)$$

The double arrow ($\rightleftharpoons$) shows that the reaction is reversible.

Equilibrium

The decomposition of $CaCO_3$ is reversible, but what happens if we put solid calcium carbonate in an open container and keep it at a constant high temperature for an extended period of time (Figure **7.1**)?

All the calcium carbonate is converted to calcium oxide because the carbon dioxide escapes and is not available to react with the calcium oxide to re-form calcium carbonate.

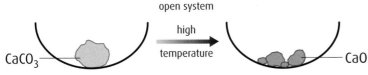

Figure 7.1 In an open container, all the calcium carbonate is converted to calcium oxide.

If we do exactly the same experiment, at the same temperature, but with the calcium carbonate in a sealed container (Figure **7.2**), we find that after the same amount of time we still have some calcium carbonate present. No matter how long we continue the experiment (keeping it at a constant temperature), the amount of calcium carbonate, calcium oxide and carbon dioxide stay the same. The reaction appears to have stopped, and we say that the system has reached a state of **equilibrium**.

The reaction has not actually stopped but is proceeding in both directions at equal rates. In other words, the calcium carbonate is

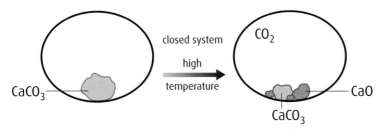

Figure 7.2 In a closed system, a state of equilibrium is attained.

Learning objectives

- Understand that a reversible reaction can come to a state of equilibrium
- Explain what is meant by **dynamic equilibrium**

Extension

On a microscopic level all reactions are reversible, i.e. if two molecules come together with the formation of a bond, that bond could also break as the two components move apart. This is often likened to the idea of running a film backwards, so that, on a molecular level, the 'film of a reaction' can always be run backwards.

Calcium oxide is also known as quicklime or lime. When heated strongly it glows bright white. This was used as theatre lighting, which gave rise to the phrase *in the limelight*.

A system has reached equilibrium when no further change appears to occur – macroscopic properties remain constant.

$$CaCO_3 \xrightarrow{\text{forward}} CaO + CO_2$$
$$CaCO_3 \xleftarrow{\text{reverse}} CaO + CO_2$$

$Rate_{forward} = Rate_{reverse}$

decomposing to give calcium oxide and carbon dioxide at exactly the same rate as the calcium oxide and carbon dioxide are recombining to form calcium carbonate. This type of equilibrium is called a **dynamic equilibrium**. All equilibria in chemistry are dynamic.

> In **dynamic equilibrium**, macroscopic properties are constant (concentrations of all reactants and products remains constant) and the rate of the forward reaction is equal to the rate of the reverse reaction.

Examiner's tip
When asked to define **dynamic equilibrium** you must address both the **dynamic** part and the **equilibrium** part.

Equilibrium and rate of reaction

Consider the reaction $H_2(g) + I_2(g) \rightleftharpoons 2HI(g)$

If we start with just hydrogen and iodine vapour in a closed container at a certain temperature and follow how the concentration of hydrogen and hydrogen iodide change with time, we should obtain a graph of the form shown in Figure **7.3**.

The concentration of H_2 decreases at first, until it levels off as equilibrium is reached. The concentration of HI is initially zero, but it increases until it flattens off and does not change any more as equilibrium is reached. If we plot a graph of rate against time for the forward and reverse reactions we get a graph of the form shown in Figure **7.4**.

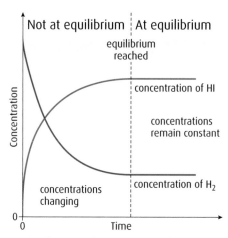

Figure 7.3 Graph showing how the concentration of hydrogen and hydrogen iodide change with time.

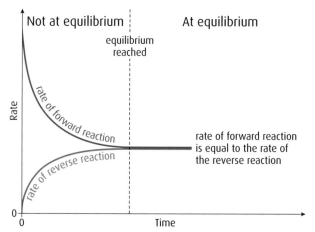

Figure 7.4 Graph showing how the rates of the forward and reverse reactions change as a reversible reaction comes to equilibrium.

Animation 1

The characteristics of the equilibrium state

Some of these have been discussed above.

1 **Macroscopic properties are constant at equilibrium**: at equilibrium the concentrations of all reactants and products remain constant.

2 **At equilibrium the rate of the forward reaction is equal to the rate of the reverse reaction**.

3 **Equilibrium can be attained only in a closed system**. As we saw above, if calcium carbonate is heated in an open container, equilibrium is never reached, as the carbon dioxide escapes and has no opportunity to recombine with the calcium oxide. In effect, a reaction going on in solution, and not involving the production of a gas, represents a closed system.

4 **All species in the chemical equation are present in the equilibrium reaction mixture**. For example, if nitrogen and hydrogen are allowed to come to equilibrium according to the equation $N_2(g) + 3H_2(g) \rightleftharpoons 2NH_3(g)$, the reaction mixture at equilibrium contains nitrogen, hydrogen and ammonia.

5 **Equilibrium can be attained from either direction**.

Consider the equilibrium:

$$CH_3COOH(l) + C_2H_5OH(l) \rightleftharpoons CH_3COOCH_2CH_3(l) + H_2O(l)$$

ethanoic acid   ethanol   ethyl ethanoate   water

If we mix together ethanoic acid and ethanol in the presence of an acid catalyst and incubate them at 60 °C, they come to equilibrium. If we do the same starting with ethyl ethanoate and water, they also come to equilibrium. A state of equilibrium, in which all four species are present, can be reached by mixing:

- ethanoic acid and ethanol
- ethyl ethanoate and water
- all four substances
- any three substances

In each case equilibrium is reached, but the actual concentrations present at equilibrium depend on how much of each substance we started with.

7.2 Position of equilibrium

The position of equilibrium refers to the relative amounts of reactants and products present at equilibrium. Some reactions go almost to completion, e.g.

$$2NO(g) \rightleftharpoons N_2(g) + O_2(g)$$

At 700 K, the position of equilibrium lies a long way to the **right**. There is a large amount of N_2 and O_2 and not very much NO at equilibrium: roughly one and a half million times as many N_2 and O_2 molecules as NO molecules. However, for

$$H_2(g) + CO_2(g) \rightleftharpoons H_2O(g) + CO(g)$$

at 1100 K, the total number of H_2 and CO_2 molecules at equilibrium is roughly equal to the total number of H_2O and CO molecules: the equilibrium is evenly balanced.

In a **closed system** there is no exchange of matter with the surroundings.

Learning objectives

- Understand what is meant by the position of equilibrium
- Apply Le Chatelier's principle to predict the effect of changes in conditions on the position of equilibrium

Equilibrium does **not** imply 50% reactants and 50% products.

The position of this equilibrium lies a long way to the **left**. Not much H^+ and OH^- are present at equilibrium.

Henri Louis Le Chatelier (1850–1936) was a French chemist. His original statement on his principle is:

Every system in stable equilibrium submitted to the influence of an exterior force which tends to cause variation, either in its temperature or its condensation (pressure, concentration, number of molecules in the unit of volume) in its totality or only in some one of its parts can undergo only those interior modifications which, if they occur alone, could produce a change of temperature, or of condensation, of a sign contary to that resulting from the exterior force.

Water dissociates according to the equation:

$$H_2O(l) \rightleftharpoons H^+(aq) + OH^-(aq)$$

At 298 K the number of water molecules present at equilibrium is over 250 million times greater than the total number of H^+ and OH^- ions present.

The effect of changing conditions on the position of equilibrium

Le Chatelier's principle

If a system at equilibrium is subjected to some change, the position of equilibrium will shift in order to minimise the effect of the change.

This means that, if we take a particular system at equilibrium under a certain set of conditions and change one of those conditions, such as the temperature or the pressure, the system will move to a new position of equilibrium. Le Chatelier's principle allows us to predict in which direction the position of equilibrium will shift, and this is considered in the next sections.

The effect of temperature

Consider the equilibrium:

$$2HI(g) \rightleftharpoons H_2(g) + I_2(g) \qquad \Delta H = +10\,kJ\,mol^{-1}$$

At room temperature (298 K), the number of molecules of HI is roughly 28 times the total number of molecules of H_2 and I_2.

$$2HI(g) \rightleftharpoons H_2(g) + I_2(g)$$
96.6%   3.4%

However, when the system reaches equilibrium at 700 K, the number of HI molecules is only approximately seven times the total number of H_2 and I_2 molecules.

$$2HI(g) \rightleftharpoons H_2(g) + I_2(g)$$
88%   12%

This means that there are relatively more H_2 and I_2 molecules present at equilibrium at 700 K than at 298 K. In this case, as the temperature increases, the position of equilibrium shifts to the right (there is more H_2 and I_2 present).

Consider another reaction:

$$N_2(g) + 3H_2(g) \rightleftharpoons 2NH_3(g) \qquad \Delta H = -92\,kJ\,mol^{-1}$$

This time, at 300 K and 10 atmosphere pressure we have:

$$N_2(g) + 3H_2(g) \rightleftharpoons 2NH_3(g)$$
$$ 85\% 15\%$$

At 700 K and the same pressure:

$$N_2(g) + 3H_2(g) \rightleftharpoons 2NH_3(g)$$
$$ 99.8\% 0.2\%$$

In this case, increasing the temperature causes the position of equilibrium to be shifted to the left, i.e. there is less ammonia present at equilibrium at the higher temperature.

The effect of a temperature change on a system at equilibrium can be now considered in terms of Le Chatelier's principle. Going back to the first reaction, the value of ΔH here refers to the forward direction; so in this case the forward reaction is endothermic and the reverse reaction is exothermic. As the temperature is increased, the position of equilibrium shifts in the direction that will minimise the effect of the change. So in this case, in order to minimise the effect of the increase in temperature, the position of equilibrium shifts in the endothermic direction to take in the heat that is added (heat energy converted to chemical energy). The endothermic direction is to the right, and therefore as the temperature is increased the position of equilibrium shifts to the right to produce relatively more H_2 and I_2.

Now consider the second reaction. As above, the position of equilibrium shifts in the endothermic direction to take in heat and minimise the effect of the change as the temperature is increased. This time the endothermic direction is to the left and, therefore, as the temperature is increased the position of equilibrium shifts to the left.

> **HEAT reaction mixture:** position of equilibrium is shifted in the **endo**thermic direction.
> **COOL reaction mixture:** position of equilibrium is shifted in the **exo**thermic direction.

The difference between these two reactions is that the first one is endothermic (ΔH positive) and the second one is exothermic (ΔH negative)

$$2HI(g) \underset{\text{exothermic}}{\overset{\text{endothermic}}{\rightleftharpoons}} H_2(g) + I_2(g)$$

This is analogous to the idea that, if the heating is turned up you might take off your jacket in order to minimise the change and keep your temperature roughly the same as it was before.

$$N_2(g) + 3H_2(g) \underset{\text{endothermic}}{\overset{\text{exothermic}}{\rightleftharpoons}} 2NH_3(g)$$

The effect of pressure

Consider the following equilibrium:

$$2NO_2(g) \rightleftharpoons N_2O_4(g)$$
$$\text{brown} \text{colourless}$$

Some NO_2 (brown) is put into a sealed gas syringe (Figure **7.5**). As the pressure is increased, the colour initially gets slightly darker, as the same number of molecules are squeezed into a smaller space. The mixture then becomes more colourless as a new position of equilibrium is established. At higher pressure there is less NO_2 (brown) and more N_2O_4 (colourless) present in the equilibrium mixture, and therefore it is paler brown than at lower pressure. Thus it can be seen that, in this case, as the pressure increases the position of equilibrium shifts to the right (more N_2O_4 is present at equilibrium).

Animation 2

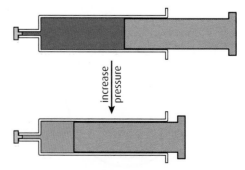

Figure 7.5 The effect of increasing pressure on the $2NO_2(g) \rightleftharpoons N_2O_4(g)$ equilibrium.

$PV = nRT$, so the number of moles of gas is proportional to the volume and pressure of the gas.

This reaction involves a decrease in the number of **gaseous** molecules, from two on the left-hand side to one on the right-hand side. Two moles of gas take up more space than one mole of gas, so as the pressure is increased the position of equilibrium shifts in order to minimise the effect of this pressure change. This is achieved by the position of equilibrium shifting to the side with fewer gaseous molecules and therefore lower volume – that is, the right-hand side.

If we imagine this reaction going to completion and two moles of $NO_2(g)$ being completely converted to 1 mole of $N_2O_4(g)$, the volume of gas at the end would be half what we started with. If this reaction were carried out in a vessel of constant volume, the conversion of 2 moles of $NO_2(g)$ to 1 mole of $N_2O_4(g)$ would involve the pressure decreasing to half its original value.

Consider the following reaction:

$$2SO_3(g) \rightleftharpoons 2SO_2(g) + O_2(g)$$

This reaction involves the conversion of two molecules of **gas** (on the left-hand side) to three molecules of **gas** (on the right-hand side). As the pressure is increased, the position of equilibrium shifts to the **left**-hand side – i.e. the side with **fewer gas molecules** – to minimise the effect of the change.

Consider the following equilibrium:

$$2HI(g) \rightleftharpoons H_2(g) + I_2(g)$$

If a reaction involves a change in the number of **gas** molecules, an increase in pressure results in the position of equilibrium shifting in the direction that gives a decrease in the number of gas molecules.

As there is the **same number** of molecules of **gas** on both sides, changing the pressure has **no effect** on the position of equilibrium.

In these three examples, it has been stressed that we are considering the number of molecules of **gas** when predicting the effect of a change in pressure on the position of equilibrium.

Consider once again the decomposition of calcium carbonate:

$$CaCO_3(s) \rightleftharpoons CaO(s) + CO_2(g)$$

There is one molecule of **gas** on the right-hand side but none on the left-hand side; therefore increasing the pressure causes the position of equilibrium to shift to the left.

The effect of concentration

Consider the following system at equilibrium:

$$\underset{\substack{\text{chromate(VI) ion} \\ \text{yellow}}}{2[CrO_4]^{2-}(aq)} + \underset{\text{from acid}}{2H^+(aq)} \rightleftharpoons \underset{\substack{\text{dichromate(VI) ion} \\ \text{orange}}}{[Cr_2O_7]^{2-}(aq)} + H_2O(l)$$

The fact that the colour of the solution on the left of Figure **7.6** is yellow indicates that the position of equilibrium lies to **left**, so that there is significantly more of the yellow ion present than the orange ion.

When acid (H^+) is added to the flask, the colour of the solution changes to orange. There is now much more of the orange dichromate(VI)

Examiner's tip
You must remember the word **gas** – solids and liquids are affected very little by changes in pressure.

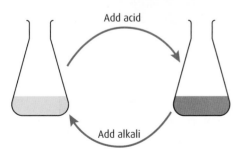

Figure 7.6 The chromate(VI)/dichromate(VI) equilibrium.

ion present, which means that the position of equilibrium has shifted to the **right**. This can be explained in terms of Le Chatelier's principle: as more acid is added, the position of equilibrium shifts to the right to use up the excess acid and so minimise the effect of the change.

If we now add alkali (OH^-) to the solution, the colour changes back to yellow. The OH^- ions react with the H^+ ions to form water. Adding alkali thus reduces the concentration of H^+ ions in the solution and the position of equilibrium must shift to the left in order to minimise the effect of the change by replacing the H^+ ions.

$$H^+(aq) + OH^-(aq) \rightleftharpoons H_2O(l)$$

In general, if the concentration of one of the species in an equilibrium mixture is increased, the position of equilibrium shifts to the opposite side to reduce the concentration of this species.

Self-test 1

Test yourself

1 Predict the effect of increasing pressure on the position of equilibrium in the following systems:
 a $CH_4(g) + 2H_2O(g) \rightleftharpoons CO_2(g) + 4H_2(g)$
 b $N_2O_5(g) + NO(g) \rightleftharpoons 3NO_2(g)$
 c $NO(g) + NO_2(g) \rightleftharpoons N_2O_3(g)$

2 Predict the effect of increasing temperature on the position of equilibrium in the following systems:
 a $NO(g) + NO_2(g) \rightleftharpoons N_2O_3(g)$
 $$\Delta H = -40 \, kJ \, mol^{-1}$$
 b $CH_4(g) + H_2O(g) \rightleftharpoons CO(g) + 3H_2(g)$
 $$\Delta H = +206 \, kJ \, mol^{-1}$$
 c $CO(g) + 2H_2(g) \rightleftharpoons CH_3OH(g)$
 $$\Delta H = -90 \, kJ \, mol^{-1}$$

3 Predict the effect of the following changes on the position of equilibrium:
 a Removing the CO_2 from the equilibrium:
 $$CaCO_3(s) \rightleftharpoons CaO(s) + CO_2(g)$$
 b Adding acid (H^+) to the system:
 $$NH_4^+ \rightleftharpoons H^+ + NH_3$$
 c Adding sodium hydroxide to the following system:
 $$CH_3COOH(aq) \rightleftharpoons CH_3COO^-(aq) + H^+(aq)$$
 d Adding sodium hydroxide to the following system:
 $$3I_2(aq) + 3H_2O(l) \rightleftharpoons 5HI(aq) + HIO_3(aq)$$

7.3 The equilibrium constant

A series of experiments is carried out on the reaction:

$$CH_3COOH(l) + C_2H_5OH(l) \rightleftharpoons CH_3COOCH_2CH_3(l) + H_2O(l)$$
ethanoic acid   ethanol   ethyl ethanoate   water

Various known amounts of ethanol and ethanoic acid are reacted together and allowed to come to equilibrium at the same temperature. The **equilibrium concentrations** of each component of the reaction mixture are determined and it is found that the ratio

$$\frac{[CH_3COOCH_2CH_3(l)][H_2O(l)]}{[CH_3COOH(l)][C_2H_5OH(l)]}$$

is constant for all the experiments.

Learning objectives

- Write the expression for the equilibrium constant for a given reversible reaction
- Understand the connection between the size of the equilibrium constant and the extent of reaction
- Understand how changing conditions affects the value of the equilibrium constant and the position of equilibrium

where $[CH_3COOH(l)]$ represents the concentration of CH_3COOH **at equilibrium**

All concentrations measured at equilibrium.

[A] represents the concentration of A **at equilibrium**.

$$2SO_2(g) + O_2(g) \rightleftharpoons 2SO_3(g)$$

$$K_c = \frac{[SO_3(g)]^2}{[SO_2(g)]^2[O_2(g)]} \begin{array}{l} \longleftarrow \text{ products} \\ \longleftarrow \text{ reactants} \end{array}$$

Extension

The equilibrium constant K_p is often calculated. This is the equilibrium constant in terms of partial pressures. The partial pressure of a gas in a mixture of gases is the pressure that the gas would exert if it were present in the container by itself.

If the same procedure is repeated for the reaction $N_2(g) + 3H_2(g) \rightleftharpoons 2NH_3(g)$, it is found that the following ratio is constant at a particular temperature:

$$\frac{[NH_3(g)]^2}{[N_2(g)][H_2(g)]^3}$$

This leads us to the general **equilibrium law**. For the reaction $aA + bB \rightleftharpoons cC + dD$ (where all reactants are in the same phase), the value of the following ratio is constant at a **particular temperature**:

$$\frac{[C]^c[D]^d}{[A]^a[B]^b}$$

As this ratio is constant at a particular temperature we can write:

$$K_c = \frac{[C]^c[D]^d}{[A]^a[B]^b}$$

where K_c is the **equilibrium constant**. The 'c' indicates that this equilibrium constant is in terms of concentrations.

> K_c **is constant for a particular reaction at a particular temperature.**

We only need to write equilibrium constants for **homogeneous** equilibria (all reactants and products in the same physical state). Reactions involving solids and gases, for example, are more complicated, and the concentrations of pure solids do not appear in the equilibrium constant expression. The equilibrium constant for the decomposition of $CaCO_3$ (page **280**) is thus $K_c = [CO_2]$.

The expressions for the equilibrium constant for some reactions are given below:

$$N_2O_4(g) \rightleftharpoons 2NO_2(g) \qquad\qquad K_c = \frac{[NO_2(g)]^2}{[N_2O_4(g)]}$$

$$N_2O_5(g) + NO(g) \rightleftharpoons 3NO_2(g) \qquad\qquad K_c = \frac{[NO_2(g)]^3}{[N_2O_5(g)][NO(g)]}$$

$$CO(g) + 3H_2(g) \rightleftharpoons CH_4(g) + H_2O(g) \qquad\qquad K_c = \frac{[CH_4(g)][H_2O(g)]}{[CO(g)][H_2(g)]^3}$$

What use is the equilibrium constant?

The equilibrium constant provides information about how far a reaction proceeds at a particular temperature.

The values of the equilibrium constants for a series of reactions at 298 K are given in Table **7.1**. These equilibrium constants are all very much greater than 1. These reactions proceed almost totally towards the products, so that there is virtually no hydrogen and halogen in the equilibrium mixture. However, for the reaction $N_2(g) + O_2(g) \rightleftharpoons 2NO(g)$ the value of the equilibrium constant is 10^{-31} at 298 K. This value is very much less than 1, indicating that the reaction hardly proceeds at all towards the products – that is, the position of equilibrium lies a long way to the left.

$K_c \gg 1$ – the reaction proceeds almost totally towards the products.
$K_c \ll 1$ – the reaction hardly proceeds at all towards the products.

Reaction	K_c
$H_2(g) + F_2(g) \rightleftharpoons 2HF(g)$	10^{95}
$H_2(g) + Cl_2(g) \rightleftharpoons 2HCl(g)$	10^{33}
$H_2(g) + Br_2(g) \rightleftharpoons 2HBr(g)$	10^{19}

Table 7.1 Equilibrium constants for reactions at 298 K.

Self-test 2

Test yourself

4 Write expressions for the equilibrium constant for the following reactions:
a $NO(g) + NO_2(g) \rightleftharpoons N_2O_3(g)$
b $CH_4(g) + H_2O(g) \rightleftharpoons CO(g) + 3H_2(g)$
c $2H_2O(g) \rightleftharpoons 2H_2(g) + O_2(g)$
d $4NH_3(g) + 5O_2(g) \rightleftharpoons 4NO(g) + 6H_2O(g)$
e $2NO(g) + O_2(g) \rightleftharpoons 2NO_2(g)$

How changing the conditions affects the value of the equilibrium constant

The effects of various changes in conditions are considered below.

The effect of pressure

The value of the equilibrium constant is **not** affected by a change in pressure.

Let us consider the equilibrium:

$N_2O_4(g) \rightleftharpoons 2NO_2(g)$

At 400 K, the value of the equilibrium constant for the reaction is $1.46\,mol\,dm^{-3}$.
If we consider a system at equilibrium, in which the equilibrium concentrations are as follows:

$$N_2O_4(g) \rightleftharpoons 2NO_2(g)$$

	N_2O_4	NO_2
Equilibrium concentration/mol dm^{-3}:	2.00	1.71
Percentage of each substance:	53.9%	46.1%

The value of the equilibrium constant for a particular reaction is affected only by a change in **temperature**.

If we now double the pressure by compressing the gaseous mixture to half its original volume, all the concentrations will be doubled, as there is the same number of molecules in half the volume.

$$N_2O_4(g) \rightleftharpoons 2NO_2(g)$$

Equilibrium concentration/mol dm^{-3}:   4.00   3.42

When we work out the value of the ratio:

$$\frac{[NO_2(g)]^2}{[N_2O_4(g)]} = \frac{3.42^2}{4.00} = 2.92 \, \text{mol dm}^{-3}$$

This value is higher than the equilibrium constant at this temperature, and so we must draw the conclusion that the system is **not at equilibrium**. As the value of this ratio is higher than the value of K_c, NO$_2$ (on the top of the expression) must react to produce more N$_2$O$_4$ (on the bottom of the expression). NO$_2$ will thus react to form N$_2$O$_4$ until the value of this ratio is equal to the value of K_c – that is until a new equilibrium is established. The concentrations in this new equilibrium mixture will be:

$$N_2O_4(g) \rightleftharpoons 2NO_2(g)$$

Equilibrium concentration/mol dm^{-3}:   4.44   2.55
Percentage of each substance: 63.5%   36.5%

$$\frac{[NO_2(g)]^2}{[N_2O_4(g)]} = \frac{2.55^2}{4.44} = 1.46 \, \text{mol dm}^{-3}, \text{ which equals } K_c \text{ at this temperature.}$$

If we consider the percentage of each substance at equilibrium, we can see that at the higher pressure the percentage of N$_2$O$_4$ in the equilibrium mixture is greater. This means that as the pressure increases, the position of equilibrium shifts to the left – i.e. to the side with fewer molecules of gas – but the value of K_c stays the same. We could thus re-state Le Chatelier's principle for change in pressure as: 'if a system at equilibrium is subjected to a change in pressure, the position of equilibrium will shift to restore the value of K_c'.

The effect of concentration

The value of the equilibrium constant is **not** affected by a change in concentration.

Let us consider the equilibrium:

$$CH_3COOH(l) + C_2H_5OH(l) \rightleftharpoons CH_3COOCH_2CH_3(l) + H_2O(l)$$
ethanoic acid   ethanol   ethyl ethanoate   water

At 373 K the equilibrium constant is about 4.0. An equilibrium mixture at this temperature could be:

$$CH_3COOH(l) + C_2H_5OH(l) \rightleftharpoons CH_3COOCH_2CH_3(l) + H_2O(l)$$

Equilibrium concentration/mol dm^{-3}:   2.88   2.88   5.76   5.76

If some water is now added so that the concentration of water in the mixture changes to $10.4\,mol\,dm^{-3}$, the concentrations of the other species in the mixture will drop slightly, as the total volume has increased. The new values for the concentrations are:

$$CH_3COOH(l) + C_2H_5OH(l) \rightleftharpoons CH_3COOCH_2CH_3(l) + H_2O(l)$$

Equilibrium concentration/mol dm^{-3}:	2.61	2.61	5.22	10.4

When we work out the value of the ratio:

$$\frac{[CH_3COOCH_2CH_3(l)][H_2O(l)]}{[CH_3COOH(l)][C_2H_5OH(l)]} = 8.0$$

This value is higher than the equilibrium constant at this temperature, and so the system is **not** at equilibrium. The value of this ratio must decrease to bring the value back to 4.0, so ethyl ethanoate must react with water. The reverse reaction is favoured over the forward reaction until a new equilibrium is established.

> The position of equilibrium shifts to the left to use up the added water.

The concentration in this equilibrium mixture will be:

$$CH_3COOH(l) + C_2H_5OH(l) \rightleftharpoons CH_3COOCH_2CH_3(l) + H_2O(l)$$

Equilibrium concentration/mol dm^{-3}:	3.31	3.31	4.52	9.70

$$\frac{[CH_3COOCH_2CH_3(l)][H_2O(l)]}{[CH_3COOH(l)][C_2H_5OH(l)]} = 4.0$$

Thus, a change in concentration has affected the position of equilibrium, but the value of K_c is the same.

The effect of temperature

Exothermic reactions

$$CO(g) + 2H_2(g) \rightleftharpoons CH_3OH(g) \qquad \Delta H^{\ominus} = -90\,kJ\,mol^{-1}$$

Temperature / K	K_c / mol^{-2} dm^6
298	1.7×10^{17}
500	1.1×10^{11}
1000	2.1×10^6

The equilibrium constant expression for this reaction is:

$$K_c = \frac{[CH_3OH(g)]}{[CO(g)][H_2(g)]^2}$$

$$\frac{[CH_3OH(g)] \quad \downarrow \text{ concentration decreases}}{[CO(g)][H_2(g)]^2 \quad \uparrow \text{ concentration increases}}$$

> For an exothermic reaction, the value of the equilibrium constant decreases as the temperature is increased.

We use Le Chatelier's principle to explain the effect of temperature on the equilibrium. The reaction is exothermic in the forward direction, and therefore, according to Le Chatelier's principle, an increase in temperature causes the position of equilibrium to shift in the endothermic direction – that is, the position of equilibrium shifts to the left. The concentration at the top of the expression for K_c decreases and the concentration at the bottom increases. Therefore, the overall value of K_c decreases.

Temperature / K	K_c / $mol^{-2} dm^6$
298	4.3×10^{-31}
500	2.7×10^{-18}
1000	7.5×10^{-9}
2000	4.0×10^{-4}
3000	0.015

For an endothermic reaction, the value of the equilibrium constant increases as the temperature is raised.

Endothermic reactions

$$N_2(g) + O_2(g) \rightleftharpoons 2NO(g) \qquad \Delta H^\ominus = +181\,kJ\,mol^{-1}$$

$$K_c = \frac{[NO(g)]^2}{[N_2(g)][O_2(g)]}$$

As the temperature increases, the value of the equilibrium constant increases. This is an endothermic reaction, so, according to Le Chatelier's principle, as the temperature increases, the position of equilibrium shifts in the endothermic direction in order to take in heat and reduce the effect of the change. The position of equilibrium is thus shifted to the right so that more NO and less N_2 and O_2 are present at equilibrium. This results in the value of the equilibrium constant increasing.

Catalysts and the equilibrium constant

Catalysts are substances that increase (or decrease) the rate of a chemical reaction without being permanently changed in the process. Because they are the same at the beginning as at the end of the reaction, catalysts do not appear in the chemical equation.

An energy level diagram for a reversible reaction is shown in Figure **7.7**.

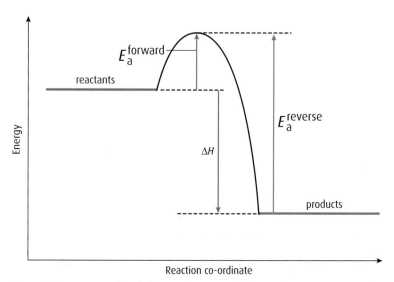

Figure 7.7 An energy level diagram for a reversible reaction.

Catalysts work by providing an alternative pathway of lower activation energy (E_a) for the reaction (Figure **7.8**). In a reversible reaction, a catalyst not only reduces the activation energy for the forward reaction but also that for the reverse reaction. The lowering of the activation energy is the same for both forward and reverse reactions. This means that a catalyst speeds up forward and reverse reactions equally and reduces the time taken to reach equilibrium. This is the only change that results from the introduction of a catalyst, and therefore a catalyst has no effect on the position of equilibrium or on the value of the equilibrium constant.

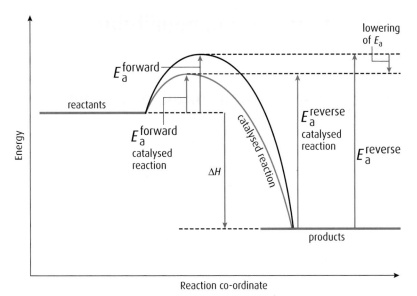

Figure 7.8 Energy level diagrams for catalysed and uncatalysed reactions.

The presence of a catalyst does **not** affect the position of equilibrium or the value of the equilibrium constant, it only reduces the time taken to reach equilibrium.

A catalyst increases the rate of forward and reverse reactions **equally**.

The equilibrium constant and rate

The equilibrium constant gives us information about how far a reaction goes towards completion (that is, about the extent of the reaction). It gives us absolutely no information about how quickly the reaction occurs. Kinetic data, such as the rate constant, indicates how quickly equilibrium is attained but provides no information whatsoever about the position of equilibrium and how far the reaction proceeds.

Test yourself

5 Explain the effect of the stated changes in conditions on the position of equilibrium and the value of the equilibrium constant. In each case state whether the value of the equilibrium constant increases, decreases or stays the same.

  a Increasing pressure in: $CH_4(g) + H_2O(g) \rightleftharpoons CO(g) + 3H_2(g)$ $\Delta H = +206\,kJ\,mol^{-1}$
  b Increasing temperature in: $CH_4(g) + H_2O(g) \rightleftharpoons CO(g) + 3H_2(g)$ $\Delta H = +206\,kJ\,mol^{-1}$
  c Decreasing temperature in: $H_2O(g) + CO(g) \rightleftharpoons H_2(g) + CO_2(g)$ $\Delta H = -40\,kJ\,mol^{-1}$
  d Increasing concentration of H_2 in: $N_2(g) + 3H_2(g) \rightleftharpoons 2NH_3(g)$ $\Delta H = -92\,kJ\,mol^{-1}$
  e Increasing pressure in: $N_2(g) + 3H_2(g) \rightleftharpoons 2NH_3(g)$ $\Delta H = -92\,kJ\,mol^{-1}$
  f Introducing a catalyst into the reaction: $2SO_2(g) + O_2(g) \rightleftharpoons 2SO_3(g)$ $\Delta H = -197\,kJ\,mol^{-1}$

Learning objectives

- Solve problems involving equilibrium constants

HL 7.4 Calculations using equilibrium constants

How to calculate the units of the equilibrium constant

The units for K_c can be calculated from the expression for the equilibrium constant. For example, for the reaction

$$CH_3COOH(l) + C_2H_5OH(l) \rightleftharpoons CH_3COOCH_2CH_3(l) + H_2O(l)$$

$$K_c = \frac{[CH_3COOCH_2CH_3(l)][H_2O(l)]}{[CH_3COOH(l)][C_2H_5OH(l)]}$$

If all concentrations are in $mol\,dm^{-3}$, the units can be substituted into the equilibrium constant expression:

$$\text{units of } K_c = \frac{\cancel{mol\,dm^{-3}} \times \cancel{mol\,dm^{-3}}}{\cancel{mol\,dm^{-3}} \times \cancel{mol\,dm^{-3}}}$$

Thus, as all the units cancel out, K_c has **no units**. This is always the case when there is the same number of species on the left-hand side and right-hand side of the equation. However, let us consider another example:

$$N_2(g) + 3H_2(g) \rightleftharpoons 2NH_3(g)$$

$$K_c = \frac{[NH_3(g)]^2}{[N_2(g)][H_2(g)]^3}$$

$$\text{units of } K_c = \frac{(\cancel{mol\,dm^{-3}})^2}{(mol\,dm^{-3}) \times (mol\,dm^{-3})^{\cancel{3}}} = \frac{1}{mol\,dm^{-3} \times mol\,dm^{-3}}$$

$$= \frac{1}{(mol\,dm^{-3})^2} = (mol\,dm^{-3})^{-2} = mol^{-2}\,dm^6$$

A shortcut is to consider the difference in the number of molecules on the top and bottom of the equilibrium constant expression. In

$$K_c = \frac{[NH_3(g)]^2}{[N_2(g)][H_2(g)]^3}$$

the total power on the top of the expression for K_c is 2. If we ignore the fact that the species on the bottom are different, the total power on the bottom is $1 + 3 = 4$.

| Δn = **total power on top – total power on bottom**

$$\Delta n = 2 - (1 + 3) = -2$$

$$\text{units of } K_c = (mol\,dm^{-3})^{-\Delta n}$$
$$\text{i.e. } (mol\,dm^{-3})^{-2} = mol^{-2}\,dm^6$$

$$\frac{1}{x^2} = x^{-2}$$

$$(x^{-3})^{-2} = x^{-3 \times -2} = x^6$$

$$\frac{x^2}{x^4} = x^{2-4} = x^{-2}$$

Note: the equilibrium constant, K_c, may also be expressed relative to a standard state of $1\,mol\,dm^{-3}$, and so it is often quoted with no units.

288

The units for some equilibrium constants are given in Table **7.2**.

Reaction	Expression for K_c	Units of K_c
$N_2O_4(g) \rightleftharpoons 2NO_2(g)$	$K_c = \dfrac{[NO_2(g)]^2}{[N_2O_4(g)]}$	$mol\,dm^{-3}$
$CO(g) + 3H_2(g) \rightleftharpoons CH_4(g) + H_2O(g)$	$K_c = \dfrac{[CH_4(g)][H_2O(g)]}{[CO(g)][H_2(g)]^3}$	$mol^{-2}\,dm^6$
$2HI(g) \rightleftharpoons H_2(g) + I_2(g)$	$K_c = \dfrac{[H_2(g)][I_2(g)]}{[HI(g)]^2}$	no units
$2SO_2(g) + O_2(g) \rightleftharpoons 2SO_3(g)$	$K_c = \dfrac{[SO_3(g)]^2}{[SO_2(g)]^2[O_2(g)]}$	$mol^{-1}\,dm^3$

Table 7.2 The units for some equilibrium constants.

Self-test 3

Test yourself

6 Work out the units of the equilibrium constants for the following reactions:

  a $N_2O_3(g) \rightleftharpoons NO(g) + NO_2(g)$
  b $CO(g) + 3H_2(g) \rightleftharpoons CH_4(g) + H_2O(g)$
  c $2H_2(g) + O_2(g) \rightleftharpoons 2H_2O(g)$
  d $4NO(g) + 6H_2O(g) \rightleftharpoons 4NH_3(g) + 5O_2(g)$
  e $2NO(g) + O_2(g) \rightleftharpoons 2NO_2(g)$

Calculation of equilibrium constants

If the concentrations of all reaction components at equilibrium are given, calculating a value for the equilibrium constant simply involves putting these values into the equilibrium constant expression.

Worked example

Use the data given to calculate the value of the equilibrium constant at 700 K for the reaction:

$$H_2(g) + I_2(g) \rightleftharpoons 2HI(g)$$

Substance	$H_2(g)$	$I_2(g)$	$HI(g)$
Equilibrium concentration / $mol\,dm^{-3}$	0.18	0.39	1.95

$$K_c = \frac{[HI(g)]^2}{[H_2(g)][I_2(g)]}$$

Substituting in the equilibrium concentrations we get:

$$K_c = \frac{1.95^2}{0.18 \times 0.39} = 54 \text{ (no units)}$$

HL If we are given a value for the equilibrium constant, we can work out the concentration of any one of the species at equilibrium.

Worked examples

Given that the equilibrium constant for the reaction $H_2(g) + I_2(g) \rightleftharpoons 2HI(g)$ at 700 K is 54 and that the concentrations of H_2 and I_2 at equilibrium are $0.25\,\text{mol}\,\text{dm}^{-3}$ and $0.50\,\text{mol}\,\text{dm}^{-3}$, respectively, what is the equilibrium concentration of HI?

$$K_c = \frac{[HI(g)]^2}{[H_2(g)][I_2(g)]}$$

Substituting in the equilibrium concentrations we get: $54 = \dfrac{[HI(g)]^2}{0.25 \times 0.50}$

Rearranging this we get: $[HI(g)]^2 = 54 \times 0.25 \times 0.50$

$[HI(g)] = 2.6\,\text{mol}\,\text{dm}^{-3}$

Therefore, the equilibrium concentration of hydrogen iodide is $2.6\,\text{mol}\,\text{dm}^{-3}$.

A variation on this calculation is given in the next example.

Equal concentrations of hydrogen and iodine are mixed together in a closed container at 700 K and allowed to come to equilibrium. If the concentration of HI at equilibrium is $0.85\,\text{mol}\,\text{dm}^{-3}$, what are the equilibrium concentrations of H_2 and I_2? $K_c = 54$ at this temperature.

$$H_2(g) + I_2(g) \rightleftharpoons 2HI(g)$$

$$K_c = \frac{[HI(g)]^2}{[H_2(g)][I_2(g)]}$$

We can substitute in the values we know: $54 = \dfrac{0.85^2}{[H_2(g)][I_2(g)]}$

However, we also know that the initial concentration of H_2 and I_2 were equal, and because, from the chemical equation, we know that 1 mole of H_2 reacts with 1 mole of I_2, they must remain equal. This means that the equilibrium concentration of H_2 is the same as that of I_2 and we can write:

$$54 = \frac{0.85^2}{[H_2(g)]^2}$$

Rearranging this we get: $[H_2(g)]^2 = \dfrac{0.85^2}{54}$

$[H_2(g)] = 0.12\,\text{mol}\,\text{dm}^{-3}$

Therefore the equilibrium concentrations of H_2 and I_2 are both $0.12\,\text{mol}\,\text{dm}^{-3}$.

Note: if we had the equation $2SO_2(g) + O_2(g) \rightleftharpoons 2SO_3(g)$ and started off with equal concentrations of SO_2 and O_2, the concentrations would not be equal at equilibrium, as 2 mol SO_2 react with 1 mol O_2 and therefore, as the reaction proceeds to equilibrium, the concentration of SO_2 drops twice as much as the concentration of O_2.

Next we will look at questions in which we need to find the value of the equilibrium constant but have not been given all the equilibrium concentrations.

HL

5.00 mol H_2 and 3.00 mol I_2 are mixed together in a vessel of volume 10.0 dm³ and allowed to come to equilibrium at 1100 K. At equilibrium there were 0.43 mol I_2 present in the reaction mixture. Calculate the value of the equilibrium constant.

We need to consider the initial situation and see how the concentrations change as the system reaches equilibrium.

$$H_2(g) + I_2(g) \rightleftharpoons 2HI(g)$$

initial no. moles / mol	5.00	3.00	0.00
equilibrium no. moles / mol	?	0.43	?

The numbers of moles at equilibrium can be worked out as follows: 3.00 mol I_2 were originally present, and this became 0.43 mol I_2 at equilibrium. This means that $3.00 - 0.43$, i.e. 2.57, mol I_2 reacted. From the chemical equation we can see that 1 mol I_2 reacts with 1 mol H_2, so 2.57 mol I_2 reacts with 2.57 mol H_2. If there were 5.00 mol H_2 originally present and 2.57 mol H_2 react, this leaves $5.00 - 2.57$, i.e. 2.43, mol H_2 present at equilibrium. From the chemical equation, 1 mol I_2 reacts to form 2 mol HI. Therefore, 2.57 mol I_2 will react to form 2×2.57, i.e. 5.14, mol HI.

This can be summarised as:

	$H_2(g)$	$+$	$I_2(g)$	$\rightleftharpoons$	$2HI(g)$
initial number of moles / mol	5.00		3.00		0.00
	2.57 mol H_2 react		2.57 mol I_2 react		2×2.57 mol HI formed
equilibrium number of moles / mol	2.43		0.43		5.14

Now that we have the equilibrium number of moles, we must work out the equilibrium **concentration** of each species. To do this we use the equation:

$$\text{concentration} = \frac{\text{no. moles}}{\text{volume}}$$

In this case, as there is the same number of molecules on both sides of the equation, all the concentrations will cancel, and so this step makes no difference to the overall answer.

As the volume of the vessel is 10.0 dm³, we must divide each number of moles by 10.0, and therefore the equilibrium concentrations are:

$$H_2(g) + I_2(g) \rightleftharpoons 2HI(g)$$

equilibrium no. moles / mol	2.43	0.43	5.14
equilibrium concentration / mol dm⁻³	0.243	0.043	0.514

The expression for K_c is: $K_c = \dfrac{[HI(g)]^2}{[H_2(g)][I_2(g)]}$

The equilibrium concentrations are substituted into this equation:

$$K_c = \frac{0.514^2}{0.243 \times 0.043} = 25.3$$

The units all cancel in this case:

$$\frac{(\cancel{\text{mol dm}^{-3}})^2}{\cancel{\text{mol dm}^{-3}} \times \cancel{\text{mol dm}^{-3}}}$$

Therefore K_c has no units.

The equilibrium constant for this reaction at 1100 K is thus 25.3.

3.00 mol NO_2 and 1.00 mol N_2O_4 are mixed together in a vessel of volume 1.00 dm^3 and allowed to come to equilibrium at 398 K. At equilibrium there were 1.74 mol N_2O_4 present in the reaction mixture. Calculate the value of the equilibrium constant. The equation for the reaction is: $2NO_2(g) \rightleftharpoons N_2O_4(g)$.

	$2NO_2(g) \rightleftharpoons N_2O_4(g)$	
initial no. moles / mol	3.00	1.00
equilibrium no. moles / mol	?	1.74

The equilibrium numbers of moles can be worked out as follows: 1.00 mol N_2O_4 was originally present, and this became 1.74 mol N_2O_4 at equilibrium. This means that 1.74 − 1.00, i.e. 0.74, mol N_2O_4 were formed by NO_2 reacting. From the chemical equation we can see that 2 mol NO_2 reacts to form 1 mol N_2O_4. This means that 2×0.74, i.e. 1.48, mol NO_2 must have reacted to form 0.74 mol N_2O_4. There were 3.00 mol NO_2 originally present and 1.48 mol NO_2 reacted, so this leaves 3.00 − 1.48, i.e. 1.52, mol NO_2 present at equilibrium.

	$2NO_2(g) \rightleftharpoons N_2O_4(g)$	
initial no. moles / mol	3.00	1.00
equilibrium no. moles / mol	**1.52**	1.74

Equilibrium concentrations are worked out using the equation:

$$\text{concentration} = \frac{\text{no. moles}}{\text{volume}}$$

As the volume of the vessel is 1.00 dm^3, we must simply divide the numbers of moles by 1, and therefore the equilibrium concentrations are:

	$2NO_2(g) \rightleftharpoons N_2O_4(g)$	
equilibrium concentration / mol dm^{-3}	1.52	1.74

The expression for K_c is:

$$K_c = \frac{[N_2O_4(g)]}{[NO_2(g)]^2}$$

The equilibrium concentrations are substituted into this equation:

$$K_c = \frac{1.74}{1.52^2} = 0.753$$

The units of K_c are worked out by substituting units into the K_c expression:

$$K_c = \frac{\cancel{\text{mol dm}^{-3}}}{(\text{mol dm}^{-3})^{\cancel{2}}} = \frac{1}{\text{mol dm}^{-3}} = \text{mol}^{-1}\,\text{dm}^3$$

Therefore the equilibrium constant for this reaction at 398 K is 0.753 mol^{-1} dm^3.

Given the initial number of moles and the equilibrium constant it is also possible to work out the number of moles at equilibrium.

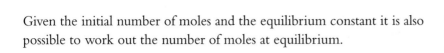

Worked example

Consider the reaction: $H_2(g) + CO_2(g) \rightleftharpoons H_2O(g) + CO(g)$. In this reaction, 2.00 mol of H_2 and 2.00 mol of CO_2 are put into a container of volume 10.0 dm^3 together with 1.00 mol H_2O and 1.00 mol CO. They are allowed to come to equilibrium at 1200 K. Given that the value of the equilibrium constant at 1200 K is 2.10, work out the composition of the equilibrium mixture in terms of concentrations.

$$H_2(g) \quad + \quad CO_2(g) \quad \rightleftharpoons \quad H_2O(g) \quad + \quad CO(g)$$

initial no. moles / mol   2.00   2.00   1.00   1.00

We will assume that x mol H_2 react with x mol CO_2 to form x mol H_2O and x mol CO.

equilibrium no. moles / mol $2.00 - x$ $2.00 - x$ $1.00 + x$ $1.00 + x$

We must divide each of these values by 10.0 to get equilibrium concentrations:

equilibrium concentration / mol dm^{-3} $\dfrac{2.00 - x}{10.0}$ $\dfrac{2.00 - x}{10.0}$ $\dfrac{1.00 + x}{10.0}$ $\dfrac{1.00 + x}{10.0}$

The equilibrium concentrations and the value of K_c must be substituted into the expression for K_c:

$$K_c = \frac{[H_2O(g)][CO(g)]}{[H_2(g)][CO_2(g)]}$$

$$2.10 = \frac{\dfrac{1.00 + x}{10.0} \times \dfrac{1.00 + x}{10.0}}{\dfrac{2.00 - x}{10.0} \times \dfrac{2.00 - x}{10.0}}$$

> As the number of species on both sides of the equation are the same, the volumes cancel.

$$2.10 = \frac{(1.00 + x)(1.00 + x)}{(2.00 - x)(2.00 - x)}$$

$$2.10 = \frac{(1.00 + x)^2}{(2.00 - x)^2}$$

The right-hand side is a perfect square, and so the square root of each side can be taken:

$$\sqrt{2.10} = \frac{(1.00 + x)}{(2.00 - x)}$$

$$1.45 = \frac{(1.00 + x)}{(2.00 - x)}$$

Examiner's tip

It is stated specifically on the IB syllabus that you should not have to solve quadratic equations, but this way of finding the square root of each side seems to be acceptable – remember this method.

This can be rearranged to give:

$$1.45(2.00 - x) = 1.00 + x$$
$$2.90 - 1.45x = 1.00 + x$$
$$1.90 = 2.45x$$

Therefore, $x = 0.776$ mol.

The equilibrium concentrations are worked out from:

$$H_2(g) + CO_2(g) \rightleftharpoons H_2O(g) + CO(g)$$

equilibrium concentration / mol dm^{-3}	$\dfrac{2.00-x}{10.0}$	$\dfrac{2.00-x}{10.0}$	$\dfrac{1.00+x}{10.0}$	$\dfrac{1.00+x}{10.0}$

Substituting in the value of x we get:

equilibrium concentration / mol dm^{-3}	0.122	0.122	0.178	0.178

Two different values of the equilibrium constant for the same reaction under the same conditions?

Consider the equilibrium: $2NO_2(g) \rightleftharpoons N_2O_4(g)$. The expression for the equilibrium constant is:

$$K_c = \frac{[N_2O_4(g)]}{[NO_2(g)]^2}$$

and the value for the equilibrium constant at 400 K is 0.69 mol^{-1} dm^3.

However, the reaction could also have been written the other way round:

$$N_2O_4(g) \rightleftharpoons 2NO_2(g)$$

The expression for the equilibrium constant in this case is:

$$K_c' = \frac{[NO_2(g)]^2}{[N_2O_4(g)]}$$

The value of the equilibrium constant at 400 K for this reaction is 1.46 mol dm^{-3}.

It can be seen then that the value of the equilibrium constant depends on how the reaction is written, and therefore an equilibrium constant is only useful when quoted in conjunction with the equilibrium reaction.

Consider the equilibrium: $\quad H_2(g) + I_2(g) \rightleftharpoons 2HI(g)$
which could also have been written: $\quad \frac{1}{2}H_2(g) + \frac{1}{2}I_2(g) \rightleftharpoons HI(g)$
Both are completely valid and accurate representations of the reaction.

The equilibrium constant expression for the first reaction is:

$$K_c = \frac{[HI(g)]^2}{[H_2(g)][I_2(g)]}$$

whereas for the second reaction it is:

$$K_c' = \frac{[HI(g)]}{[H_2(g)]^{\frac{1}{2}}[I_2(g)]^{\frac{1}{2}}}$$

The value of the equilibrium constant for the first reaction at 700 K is 54, whereas for the second reaction at the same temperature it is 7.3. The relationship between the two equilibrium constants is $K_c' = \sqrt{K_c}$.

$$K_c' = \frac{1}{K_c}$$

The principal use of HI is to make hydriodic acid, which is used to make iodides and as a reducing agent. Hydriodic acid is a controlled chemical in the USA as it can be used in the production of methamphetamine (crystal meth).

7 Given the equilibrium concentrations, calculate the value of the equilibrium constant for each reaction:

  a $2A(g) \rightleftharpoons Z(g)$

    equilibrium concentrations are:

    [A] $0.150 \, mol \, dm^{-3}$ [Z] $0.500 \, mol \, dm^{-3}$

  b $2Q(g) + 3X(g) \rightleftharpoons 2Z(g) + 4E(g)$

    equilibrium concentrations are:

    [Q] $1.50 \times 10^{-3} \, mol \, dm^{-3}$

    [X] $2.75 \times 10^{-3} \, mol \, dm^{-3}$

    [Z] $7.86 \times 10^{-4} \, mol \, dm^{-3}$

    [E] $9.37 \times 10^{-5} \, mol \, dm^{-3}$

8 In each of the following reactions use the given data to calculate equilibrium number of moles of each substance.

  a $2A(g) \rightleftharpoons Z(g)$

    initial no. moles of A = 0.100 mol

    initial no. moles of Z = 0.500 mol

    no. moles of A at equilibrium = 0.0600 mol

  b $2A(g) + X(g) \rightleftharpoons 2Z(g)$

    initial no. moles of A = 1.00 mol

    initial no. moles of X = 2.00 mol

    initial no. moles of Z = 0.00 mol

    no. moles of Z at equilibrium = 0.400 mol

9 Consider the reversible reaction:

$A(g) + X(g) \rightleftharpoons Q(g)$

  a Write the expression for K_c for this reaction.

  b In each of the following situations calculate a value for the equilibrium constant from the data given:

    i initial no. moles of A = 0.200 mol

      initial no. moles of X = 0.400 mol

      initial no. moles of Q = 0.000 mol

      no. moles of A at equilibrium = 0.100 mol

      volume of container = $1.00 \, dm^3$

      temperature = 300 K

    ii initial no. moles of A = 0.200 mol

      initial no. moles of X = 0.100 mol

      initial no. moles of Q = 0.100 mol

      no. moles of A at equilibrium = 0.150 mol

      volume of container = $10.0 \, dm^3$

      temperature = 400 K

  c Use the values of K_c that you have calculated to work out whether this reaction is exothermic or endothermic.

10 Consider the reversible reaction:

$2A(g) + X(g) \rightleftharpoons 4Q(g) + Z(g)$

  a Write the expression for K_c for this reaction.

  b In each of the following situations calculate a value for the equilibrium constant from the data given:

    i initial no. moles of A = 0.800 mol

      initial no. moles of X = 0.400 mol

      initial no. moles of Q = 0.000 mol

      initial no. moles of Z = 0.000 mol

      no. moles of Z at equilibrium = 0.100 mol

      volume of container = $10.0 \, dm^3$

      temperature = 800 K

    ii initial no. moles of A = 0.000 mol

      initial no. moles of X = 0.000 mol

      initial no. moles of Q = 1.000 mol

      initial no. moles of Z = 2.000 mol

      no. moles of A at equilibrium = 0.200 mol

      volume of container = $20.0 \, dm^3$

      temperature = 500 K

  c Use the values of K_c that you have calculated to work out whether this reaction is exothermic or endothermic.

11 Consider the equilibrium:

$A(g) + Z(g) \rightleftharpoons X(g) + Q(g)$

  a At a certain temperature, the value of the equilibrium constant for this reaction is 9.00. At this temperature 0.100 mol of A and 0.100 mol of Z are placed in a container of volume $1.00 \, dm^3$ and allowed to come to equilibrium. Calculate the no. moles of X present at equilibrium.

  b At a different temperature, the value of the equilibrium constant for this reaction is 16.0. At this temperature 0.200 mol of A, 0.200 mol of Z, 0.200 mol of X and 0.200 mol of Q are placed in a container of volume $2.00 \, dm^3$ and allowed to come to equilibrium. Calculate the concentration of A at equilibrium.

12 a Consider the equilibrium:
$2SO_2(g) + O_2(g) \rightleftharpoons 2SO_3(g)$
The value of the equilibrium constant at
$500\,K$ is $1.03 \times 10^{12}\,mol^{-1}\,dm^3$. What is the
value of the equilibrium constant for the
reaction: $2SO_3(g) \rightleftharpoons 2SO_2(g) + O_2(g)$ at $500\,K$?

b The value of the equilibrium constant for the
reaction $N_2(g) + 3H_2(g) \rightleftharpoons 2NH_3(g)$ at $500\,K$
is $59.8\,mol^{-2}\,dm^6$. What is the value of the
equilibrium constant for the reaction:
$\frac{1}{2}N_2(g) + \frac{3}{2}H_2(g) \rightleftharpoons NH_3(g)$ at the same
temperature?

7.5 Industrial processes

Applying the ideas of rates and equilibrium to industrial processes

When considering how to make an industrial process as efficient – and hence profitable – as possible, two main factors must be considered:

1 How much product is obtained?

2 How quickly is the product obtained?

We will now consider how changing the conditions in industrial processes affects these two factors.

The Haber process

The Haber process (or Haber–Bosch process) is for the industrial preparation of ammonia (Figure **7.9**). The main reaction in the process is:

$$N_2(g) + 3H_2(g) \rightleftharpoons 2NH_3(g) \qquad\qquad \Delta H = -92\,kJ\,mol^{-1}$$

The nitrogen is obtained from the air and one of the sources of the hydrogen is from natural gas (methane).

The yield of ammonia is about 15–20% per pass, and, once the ammonia has been removed by refrigeration, the remaining gases are recycled to pass over the catalyst once more.

Learning objectives

- Understand the conditions used in some industrial processes by the application of kinetic and equilibrium principles

The gases are reacted together in stoichiometric ratio ($N_2 : H_2$, $1 : 3$) at a pressure of $200\,atm$ and about $500\,°C$ over an iron catalyst.

Ammonia is an important chemical, as it is used, among other things, for making fertilisers.

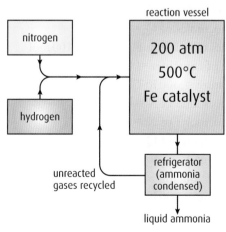

Figure 7.9 A schematic diagram showing the industrial production of ammonia.

Pressure

How the percentage of ammonia in an equilibrium mixture at 700 K (427 °C) varies with pressure is shown in Table **7.3** and in Figure **7.10**. It can be seen clearly that increasing the pressure increases the percentage of ammonia at equilibrium. This can be understood on the basis of Le Chatelier's principle, as the reaction involves a decrease in the number of moles of gas from the left-hand side to the right-hand side:

$$N_2(g) + 3H_2(g) \rightleftharpoons 2NH_3(g)$$

As the pressure increases, the position of equilibrium shifts to the side with fewer moles of gas, i.e. to the right-hand side. Therefore, the percentage of ammonia at equilibrium increases as the pressure increases.

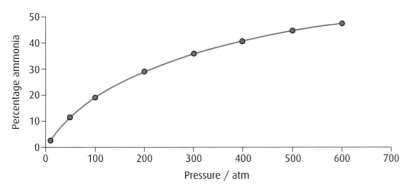

Figure 7.10 The variation of the equilibrium yield of ammonia with pressure at a constant temperature of 700 K.

Pressure / atm	Percentage ammonia at equilibrium
10	2.71
50	11.3
100	18.8
200	28.9
300	35.6
400	40.5
500	44.3
600	47.4

Table 7.3 The variation of the equilibrium yield of ammonia with pressure.

High pressure increases the yield of ammonia and increases the rate of reaction. Extremely high pressure is difficult to achieve – we have to balance increased yield against increased expense of building and maintaining plants.

It would be expected from these data that the reaction should be carried out at the highest possible pressure, and indeed a pressure of 1000 atm would produce a greater yield of ammonia (55.8%) than at 200 atm. However, the advantage of having a better yield has to be balanced against the increased capital costs of building a plant able to operate at much higher pressures, and all the extra safety and maintenance considerations that accompany it.

Increasing the pressure also speeds up the rate of reaction – the particles are forced closer together and therefore collide more often.

Temperature

How the percentage of ammonia in an equilibrium mixture at 200 atm varies with temperature is shown in Table **7.4** and in Figure **7.11**, overleaf.

These data can be rationalised using Le Chatelier's principle. The reaction is exothermic in the forward direction and therefore endothermic in the reverse direction:

$$N_2(g) + 3H_2(g) \rightleftharpoons 2NH_3(g) \qquad \Delta H = -92\,kJ\,mol^{-1}$$

As the temperature increases at constant pressure, the position of equilibrium shifts in the endothermic direction – that is, to the left – so the percentage of ammonia at equilibrium drops.

Temperature / °C	Percentage ammonia at equilibrium
25	99.6
127	95.2
227	75.2
327	54.6
427	28.9
527	12.9
627	5.77
827	1.41

Table 7.4 The variation of the equilibrium yield of ammonia with temperature.

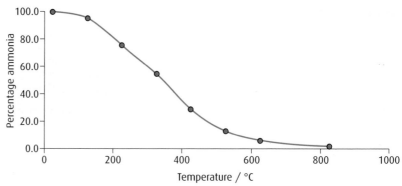

Figure 7.11 The variation of the equilibrium yield of ammonia with temperature at a constant pressure of 200 atm.

Compromise temperature – a balance between yield and rate.

From these data it would be expected that the reaction should be run at the lowest possible temperature – and, indeed, 25 °C looks ideal, with conversion to ammonia approaching 100%. However, the rate of reaction at 25 °C would be much lower than at 500 °C (the rate at 500 °C is likely to be about 1×10^{12} times greater than the rate at 25 °C!). A compromise temperature must therefore be used, at which a reasonable yield of ammonia is obtained at a reasonable rate.

Catalyst

A catalyst (iron) is used to speed up the rate of the reaction without having to heat up the reaction mixture further. Although the catalyst does not affect the position of equilibrium, and hence the yield of ammonia, it does allow the ammonia to be produced more quickly and improve the overall cost-effectiveness of the process.

Removal of product

The ammonia is removed from the reaction mixture by cooling it so that it liquefies (NH_3 has a much higher boiling point than N_2 and H_2). The position of equilibrium thus shifts to the right to replace the ammonia that has been removed.

The Contact process

The Contact process is for the production of sulfuric acid. Uses of sulfuric acid include making detergents and fertilisers. The process involves the following reactions:

Sulfuric acid is one of the most-produced chemicals worldwide. Its single largest use is in the manufacture of phosphate fertilisers.

$$S(s) + O_2(g) \rightarrow SO_2(g) \qquad \Delta H = -297 \, kJ \, mol^{-1}$$
$$2SO_2(g) + O_2(g) \rightleftharpoons 2SO_3(g) \qquad \Delta H = -197 \, kJ \, mol^{-1}$$
$$SO_3(g) + H_2O(l) \rightleftharpoons H_2SO_4(l) \qquad \Delta H = -130 \, kJ \, mol^{-1}$$

The first stage involves burning sulfur in air. The reaction goes essentially to completion and can be regarded as non-reversible. The second stage takes place in the presence of a vanadium(V) oxide (V_2O_5) catalyst. The catalyst is inactive below 400 °C and breaks down above 620 °C. The reaction involves a reversible reaction, and the conditions are critical. It is the choice of conditions for this reaction that is considered here.

The reaction is exothermic:
$$2SO_2(g) + O_2(g) \rightleftharpoons 2SO_3(g)$$
$$\Delta H = -197 \, kJ \, mol^{-1}$$

Fritz Haber – hero or villain? Saviour of humankind or war criminal?

Haber was born in 1868 in Silesia, which was then part of Germany but is now part of Poland. His parents were Jewish, but Haber later renounced his religion in favour of Christianity, as the opportunities available to Jews in Germany in the late 19th century were limited. He is most famous for developing a process for fixing nitrogen (taking nitrogen from the air and converting it into a much more reactive chemical, ammonia).

Nitrogen is an important element for plant growth and, as most plants are unable to fix nitrogen from the air, they rely on absorbing it in some soluble form from the soil. At the beginning of the 20th century scientists were struggling to come up with a method to produce ammonia from nitrogen and Germany was reliant on imported guano as a fertiliser. It was Haber and his co-workers who came up with a solution. Their process was scaled up to industrial level by Carl Bosch of BASF, and the first industrial ammonia production plant opened in Germany in 1913. Ammonia can be further converted into fertilisers such as ammonium nitrate. Without artificial fertilisers it is likely that, in the last hundred years, millions of people around the world would have died of starvation. For his work on this process, which was regarded as benefiting the 'whole of humanity', Haber was awarded the Nobel Prize for Chemistry in 1918.

There is, however, another side to Fritz Haber and ammonia. As well as being the basis of artificial fertilisers, ammonia can be used to make explosives. Without Haber's process, Germany would have very quickly run out of explosives in World War I, the war would almost certainly have been shorter and millions of lives might have been saved. To what extent is Haber personally responsible for lengthening the war? How far does the responsibility of a scientist stretch? Can he or she be expected to foresee all possible uses of their discoveries?

Haber also developed and supervised the use of chemical weapons, such as chlorine gas, in World War I and could perhaps be regarded as the founder of chemical warfare. He was a staunch patriot, who fully supported the German war effort, but he did not take the ultimate decision to use these weapons. How far was Haber responsible for the deaths of people

Figure 7.12 Fritz Haber.

through the use of poison gas? Is he more responsible here than for the deaths that arose due to the lengthening of the war through the use of ammonia to make explosives?

After World War I, Germany had to pay huge sums of money as war reparations and Haber yet again tried to use chemistry to save his country. He investigated processes for extracting gold from sea water but eventually had to abandon the project when it became apparent that the concentration of gold in sea water was substantially lower than had been originally estimated.

When the Nazis took control of Germany in 1933, laws were passed to prevent Jews from holding positions in universities. Although Haber could have remained in his position as head of the Kaiser Wilhelm Institute, he resigned his post. Shortly afterwards he left Germany and died a few months later in Switzerland. It is a sad postscript to the life of a talented chemist that Zyklon B, which was developed as an insecticide at Haber's institute, was used in the gas chambers of the Nazi concentration camps in World War II. Could Haber be held in any way responsible for this?

I will leave it up to you to decide whether Haber was a saviour of humankind or a war criminal.

Compromise temperature – a balance between yield and rate.

Increasing pressure increases yield, but the extra expense is not justified in this case.

SO_3 is sulfur(VI) oxide.
SO_2 is sulfur(IV) oxide – see Chapter **9**.

Le Chatelier's principle suggests the use of as low a temperature as possible for the Contact process. However, at lower temperatures the rate of the reaction is also lower, and so a compromise temperature of 420 °C is used. Other important reasons for keeping the temperature as low as possible are that fuel costs and corrosion of reaction vessels increase rapidly as the temperature is increased.

Le Chatelier's principle suggests that increasing the pressure would increase the yield of SO_3 because there is a decrease in the number of gaseous molecules from left to right. However, the equilibrium constant for this reaction at 420 °C is about $2 \times 10^6 \, mol^{-1} \, dm^3$, and the percentage SO_3 in the equilibrium mixture is very high. The extra expense of designing the plant for high pressures would not be justified.

The yield is also increased by having an excess of oxygen present ($SO_2 : O_2$, 1 : 1) and by removing the SO_3 from the reaction vessel. Both of these factors can be understood in term of Le Chatelier's principle. If the concentration of O_2 increases, the position of equilibrium shifts to the right to use up the extra O_2. If SO_3 is removed, the position of equilibrium shifts to the right to replace the SO_3.

The SO_3 cannot be absorbed directly in water because a fine mist of sulfuric acid is formed, which can pass into the atmosphere. The SO_3 is, therefore, absorbed into 98% sulfuric acid to produce oleum ($H_2S_2O_7$), which reacts with further water to form sulfuric acid that is slightly more concentrated than 98%.

$$SO_3(g) + H_2SO_4(l) \rightleftharpoons H_2S_2O_7(l)$$

$$H_2S_2O_7(l) + H_2O(l) \rightleftharpoons 2H_2SO_4(l)$$

$$\text{Overall: } SO_3(g) + H_2O(l) \rightleftharpoons H_2SO_4(l)$$

Self-test 5

Test yourself

13 Hydrogen for the Haber process can be produced by the reaction between methane and steam:

$$CH_4(g) + H_2O(g) \rightleftharpoons CO(g) + 3H_2(g) \qquad \Delta H = +206 \, kJ \, mol^{-1}$$

State whether each of the following changes in conditions would: (**i**) increase, decrease or have no effect on the yield of hydrogen; and (**ii**) increase, decrease or not change the rate of the reaction.

a increasing the pressure
b increasing the temperature
c introducing a catalyst

7.6 Phase equilibria

Physical equilibria

All the previous discussion was regarding chemical equilibria – that is, equilibria established as a result of chemical reactions. We will now discuss physical equilibria (equilibria involving a change in state), and specifically the equilibrium between a liquid and its vapour.

Evaporation

When a liquid is placed in an **open** container it evaporates. On a molecular level, the particles must overcome the forces holding them in the liquid (intermolecular forces) in order to escape into the gas phase. Evaporation is thus an endothermic process.

The spread of molecular velocities in a liquid is shown in Figure **7.13**. Molecules in the shaded region have sufficient energy to escape and evaporate. The faster-moving molecules are able to break free from the intermolecular forces, so they escape first and the average kinetic energy of the particles in the liquid phase drops. Average kinetic energy is an indication of the temperature, and therefore the temperature of the liquid falls. Heat is drawn from the surroundings to allow further molecules to evaporate. If the container is open then all the liquid will eventually evaporate.

Liquid–vapour equilibrium

Consider a volatile liquid, such as bromine, in a **closed** container (Figure **7.14**). At the beginning there are no molecules of vapour above the liquid – molecules are evaporating, but there is no condensation (Figure **7.14a**). As molecules of vapour appear, these strike the surface of the liquid and some re-enter it – this process is condensation. At first the rate of condensation is low, but as the number of molecules in the vapour phase increases the rate of condensation increases (Figure **7.14b**). Eventually the rate of condensation becomes equal to the rate of evaporation and nothing more appears to change (Figure **7.14c**).

Learning objectives

- Understand that dynamic equilibrium is also attained in a process involving a change in state
- **HL** Understand what is meant by vapour pressure
- Describe and explain the relationship between vapour pressure of a liquid and temperature
- Understand the relationship between vapour pressure, strength of intermolecular forces and boiling point for a liquid–vapour system

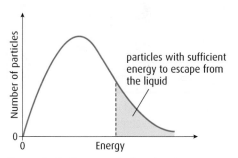

Figure 7.13 The spread of molecular velocities in a sample of liquid.

As the rate of vaporisation and the rate of condensation are equal, this is a **dynamic equilibrium**.

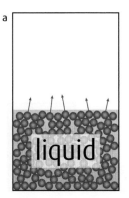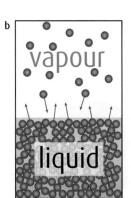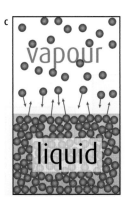

Figure 7.14 Equilibrium is attained when the rate of evaporation equals the rate of condensation.

This is known as **phase equilibrium**, as it involves a change of phase (state).

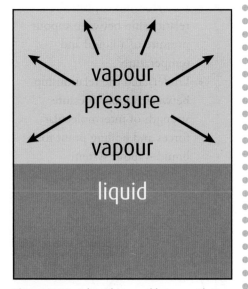

Figure 7.15 A liquid in equilibrium with its vapour exerts a vapour pressure.

> **The vapour pressure depends only on the nature of the liquid and the temperature.**

Note: sufficient liquid must be present to attain equilibrium – if all the liquid evaporates, then the equilibrium vapour pressure will not be attained.

When the rate of evaporation (vaporisation) is equal to the rate of condensation, the colour of the vapour remains constant (it does not get any darker or lighter) and a state of equilibrium has been reached. As for a chemical equilibrium, this is a **dynamic** equilibrium, as it involves two opposing processes happening at the same rate.

⒣ Vapour pressure

The vapour above a liquid exerts a pressure on the walls of the container. If the vapour is in equilibrium with the liquid, this pressure is called the vapour pressure (or 'equilibrium vapour pressure' or 'saturated vapour pressure') (Figure **7.15**).

> **Vapour pressure**: the pressure exerted by the vapour in equilibrium with a liquid (or a solid).

Vapour pressure only depends on the nature of the liquid, as this determines the size of the intermolecular forces that hold the molecules in the liquid state, and on the temperature, as the higher the temperature the more energy the molecules have to enable them to break free from the intermolecular forces. These points will be considered in more detail below.

The vapour pressure of the liquid is identical in each of the containers in Figure **7.16**. We can think about why these are all the same in the following way. If we look at the first two containers, the surface area of the liquid is larger in the second container. With a greater liquid surface area it would be expected that the rate of evaporation from the surface would be higher; however, the surface area available for the molecules of the vapour to collide with and condense into is also greater, and therefore the rate of condensation is also higher. These two effects balance out, and the vapour pressure is the same in both containers.

Vapour pressure is independent of the:
- volume of the container
- volume of the liquid
- volume of the vapour
- shape of the container
- surface area of the liquid.

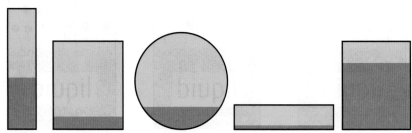

Figure 7.16 A liquid in equilibrium with its vapour in different-sized containers, all at the same temperature.

Variation of vapour pressure with temperature

HL

The effect of temperature on vapour pressure is a large one (Figure **7.17**) – the relationship between the two is exponential. Between 0 °C and 20 °C the vapour pressure of water approximately doubles as the temperature is increased by 10 °C.

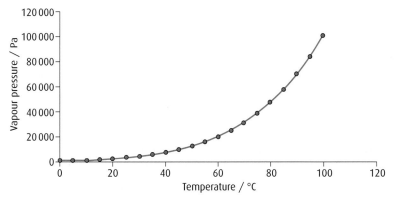

Figure 7.17 Variation of vapour pressure of water with temperature.

As the temperature increases, the molecules move faster and more of them have sufficient energy to break free from the intermolecular forces and escape from the liquid.

As the temperature increases, fewer particles have lower energies and more particles have higher energies (Figure **7.18**). More particles thus have sufficient energy to break free from the intermolecular forces holding them in the liquid and will escape into the vapour phase.

The proportion of molecules that have sufficient energy to escape from the liquid at the lower temperature is shown in yellow in Figure **7.18**, and the checked area represents the number of molecules that have sufficient energy to escape from the liquid at the higher temperature.

The boiling point of a liquid

Boiling occurs when bubbles of vapour form in a liquid and escape. Bubbles of vapour cannot be formed until the vapour pressure equals the external pressure.

> **A liquid boils when its vapour pressure equals the external pressure**. Thus the normal boiling point of a liquid is the temperature at which the vapour pressure of the liquid is 1 atmosphere.

The boiling point of butan-1-ol (117 °C) at normal atmospheric pressure can be read off the graph in Figure **7.19** (overleaf) by drawing a line across at 1 atm pressure (101 325 Pa) and seeing where it intersects the vapour pressure curve.

It can also be seen from the graph that the boiling point is dependent on the external atmospheric pressure. This is the reason why liquids boil at lower temperatures at high altitude – the external atmospheric pressure is lower at higher altitude.

Vapour pressure increases as temperature increases.

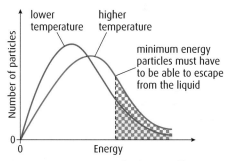

Figure 7.18 More particles have sufficient energy to escape from the liquid at a higher temperature.

Water will boil at about 70 °C on top of Mount Everest.

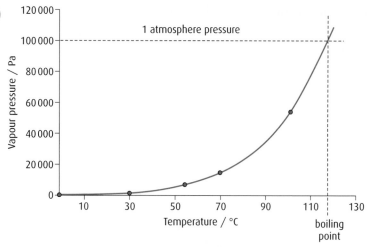

Figure 7.19 Variation of vapour pressure with temperature for butan-1-ol. A liquid boils when its vapour pressure equals atmospheric pressure.

Variation of vapour pressure with the strength of intermolecular forces

At all temperatures butan-1-ol has lower vapour pressure than ethoxyethane (Figure **7.20**). The reason for this is that butan-1-ol has stronger intermolecular forces than ethoxyethane, so it must be heated to a higher temperature to give the same number of molecules sufficient energy to break free from these intermolecular forces.

Butan-1-ol ($CH_3CH_2CH_2CH_2OH$) and ethoxyethane ($CH_3CH_2OCH_2CH_3$) have the same relative molecular mass, so van der Waals' forces would be expected to be approximately the same. However, butan-1-ol has hydrogen bonding between molecules, whereas ethoxyethane has only dipole–dipole interactions between molecules. Hydrogen bonding is a stronger intermolecular force than dipole–dipole interactions, so the intermolecular forces are stronger in butan-1-ol and it has less tendency to enter the vapour phase.

A liquid that evaporates readily and hence has a high vapour pressure is described as **volatile**.

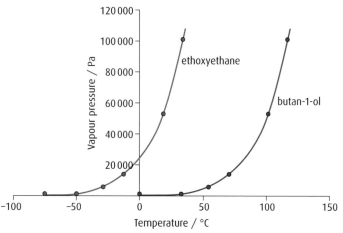

Figure 7.20 Variation of vapour pressure with temperature for ethoxyethane and butan-1-ol. Ethoxyethane has a higher vapour pressure than butan-1-ol at all temperatures.

In general, liquids with weaker intermolecular forces evaporate more easily than liquids with stronger intermolecular forces. If the intermolecular forces are weaker, the particles are better able to break free from these forces and enter the vapour phase at a certain temperature. Therefore liquids with weaker intermolecular forces have higher vapour pressure at the same temperature.

This means that for liquids with weaker intermolecular forces, less heating is required to cause the vapour pressure to equal 1 atmosphere, and therefore they tend to boil at lower temperatures.

Enthalpy of vaporisation

The standard enthalpy change of vaporisation ($\Delta H_{vap}^{\ominus}$) is the energy needed to convert 1 mole of a liquid to vapour under standard conditions.

The value of the enthalpy change of vaporisation depends on the strength of the intermolecular forces. Liquids with stronger intermolecular forces have higher enthalpy changes of vaporisation, as more energy has to be supplied to break the intermolecular forces and allow the molecules to enter the vapour phase. Thus water (stronger intermolecular forces) has a ΔH_{vap} of 41 kJ mol^{-1}, whereas ethoxyethane (weaker intermolecular forces) has a ΔH_{vap} of 28 kJ mol^{-1}.

Liquids with high values of ΔH_{vap} will have little tendency to evaporate and thus have lower vapour pressures at a certain temperature than substances with lower values of ΔH_{vap}. For example, under the same conditions water has a much lower vapour pressure than ethoxyethane.

Liquids with lower ΔH_{vap} tend to have higher vapour pressure at a certain temperature (Table **7.5**). Less heating is therefore required to cause the vapour pressure to equal 1 atmosphere and liquids with lower ΔH_{vap} tend to boil at lower temperatures.

In summary:

Intermolecular forces	Vapour pressure	Boiling point	Enthalpy of vaporisation
weak	high	low	low
strong	low	high	high

Values are often quoted for ΔH_{vap} measured at temperatures other than 298 K.

Alkane	ΔH_{vap} / kJ mol^{-1}	Boiling point / °C
pentane	25.9	36
hexane	28.6	69
heptane	32.6	99
octane	33.3	126

Table 7.5 The enthalpy change of vaporisation of some alkanes, measured under the same conditions.

Using ΔH_{vap} to compare boiling points is most useful when similar substances are being compared.

Self-test 6

Test yourself

14 Arrange the following in order of increasing vapour pressure:
  propanoic acid at 20 °C   **pentane at 20 °C**
  pentane at 30 °C   **butanal at 20 °C**

15 Describe how and why the vapour pressure of propan-1-ol changes between its melting point and its boiling point.

Exam-style questions

1 Which of the following is a property of a system at equilibrium?

    A The concentrations of reactants and products are equal.
    B The rate of the forward reaction is zero.
    C The rate of the forward reaction is equal to the rate of the reverse reaction.
    D The rate of the reverse reaction is a maximum.

2 Consider the reaction:

$$CO_2(g) + 4H_2(g) \rightleftharpoons CH_4(g) + 2H_2O(g)$$

What is the expression for the equilibrium constant?

    A $K_c = \dfrac{[CO_2][H_2]}{[CH_4][H_2O]}$ **C** $K_c = \dfrac{[CH_4][2H_2O]}{[CO_2][4H_2]}$

    B $K_c = \dfrac{[CH_4][H_2O]^2}{[CO_2][H_2]^4}$ **D** $K_c = \dfrac{[CH_4] + [H_2O]^2}{[CO_2] + [H_2]^4}$

3 In which system will decreasing the pressure increase the equilibrium concentration of the species in bold?

    A $CH_4(g) + 2H_2O(g) \rightleftharpoons CO_2(g) + 4\mathbf{H_2(g)}$
    B $N_2O_5(g) + \mathbf{NO(g)} \rightleftharpoons 3NO_2(g)$
    C $H_2(g) + I_2(g) \rightleftharpoons 2\mathbf{HI(g)}$
    D $NO(g) + NO_2(g) \rightleftharpoons \mathbf{N_2O_3(g)}$

4 What is the effect of increasing the temperature on the position of equilibrium and the value of the equilibrium constant for the reaction:

$$CO(g) + 3H_2(g) \rightleftharpoons CH_4(g) + H_2O(g) \qquad\qquad \Delta H = -206\,kJ\,mol^{-1}$$

	Position of equilibrium	Value of equilibrium constant
A	shifts to left	decreases
B	shifts to right	decreases
C	shifts to right	increases
D	shifts to left	increases

5 Consider the system:

$$A(g) \rightleftharpoons B(g)$$

What is the effect of introducing a catalyst?

    A The rate of the forward reaction increases but the rate of the reverse reaction remains the same.
    B The position of equilibrium is shifted to the right.
    C The time taken to reach equilibrium is decreased.
    D The value of the equilibrium constant is reduced.

6   Which of the following changes will increase the equilibrium yield of ammonia according to the following equation?

$$N_2(g) + 3H_2(g) \rightleftharpoons 2NH_3(g) \qquad\qquad \Delta H = -92\,kJ\,mol^{-1}$$

    A   decreasing the temperature from 200 °C to 100 °C
    B   introducing a catalyst
    C   decreasing the pressure from 200 atm to 100 atm
    D   increasing the temperature from 100 °C to 200 °C

7   The equilibrium concentrations at a certain temperature for the reaction

$$2SO_2(g) + O_2(g) \rightleftharpoons 2SO_3(g)$$

are $0.20\,mol\,dm^{-3}$ for $[SO_2]$, $0.40\,mol\,dm^{-3}$ for $[O_2]$, $0.80\,mol\,dm^{-3}$ for $[SO_3]$.

The value of the equilibrium constant at this temperature is:

    A 0.025   **B** 2   **C** 10   **D** 40

8   Consider the equilibrium:

$$A(g) + X(g) \rightleftharpoons 2Z(g)$$

$0.20\,mol\,Z$ are placed in a sealed $10\,dm^3$ container and allowed to come to equilibrium at $500\,K$. At equilibrium, $0.040\,mol$ of X were present in the reaction vessel. The value of the equilibrium constant at this temperature is:

    A 5   **B** 9   **C** 16   **D** 25

9   $20\,cm^3$ of water is put into a sealed $1.00\,dm^3$ container at $300\,K$ and allowed to come to equilibrium. Which of the following will change the equilibrium vapour pressure?

    A   increasing the volume of the container to $1.50\,dm^3$
    B   increasing the temperature to $320\,K$
    C   increasing the volume of water to $50\,cm^3$
    D   changing the shape of the container but keeping the volume constant

10 The relationship between the boiling point, vapour pressure and strength of intermolecular forces is:

	Boiling point	Vapour pressure	Intermolecular forces
A	high	low	strong
B	high	high	strong
C	low	high	strong
D	low	low	weak

11 **a** Explain what is meant by **dynamic equilibrium**. [2]

b Consider the following system at equilibrium:

$$H_2(g) + CO_2(g) \rightleftharpoons H_2O(g) + CO(g) \qquad \Delta H = +41\,kJ\,mol^{-1}$$

State and explain the effect of the following changes on the position of equilibrium and the value of the equilibrium constant.

    i Increasing the temperature at constant pressure. [3]
    ii Increasing the pressure at constant temperature. [2]
    iii Introducing a catalyst at constant temperature and pressure. [2]

12 Consider the reaction:

$$N_2(g) + O_2(g) \rightleftharpoons 2NO(g)$$

a Write an expression for the equilibrium constant for this reaction. [1]

b The value of the equilibrium constant for this reaction at 700 K is 5×10^{-13}, but the value at 1100 K is 4×10^{-8}. Use these values to state and explain whether this reaction is exothermic or endothermic in the forward direction as written. [3]

13 Consider the reversible reaction between colourless N_2O_4 and brown NO_2:

$$N_2O_4(g) \rightleftharpoons 2NO_2(g) \qquad \Delta H^\ominus = +58\,kJ\,mol^{-1}$$

a Write an expression for the equilibrium constant for this reaction. [1]

b State and explain how the colour of the mixture will change as the temperature is increased. [3]

c State and explain the effect of increasing the pressure on the colour of the equilibrium mixture and the value of the equilibrium constant. [4]

d 0.200 mol N_2O_4 is placed in a container of volume 4.00 dm³ at a certain temperature and allowed to come to equilibrium. At equilibrium there were 0.140 mol N_2O_4 present. Calculate the equilibrium concentrations of N_2O_4 and NO_2 and hence the value of the equilibrium constant at this temperature. [4]

14 The following reaction is an important stage in the Contact process for the production of sulfuric acid:

$$2SO_2(g) + O_2(g) \rightleftharpoons 2SO_3(g)$$

a Which catalyst is used for this reaction in the industrial process? [1]

b 0.120 mol SO_2 and 0.120 mol O_2 are introduced into a reaction vessel of volume 2.00 dm³ and allowed to come to equilibrium at 1100 K. At equilibrium there were 0.060 mol SO_3 present.
    i Write an expression for the equilibrium constant for this reaction. [1]
    ii Calculate the concentration of O_2 at equilibrium. [2]
    iii Calculate a value for the equilibrium constant for this reaction at 1100 K. [3]
    iv What are the units of the equilibrium constant in **iii**? [1]

c The standard enthalpy changes of formation of $SO_2(g)$ and $SO_3(g)$ are $-297\,kJ\,mol^{-1}$ and $-395\,kJ\,mol^{-1}$, respectively.
    i Calculate a value for the enthalpy change for the conversion of 2 moles of SO_2 to 2 moles of SO_3. [2]
    ii State and explain whether the value of the equilibrium constant for this reaction at 1500 K will be higher or lower than the value you found in **b iii**. [2]

HL **15** Consider the reaction $H_2(g) + I_2(g) \rightleftharpoons 2HI(g)$

    a Write an expression for the equilibrium constant for this reaction. [1]

    b The value of the equilibrium constant for this reaction at 700 K is 54.0. What is the value of the equilibrium constant for the following reaction?

    $2HI(g) \rightleftharpoons H_2(g) + I_2(g)$ [1]

    c 2.00 mol of HI are introduced into a closed reaction vessel of volume 4.00 dm^3 and allowed to come to equilibrium at 700 K. Calculate the equilibrium concentration of H_2. [3]

16 When a volatile liquid such as hexane is introduced into a closed container and left for some time, equilibrium is established.

    a Explain, with reference to this system, what is meant by **dynamic equilibrium**. [2]

    b Hexane melts at −95 °C and boils at 69 °C at 1 atmosphere pressure. Sketch a graph showing how the vapour pressure of hexane varies between −50 °C and +50 °C [2]

    c State and explain the value of the vapour pressure (in Pa) of hexane at 69 °C. [2]

    d State and explain how the vapour pressure of pentan-1-ol at 50 °C would compare with that of hexane at the same temperature. [3]

Summary

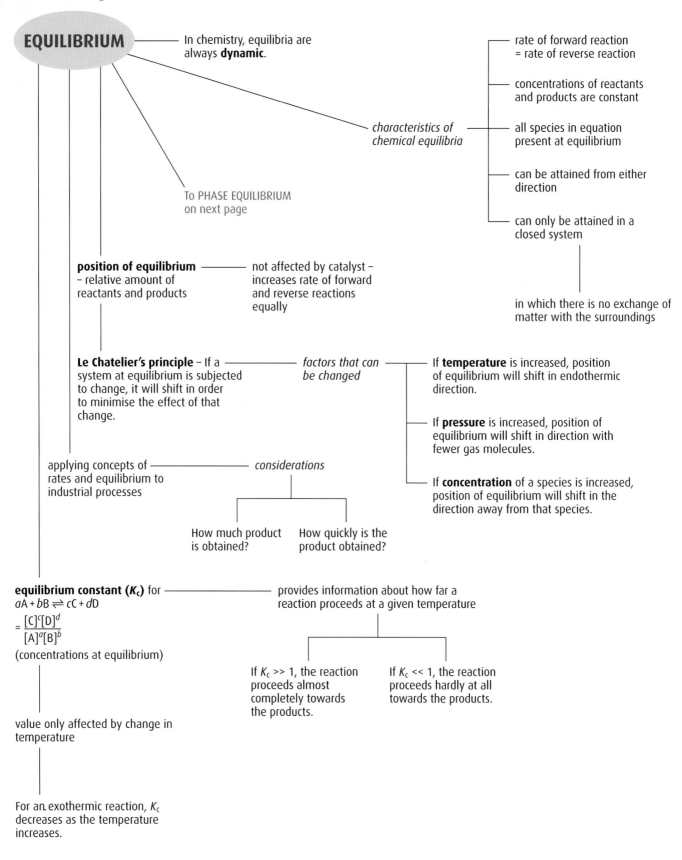

EQUILIBRIUM

In chemistry, equilibria are always **dynamic**.

characteristics of chemical equilibria
- rate of forward reaction = rate of reverse reaction
- concentrations of reactants and products are constant
- all species in equation present at equilibrium
- can be attained from either direction
- can only be attained in a closed system

in which there is no exchange of matter with the surroundings

To PHASE EQUILIBRIUM on next page

position of equilibrium – relative amount of reactants and products

not affected by catalyst – increases rate of forward and reverse reactions equally

Le Chatelier's principle – If a system at equilibrium is subjected to change, it will shift in order to minimise the effect of that change.

factors that can be changed
- If **temperature** is increased, position of equilibrium will shift in endothermic direction.
- If **pressure** is increased, position of equilibrium will shift in direction with fewer gas molecules.
- If **concentration** of a species is increased, position of equilibrium will shift in the direction away from that species.

applying concepts of rates and equilibrium to industrial processes

considerations
- How much product is obtained?
- How quickly is the product obtained?

equilibrium constant (K_c) for $a\text{A} + b\text{B} \rightleftharpoons c\text{C} + d\text{D}$

$$= \frac{[\text{C}]^c[\text{D}]^d}{[\text{A}]^a[\text{B}]^b}$$

(concentrations at equilibrium)

provides information about how far a reaction proceeds at a given temperature

- If $K_c \gg 1$, the reaction proceeds almost completely towards the products.
- If $K_c \ll 1$, the reaction proceeds hardly at all towards the products.

value only affected by change in temperature

For an exothermic reaction, K_c decreases as the temperature increases.

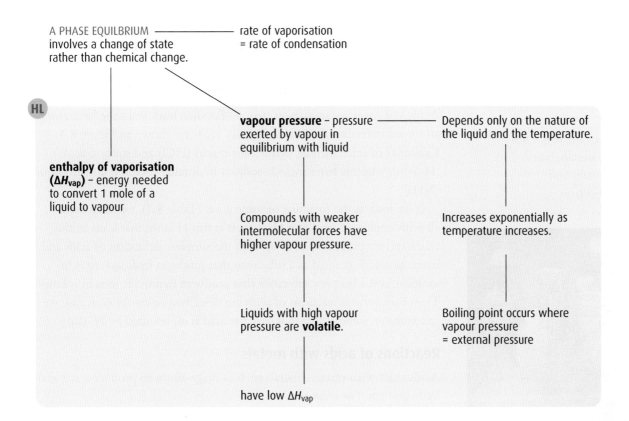

A PHASE EQUILBRIUM involves a change of state rather than chemical change.

rate of vaporisation = rate of condensation

HL

enthalpy of vaporisation (ΔH_{vap}) – energy needed to convert 1 mole of a liquid to vapour

vapour pressure – pressure exerted by vapour in equilibrium with liquid

Depends only on the nature of the liquid and the temperature.

Compounds with weaker intermolecular forces have higher vapour pressure.

Increases exponentially as temperature increases.

Liquids with high vapour pressure are **volatile**.

Boiling point occurs where vapour pressure = external pressure

have low ΔH_{vap}

8 Acids and bases

Learning objectives

- Understand how to distinguish between an acid and a base using an indicator
- Give equations for reactions of acids with metals, bases, alkalis, carbonates and hydrogencarbonates

Figure 8.1 These all contain acids. Cola is a solution of phosphoric acid, among other things.

metal + acid → salt + hydrogen

Acid	Formula
hydrochloric	HCl
sulfuric	H_2SO_4
nitric	HNO_3
carbonic	H_2CO_3
ethanoic	CH_3COOH
benzoic	C_6H_5COOH

Table 8.1 The formulas for some common acids, with the H that is lost as H⁺ shown in red.

8.1 Reactions of acids and bases

The reactions of acids and bases

Acids and bases are substances that are familiar, both from the laboratory and from everyday life. A few everyday acids are shown in Figure **8.1**. Examples of acids include hydrochloric acid (HCl) and sulfuric acid (H_2SO_4), whereas bases include sodium hydroxide (NaOH) and ammonia (NH_3).

If we look at the formulas of some acids (Table **8.1**), we can see that all acids contain at least one H atom. It is this H atom that leads to the characteristic properties of an acid. In the simplest definition of acids and bases, an acid is defined as a substance that produces hydrogen ions in solution, and a base is a substance that produces hydroxide ions in solution. The characteristic reactions of acids are described below. In each case we can write an ionic equation where the acid is represented by H^+(aq).

Reactions of acids with metals

Acids react with reactive metals such as magnesium to produce a salt and hydrogen gas. For example:

$$Mg(s) + 2HCl(aq) \rightarrow MgCl_2(aq) + H_2(g)$$

Ionic equation: $Mg(s) + 2H^+(aq) \rightarrow Mg^{2+}(aq) + H_2(g)$

Unreactive metals such as copper do not react with dilute acids.

Reactions of acids with carbonates and hydrogencarbonates

acid + carbonate/hydrogencarbonate → salt + carbon dioxide + water

Acids react with carbonates and hydrogencarbonates to produce a salt, carbon dioxide and water. For example:

$$Na_2CO_3(aq) + H_2SO_4(aq) \rightarrow Na_2SO_4(aq) + H_2O(l) + CO_2(g)$$

(ionic equation: $CO_3{}^{2-}(aq) + 2H^+(aq) \rightarrow H_2O(l) + CO_2(g)$)

and $NaHCO_3(aq) + HCl(aq) \rightarrow NaCl(aq) + H_2O(l) + CO_2(g)$
    sodium hydrogencarbonate

Reactions of acids with bases and alkalis

Bases are metal oxides, such as copper(II) oxide. These react with acids to form a salt and water. This is called a neutralisation reaction.

For example:

$$CuO(s) + H_2SO_4(aq) \rightarrow CuSO_4(aq) + H_2O(l)$$

Alkalis are bases that dissolve in water, and the reaction between an acid and alkali is the same as that between an acid and a base. For example:

$$NaOH(aq) + HNO_3(aq) \rightarrow NaNO_3(aq) + H_2O(l)$$

Ionic equation: $OH^-(aq) + H^+(aq) \rightarrow H_2O(l)$

The reactions of acids with ammonia solution, an alkali, are often written slightly differently, e.g.

$$NH_3(aq) + HCl(aq) \rightarrow NH_4Cl(aq)$$

Ammonia solution is equivalent to ammonium hydroxide (NH_4OH); in some laboratories bottles are labelled 'ammonia solution' and in others they are labelled 'ammonium hydroxide'. Ammonia is in equilibrium with the ammonium ion and the hydroxide ion:

$$NH_3(aq) + H_2O(l) \rightleftharpoons NH_4^+(aq) + OH^-(aq)$$

The reaction with hydrochloric acid could also have been written:

$$NH_4OH(aq) + HCl(aq) \rightarrow NH_4Cl(aq) + H_2O(l)$$

which corresponds to the general equation of alkali + acid → salt + water.

8.2 Definitions of acids and bases

The Brønsted–Lowry definition of acids and bases

We have considered one definition of acids and bases above, but a slightly more general definition is that due to Brønsted and Lowry.

> The Brønsted–Lowry definition of acids and bases is:
> **Acid** = proton (H^+) **donor**
> **Base**/alkali = proton (H^+) **acceptor**

Consider the reaction of ethanoic acid with water (Figure **8.2**, overleaf). In the forward direction, the CH_3COOH donates a proton (H^+) to the H_2O – the CH_3COOH is thus an acid, as it donates a proton. The H_2O accepts a proton and therefore acts as a base. In the reverse direction, H_3O^+ donates a proton to CH_3COO^-; H_3O^+ is thus an acid and CH_3COO^- is a base.

When CH_3COOH acts as an acid and donates a proton, it forms a base: CH_3COO^-. CH_3COO^- is called the **conjugate base** of CH_3COOH. CH_3COOH and CH_3COO^- are called a **conjugate acid–base pair**. Similarly, when H_2O acts as a base and accepts a proton, it forms H_3O^+, which acts as an acid in the reverse direction. H_3O^+ is the **conjugate acid** of H_2O, and H_3O^+ and H_2O are a conjugate acid–base pair.

base + acid → salt + water

alkali + acid → salt + water

An alkali is obtained when a base dissolves in water.

Learning objectives

- Understand the Brønsted–Lowry and Lewis definitions of acids and bases
- Recognise Brønsted–Lowry and Lewis acids and bases

Conjugate acid and base pairs always differ by one proton (H^+).

It was originally thought that all acids contain oxygen, and the names of this element in English, German (Sauerstoff) and several other languages reflect this mistaken assumption.

$$\text{a} \quad CH_3COOH(aq) + H_2O(l) \longrightarrow CH_3COO^-(aq) + H_3O^+(aq)$$

H⁺ donated

$$\text{b} \quad CH_3COOH(aq) + H_2O(l) \longleftarrow CH_3COO^-(aq) + H_3O^+(aq)$$

H⁺ donated

Figure 8.2 The reaction of ethanoic acid with water. (**a**) In the forward direction ethanoic acid acts as an acid, as it donates a proton to water; (**b**) in the reverse direction, H_3O^+ acts as an acid, as it donates a proton to CH_3COO^-.

We can label the conjugate acid–base pairs in the equation:

$$CH_3COOH(aq) + H_2O(l) \rightleftharpoons CH_3COO^-(aq) + H_3O^+(aq)$$

acid 1   base 2   base 1   acid 2

Species with the same number form a conjugate pair.

Some more examples of acid–base reactions

Let us look at another example:

$$NH_3(aq) + H_2O(l) \rightleftharpoons NH_4^+(aq) + OH^-(aq)$$

base 1   acid 2   acid 1   base 2

> **In the forward direction:** H_2O donates a proton to NH_3. H_2O therefore acts as an acid, and as NH_3 accepts the proton, it acts as a base.

When H_2O donates the proton, it forms OH^-. OH^- is the conjugate base of H_2O, and H_2O and OH^- are a conjugate acid–base pair. We could also say that H_2O is the conjugate acid of OH^-.

> **In the reverse direction:** NH_4^+ donates a proton to OH^-. NH_4^+ therefore acts as an acid, and as OH^- accepts the proton, it acts as a base.

When NH_3 accepts a proton it forms NH_4^+. NH_4^+ is the conjugate acid of NH_3, and NH_3 and NH_4^+ are a conjugate acid–base pair. We could also say that NH_3 is the conjugate base of NH_4^+.

The Lewis theory of acids and bases

The Brønsted–Lowry definition of acids and bases is only one of several definitions of acids and bases, and we will now consider the Lewis definition.

The hydrated proton may be written as $H^+(aq)$ or $H_3O^+(aq)$. H_3O^+ (called the hydronium ion, hydroxonium ion or oxonium ion) has the structure shown in Figure **8.3**.

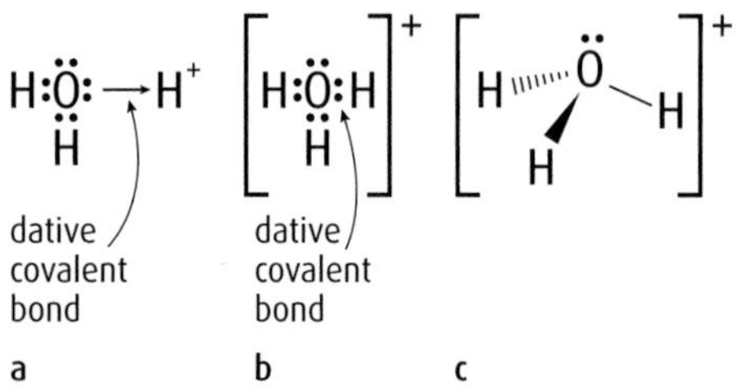

Figure 8.3 Three different representations of the structure of H_3O^+. (**a,b**) The electronic structure; (**c**) the trigonal pyramidal shape.

Water is sometimes described as **amphiprotic**, as it can accept or donate a proton.

> **Brønsted–Lowry**
> An **acid** is a proton (H^+) **donor**
> A **base**/alkali is a proton (H^+) **acceptor**

> **Lewis**
> An **ACid** is an electron **pair ACceptor**
> A **base** is an electron **pair donor**

The Lewis definition is more general than the Brønsted–Lowry definition and can be applied to reactions that do not involve the transfer of a proton. It is also useful when considering acid–base reactions in solvents other than water.

The Lewis definition of acids and bases encompasses all the Brønsted–Lowry reactions, as acceptance of a proton by a base must involve donation of an electron pair to the proton. Thus, if we consider the protonation of ammonia:

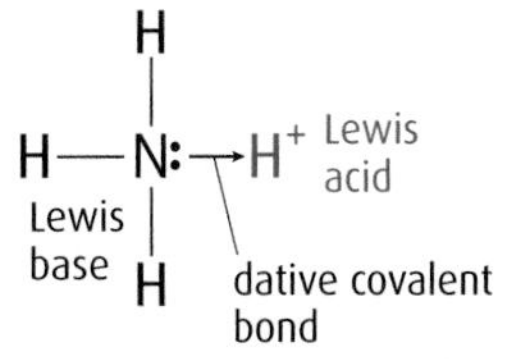

$$NH_3 + H^+ \rightleftharpoons NH_4^+$$

NH_3 is the Lewis base, as it donates an electron pair to H^+, which is the electron pair acceptor, i.e. Lewis acid.

The reaction between BF_3 and NH_3 (Figure **8.4**) is a Lewis acid–base reaction that does not involve the transfer of a proton:

$$NH_3 + BF_3 \rightleftharpoons H_3N{:}BF_3$$

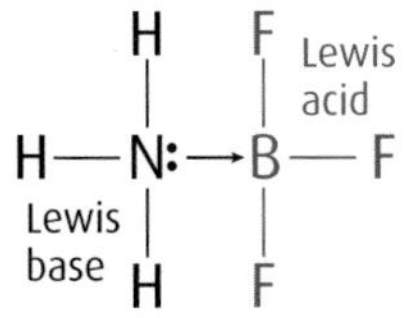

> A dative covalent bond is always formed in a Lewis acid–base reaction.

Formation of a complex ion by a transition metal ion (Figure **8.5**) is another example of a Lewis acid–base reaction. The transition metal ion is the Lewis acid, and the ligand is the Lewis base. The ligands bond to the transition metal ion through the formation of dative covalent bonds. For example:

$$Fe^{2+} + 6H_2O \rightleftharpoons [Fe(H_2O)_6]^{2+}$$

The last two reactions would not be described as acid–base according to the Brønsted–Lowry theory.

> For a substance to act as a Lewis base, it must have a lone pair of electrons. For a substance to act as a Lewis acid, it must have space to accept a pair of electrons in its outer shell.

For example, NH_3 and H_2O can both act as Lewis bases, as they have a lone pair of electrons, and H^+ and BX_3 (where X is a halogen) can act as Lewis acids because they have space in their outer shells to accept a pair of electrons.

In all further discussion of the behaviour and properties of acids, we will be using the Brønsted–Lowry definition.

Figure 8.4 An **adduct** is formed when NH_3 and BF_3 react together.

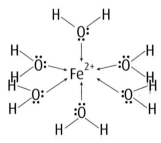

Figure 8.5 A transition metal complex ion.

Only Higher Level students should encounter transition metal complex ions.

The relationship between depth and simplicity

There are various theories of acids and bases. We have encountered the Brønsted–Lowry and Lewis theories. The Lewis theory is a more sophisticated theory and extends the Brønsted–Lowry theory, which is limited to describing acid–base behaviour of species in aqueous solution. The Lewis theory can be used to describe the acid–base reactions of substances, including those not containing H atoms, in a variety of different solvents. The Lewis theory can be applied to reactions in organic chemistry – a nucleophile is a Lewis base, and the reaction between an electrophile and a nucleophile is a Lewis acid–base reaction. The reaction of a transition metal with a ligand such as CO is a Lewis acid–base reaction. To what extent is it useful to describe these reactions as acid–base reactions? Before we knew about the Lewis theory, we probably had a fairly good picture in our minds as to what an acid–base reaction is. Have we got a more sophisticated theory at the expense of losing an understanding of what an acid–base reaction is?

Self-tests 1 & 2

Test yourself

1 Define an acid according to the Brønsted–Lowry and Lewis definitions.

2 Write an equation for the reaction between ammonia and ethanoic acid, classifying each species as either an acid or base.

3 Give the formula of the conjugate acid of each of the following:

   a NH_3 **d** CN^-
   b OH^- **e** HPO_4^{2-}
   c HSO_4^-

4 Give the formula of the conjugate base of each of the following:

   a HCO_3^- **c** $HCOOH$
   b H_2O **d** NH_3

5 In each of the following reactions state whether the species in **bold** is acting as an acid or a base according to the Brønsted–Lowry definition:

   a $\mathbf{HSO_4^-}(aq) + H_2O(l) \rightleftharpoons SO_4^{2-}(aq) + H_3O^+(aq)$
   b $\mathbf{HCO_3^-}(aq) + HSO_4^-(aq)$
       $\rightleftharpoons H_2CO_3(aq) + SO_4^{2-}(aq)$
   c $\mathbf{CH_3COOH}(aq) + H_2SO_4(aq)$
       $\rightleftharpoons CH_3COOH_2^+(aq) + HSO_4^-(aq)$

6 Classify each of the following as a substance that can act as a Lewis acid or as a Lewis base:

   H_2O BF_3 HCO_3^- H^+ $AlCl_3$ NH_3 CO

7 Complete and balance the following equations:

   a $Zn + H_2SO_4 \rightarrow$ **e** $Mg(OH)_2 + H_2SO_4 \rightarrow$
   b $CuO + HNO_3 \rightarrow$ **f** $Cu + H_2SO_4 \rightarrow$
   c $NH_3 + H_2SO_4 \rightarrow$ **g** $CaO + HCl \rightarrow$
   d $Ca(HCO_3)_2 + HCl \rightarrow$

Learning objectives

- Understand the difference between **strong** and **weak** acids and bases
- Recognise and give examples of strong and weak acids and bases
- Describe and explain experiments to distinguish between strong and weak acids (or bases)

8.3 Strong and weak acids and bases

Strong and weak acids and bases

When an acid reacts with water it **dissociates**, or **ionises**. This dissociation can be shown as:

$$HA(aq) + H_2O(l) \rightleftharpoons H_3O^+(aq) + A^-(aq)$$

This can be understood from the Brønsted–Lowry theory: the acid donates a proton to water. Basically, though, what has happened is that the acid has dissociated into H^+ and A^- ions. This reaction is, therefore, often simplified as:

$$HA(aq) \rightleftharpoons H^+(aq) + A^-(aq)$$

This reaction is exactly the same as the one above, and the H^+ from the acid is still actually donated to H_2O, but the H_2O has been omitted for simplicity ($H^+(aq)$ is equivalent to $H_3O^+(aq)$).

We can classify acids as strong or weak according to how much they dissociate.

Strong acids

Strong acids such as hydrochloric (HCl), sulfuric (H_2SO_4) and nitric (HNO_3) acid dissociate completely in aqueous solution (see Figure **8.6**).

Extension

Actually, nothing ever dissociates **completely**, as all these reactions involve an equilibrium. However, for strong acids this equilibrium lies a very long way to the right.

This can be represented as:

$$HA(aq) \rightarrow H^+(aq) + A^-(aq)$$

The non-reversible arrow ($\rightarrow$) is used to indicate that dissociation is essentially complete.

HCl is a **monoprotic** acid – it dissociates to form one proton per molecule – but H_2SO_4 is a **diprotic** acid – it can dissociate to form two protons per molecule:

$$H_2SO_4(aq) + H_2O(l) \rightarrow HSO_4^-(aq) + H_3O^+(aq)$$

$$HSO_4^-(aq) + H_2O(l) \rightleftharpoons SO_4^{2-}(aq) + H_3O^+(aq)$$

Sulfuric acid is a strong acid for the first dissociation only.

complete dissociation

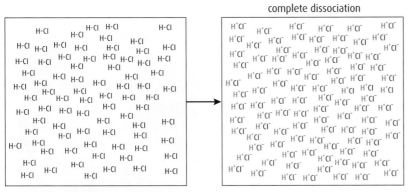

Figure 8.6 HCl dissociates completely in aqueous solution.

Weak acids

Weak acids dissociate only partially in aqueous solution (see Figure **8.7**, overleaf).

The dissociation of a weak acid is represented as:

$$HA(aq) \rightleftharpoons H^+(aq) + A^-(aq)$$

The **equilibrium arrow** here is essential and indicates that the reaction is reversible and does not go to completion.

Examples of weak acids are carbonic acid (H_2CO_3) and carboxylic acids such as ethanoic acid (CH_3COOH).

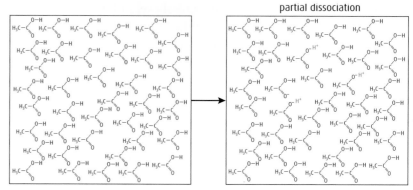

partial dissociation

Figure 8.7 Only a few of the ethanoic acid molecules dissociate.

The dissociation of ethanoic acid is represented as:

$$CH_3COOH(aq) \rightleftharpoons CH_3COO^-(aq) + H^+(aq)$$

$$or\ CH_3COOH(aq) + H_2O(l) \rightleftharpoons CH_3COO^-(aq) + H_3O^+(aq)$$

Carbonic acid is formed when carbon dioxide dissolves in water (see Figure **8.8**):

$$H_2O(l) + CO_2(g) \rightarrow H_2CO_3(aq)$$

It is a diprotic acid, and its dissociation can be shown as:

$$H_2CO_3(aq) \rightleftharpoons HCO_3^-(aq) + H^+(aq)$$

$$HCO_3^-(aq) \rightleftharpoons CO_3^{2-}(aq) + H^+(aq)$$

Figure 8.8 Carbonated water is acidic because of dissolved CO_2.

HCO_3^- is the hydrogencarbonate ion – it acts as a base in the first equation and as an acid in the second one.

Many scientists believe that increasing levels of CO_2 in the atmosphere resulting from human activity, such as the burning of fossil fuels, are making the oceans more acidic as more CO_2 dissolves in them. Some scientists believe that the pH of the oceans could drop by up to 0.5 units by the end of the century, and this could have a disastrous effect on coral reefs, as these are limestone ($CaCO_3$) structures.

Bases

When a base reacts with water, it accepts a proton from the water and ionises according to the equation:

$$B(aq) + H_2O(l) \rightleftharpoons BH^+(aq) + OH^-(aq)$$

Bases are defined as strong or weak, depending on how much they ionise in aqueous solution.

All rain is acidic as a result of dissolved CO_2. However, what we normally refer to as acid rain (a form of acid deposition) results when SO_2 and nitrogen oxides such as NO/NO_2 are converted to acids such as sulfuric acid or nitric acid by various processes in the atmosphere. SO_2 and NO_x can be produced when fossil fuels are burnt or in the internal combustion engine. This can kill trees (**a**) and fish in lakes and react with limestone buildings to cause erosion (**b**).

Strong bases

> Strong bases ionise completely in aqueous solution.

For example, sodium hydroxide ionises completely to produce OH^- ions:

$$NaOH(aq) \rightarrow Na^+(aq) + OH^-(aq)$$

Strong bases include the group 1 hydroxides (LiOH, NaOH, etc.) and $Ba(OH)_2$.

Weak bases

> Weak bases ionise only partially in aqueous solution.

Ammonia is a typical weak base and ionises according to the equation:

$$NH_3(aq) + H_2O(l) \rightleftharpoons NH_4^+(aq) + OH^-(aq)$$

At 25 °C in a $0.10\,mol\,dm^{-3}$ solution of ammonia about 1.3% of the molecules are ionised.

Other weak bases are amines such as ethylamine (ethanamine) ($CH_3CH_2NH_2$). Ethylamine ionises according to the equation:

$$CH_3CH_2NH_2(aq) + H_2O(l) \rightleftharpoons CH_3CH_2NH_3^+(aq) + OH^-(aq)$$

At 25 °C in a $0.10\,mol\,dm^{-3}$ solution of ethylamine about 7.1% of the molecules are ionised. Ethylamine is thus a stronger base than ammonia.

Examiner's tip
$Ba(OH)_2$ dissociates to give $2OH^-$.

$$Ba(OH)_2(aq) \rightarrow Ba^{2+}(aq) + 2OH^-(aq)$$

Thus $1\,mol\,dm^{-3}$ $Ba(OH)_2$ produces $2\,mol\,dm^{-3}$ OH^-.

Extension

The higher basic strength of ethylamine can be understood in terms of the electron-releasing effect (positive inductive effect) of the alkyl group attached to the N (see Option **G** on the CD-ROM).

When comparing strong and weak acids, it is essential that the solutions are of the **same concentration**, as it is possible that the total concentration of H⁺ ions in a concentrated solution of a weak acid could be more than in a dilute solution of a strong acid – this will be discussed further in Section **8.4**.

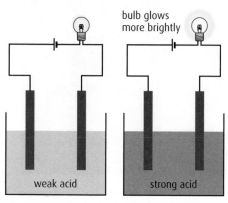

Figure 8.9 The bulb glows more brightly with a solution of a strong acid than it does with a solution of weak acid.

Figure 8.10 Magnesium reacting with a strong acid (hydrochloric acid, left) and a weak acid (ethanoic acid, right). The more violent reaction with the strong acid causes larger hydrogen bubbles, which keeps the magnesium at the surface of the fluid. The much smaller bubbles caused by the weaker reaction spread through the acid, making it appear milky.

Distinguishing experimentally between strong and weak acids and between strong and weak bases

In this section we will look at how we can distinguish between a strong acid and a weak acid in the laboratory. The methods for distinguishing between the acids rely on the fact that strong acids dissociate more than weak acids.

In the following examples we will be comparing solutions of strong and weak acids of equal concentrations.

Solutions of strong acids conduct electricity better than solutions of weak acids

A strong acid dissociates fully so the concentration of ions is high and the solution is a good conductor of electricity. A weak acid dissociates only partially, and so the concentration of ions is lower and the solution does not conduct electricity as well.

The conductivity of the solutions can be measured using a conductivity meter or by looking at the brightness of a bulb in the experimental set-up shown in Figure **8.9**.

Strong acids may be described as **strong electrolytes**, whereas weak acids are **weak electrolytes**. This also applies to strong and weak bases – strong bases conduct electricity better than weak bases.

Strong acids have a lower pH than weak acids

pH is a measure of the concentration of H⁺ ions in solution – the lower the pH, the higher the concentration of H⁺ ions. Strong acids dissociate more, producing a higher concentration of H⁺ ions in solution (that is, a lower pH). This can be tested using universal indicator or a pH meter. Again, this method could be used for distinguishing between strong and weak bases. Strong bases have a higher pH than weak bases of the same concentration.

Strong acids react more violently with metals or carbonates

Strong acids have a higher concentration of free H⁺ ions and therefore react more rapidly with a metal such as magnesium to form hydrogen – this can be shown by more rapid bubbling (effervescence) when the metal is added (see Figure **8.10**). A similar effect is seen when a carbonate is added to an acid.

Strength vs concentration

It is important to be aware of the difference between the concentration and the strength of an acid (or base). The concentration of an acid refers to the number of moles of acid in a certain volume, e.g. in a solution of ethanoic acid of concentration $0.100\,\text{mol}\,\text{dm}^{-3}$, the total number of moles of ethanoic acid before dissociation is $0.100\,\text{mol}$ in every cubic decimetre (litre). The strength of an acid refers to how much it dissociates.

A solution of ethanoic acid of concentration $1.00\,mol\,dm^{-3}$ is a more concentrated solution than $0.100\,mol\,dm^{-3}$ ethanoic acid. No matter how concentrated the solution of ethanoic acid is, it will never become a strong acid, as it always dissociates partially. Similarly, diluting a strong acid such as hydrochloric acid does not make it anything other than a strong acid, as it always dissociates fully.

8.4 pH

pH

Not everything covered in this section is strictly on the Standard Level syllabus, but a more in-depth knowledge of pH can be helpful in answering exam questions.

The pH scale can be used to indicate whether a solution is acidic, alkaline or neutral. At 25 °C, a solution with pH less than 7 is acidic, a solution with pH 7 is neutral and a solution with pH greater than 7 is alkaline (Figure **8.11**).

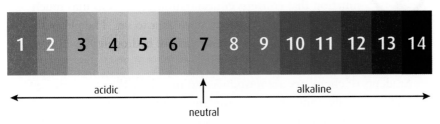

Figure 8.11 The pH scale, showing the colours of universal indicator.

The pH of a solution may be determined by using a pH meter or by using universal indicator solution or paper.

pH is a measure of the concentration of $H^+(aq)$ ions in a solution. The concentration of H^+ ions can be stated in $mol\,dm^{-3}$, but the use of the $\log_{10}$ function simplifies the numbers involved.

> Definition: pH is the negative logarithm to base 10 of the hydrogen ion concentration in aqueous solution.
>
> $$pH = -\log_{10}[H^+(aq)]$$

Note: the 10 is often omitted in '$\log_{10}$', i.e. $pH = -\log[H^+(aq)]$. To work out pH, use the 'log' button on a calculator.

Thus, if the concentration of H^+ ions in a solution is $1.57 \times 10^{-5}\,mol\,dm^{-3}$, the pH is worked out as:

$$pH = -\log_{10}(1.57 \times 10^{-3}) = 2.80$$

Titration using an indicator cannot be used to distinguish between a weak and a strong acid – if they have the same concentration they will have the same end point – this will be discussed further in Section **8.6**.

Learning objectives

- Use pH values to distinguish between acidic, neutral and alkaline solutions
- Use pH values to arrange solutions of equal concentrations in terms or acid or base strength
- Understand that pH can be measured using universal indicator or a pH meter
- Understand that pH provides a measure of the concentration of H^+ ions in aqueous solution
- Understand the consequences of pH being a log scale
- Given whole number pH values, work out the concentration of $H^+(aq)$ in a solution

pH has no units.

The pH for solutions in which the concentration of H^+ ions is a power of 10 can be worked out without using a calculator by understanding how the $\log_{10}$ function works.

$$\log_{10} 100 = 2 \qquad\qquad 10^2 = 100$$

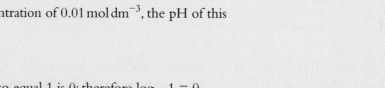

The log of a number is thus the power that 10 must be raised to in order to equal that number.

0.01 can be written as a power of **10**: $\qquad 0.01 = 10^{-2}$

so $\log_{10} 0.01 = -2$

Therefore, if a solution has an $H^+(aq)$ concentration of $0.01\,mol\,dm^{-3}$, the pH of this solution is given by:

$$pH = -\log_{10} 0.01 = 2$$

Note: the power 10 must be raised in order to equal 1 is 0; therefore $\log_{10} 1 = 0$.

Examiner's tip

Higher Level students must be able to work out the log of a simple power of 10, such as 1×10^{-3} without using a calculator.

As pH is a log scale (to base 10), a 1 unit change in pH indicates a tenfold change in the H^+ ion concentration (see Table **8.2**).

pH is an artificial scale developed using a mathematical function that converts concentration of H^+ ions into much simpler numbers. It is definitely easier to say 'The pH of the solution is 6' rather than 'the concentration of hydrogen ions in the solution is $1.0 \times 10^{-6}\,mol\,dm^{-3}$'.

Students of chemistry are introduced to the pH scale at an early age and are usually content to compare 'the acidity of solutions' in terms of pH and work out whether these solutions are acidic, alkaline or neutral. Most students do this without ever really understanding anything about what pH means. The idea of concentration of H^+ ions could not be introduced at such an early age; if it were, far fewer students would be able to work out whether a solution were acidic, alkaline or neutral and would almost certainly not have such a clear picture in their minds about the relative acidities/alkalinities of substances.

So is it better to have a scale that most people can use but do not understand or to have a more accurate and in-depth description of the acidity of solutions that most people will not be able to understand? Do we lose or gain understanding by using the pH scale?

$[H^+(aq)]\,/\,mol\,dm^{-3}$	pH
1	0
0.1	1
0.01	2
1×10^{-3}	3
1×10^{-4}	4
1×10^{-5}	5
1×10^{-6}	6
1×10^{-7}	7
1×10^{-8}	8

Table 8.2 pH values and the corresponding concentration of H^+ ions.

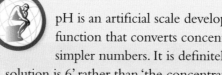

$$[H^+(aq)] = 10^{-pH}$$

To calculate $[H^+(aq)]$ from the pH

In order to calculate $[H^+(aq)]$ from the pH, the inverse function of $\log_{10}$ must be used. Thus 10 must be raised to the power of $-pH$.

This is usually done using the '2nd' (or 'shift') and 'log' key combination on a calculator.

Calculating the pH of a strong acid

As strong acids can be assumed to dissociate fully in aqueous solution, the concentration of H^+ ions is the same as the concentration of the acid.

Example

Let us calculate the pH of a $0.001\,50\,mol\,dm^{-3}$ solution of hydrochloric acid. The acid is strong, so full dissociation produces an $H^+(aq)$ concentration of $0.001\,50\,mol\,dm^{-3}$:

$$pH = -\log_{10}[H^+(aq)] = -\log_{10}[0.001\,50] = 2.82$$

Worked example

a What is the pH of $10\,cm^3$ of $0.10\,mol\,dm^{-3}$ hydrochloric acid?

b If $90\,cm^3$ of water is added to the acid, what happens to the pH?

c If the solution from part **b** is now diluted by a factor of a million (10^6), what is the approximate pH of the final solution?

a HCl is a strong acid and dissociates fully. The concentration of $H^+(aq)$ is thus $0.10\,mol\,dm^{-3}$:

$$pH = -\log_{10}[H^+(aq)] = -\log_{10}[0.10] = 1.0$$

b If $90\,cm^3$ of water is added to $10\,cm^3$ of acid, the total volume of the solution becomes $100\,cm^3$. There are thus the same number of H^+ ions in ten times the volume, i.e. the concentration of H^+ ions has been reduced by a factor of 10. As pH is a log scale, a reduction in the $[H^+(aq)]$ by a factor of 10 results in the pH of the solution increasing by 1. The pH of the diluted solution is thus 2.0.

We can also consider this in terms of numbers. The initial concentration of $H^+(aq)$ is $0.10\,mol\,dm^{-3}$. When this is diluted by a factor of 10, the concentration of $H^+(aq)$ drops to $0.010\,mol\,dm^{-3}$.

$$pH = -\log_{10}[H^+(aq)] = -\log_{10}[0.010] = 2.0$$

c Diluting a solution by a factor of 10 causes the pH to increase by 1 unit, so diluting the solution in part **b** by a factor of 10^6 would cause its pH to increase by 6 to 8.0. However, it is not possible to dilute an acidic solution so that it becomes an alkaline solution; we have ignored the dissociation of water molecules into H^+ and OH^- ions (this will be considered in more detail in the Higher Level section below). The actual pH of this solution will be slightly less than 7. If the solution is diluted further, the pH will get closer and closer to 7 but never reach it.

pH is not a measure of acid strength

pH is not a measure of acid strength; it is simply a measure of the concentration of $H^+(aq)$ ions. It is possible for a dilute solution of a strong acid to have a higher pH than a concentrated solution of a weak acid. $1.00\,mol\,dm^{-3}$ ethanoic acid has a pH of 2.38, but $1.00 \times 10^{-3}\,mol\,dm^{-3}$ hydrochloric acid has a pH of 3.00. Because the solution of ethanoic acid is much more concentrated, the partial dissociation of the weak acid produces a higher concentration of $H^+(aq)$ than the complete dissociation of the strong acid HCl.

pH can be used to compare acid strength only if equal concentrations of acids are being compared.

Test yourself

8 Classify the following as (i) strong acid, (ii) weak acid, (iii) strong base, (iv) weak base or (v) salt:

HCl	H_2SO_4	NH_4NO_3	NaOH
NH_3	HNO_3	Na_2SO_4	H_2CO_3
$Ba(OH)_2$	KNO_3	CH_3NH_2	HCOOH

9 For each pair of solutions, state which will have the higher electrical conductivity:

a $0.10\,mol\,dm^{-3}$ HCOOH and $0.10\,mol\,dm^{-3}$ HCl

b $0.10\,mol\,dm^{-3}$ NH_3 and $0.10\,mol\,dm^{-3}$ KOH

c $0.10\,mol\,dm^{-3}$ HCl and $0.10\,mol\,dm^{-3}$ H_2SO_4

d $0.10\,mol\,dm^{-3}$ HNO_3 and $0.010\,mol\,dm^{-3}$ HCl

10 Arrange the following in order of increasing pH:

$1.0\,mol\,dm^{-3}$ NH_3

$0.010\,mol\,dm^{-3}$ HCl

$1.0\,mol\,dm^{-3}$ NaOH

$0.001\,mol\,dm^{-3}$ CH_3CH_2COOH

$0.10\,mol\,dm^{-3}$ H_2SO_4

$0.010\,mol\,dm^{-3}$ CH_3CH_2COOH

$0.0010\,mol\,dm^{-3}$ NH_3

$0.10\,mol\,dm^{-3}$ HCl

11 State whether each of the following statements is **true** or **false**:

a The pH of $0.10\,mol\,dm^{-3}$ HCl is 2.

b The $[H^+]$ in a solution of pH = 3 is 100 times the $[H^+]$ in a solution of pH = 5.

c The $[H^+]$ in a solution of pH = 13 is $1.0 \times 10^{13}\,mol\,dm^{-3}$.

d The pH of $0.010\,mol\,dm^{-3}$ H_2SO_4 is 2.

12 A solution of $0.2\,mol\,dm^{-3}$ HCl has a pH of 0.7. Of this solution, $25.0\,cm^3$ is taken and made up to a total volume of $250\,cm^3$ with distilled water in a volumetric flask to form solution **X**. $10.0\,cm^3$ of solution **X** is taken and made up to a total volume of $1.00\,dm^3$ with distilled water in a volumetric flask; this is solution **Y**.

a Work out the pH value for each solution.

b Suggest an experimental method, other than measuring the pH or using universal indicator, that could be used to distinguish between solution **X** and solution **Y**.

13 A solution of $0.000\,100\,mol\,dm^{-3}$ hydrochloric acid has a pH of 4.00, whereas a solution of $0.100\,mol\,dm^{-3}$ ethanoic acid has a pH of 2.88. Explain what these values tell you about the usefulness of pH as a measure of acid strength.

Learning objectives

- Write an equation for the dissociation of water and state the expression for K_w
- Use K_w or pK_w values to work out the concentrations of $H^+(aq)$ and $OH^-(aq)$ and pH of water at various temperatures
- Arrange acids/bases in order of strength based on K_a, pK_a, K_b or pK_b values
- Carry out calculations involving K_a, K_b, pK_a, pK_b, pH and pOH
- Use the relationships $K_w = K_a \times K_b$, $pK_a + pK_b = pK_w$, and $pH + pOH = pK_w$ in calculations

HL 8.5 Calculations involving acids and bases

The acid dissociation constant

Consider the dissociation of ethanoic acid:

$$CH_3COOH(aq) + H_2O(l) \rightleftharpoons CH_3COO^-(aq) + H_3O^+(aq)$$

We can write an equilibrium constant for the dissociation of an acid as:

$$K_c = \frac{[CH_3COO^-(aq)][H_3O^+(aq)]}{[CH_3COOH(aq)][H_2O(l)]}$$

However, the reaction occurs in aqueous solution, and so the concentration of water is very much greater than the other concentrations and essentially constant ($55.5\,mol\,dm^{-3}$). This is then incorporated into the equilibrium constant:

$$K_c \times [H_2O(l)] = \frac{[CH_3COO^-(aq)][H_3O^+(aq)]}{[CH_3COOH(aq)]}$$

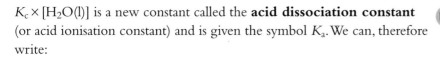

$K_c \times [H_2O(l)]$ is a new constant called the **acid dissociation constant** (or acid ionisation constant) and is given the symbol K_a. We can, therefore write:

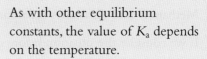

$$K_a = \frac{[CH_3COO^-(aq)][H_3O^+(aq)]}{[CH_3COOH(aq)]}$$

The value of K_a for ethanoic acid at $25\,^{\circ}C$ is $1.74 \times 10^{-5}\,mol\,dm^{-3}$.

The units can be worked out by substituting the units into the expression for K_a.

$$K_a = \frac{[\cancel{mol\,dm^{-3}}][mol\,dm^{-3}]}{[\cancel{mol\,dm^{-3}}]}$$

The units for K_a are $mol\,dm^{-3}$, but they are often omitted.

If we write the dissociation of ethanoic acid as:

$$CH_3COOH(aq) \rightleftharpoons CH_3COO^-(aq) + H^+(aq)$$

we can write an equilibrium constant for the dissociation of the acid as:

$$K_a = \frac{[CH_3COO^-(aq)][H^+(aq)]}{[CH_3COOH(aq)]}$$

This is entirely equivalent to the expression above.

Weak acids dissociate partially, but different weak acids dissociate to different extents. The more an acid dissociates, the stronger it is. The acid dissociation constant is a measure of the extent to which the acid dissociates. The higher the value of K_a, the more the acid dissociates and the stronger it is. The K_a values for some acids are shown in Table **8.3**.

> As with other equilibrium constants, the value of K_a depends on the temperature.

> In general, for the dissociation of acid, HA:
>
> $$HA(aq) \rightleftharpoons H^+(aq) + A^-(aq)$$
>
> The expression for the acid dissociation constant is:
>
> $$K_a = \frac{[A^-(aq)][H^+(aq)]}{[HA(aq)]}$$

> The higher the value of K_a, the stronger the acid.

Acid	Formula	$K_a\,/\,mol\,dm^{-3}$
hydrofluoric acid	HF	5.62×10^{-4}
benzoic acid	C_6H_5COOH	6.31×10^{-5}
propanoic acid	CH_3CH_2COOH	1.35×10^{-5}
chloric(I) acid	HOCl	3.72×10^{-8}
hydrocyanic acid	HCN	3.98×10^{-10}

increasing strength

Table 8.3 The formula and K_a value of some acids.

The acids in Table **8.3** are arranged in order of strength: HF is the strongest acid and dissociates to the greatest extent; HCN is the weakest acid and dissociates to the smallest extent in aqueous solution.

> K_a is a better measure of acid strength than pH, as it does not depend on the concentration of the acid – K_a depends only on temperature.

> K_a is usually not quoted for strong acids, because the values are so large. Strong acids dissociate essentially completely, so the denominator in the K_a expression would be very close to zero.

Worked examples

Calculate the K_a value for methanoic acid at 25 °C if a 0.100 mol dm^{-3} solution dissociates to give a hydrogen ion concentration of 4.13×10^{-3} mol dm^{-3}.

Methanoic acid dissociates according to the equation: $HCOOH(aq) \rightleftharpoons HCOO^-(aq) + H^+(aq)$

If we consider the situation before dissociation occurs we have:

$$HCOOH(aq) \rightleftharpoons HCOO^-(aq) + H^+(aq)$$

initial concentration / mol dm^{-3}:   0.100   0   0

At equilibrium the concentration of H^+ ions is 4.13×10^{-3} mol dm^{-3}. To produce 4.13×10^{-3} mol dm^{-3} H^+, 4.13×10^{-3} mol dm^{-3} HCOOH must dissociate. The concentration of HCOOH at equilibrium is thus $0.100 - 4.13 \times 10^{-3}$, i.e. 9.59×10^{-2} mol dm^{-3}.

As one molecule of HCOOH dissociates to produce one H^+ ion and one $HCOO^-$ ion, the concentration of $HCOO^-$ at equilibrium is the same as that of H^+.

The equilibrium concentrations are thus:

$$HCOOH(aq) \rightleftharpoons HCOO^-(aq) + H^+(aq)$$

equilibrium concentration / mol dm^{-3}: 9.59×10^{-2} 4.13×10^{-3} 4.13×10^{-3}

These values can be put into the expression for K_a:

$$K_a = \frac{[HCOO^-(aq)][H^+(aq)]}{[HCOOH(aq)]} = \frac{(4.13 \times 10^{-3}) \times (4.13 \times 10^{-3})}{(9.59 \times 10^{-2})} = 1.78 \times 10^{-4} \text{ mol dm}^{-3}$$

If the degree of dissociation is very small compared with the concentration of the acid, the above calculation may be simplified, as shown in the next example.

Calculate the K_a value for HCN(aq) at 25 °C if a 0.500 mol dm^{-3} solution dissociates to give a hydrogen ion concentration of 1.41×10^{-5} mol dm^{-3}.

The dissociation of HCN is represented by the equation: $HCN(aq) \rightleftharpoons H^+(aq) + CN^-(aq)$

The concentration of CN^- at equilibrium will be the same as that of H^+. We will make the assumption that, as the dissociation of the acid is so small, the concentration of HCN at equilibrium is essentially the same as the initial concentration. We can now substitute these values into the expression for K_a:

$$K_a = \frac{[CN^-(aq)][H^+(aq)]}{[HCN(aq)]} = \frac{(1.41 \times 10^{-5}) \times (1.41 \times 10^{-5})}{(0.500)} = 3.98 \times 10^{-10} \text{ mol dm}^{-3}$$

This is the same as the literature value for K_a, and so it can be seen that the approximation works well in this case as the degree of dissociation is so small. If we had made the same approximation in the calculation above on methanoic acid, the value obtained for K_a would have been 1.71×10^{-4} mol dm^{-3}, which is reasonably close to the accepted value. This approximation will be discussed further below.

The base ionisation constant (K_b)

Consider the ionisation of a weak base:

$$B(aq) + H_2O(l) \rightleftharpoons BH^+(aq) + OH^-(aq)$$

We can write an equilibrium constant for the ionisation of the base as:

$$K_c = \frac{[BH^+(aq)][OH^-(aq)]}{[B(aq)][H_2O(l)]}$$

As above, the reaction occurs in aqueous solution, so the concentration of water is very much greater than the other concentrations and essentially constant. This is then incorporated into the equilibrium constant:

$$K_c \times [H_2O(l)] = \frac{[BH^+(aq)][OH^-(aq)]}{[B(aq)]}$$

$K_c \times [H_2O(l)]$ is a new constant called the **base ionisation constant** (base dissociation constant) and is given the symbol K_b. We can, therefore, write:

$$K_b = \frac{[BH^+(aq)][OH^-(aq)]}{[B(aq)]}$$

The value of K_b for ammonia is $1.78 \times 10^{-5}\,mol\,dm^{-3}$.

Similarly to K_a for acids, the base ionisation constant provides a measure of the extent to which the base ionises, and hence the strength of the base. The higher the value of K_b, the more the base ionises and the stronger it is. The K_b values for some bases are shown in Table **8.4**.

Base	Formula	K_b / mol dm^{-3}
dimethylamine	$(CH_3)_2NH$	5.25×10^{-4}
methylamine	CH_3NH_2	4.37×10^{-4}
sodium carbonate	Na_2CO_3	2.09×10^{-4}
ammonia	NH_3	1.78×10^{-5}
phenylamine	$C_6H_5NH_2$	4.17×10^{-10}

Table 8.4 The formula and K_b value for some bases.

increasing strength

The bases in Table **8.4** are arranged in order of strength: dimethylamine is the strongest base and ionises to the greatest extent; phenylamine is the weakest base and ionises to the smallest extent in aqueous solution.

> The units for K_b are mol dm^{-3}, but they are often omitted.

> The higher the value of K_b, the stronger the base.

Worked example

Calculate the K_b value for ethylamine at 25 °C if a 0.100 mol dm^{-3} solution ionises to give a hydroxide ion concentration of 7.06×10^{-3} mol dm^{-3}.

The equation for the ionisation of ethylamine is:

$$CH_3CH_2NH_2(aq) + H_2O(l) \rightleftharpoons CH_3CH_2NH_3^+(aq) + OH^-(aq)$$

When one molecule of $CH_3CH_2NH_2$ reacts with water, it ionises to form one $CH_3CH_2NH_3^+$ ion and one OH^- ion. This means that, if 7.06×10^{-3} mol dm^{-3} of OH^- are present at equilibrium, they must have come from the ionisation of 7.06×10^{-3} mol dm^{-3} $CH_3CH_2NH_2$. The concentration of $CH_3CH_2NH_2$ at equilibrium is therefore $0.100 - 7.06 \times 10^{-3} = 9.29 \times 10^{-2}$ mol dm^{-3}. The concentration of OH^- formed is the same as that of $CH_3CH_2NH_3^+$.

Thus, at equilibrium, the concentrations are:

$$CH_3CH_2NH_2(aq) + H_2O(l) \rightleftharpoons CH_3CH_2NH_3^+(aq) + OH^-(aq)$$

equilibrium concentration / mol dm^{-3}: 9.29×10^{-2} $\qquad$ 7.06×10^{-3} $\qquad$ 7.06×10^{-3}

The expression for K_b is:

$$K_b = \frac{[CH_3CH_2NH_3^+(aq)][OH^-(aq)]}{[CH_3CH_2NH_2(aq)]}$$

The equilibrium concentrations can be substituted into this equation:

$$K_b = \frac{[7.06 \times 10^{-3}][7.06 \times 10^{-3}]}{[9.29 \times 10^{-2}]} = 5.37 \times 10^{-4} \text{ mol dm}^{-3}$$

As for the K_a calculation above, this calculation can be simplified by making the approximation that the amount of ionisation of the base is small compared with its concentration, so the original concentration of the base is used in the K_b expression.

Calculating the pH of a weak acid

A weak acid dissociates only partially, and therefore in order to calculate the pH we need to know how much the acid dissociates. This can be worked out using the K_a value of the acid.

Worked example

Calculate the pH of a 0.200 mol dm^{-3} solution of propanoic acid at 25 °C. The K_a of propanoic acid at 25 °C is 1.35×10^{-5} mol dm^{-3}.

The equation for the dissociation of propanoic acid is:

$$CH_3CH_2COOH(aq) \rightleftharpoons CH_3CH_2COO^-(aq) + H^+(aq)$$

$$K_a = \frac{[CH_3CH_2COO^-(aq)][H^+(aq)]}{[CH_3CH_2COOH(aq)]}$$

As one molecule of CH_3CH_2COOH dissociates to form one $CH_3CH_2COO^-$ ion and one H^+ ion, the concentration of $CH_3CH_2COO^-$ and H^+ ions in the solution will be equal, i.e.:

$$[CH_3CH_2COO^-(aq)] = [H^+(aq)]$$

We will make the assumption that the dissociation of the acid is negligible compared with the concentration of the acid – that is, we will assume that the concentration of the acid at equilibrium is the same as the initial concentration, i.e. $0.200\,mol\,dm^{-3}$ in this case.

Application 1

The validity of the approximation that the dissociation of the acid can be ignored can be investigated in Application 1 on the CD-ROM.

These terms, together with the K_a value, will now be substituted into the K_a expression:

$$1.35 \times 10^{-5} = \frac{[H^+(aq)]^2}{0.200}$$

$$[H^+(aq)]^2 = 1.35 \times 10^{-5} \times 0.200 = 2.70 \times 10^{-6}$$

$$[H^+(aq)] = \sqrt{(2.70 \times 10^{-6})} = 1.64 \times 10^{-3}\,mol\,dm^{-3}$$

$$pH = -\log_{10}[H^+(aq)]$$

$$pH = -\log_{10}(1.64 \times 10^{-3}) = 2.78$$

The hydrogen ion concentration could also be worked out using the equation:

$$[H^+(aq)] = \sqrt{(c \times K_a)}$$

or pH could be worked out using the equation:

$$pH = -\tfrac{1}{2}\log_{10}(c \times K_a)$$

where c is the concentration of the acid.

Extension

We can avoid using the approximation by solving the quadratic equation:

$$1.35 \times 10^{-5} = \frac{[H^+(aq)]^2}{(0.200 - [H^+(aq)])}$$

Calculating K_a for an acid from the pH

Worked example

Calculate the value of the acid dissociation constant for benzoic acid if a $0.250\,mol\,dm^{-3}$ solution has a pH of 2.40.

The equation for the dissociation of benzoic acid is:

$$C_6H_5COOH(aq) \rightleftharpoons C_6H_5COO^-(aq) + H^+(aq)$$

$$K_a = \frac{[C_6H_5COO^-(aq)][H^+(aq)]}{[C_6H_5COOH(aq)]}$$

The $[H^+(aq)]$ can be worked out from the pH as:

$$[H^+(aq)] = 10^{-pH}$$

$$[H^+(aq)] = 10^{-2.40} = 3.94 \times 10^{-3}\,mol\,dm^{-3}$$

To produce $3.94 \times 10^{-3}\,mol\,dm^{-3}\,H^+$, $3.94 \times 10^{-3}\,mol\,dm^{-3}\,C_6H_5COOH$ must dissociate. The concentration of C_6H_5COOH at equilibrium is thus $0.250 - 3.94 \times 10^{-3}\,mol\,dm^{-3}$, i.e. $0.246\,mol\,dm^{-3}$.

As one molecule of C_6H_5COOH dissociates to produce one H^+ ion and one $C_6H_5COO^-$ ion, the concentration of $C_6H_5COO^-$ at equilibrium is the same as that of H^+.

The equilibrium concentrations are thus:

$$C_6H_5COOH(aq) \rightleftharpoons C_6H_5COO^-(aq) + H^+(aq)$$

equilibrium concentration / $mol\,dm^{-3}$:   0.246 3.94×10^{-3} 3.94×10^{-3}

These values can be put into the expression for K_a:

$$K_a = \frac{[C_6H_5COO^-(aq)][H^+(aq)]}{[C_6H_5COOH(aq)]}$$

$$K_a = \frac{(3.94 \times 10^{-3}) \times (3.94 \times 10^{-3})}{(0.246)}$$

$$K_a = 6.44 \times 10^{-5}\,mol\,dm^{-3}$$

If the approximation had been made that the effect of the dissociation of the acid on concentration of the acid at equilibrium can be ignored, the answer $6.34 \times 10^{-5}\,mol\,dm^{-3}$ would have been obtained.

The answer $6.34 \times 10^{-5}\,mol\,dm^{-3}$ could also have been obtained using the equation:

$$K_a = \frac{10^{-2pH}}{c}$$

where c is the concentration of the acid.

Self-tests 4 & 5

Test yourself

14 Copy and complete the following table by working out pH values. The first three should be done without using a calculator.

a solution containing $0.001\,00\,mol\,dm^{-3}\,H^+(aq)$	
a solution containing $1.00 \times 10^{-12}\,mol\,dm^{-3}\,H^+(aq)$	
a solution of $1.00\,mol\,dm^{-3}\,HCl(aq)$	
a solution of $2.00 \times 10^{-4}\,mol\,dm^{-3}\,HNO_3(aq)$	
a solution of CH_3COOH of concentration $0.100\,mol\,dm^{-3}$ assuming 5% dissociation of the acid	

15 Calculate the concentration of H^+ ions in each of the following solutions:
a pH = 3.5
b pH = 7.9
c pH = 12.8

16 HA to HF are all weak acids.

a Copy and complete the following table:

Acid	Concentration of acid / $mol\,dm^{-3}$	$[H^+]$ / $mol\,dm^{-3}$	pH	K_a / $mol\,dm^{-3}$
HA	0.0100	2.00×10^{-6}		
HB	0.200		4.70	
HC	0.500	2.50×10^{-4}		
HD	2.20×10^{-2}		5.20	
HE	0.250			3.72×10^{-8}
HF	0.0300			4.96×10^{-6}

b Use the K_a values in part **a** to arrange the acids in order of acid strength (strongest first).

17 B_1, B_2 and B_3 are weak bases.

a Copy and complete the table:

Base	Concentration of base / $mol\,dm^{-3}$	$[OH^-]$ / $mol\,dm^{-3}$	K_b / $mol\,dm^{-3}$
B_1	0.100	1.33×10^{-3}	
B_2	0.250		5.75×10^{-5}
B_3	0.0200	4.70×10^{-4}	

b Arrange the bases in order of increasing strength (weakest first).

The dissociation (ionisation) of water

Water dissociates according to the equation:

$$H_2O(l) \rightleftharpoons H^+(aq) + OH^-(aq)$$

The degree of dissociation is very small, and at 25 °C in pure water the concentration of H^+ and OH^- ions are equal, at $1.0 \times 10^{-7}\,mol\,dm^{-3}$.

An equilibrium constant, K_w, can be derived for this reaction:

$K_w = [H^+(aq)][OH^-(aq)]$
K_w is called the **ionic product constant** (ionic product) for water.
K_w has a value of $1.0 \times 10^{-14}\,mol^2\,dm^{-6}$ at 25 °C.
K_w refers to the $H_2O(l) \rightleftharpoons H^+(aq) + OH^-(aq)$ equilibrium in **all aqueous solutions** – the product of H^+ and OH^- concentrations in any aqueous solution at 25 °C is always $1.0 \times 10^{-14}\,mol^2\,dm^{-6}$.

Let us consider what happens to the equilibrium when acid or alkali is added to water.

If hydrogen chloride gas is bubbled in to water it will dissolve and dissociate to form H^+ ions:

$$HCl(aq) \rightarrow H^+(aq) + Cl^-(aq)$$

As the concentration of H^+ ions in the solution increases, according to Le Chatelier's principle, the position of equilibrium for the dissociation of water will shift to the left to use up the H^+ added and restore the value of the equilibrium constant. H^+ ions will thus react with OH^- ions to form water and the concentration of OH^- ions will drop below $1.0 \times 10^{-7}\,mol\,dm^{-3}$.

This equation may also be written as:

$$2H_2O(l) \rightarrow H_3O^+(aq) + OH^-(aq)$$

As with the dissociation constants derived above, any terms relating to the concentration of water are incorporated into the equilibrium constant, as the concentration of water is essentially constant.

HL

If sufficient acid is added to make the concentration of H^+ ions $0.10\,mol\,dm^{-3}$, the concentration of OH^- ions will drop to $1.0 \times 10^{-13}\,mol\,dm^{-3}$, as:

$$0.10 \times 1.0 \times 10^{-13} = 1.0 \times 10^{-14}$$

which is the value of K_w at this temperature.

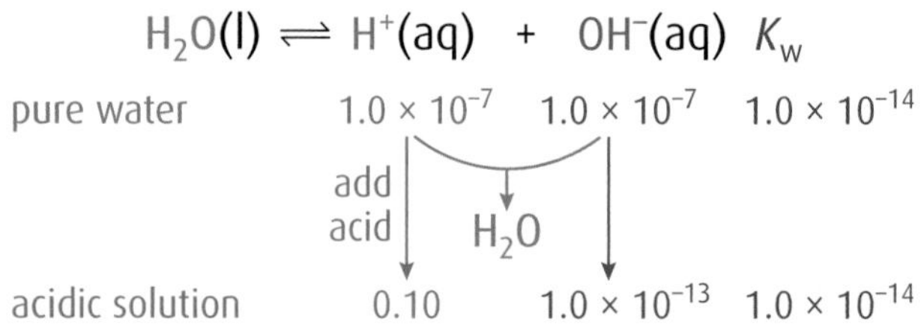

$$H_2O(l) \rightleftharpoons H^+(aq) + OH^-(aq) \quad K_w$$

pure water	1.0×10^{-7}	1.0×10^{-7}	1.0×10^{-14}

add acid → H_2O

acidic solution	0.10	1.0×10^{-13}	1.0×10^{-14}

Similarly, if ammonia is bubbled into water, the concentration of OH^- ions will increase. The product $[H^+(aq)][OH^-(aq)]$ will be greater than 1.0×10^{-14}, and therefore H^+ ions must react with some of the OH^- ions to bring the value of $[H^+(aq)][OH^-(aq)]$ back down to 1.0×10^{-14}, i.e. the position of equilibrium shifts to the left. The concentration of the H^+ ions will thus drop below $1.0 \times 10^{-7}\,mol\,dm^{-3}$. For instance, if the concentration of OH^- ions in an ammonia solution is $1.0 \times 10^{-4}\,mol\,dm^{-3}$, the concentration of H^+ ions in this solution will be $1.0 \times 10^{-10}\,mol\,dm^{-3}$, as $1.0 \times 10^{-4} \times 1.0 \times 10^{-10} = 1.0 \times 10^{-14}$.

The variation of K_w with temperature

Like other equilibrium constants, the value of K_w varies with temperature (Table **8.5** and Figure **8.12**). We can use the data in Table **8.5** to work out the pH of water at any temperature.

Temperature / °C	K_w / $mol^2\,dm^{-6}$
0	1.14×10^{-15}
5	1.86×10^{-15}
10	2.93×10^{-15}
15	4.52×10^{-15}
20	6.81×10^{-15}
25	1.01×10^{-14}
30	1.47×10^{-14}
35	2.09×10^{-14}
40	2.92×10^{-14}
45	4.02×10^{-14}
50	5.48×10^{-14}

Table 8.5 The variation of K_w with temperature.

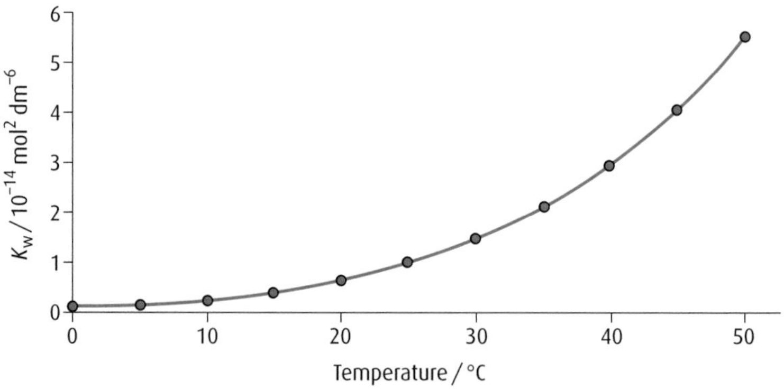

Figure 8.12 The variation of K_w with temperature.

Worked example

Calculate the pH of water at 40 °C.

Water dissociates according to the equation:

$$H_2O(l) \rightleftharpoons H^+(aq) + OH^-(aq) \qquad K_w = [H^+(aq)][OH^-(aq)]$$

As one H_2O molecule dissociates to form one H^+ and one OH^-, in pure water the concentration of H^+ ions is equal to the concentration of OH^- ions. We can therefore write $K_w = [H^+(aq)]^2$ for pure water. Thus, at 40 °C:

$$2.92 \times 10^{-14} = [H^+(aq)]^2$$

$$[H^+(aq)] = \sqrt{(2.92 \times 10^{-14})} = 1.71 \times 10^{-7}\,mol\,dm^{-3}$$

$$pH = -\log_{10}[H^+(aq)]$$

$$pH = -\log_{10}(1.71 \times 10^{-7}) = 6.77$$

Therefore the pH of pure water at 40 °C is 6.77.

This can also be worked out using the equation:

$$pH\ of\ water = \frac{pK_w}{2}$$

(see below for pK_w).

This does not, however, mean that the water is acidic at 40 °C, and we must now modify our definition of 'neutral'. Pure water is neutral because $[H^+(aq)] = [OH^-(aq)]$. As K_w only equals $1.0 \times 10^{-14}\,mol^2\,dm^{-6}$ at 25 °C, we can also see that pH 7 is neutral only at 25 °C!

The graph in Figure **8.13** shows the variation of the pH of pure water with temperature. This is the same as the variation of the neutral pH with temperature (Figure **8.14**). Any pH above the red line in Figure **8.14** indicates an alkaline pH at that temperature and any pH below the line indicates an acidic pH at that temperature. Thus, at 10 °C a pH of 7.1 is in the acidic region, below the line, and would represent an acidic pH at this temperature!

A solution is neutral if $[H^+(aq)] = [OH^-(aq)]$.
A solution is acidic if $[H^+(aq)] > [OH^-(aq)]$.
A solution is alkaline if $[OH^-(aq)] > [H^+(aq)]$.

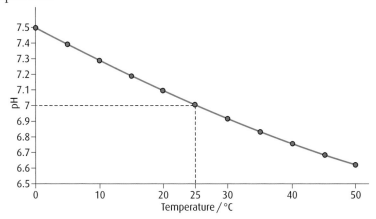

Figure 8.13 The variation of the pH of water with temperature.

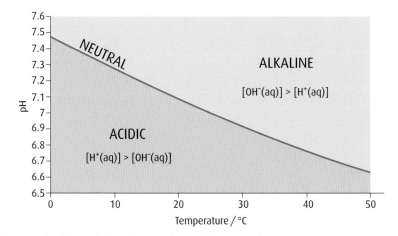

Figure 8.14 The variation of neutral pH with temperature.

When students first come across the idea of water having a pH of less than 7 at 40 °C and they are asked about it, the following piece of deductive reasoning usually goes on:

- all liquids with pH less than 7 are acidic
- water at 40 °C is a liquid with a pH of less than 7
- therefore water is acidic at 40 °C.

The conclusion of this reasoning is incorrect, but the argument is valid. The problem is, of course, with the first premise, which, we have just learnt, is incorrect. Can you reword the first premise to make it true and construct a valid argument?

We also have another problem here: when I first thought about demonstrating this argument I wanted to write the first premise as 'all solutions with pH less than 7 are acidic'. Why did I choose the word 'liquid' instead and does this introduce any extra difficulties with trying to come up with a completely true version of the first premise?

Another problem we encounter the first time we come across the idea of water having a pH other than 7 is, of course, that we 'know' that the neutral pH is 7 because we have been told it from an early age; it is even stated earlier in this chapter! The idea of water having a pH of anything other than 7 goes against everything we have learnt. If you obtained this result experimentally using a pH meter before you learnt about the theory of pH, would you dismiss the result as wrong (the pH meter had been poorly calibrated!) and ignore it?

Calculating the pH of a solution of a strong base

Alkalis or bases react with water to produce OH^- ions; it is therefore difficult initially to see why these solutions should have a pH, as pH is a measure of the H^+ ions present. However, all aqueous solutions contain H^+ ions, owing to the dissociation of water. The pH of an alkaline solution can therefore be worked out by using the ionic product constant, K_w.

Worked example

Calculate the pH of a 0.250 mol dm^{-3} solution of potassium hydroxide at 25 °C.

KOH is a strong base and will ionise completely in aqueous solution:

$$KOH(aq) \rightarrow K^+(aq) + OH^-(aq)$$

The concentration of the OH^- is thus the same as that of the original base, i.e. 0.250 mol dm^{-3}.

At 25 °C, $K_w = 1.00 \times 10^{-14}$ mol dm^{-3}

$$K_w = [H^+(aq)][OH^-(aq)]$$

Substituting the OH^- concentration and the value of K_w into this expression we obtain:

$$1.00 \times 10^{-14} = [H^+(aq)] \times 0.250$$

$$[H^+(aq)] = 4.00 \times 10^{-14} \text{ mol dm}^{-3}$$

$$pH = -\log_{10}[H^+(aq)] = -\log_{10}(4.00 \times 10^{-14}) = 13.4$$

Therefore, the pH of 0.250 mol dm^{-3} KOH at 25 °C is 13.4.

pOH

The calculation of pH of a base can be simplified by using pOH.

$$pOH = -\log_{10}[OH^-(aq)]$$

Let us consider the expression for the ionic product constant for water:

$$K_w = [H^+(aq)][OH^-(aq)]$$

$-\log_{10}$ of both sides is taken to give:

$$-\log_{10} K_w = -\log_{10}([H^+(aq)][OH^-(aq)])$$

$$-\log_{10} K_w = -\log_{10}[H^+(aq)] + -\log_{10}[OH^-(aq)]$$

We can re-write this as:

$$pK_w = pH + pOH$$

'p' stands for '$-\log_{10}$'

The value of pK_w at $25\,°C$ is $-\log_{10} 1.0 \times 10^{-14}$, i.e. 14.
We can therefore re-write the above equation as:

$$pH + pOH = 14 \qquad \text{at } 25\,°C$$

Worked example

Calculate the pH of $0.0500\,\text{mol}\,\text{dm}^{-3}$ sodium hydroxide solution at $25\,°C$.

NaOH is a strong base and ionises completely to form $0.0500\,\text{mol}\,\text{dm}^{-3}$ $OH^-(aq)$.

$$pOH = -\log_{10}(0.0500) = 1.30$$

At $25\,°C$: $pH + pOH = 14$

$$pH + 1.30 = 14$$

$$pH = 12.7$$

Calculating the pH and pOH of a solution of a weak base

Because a weak base only partially ionises in aqueous solution, we must use K_b to work out the concentration of OH^- ions present in a solution.

Worked example

Calculate pH and pOH for a $0.120\,\text{mol}\,\text{dm}^{-3}$ solution of ammonia at $25\,°C$, given that K_b is $1.78 \times 10^{-5}\,\text{mol}\,\text{dm}^{-3}$ at $25\,°C$.

The ionisation of ammonia is shown by the equation:

$$NH_3(aq) + H_2O(l) \rightleftharpoons NH_4^+(aq) + OH^-(aq)$$

$$K_b = \frac{[NH_4^+(aq)][OH^-(aq)]}{[NH_3(aq)]}$$

1 NH_3 molecule ionises to produce 1 NH_4^+ ion and 1 OH^- ion. This means that the concentration of NH_4^+ is equal to the OH^- concentration and we can write:

$$K_b = \frac{[OH^-(aq)]^2}{[NH_3(aq)]}$$

We will make the approximation that the concentration of NH_3 at equilibrium is equal to the initial concentration, i.e. that the ionisation of the base is negligible compared with its concentration. Therefore we take $[NH_3(aq)]$ as $0.120\,mol\,dm^{-3}$. If we substitute this value and the value for K_b into the expression for K_b, we get:

$$1.78 \times 10^{-5} = \frac{[OH^-(aq)]^2}{0.120}$$

$$[OH^-(aq)]^2 = 1.78 \times 10^{-5} \times 0.120 = 2.14 \times 10^{-6}$$

Therefore, $[OH^-(aq)] = 1.46 \times 10^{-3}\,mol\,dm^{-3}$.

$$pOH = -\log_{10}[OH^-(aq)]$$

$$pOH = -\log_{10}(1.46 \times 10^{-3}) = 2.84$$

$$pOH + pH = pK_w$$

At 25 °C, $pOH + pH = 14$.
Therefore, $pH = 14 - 2.84$, i.e. 11.16.

The hydroxide ion concentration could also be worked out using the equation:

$$[OH^-(aq)] = \sqrt{(c \times K_b)}$$

where c is the concentration of the base.

pOH could be worked out using the equation:

$$pOH = -\tfrac{1}{2}\log_{10}(c \times K_b)$$

pH could be worked out by using the equation:

$$pH = 14 + \tfrac{1}{2}\log_{10}(c \times K_b)$$

where c is the concentration of the base

Calculating pOH of an acid

Just as the pH of a base may be worked out, pOH for an acid may also be calculated. The OH^- in an acidic solution comes from the dissociation of water.

Worked example

Calculate the pOH of $0.0225\,mol\,dm^{-3}$ hydrochloric acid at 25 °C.

HCl is a strong acid and dissociates completely. The concentration of H^+ ions produced is thus $0.0225\,mol\,dm^{-3}$.

$$pH = -\log_{10}[H^+(aq)] = -\log_{10}0.0225 = 1.65$$

$$pOH + pH = pK_w$$

At 25 °C, $pOH + pH = 14$.

$$pOH = 14 - 1.65 = 12.35$$

Therefore the pOH of $0.0225\,mol\,dm^{-3}$ hydrochloric acid is 12.35.

pH, pOH and neutrality

At 25 °C, neutral pH is 7. At 25 °C, solutions that have a pH of less than 7 are acidic and those that have a pH of greater than 7 are alkaline. For pOH the situation is reversed: solutions that have a pOH of less than 7 are alkaline and those that have a pOH of greater than 7 are acidic.

$$pH + pOH = pK_w$$

If pH < pOH, the solution is acidic, and if pOH < pH, the solution is alkaline.

In **pure water** (or a neutral solution), pH = pOH, which leads to the relationship:

$$pH = pOH = \frac{pK_w}{2}$$

Self-test 6

Test yourself

18 Copy and complete the table for aqueous solutions at 25 °C. Try to do it without using a calculator. The first row has been done for you.

$[H^+(aq)]$/ mol dm^{-3}	$[OH^-(aq)]$/ mol dm^{-3}	pH	pOH	Acidic or alkaline?
1×10^{-3}	1×10^{-11}	3	11	acidic
1×10^{-5}				
	0.01			
		11		
			1	

19 Calculate the pH of pure water at each of the following temperatures
   a at 5 °C, K_w is 1.86×10^{-15} mol^2 dm^{-6}
   b at 35 °C, K_w is 2.09×10^{-14} mol^2 dm^{-6}
   c at 100 °C, K_w is 5.13×10^{-13} mol^2 dm^{-6}

20 Calculate the pOH of the following solutions:
   a 0.0300 mol dm^{-3} KOH
   b 0.500 mol dm^{-3} NaOH
   c 0.0200 mol dm^{-3} HCl

21 Calculate the pH of the following solutions:
   a 0.0150 mol dm^{-3} NaOH
   b 0.0500 mol dm^{-3} Ba(OH)$_2$

22 Calculate the pH values for the following solutions:
   a a 0.0500 mol dm^{-3} solution of ethylamine (CH$_3$CH$_2$NH$_2$) at 25 °C, given that the K_b value is 5.37×10^{-4} mol dm^{-3} at that temperature.
   b a 0.0100 mol dm^{-3} solution of phenylamine (C$_6$H$_5$NH$_2$) at 25 °C, given that the K_b value is 4.17×10^{-10} mol dm^{-3} at that temperature.

pK_a and pK_b

The acid and base ionisation constants may be expressed in a more convenient form by taking the negative logarithm to base 10 of them.

$$pK_a = -\log_{10} K_a \qquad K_a = 10^{-pK_a}$$
$$pK_b = -\log_{10} K_b \qquad K_b = 10^{-pK_b}$$

You can think about this in the same way as pH – the lower the pH value, the higher the $[H^+(aq)]$.

The lower the value of pK_a, the stronger the acid.

HL A low value of K_a corresponds to a high value of pK_a and vice versa, so that the lower the pK_a value, the stronger the acid. Similarly for pK_b: the lower the value, the stronger the base.

The acids in Table **8.6** are arranged in order of strength, i.e. from HF, which has the lowest pK_a value and is the strongest acid, to HCN, which has the highest pK_a value and is the weakest acid.

Acid	Formula	K_a / mol dm^{-3}	pK_a
hydrofluoric acid	HF	5.62×10^{-4}	3.25
benzoic acid	C_6H_5COOH	6.31×10^{-5}	4.20
propanoic acid	CH_3CH_2COOH	1.35×10^{-5}	4.87
chloric(I) acid	HOCl	3.72×10^{-8}	7.43
hydrocyanic acid	HCN	3.98×10^{-10}	9.40

increasing strength

Table 8.6 K_a and pK_a values for some acids.

The bases in Table **8.7** are arranged in order of strength, i.e. from dimethylamine, which has the lowest pK_b value and is the strongest base, to phenylamine, which has the highest pK_b value and is the weakest base.

Base	Formula	K_b / mol dm^{-3}	pK_b
dimethylamine	$(CH_3)_2NH$	5.25×10^{-4}	3.28
methylamine	CH_3NH_2	4.37×10^{-4}	3.36
sodium carbonate	Na_2CO_3	2.09×10^{-4}	3.68
ammonia	NH_3	1.78×10^{-5}	4.75
phenylamine	$C_6H_5NH_2$	4.17×10^{-10}	9.38

increasing strength

The lower the value of pK_b, the stronger the base.

Table 8.7 K_b and pK_b values for some acids.

Calculating the pH of an acid given the concentration and pK_a value

This is identical to the method above for working out pH from the K_a value, except that K_a must first be calculated from pK_a using the equation:

$$K_a = 10^{-pK_a}$$

Worked example

Calculate the pH of a 0.100 mol dm^{-3} solution of ethanoic acid at 25 °C. The pK_a of ethanoic acid at 25 °C is 4.76.

$$K_a = 10^{-pK_a}$$

$$K_a = 10^{-4.76} = 1.74 \times 10^{-5}\,\text{mol}\,\text{dm}^{-3}$$

2nd log −4.76 on the calculator

The equation for the dissociation of ethanoic acid is:

$$CH_3COOH(aq) \rightleftharpoons CH_3COO^-(aq) + H^+(aq)$$

$$K_a = \frac{[CH_3COO^-(aq)][H^+(aq)]}{[CH_3COOH(aq)]}$$

As one molecule of CH_3COOH dissociates to form one CH_3COO^- ion and one H^+ ion, the concentration of CH_3COO^- and H^+ ions in the solution will be equal:

$$[CH_3COO^-(aq)] = [H^+(aq)]$$

We will make the assumption that the dissociation of the acid is negligible compared with the concentration of the acid – that is, we will assume that the concentration of the acid at equilibrium is the same as the initial concentration, i.e. $0.100\,\text{mol}\,\text{dm}^{-3}$ in this case.

These terms, together with the K_a value, will now be substituted into the K_a expression:

$$1.74 \times 10^{-5} = \frac{[H^+(aq)]^2}{0.100}$$

$$[H^+(aq)]^2 = 1.74 \times 10^{-5} \times 0.100 = 1.74 \times 10^{-6}$$

$$[H^+(aq)] = \sqrt{(1.74 \times 10^{-6})} = 1.32 \times 10^{-3}\,\text{mol}\,\text{dm}^{-3}$$

$$pH = -\log_{10}[H^+(aq)]$$

$$pH = -\log_{10}(1.32 \times 10^{-3}) = 2.88$$

pH could be worked out using the equation:

$$pH = \tfrac{1}{2}(pK_a - \log_{10} c)$$

where c is the concentration of the acid

Equations for working out pH and pOH for weak bases

pOH and pH for a weak base are worked out using a similar approach to that above or using the following equations:

$$pOH = \tfrac{1}{2}(pK_b - \log_{10} c)$$

$$pH = 14 - \tfrac{1}{2}(pK_b - \log_{10} c) \text{ at } 25\,°C$$

where c is the concentration of the base.

The relationship between K_a and K_b

Consider the equilibria for an acid HA and its conjugate base A^-:

$$HA(aq) \rightleftharpoons A^-(aq) + H^+(aq) \qquad\qquad \textbf{Equation 1}$$

$$A^-(aq) + H_2O(l) \rightleftharpoons HA(aq) + OH^-(aq) \qquad\qquad \textbf{Equation 2}$$

We can write the K_a expression for Equation 1:

$$K_a = \frac{[A^-(aq)][H^+(aq)]}{[HA(aq)]}$$

and the K_b expression for Equation 2:

$$K_b = \frac{[HA(aq)][OH^-(aq)]}{[A^-(aq)]}$$

If we multiply K_a by K_b we get:

certain terms cancel

$$K_a \times K_b = \frac{[\cancel{A^-}(aq)][H^+(aq)]}{[\cancel{HA}(aq)]} \times \frac{[\cancel{HA}(aq)][OH^-(aq)]}{[\cancel{A^-}(aq)]}$$

$$K_a \times K_b = [H^+(aq)] \times [OH^-(aq)]$$

But $[H^+(aq)] \times [OH^-(aq)] = K_w$, so we can write:

$$K_a \times K_b = K_w$$

This relationship works only for a **conjugate acid–base pair**, e.g. for NH_4^+ ($K_a = 5.62 \times 10^{-10}\,mol\,dm^{-3}$) and for NH_3 ($K_b = 1.78 \times 10^{-5}\,mol\,dm^{-3}$):

$$K_a \times K_b = 5.62 \times 10^{-10} \times 1.78 \times 10^{-5} = 1.00 \times 10^{-14}\,mol^2\,dm^{-6}$$

which is the value for K_w at $25\,°C$.

If we take negative logarithms to base 10 of each side in the expression $K_a \times K_b = K_w$, we get the relationship:

$$pK_a + pK_b = pK_w$$

4.76 + 9.24 = 14

At $25\,°C$ the value of pK_w is 14, so, at $25\,°C$ $pK_a + pK_b = 14$.

The pK_a for ethanoic acid (CH_3COOH) is 4.76 and the pK_b for its conjugate base, the ethanoate ion (CH_3COO^-), is 9.24 at $25\,°C$.

The relationship between the strength of an acid and the strength of its conjugate base

For a conjugate acid–base pair, $pK_a + pK_b = pK_w$ (or $K_a \times K_b = K_w$). This means that the lower the value of pK_a for an acid the higher the value of pK_b for its conjugate base. A lower value of pK_a indicates a stronger acid and a higher value of pK_b indicates a weaker base. This leads to the conclusion:

the stronger the acid, the weaker its conjugate base.

This can be seen with a strong acid such as HCl. HCl dissociates completely in aqueous solution:

$$HCl(aq) \rightarrow H^+(aq) + Cl^-(aq)$$

The conjugate base of HCl is Cl^-, and this is a very weak base, as it has virtually no tendency to react with H_2O to reform HCl:

$$Cl^-(aq) + H_2O(l) \rightleftharpoons HCl(aq) + OH^-(aq)$$

Let us consider the acids in Table **8.8**.

Acid	pK_a		Conjugate Base	pK_b
HF	3.25		F^-	10.75
C_6H_5COOH	4.20	increasing strength	$C_6H_5COO^-$	9.80
CH_3CH_2COOH	4.87		$CH_3CH_2COO^-$	9.13
HOCl	7.43		OCl^-	6.57
HCN	9.40		CN^-	4.60

Table 8.8 The relationship between the strength of an acid and its conjugate base.

HCN is the weakest acid in Table **8.8** and has the strongest conjugate base. HCN has very little tendency to dissociate, according to the equation:

$$HCN(aq) \rightarrow H^+(aq) + CN^-(aq)$$

and CN^- has a strong tendency to react with water to re-form the parent acid:

$$CN^-(aq) + H_2O(l) \rightarrow HCN(aq) + OH^-(aq)$$

Self-test 7

Test yourself

23 Arrange the following acids in order of increasing strength (weakest first):

Acid	pK_a
HOCl	7.4
$HClO_2$	2.0

Acid	$K_a / mol\,dm^{-3}$
HOI	3.0×10^{-11}
HNO_2	4.6×10^{-4}

24 Copy and complete the following table, which contains values measured at 25 °C. The first row has been done for you.

Acid	$K_a / mol\,dm^{-3}$	pK_a	Conjugate base	$K_b / mol\,dm^{-3}$	pK_b
HCN	3.98×10^{-10}	9.40	CN^-	2.51×10^{-5}	4.60
HF	5.62×10^{-4}				
HIO_3		0.8			
NH_4^+					4.75
			CH_3COO^-	5.75×10^{-10}	
		10.64	CH_3NH_2		

25 Calculate pH values for the following solutions:
  a a $0.0200\,mol\,dm^{-3}$ solution of propanoic acid, given that the pK_a value at 25 °C is 4.87.
  b a $0.500\,mol\,dm^{-3}$ solution of HCN, given that the pK_a value at 25 °C is 9.40.
  c a $0.00250\,mol\,dm^{-3}$ solution of phenol (C_6H_5OH), given that the pK_a value at 25 °C is 10.00.

The lower the value of pK_a, the stronger the acid.

The lower the value of pK_b, the stronger the base.

Learning objectives

- Sketch titration curves for titrations involving any combination of strong and weak acids and bases
- Explain the important features of titration curves
- Understand how to work out pK_a or pK_b values from a titration curve
- Explain how an acid–base indicator works
- Understand what is meant by the pH range of an indicator
- Select a suitable indicator for a titration

Acid–base titrations

Titration as a technique for determining the concentration of a solution has already been discussed on page **38**. Here we will look at **titration curves**, which show how pH varies during titrations involving different combinations of strong and weak acids and bases. The pH can be monitored during a titration by using a pH meter or a pH probe attached to a data logger (Figure **8.15**).

Strong acid–strong base titration

The titration curve for adding $0.100 \, mol \, dm^{-3}$ sodium hydroxide solution to $25.0 \, cm^3$ of $0.100 \, mol \, dm^{-3}$ hydrochloric acid is shown in Figure **8.16**.

The reaction that occurs is:

$$HCl(aq) + NaOH(aq) \rightarrow NaCl(aq) + H_2O(l)$$

The initial pH is 1.0, as the initial solution is $0.100 \, mol \, dm^{-3}$ hydrochloric acid. Hydrochloric acid is a strong acid and dissociates completely:

$$HCl(aq) \rightarrow H^+(aq) + Cl^-(aq)$$

The concentration of H^+ ions is $0.100 \, mol \, dm^{-3}$ and the pH = $-\log_{10}$ 0.10, i.e. 1.00.

From Figure **8.16** it can be seen that as the NaOH is added the pH initially changes very little. The pH after $20.0 \, cm^3$ of NaOH has been added is 1.95, so adding $20.0 \, cm^3$ of the sodium hydroxide has changed the pH of the solution by less than 1 unit. This is partly a consequence of the fact that the $H^+(aq)$ ion concentration is reasonably high in this region and therefore adding NaOH does not affect the overall pH very much. However, it also arises from the nature of the log scale: the $[H^+(aq)]$ in this region decreases by about $0.09 \, mol \, dm^{-3}$ from $0.100 \, mol \, dm^{-3}$ to $0.010 \, mol \, dm^{-3}$, but a 10-fold change in the $[H^+(aq)]$ corresponds to a change in pH of only 1 unit.

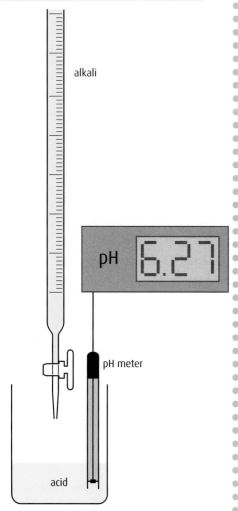

Figure 8.15 This experimental set-up could be used to track the pH of a solution in a titration.

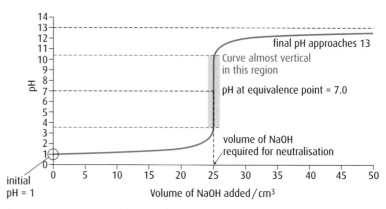

Figure 8.16 A strong acid–strong base titration curve.

The pH then rises much more rapidly, and between a pH of about 3.5 and 10.5 the curve is virtually vertical. In this region (shaded on the graph), addition of about $0.3\,cm^3$ of NaOH causes the pH to change by 7 units. In this region the $[H^+(aq)]$ is low and adding NaOH has a larger effect on the pH. The fact that this is a log scale, however, magnifies the effect – in this region the $[H^+(aq)]$ actually decreases only by about $0.000\,31\,mol\,dm^{-3}$, but as it decreases from $3.15 \times 10^{-4}\,mol\,dm^{-3}$ to $3.15 \times 10^{-11}\,mol\,dm^{-3}$, the pH changes by 7 units.

After this region, the pH changes only gradually again, and as more and more NaOH is added the pH gets closer to 13, which is the pH of $0.100\,mol\,dm^{-3}$ NaOH(aq). All the acid has been neutralised and the OH^- ions are in excess in this region. As more and more NaOH is added, the solution resembles more and more closely the original NaOH solution (when $200\,cm^3$ have been added the pH is 12.89).

> The pH at the equivalence point for a strong acid–strong alkali titration is 7.0.

> The **equivalence point** is the point at which equivalent numbers of moles of acid and alkali have been added.

If, instead of adding $0.100\,mol\,dm^{-3}$ NaOH to the acid ($25\,cm^3$ of $0.100\,mol\,dm^{-3}$ HCl), we had added $0.200\,mol\,dm^{-3}$ NaOH, we would get the titration curve shown in Figure **8.17**. The equivalence point would now occur once $12.5\,cm^3$ of the alkali has been added.

In this case, as the concentrations of the acid and alkali are equal, the equivalence point occurs when equal volumes of the acid and alkali have been added.

Note: the equivalence point is not the same as the end point – the end point will be discussed later in the section on indicators (pages **350–354**).

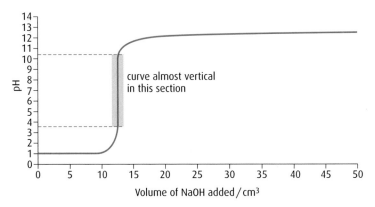

Figure 8.17 A titration curve for adding $0.200\,mol\,dm^{-3}$ NaOH to $25\,cm^3$ of $0.100\,mol\,dm^{-3}$ HCl.

If we had used $1.00\,mol\,dm^{-3}$ HCl and $1.00\,mol\,dm^{-3}$ NaOH for the titration, the initial pH would be lower and the steep part would be longer (Figure **8.18**).

If we had performed the original titration the other way round, i.e. by adding the acid to the alkali, the curve would have been reversed, as shown in Figure **8.19** (overleaf).

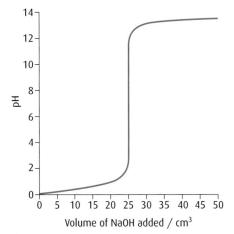

Figure 8.18 A titration curve for adding $1.00\,mol\,dm^{-3}$ NaOH to $25\,cm^3$ of $1.00\,mol\,dm^{-3}$ HCl.

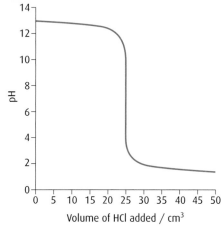

Figure 8.19 A titration curve for adding 0.100 mol dm^{-3} HCl to 25 cm^3 of 0.100 mol dm^{-3} NaOH.

HL How to calculate the points on the strong acid–strong base titration curve

Consider again the original titration, i.e. the addition of 0.100 mol dm^{-3} sodium hydroxide solution to 25.0 cm^3 of 0.100 mol dm^{-3} hydrochloric acid (Figure **8.16**, page **342**). We will look at how each point on the titration curve can be calculated.

Initial pH (no NaOH added)

The initial pH is 1.00, as the initial solution is 0.100 mol dm^{-3} hydrochloric acid. Hydrochloric acid is a strong acid and dissociates completely:

$$HCl(aq) \rightarrow H^+(aq) + Cl^-(aq)$$

The concentration of H$^+$ ions is 0.100 mol dm^{-3} and the pH = $-\log_{10}$ 0.100, i.e. 1.00.

In 25.0 cm^3 of 0.100 mol dm^{-3} HCl, the number of moles of H$^+$ ions is given by:

$$\text{no. moles} = \text{concentration} \times \text{volume in dm}^3$$

$$\text{no. moles of H}^+ = 0.100 \times \frac{25.0}{1000} = 2.50 \times 10^{-3} \text{ mol}$$

Addition of 5.0 cm^3 of NaOH to 25.0 cm^3 of the acid

The total volume of the solution is now:

$$25.0 + 5.0 = 30.0 \text{ cm}^3$$

The number of moles of OH$^-$ ions in 5.0 cm^3 of solution is given by:

$$\text{no. moles of OH}^- = 0.100 \times \frac{5.0}{1000} = 5.0 \times 10^{-4} \text{ mol}$$

These OH$^-$ ions react with the H$^+$ ions in the acid solution according to the equation:

$$H^+(aq) + OH^-(aq) \rightarrow H_2O(l)$$

H$^+$ ions are in excess and 5.0×10^{-4} mol OH$^-$ react with 5.0×10^{-4} mol H$^+$. The original number of moles of H$^+$ ions was 2.50×10^{-3}; therefore, if 5.0×10^{-4} mol react, the number of moles of H$^+$ ions left over in the solution is $2.50 \times 10^{-3} - 5.0 \times 10^{-4}$, i.e. 2.00×10^{-3} mol.

This number of moles of H$^+$ is present in 30.0 cm^3 of solution; therefore the concentration of H$^+$ ions in the solution is given by:

$$\text{concentration} = \frac{\text{no. moles}}{\text{volume in dm}^3}$$

$$[H^+(aq)] = \frac{2.00 \times 10^{-3}}{0.0300} = 6.67 \times 10^{-2} \text{ mol dm}^{-3}$$

$$pH = -\log_{10}[H^+(aq)] = -\log_{10} 6.67 \times 10^{-2} = 1.18$$

This technique can be used to work out the pH of all solutions up to the addition of just less than $25.0\,cm^3$ NaOH.

If the calculation is attempted for $25.0\,cm^3$ of NaOH added, a problem is encountered, as the number of moles of H^+ ions in the original solution was $2.50 \times 10^{-3}\,mol\,dm^{-3}$ and the number of moles of OH^- that is added is $2.50 \times 10^{-3}\,mol\,dm^{-3}$. These will react together completely so that the number of moles of H^+ left will be zero, but $-\log_{10} 0$ does not exist! The problem has arisen because, in all of the above calculations, we have ignored any H^+ in the solution from the dissociation of water. In most cases we are totally justified in ignoring this. For instance, at $20.0\,cm^3$ of NaOH added, the concentration of H^+ ions in the solution from the hydrochloric acid is $0.0111\,mol\,dm^{-3}$, whereas that from the dissociation of water is $9.00 \times 10^{-13}\,mol\,dm^{-3}$, i.e. the dissociation of water accounts for $8.1 \times 10^{-9}\%$ of the H^+ ion concentration of the solution. Even at $24.999\,cm^3$ of NaOH added this percentage has only risen to about 0.25%.

However, at $25.0\,cm^3$ of NaOH added, the H^+ ion concentration of the solution is entirely due to the dissociation of water and the H^+ ion concentration is $1.00 \times 10^{-7}\,mol\,dm^{-3}$. The pH of the solution is thus 7.0.

After $25.0\,cm^3$ of NaOH has been added, the calculation changes slightly, as the NaOH is in excess. Let us consider $30.0\,cm^3$ of NaOH added. The total volume of the solution is:

$$25.0 + 30.0 = 55.0\,cm^3$$

The number of moles of OH^- ions in $30.0\,cm^3$ of solution is given by:

$$\text{no. moles of } OH^- = 0.100 \times \frac{30.0}{1000} = 3.00 \times 10^{-3}\,mol$$

These OH^- ions reacts with the H^+ ions in the solution according to the equation:

$$H^+(aq) + OH^-(aq) \rightarrow H_2O(l)$$

The original number of moles of H^+ ions was $2.50 \times 10^{-3}\,mol$.
The number of moles of OH^- in excess is:

$$3.00 \times 10^{-3} - 2.50 \times 10^{-3} = 5.0 \times 10^{-4}\,mol$$

$$\text{concentration} = \frac{\text{no. moles}}{\text{volume in dm}^3}$$

$$[OH^-(aq)] = \frac{5.0 \times 10^{-4}}{0.0550} = 9.09 \times 10^{-3}\,mol\,dm^{-3}$$

$$pOH = -\log_{10}[OH^-(aq)]$$

$$pOH = -\log_{10} 9.09 \times 10^{-3} = 2.04$$

At $25\,°C$, $pH + pOH = 14$. Therefore, $pH = 12.0$ (to three significant figures).

pH values when $25.0\,cm^3$ of $0.100\,mol\,dm^{-3}$ HCl is titrated with $0.100\,mol\,dm^{-3}$ NaOH	
Volume of NaOH added / cm^3	pH
0.00	1.000
5.00	1.176
10.00	1.368
15.00	1.602
20.00	1.954
21.00	2.061
22.00	2.195
23.00	2.380
24.00	2.690
24.50	2.996
24.90	3.698
24.95	4.000
24.99	4.699
24.995	5.000
24.999	5.699
25.00	7.000
25.01	9.301
25.10	10.300
25.50	10.996
26.00	11.292
30.00	11.959
35.00	12.222
40.00	12.363
50.00	12.523
60.00	12.615
100.00	12.778
200.00	12.891

HL Titration of a weak acid with a strong base

Let us consider adding $0.100 \text{ mol dm}^{-3}$ NaOH to 25 cm^3 of $0.100 \text{ mol dm}^{-3}$ CH$_3$COOH (ethanoic acid) ($K_a = 1.74 \times 10^{-5} \text{ mol dm}^{-3}$). The titration curve is shown in Figure **8.20**.

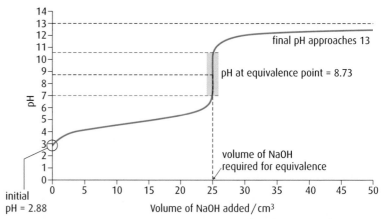

Figure 8.20 A titration curve for adding $0.100 \text{ mol dm}^{-3}$ NaOH to 25 cm^3 of $0.100 \text{ mol dm}^{-3}$ CH$_3$COOH.

The initial pH may be calculated using the K_a value for ethanoic acid and the method given on pages **338** and **339**.

The equivalence point is reached when equal numbers of moles of acid and alkali have been added. As the concentrations of the acid and alkali are the same, this occurs when the same volumes have been added (that is, when 25.0 cm^3 of sodium hydroxide has been added). The pH at the equivalence point is not 7, however; it is greater than 7.

The equation for the reaction is:

$$CH_3COOH(aq) + NaOH(aq) \rightarrow CH_3COONa(aq) + H_2O(l)$$

When equivalent amounts of ethanoic acid and sodium hydroxide have been added, a solution of sodium ethanoate (CH$_3$COONa(aq)) has been formed. The CH$_3$COO$^-$ ion is the conjugate base of the weak acid ethanoic acid, and so, acting as a base, will react with some water molecules to accept a proton according to the equilibrium:

$$CH_3COO^-(aq) + H_2O(l) \rightleftharpoons CH_3COOH(aq) + OH^-(aq)$$

The concentration of OH$^-$ ions in the solution is thus increased and the pH at the equivalence point is greater than 7.

The steep part of the curve, where it is virtually vertical, is more in the alkaline region than in the acidic region of the graph. As more and more NaOH is added, the pH approaches 13, which is the pH of pure $0.100 \text{ mol dm}^{-3}$ NaOH.

In Figure **8.21**, the weak acid–strong base titration curve is compared with a strong acid–strong base titration curve.

The equivalence point is the **point of inflexion** on the curve. A point of inflexion is where the gradient (slope) of the curve stops increasing (or decreasing) and starts decreasing (or increasing).

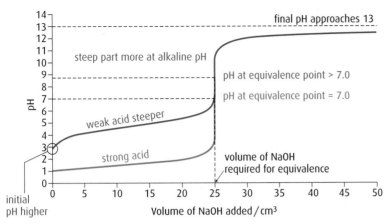

Figure 8.21 Comparison of a weak acid–strong base titration curve (blue) with a strong acid–strong base titration curve (red).

There are some important differences between the strong acid–strong base titration curve and the weak acid–strong base titration curve.

- The initial pH is higher for the weak acid. The weak acid is only partially dissociated.
- The initial part of the curve, up to a volume of about $24\,cm^3$ NaOH added, is steeper for the weak acid–strong base titration. Because the weak acid is only partially dissociated, the concentration of H^+ ions in the solution is lower, and adding a certain volume of NaOH has a greater relative effect on the pH than for a strong acid, in which the concentration of H^+ ions is higher.
- The steep part of the curve is more in the alkaline region.
- The pH at the equivalence point is greater than 7.

Determination of pK_a from a titration curve

The pK_a value for a weak acid may be determined experimentally by constructing a titration curve.

Consider the above example of the titration of $0.100\,mol\,dm^{-3}$ ethanoic acid with $0.100\,mol\,dm^{-3}$ NaOH; $25.0\,cm^3$ of NaOH is required to reach the equivalence point. Here we will consider the point in the titration when half this amount of NaOH has been added, i.e. $12.5\,cm^3$.

The equation for the reaction is:

$$CH_3COOH(aq) + NaOH(aq) \rightarrow CH_3COONa(aq) + H_2O(l)$$

When $12.5\,cm^3$ of NaOH has been added, half of the CH_3COOH has been converted to CH_3COONa, and therefore the concentrations of CH_3COOH and CH_3COONa are equal. This can be seen if we work out the number of moles of each species:

no. moles of CH_3COOH originally in solution $= \dfrac{25.0}{1000} \times 0.1$

$$= 2.50 \times 10^{-3}\,mol$$

no. moles of NaOH added $= \dfrac{12.5}{1000} \times 0.1 = 1.25 \times 10^{-3}\,mol$

Examiner's tip
This seems to come up a lot in examinations!

HL 1.25×10^{-3} mol NaOH will react with 1.25×10^{-3} mol CH$_3$COOH to form 1.25×10^{-3} mol CH$_3$COONa. There were originally 2.50×10^{-3} mol CH$_3$COOH, and if 1.25×10^{-3} mol reacted that leaves 1.25×10^{-3} mol CH$_3$COOH in the reaction mixture, i.e. the same number of moles as CH$_3$COONa.

The expression for K_a is:

$$K_a = \frac{[CH_3COO^-(aq)][H^+(aq)]}{[CH_3COOH(aq)]}$$

As the concentration of CH$_3$COO$^-$ is equal to the concentration of CH$_3$COOH, we can write:

$$K_a = \frac{[\cancel{CH_3COOH(aq)}][H^+(aq)]}{[\cancel{CH_3COOH(aq)}]} = [H^+(aq)]$$

or, if we take $-\log_{10}$ of both sides, we get: $pK_a = pH$. Thus, at the half equivalence point we can read the value of pK_a off the graph in Figure **8.22**.

> Note: [CH$_3$COONa(aq)] is equal to [CH$_3$COO$^-$(aq)], as the ionic salt is fully dissociated in solution.

> pH = pK_a at half equivalence point.

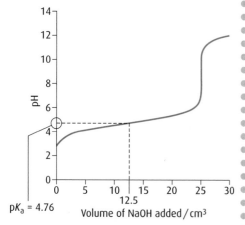

Figure 8.22 The pK_a value of the acid is equal to the pH at the half equivalence point.

Different strength acids

The strength of the acid does not affect the volume of alkali required to reach the equivalence point for a titration. The titration curves for adding $0.100 \, \text{mol dm}^{-3}$ NaOH to separate samples of $25.0 \, \text{cm}^3$ of $0.100 \, \text{mol dm}^{-3}$ ethanoic acid ($pK_a = 4.76$) and $25.0 \, \text{cm}^3$ of $0.100 \, \text{mol dm}^{-3}$ methanoic acid ($pK_a = 3.75$) are shown in Figure **8.23**.

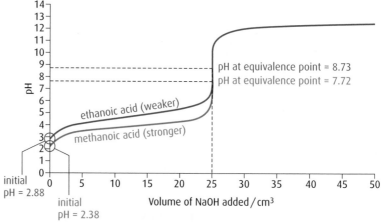

Figure 8.23 Titration curves for adding sodium hydroxide solution to different strength weak acids.

The strength of the acid affects the initial pH and the pH at the equivalence point. The initial pH gets closer to 1 (the pH of a $0.100 \, \text{mol dm}^{-3}$ solution of a strong acid), and the pH at the equivalence point gets closer to 7.0, if a stronger acid is used in the titration. The volume of alkali required for equivalence stays the same; this just depends on the concentration of the acid, and as the same concentration of the acid is used in each case, the same volume of NaOH is required to reach equivalence.

Titration of a strong acid with a weak base

HL

Let us consider adding $0.100 \, mol \, dm^{-3}$ $NH_3(aq)$ (ammonium hydroxide) to $25 \, cm^3$ $0.100 \, mol \, dm^{-3}$ $HCl(aq)$ (Figure **8.24**). The pH at the equivalence point for a strong acid–weak base titration is at a pH lower than 7. This is because at the equivalence point the NH_3 has reacted with HCl to form NH_4Cl:

$$NH_3(aq) + HCl(aq) \rightarrow NH_4Cl(aq)$$

The ammonium ion is, however, the conjugate acid of a weak base and as such will dissociate to a certain extent in aqueous solution according to the equation:

$$NH_4^+(aq) \rightleftharpoons NH_3(aq) + H^+(aq)$$

The concentration of H^+ ions in the solution is thus increased, and the pH is less than 7.

The titration could also have been performed the other way around, that is, by adding hydrochloric acid to the ammonia solution. The titration curve obtained is shown in Figure **8.25**.

The initial pH can be worked out using the K_b value of ammonia, as already described. At the half equivalence point of this titration, $12.5 \, cm^3$ of HCl has been added. The equilibrium that exists in this solution is:

$$NH_3(aq) + H_2O(l) \rightleftharpoons NH_4^+(aq) + OH^-(aq)$$

The expression for K_b is:

$$K_b = \frac{[NH_4^+(aq)][OH^-(aq)]}{[NH_3(aq)]}$$

When $12.5 \, cm^3$ of HCl has been added, half of the NH_3 will have been converted into NH_4^+, and so the concentration of NH_3 will be equal to the concentration of NH_4^+.

$$K_b = \frac{[\cancel{NH_4^+(aq)}][OH^-(aq)]}{[\cancel{NH_3(aq)}]}$$

Therefore, at the half equivalence point: $K_b = [OH^-]$.

Taking $-\log_{10}$ of both side we get: $pK_b = pOH$.

At $25 \, ^{\circ}C$, $pH + pOH = 14$, so, at the half equivalence point, $14 - pH = pK_b$. We can thus work out the pK_b for ammonia from the graph in Figure **8.26**.

The pH at the half equivalence point is 9.25, so the pK_b of ammonia is given by:

$$14 - 9.25 = pK_b$$

i.e. the pK_b for ammonia is 4.75.

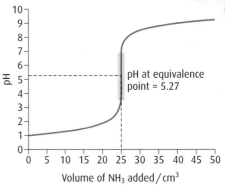

Figure 8.24 A strong acid–weak base titration curve.

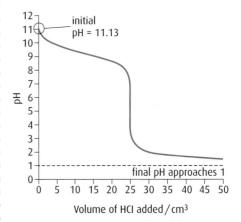

Figure 8.25 Titration curve for adding a weak base to a strong acid.

> When a strong acid is added to a weak base, $pK_b = pOH$ at the half equivalence point.

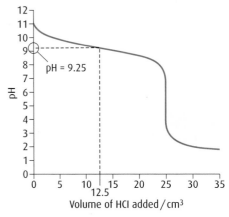

Figure 8.26 pK_b can be obtained from a strong acid–weak base titration curve.

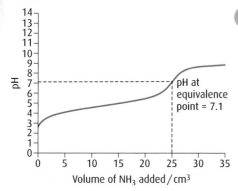

Figure 8.27 A weak acid–weak base titration curve.

The equivalence point of a titration is the point at which equivalent numbers of moles of acid and alkali have been added. The end point of a titration is the point at which the indicator changes colour – these are not necessarily the same.

Both colours are present, but we see the solution as if only one colour were present. Scientific reality is different to our everyday reality.

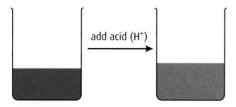

Figure 8.28 The indicator changes from colour II to colour I as acid is added.

HL Titration of a weak acid with a weak base

An example of titration of a weak acid and a weak base is the addition of $0.100 \, mol \, dm^{-3}$ $NH_3(aq)$ to $25.0 \, cm^3$ of $0.100 \, mol \, dm^{-3}$ CH_3COOH (Figure **8.27**).

There is no very steep (almost vertical) part in this titration curve, and the change in pH throughout the experiment is more gradual than in the other experiments we have seen.

The pH at the equivalence point may be less than 7 or greater than 7, depending on the relative strength of the acid and the base. In this case, the ethanoic acid ($K_a = 1.74 \times 10^{-5} \, mol \, dm^{-3}$) is very similar in strength to the ammonia ($K_b = 1.78 \times 10^{-5} \, mol \, dm^{-3}$), and the pH at the equivalence point is very close to 7.0 (it is just slightly greater than 7.0, as the base is very slightly stronger than the acid). If we had used a different acid, such as methanoic acid ($K_a \, 1.78 \times 10^{-4} \, mol \, dm^{-3}$), the pH at the equivalence point would have been less than 7, as the acid is relatively stronger than the base.

Indicators

Acid–base titrations are carried out in order to establish the equivalent amounts of acid and base that react with each other, and hence the concentration of the acid or the alkali. We need some way of determining when equivalent amounts of acid and alkali have been added, and this can be done either using a pH meter and looking for the point of inflection in the titration curve or, more usually and more conveniently, by using an acid–base indicator.

Indicators are usually weak acids and may be represented as HIn. They dissociate according to the equation:

$$HIn(aq) \rightleftharpoons H^+(aq) + In^-(aq)$$
Colour I   Colour II

The ionised (**In⁻**) and un-ionised (**HIn**) forms must have **different colours** for the substance to function as an indicator. In this case, we will take the colours as **red** and **blue**, as shown in the equation.

If we add indicator to a solution and the colour of the indicator is blue, this indicates that the position of the above equilibrium lies mostly to the right, i.e. there is so much more of the blue form than the red form that the solution appears blue to our eyes.

If we now add acid to the solution, the colour of the indicator changes to red (Figure **8.28**).

This can be understood in terms of Le Chatelier's principle. If acid (H^+) is added to the system at equilibrium, the position of equilibrium will shift to the left to use up, as far as possible, the H^+ that has been added. As the position of equilibrium shifts to the left, there is now significantly more HIn (red) than In⁻ (blue) present, and the colour of the indicator appears red.

If we now add some alkali to this solution, the colour changes to blue (Figure **8.29**). When we add alkali, the OH⁻ from the alkali reacts with the H⁺ on the right-hand side of the equilibrium to produce water. The position of equilibrium thus shifts to the right to replace the H⁺ as far as possible and restore the value of K_c.

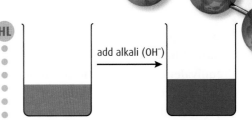

Figure 8.29 The indicator changes colour from colour I to colour II as alkali is added.

The pH range of an indicator

If we imagine a different indicator, for which the colours of the un-ionised and ionised forms are yellow and blue, respectively:

$HIn(aq) \rightleftharpoons H+(aq) + In-(aq)$
Colour I   Colour **II**

Let us consider increasing the pH gradually from 1. We could get the results for the colour of the indicator shown in Figure **8.30**.

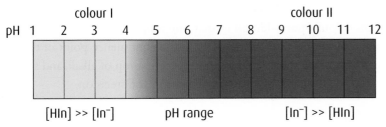

Figure 8.30 The variation of colour with pH for an indicator that is yellow in acidic solutions and blue in alkaline solution.

Up to pH 5 the concentration of HIn (yellow) is so much greater than the concentration of In⁻ (blue) that the indicator appears yellow. From pH 7 onwards, the concentration of In⁻ is so much greater than the concentration of HIn that the colour appears blue. Between pH 5 and 7 the concentrations of HIn and In⁻ are fairly evenly balanced, and the indicator is various shades of green in this region (green is a mixture of yellow and blue). In this region, if we gradually change the pH, we can **see** the indicator changing colour, and this is called the pH range of the indicator. In this case the pH range of the indicator would be quoted as 5–7.

The ranges of various indicators are given in Table **8.9**.

Indicator	pH range	Acid colour	Alkali colour
thymol blue	1.2–2.8	red	yellow
methyl orange	3.1–4.4	red	yellow
bromophenol blue	2.9–4.6	yellow	blue
bromocresol green	3.8–5.4	yellow	blue
methyl red	4.2–6.3	red	yellow
bromothymol blue	6.0–7.6	yellow	blue
phenol red	6.8–8.4	yellow	red
phenolphthalein	8.2–10.0	colourless	red

Table 8.9 The pH ranges and colours of some indicators.

Indicators can be made from natural substances, for example red cabbage and some types of flowers. Litmus is extracted from lichen.

The pH range of an indicator: the pH values between which the indicator can be seen to change colour because comparable amounts of the unionised and ionised forms are present.

Universal indicator solution and pH paper contain a mixture of indicators that change colour over different pH ranges.

The point at which an indicator changes colour in a titration is called the **end point**.

Where possible, the indicator should be chosen so that the equivalence point of the titration occurs within the pH range of the indicator.

HL If an indicator is to be suitable for a titration, we require that one drop of the solution being added from the burette (either the acid or the alkali) should change the indicator from colour I to colour II. An indicator is no good for a titration if it can be seen to change colour gradually. Another way of saying that is that the indicator must be chosen to give a sharp **end point**. In order to have a clear end point for a titration, the range of the indicator must occur completely within the very steep part of the titration curve.

Consider a strong acid–strong base titration, as shown in Figure **8.31**. In the vertical region of the curve, approximately one drop of alkali causes the pH to change by about 6–7 units. Therefore, if an indicator has its range in this part of the curve, adding one drop of alkali will cause the indicator to change colour from the acid colour to the alkali colour.

Let us consider what happens if we use bromothymol blue for this titration. This is a suitable indicator for the titration, as the pH range is entirely within the steep part of the titration curve. Adding one drop of alkali causes the pH to change from about 4 to 10 and the indicator changes colour upon addition of that one drop. A sharp end point is thus obtained in this titration. We know that the equivalence point of the titration occurred somewhere within that one drop of alkali, and so we know the equivalence point to a good degree of precision.

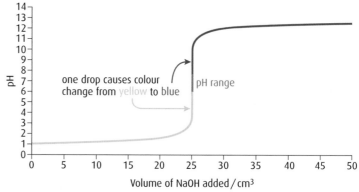

Figure 8.31 The colour changes of bromothymol blue during a strong acid–strong base titration.

If, however, we do the same titration using thymol blue, we get the colour changes shown in Figure **8.32**. The indicator is red in the acid solution, but as we add alkali we see the colour changing gradually from red, through orange to yellow. It would have changed colour to yellow before the equivalence point and so we would not be able to detect the equivalence point using this indicator.

Depending on the concentrations of the solutions used, all the indicators in Table **8.9**, with the exception of thymol blue, could be suitable for a strong acid–strong base titration.

Let us now consider a weak acid–strong base titration, as shown in Figure **8.33**. The pH ranges of various indicators are shown on the curve for a weak acid–strong base titration, and it can be seen that phenolphthalein is the most suitable indicator for this type of titration, with its pH range occurring entirely within the steep part of the curve.

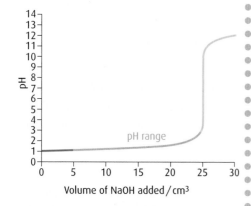

Figure 8.32 The colour changes of thymol blue during a strong acid–strong base titration.

Phenol red is also suitable as an indicator for this titration. Although bromothymol blue is not a suitable indicator for the titration shown, it may be suitable for other weak acid–strong base titrations.

For titrating a strong acid with a weak base, methyl red will generally be the most suitable indicator, but bromocresol green, methyl orange or bromophenol may also be suitable, depending on the weak base used and the concentration of the acid.

Because the change in pH is gradual for titrating a weak acid with a weak base (no very steep part in the curve), it is not generally possible to carry out this titration with an indicator and obtain a good estimate of the equivalence point, as it is difficult to judge the end point of the indicator. The indicator is seen to change colour gradually during the titration.

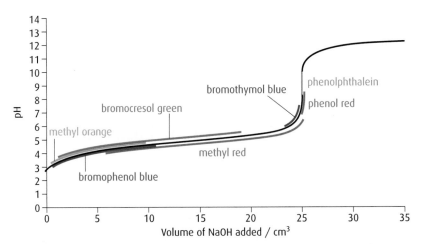

Figure 8.33 The ranges of various indicators superimposed on a weak acid–strong base titration curve.

pK_a for an indicator

Consider the dissociation of the indicator:

$$HIn(aq) \rightleftharpoons H^+(aq) + In^-(aq)$$

The K_a expression for the indicator is:

$$K_a = \frac{[In^-(aq)][H^+(aq)]}{[HIn(aq)]}$$

At the midpoint of the pH range, half of the HIn will have dissociated and the concentrations of HIn and In$^-$ will be equal, i.e. [HIn(aq)] = [In$^-$(aq)].

$$K_a = \frac{[\cancel{In^-(aq)}][H^+(aq)]}{[\cancel{HIn(aq)}]} = [H^+(aq)]$$

Taking $-\log_{10}$ of each side we get: pK_a = pH. Therefore, the pK_a of the indicator is equal to the pH at the midpoint of its pH range. As a rough rule of thumb, we can take the pH range of the indicator to be p$K_a \pm 1$.

HL

As only strong acid–strong base titrations have pH = 7.0 at the end point, it is important to remember that the indicator is being used to determine the point at which equivalent numbers of moles of acid and alkali have been added, and not the point at which pH = 7.

Note: titration using an indicator cannot be used to distinguish between a weak and a strong acid – if they have the same concentration, they will require the same amount of alkali to reach the equivalence point.

pK_a for an indicator is sometimes given the symbol pK_{in}.

This is a theoretical derivation of the pH range of an indicator. In practice, due to our eye's ability to detect various colours and colour changes, the midpoint of the working pH range of an indicator may not correspond exactly to the pK_a of the indicator.

We can now decide the best indicator for a particular titration using the pK_a value for the indicator. The indicator will be suitable if its pK_a value is close to the pH at the equivalence point of the titration.

8.7 Salt hydrolysis

A salt may be formed when an acid reacts with a base:

$$acid + base \rightarrow salt + water$$

$$HNO_3 + NaOH \rightarrow NaNO_3 + H_2O$$

Sodium nitrate is thus the salt of a strong acid (HNO_3) and a strong base (NaOH).

When a solid salt is dissolved in water, the resulting solution may be acidic, basic or neutral, depending on the particular salt used.

Salt of a weak acid and a strong base (pH > 7)

Consider the salt sodium ethanoate ($CH_3COO^-Na^+$), formed when NaOH reacts with ethanoic acid (CH_3COOH):

$$CH_3COOH(aq) + NaOH(aq) \rightarrow CH_3COONa(aq) + H_2O(l)$$

If some solid sodium ethanoate is dissolved in water, the pH will be greater than 7. A $0.500 \, mol \, dm^{-3}$ solution will have a pH of 9.23 (Figure **8.34**).

When the salt dissolves in water, the two ions separate from each other – that is, the solution contains $CH_3COO^-(aq)$ and $Na^+(aq)$ ions.

The CH_3COO^- ion is the conjugate base of ethanoic acid (a weak acid) and so, acting as a base, will react with some water molecules to accept a proton according to the equilibrium:

$$CH_3COO^-(aq) + H_2O(l) \rightleftharpoons CH_3COOH(aq) + OH^-(aq)$$

The concentration of OH^- ions in the solution has thus been increased and the solution is alkaline. This process is called salt hydrolysis – the salt has reacted with water.

The other ion from CH_3COONa present in this solution, the Na^+ ion, is derived from a strong base (NaOH), which is fully ionised. There is therefore no tendency for Na^+ to react with the OH^- ions produced.

$$Na^+(aq) + OH^-(aq) \rightleftharpoons\!\!\!\!\times NaOH(aq)$$

The pH of a $0.500 \, mol \, dm^{-3}$ solution of sodium ethanoate may be calculated as follows.

Learning objectives

- Work out whether a solution of a salt will have a pH of less than, equal to or greater than 7
- Understand that the pH of a solution of a salt will depend on the charge (and size) of the cation

Examiner's tip

A way of **thinking** about this is that the base is stronger than the acid, so the pH will be basic.

The reason given here is the same reason why the pH at the equivalence point in a weak acid–strong base titration is greater than 7.

The pK_a of ethanoic acid is 4.76. pK_b for its conjugate base, the ethanoate ion, is given by:

$$pK_a + pK_b = pK_w$$

Therefore, at 25 °C, $pK_b = 14 - 4.76 = 9.24$. K_b for the ethanoate ion is thus $10^{-9.24}$, i.e. $5.75 \times 10^{-10} \, mol \, dm^{-3}$.

The ethanoate ion reacts with water according to the equation:

$$CH_3COO^-(aq) + H_2O(l) \rightleftharpoons CH_3COOH(aq) + OH^-(aq)$$

The K_b for CH_3COO^- is:

$$K_b = \frac{[CH_3COOH(aq)][OH^-(aq)]}{[CH_3COO^-(aq)]}$$

One CH_3COO^- ion reacts with one H_2O molecule to form one CH_3COOH and one OH^-; therefore:

$$[CH_3COOH(aq)] = [OH^-(aq)]$$

We will use the approximation that the extent to which the CH_3COO^- reacts is negligible compared with its concentration and take $[CH_3COO^-(aq)]$ to be $0.500 \, mol \, dm^{-3}$.

Substituting known values into the K_b expression:

$$5.75 \times 10^{-10} = \frac{[OH^-(aq)]^2}{0.500}$$

$$[OH^-] = 1.70 \times 10^{-5} \, mol \, dm^{-3}$$

$$pOH = -\log_{10}[OH^-(aq)] = -\log_{10} 1.70 \times 10^{-5} = 4.77$$

$$pOH + pH = pK_w$$

At 25 °C, $pOH + pH = 14$, so $pH = 14 - 4.77 = 9.23$. Therefore the pH of a $0.500 \, mol \, dm^{-3}$ solution of sodium ethanoate is 9.23.

Salt of a strong acid and weak base (pH < 7)

Consider ammonium chloride (NH_4Cl). This is the salt of a strong acid (HCl) and a weak base (NH_3):

$$NH_3(aq) + HCl(aq) \rightarrow NH_4Cl(aq)$$

When this is dissolved in water, an acidic solution is formed (Figure **8.35**).

The NH_4^+ is the conjugate acid of the weak base NH_3 and will therefore dissociate according to the equation:

$$NH_4^+(aq) \rightleftharpoons NH_3(aq) + H^+(aq)$$

H^+ is generated, and the solution of NH_4Cl is acidic. The pH of a $0.500 \, mol \, dm^{-3}$ solution of NH_4Cl is 4.78.

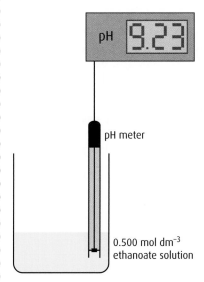

Figure 8.34 A solution of sodium ethanoate will have a pH > 7.

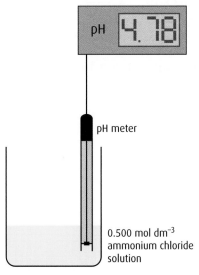

Figure 8.35 The pH of ammonium chloride solution is < 7.

Cl⁻ is the conjugate base of the strong acid, HCl. It is therefore an extremely weak base (the stronger the acid, the weaker the conjugate base). There is thus virtually no tendency for the following reaction to occur:

$$Cl^-(aq) + H_2O(l) \rightleftharpoons HCl(aq) + OH^-(aq)$$

The pH of a solution of ammonium chloride can be worked out using a similar method to that used to work out the pH of a sodium ethanoate solution above.

Worked example

What is the pH of a $0.200\,mol\,dm^{-3}$ solution of ammonium chloride? The pK_b of ammonia is 4.75.

The ammonium ion acts as an acid in the solution according to the equation:

$$NH_4^+(aq) \rightleftharpoons NH_3(aq) + H^+(aq)$$

We can work out pK_a for the ammonium ion from the pK_b value for ammonia.

At 25 °C, $pK_a + pK_b = 14.00$.

$pK_a = 9.25$

$K_a = 10^{-pK_a}$

Therefore K_a for the ammonium ion is given by:

$K_a = 10^{-9.25} = 5.63 \times 10^{-10}\,mol\,dm^{-3}$

$$K_a = \frac{[NH_3(aq)][H^+(aq)]}{[NH_4^+(aq)]}$$

$[NH_3] = [H^+]$, and assuming that the amount of ionisation of NH_4^+ is small compared with its concentration, we get:

$$5.63 \times 10^{-10} = \frac{[H^+(aq)]^2}{0.200}$$

Rearranging this we get:

$[H^+(aq)] = 1.06 \times 10^{-5}\,mol\,dm^{-3}$

$pH = -\log_{10}(1.06 \times 10^{-5}) = 4.97$

Salt of a strong acid and strong base (pH = 7)

Consider sodium chloride, NaCl. This is derived from the strong acid HCl and the strong base NaOH. These are both fully dissociated in aqueous solution, so a solution of NaCl is neutral (pH 7 at 25 °C). There is virtually no tendency for either of these reactions to occur:

$$Na^+(aq) + OH^-(aq) \rightleftharpoons NaOH(aq)$$

$$Cl^-(aq) + H_2O(l) \rightleftharpoons HCl(aq) + OH^-(aq)$$

Salt of a weak acid and a weak base (pH = ?)

Consider ammonium ethanoate [$CH_3COO^-NH_4^+$]. This is the salt of the weak acid (CH_3COOH) and the weak base ($NH_3(aq)$). It is not possible to predict whether the solution is acidic or alkaline without looking at the pK_a values.

When ammonium ethanoate is dissolved in water, CH_3COO^- acts as a base and NH_4^+ acts as an acid:

$$CH_3COO^-(aq) + H_2O(l) \rightleftharpoons CH_3COOH(aq) + OH^-(aq) \qquad pK_b = 9.24$$

$$NH_4^+(aq) \rightleftharpoons NH_3(aq) + H^+(aq) \qquad pK_a = 9.25$$

Because the pK_b value is slightly lower (lower value = stronger) than the pK_a value, the solution will be slightly alkaline. However, the values are very close together, so the pH of a solution of ammonium ethanoate will be very close to 7.0.

A solution of ammonium methanoate would have a pH of less than 7:

$$HCOO^-(aq) + H_2O(l) \rightleftharpoons HCOOH(aq) + OH^-(aq) \qquad pK_b = 10.25$$

$$NH_4^+(aq) \rightleftharpoons NH_3(aq) + H^+(aq) \qquad pK_a = 9.25$$

as pK_a for the ammonium ion (stronger acid) is lower than pK_b for the methanoate ion.

A solution of ethylammonium ethanoate ($C_2H_5NH_3^+CH_3COO^-$) will have a pH greater than 7.

$$CH_3COO^-(aq) + H_2O(l) \rightleftharpoons CH_3COOH(aq) + OH^-(aq) \qquad pK_b = 9.24$$

$$C_2H_5NH_3^+(aq) \rightleftharpoons C_2H_5NH_2(aq) + H^+(aq) \qquad pK_a = 10.73$$

as pK_b is lower (stronger base) than pK_a.

The acidity due to positive ions in solution

Let us consider a solution of iron(III) chloride. A $0.100\,mol\,dm^{-3}$ solution of iron(III) will have a pH of less than 2 (Figure **8.36**).

Positive ions in solution are hydrated to form aqueous ions, e.g. $Fe^{3+}(aq)$. The formula of $Fe^{3+}(aq)$ is $[Fe(H_2O)_6]^{3+}$. This ion dissociates in solution according to the equation:

$$[Fe(H_2O)_6]^{3+}(aq) \rightleftharpoons [Fe(H_2O)_5(OH)]^{2+}(aq) + H^+(aq)$$

Hence the solution is acidic due to the H^+ ions produced.

The reason that this occurs with 3+ ions is because of the high charge density (or charge to radius ratio) of the ion, which causes the water molecule to be sufficiently **polarised** for H^+ to dissociate. The Fe^{3+} ion pulls electrons away from the H_2O molecules, which increases the $\delta+$ charge on the H so that it is more readily lost as H^+ (Figure **8.37**).

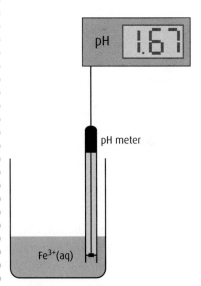

Figure 8.36 A solution containing a 3+ ion has a pH < 7.

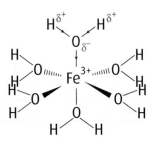

Figure 8.37 The polarisation of one of the water ligands in [$Fe(H_2O)_6$]$^{3+}$.

The effect of charge on the metal ion on the pH of a solution

The higher the charge and the smaller the radius, the greater the charge density.

The larger an ion is and the lower the charge, then the smaller the charge density of the ion and the lower its tendency to polarise water molecules. Na^+ is relatively large and only has a 1+ charge so causes essentially no polarisation of water, and the pH of a solution will be 7. Mg^{2+} causes a small amount of polarisation, as it is more highly charged and smaller than Na^+. Al^{3+} is the smallest ion and the most highly charged; therefore it causes the greatest amount of polarisation of water.

Examiner's tip
All 3+ ions in solution are acidic. This seems to come up a lot in questions and should be remembered.

> Ions with a greater charge density cause more polarisation of water, resulting in a more acidic solution.

Ion	Na^+(aq)	Mg^{2+}(aq)	Al^{3+}(aq)
charge	+1	+2	+3
ionic radius / 10^{-12} m	98	65	45
approximate pH of a 0.100 mol dm^{-3} solution	7.0	6.2	3.0

increasing charge density →

Self-test 8

Test yourself

26 Predict whether the pH of each of the following solutions will be equal to 7, greater than 7 or less than 7.

	pH
0.100 mol dm^{-3} $CH_3CH_2CH_2CH_2COONa$	
0.500 mol dm^{-3} KNO_3	
0.100 mol dm^{-3} Na_2CO_3	
0.100 mol dm^{-3} $CH_3CH_2NH_3^+Cl^-$	
0.200 mol dm^{-3} $CrCl_3$	

27 Select a suitable indicator, from the list given, for each of the following titrations in which the alkali is added to 25.0 cm^3 of acid.
phenolphthalein $pK_a = 9.3$
bromocresol green $pK_a = 4.7$
bromothymol blue $pK_a = 7.0$
thymol blue $pK_a = 1.7$

Acid	Alkali	Indicator
0.100 mol dm^{-3} CH_3COOH	0.100 mol dm^{-3} NaOH	
0.010 mol dm^{-3} HNO_3	0.020 mol dm^{-3} KOH	
0.010 mol dm^{-3} HCl	0.010 mol dm^{-3} NH_3	

28 Consider adding 0.0100 mol dm^{-3} sodium hydroxide solution to 25.0 cm^3 of 0.0200 mol dm^{-3} ethanoic acid ($pK_a = 4.76$). Suggest values for the following important points on the titration curve.

initial pH	
volume of NaOH required to reach the equivalence point	
approximate pH at equivalence point	
approximate final pH (after approximately 200 cm^3 of NaOH has been added)	

29 Calculate pH values for the following salt solutions:
a a 0.100 mol dm^{-3} solution of potassium cyanide (KCN), given that pK_a for hydrocyanic acid (HCN) is 9.40
b a 0.200 mol dm^{-3} solution of sodium propanoate (CH_3CH_2COONa), given that the pK_a for propanoic acid is 4.87

30 In the titration of 20.0 cm^3 of a 0.100 mol dm^{-3} solution of a weak acid, HA, with 0.100 mol dm^{-3} sodium hydroxide solution, the pH when 10.0 cm^3 of NaOH had been added was 4.80 and the pH when 20.0 cm^3 of NaOH had been added was 8.80. What is the value of pK_a for HA?

8.8 Buffer solutions

HL

Buffer solutions

The blue line on the graph in Figure **8.38** shows the result of adding $10\,cm^3$ of $0.100\,mol\,dm^{-3}$ hydrochloric acid in stages to $100\,cm^3$ of water.

The orange line shows the effect of adding the hydrochloric acid to $100\,cm^3$ of buffer solution formed by mixing $50\,cm^3$ of $1.00\,mol\,dm^{-3}$ ethanoic acid and $50\,cm^3$ of $0.100\,mol\,dm^{-3}$ sodium ethanoate. The pH of the water changes from 7.00 to 2.04 when $10\,cm^3$ of hydrochloric acid is added. The pH of the buffer solution changes from 4.76 to 4.74. When $10\,cm^3$ of $0.100\,mol\,dm^{-3}$ sodium hydroxide is added to $100\,cm^3$ of the ethanoic acid/sodium ethanoate buffer solution, the pH changes from 4.76 to 4.78. The pH of the buffer solution remains virtually constant when acid and alkali are added, which leads to the definition of a buffer solution as:

> a solution that resists changes in pH when **small amounts** of acid or alkali are added.

The 'small amount' in this definition is important. If, for instance, $33.3\,cm^3$ of $2.00\,mol\,dm^{-3}$ hydrochloric acid is added to $100\,cm^3$ of the ethanoic acid/sodium ethanoate buffer solution we have just considered, the pH will change by about 4.5 units!

A buffer solution consists of two components and must always contain something to react with any acid added and something to react with any base added. In other words, a buffer solution always contains an acid and a base.

Buffers are important in many industrial processes and biological systems (for example, the blood – the pH of blood is about 7.4, and if it changes by about 0.5 in either direction you would die!). They also crop up in products such as contact lens solutions, cosmetics and shampoos.

Acid buffer solution

An acid buffer solution consists of a weak acid (e.g. ethanoic acid) and the salt of that weak acid (e.g. sodium ethanoate). The equilibrium that exists in this solution is:

$$CH_3COOH(aq) \rightleftharpoons CH_3COO^-(aq) + H^+(aq)$$

If some hydrochloric acid is added to this solution, the extra H^+ added reacts with the CH_3COO^- in the solution:

$$CH_3COO^-(aq) + H^+(aq) \rightarrow CH_3COOH(aq)$$

If some sodium hydroxide is added to the solution, the extra OH^- added reacts with the CH_3COOH in the solution:

$$CH_3COOH(aq) + OH^-(aq) \rightarrow CH_3COO^-(aq) + H_2O(l)$$

Learning objectives

- Understand what is meant by a buffer solution and how both acidic and basic buffers can be made
- Describe how a buffer solution works when small amounts of acid/alkali are added
- Work out the pH of a buffer solution given its composition, and vice versa

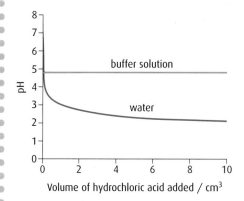

Figure 8.38 The pH of a buffer solution changes very little when hydrochloric acid is added. Water is not a good buffer.

The H^+ added is 'mopped up' by reaction with the ethanoate ion (a base).

The OH^- added is 'mopped up' by reaction with the ethanoic acid.

If we consider the expression for K_a we can understand why the pH changes so little:

$$K_a = \frac{[CH_3COO^-(aq)][H^+(aq)]}{[CH_3COOH(aq)]}$$

This can be rearranged as:

$$[H^+(aq)] = \frac{[CH_3COOH(aq)] \times K_a}{[CH_3COO^-(aq)]}$$

As K_a is a constant, this means that the H^+ concentration in the solution is proportional to the ratio between the ethanoic acid concentration and the ethanoate ion concentration.

For the solution to function as a buffer, both $[CH_3COO^-(aq)]$ and $[CH_3COOH(aq)]$ must be large so that any changes in their concentration that occur when acid or alkali are added are small compared with these concentrations. This means that the value of the ratio $([CH_3COOH(aq)]:[CH_3COO^-(aq)])$ changes very little and the $[H^+(aq)]$ (and thus pH) changes very little.

Let us consider a buffer solution in which the concentration of ethanoic acid and sodium ethanoate are both $0.500\,mol\,dm^{-3}$. If we take $100.0\,cm^3$ of this solution, the number of moles of CH_3COOH and CH_3COO^- are given by:

$$no.\ moles = concentration \times volume\ (in\ dm^3)$$

$$no.\ moles\ of\ CH_3COOH = no.\ moles\ of\ CH_3COO^-$$

$$= 0.500 \times \frac{100.0}{1000} = 0.0500\,mol$$

If $1.00\,cm^3$ of $0.100\,mol\,dm^{-3}$ HCl is added to this solution:

$$no.\ moles\ of\ HCl = 0.100 \times \frac{1.00}{1000} = 1.00 \times 10^{-4}\,mol$$

The HCl will react with the ethanoate ion:

$$CH_3COO^-(aq) + H^+(aq) \rightleftharpoons CH_3COOH(aq)$$

	CH_3COO^-	CH_3COOH
initial no. moles / mol	0.0500	0.0500
no. moles after HCl added / mol	$0.0500 - 1.00 \times 10^{-4}$	$0.0500 + 1.00 \times 10^{-4}$
i.e.	0.0499	0.0501

The concentrations after the HCl has been added may be worked out by dividing the number of moles by the new volume ($100\,cm^3 + 1\,cm^3 = 101\,cm^3 = 0.101\,dm^3$)

$$CH_3COO^-(aq) + H^+(aq) \rightleftharpoons CH_3COOH(aq)$$

	CH_3COO^-	CH_3COOH
concentration after HCl added / mol dm^{-3}	0.494	0.496

We can now compare the ratio $\frac{[CH_3COOH(aq)]}{[CH_3COO^-(aq)]}$ before and after adding the HCl:

	$\dfrac{[CH_3COOH(aq)]}{[CH_3COO^-(aq)]}$	K_a / mol dm^{-3}	$\dfrac{[CH_3COOH(aq)]\ K_a}{[CH_3COO^-(aq)]}$	$[H^+(aq)]$ / mol dm^{-3}	pH
Before adding HCl	1.000	1.738×10^{-5}	1.738×10^{-5}	1.738×10^{-5}	4.760
After adding HCl	1.004	1.738×10^{-5}	1.745×10^{-5}	1.745×10^{-5}	4.758

It can thus be seen that as the concentrations of both CH_3COOH and CH_3COO^- are large compared with the amount of acid added, the addition of a small amount of HCl hardly changes the $[CH_3COOH(aq)] : [CH_3COO^-(aq)]$ ratio at all, and, to three significant figures, the pH has not changed.

If we do the same calculation but with adding the hydrochloric acid to a solution of 0.500 mol dm^{-3} ethanoic acid (i.e. no ethanoate present).

$$CH_3COOH(aq) \rightleftharpoons CH_3COO^-(aq) + H^+(aq)$$

initial equilibrium concentration / mol dm^{-3} 0.497 2.94×10^{-3} 2.94×10^{-3}
concentration after HCl added / mol dm^{-3} 0.493 1.92×10^{-3}

	$\dfrac{[CH_3COOH(aq)]}{[CH_3COO^-(aq)]}$	K_a / mol dm^{-3}	$\dfrac{[CH_3COOH(aq)]\ K_a}{[CH_3COO^-(aq)]}$	$[H^+(aq)]$ / mol dm^{-3}	pH
Before adding HCl	169	1.738×10^{-5}	2.93×10^{-3}	2.93×10^{-3}	2.53
After adding HCl	257	1.738×10^{-5}	4.47×10^{-3}	4.47×10^{-3}	2.35

In this case, for the same addition of HCl, the pH has changed by almost 100 times as much. This is because the initial concentration of the ethanoate ion was so small that any small change in concentration causes a significant percentage change in its concentration, and hence in the value of the ratio $\dfrac{[CH_3COOH(aq)]}{[CH_3COO^-(aq)]}$ and therefore in the pH.

A basic buffer solution

A basic buffer solution consists of a weak base (e.g. ammonia) and the salt of that weak base (e.g. ammonium chloride). The equilibrium that exists in this solution is:

$$NH_3(aq) + H_2O(l) \rightleftharpoons NH_4^+(aq) + OH^-(aq)$$

If some hydrochloric acid is added to this solution, the extra H^+ added reacts with the NH_3 in the solution:

$$NH_3(aq) + H^+(aq) \rightarrow NH_4^+(aq)$$

If some sodium hydroxide is added to the solution, the extra OH^- added reacts with the NH_4^+ in the solution:

$$NH_4^+(aq) + OH^-(aq) \rightarrow NH_3(aq) + H_2O(l)$$

As above, because the concentrations of NH_3 and NH_4^+ in the solution are both high, any small changes in their concentrations have very little effect on the $[NH_4^+(aq)] : [NH_3(aq)]$ ratio in the K_b expression.

The H^+ added is 'mopped up' by reaction with the ammonia.

The OH^- added is 'mopped up' by reaction with the ammonium ion.

$$\text{HL} \quad K_b = \frac{[NH_4^+(aq)][OH^-(aq)]}{[NH_3(aq)]}$$

The value of the OH^- concentration and hence the pH therefore change very little.

How to calculate the pH of a buffer solution

Worked example

Calculate the pH of a solution containing $0.200\,mol\,dm^{-3}$ ethanoic acid ($K_a = 1.74 \times 10^{-5}\,mol\,dm^{-3}$) and $0.250\,mol\,dm^{-3}$ sodium ethanoate.

The equilibrium that exists in this solution is:

$$CH_3COOH(aq) \rightleftharpoons CH_3COO^-(aq) + H^+(aq)$$

K_a for this equilibrium is given by:

$$K_a = \frac{[CH_3COO^-(aq)][H^+(aq)]}{[CH_3COOH(aq)]}$$

Sodium ethanoate is a salt and therefore breaks apart completely into its ions in aqueous solution. The concentration of ethanoate ions is therefore the same as that of sodium ethanoate.

We will make the approximation that the equilibrium concentrations of ethanoic acid and the ethanoate ion are the same as their initial concentrations. This is a reasonable assumption, as the dissociation of ethanoic acid in pure water is very low, and therefore the dissociation is going to be even lower if some CH_3COO^- is already present (Le Chatelier's principle – the position of dissociation equilibrium shifts to the left if CH_3COO^- is added).

We can therefore substitute values into the K_a expression:

$$1.74 \times 10^{-5} = \frac{(0.250)[H^+(aq)]}{(0.200)}$$

Rearranging this we get:

$$[H^+(aq)] = 1.39 \times 10^{-5}\,mol\,dm^{-3}$$

$$pH = -\log_{10}[H^+(aq)] = -\log_{10}(1.39 \times 10^{-5}) = 4.86$$

Therefore the pH of this buffer solution is 4.86.

The Henderson–Hasselbalch equation

Examiner's tip

The equation is a quick and easy way of solving problems involving buffers but must be remembered correctly!

The pH of a buffer can also be worked out by using the Henderson–Hasselbalch equation:

$$pH = pK_a + \log_{10}\frac{[salt]}{[acid]}$$

Worked example

Calculate the pH of a buffer solution containing $0.550\,mol\,dm^{-3}$ propanoic acid and $0.450\,mol\,dm^{-3}$ sodium propanoate. The pK_a for propanoic acid is 4.87.

$[\text{salt}] = 0.450\,\text{mol}\,\text{dm}^{-3}$

$[\text{acid}] = 0.550\,\text{mol}\,\text{dm}^{-3}$

$$\text{pH} = \text{p}K_a + \log_{10}\frac{[\text{salt}]}{[\text{acid}]}$$

$$\text{pH} = 4.87 + \log_{10}\left(\frac{0.450}{0.550}\right) = 4.87 - 0.0872 = 4.78$$

Therefore the pH of this buffer solution is 4.78.

Calculating the pH of a basic buffer solution

Worked example

Calculate the pH of a solution containing $0.400\,\text{mol}\,\text{dm}^{-3}$ ammonia ($\text{p}K_b = 4.75$) and $0.200\,\text{mol}\,\text{dm}^{-3}$ ammonium chloride.

$$K_b = 10^{-4.75} = 1.78 \times 10^{-5}\,\text{mol}\,\text{dm}^{-3}$$

The expression for the ionisation is:

$$NH_3(aq) + H_2O(l) \rightleftharpoons NH_4^+(aq) + OH^-(aq)$$

$$K_b = \frac{[NH_4^+(aq)][OH^-(aq)]}{[NH_3(aq)]}$$

Again, making the approximation that the degree of ionisation is negligible compared with the original concentrations of the base and the salt, we can put values into the K_b expression:

$$1.78 \times 10^{-5} = \frac{(0.200)[OH^-(aq)]}{(0.400)}$$

$$[OH^-(aq)] = 3.56 \times 10^{-5}\,\text{mol}\,\text{dm}^{-3}$$

$$\text{pOH} = -\log_{10}[OH^-(aq)] = 4.45$$

At $25\,^\circ\text{C}$, $\text{pH} + \text{pOH} = 14$, i.e. $\text{pH} = 9.55$.

This can also be worked out using an equation similar to the Henderson–Hasselbalch equation:

$$\text{pOH} = \text{p}K_b + \log_{10}\frac{[\text{salt}]}{[\text{base}]}$$

or

$$\text{pH} = \text{p}K_w - \text{p}K_b - \log_{10}\frac{[\text{salt}]}{[\text{base}]}$$

or

$$\text{pH} = \text{p}K_w - \text{p}K_b + \log_{10}\frac{[\text{base}]}{[\text{salt}]}$$

Worked example

A buffer solution is formed when $30.0\,cm^3$ of $1.00\,mol\,dm^{-3}$ ethanoic acid is added to $40.0\,cm^3$ of $1.10\,mol\,dm^{-3}$ sodium ethanoate.

The total volume of the solution is $70.0\,cm^3$. As the same number of moles of ethanoic acid are now present in $70.0\,cm^3$ instead of $30.0\,cm^3$, the concentration of the ethanoic acid has decreased by a factor of $\frac{30}{70}$.

The concentration of ethanoic acid in this solution will be:

$\frac{30.0}{70.0} \times 1.00$, i.e. $0.429\,mol\,dm^{-3}$

The concentration of sodium ethanoate in this solution will be:

$\frac{40.0}{70.0} \times 1.10 = 0.629\,mol\,dm^{-3}$

The rest of the process for working out the pH of the buffer is exactly the same as above, i.e.

$CH_3COOH(aq) \rightleftharpoons CH_3COO^-(aq) + H^+(aq)$

$K_a = \dfrac{[CH_3COO^-(aq)][H^+(aq)]}{[CH_3COOH(aq)]}$

$1.74 \times 10^{-5} = \dfrac{(0.629)\,[H^+(aq)]}{(0.429)}$

Rearranging this we get:

$[H^+(aq)] = 1.19 \times 10^{-5}\,mol\,dm^{-3}$

$pH = -\log_{10}[H^+(aq)] = -\log_{10}(1.19 \times 10^{-5}) = 4.93$

Therefore the pH of this buffer solution is 4.93.

This can also be worked out by calculating the number of moles of ethanoic acid in $30.0\,cm^3$:

$\frac{30.0}{1000} \times 1.00 = 0.0300\,mol$

So the concentration of the ethanoic acid in the buffer solution is:

$\frac{(0.0300)}{(70/1000)} = 0.429\,mol\,dm^{-3}$

Determining the composition of a buffer solution given its pH

Worked examples

Determine the ratio of the concentration of ammonium chloride to ammonia in a buffer of pH 9.00 at 25 °C. The K_b for ammonia is $1.78 \times 10^{-5}\,mol\,dm^{-3}$.

The expression for the ionisation is:

$NH_3(aq) + H_2O(l) \rightleftharpoons NH_4^+(aq) + OH^-(aq)$

$K_b = \dfrac{[NH_4^+(aq)][OH^-(aq)]}{[NH_3(aq)]}$

pH = 9.00, so at 25 °C, pOH = 14.00 − 9.00 = 5.00.

$[OH^-(aq)] = 10^{-pOH}$, so $[OH^-(aq)] = 1.00 \times 10^{-5}\,mol\,dm^{-3}$.

Substituting this into the expression for K_b we get:

$$1.78 \times 10^{-5} = \frac{[NH_4^+(aq)][1.00 \times 10^{-5}]}{[NH_3(aq)]}$$

Rearranging this we get:

$$\frac{1.78 \times 10^{-5}}{1.00 \times 10^{-5}} = \frac{[NH_4^+(aq)]}{[NH_3(aq)]}$$

$$\frac{[NH_4^+(aq)]}{[NH_3(aq)]} = 1.78$$

Therefore, in order to produce a buffer of pH 9.00, the ratio of the ammonium chloride concentration to the ammonia concentration must be 1.78 : 1.00.

This calculation could have been carried out more rapidly using the equation:

$$pH = pK_w - pK_b - \log_{10}\frac{[salt]}{[base]}$$

What mass of solid sodium ethanoate must be added to $100.0\,cm^3$ of $0.200\,mol\,dm^{-3}$ ethanoic acid to produce a buffer of pH = 4.00? Assume there is no change in volume when the sodium ethanoate is added. The pK_a for ethanoic acid is 4.76.

We will use the equation:

$$pH = pK_a + \log_{10}\frac{[salt]}{[acid]}$$

Substituting in the values for pH and pK_a we get:

$$4.00 = 4.76 + \log_{10}\frac{[CH_3COONa(aq)]}{[CH_3COOH(aq)]}$$

$$-0.76 = \log_{10}\frac{[CH_3COONa(aq)]}{[CH_3COOH(aq)]}$$

$$10^{-0.76} = \frac{[CH_3COONa(aq)]}{[CH_3COOH(aq)]}$$

$$0.174 = \frac{[CH_3COONa(aq)]}{[CH_3COOH(aq)]}$$

The concentration of ethanoic acid is $0.200\,mol\,dm^{-3}$. Substituting this into the above equation we get:

$$0.174 = \frac{[CH_3COONa(aq)]}{0.200}$$

$$[CH_3COONa(aq)] = 0.0348\,mol\,dm^{-3}$$

The concentration of the sodium ethanoate in the solution must be $0.0348\,mol\,dm^{-3}$ but, as we are making up $100\,cm^3$ of buffer solution, the number of moles of sodium ethanoate that must be used is given by:

no. moles = concentration × volume (in dm^3)

no. moles = $0.0348 \times \dfrac{100.0}{1000} = 0.003\,48\,mol$

The molar mass of sodium ethanoate is $82.04\,g\,mol^{-1}$. Therefore the mass of $0.003\,48\,mol$ is given by:

mass = no. moles × molar mass

mass = $0.003\,48 \times 82.04 = 0.285\,g$

Therefore $0.285\,g$ of sodium ethanoate must be dissolved in the ethanoic acid to produce a buffer of pH = 4.00.

Calculating the change in pH of a buffer solution when acid or alkali are added

Worked example

a Calculate the pH of a buffer solution containing $0.750\,mol\,dm^{-3}$ ethanoic acid ($pK_a = 4.76$) and $0.750\,mol\,dm^{-3}$ sodium ethanoate.

b What is the pH of the solution formed when $10.0\,cm^3$ of $0.100\,mol\,dm^{-3}$ hydrochloric acid is added to $50.0\,cm^3$ of the buffer solution in **a**?

a [salt] = $0.750\,mol\,dm^{-3}$
   [acid] = $0.750\,mol\,dm^{-3}$

$pH = pK_a + \log_{10} \dfrac{[salt]}{[acid]}$

$pH = 4.76 + \log_{10}\left(\dfrac{0.750}{0.750}\right) = 4.76$

Examiner's tip
When [salt] = [acid], the pH of the buffer is equal to the pK_a of the acid.

b When acid is added to the buffer, the following reaction occurs:

$CH_3COO^-(aq) + H^+(aq) \rightarrow CH_3COOH(aq)$

This means that the concentration of the ethanoate ion decreases and the concentration of ethanoic acid increases. In order to work out by how much they change we need to work out the initial number of moles of CH_3COO^- and CH_3COOH and how many moles of acid were added.

The number of moles of ethanoic acid in $50.0\,cm^3$ of $0.750\,mol\,dm^{-3}$ solution is given by:

no. moles = concentration × volume in dm^3

no. moles = $0.750 \times \dfrac{50.0}{1000} = 0.0375\,mol$

This is the same as the number of moles of ethanoate ion.

The number of moles of hydrochloric acid in $10.0 \, cm^3$ of $0.100 \, mol \, dm^{-3}$ solution is:

$$\text{no. moles} = 0.100 \times \frac{10.0}{1000} = 1.00 \times 10^{-3} \, mol$$

We will assume that the H^+ from the hydrochloric acid reacts with the equivalent amount of CH_3COO^- and that there is no further change in the number of moles as equilibrium is established.

The number of moles of CH_3COO^- thus decreases by $1.00 \times 10^{-3} \, mol$ and the number of moles of CH_3COOH increases by $1.00 \times 10^{-3} \, mol$.

	$CH_3COO^-(aq)$	$+ H^+(aq) \rightarrow CH_3COOH(aq)$
initial no. moles / mol	0.0375	0.0375
no. moles after HCl added / mol	$0.0375 - 1.00 \times 10^{-3}$	$0.0375 + 1.00 \times 10^{-3}$
i.e.	0.0365	0.0385

The concentration of each species can now be worked out by dividing the number of moles by the total volume in dm^3.

$$\text{total volume} = 50.0 + 10.0 = 60.0 \, cm^3 = 0.0600 \, dm^3$$

	$CH_3COO^-(aq) + H^+(aq) \rightarrow CH_3COOH(aq)$	
concentration after HCl added / mol dm^{-3}	$\dfrac{0.0365}{0.0600}$	$\dfrac{0.0385}{0.0600}$
concentration / mol dm^{-3}	0.608	0.642

$$pH = pK_a + \log_{10} \frac{[\text{salt}]}{[\text{acid}]}$$

$$pH = 4.76 + \log_{10} \left(\frac{0.608}{0.642} \right) = 4.74$$

Therefore, upon addition of $10.0 \, cm^3$ of the hydrochloric acid the pH of the solution drops by 0.02 to 4.74.

Buffers and titration

The graph in Figure **8.39** shows the titration curve of a weak acid (ethanoic acid) with a strong base (NaOH).

The shaded region in Figure **8.39** represents where this solution acts as buffer. In this region adding sodium hydroxide is not causing the pH to change very much and addition of $20 \, cm^3$ of NaOH in this region only causes the pH to change by about 1.5 units. Although this seems to be a much more significant increase than we have seen above, it must be remembered here that we are adding sodium hydroxide of the same concentration as the ethanoic acid to a similar volume of solution (i.e. we are not just adding **small** amounts).

Let us consider how this solution can act as a buffer. The reaction that occurs when sodium hydroxide is added to ethanoic acid is:

$$CH_3COOH(aq) + NaOH(aq) \rightarrow CH_3COONa(aq) + H_2O$$

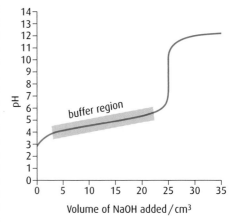

Figure 8.39 The buffering region in a weak acid–strong base titration curve.

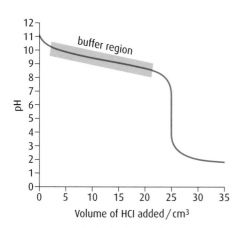

When 10 cm³ of 0.100 mol dm⁻³ NaOH is added to 25 cm³ of 0.100 mol dm⁻³ CH₃COOH some of the ethanoic acid will be converted to sodium ethanoate but there will still be some ethanoic acid left. The solution thus contains both ethanoic acid and sodium ethanoate, which are the components of a buffer.

As long as the number of moles of sodium hydroxide added is fewer than the number of moles of ethanoic acid present in the original solution, the solution will contain both ethanoic acid and sodium ethanoate and act as a buffer.

The same effect is seen in a strong acid–weak base titration. The titration curve for adding 0.100 mol dm⁻³ HCl to 25 cm³ of 0.100 mol dm⁻³ ammonia solution is shown in Figure **8.40**. The reaction that occurs is:

$$NH_3(aq) + HCl(aq) \rightarrow NH_4Cl(aq)$$

If HCl is added to ammonia solution, as long as the number of moles of hydrochloric acid is lower than the number of moles of ammonia in the solution, the solution will contain some NH_3 and some NH_4Cl and will act as a buffer.

pH

Volume of HCl added / cm³

Figure 8.40 The buffering region in a strong acid–weak base titration curve.

Self-tests 9 & 10; Applications 2 & 3

Test yourself

31 State whether each of the following mixtures would constitute a buffer solution?
  a 50 cm³ 0.100 mol dm⁻³ CH₃CH₂COOH(aq) and
  25 cm³ 0.100 mol dm⁻³ CH₃CH₂COONa(aq)
  b 50 cm³ 0.100 mol dm⁻³ CH₃CH₂COOH(aq) and
  25 cm³ 0.100 mol dm⁻³ HCOONa(aq)
  c 50 cm³ 0.100 mol dm⁻³ HCOOH(aq) and
  75 cm³ 0.100 mol dm⁻³ HCOONa(aq)
  d 25 cm³ 0.010 mol dm⁻³ NaOH(aq) and
  25 cm³ 0.020 mol dm⁻³ CH₃COOH(aq)
  e 50 cm³ 0.200 mol dm⁻³ HCl(aq) and
  25 cm³ 0.400 mol dm⁻³ NaCl(aq)
  f 50 cm³ 0.100 mol dm⁻³ NH₃(aq) and
  50 cm³ 0.100 mol dm⁻³ NH₄NO₃(aq)
  g 50 cm³ 0.100 mol dm⁻³ NH₃(aq) and
  25 cm³ 0.100 mol dm⁻³ HCl(aq)

32 Calculate the pH values for the following buffer solutions:
  a a solution containing 0.0200 mol dm⁻³ butanoic acid (pK_a = 4.82) and 0.0200 mol dm⁻³ sodium butanoate
  b a solution containing 0.0500 mol dm⁻³ propanoic acid (pK_a = 4.87) and 0.0200 mol dm⁻³ sodium propanoate
  c a solution containing 0.300 mol dm⁻³ ethanoic acid (pK_a = 4.76) and 0.500 mol dm⁻³ sodium ethanoate
  d a solution made up by mixing together 25.0 cm³ of 0.200 mol dm⁻³ ethanoic acid (pK_a = 4.76) and 50 cm³ of 0.100 mol dm⁻³ sodium ethanoate
  e a solution obtained when 10.0 cm³ of 0.100 mol dm⁻³ sodium hydroxide is added to 20.0 cm³ of 0.100 mol dm⁻³ ethanoic acid (pK_a = 4.76)
  f a solution obtained when 20.0 cm³ of 0.100 mol dm⁻³ ammonia solution (pK_b = 4.75) is added to 40.0 cm³ of 0.100 mol dm⁻³ ammonium chloride solution

33 a A buffer solution contains ethanoic acid (pK_a = 4.76) at a concentration of $1.00\,mol\,dm^{-3}$ and sodium ethanoate. If the pH of the buffer solution is 4.20, what is the concentration of the sodium ethanoate?

b $20.0\,cm^3$ of $0.0100\,mol\,dm^{-3}$ hydrochloric acid is added to $50\,cm^3$ of the buffer solution in part **a**. Calculate the new pH of the buffer solution.

34 What mass of solid sodium propanoate must be added to $50.0\,cm^3$ of $0.100\,mol\,dm^{-3}$ propanoic acid (pK_a= 4.87) to produce a buffer of pH = 5.00? Assume there is no change in volume when the sodium propanoate is added.

Exam-style questions

1 According to the Lewis definition, an acid is:

    A a proton donor

    B an electron pair donor

    C an electron acceptor

    D an electron pair acceptor

2 Consider the dissociation of carbonic acid in aqueous solution:

$$H_2CO_3 + H_2O \rightarrow HCO_3^- + H_3O^+ \qquad \textbf{equation 1}$$

$$HCO_3^- + H_2O \rightarrow CO_3^{2-} + H_3O^+ \qquad \textbf{equation 2}$$

Which of the following is correct?

    A HCO_3^- acts as an acid in equation 1 but as a base in equation 2

    B HCO_3^- is the conjugate base of H_2O

    C HCO_3^- is the conjugate acid of CO_3^{2-}

    D H_2CO_3 and CO_3^{2-} are a conjugate acid–base pair

3 The pH of a solution of $0.0100\,mol\,dm^{-3}$ hydrochloric acid is 2; $10\,cm^3$ of the acid is measured out and distilled water added to dilute it to a total volume of $100\,cm^3$. How do the hydrogen ion concentration and the pH change as this solution is diluted?

	hydrogen ion concentration	pH
A	decreases by a factor of 10	increases by 1
B	decreases by a factor of 100	decreases by 2
C	increases by a factor of 10	increases by 1
D	decreases by a factor of 10	decreases by 1

4 The electrical conductivity of five aqueous solutions is measured:

> **I** $0.100 \, \text{mol} \, \text{dm}^{-3}$ NaOH(aq)
> **II** $0.100 \, \text{mol} \, \text{dm}^{-3}$ CH_3COOH(aq)
> **III** $0.100 \, \text{mol} \, \text{dm}^{-3}$ NH_4Cl(aq)
> **IV** $0.100 \, \text{mol} \, \text{dm}^{-3}$ NH_3(aq)
> **V** $0.100 \, \text{mol} \, \text{dm}^{-3}$ HCl(aq)

Which of the following is correct?

> **A**   The conductivity of **I** is higher than that of **II** but lower than that of **IV**.
> **B**   The conductivity of **III** is higher than that of **II** and higher than that of **IV**.
> **C**   The conductivity of **V** is lower than that of **II** but higher than that of **III**.
> **D**   The conductivity of **I** is lower than that of **III** and lower than that of **IV**.

5 HCN is a weak acid and dissociates in water according to the following equilibrium:

$$HCN(aq) + H_2O(l) \rightleftharpoons H_3O^+(aq) + CN^-(aq)$$

Which of the following statements is correct?

> **A**   HCN dissociates completely in solution.
> **B**   The concentration of CN^- ions is greater than that of HCN.
> **C** CN^- is a stronger base than H_2O.
> **D** H_3O^+ acts as a Brønsted–Lowry base.

HL 6 What is the pH of a $1.00 \times 10^{-5} \, \text{mol} \, \text{dm}^{-3}$ solution of sodium hydroxide?

> **A** 5   **B** 9   **C** 13   **D** 14

7 The acid HA has a K_a value of $1.00 \times 10^{-7} \, \text{mol} \, \text{dm}^{-3}$. What is the pH of a $0.100 \, \text{mol} \, \text{dm}^{-3}$ solution of HA?

> **A** 7   **B** 4   **C** 8   **D** 3

8 The following salts are dissolved in water:

> **I**   NaCl
> **II** CH_3COONa
> **III** Na_2CO_3
> **IV** $FeCl_3$

Which of these solutions will have a pH greater than 7?

> **A** **I** and **IV** only   **C** **IV** only
> **B** **II** and **III** only   **D** **II** only

9 A series of solutions are made up:

> **I** $50 \, \text{cm}^3$ $0.100 \, \text{mol} \, \text{dm}^{-3}$ CH_3COOH and $25 \, \text{cm}^3$ $0.100 \, \text{mol} \, \text{dm}^{-3}$ NaOH
> **II** $50 \, \text{cm}^3$ $0.050 \, \text{mol} \, \text{dm}^{-3}$ CH_3COOH and $25 \, \text{cm}^3$ $0.100 \, \text{mol} \, \text{dm}^{-3}$ NaOH
> **III** $25 \, \text{cm}^3$ $0.100 \, \text{mol} \, \text{dm}^{-3}$ CH_3COOH and $50 \, \text{cm}^3$ $0.100 \, \text{mol} \, \text{dm}^{-3}$ NaOH
> **IV** $25 \, \text{cm}^3$ $0.100 \, \text{mol} \, \text{dm}^{-3}$ CH_3COOH and $50 \, \text{cm}^3$ $0.100 \, \text{mol} \, \text{dm}^{-3}$ CH_3COONa

Which solution(s) is/are buffer solutions?

    A **I** and **IV** only

    B **III** and **IV** only

    C **II**, **III** and **IV** only

    D **I** and **II** only

10 The pK_a values for four indicators are shown here.

Indicator	pK_a
thymol blue	1.7
bromocresol green	4.7
phenol red	7.9
phenolphthalein	9.3

Which indicator would be most suitable for a titration in which $0.0100\,mol\,dm^{-3}$ ammonia is added gradually to $25.00\,cm^3$ of $0.0100\,mol\,dm^{-3}$ hydrochloric acid?

    A thymol blue

    B bromocresol green

    C phenol red

    D phenolphthalein

11 Ethanoic acid is a weak acid and hydrochloric acid is a strong acid.

  a Write an equation for the reaction of ethanoic acid with water, and identify the conjugate base of ethanoic acid. **[2]**

  b Explain the difference between a strong acid and a weak acid. **[2]**

  c A $1.00 \times 10^{-3}\,mol\,dm^{-3}$ solution of hydrochloric acid has a pH of 3. Suggest values for the pH of:

    i a $0.100\,mol\,dm^{-3}$ solution of hydrochloric acid

    ii a $1.00 \times 10^{-3}\,mol\,dm^{-3}$ solution of ethanoic acid **[2]**

  d State and explain **two** methods, other than measuring pH, that could be used to distinguish between $0.100\,mol\,dm^{-3}$ ethanoic acid and $0.100\,mol\,dm^{-3}$ hydrochloric acid. **[2]**

12 **a** Define pH. **[1]**

  b The pK_a value of butanoic acid is 4.82. Determine the pH of a $0.150\,mol\,dm^{-3}$ solution of butanoic acid. **[4]**

  c Explain, using an equation, whether the pH of a $0.100\,mol\,dm^{-3}$ solution of sodium butanoate will be less that 7, greater than 7 or equal to 7. **[3]**

  d $25.00\,cm^3$ of $0.150\,mol\,dm^{-3}$ butanoic acid is titrated with sodium hydroxide solution. $27.60\,cm^3$ of sodium hydroxide is required to reach the equivalence point.

    i Calculate the concentration of the sodium hydroxide. **[3]**

    ii Calculate the pH of the sodium hydroxide solution. **[3]**

    iii Sketch a graph to show how the pH changes as the sodium hydroxide is added to the butanoic acid up to a total volume of $50\,cm^3$ of sodium hydroxide. **[3]**

    iv Suggest, with a reason, a suitable indicator for the titration. **[2]**

13 Propanoic acid has a pK_a of 4.87 and ethanoic acid has a pK_a of 4.76.

    a Write an equation for the ionisation of propanoic acid in water.   **[2]**

    b Calculate the values for K_a for propanoic acid and ethanoic acid and use these values to explain which is the stronger acid.   **[4]**

    c Calculate the concentration of H^+ ions and pH of a $0.250\,mol\,dm^{-3}$ solution of propanoic acid, stating any assumptions you make.   **[4]**

    d Write an equation for the reaction of the propanoate ion ($CH_3CH_2COO^-$) with water.   **[1]**

    e Calculate the K_b value for the propanoate ion.   **[2]**

    f Calculate the pOH and pH of a $0.200\,mol\,dm^{-3}$ solution of sodium propanoate.   **[4]**

14 The pK_b value for ammonia is 4.75.

    a Calculate the pOH of a $0.125\,mol\,dm^{-3}$ solution of ammonia.   **[3]**

    b State and explain how much hydrochloric acid of concentration $0.125\,mol\,dm^{-3}$ you would need to add to $50.0\,cm^3$ of $0.125\,mol\,dm^{-3}$ ammonia solution to produce a buffer solution of pH 9.25.   **[3]**

15 The value of the ionic product constant for water, K_w, is $5.48 \times 10^{-14}\,mol^2\,dm^{-6}$ at 323 K.

    a Write an equation for the ionisation of water.   **[1]**

    b Calculate the pH of water at 323 K.   **[3]**

    c A solution has a pOH of 7.0 at 323 K. State and explain whether this solution is acidic, alkaline or neutral.   **[3]**

    d pK_w for water is 14.34 at 288 K. Explain whether the ionisation of water is exothermic or endothermic.   **[3]**

16 A buffer solution can be made by mixing together ammonia solution and ammonium chloride solution.

    a State what is meant by a **buffer solution**.   **[2]**

    b Explain, using equations, what happens when sodium hydroxide and hydrochloric acid are added separately to separate samples of this buffer solution.   **[2]**

    c Calculate the pH of the buffer solution, **Q**, made by mixing $50.0\,cm^3$ of $0.100\,mol\,dm^{-3}$ ammonia solution with $50.0\,cm^3$ of $0.0500\,mol\,dm^{-3}$ ammonium chloride solution. pK_b of ammonia is 4.75.   **[3]**

    d $10\,cm^3$ of $0.100\,mol\,dm^{-3}$ HCl is added to the buffer solution **Q** in part **c** and to another buffer, **X**, made by mixing $50.0\,cm^3$ of $1.00\,mol\,dm^{-3}$ ammonia solution of concentration with $50.0\,cm^3$ of $0.500\,mol\,dm^{-3}$ ammonium chloride solution. With which buffer will the larger pH change occur? Explain your answer.   **[2]**

Summary

A base must have a lone pair of electrons; an acid must have space to accept a lone pair.

Lewis:
an ACid is an electron pair ACceptor
a base is an electron pair donor

Brønsted–Lowry:
– an acid is a proton (H^+) donor
– a base/alkali is a proton acceptor

definitions

reactions

alkali + acid → salt + H_2O

base + acid → salt + H_2O

acid + carbonate/hydrogencarbonate → salt + CO_2 + H_2O

metal + acid → salt + H_2

examples: HCl, H_2SO_4 (first dissociation only), HNO_3

examples: group 1 hydroxides, $Ba(OH)_2$

Strong acids dissociate completely in aqueous solution

Strong bases ionise completely in aqueous solution

pH < 7
acidic

pH = 7
neutral

pH > 7
basic

$pH = -\log_{10}[H^+]$ —— no units

If $[H^+]$ decreases by a factor of 10, the pH increases by 1.

strong and weak acids and bases

ACIDS AND BASES

distinguishing between strong and weak acids experimentally

Weak acids dissociate only partially in aqueous solution

Weak bases ionise only partially in aqueous solution

examples: carboxylic acids (such as CH_3COOH) and H_2CO_3

examples: NH_3 and amines

at equal concentration

strong acids conduct electricity better

strong acids have lower pH

strong acids react more violently with metals or carbonates

To TITRATION, SALT HYDROLYSIS and BUFFER SOLUTIONS on the next page

ionic product constant for water
$K_w = [H^+(aq)][OH^-(aq)]$
$= 1.0 \times 10^{-14}\,mol^2\,dm^{-6}$
at 25 °C

refers to
$H_2O \rightleftharpoons H^+ + OH^-$
for any aqueous solution

for pure water:
$pH = pOH = \dfrac{pK_w}{2}$

$pH + pOH = pK_w$

HL

Stronger acids have higher K_a.

acid dissociation constant
$K_a = \dfrac{[A^-][H^+]}{[HA]}$
for $HA \rightleftharpoons H^+ + A^-$

$pH = \frac{1}{2}(pK_a - \log_{10}[acid])$

$K_w = K_a \times K_b$
and
$pK_w = pK_a + pK_b$
for a conjugate acid–base pair

Stronger bases have higher K_b.

base ionisation constant
$K_b = \dfrac{[BH^+][OH^-]}{[B]}$
for $B + H_2O \rightleftharpoons BH^+ + OH^-$

$pOH = \frac{1}{2}(pK_b - \log_{10}[base])$

TITRATION —— A **titration curve** shows how the pH varies in the titration of an acid with a base, or vice versa

indicator: (usually) weak acid in which the ionised and un-ionised forms have different colours

equivalence point: point at which equivalent amounts of acid and alkali have been added

At this point on the titration curve, the gradient stops decreasing and starts increasing, or vice versa.

acid	base	pH at equivalence point
strong	strong	7
strong	weak	<7
weak	strong	>7
weak	weak	?

$HIn \rightleftharpoons H^+ + In^-$
colour 1   colour 2

If acid is added, the equilibrium shifts towards the un-ionised form (colour 1).

$pH = pK_a$ at half equivalence point

pH range of an indicator: range in which intermediate colours are seen

The indicator should be chosen so that its pH range lies within the steep part of the titration curve.

$pOH = pK_b$ at half equivalence point

SALT HYDROLYSIS —— A salt dissolves in water to produce a solution that is acidic, basic or neutral, depending on the strength of the acid/base used to make the salt.

3+ ions polarise H_2O molecules sufficiently for them to dissociate, therefore they produce an acidic solution.

Ions with higher charge density are more acidic.

acid	base	pH of solution	example
strong	strong	7	NaCl
strong	weak	<7	NH_4Cl
weak	strong	>7	CH_3COONa
weak	weak	?	CH_3COONH_4

BUFFER SOLUTION —— made using a weak acid and its salt or a weak base and its salt
solution that resists changes in pH when **small** amounts of acid or base are added

$pH = pK_a + \log_{10}\dfrac{[salt]}{[acid]}$

$pH = pK_w - pK_b - \log_{10}\dfrac{[salt]}{[base]}$

CH_3COOH/CH_3COONa

NH_3/NH_4Cl

add acid
$CH_3COO^- + H^+ \rightarrow CH_3COOH$

add alkali
$CH_3COOH + OH^- \rightarrow CH_3COO^- + H_2O$

add acid
$NH_3 + H^+ \rightarrow NH_4^+$

add alkali
$NH_4^+ + OH^- \rightarrow NH_3 + H_2O$

Redox 9

9.1 Oxidation and reduction

Oxidation and reduction may be defined in many ways, such as 'oxidation is the loss of hydrogen or the gain of oxygen, and reduction is the gain of hydrogen or the loss of oxygen'. For instance, in the equation

$$C_2H_5OH + [O] \rightarrow CH_3CHO + H_2O$$

we can see that the C_2H_5OH (ethanol) has been oxidised, as it has lost H to form CH_3CHO (ethanal).

[O] indicates oxygen added in an oxidation reaction.

Or, in the equation

$$C_6H_5NO_2 + 6[H] \rightarrow C_6H_5NH_2 + 2H_2O$$

$C_6H_5NO_2$ has been reduced, as it has lost oxygen/gained hydrogen.

[H] indicates hydrogen added in a reduction reaction.

These definitions are, however, only useful in a limited number of reactions and a more fundamental definition of oxidation and reduction is:

Oxidation – loss of electrons
Reduction – gain of electrons (Figure **9.1**)

For instance, in the equation

$$Zn(s) + Cu^{2+}(aq) \rightarrow Zn^{2+}(aq) + Cu(s)$$

the Zn has been oxidised to Zn^{2+}, as it has lost electrons, and the Cu^{2+} has been reduced to Cu, as it has gained electrons. This can be seen more clearly by splitting the overall reaction into **half equations**, as shown in Figure **9.2**.

If something loses electrons, something else must gain them, so oxidation and reduction always occur together – that is, if something is oxidised, something else must be reduced. Reactions such as the one described above are called **redox** reactions, indicating that both oxidation and reduction occur.

Although it is fairly easy to understand which species has been oxidised and reduced in ionic equations such as $Zn(s) + Cu^{2+}(aq) \rightarrow Zn^{2+}(aq) + Cu(s)$, it is more difficult to see where electrons are being transferred and what is going on in redox reactions such as $PCl_3 + Cl_2 \rightarrow PCl_5$. For discussing reactions such as this in terms of oxidation and reduction, we use the concept of oxidation number (oxidation state).

Learning objectives

- Define **oxidation** and **reduction** in terms of the loss and gain of electrons
- Work out oxidation numbers for elements in compounds
- Understand what is meant by a **redox** reaction
- Work out whether an element has been oxidised or reduced in a given equation
- Understand what is meant by an **oxidising agent** and a **reducing agent**

Oxidation
Is
Loss of electrons
Reduction
Is
Gain of electrons

Figure 9.1 A mnemonic to help you remember the definition of oxidation and reduction.

$$Zn(s) \longrightarrow Zn^{2+}(aq) + \widehat{2e^-} \; \text{OXIDATION}$$
electrons lost

$$Cu^{2+}(aq) + \widehat{2e^-} \longrightarrow Cu(s) \; \text{REDUCTION}$$
electrons gained

Figure 9.2 Breaking an oxidation–reduction reaction into two half equations.

Oxidation number

Oxidation number is a purely formal concept, which regards all compounds as ionic and assigns charges to the components accordingly. It provides a guide to the distribution of electrons and relative charges on atoms in covalent compounds and allows us to understand redox processes more easily.

General rules for working out oxidation numbers:

1 treat the compound as totally ionic (if the compound **is** ionic then the charges on the ions are the oxidation numbers)

2 the most electronegative atom in a molecule is assigned a negative charge according to its valency to give a full outer shell (see Table **9.1**)

3 assign oxidation numbers (charges) accordingly to give the overall charge on the molecule/ion; that is, the sum of the oxidation numbers, taking into account signs and coefficients, is equal to the overall charge on the molecule/ion

4 the oxidation number of atoms in an element is zero

5 the elements in groups 1–3 virtually always have the group number as their oxidation number

6 the maximum possible oxidation number for an element will be its group number (see Table **9.2**)

Examiner's tip

Oxidation number is written with the sign first, i.e. −2, but a charge is written with the number first, i.e. 2−. This may seem like a trivial point, but if you get it the wrong way round you could lose a mark in the exam!

It is not possible to lose more electrons than there are in the outer shell – the maximum possible oxidation number for group 6 is +6, because there are six electrons in the outer shell.

Atom	Ionic charge	Oxidation number	Comment
F	F^-	−1	always, as most electronegative element
O	O^{2-}	−2	virtually always, but not in compounds with F or in peroxides and superoxides
Cl	Cl^-	−1	not in compounds with O and F; other oxidation numbers include +1, +3, +5, +7
H	H^+	+1	not in metal hydrides, e.g. NaH, where oxidation number is −1

Table 9.1 Assigning negative charge according to valency.

	Group 1	Group 2	Group 3	Group 4	Group 5	Group 6	Group 7
Maximum oxidation number	+1	+2	+3	+4	+5	+6	+7

Table 9.2 Group number as maximum possible oxidation number.

Examples

SO_2

SO_2 is a covalent compound, but we will assign oxidation numbers as if it were an ionic compound. The more electronegative atom is O, and therefore this is assigned its normal valency (the charge it would have in an ionic compound). The oxidation number of oxygen is thus −2. The overall charge on the molecule is zero, and therefore the oxidation number of S must be +4 to cancel out the total oxidation number of two O atoms (−4) (Figure **9.3**).

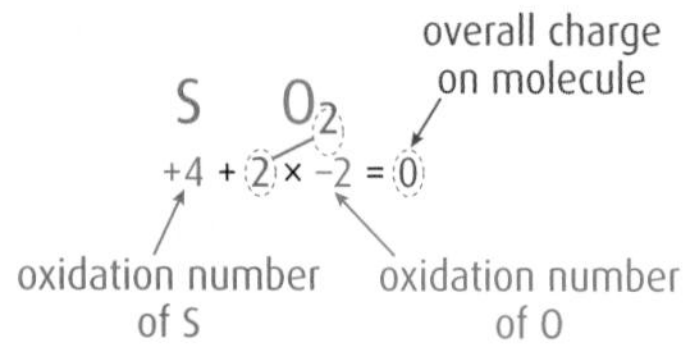

Figure 9.3 Assigning oxidation numbers to sulfur dioxide.

SO_4^{2-}

The more electronegative atom is O, and therefore this is assigned its normal valency. The oxidation number of oxygen is thus -2. The total oxidation number of four O atoms is 4×-2, i.e. -8. As the overall charge on the ion is $2-$, the oxidation number of S must be $+6$ to cancel out all but 2 of the total oxidation number of the four O atoms (Figure **9.4**).

$Cr_2O_7^{2-}$

The more electronegative atom is O, and therefore the oxidation number of oxygen is -2. The total oxidation number of seven O atoms is 7×-2, i.e. -14. As the overall charge on the ion is $2-$, the total oxidation number of two Cr atoms must be $+12$ to cancel out all but 2 of the total oxidation number of the seven O atoms. Therefore the oxidation number of Cr is $+12/2$, i.e. $+6$ (Figure **9.5**).

Some other oxidation numbers are shown in Table **9.3**.

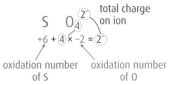

Figure 9.4 Assigning oxidation number to the sulfate ion.

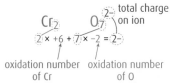

Figure 9.5 Assigning oxidation number to the dichromate ion.

	Oxidation numbers			
SO₃	S: +6		O: −2	
PCl₃	P: +3		Cl: −1	
Cl₂	Cl: 0		Cl: 0	
PO₄³⁻	P: +5		O: −2	
OF₂	O: +2		F: −1	
H₂O₂	H: +1		O: −1	
CO₂	C: +4		O: −2	
C₂H₆	C: −3		H: +1	
NaH	Na: +1		H: −1	
CaF₂	Ca: +2		F: −1	
HNO₃	H: +1	N: +5		O: −2
H₂SO₄	H: +1	S: +6		O: −2
KMnO₄	K: +1	Mn: +7		O: −2
NaClO₃	Na: +1	Cl: +5		O: −2

Table 9.3 The oxidation numbers of some elements in a variety of compounds.

Examiner's tip

In most cases, we will be able to work out the oxidation number of an atom in a molecule/ion by assuming that O has an oxidation number of -2 and that H has an oxidation number of $+1$.

H_2O_2 is hydrogen peroxide. The oxidation number of O cannot be -2 in this case as the oxidation number of H would have to be $+2$. This is not possible, as H has only one electron – its maximum oxidation number is $+1$.

$KMnO_4$ contains the ions K^+ and MnO_4^-.

HL Transition metals

The oxidation number of a transition metal in a complex ion is worked out from the charges on the ligands. Ligands may be either neutral or negatively charged. Examples of each type of ligand are shown in Table **9.4**.

Let us consider $[Fe(H_2O)_6]^{2+}$. All the ligands are neutral, so the overall charge on the ion is just due to the Fe, and thus the oxidation number of Fe must be $+2$.

Neutral ligands	1− ligands
H₂O	Cl⁻
NH₃	CN⁻

Table 9.4 Examples of neutral and negatively charged ligands in transition metals.

Let us also consider $[Ni(CN)_4]^{2-}$. All the ligands have a 1− charge, so the total charge on all four ligands is 4−. The overall charge on the ion is 2−, so the oxidation state of Ni must be +2 to cancel out 2− from the 4− charge.

Naming compounds using oxidation numbers

SO_2 and SO_3 are commonly referred to as sulfur dioxide and sulfur trioxide, respectively. They are, however, more correctly named using the oxidation number of the sulfur atom. Thus SO_2 is sulfur(IV) oxide and SO_3 is sulfur(VI) oxide. Strangely enough, no-one ever calls carbon dioxide carbon(IV) oxide or carbon monoxide carbon(II) oxide!

> Roman numerals are used for the oxidation numbers in the names of compounds.

Some other names of compounds or ions are shown in Table **9.5**.

Compound/ion	Name
H_2SO_3	sulfuric(IV) acid
H_2SO_4	sulfuric(VI) acid
PCl_3	phosphorus(III) chloride
PCl_5	phosphorus(V) chloride
N_2O	nitrogen(I) oxide
NO_2	nitrogen(IV) oxide
$HClO_3$	chloric(V) acid
PO_4^{3-}	phosphate(V) ion
$CuSO_4$	copper(II) sulfate
SO_4^{2-}	sulfate(VI) ion
$Cr_2O_7^{2-}$	dichromate(VI) ion
CrO_4^{2-}	chromate(VI) ion
MnO_4^-	manganate(VII) ion

Table 9.5 These compounds/ions are named systematically using oxidation numbers.

What exactly are oxidation numbers? The sulfur atom in SO_2 definitely does not have a charge of 4+, so what does the oxidation number actually represent?

Why have scientists developed this systematic way of naming compounds; what has been gained by this? The old name for H_2SO_3 was **sulfurous acid** and that for $KMnO_4$ was **potassium permanganate**. Why do some people still prefer to use the old names? Will anything be lost when the old names become obsolete?

Examiner's tip
Although you need to know how to name substances using oxidation numbers, it is still usually acceptable to use their more common names, e.g. sulfur dioxide for SO_2 and sulfuric acid for H_2SO_4.

Self-test 1

Test yourself

1 Work out oxidation numbers for nitrogen in the following molecules/ions:
  a NF_3 **c** N_2O **e** N_2H_4
  b NO **d** N_2O_4 **f** NO_2^-

2 Work out the oxidation number of chlorine in the following species:
  a Cl_2O **c** ClO_4^- **e** $HClO_3$
  b HCl **d** ClF_3

3 Work out the oxidation number of the species in bold in each of the following compounds:
  a $\mathbf{Na}_2O$ **c** $Na_2\mathbf{S}O_3$ **e** $\mathbf{N}H_4\mathbf{N}O_3$
  b $K\mathbf{Br}O_3$ **d** $K_2\mathbf{Cr}O_4$

4 Name the following compounds using oxidation numbers:
  a NO **c** SeO_2 **e** Cr_2O_3
  b Cl_2O_7 **d** KIO_3

5 Work out the oxidation number of the transition metal in each of the following complex ions or compounds:
a $[CuCl_4]^{2-}$
b $[Co(H_2O)_6]^{3+}$
c $[MnBr_4]^{2-}$
d $[Fe(CN)_6]^{4-}$
e $[Ag(NH_3)_2]^+$
f $[Co(H_2O)_6]Cl_2$

Oxidation and reduction in terms of oxidation numbers

If an atom gains electrons, its oxidation number will become more negative. Therefore reduction involves a decrease in oxidation number. If an atom loses electrons, its oxidation number increases. Therefore oxidation involves an increase in oxidation number.

We can work out which species is oxidised or reduced in a redox reaction by analysing the oxidation numbers of the substances in the reaction.

Reduction – decrease in oxidation number
Oxidation – increase in oxidation number

Examples

$Br_2 + SO_2 + 2H_2O \rightarrow H_2SO_4 + 2HBr$

Br_2 is reduced, as the oxidation number decreases from 0 to −1 and the S in SO_2 is oxidised as its oxidation number increases from +4 to +6 (Figure **9.6**). We would usually say that the SO_2 is oxidised.

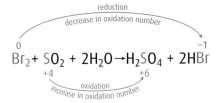

Figure 9.6 Reduction of Br_2 and oxidation of S.

$6OH^- + 3Cl_2 \rightarrow 5Cl^- + ClO_3^- + 3H_2O$

In this reaction, five Cl atoms have been reduced and one has been oxidised; therefore Cl_2 has been oxidised and reduced (Figure **9.7**). This type of reaction, in which the same species has been oxidised and reduced, is called a **disproportionation** reaction.

$Cr_2O_7^{2-} + H_2O \rightarrow 2CrO_4^{2-} + 2H^+$

The oxidation number of Cr on both sides of the equation is +6, and no other atom undergoes a change in oxidation number. This reaction is, therefore, **not** a redox reaction.

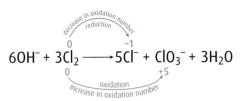

Figure 9.7 Oxidation and reduction of Cl_2, an example of a disproportionation reaction.

For a reaction to be a redox reaction, the reaction must involve a change in oxidation state.

Oxidising and reducing agents

An oxidising agent is a substance that oxidises something else. A reducing agent is a substance that reduces something else.

Examples

$2Br^- + Cl_2 \rightarrow 2Cl^- + Br_2$

Cl_2 is the oxidising agent, as it oxidises the Br^- to Br_2. In terms of electrons, an oxidising agent oxidises a substance by removing electrons

Oxidising agents (oxidants) oxidise other species and, in the process, are, themselves, reduced. An oxidising agent takes electrons away from something.

from it. So the Cl_2 removes electrons from the bromide ions, oxidising them. The Cl_2 has thus gained electrons and has been reduced.

The Br^- in this reaction causes the Cl_2 to be reduced, by giving electrons to it to form Cl^-. Therefore the Br^- acts as a reducing agent in this reaction. The Br^- ions have thus lost electrons and been oxidised.

$$Cr_2O_7^{2-}(aq) + 6Fe^{2+}(aq) + 14H^+(aq) \rightarrow 2Cr^{3+}(aq) + 6Fe^{3+}(aq) + 7H_2O(l)$$

The Fe^{2+} is oxidised to Fe^{3+} by the $Cr_2O_7^{2-}$, so $Cr_2O_7^{2-}$ is the oxidising agent. We can tell that $Cr_2O_7^{2-}$ is the oxidising agent, as it has been reduced in the reaction. The $Cr_2O_7^{2-}$ has been reduced by the Fe^{2+}, which means that Fe^{2+} is the reducing agent in this reaction. We can tell that Fe^{2+} is a reducing agent, as it has been oxidised.

Reducing agents (reductants) reduce other species and are, in the process, themselves, oxidised. A reducing agent gives electrons to something.

Self-test 2

Test yourself

6 State whether the following half equations involve oxidation or reduction:
   a $Cl_2 + 2e^- \rightarrow 2Cl^-$
   b $Mn^{3+} + e^- \rightarrow Mn^{2+}$
   c $Cu^+ \rightarrow Cu^{2+} + e^-$
   d $I_2 + 6H_2O \rightarrow 2IO_3^- + 12H^+ + 10e^-$
   e $Cr_2O_7^{2-} + 14H^+ + 6e^- \rightarrow 2Cr^{3+} + 7H_2O$

7 State which of the following reactions are redox reactions and, for each redox reaction, identify the element that has been oxidised and the element that has been reduced.
   a $Cu^{2+}(aq) + 2OH^-(aq) \rightarrow Cu(OH)_2(s)$
   b $2ZnS + 3O_2 \rightarrow 2ZnO + SO_2$
   c $2Na + 2H_2O \rightarrow 2NaOH + H_2$
   d $SO_3 + H_2O \rightarrow H_2SO_4$
   e $Na_2CO_3 + 2HCl \rightarrow 2NaCl + H_2O + CO_2$

   f $2FeSO_4 + H_2SO_4 + H_2O_2 \rightarrow Fe_2(SO_4)_3 + 2H_2O$
   g $3HgSO_4 \rightarrow Hg_2SO_4 + Hg + 2SO_2 + 2O_2$
   h $2I^- + H^+ + HOCl \rightarrow I_2 + H_2O + Cl^-$

8 In each of the following redox reactions, identify the oxidising agent and the reducing agent:
   a $Zn + CuSO_4 \rightarrow ZnSO_4 + Cu$
   b $Cl_2 + 2Br^- \rightarrow 2Cl^- + Br_2$
   c $I_2O_5 + 5CO \rightarrow 5CO_2 + I_2$
   d $S + 6HNO_3 \rightarrow 2H_2O + H_2SO_4 + 6NO_2$
   e $2Na_2S_2O_3 + I_2 \rightarrow Na_2S_4O_6 + 2NaI$
   f $2KMnO_4 + 5Na_2C_2O_4 + 8H_2SO_4$
$$\rightarrow 2MnSO_4 + 10CO_2 + K_2SO_4$$
$$+ 5Na_2SO_4 + 8H_2O$$
   g $6FeSO_4 + K_2Cr_2O_7 + 7H_2SO_4$
$$\rightarrow 3Fe_2(SO_4)_3 + K_2SO_4 + Cr_2(SO_4)_3 + 7H_2O$$

Learning objectives

• Understand what is meant by half equations and be able to balance them
• Combine half equations to produce an overall redox equation

9.2 Redox equations

Half equations

As already mentioned above, a redox equation may be broken down into two **half** equations. These half equations show the oxidation and reduction processes separately.

For instance, in the equation

$$2Br^-(aq) + Cl_2(aq) \rightarrow 2Cl^-(aq) + Br_2(aq)$$

we can separate the two processes as:

$$2Br^-(aq) \rightarrow Br_2(aq) + 2e^- \qquad \textbf{Oxidation}$$
$$Cl_2(aq) + 2e^- \rightarrow 2Cl^-(aq) \qquad \textbf{Reduction}$$

The number of electrons is the same in both equations.

Examples

$$Cr_2O_7^{2-}(aq) + 6Fe^{2+}(aq) + 14H^+(aq) \rightarrow 2Cr^{3+}(aq) + 6Fe^{3+}(aq) + 7H_2O(l)$$

This reaction can be separated as:

$$Cr_2O_7^{2-}(aq) + 14H^+(aq) + 6e^- \rightarrow 2Cr^{3+}(aq) + 7H_2O(l) \qquad \textbf{Reduction}$$
$$6Fe^{2+}(aq) \rightarrow 6Fe^{3+}(aq) + 6e^- \qquad \textbf{Oxidation}$$

The dichromate half equation is discussed in more detail on the next page.

This second half equation can be simplified as:

$$Fe^{2+}(aq) \rightarrow Fe^{3+}(aq) + e^- \qquad \textbf{Oxidation}$$

$Br_2 + SO_2 + 2H_2O \rightarrow H_2SO_4 + 2HBr$

This reaction can be separated as:

$$Br_2 + 2H^+ + 2e^- \rightarrow 2HBr \qquad \textbf{Reduction}$$
$$SO_2 + 2H_2O \rightarrow H_2SO_4 + 2H^+ + 2e^- \qquad \textbf{Oxidation}$$

Although $2H^+$ and $2e^-$ were required to balance the individual half equations, these cancel out when the half equations are combined to give the overall redox equation.

It can be seen that all of these half equations balance, both in terms of number of atoms on both sides and the total charge on both sides. This must be true for all half equations.

It should also be noted that the number of electrons lost in the oxidation reaction is equal to the number of electrons gained in the reduction reaction. This must be true, as the electrons cannot simply disappear or be created from nothing.

Balancing half equations

Half equations must balanced in terms of the number of atoms on both sides and in terms of the total charge on both sides. In some cases it is very straightforward to balance half equations, and electrons must simply be added to one side or the other.

For example, consider the half equation:

$$Ni^{2+} \rightarrow Ni$$

Although the number of nickel atoms on each side is the same, the total charge on the left-hand side is 2+ but the total charge on the right-hand side is 0. In order to balance the charges, we must simply add $2e^-$ to the left-hand side:

$$Ni^{2+} + 2e^- \rightarrow Ni$$

Now the number of atoms and the charges balance on each side.

Now, let's look at the following half-equation:

$$Br_2 \rightarrow Br^-$$

In this example, neither the number of atoms nor the total charge balance. First of all we balance the atoms to get:

$$Br_2 \rightarrow 2Br^-$$

The total charge on the left-hand side is zero, but that on the right-hand side is 2−. In order to balance the charges we need to add $2e^-$ to the left-hand side so that the charge is equal on both sides:

$$Br_2 + 2e^- \rightarrow 2Br^-$$

This is now balanced.

These were both fairly straightforward examples, but the process becomes a bit more difficult in some cases, and we will now consider balancing more complex half equations in acidic solution.

Balancing half equations in acidic solution

Examples

$Cr_2O_7{}^{2-} \rightarrow Cr^{3+}$

1 Balance all atoms except H and O – the Cr atoms must be balanced:

$$Cr_2O_7{}^{2-} \rightarrow 2Cr^{3+}$$

2 Add H_2O to side deficient in O to balance O – there are **7** O atoms on the left-hand side and none on the right-hand side, so **7**H_2O must be added to the right-hand side:

$$Cr_2O_7{}^{2-} \rightarrow 2Cr^{3+} + 7H_2O$$

3 Add H^+ to side deficient in H to balance H – there are **14** H atoms on the right-hand side but none on the left-hand side, so **14**H^+ must be added to the left-hand side:

$$Cr_2O_7{}^{2-} + 14H^+ \rightarrow 2Cr^{3+} + 7H_2O$$

4 Add e^- to side deficient in negative charge to balance charge – the total charge on the left-hand side is 2− + 14+ = 12+, and the total charge on the right-hand side is 2 × 3+ = 6+, so $6e^-$ must be added to the left-hand side to balance the charges:

$$Cr_2O_7{}^{2-} + 14H^+ + 6e^- \rightarrow 2Cr^{3+} + 7H_2O$$

The total charge on the left-hand side is now 2− + 14+ + 6− = 6+, which is equal to the total charge on the right-hand side.

$S_4O_6{}^{2-} + H_2O \rightarrow H_2SO_3 + H^+ + e^-$

In this case, the H_2O, H^+ and e^- have already been included on their correct sides. However, the overall process of balancing the equation is the same.

The following procedure should be followed for balancing these equations.

1 Balance all atoms except H and O
2 Add H_2O to side deficient in O to balance O
3 Add H^+ to side deficient in H to balance H
4 Add e^- to side deficient in negative charge to balance charge

1 There are four S atoms on the left-hand side but only one on the right-hand side, so H_2SO_3 must be multiplied by **4**:

$$S_4O_6{}^{2-} + H_2O \rightarrow \mathbf{4}H_2SO_3 + H^+ + e^-$$

2 There are seven O atoms on the left-hand side and 12 on the right-hand side, so another five H_2O must be added to the left-hand side:

$$S_4O_6{}^{2-} + 6H_2O \rightarrow 4H_2SO_3 + H^+ + e^-$$

There are now 12 O atoms on each side.

3 There are 12 H atoms on the left-hand side and nine on the right-hand side, so another three H^+ must be added to the right-hand side:

$$S_4O_6{}^{2-} + 6H_2O \rightarrow 4H_2SO_3 + 4H^+ + e^-$$

There are now 12 H atoms on each side.

4 The total charge on the left-hand side is 2− and the total charge on the right-hand side is $4 \times 1+ \; + 1- = 3+$, so five more e^- must be added to the right-hand side to give a total of $6e^-$ on that side and therefore to balance the charges:

$$S_4O_6{}^{2-} + 6H_2O \rightarrow 4H_2SO_3 + 4H^+ + 6e^-$$

The total charge on both sides is now 2−.

Combining half equations to produce an overall redox equation

An oxidation half equation may be combined with a reduction half equation to produce an overall redox equation. When the half equations are combined, the number of electrons lost in the oxidation reaction must be the same as the number gained in the reduction reaction.

Let us consider the two half equations:

$$MnO_4{}^-(aq) + 8H^+(aq) + 5e^- \rightarrow Mn^{2+}(aq) + 4H_2O(l) \qquad \textbf{Reduction}$$
$$Fe^{2+}(aq) \rightarrow Fe^{3+}(aq) + e^- \qquad \textbf{Oxidation}$$

Five electrons are gained in the reduction half equation, but only one is lost in the oxidation half equation. The oxidation half equation must therefore be multiplied by 5:

$$MnO_4{}^-(aq) + 8H^+(aq) + 5e^- \rightarrow Mn^{2+}(aq) + 4H_2O(l) \qquad \textbf{Reduction}$$
$$5Fe^{2+}(aq) \rightarrow 5Fe^{3+}(aq) + 5e^- \qquad \textbf{Oxidation}$$

The number of electrons now balance and the two half equations are simply added together:

$$MnO_4{}^-(aq) + 8H^+(aq) + \mathbf{5e^-} \rightarrow Mn^{2+}(aq) + 4H_2O(l)$$
$$5Fe^{2+}(aq) \rightarrow 5Fe^{3+}(aq) + \mathbf{5e^-}$$

$$\overline{MnO_4{}^-(aq) + 8H^+(aq) + \cancel{\mathbf{5e^-}} + 5Fe^{2+}(aq) \rightarrow Mn^{2+}(aq) + 4H_2O(l) + 5Fe^{3+}(aq) + \cancel{\mathbf{5e^-}}}$$

A final check can be done to see that this is, indeed, balanced by checking that the number of atoms of each type is the same on both sides and also that the total charge is the same on both sides.

The electrons are cancelled from each side to give the overall redox equation:

$$MnO_4^-(aq) + 8H^+(aq) + 5Fe^{2+}(aq) \rightarrow Mn^{2+}(aq) + 4H_2O(l) + 5Fe^{3+}(aq)$$

Worked example

What is the overall redox equation when the following two half equations are combined?

$$MnO_4^-(aq) + 8H^+(aq) + 5e^- \rightarrow Mn^{2+}(aq) + 4H_2O(l) \qquad \textbf{Reduction}$$
$$Re^{3+}(aq) + 4H_2O(l) \rightarrow ReO_4^{2-}(aq) + 8H^+(aq) + 3e^- \qquad \textbf{Oxidation}$$

Five electrons are gained in the reduction half equation, but only three are lost in the oxidation half equation. Therefore, in order to balance the number of electrons lost with the number of electrons gained, the oxidation half equation must be multiplied by 3 and the reduction half equation by 5:

$$3MnO_4^-(aq) + 24H^+(aq) + \textbf{15e}^- \rightarrow 3Mn^{2+}(aq) + 12H_2O(l) \qquad \textbf{Reduction}$$
$$5Re^{3+}(aq) + 20H_2O(l) \rightarrow 5ReO_4^{2-}(aq) + 40H^+(aq) + \textbf{15e}^- \qquad \textbf{Oxidation}$$

The number of electrons now balance and the two half equations are added together:

$$3MnO_4^-(aq) + 24H^+(aq) + \textbf{15e}^- \rightarrow 3Mn^{2+}(aq) + 12H_2O(l)$$
$$5Re^{3+}(aq) + 20H_2O(l) \rightarrow 5ReO_4^{2-}(aq) + 40H^+(aq) + \textbf{15e}^-$$
$$\overline{5Re^{3+}(aq) + 20H_2O(l) + 3MnO_4^-(aq) + 24H^+(aq) + \cancel{\textbf{15e}^-} \rightarrow 3Mn^{2+}(aq) + 12H_2O(l) + 5ReO_4^{2-}(aq) + 40H^+(aq) + \cancel{\textbf{15e}^-}}$$

The electrons are cancelled from each side to give:

$$5Re^{3+}(aq) + 20H_2O(l) + 3MnO_4^-(aq) + 24H^+(aq) \rightarrow 3Mn^{2+}(aq) + 12H_2O(l) + 5ReO_4^{2-}(aq) + 40H^+(aq)$$

It can be seen that there are H_2O molecules and H^+ ions on both sides. These can also be cancelled to give:

$$5Re^{3+}(aq) + 8H_2O(l) + 3MnO_4^-(aq) \rightarrow 3Mn^{2+}(aq) + 5ReO_4^{2-}(aq) + 16H^+(aq)$$

This is the final redox equation.

Balancing redox equations in acidic solution using half equations

We can combine the above techniques to allow us to balance overall redox equations. The equation is first split up into half equations, which are balanced separately and then combined to give the overall redox equation.

The procedure for doing this is as follows.

1 Separate the reaction into oxidation and reduction half equations
2 Balance each half equation separately
3 Combine the two half equations by multiplying by appropriate numbers to balance the electrons between each
4 Subtract any duplications on left- and right-hand sides

Example

$MnO_4^-(aq) + C_2O_4^{2-}(aq) \rightarrow CO_2(g) + Mn^{2+}(aq)$

Balance the above redox equation in acidic solution.

The two half equations are:

$MnO_4^-(aq) \rightarrow Mn^{2+}(aq)$
$C_2O_4^{2-}(aq) \rightarrow CO_2(g)$

1 Balance all atoms except H and O:
$MnO_4^- \rightarrow Mn^{2+}$
$C_2O_4^{2-} \rightarrow 2CO_2$

2 Add H_2O to side deficient in O to balance O:
$MnO_4^- \rightarrow Mn^{2+} + 4H_2O$
$C_2O_4^{2-} \rightarrow 2CO_2$

3 Add H^+ to side deficient in H to balance H:
$MnO_4^- + 8H^+ \rightarrow Mn^{2+} + 4H_2O$
$C_2O_4^{2-} \rightarrow 2CO_2$

4 Add e^- to side deficient in negative charge to balance charge:
$MnO_4^- + 8H^+ + 5e^- \rightarrow Mn^{2+} + 4H_2O$
$C_2O_4^{2-} \rightarrow 2CO_2 + 2e^-$

5 These must be combined so that the electrons balance. This is achieved by multiplying the reduction equation by 2 and the oxidation equation by 5:
$2MnO_4^- + 16H^+ + 10e^- \rightarrow 2Mn^{2+} + 8H_2O(l)$
$5C_2O_4^{2-} \rightarrow 10CO_2 + 10e^-$

The numbers of electrons now balance. The two half equations are added together and the electrons cancelled:

$$2MnO_4^- + 16H^+ + 10e^- \rightarrow 2Mn^{2+} + 8H_2O(l)$$
$$5C_2O_4^{2-} \rightarrow 10CO_2 + 10e^-$$
$$\overline{5C_2O_4^{2-}(aq) + 2MnO_4^-(aq) + 16H^+ \rightarrow 2Mn^{2+}(aq) + 8H_2O(l) + 10CO_2(g)}$$

There are no species the same on both sides, so this is the final equation.

Worked examples

Balance the redox equation:

$HAsO_2(aq) + BrO_3^-(aq) \rightarrow Br_2(aq) + H_3AsO_4(aq)$

The two half equations are:

$HAsO_2(aq) \rightarrow H_3AsO_4(aq)$ $BrO_3^-(aq) \rightarrow Br_2(aq)$

1 Balance all atoms except H and O:
$HAsO_2 \rightarrow H_3AsO_4$ $2BrO_3^- \rightarrow Br_2$

2 Add H_2O to side deficient in O to balance O:
$2H_2O + HAsO_2 \rightarrow H_3AsO_4$ $2BrO_3^- \rightarrow Br_2 + 6H_2O$

3 Add H^+ to side deficient in H to balance H:

$$2H_2O + HAsO_2 \rightarrow H_3AsO_4 + 2H^+ \qquad\qquad 2BrO_3^- + 12H^+ \rightarrow Br_2 + 6H_2O$$

4 Add e^- to side deficient in negative charge to balance charge:

$$2H_2O + HAsO_2 \rightarrow H_3AsO_4 + 2H^+ + 2e^- \qquad 2BrO_3^- + 12H^+ + 10e^- \rightarrow Br_2 + 6H_2O$$

5 Multiply by 5:

$$10H_2O + 5HAsO_2 \rightarrow 5H_3AsO_4 + 10H^+ + 10e^-$$

Multiply by 1:

$$2BrO_3^- + 12H^+ + 10e^- \rightarrow Br_2 + 6H_2O$$

The two half equations can now be added together and the electrons cancelled:

$$10H_2O + 5HAsO_2 \rightarrow 5H_3AsO_4 + 10H^+ + 10e^-$$
$$\underline{2BrO_3^- + 12H^+ + 10e^- \rightarrow Br_2 + 6H_2O}$$
$$10H_2O + 5HAsO_2 + 2BrO_3^- + 12H^+ \rightarrow 5H_3AsO_4 + 10H^+ + Br_2 + 6H_2O$$

There are H_2O molecules and H^+ ions on both sides, and these can be cancelled to give the overall equation:

$$4H_2O(l) + 5HAsO_2(aq) + 2BrO_3^-(aq) + 2H^+(aq) \rightarrow 5H_3AsO_4(aq) + Br_2(aq)$$

A final check can be done to see that this is, indeed, balanced by checking that the number of atoms of each type is the same on both sides and also that the total charge is the same on both sides.

Self-test 3

Test yourself

9 Balance the following half equations:

   a $Fe^{3+} \rightarrow Fe$ **d** $S_2O_3^{2-} \rightarrow S_4O_6^{2-}$

   b $Pb^{2+} \rightarrow Pb^{4+}$ **e** $C_2O_4^{2-} \rightarrow CO_2$

   c $I_2 \rightarrow I^-$

10 Balance the following half equations in acidic solution:

   a $I_2 + H_2O \rightarrow OI^- + H^+ + e^-$

   b $MnO_4^- + H^+ + e^- \rightarrow MnO_2 + H_2O$

   c $IO_3^- + H^+ + e^- \rightarrow I_2 + H_2O$

   d $N_2 + H_2O \rightarrow NO_3^- + H^+ + e^-$

   e $SO_4^{2-} + H^+ + e^- \rightarrow H_2SO_3 + H_2O$

11 Balance the following half equations in acidic solution:

   a $VO^{2+} \rightarrow V^{3+}$ **d** $NO_3^- \rightarrow N_2O$

   b $Xe \rightarrow XeO_3$ **e** $VO_2^+ \rightarrow VO^{2+}$

   c $NO_3^- \rightarrow NO$

12 Balance the following redox equations in acidic solution:

   a $Fe^{2+} + Cr_2O_7^{2-} + H^+ \rightarrow Fe^{3+} + Cr^{3+} + H_2O$

   b $I^- + Cr_2O_7^{2-} + H^+ \rightarrow I_2 + Cr^{3+} + H_2O$

   c $Zn + VO^{2+} + H^+ \rightarrow V^{3+} + H_2O + Zn^{2+}$

   d $BrO_3^- + I^- \rightarrow Br_2 + I_2$

   e $NpO_2^{2+} + U^{4+} \rightarrow NpO_2^+ + UO_2^+$

9.3 Reactivity series

Metals may be arranged in a reactivity series such as this:

decreasing reactivity

magnesium

zinc

iron

nickel

copper

silver

Learning objectives

- Understand what is meant by a reactivity series
- Construct reactivity series based on displacement reactions of metals and halogens
- Explain reactivity series in terms of the oxidising and reducing ability of the species involved

There are various ways of arriving at this reactivity series: for instance, the reactions of the metals with oxygen, water or acids can be investigated and the metals arranged in order of reactivity based on the nature and/or vigour of the reaction.

The metals higher in the reactivity series displace those lower in the reactivity series from solutions of their salts. For instance, when a piece of zinc is placed in a solution containing copper ions, the zinc becomes coated with copper and gets smaller, the blue colour of the solution fades and the solution gets warmer (see Figure **9.8**).

The zinc is more reactive than copper and therefore displaces copper ions from solution. The reaction that occurs is:

$$Zn(s) + Cu^{2+}(aq) \rightarrow Zn^{2+}(aq) + Cu(s)$$

The Zn reduces the copper ions.

Sometimes hydrogen is also included in these reactivity series:

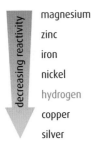

decreasing reactivity

magnesium

zinc

iron

nickel

hydrogen

copper

silver

Metals above hydrogen in the reactivity series are stronger reducing agents than hydrogen and should displace it from a solution of its ions. Thus the reaction between magnesium and hydrogen ions is:

$$Mg(s) + 2H^+(aq) \rightarrow Mg^{2+}(aq) + H_2(g)$$

Acids produce hydrogen ions in solution, and therefore we can conclude that metals above hydrogen in the reactivity series should liberate hydrogen gas from acids.

These reactions are known as displacement reactions.

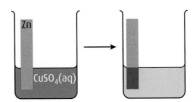

Figure 9.8 Zinc displaces copper from solution.

Animation 1

Metals higher in the reactivity series are stronger reducing agents than metals lower in the reactivity series. Thus magnesium will reduce Zn^{2+} ions, zinc will reduce Fe^{2+} ions, iron will reduce Ni^{2+} ions, etc.

The reaction of magnesium with hydrochloric acid is:

$$Mg(s) + 2HCl(aq) \rightarrow MgCl_2(aq) + H_2(g)$$

Metals lower than hydrogen in the reactivity series will not react with acids, so copper and silver do not react with hydrochloric acid.

Reactivity of halogens

A reactivity series for the halogens may be arrived at by carrying out the following series of experiments: $1\,cm^3$ of potassium chloride solution is put into each of three test tubes. To the first test tube we add chlorine solution, to the second we add bromine solution and to the third iodine solution. Any colour change is observed. The experiment is then repeated using potassium bromide solution and then potassium iodide solution instead of potassium chloride solution.

Potassium chloride, potassium bromide and potassium iodide solutions are all colourless. The colours of chlorine, bromine and iodine solutions are shown in Figure **9.9**, and the results of the experiments are shown in Table **9.6**.

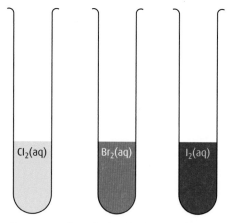

Figure 9.9 The colours of solutions of chlorine, bromine and iodine.

	KCl(aq)	KBr(aq)	KI(aq)
Cl₂(aq)	no reaction	orange solution	dark red/brown solution
Br₂(aq)	no reaction	no reaction	dark red/brown solution
I₂(aq)	no reaction	no reaction	no reaction

Table 9.6 Displacement reactions of halogens.

The reactions that occur are:

- $Cl_2(aq) + 2KBr(aq) \rightarrow 2KCl(aq) + Br_2(aq)$
  Ionic equation: $Cl_2(aq) + 2Br^-(aq) \rightarrow 2Cl^-(aq) + Br_2(aq)$

- $Cl_2(aq) + 2KI(aq) \rightarrow 2KI(aq) + I_2(aq)$
  Ionic equation: $Cl_2(aq) + 2I^-(aq) \rightarrow 2Cl^-(aq) + I_2(aq)$

- $Br_2(aq) + 2KI(aq) \rightarrow 2KBr(aq) + I_2(aq)$
  Ionic equation: $Br_2(aq) + 2I^-(aq) \rightarrow 2Br^-(aq) + I_2(aq)$

The above reactions are all **redox** reactions, in which the more reactive halogen oxidises the less reactive halide ion.

These reactions allow us to put these three halogens into a reactivity series:

orange colour due to the production of bromine

red/brown colour due to the production of iodine

chlorine

bromine

iodine

decreasing reactivity

Chlorine is a stronger oxidising agent than bromine and iodine and will oxidise the bromide ions to bromine and the iodide ions to iodine. Bromine is a stronger oxidising agent than iodine and will oxidise iodide ions to iodine. In terms of electrons, chlorine has the strongest affinity for electrons and will remove electrons from bromide ions and iodide ions.

9.4 Voltaic cells

Voltaic cells (electrochemical cells) provide us with a way of harnessing redox reactions to generate electricity. This is the basis of cells (batteries).

When a piece of zinc is put into a solution of copper sulfate, the piece of zinc becomes coated with copper and the blue colour of the copper sulfate solution fades (Figure **9.10**).

The overall reaction is:

$$Zn(s) + Cu^{2+}(aq) \rightarrow Zn^{2+}(aq) + Cu(s)$$

The half equations involved are:

$$Zn(s) \rightarrow Zn^{2+}(aq) + 2e^-$$ **Oxidation**
$$Cu^{2+}(aq) + 2e^- \rightarrow Cu(s)$$ **Reduction**

Thus, when zinc metal is added to a solution of Cu^{2+} ions, the electrons are transferred from the zinc to the Cu^{2+} – i.e. the Cu^{2+} is reduced and the Zn is oxidised.

However, if the two reactions are separated, as in Figure **9.11**, exactly the same reaction occurs except that instead of the electrons being transferred directly from the Zn to the Cu^{2+} they are transferred via the external circuit.

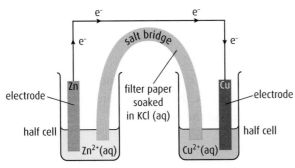

Figure 9.11 A voltaic cell.

Learning objectives

- Understand how electricity is produced in a voltaic cell

Voltaic cells are also called Galvanic cells.

The blue colour of the solution is due to the presence of $Cu^{2+}(aq)$ ions.

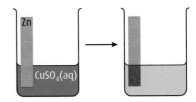

Figure 9.10 Zinc is oxidised and copper ions are reduced to form copper when a piece of zinc is put into a solution of copper sulfate.

$$Zn(s) \rightarrow Zn^{2+}(aq) + 2e^-$$
$$Cu^{2+}(aq) + 2e^- \rightarrow Cu(s)$$

Reactivity decreases down the group.

The more reactive halogen is a stronger oxidising agent.

In the left-hand beaker, Zn atoms are oxidised to Zn^{2+} ions and the electrons that are lost flow around the circuit to the other beaker, where they are gained by copper ions to form Cu. If the reaction was allowed to keep going, we would see the zinc electrode getting smaller (as the zinc goes into solution as Zn^{2+}), the Cu electrode getting larger (as it is coated with copper) and the colour of the solution in the right-hand beaker becoming paler (as the copper ions are converted to copper atoms).

Why is the salt bridge necessary?

In the cell shown in Figure **9.11**, the current will not flow unless the salt bridge is present. If the salt bridge were not present and the reaction were to proceed, there would be a build up of Zn^{2+} ions in the left-hand beaker, the solution would become positively charged overall and any further oxidation of Zn atoms to Zn^{2+} would be opposed. Similarly, there would be a decrease in the concentration of Cu^{2+} ions in the right-hand beaker, which would mean that this solution would have a negative charge and any further reduction of Cu^{2+} ions would be opposed. The flow of electrons from the positively charged half cell to the negatively charged half cell would not occur. The salt bridge contains ions that can flow out of the salt bridge into the individual half cell to prevent any build up of charge (Figure **9.12**). Similarly, any excess ions in the individual half cells can flow into the salt bridge to prevent any build up of charge.

> The salt bridge provides an electrical connection between the two half cells to complete the circuit. It allows ions to flow into or out of the half cells to balance out the charges in the half cells.

> The salt bridge contains a concentrated solution of an ionic salt such as KCl.

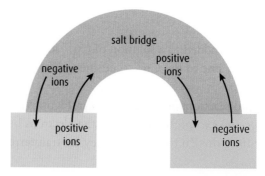

Figure 9.12 Ions flow into and out of the salt bridge to balance the charges in the half cells.

Details of the cell

Negative charge always flows in the same continuous direction around a complete circuit – in this case the electrons and the negative ions are all travelling clockwise around the circuit:

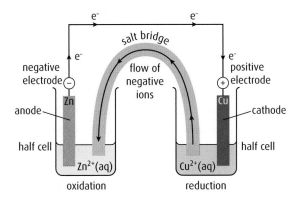

In the zinc half cell an oxidation reaction occurs:

$$Zn(s) \rightarrow Zn^{2+}(aq) + 2e^-$$

As electrons are produced at this electrode, this is the negative electrode. Because this is the electrode at which oxidation occurs, the negative electrode is the **anode** in this type of cell.

In the copper half cell, a reduction reaction occurs:

$$Cu^{2+}(aq) + 2e^- \rightarrow Cu(s)$$

As electrons are used up at this electrode, this is the positive electrode. As reduction occurs at the copper electrode, this is the **cathode** in this cell.

> Electrons always flow around the external circuit from the negative electrode to the positive electrode.

> Oxidation occurs at the negative electrode.

> The electrode at which oxidation occurs is called the **anode**.

> Reduction occurs at the positive electrode.

> The electrode at which reduction occurs is called the **cathode**.

The size of the voltage

If a voltmeter is inserted across the above cell, it will read a voltage of just over 1 volt (Figure **9.13a**). However, if the zinc electrode is replaced by a magnesium electrode, the voltage is much higher (Figure **9.13b**). This is because there is a bigger difference in reactivity between magnesium and copper than between zinc and copper. The magnesium has a greater tendency than zinc to donate electrons to copper ions.

> The reactions in a cell are sometimes described using notation such as $Zn|Zn^{2+}||Cu^{2+}|Cu$. The single vertical line represents a phase boundary and the double line indicates the salt bridge.

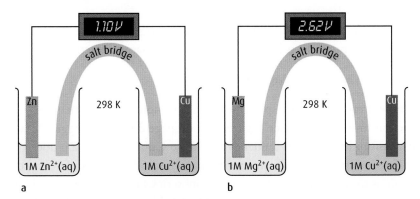

> The bigger the difference in reactivity between the metal electrodes, the larger the voltage of the cell.

Figure 9.13 The voltage in a $Zn|Zn^{2+}||Cu^{2+}|Cu$ cell (**a**) is less than in a $Mg|Mg^{2+}||Cu^{2+}|Cu$ cell (**b**). Note: $1\,M = 1\,mol\,dm^{-3}$.

13 Consider four imaginary metals, X, Z, A and Q.

a On the basis of the following data, arrange the metals X, Z and Q in order of reactivity (most reactive first):

Z reduces Q^{2+} to Q

X reduces Z^{2+} to Z

b The following reactions also occur:

$$A + Q^{2+} \rightarrow A^{2+} + Q$$
$$Z + A^{2+} \rightarrow Z^{2+} + A$$

i Is A a stronger or weaker reducing agent than Q?

ii Arrange all four metals in order of reducing ability (strongest reducing agent first).

iii Which of the species, A, A^{2+}, Z, Z^{2+}, Q, Q^{2+}, X, X^{2+} is the strongest oxidising agent?

c An electrochemical cell is set up with a piece of A dipping into a solution of $A(NO_3)_2$ in one half cell and a piece of X dipping into a solution of XSO_4 in the other half cell.

i Which way do electrons flow in the external circuit?

ii Which is the anode in the cell?

iii The X/XSO_4 half cell is replaced by a Z/ZSO_4 half cell. Will the voltage be higher or lower than that in the original cell?

Learning objectives

- Describe the features of the standard hydrogen electrode
- Understand the term **standard electrode potential**
- Calculate the cell potential for a given redox reaction
- Use the cell potential to predict whether a redox reaction will be spontaneous

The Zn/Cu^{2+} reaction has been shown with reversible, equilibrium arrows here; indeed, $E^{\ominus}$ is related to the equilibrium constant, and these systems will reach a state of equilibrium. However, in most cases the position of equilibrium lies a very long way to the right, and the reaction will go essentially to completion – K_c for the Zn/Cu^{2+} system at 298 K is about 1×10^{37}!

HL 9.5 Standard electrode potentials

Cell potentials

The voltmeter in the $Zn|Zn^{2+}||Cu^{2+}|Cu$ cell will read 1.10 V if the concentrations of both solutions are $1 \, mol \, dm^{-3}$ and the temperature is 298 K. This value is called the standard cell potential and gives us some idea of the favourability of the redox reaction:

$$Zn(s) + Cu^{2+}(aq) \rightleftharpoons Zn^{2+}(aq) + Cu(s)$$

The standard cell potential ($E^{\ominus}_{cell}$) is related to the value of $\Delta G^{\ominus}$ and K_c for the reaction. The higher the value (more positive) of the standard cell potential, the more favourable the reaction (ΔG is more negative and the value of K_c is larger).

When the zinc in this cell is replaced with magnesium, the value of the standard cell potential is larger, which indicates that the reaction

$$Mg(s) + Cu^{2+}(aq) \rightarrow Mg^{2+}(aq) + Cu(s)$$

is more favourable (more spontaneous/ΔG is more negative) than the reaction involving zinc (see Figure **9.13** on page **391**). This suggests that magnesium has a greater tendency to reduce Cu^{2+} ions than Zn does.

Thus, using various cells we can measure the tendency for different redox reactions to occur and build up a reactivity series. However, what would be more useful is being able to predict the favourability of a particular redox reaction from a knowledge of the favourability of the individual oxidation and reduction half reactions making up the redox reaction – that is, a way of predicting in which direction a particular redox reaction will occur and how favourable it will be without setting up each cell.

It is not, however, possible to measure the tendency for reactions such as

$$Cu^{2+}(aq) + 2e^- \rightarrow Cu(s)$$

to occur in isolation, because if something is reduced, something else must be oxidised. The tendency of these reactions to occur can be measured only by connecting one half cell to another half cell and measuring the cell potential. However, if we always choose one particular half cell as a reference half cell in the system, then by measuring the cell potentials of lots of cells relative to this half cell we will be able to build up a set of values that allow us to judge the relative oxidising and reducing ability of various species. The reference half cell that we choose is called the standard hydrogen electrode.

The standard hydrogen electrode

Individual half-cell electrode potentials cannot be measured in isolation, and so they are measured relative to a standard. The standard that is chosen is the standard hydrogen electrode (Figure **9.14**).

In the standard hydrogen electrode, hydrogen gas at 1 atm pressure is bubbled around a platinum electrode of very high surface area in a solution of H^+ ions of concentration $1 \, mol \, dm^{-3}$. Platinum is chosen as it is an inert metal, has very little tendency to be oxidised and does not react with acid. The reaction occurring in this half cell is:

$$2H^+(aq) + 2e^- \rightleftharpoons H_2(g)$$

and this is **assigned** a standard electrode potential ($E^\ominus$) of 0.00 V.

Standard electrode potentials

The standard electrode potential ($E^\ominus$) of copper could be measured by connecting a standard copper half cell ($1 \, mol \, dm^{-3} \, Cu^{2+}(aq)/Cu(s)$) to the standard hydrogen electrode (Figure **9.15**, overleaf).

Reactions that go on in the half cells are:

$$H_2(g) \rightarrow 2H^+(aq) + 2e^- \qquad\qquad Cu^{2+}(aq) + 2e^- \rightarrow Cu(s)$$

The hydrogen is oxidised and the Cu^{2+} ions are reduced.

The cell potential when copper is attached to the standard hydrogen electrode is 0.34 V and we can write:

$$Cu^{2+}(aq) + 2e^- \rightleftharpoons Cu(s) \qquad\qquad E^\ominus = +0.34 \, V$$

The standard electrode potential of copper is +0.34 V. The half equations for standard electrode potentials are always written as reduction reactions and, as the reduction of Cu^{2+} occurs when it is attached to the standard hydrogen electrode, the standard electrode potential has a positive sign, indicating that the reduction of copper ions is favourable compared with the standard hydrogen electrode.

HL **Extension**

$$\Delta G = -nFE$$

where n is the number of electrons transferred, F is the Faraday constant and E is the cell potential.

Examiner's tip
You will need to recall the features of the standard hydrogen electrode.

Note: the reaction could also have been written as:

$$H^+(aq) + e^- \rightleftharpoons \tfrac{1}{2}H_2(g)$$
$$E^\ominus = 0.00 \, V$$

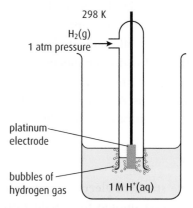

Figure 9.14 The standard hydrogen electrode. Note: $1 \, M = 1 \, mol \, dm^{-3}$.

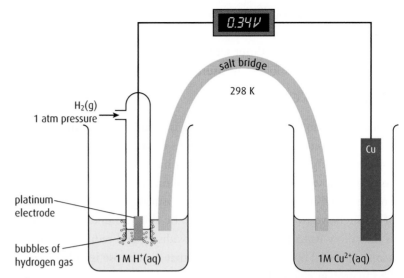

Figure 9.15 Measuring the standard electrode potential of the Cu²⁺/Cu half cell. Note: 1 M = 1 mol dm⁻³.

A very high resistance voltmeter is used so that the current is as low as possible. If current flows, the concentrations of the species in the half cells will change and the system will no longer be under standard conditions.

Figure **9.16** shows a cell in which a standard zinc half cell is connected to a standard hydrogen electrode.

$$2H^+(aq) + 2e^- \rightarrow H_2(g) \qquad\qquad Zn(s) \rightarrow Zn^{2+}(aq) + 2e^-$$

The zinc is oxidised when attached to the standard hydrogen electrode, but as the standard electrode potential is always written in terms of a reduction reaction, we write:

$$Zn^{2+}(aq) + 2e^- \rightleftharpoons Zn(s) \qquad\qquad E^\ominus = -0.76\,V$$

The negative sign indicates that it is the reverse reaction that is favourable when the zinc half cell is connected to a standard hydrogen electrode.

The **standard electrode potential** is the emf (voltage) of a half cell connected to a standard hydrogen electrode, measured under standard conditions. All solutions must be of concentration 1 mol dm⁻³.

The standard electrode potential is always quoted for a reduction reaction.

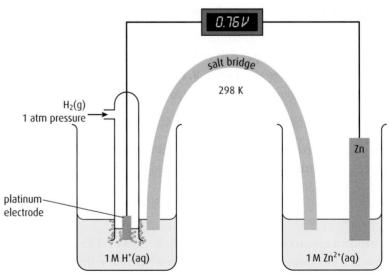

Figure 9.16 Measuring the standard electrode potential of the Zn²⁺/Zn half cell. Note: 1 M = 1 mol dm⁻³.

Some standard electrode potentials are given in Table **9.7**.

Half equation	$E^{\ominus}$/V
$K^+(aq) + e^- \rightleftharpoons K(s)$	-2.92
$Na^+(aq) + e^- \rightleftharpoons Na(s)$	-2.71
$Mg^{2+}(aq) + 2e^- \rightleftharpoons Mg(s)$	-2.36
$Zn^{2+}(aq) + 2e^- \rightleftharpoons Zn(s)$	-0.76
$Fe^{2+}(aq) + 2e^- \rightleftharpoons Fe(s)$	-0.44
$Ni^{2+}(aq) + 2e^- \rightleftharpoons Ni(s)$	-0.23
$Pb^{2+}(aq) + 2e^- \rightleftharpoons Pb(s)$	-0.13
$2H^+(aq) + 2e^- \rightleftharpoons H_2(g)$	0.00
$Cu^{2+}(aq) + 2e^- \rightleftharpoons Cu(s)$	$+0.34$
$I_2(aq) + 2e^- \rightleftharpoons 2I^-(aq)$	$+0.54$
$Br_2(aq) + 2e^- \rightleftharpoons 2Br^-(aq)$	$+1.09$
$Cr_2O_7^{2-}(aq) + 14H^+(aq) + 6e^- \rightleftharpoons 2Cr^{3+}(aq) + 7H_2O(l)$	$+1.33$
$Cl_2(aq) + 2e^- \rightleftharpoons 2Cl^-(aq)$	$+1.36$
$MnO_4^-(aq) + 8H^+(aq) + 5e^- \rightleftharpoons Mn^{2+}(aq) + 4H_2O(l)$	$+1.51$
$2BrO_3^-(aq) + 12H^+(aq) + 10e^- \rightleftharpoons Br_2(aq) + 6H_2O(l)$	$+1.52$
$F_2(g) + 2e^- \rightleftharpoons 2F^-(aq)$	$+2.87$

Table 9.7 Some standard electrode potentials.

Note, in some tables of standard electrode potentials the half equations for the F_2/F^- reaction, for example, are written as:

$$\tfrac{1}{2}F_2(g) + e^- \rightleftharpoons F^-(aq)$$

This makes absolutely no difference to the value of the standard electrode potential.

Working out cell potentials

We can use standard electrode potentials to work out the cell potential of the $Zn|Zn^{2+}||Ni^{2+}|Ni$ cell (Figure **9.17**).

The standard electrode potentials are:

$$Zn^{2+}(aq) + 2e^- \rightleftharpoons Zn(s) \qquad E^{\ominus} = -0.76\,V$$
$$Ni^{2+}(aq) + 2e^- \rightleftharpoons Ni(s) \qquad E^{\ominus} = -0.23\,V$$

However, both of these are written as reduction reactions, and in any cell there must be a reduction reaction and an oxidation reaction. One of the reactions must then occur in the reverse direction.

As the value of the standard electrode potential is more negative for the Zn^{2+}/Zn reaction, this means that the oxidation reaction is more favourable for zinc than for nickel. We therefore reverse the zinc half equation:

$$Zn(s) \rightarrow Zn^{2+}(aq) + 2e^- \qquad E^{\ominus} = +0.76\,V \qquad \textbf{Oxidation}$$
$$Ni^{2+}(aq) + 2e^- \rightarrow Ni(s) \qquad E^{\ominus} = -0.23\,V \qquad \textbf{Reduction}$$

The cell potential is just the sum of these electrode potentials:

$$E^{\ominus}_{cell} = 0.76 - 0.23 = +0.53\,V$$

An overall positive value indicates a spontaneous reaction.

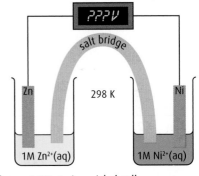

Figure 9.17 A zinc–nickel cell.

In general, the procedure for calculating a cell potential is:
1 write down the half equations and standard electrode potentials for the two reactions involved
2 change the sign of the more negative (less positive) standard electrode potential and add it to the other electrode potential

We are always looking for a cell potential that is **positive** overall, as a positive value indicates a **spontaneous** reaction.

HL The overall equation for the redox reaction is obtained by adding together the two half equations (checking first that the number of electrons balances between them):

$$Zn(s) \rightarrow Zn^{2+}(aq) + 2e^- \qquad \textbf{Oxidation}$$
$$\underline{Ni^{2+}(aq) + 2e^- \rightarrow Ni(s)} \qquad \textbf{Reduction}$$
$$Zn(s) + Ni^{2+}(aq) \rightarrow Zn^{2+}(aq) + Ni(s) \qquad \textbf{Overall redox reaction}$$

Worked example

Work out the overall reaction and calculate the cell potential for a cell consisting of an Fe^{3+}/Fe^{2+} half cell and a Zn/Zn^{2+} half cell.

The two half equations are:

$$Zn^{2+}(aq) + 2e^- \rightleftharpoons Zn(s) \qquad E^{\ominus} = -0.76\,V$$

$$Fe^{3+}(aq) + e^- \rightleftharpoons Fe^{2+}(aq) \qquad E^{\ominus} = +0.77\,V$$

The more negative value is $-0.76\,V$, and this half equation is reversed:

$$Zn(s) \rightarrow Zn^{2+}(aq) + 2e^- \qquad E^{\ominus} = +0.76\,V \qquad \textbf{Oxidation}$$
$$Fe^{3+}(aq) + e^- \rightarrow Fe^{2+}(aq) \qquad E^{\ominus} = +0.77\,V \qquad \textbf{Reduction}$$

The electrode potential values are added together to give the cell potential:

$$E^{\ominus}_{cell} = 0.76 + 0.77 = +1.53\,V \qquad \boxed{\text{positive cell potential = spontaneous}}$$

In order to combine the two half equations to produce the overall redox equation, the Fe^{3+}/Fe^{2+} half equation must be multiplied by 2 so that the number of electrons balances between the two half equations.

$$Zn(s) \rightarrow Zn^{2+}(aq) + 2e^- \qquad E^{\ominus} = +0.76\,V \qquad \textbf{Oxidation}$$
$$\underline{2Fe^{3+}(aq) + 2e^- \rightarrow 2Fe^{2+}(aq)} \qquad E^{\ominus} = +0.77\,V \qquad \textbf{Reduction}$$
$$Zn(s) + 2Fe^{3+}(aq) \rightarrow Zn^{2+}(aq) + 2Fe^{2+}(aq) \qquad E^{\ominus}_{cell} = +1.53\,V \qquad \textbf{Overall redox reaction}$$

Note: although the Fe^{3+}/Fe^{2+} half equation is multiplied by 2, the standard electrode potential is not. The standard electrode potential indicates the potential for a reaction to occur – it is never multiplied by anything when working out a standard cell potential.

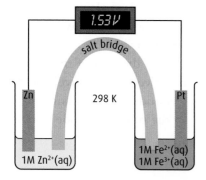

How is a cell potential such as this actually measured?

In the other reactions above there was always a metal in each half cell that could be connected to a voltmeter. However, in the Fe^{3+}/Fe^{2+} half cell there is no solid metal that can be connected to the voltmeter, and therefore an inert (platinum) electrode must be used to make an electrical connection to the half cell. This technique of using a platinum electrode is adopted whenever neither of the components of a half cell is a metal.

If one of the components of a half cell is a gas and the other an aqueous ion, as in the $Cl_2(g)/Cl^-(aq)$ half cell for example, a set-up similar to the standard hydrogen electrode is used except that Cl_2 is substituted for H_2 and the solution contains $1\,mol\,dm^{-3}$ $Cl^-(aq)$ instead of $H^+(aq)$.

The polarity of the electrodes and the direction of electron flow in the external circuit

HL

Consider again the cell made from Mg/Mg^{2+} and Zn/Zn^{2+} half cells (Figure **9.18**). In the right-hand half cell, the magnesium is oxidised and therefore electrons are lost. This means that the magnesium electrode is the negative one, as electrons are produced there. The electrons move through the external circuit from the Mg to the Zn electrode, where they combine with Zn^{2+} ions in the reduction reaction. The Zn electrode is the positive electrode as the electrons are used up there.

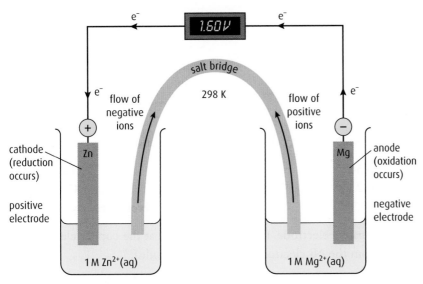

Figure 9.18 A Zn|Zn^{2+}||Mg^{2+}|Mg cell.

> The electrode at which oxidation occurs is the anode; therefore the Mg electrode is the anode. The electrode at which reduction occurs is the cathode; therefore the Zn electrode is the cathode.

Another way to determine which is the negative and positive electrode is to just look at the original electrode potentials:

$$Mg^{2+}(aq) + 2e^- \rightleftharpoons Mg(s) \qquad\qquad E^\ominus = -2.36\,V$$

$$Zn^{2+}(aq) + 2e^- \rightleftharpoons Zn(s) \qquad\qquad E^\ominus = -0.76\,V$$

The electrode potential is more negative for the Mg/Mg^{2+} half cell; therefore the Mg electrode is the negative electrode. The Zn electrode is thus the positive electrode. The electrons flow from the negative electrode to the positive electrode – that is, from Mg to Zn (Figure **9.18**). Negative charge always flows in the same continuous direction around the circuit, so negative ions will flow through the salt bridge from the zinc half cell to the magnesium half cells. Positive ions will flow in the opposite direction.

Note: these are the original standard electrode potentials (for the reduction reactions) – neither has been reversed.

Examiner's tip
Whichever half cell has the more negative standard electrode potential will be the negative electrode in the cell, and the electrons will flow from this half cell to the other one.

Worked example

Predict the cell potential for a cell made up of Cu/Cu^{2+} and Ni/Ni^{2+} half cells. Indicate which is the positive and which is the negative electrode. Give the direction of electron flow in the external circuit and write an overall equation for the reaction that occurs.

The half equations and standard electrode potentials are:

$$Cu^{2+}(aq) + 2e^- \rightleftharpoons Cu(s) \qquad E^\ominus = +0.34\,V$$

$$Ni^{2+}(aq) + 2e^- \rightleftharpoons Ni(s) \qquad E^\ominus = -0.23\,V$$

We can see immediately which is the negative and which the positive electrode. The Ni/Ni^{2+} standard electrode potential is more negative, and therefore this is the negative electrode. The electrons flow from the negative electrode (Ni) to the positive electrode (Cu).

Examiner's tip

There is more than one half equation in the data booklet involving copper – make sure that you select the correct one – you must always check that both the oxidised and reduced species are the same as in your half equation.

The more negative electrode potential is that for the Ni/Ni^{2+} half cell and so this half equation is reversed.

$Cu^{2+}(aq) + 2e^- \rightarrow Cu(s)$	$E^\ominus = +0.34\,V$	**Reduction**
$Ni(s) \rightarrow Ni^{2+}(aq) + 2e^-$	$E^\ominus = +0.23\,V$	**Oxidation**
$Cu^{2+}(aq) + Ni(s) \rightarrow Ni^{2+}(aq) + Cu(s)$	$E^\ominus_{cell} = +0.57\,V$	**Overall redox reaction**

Electrons are lost at the Ni electrode so this is this negative electrode. Electrons are gained at the copper electrode and so this is the positive electrode. Electrons flow from the Ni electrode to the Cu electrode.e

Examiner's tip

In the IBO Chemistry Data booklet the electrode potentials are arranged from negative to positive. The half equation higher up the table is therefore the one that is reversed to give the overall spontaneous reaction.

Self-test 5

Test yourself

14 Predict cell potentials for the following cells. Indicate which is the positive and which is the negative electrode. Give the direction of electron flow in the external circuit and write an overall equation for the reaction that occurs.

a $Ni^{2+}(aq) + 2e^- \rightleftharpoons Ni(s)$ $\qquad$ $Fe^{2+}(aq) + 2e^- \rightleftharpoons Fe(s)$

b $I_2(s) + 2e^- \rightleftharpoons 2I^-(aq)$ $\qquad$ $Cl_2(g) + 2e^- \rightleftharpoons 2Cl^-(aq)$

c $Ag^+(aq) + e^- \rightleftharpoons Ag(s)$ $\qquad$ $Zn^{2+}(aq) + 2e^- \rightleftharpoons Zn(s)$

d $Cr_2O_7^{2-}(aq) + 14H^+(aq) + 6e^- \rightleftharpoons 2Cr^{3+}(aq) + 7H_2O(l)$ $\qquad$ $Fe^{3+}(aq) + e^- \rightleftharpoons Fe^{2+}(aq)$

e $MnO_4^-(aq) + 8H^+(aq) + 5e^- \rightleftharpoons Mn^{2+}(aq) + 4H_2O(l)$ $\qquad$ $2Cl^-(aq) \rightleftharpoons Cl_2(g) + 2e^-$

Using standard electrode potentials to predict the feasibility of a redox reaction $\quad$ (HL)

In chemistry, rather than being concerned with generating electricity and voltaic cells, we more normally use standard electrode potentials to predict whether a particular redox reaction is likely to occur. For instance, will acidified potassium dichromate(VI) oxidise iron(II) ions? If we examine the relevant half equations we get:

$$Cr_2O_7^{2-}(aq) + 14H^+(aq) + 6e^- \rightleftharpoons 2Cr^{3+}(aq) + 7H_2O(l) \qquad E^\ominus = +1.33\,V$$

$$Fe^{3+}(aq) + e^- \rightleftharpoons Fe^{2+}(aq) \qquad E^\ominus = +0.77\,V$$

We are looking at the possibility of Fe^{2+} being oxidised to Fe^{3+}, and therefore we must reverse this half equation:

$$Cr_2O_7^{2-}(aq) + 14H^+(aq) + 6e^-$$
$$\rightarrow 2Cr^{3+}(aq) + 7H_2O(l) \qquad E^\ominus = +1.33\,V \qquad \textbf{Reduction}$$

$$Fe^{2+}(aq) \rightarrow Fe^{3+}(aq) + e^- \qquad E^\ominus = -0.77\,V \qquad \textbf{Oxidation}$$

When we add up these values we get: $E^\ominus_{cell} = 1.33 - 0.77 = +0.56\,V$.

A positive value indicates that the reaction will be spontaneous, so Fe^{2+} ions will be oxidised to Fe^{3+} ions by acidified dichromate(VI) ions.

The overall redox equation is obtained by multiplying the oxidation half equation by 6 and then adding it to the reduction half equation:

$$Cr_2O_7^{2-}(aq) + 14H^+(aq) + 6Fe^{2+}(aq) \rightarrow 2Cr^{3+}(aq) + 7H_2O(l) + 6Fe^{3+}(aq)$$

> Predictions using standard electrode potentials are valid only under standard conditions – that is, at 298 K and with $1\,mol\,dm^{-3}$ solutions. However, as long as the values are not too close to zero, the predictions are likely to be useful even when an experiment is not carried out under standard conditions.

As with using ΔG to predict the spontaneity of a reaction, the fact that a reaction is spontaneous does not tell us anything about the speed of the reaction. Although this reaction occurs relatively rapidly at room temperature, this will not always be the case and some reactions will need heating for them to occur at a significant rate.

Worked example

Predict, using standard electrode potentials, whether acidified potassium dichromate(VI) will oxidise Cl^- ions to Cl_2.

The half equations are

$$Cr_2O_7^{2-}(aq) + 14H^+(aq) + 6e^- \rightleftharpoons 2Cr^{3+}(aq) + 7H_2O(l) \qquad E^\ominus = +1.33\,V$$
$$Cl_2(aq) + 2e^- \rightleftharpoons 2Cl^-(aq) \qquad E^\ominus = +1.36\,V$$

We are looking at the possibility of Cl^- ions being oxidised and must therefore reverse this half equation:

$$Cr_2O_7^{2-}(aq) + 14H^+(aq) + 6e^- \rightarrow 2Cr^{3+}(aq) + 7H_2O(l) \qquad E^\ominus = +1.33\,V \qquad \textbf{Reduction}$$
$$2Cl^-(aq) \rightarrow Cl_2(aq) + 2e^- \qquad E^\ominus = -1.36\,V \qquad \textbf{Oxidation}$$

When the electrode potentials are added together we get: $E^{\ominus}_{\text{cell}} = 1.33 - 1.36 = -0.03\,\text{V}$. The value is negative, which indicates that the reaction will not be spontaneous under standard conditions, and acidified dichromate(VI) will not oxidise Cl^- to Cl_2.

Oxidising and reducing agents

A very **positive** value for $E^{\ominus}$, e.g.

$$Cr_2O_7^{2-}(aq) + 14H^+(aq) + 6e^- \rightarrow 2Cr^{3+}(aq) + 7H_2O(l) \quad E^{\ominus} = +1.33\,\text{V}$$

means that the reduction reaction is very favourable (relative to the standard hydrogen electrode), and the substance has a very strong tendency to pick up electrons from other species – i.e. it is a strong oxidising agent.

> **The more positive the standard electrode potential, the stronger the oxidising agent.**

> Oxidising agents have a strong tendency to remove electrons from other things, i.e. oxidise other species. Oxidising agents are substances that are readily reduced.

A very negative value of the standard electrode potential, e.g.

$$Na^+(aq) + e^- \rightleftharpoons Na(s) \qquad E^{\ominus} = -2.71\,\text{V}$$

indicates that the **reverse reaction** is very favourable:

$$Na(s) \rightarrow Na^+(aq) + e^- \qquad E^{\ominus} = +2.71\,\text{V}$$

Thus, sodium has a very strong tendency to give electrons to other species – that is, to reduce other species. Na is thus a very good reducing agent.

In general then we can say:

> **The more negative the standard electrode potential, the stronger the reducing agent.**

> a substance with a more positive electrode potential will oxidise a substance with a less positive electrode potential
>
> or
>
> a substance with a more negative electrode potential will reduce a substance with a less negative standard electrode potential.

Example 1

Let us consider the half equations:

$$Cr_2O_7^{2-}(aq) + 14H^+(aq) + 6e^- \rightleftharpoons 2Cr^{3+}(aq) + 7H_2O(l) \quad E^{\ominus} = +1.33\,\text{V}$$

$$I_2(aq) + 2e^- \rightleftharpoons 2I^-(aq) \qquad E^{\ominus} = +0.54\,\text{V}$$

$Cr_2O_7^{2-}$ has a more positive standard electrode potential than I_2, and therefore $Cr_2O_7^{2-}$ is a stronger oxidising agent than I_2 and will oxidise I^- to I_2.

Overall reaction:

$$Cr_2O_7^{2-}(aq) + 14H^+(aq) + 6I^-(aq) \rightarrow 2Cr^{3+}(aq) + 7H_2O(l) + 3I_2(aq)$$

$$E_{cell}^{\ominus} = 1.33 - 0.54 = +0.79\,V$$

In this reaction, $Cr_2O_7^{2-}$ is the oxidising agent and I^- is the reducing agent.

Example 2

Let us consider the half equations:

$$Mg^{2+}(aq) + 2e^- \rightleftharpoons Mg(s) \qquad\qquad E^{\ominus} = -2.36\,V$$

$$Pb^{2+}(aq) + 2e^- \rightleftharpoons Pb(s) \qquad\qquad E^{\ominus} = -0.13\,V$$

The standard electrode potential of the Mg/Mg^{2+} half cell is more negative than that of the Pb/Pb^{2+} half cell, which indicates that Mg is a stronger reducing agent than Pb and that Mg will therefore reduce Pb^{2+} to Pb.

The overall equation is:

$$Mg(s) + Pb^{2+}(aq) \rightarrow Mg^{2+}(aq) + Pb(s) \qquad E_{cell}^{\ominus} = +2.23\,V$$

In this reaction, Mg is the reducing agent and Pb^{2+} is the oxidising agent.

Let us consider the standard electrode potentials in Table **9.8**. Species higher in the table reduce those lower in the table. Thus, Na will reduce Mg^{2+} ions, and Zn will reduce Fe^{2+} ions. Species lower in the table oxidise those higher in the table. Thus BrO_3^- will oxidise Cl^- and Br_2 will oxidise I^-.

Half equation	$E^{\ominus}/V$
$K^+(aq) + e^- \rightleftharpoons K(s)$	−2.92
$Na^+(aq) + e^- \rightleftharpoons Na(s)$	−2.71
$Mg^{2+}(aq) + 2e^- \rightleftharpoons Mg(s)$	−2.36
$Zn^{2+}(aq) + 2e^- \rightleftharpoons Zn(s)$	−0.76
$Fe^{2+}(aq) + 2e^- \rightleftharpoons Fe(s)$	−0.44
$Ni^{2+}(aq) + 2e^- \rightleftharpoons Ni(s)$	−0.23
$Pb^{2+}(aq) + 2e^- \rightleftharpoons Pb(s)$	−0.13
$2H^+(aq) + 2e^- \rightleftharpoons H_2(g)$	0.00
$Cu^{2+}(aq) + 2e^- \rightleftharpoons Cu(s)$	+0.34
$I_2(s) + 2e^- \rightleftharpoons 2I^-(aq)$	+0.54
$Br_2(aq) + 2e^- \rightleftharpoons 2Br^-(aq)$	+1.09
$Cr_2O_7^{2-}(aq) + 14H^+(aq) + 6e^- \rightleftharpoons 2Cr^{3+}(aq) + 7H_2O(l)$	+1.33
$Cl_2(aq) + 2e^- \rightleftharpoons 2Cl^-(aq)$	+1.36
$MnO_4^-(aq) + 8H^+(aq) + 5e^- \rightleftharpoons Mn^{2+}(aq) + 4H_2O(l)$	+1.51
$2BrO_3^-(aq) + 12H^+(aq) + 10e^- \rightleftharpoons Br_2(aq) + 6H_2O(l)$	+1.52
$F_2(g) + 2e^- \rightleftharpoons 2F^-(aq)$	+2.87

Table 9.8 Some standard electrode potentials.

strongest reducing agent

decreasing strength of reducing agent

decreasing strength of oxidising agent

strongest oxidising agent

(HL) Reactivity series and electrode potentials – the electrochemical series

We saw earlier in this chapter that a more reactive metal will displace a less reactive metal from solution. For example, zinc is more reactive than copper and displaces copper ions from solution:

$$Zn(s) + Cu^{2+}(aq) \rightarrow Zn^{2+}(aq) + Cu(s) \qquad E^{\ominus}_{cell} = +1.10\,V$$

In terms of standard electrode potentials, the more reactive a metal the more negative its standard electrode potential. The more negative standard electrode potential indicates that the reduction reaction of the metal ion is very unfavourable and therefore that the oxidation of the metal is very favourable. More reactive metals have a greater tendency to be oxidised and thus give electrons to (reduce) other species.

In Table **9.9** Mg is the most reactive metal and Ag the least reactive.

Metals above hydrogen in the reactivity series are stronger reducing agents than hydrogen and should displace hydrogen from a solution of its ions – that is, from acids:

$$Mg(s) + 2H^{+}(aq) \rightarrow Mg^{2+}(aq) + H_2(g) \qquad E^{\ominus}_{cell} = +2.36\,V$$

Metals lower than hydrogen in the reactivity series will not react with acids; thus copper and silver do not react with hydrochloric acid.

In terms of standard electrode potentials, any metal with a negative standard electrode potential is a stronger reducing agent than hydrogen ($E^{\ominus} = 0.00\,V$) and reduces hydrogen ions to hydrogen gas. In other words, metals with negative standard electrode potentials should liberate hydrogen from acids.

We can consider the reactivity of the halogens in terms of their oxidising ability. Thus, chlorine is a stronger oxidising agent than bromine and iodine and will oxidise bromide ions to bromine and iodide ions to iodine. Bromine is a stronger oxidising agent than iodine and will oxidise iodide ions to iodine. In terms of electrons, chlorine has the strongest affinity for electrons and will remove electrons from bromide ions and iodide ions.

Let us consider the standard electrode potentials in Table **9.10**. Chlorine has the most positive standard electrode potential and is therefore the strongest oxidising agent.

$$Cl_2(aq) + 2Br^{-}(aq) \rightarrow 2Cl^{-}(aq) + Br_2(aq) \qquad E^{\ominus}_{cell} = +0.27\,V$$

$$Cl_2(aq) + 2I^{-}(aq) \rightarrow 2Cl^{-}(aq) + I_2(aq) \qquad E^{\ominus}_{cell} = +0.82\,V$$

$$Br_2(aq) + 2I^{-}(aq) \rightarrow 2Br^{-}(aq) + I_2(aq) \qquad E^{\ominus}_{cell} = +0.55\,V$$

These reactions all have a positive electrode potential and are therefore all spontaneous. All other possible reactions between the halogens and the halide ions would have a negative electrode potential and are therefore not spontaneous, e.g.:

$$Br_2(aq) + 2Cl^{-}(aq) \rightarrow 2Br^{-}(aq) + Cl_2(aq) \qquad E^{\ominus}_{cell} = -0.27\,V$$

	$E^{\ominus}$ / V
$Mg^{2+}(aq) + 2e^{-} \rightleftharpoons Mg(s)$	-2.36
$Zn^{2+}(aq) + 2e^{-} \rightleftharpoons Zn(s)$	-0.76
$Fe^{2+}(aq) + 2e^{-} \rightleftharpoons Fe(s)$	-0.44
$Ni^{2+}(aq) + 2e^{-} \rightleftharpoons Ni(s)$	-0.23
$Cu^{2+}(aq) + 2e^{-} \rightleftharpoons Cu(aq)$	$+0.34$
$Ag^{+}(aq) + e^{-} \rightleftharpoons Ag(s)$	$+0.80$

Table 9.9 Reactivity series and electrode potentials.

	$E^{\ominus}$ / V
$I_2(aq) + 2e^{-} \rightleftharpoons 2I^{-}(aq)$	$+0.54$
$Br_2(aq) + 2e^{-} \rightleftharpoons 2Br^{-}(aq)$	$+1.09$
$Cl_2(aq) + 2e^{-} \rightleftharpoons 2Cl^{-}(aq)$	$+1.36$

Table 9.10 Electrode potentials for halogens.

Test yourself

15 Use standard electrode potentials to predict whether the following reactions will be spontaneous. If the reaction is spontaneous, state the oxidising agent and the reducing agent.

a $Cu(s) + Mg^{2+}(aq) \rightarrow Cu^{2+}(aq) + Mg(s)$

b $Cr_2O_7^{2-}(aq) + 14H^+(aq) + 6Br^-(aq)$
  $\rightarrow 2Cr^{3+}(aq) + 7H_2O(l) + 3Br_2(l)$

c $Cr_2O_7^{2-}(aq) + 14H^+(aq) + 6F^-(aq)$
  $\rightarrow 2Cr^{3+}(aq) + 7H_2O(l) + 3F_2(g)$

d $5Fe^{3+}(aq) + Mn^{2+}(aq) + 4H_2O(l)$
  $\rightarrow 5Fe^{2+}(aq) + MnO_4^-(aq) + 8H^+(aq)$

e $Ca(s) + 2H_2O(l) \rightarrow Ca(OH)_2(aq) + H_2(g)$

16 Consider the following electrode potentials:

$U^{4+} + e^- \rightleftharpoons U^{3+}$	$E^\ominus = -0.61\,V$
$U^{3+} + 3e^- \rightleftharpoons U$	$E^\ominus = -1.79\,V$
$Eu^{3+} + e^- \rightleftharpoons Eu^{2+}$	$E^\ominus = -0.43\,V$
$Po^{2+} + 2e^- \rightleftharpoons Po$	$E^\ominus = +0.65\,V$
$In^{3+} + 3e^- \rightleftharpoons In$	$E^\ominus = -0.34\,V$
$Sm^{3+} + e^- \rightleftharpoons Sm^{2+}$	$E^\ominus = -1.15\,V$
$Np^{3+} + 3e^- \rightleftharpoons Np$	$E^\ominus = -1.86\,V$
$Np^{4+} + e^- \rightleftharpoons Np^{3+}$	$E^\ominus = +0.15\,V$

a Select from this list:
  i the strongest oxidising agent
  ii the strongest reducing agent

b Use the standard electrode potentials above to work out whether the following statements are **true** or **false**:
  i Eu^{2+} will reduce In^{3+} to In
  ii Sm^{3+} will oxidise Np to Np^{3+}
  iii Po will reduce Sm^{3+} to Sm^{2+}
  iv Np^{3+} is a stronger reducing agent than Po
  v U is a stronger reducing agent than Np
  vi Np^{3+} will reduce Po^{2+} to Po but will not oxidise Eu^{2+} to Eu^{3+}
  vii Sm^{2+} will not reduce U^{3+} to U but will reduce U^{4+} to U^{3+}

c Predict whether the following reactions will be spontaneous:
  i $3Eu^{3+} + In \rightarrow 3Eu^{2+} + In^{3+}$
  ii $2Eu^{2+} + Po^{2+} \rightarrow 2Eu^{3+} + Po$
  iii $3Np^{3+} + In \rightarrow 3Np^{4+} + In^{3+}$

9.6 Electrolysis of molten salts

Electrolysis

Electrolysis is the breaking down of a substance (in molten state or solution) by the passage of electricity through it.

Electrolysis of molten salts

The experimental set-up for electrolysis of molten lead bromide is shown in Figure **9.19**. The overall reaction is:

$$PbBr_2(l) \xrightarrow[\text{energy}]{\text{electrical}} Pb(l) + Br_2(g)$$

The lead bromide is broken down into its elements, lead and bromine, by the passage of the electricity.

Learning objectives

- Describe the features of an electrolytic cell
- Understand how current is conducted during electrolysis
- Predict the products of electrolysis of a molten salt
- Write half equations for the reactions occurring at the electrodes during electrolysis

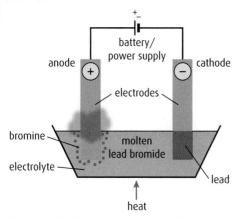

Figure 9.19 The electrolysis of molten lead bromide.

> The anode is the electrode at which oxidation occurs.

> The cathode is the electrode at which reduction occurs.

> An **electrolyte** is a solution or a molten compound that will conduct electricity, with decomposition at the electrodes as it does so. Electrolytes contain ions that are free to move towards the electrodes.

Animation 2

Negative electrode:
$M^+ + e^- \rightarrow M$ **Reduction**
Positive electrode:
$X^- \rightarrow X + e^-$ **Oxidation**

Electrons are taken from the external circuit at the negative electrode (by the positive ions) and given back to the external circuit at the positive electrode (by the negative ions). The circuit is completed, but the electrons that flow into the positive side of the battery are not the ones that flowed out of the negative side of the battery. **No electrons travel through the electrolyte**.

> The electrodes are usually made of **graphite**, a fairly inert non-metal, which conducts electricity.

Positive electrode

At the positive electrode, bromide ions are oxidised and lose electrons to form bromine:

$$2Br^- \rightarrow Br_2 + 2e^-$$ **Oxidation**

Because oxidation occurs at this electrode, the positive electrode is the **anode** in an electrolytic cell.

Negative electrode

At the negative electrode, lead ions are reduced as they gain electrons to form lead:

$$Pb^{2+} + 2e^- \rightarrow Pb$$ **Reduction**

Because reduction occurs at this electrode the negative electrode is the **cathode** in an electrolytic cell.

Conduction of electricity in an electrolytic cell

In the external circuit the current is carried by electrons (delocalised electrons in the metal wire) but in the molten salt (electrolyte) conduction involves movement of **ions** (Figure **9.20**).

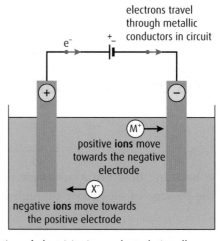

Figure 9.20 Conduction of electricity in an electrolytic cell.

Electrons travel from the negative pole of the battery to the negative electrode. The positive ions in the electrolyte move towards the negative electrode. At the negative electrode electrons are transferred to the positive ions. The negative ions move towards the positive electrode. At the positive electrode the extra electron(s) from the negative ion is/are transferred to the electrode. The electron released from the negative ion travels through the external circuit to the positive pole of the battery.

Ionic salts will not conduct electricity when solid because the ions are held tightly in the lattice structure and are therefore not free to move (Figure **9.21**).

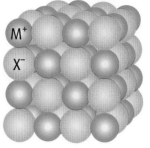

The products of electrolysis of a molten salt

When a molten salt is electrolysed, the products at the electrodes are the elements of which that salt is made up. A metal is formed at the negative electrode, because metals form positive ions, and a non-metal is formed at the positive electrode, because non-metals form negative ions.

Figure 9.21 An ionic lattice.

Electrolysis of molten aluminium oxide (Al₂O₃)

A metal is formed at the negative electrode (cathode) – in this case, aluminium:

$$Al^{3+} + 3e^- \rightarrow Al \qquad \textbf{Reduction}$$

Reduction occurs at the cathode.

A non-metal is formed at the positive electrode – in this case, oxygen:

$$2O^{2-} \rightarrow O_2 + 4e^- \qquad \textbf{Oxidation}$$

Oxidation occurs at the anode.

Electrolysis of molten potassium chloride (KCl)

Potassium is formed at the negative electrode (cathode) and chlorine is formed at the positive electrode (anode):

$$K^+ + e^- \rightarrow K \qquad \textbf{Reduction}$$
$$2Cl^- \rightarrow Cl_2 + 2e^- \qquad \textbf{Oxidation}$$

Electrolysis and ΔG

The overall equation for the electrolysis of aluminium oxide is:

$$2Al_2O_3 \rightarrow 4Al + 3O_2 \quad \Delta G \approx 2000\,kJ\,mol^{-1} \text{ at the melting point of } Al_2O_3$$

The value of ΔG at the melting point of Al_2O_3 is very positive, indicating that the reaction is definitely not spontaneous at this temperature. However, passage of a current continually through the molten salt causes the non-spontaneous reaction to occur.

The differences between an electrolytic cell and a voltaic (electrochemical) cell

The reaction that occurs in an electrolytic cell is non-spontaneous – electricity has to be supplied to cause it to occur (the ΔG for the process is positive). This can be contrasted with an electrochemical cell (voltaic cell), in which a spontaneous reaction can be used to generate electricity (ΔG negative).

Voltaic cell	Electrolytic cell
spontaneous redox reaction produces electricity	non-spontaneous redox reaction (one that would not happen by itself) is brought about by the passage of an electric current
conversion of chemical energy to electrical energy	conversion of electrical energy to chemical energy
anode is negative electrode and cathode is positive electrode	anode is positive electrode and cathode is negative electrode

Test yourself

17 State the products at the anode and cathode
   when the following molten salts are electrolysed:
   a potassium bromide
   b copper(II) chloride
   c nickel(II) oxide
   d calcium chloride

18 Write equations for the reactions at the anode
   and cathode when the following molten salts are
   electrolysed:
   a sodium chloride
   b iron(III) oxide
   c magnesium bromide

Iron is the second most abundant metal in the Earth's crust, and because it is not very reactive it can be extracted relatively easily from its ore by heating with carbon. It has been used since ancient times and, in the form of steel, is the most important construction metal. Mild steel has a very large number of uses, from building bridges to making car bodies. Although iron is not very reactive, it does undergo one very important redox reaction in the presence of air and water – rusting. Rusting of iron structures, machinery, vehicles, etc. costs the world's economies billions of dollars each year.

Aluminium is the most abundant metal in the Earth's crust. It is much more reactive than iron and so more difficult to extract from its compounds. It was not isolated until 1825. The advent of electricity allowed the commercial production of aluminium and has resulted in aluminium replacing iron for many uses. Aluminum has a low density (about one-third the density of iron) and so is useful in aeroplanes, for example. Aluminium is resistant to corrosion, because although it is significantly more reactive than iron, it has an impermeable oxide layer on the surface that prevents further reaction with air.

Learning objectives

- Understand the factors that
  affect the nature of the products
  of electrolysis of aqueous
  solutions
- Work out the relative amounts
  of products at the electrodes
  during electrolysis
- Understand how electrolysis is
  used in electroplating

HL 9.7 Electrolysis of aqueous solutions

Electrolysis of aqueous solutions

Ionic salts also conduct electricity when dissolved in water, as the ions are free to move. These solutions can then be electrolysed, but the products are not as straightforward as for electrolysis of molten salts. The general rule for the products formed at the electrodes when aqueous solutions are electrolysed is:

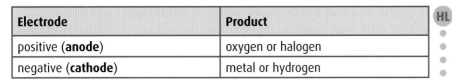

Electrode	Product
positive (**anode**)	oxygen or halogen
negative (**cathode**)	metal or hydrogen

The products obtained from the electrolysis of various $1\,mol\,dm^{-3}$ solutions using platinum electrodes are given in Table **9.11**.

Solution	Product at anode (+)	Product at cathode (−)
copper(II) chloride	chlorine gas	copper metal
copper(II) sulfate	oxygen gas	copper metal
sodium chloride	chlorine gas	hydrogen gas
hydrochloric acid	chlorine gas	hydrogen gas
water (acidified)	oxygen gas	hydrogen gas

Table 9.11 Electrolysis products of aqueous solutions using Pt electrodes.

The **acidified water** is water with a small amount of sulfuric acid added.

Factors that affect the products formed at the electrodes

There are three main factors that affect which product is formed when an aqueous solution of a salt is electrolysed:

1 the standard electrode potentials of the species in solution
2 the concentration of the electrolyte
3 the material from which the electrodes are made

Using the standard electrode potential to predict the product of electrolysis

We will first of all look at the products at the cathode. When sodium chloride solution is electrolysed, a reduction reaction occurs at the cathode and hydrogen gas is formed. The two possible species that are present in the solution that could be reduced are Na^+ and H_2O. Let us consider the standard electrode potentials for the reduction of Na^+ and water:

$$Na^+(aq) + e^- \rightleftharpoons Na(s) \qquad\qquad E^\ominus = -2.71\,V$$

$$H_2O(l) + e^- \rightleftharpoons \tfrac{1}{2}H_2(g) + OH^-(aq) \qquad\qquad E^\ominus = -0.83\,V$$

It can be seen that the standard electrode potential for the reduction of water is much more positive than that for the reduction of Na^+. Therefore the reduction of water is more favourable than the reduction of Na^+, and hydrogen will be formed from the reduction of water rather than sodium metal from the reduction of Na^+.

If we then compare this with the electrolysis of copper(II) sulfate solution, the electrode potentials for the possible reduction reactions are:

$$H_2O(l) + e^- \rightleftharpoons \tfrac{1}{2}H_2(g) + OH^-(aq) \qquad\qquad E^\ominus = -0.83\,V$$

$$Cu^{2+}(aq) + 2e^- \rightleftharpoons Cu(s) \qquad\qquad E^\ominus = +0.34\,V$$

The electrolysis of brine (sodium chloride solution) to produce chlorine, hydrogen and sodium hydroxide is one of the world's most important industrial processes. The industry that has grown up around this is called the chlor-alkali industry and is discussed in more detail in Option **C**.

This approach is perfectly valid for examination questions.

Predicting the products of electrolysis is more complex for metals between zinc and hydrogen in the reactivity series, i.e. for metals such as zinc ($E^\ominus = -0.76\,\text{V}$), nickel ($E^\ominus = -0.23\,\text{V}$) and lead ($E^\ominus = -0.13\,\text{V}$). Electrolysis of a solution of zinc sulfate produces zinc metal at the cathode, electrolysis of nickel chloride solution produces a mixture of nickel and hydrogen gas and electrolysis of lead(II) nitrate solution produces lead metal at the cathode.

You should not be asked about these metals in examination questions.

HL It can be seen that it is more favourable to reduce Cu^{2+} ions than to reduce water and therefore copper, from the reduction of Cu^{2+}, will be formed at the cathode rather than hydrogen.

An alternative approach to that discussed above is to consider the reduction of the metal ion relative to the reduction of H^+ ions, which are also present in aqueous solution at very small concentration due to the dissociation of water. The standard electrode potential for the reduction of H^+ ions is:

$$H^+(aq) + e^- \rightleftharpoons \tfrac{1}{2}H_2(g) \qquad\qquad E^\ominus = 0.00\,\text{V}$$

This approach would predict that the electrolysis of the salt of any metal with a positive standard electrode potential would produce the metal at the cathode, and the electrolysis of the salt of any metal with a negative standard electrode potential would produce hydrogen at the cathode, which does not entirely agree with experimental observations for metals of intermediate reactivity.

In general metals can be divided into three groups.

1 Very reactive metals (with very negative standard electrode potentials), such as sodium, potassium and magnesium – that is, metals above zinc in the reactivity series. These produce hydrogen when aqueous solutions of their ions are electrolysed.
2 Unreactive metals (with positive standard electrode potentials), such as copper or silver. These produce the metal when aqueous solutions of their ions are electrolysed.
3 Metals of intermediate reactivity (with standard electrode potentials between $-0.83\,\text{V}$ and $0.00\,\text{V}$), e.g. zinc, nickel, lead. For these metals it is much more difficult to make predictions and we can get either the metal or a mixture of the metal and hydrogen, depending on the metal and the conditions used.

We can see that it is possible, to a certain extent, to predict the products of electrolysis of aqueous solutions based on the reactivity of the metals and their standard electrode potentials. Problems that arise with using standard electrode potentials are that they refer to standard conditions ($1\,\text{mol}\,\text{dm}^{-3}$ concentrations) and to solutions containing both the oxidised and reduced species.

Formation of halogens at the anode during electrolysis of aqueous solutions

When a solution of sodium iodide is electrolysed iodine is produced at the anode but when a solution of sodium fluoride is electrolysed oxygen is produced at the anode. This can be explained in term of how easy it is to oxidise the halide ions to the element and standard electrode potentials can be used as a guide to this.

Consider the following standard electrode potentials:

$$I_2(s) + 2e^- \rightleftharpoons 2I^-(aq) \qquad\qquad E^\ominus = +0.54\,\text{V}$$
$$O_2(g) + 4H^+(aq) + 4e^- \rightleftharpoons 2H_2O(l) \qquad\qquad E^\ominus = +1.23\,\text{V}$$
$$F_2(s) + 2e^- \rightleftharpoons 2F^-(aq) \qquad\qquad E^\ominus = +2.87\,\text{V}$$

At the anode oxidation occurs and therefore we can reverse all these half equations to produce the oxidation reaction:

$$2I^-(aq) \rightarrow I_2(s) + 2e^- \qquad E_{ox} = -0.54\,V$$

$$2H_2O(l) \rightarrow O_2(g) + 4H^+(aq) + 4e^- \qquad E_{ox} = -1.23\,V$$

$$2F^-(aq) \rightarrow F_2(g) + 2e^- \qquad E_{ox} = -2.87\,V$$

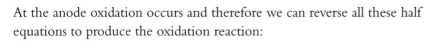

At the anode two oxidation reactions are possible; either the halide ion can be oxidised to produce the halogen, or water can be oxidised to produce oxygen. From these values it can be seen that it is more favourable to oxidise I^- ions (more positive potential for oxidation) than to oxidise water, but it is less favourable to oxidise F^- ions (more negative potential for oxidation). Thus in NaI(aq) iodide ions will be oxidised at the anode to produce iodine, but in NaF(aq), water will be oxidised in preference to fluoride ions to produce oxygen gas at the anode.

Product at the anode during the electrolysis of copper sulfate using graphite electrodes

Oxygen is produced at the anode from the oxidation of water:

$$2H_2O(l) \rightarrow O_2(g) + 4H^+(aq) + 4e^- \qquad \textbf{Oxidation}$$

Nitrates and sulfates contain the nitrogen and sulfur in their highest oxidation states and are not susceptible to oxidation.

It is actually possible to oxidise the SO_4^{2-} ion, but this is much more difficult than the oxidation of water:

$$2H_2O(l) \rightleftharpoons O_2(g) + 4H^+(aq) + 4e^- \qquad E_{ox} = -1.23\,V$$

$$SO_4^{2-}(aq) \rightleftharpoons \tfrac{1}{2}S_2O_8^{2-}(aq) + e^- \qquad E_{ox} = -2.01\,V$$

Just as the production of hydrogen at the cathode may be discussed in terms of the reduction of hydrogen ions from the dissociation of water (rather than the reduction of water), the production of oxygen at the anode may be discussed in terms of the oxidation of OH^- ions from the dissociation of water:

$$4OH^-(aq) \rightarrow O_2(g) + 2H_2O(l) + 4e^-$$

The effect of concentration of the electrolyte on the products at the electrodes

We will consider the products at the anode when a solution of sodium chloride is electrolysed. The two species in solution that can be oxidised at the anode are Cl^- and H_2O and the equations for the relevant standard electrode potentials are:

$$O_2(g) + 4H^+(aq) + 4e^- \rightleftharpoons 2H_2O(l) \qquad E^\ominus = +1.23\,V$$

$$Cl_2(g) + 2e^- \rightleftharpoons 2Cl^-(aq) \qquad E^\ominus = +1.36\,V$$

E_{ox} is the potential for oxidation.

Electrolysis of sulfates and nitrates always produces oxygen gas at the anode.

Note: $S_2O_8^{2-}$ contains a peroxo group, and so the oxidation state of S is still +6; the O is oxidised.

These are both reduction reactions.

HL

At very low chloride concentrations the product of electrolysis is mainly oxygen, but with more concentrated solutions chlorine is the major product.

Extension

The exact reasons for this are complex, but it can be explained in terms of the difficulty in transferring electrons from water across the electrode solution interface – a higher voltage is required. The voltage in excess of the expected voltage is known as the overvoltage.

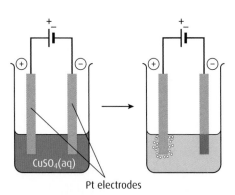

Figure 9.22 Electrolysis of copper sulfate solution using platinum electrodes.

Animation 3

The blue colour of the solution is due to the presence of $Cu^{2+}(aq)$ ions. The colour of the solution becomes paler as the Cu^{2+} ions are removed from the solution at the cathode.

Animation 4

We are, however, interested in the oxidation reactions and these equations must be reversed:

$$2H_2O(l) \rightarrow O_2(g) + 4H^+(aq) + 4e^- \qquad E_{ox} = -1.23\,V$$
$$2Cl^-(aq) \rightarrow Cl_2(g) + 2e^- \qquad E_{ox} = -1.36\,V$$

From these values it can be seen that it is slightly more favourable (E_{ox} more positive) to oxidise water to form oxygen than to oxidise Cl^- to form chlorine. If a solution of sodium chloride of low concentration is electrolysed, the major product at the anode is oxygen. However, these values are very close together, and at higher concentrations of sodium chloride chlorine becomes the major product.

How the nature of the electrodes affects the nature of the products formed

In order to illustrate this, we will consider the electrolysis of copper sulfate solution using two different sets of electrodes. Different products are obtained at the anode depending on the material of which the electrodes are made.

Electrolysis of copper sulfate solution using inert electrodes (graphite or platinum)

Electrolysis of copper sulfate solution using platinum electrodes is shown in Figure **9.22**. The products and half equations at each electrode are:

Electrode	Product	Half equation
anode (+)	oxygen	$2H_2O(l) \rightarrow O_2(g) + 4H^+(aq) + 4e^-$
cathode (−)	copper	$Cu^{2+}(aq) + 2e^- \rightarrow Cu(s)$

Experimental observations

During the experiment, the cathode (−) becomes coated in a brown metal (copper), bubbles of a colourless gas (oxygen) are given off at the anode (+), the blue colour of the solution fades and the solution becomes more acidic (test with a pH meter or pH paper).

The oxidation of water at the anode produces H^+ ions as well as O_2. This means that the solution becomes acidic.

The sulfate ions remain unchanged in the solution, and, as H^+ ions are also produced, the remaining solution after all the copper ions have been removed by electrolysis is sulfuric acid (H_2SO_4).

Electrolysis of copper sulfate solution using copper electrodes

Electrolysis of copper sulfate solution using copper electrodes is shown in Figure **9.23**.

Experimental observations

The positive electrode (anode) becomes smaller, the negative electrode (cathode) becomes coated with a brown metal (copper) and the solution remains the same colour.

The reaction at the cathode is exactly the same as when inert electrodes are used. However, at the anode the reaction is different and no oxygen is given off. The reaction at the anode is oxidation and two possible oxidation reactions are possible:

$$Cu(s) \rightarrow Cu^{2+}(aq) + 2e^- \qquad E_{ox} = -0.34\,V$$

$$2H_2O(l) \rightarrow O_2(g) + 4H^+(aq) + 4e^- \qquad E_{ox} = -1.23\,V$$

The potential for oxidation of copper is more positive than that for the oxidation of water, and therefore the oxidation of copper is more favourable than the oxidation of water. Thus copper ions pass into solution from the anode and oxygen is not produced. The oxidation of copper at the anode was not possible when inert electrodes were used.

The overall processes that occur can be summarised as:

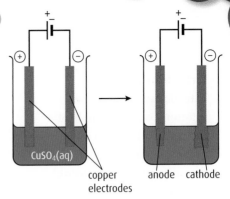

Figure 9.23 Electrolysis of copper sulfate solution using copper electrodes.

Electrode	Product	Half equation
anode (+)	copper ions pass into solution	$Cu(s) \rightarrow Cu^{2+}(aq) + 2e^-$
cathode (−)	copper	$Cu^{2+}(aq) + 2e^- \rightarrow Cu(s)$

The net process is therefore a transfer of copper from the anode to the cathode. If pure copper electrodes are used, the mass of copper lost from the anode will be equal to the mass of copper deposited on the cathode.

As one Cu^{2+} ion is removed from the solution at the cathode for every Cu^{2+} ion added to the solution at the anode, the overall concentration of Cu^{2+} ions in the electrolyte does not change and the blue colour of the solution remains constant.

This process is used in the purification of copper. The anode is then made of impure copper and the cathode of pure copper. Copper dissolves from the anode and is deposited as pure copper at the cathode. Impurities are left as a sludge below the anode or go into solution. The gain in mass of the cathode is less than the loss in mass of the anode as a result of the impurities.

Electroplating

Electroplating is the process of coating an object with a thin layer of a metal using electrolysis. The object to be coated should be used as the cathode, the anode should be made of the metal with which the object is to be plated and the electrolyte will normally be a solution containing the ions of the coating metal. The object to be plated must be thoroughly cleaned before electroplating, otherwise the coating will not stick properly to the surface. Figure **9.24** shows the experimental set-up for coating a key with copper.

Animation 5

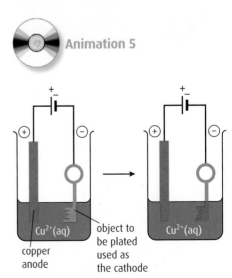

Figure 9.24 Experimental set-up for coating a key with copper.

The reactions involved are:

Electrode	Half equation
anode (+)	$Cu(s) \rightarrow Cu^{2+}(aq) + 2e^-$
cathode (−)	$Cu^{2+}(aq) + 2e^- \rightarrow Cu(s)$

The processes here are essentially the same as for the electrolysis of copper sulfate solution using copper electrodes. The copper anode gets smaller as copper ions go into solution and the colour of the electrolyte remains constant as the concentration of $Cu^{2+}(aq)$ ions remains constant.

Electrolysis of water

Distilled water is a very poor conductor of electricity, and so the electrolysis of water is usually carried out on water to which small amount of sulfuric acid has been added (acidified water). Universal indicator has also been added to the water in Figure **9.25**.

The reaction that occurs at the anode (+) is oxidation of water:

$$2H_2O(l) \rightarrow O_2(g) + 4H^+(aq) + 4e^-$$

The product at the anode is oxygen gas. H^+ ions are also produced in this reaction, and the universal indicator is redder around the anode.

The reaction that occurs at the cathode (−) is reduction of water:

$$H_2O(l) + e^- \rightarrow \tfrac{1}{2}H_2(g) + OH^-(aq)$$

The product at the cathode is hydrogen gas. OH^- ions are also produced at the cathode, and the universal indicator is blue around the cathode.

The H^+ ions produced at the anode combined with the OH^- ions formed at the cathode so that the overall reaction when water is electrolysed is:

$$2H_2O(l) \rightarrow 2H_2(g) + O_2(g)$$

It can be seen from this equation that twice as much hydrogen as oxygen should be collected. Why this occurs may be understood by looking at the half equations:

$$2H_2O(l) \rightarrow O_2(g) + 4H^+(aq) + \mathbf{4e^-} \qquad \textbf{Anode}$$
$$4H_2O(l) + \mathbf{4e^-} \rightarrow 2H_2(g) + 4OH^-(aq) \qquad \textbf{Cathode}$$

The half equations have been written here so that the number of electrons is the same in each.

When four electrons are lost at the anode, one molecule of O_2 is formed, but when four electrons are gained at the cathode, two molecules of H_2 are formed. Electrons must be lost from the anode at the same rate at which they are gained at the cathode (continuous flow of electrons in the external circuit), so two molecules of H_2 are formed for every molecule of O_2 formed.

Examiner's tip
The electrolyte must be a solution containing ions of the plating metal. To select a suitable solution, remember that **all nitrates are soluble in water**.

Steel objects can be electroplated with chromium to prevent rusting and to provide a decorative finish.

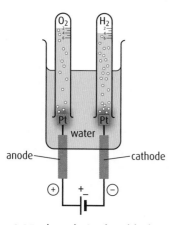

Figure 9.25 Electrolysis of acidified water.

Quantitative electrolysis

HL

In this section we will investigate the factors that affect the amount of product formed at the electrodes.

The factors that affect the amount of product formed at the electrodes are:

- current
- time of electrolysis
- charge on the ion

Current

As you can see from the equation, the current is directly proportional to the charge, and hence to the number of electrons, that flows around the circuit. If twice the current flows in a certain time, then twice as much charge will pass and twice as many electrons will be transferred to/from ions; therefore twice as many moles of substance will be produced.

Let us consider the half equation:

$$Cu^{2+}(aq) + 2e^- \rightarrow Cu(s)$$

To produce 1 mole of copper, 2 moles of electrons must flow around the circuit. A current of about 2.23 A must flow for 24 hours to produce 1 mol Cu. If a current of 4.46 A flows for 24 hours, twice as many electrons (4 mol) will flow around the circuit, and 2 mol Cu will be formed.

Time of electrolysis

If current flows for twice the time, then twice as many electrons will be transferred and twice as much product will be formed.

Time, like current, is directly proportional to the charge, and hence number of electrons, that flows around the circuit.

Charge on the ion

Consider electrolysis of molten samples containing Na^+, Mg^{2+} and Al^{3+} ions. These ions will be reduced according to the equations:

$$Na^+ + e^- \rightarrow Na$$

$$Mg^{2+} + 2e^- \rightarrow Mg$$

$$Al^{3+} + 3e^- \rightarrow Al$$

Therefore if three moles of electrons are passed through each electrolyte, 3 mol Na, 1.5 mol Mg and 1 mol Al will be obtained. This can also be seen if we re-write the above half equations using $3e^-$ in each:

$$3Na^+ + 3e^- \rightarrow 3Na$$

$$\tfrac{3}{2}Mg^{2+} + 3e^- \rightarrow \tfrac{3}{2}Mg$$

$$Al^{3+} + 3e^- \rightarrow Al$$

$$Q = It$$

Q = charge (in coulombs, C)
I = current (in amperes, A)
t = time (in seconds, s)

The number of moles of substance produced at the electrodes is proportional to the current and the time and inversely proportional to the charge on the ion.

Worked examples

How much copper and how much oxygen are formed when 0.80 mol of electrons are passed through aqueous copper sulfate solution using platinum electrodes?

The equations for the reactions at the electrodes are:

$$2H_2O(l) \rightarrow O_2(g) + 4H^+(aq) + 4e^- \qquad \textbf{Anode}$$
$$Cu^{2+}(aq) + 2e^- \rightarrow Cu(s) \qquad \textbf{Cathode}$$

Four moles of electrons are required to produce one mole of O_2 at the anode, so the number of moles of oxygen produced when 0.80 mol of electrons are passed is $\frac{0.80}{4}$, i.e. 0.20 mol.

Two moles of electrons are required to produce one mole of Cu at the cathode, so the number of moles of copper produced when 0.80 mol of electrons are passed is $\frac{0.80}{2}$, i.e. 0.40 mol.

> This is essentially the same approach as working out the number of moles of product formed in a moles question.

The same amount of current is passed for the same amount of time through aqueous sodium chloride, and aqueous copper sulfate. Platinum electrodes were used throughout. Compare the volumes of all gases produced and the volume of gas produced in each cell.

The products formed at the electrodes and the half equations for their formation are as follows:

NaCl(aq)

$$2Cl^-(aq) \rightarrow Cl_2(g) + 2e^- \qquad \textbf{Anode}$$
$$2H_2O(l) + 2e^- \rightarrow H_2(g) + 2OH^-(aq) \qquad \textbf{Cathode}$$

CuSO$_4$(aq)

$$2H_2O(l) \rightarrow O_2(g) + 4H^+(aq) + 4e^- \qquad \textbf{Anode}$$
$$Cu^{2+}(aq) + 2e^- \rightarrow Cu(s) \qquad \textbf{Cathode}$$

If we now re-write the equations involving gases so that the same number of electrons is transferred in each we get:

$$4Cl^-(aq) \rightarrow 2Cl_2(g) + 4e^- \qquad \textbf{Chlorine}$$
$$4H_2O(l) + 4e^- \rightarrow 2H_2(g) + 4OH^-(aq) \qquad \textbf{Hydrogen}$$
$$2H_2O(l) \rightarrow O_2(g) + 4H^+(aq) + 4e^- \qquad \textbf{Oxygen}$$

From this it can be seen that the volume of chlorine and hydrogen produced would be the same, but the volume of oxygen produced would be half that of either of the other two gases. Therefore, for every mole of oxygen gas produced, two moles of hydrogen and two moles of chlorine are produced.

The total volume of gas produced in the first cell (chlorine and hydrogen) is thus four times the amount of gas produced in the second cell (oxygen).

> Actually, if the experiment is carried out in the laboratory, the results will not match this exactly, as the gases are soluble to different extents in water.

Test yourself •

19 Predict the products at the anode and cathode when the following aqueous solutions are electrolysed using platinum electrodes:
  a potassium iodide solution
  b calcium nitrate solution
  c concentrated potassium chloride solution
  d magnesium sulfate solution
  e silver nitrate solution

20 Write equations for the reactions at the anode and cathode when the following solutions are electrolysed using platinum electrodes:

  a sodium sulfate solution
  b copper fluoride solution
  c magnesium nitrate solution

21 0.20 mol of electrons are passed through each of the following electrolytic cells. In each case state the number of moles of each product formed.
  a molten sodium chloride
  b aqueous coppe chloride solution
  c aqueous potassium sulfate solution

Exam-style questions

1 Which compound contains chlorine with the lowest oxidation number?

  A $NaCl$ **B** $HOCl$ **C** Cl_2O_7 **D** ClF

2 Which of the following is **not** a redox reaction?

  A $Zn(NO_3)_2(aq) + Mg(s) \rightarrow Mg(NO_3)_2(aq) + Zn(s)$
  B $U(s) + 6ClF(l) \rightarrow UF_6(l) + 3Cl_2(g)$
  C $2NO_2(g) \rightarrow N_2O_4(g)$
  D $2SO_2(g) + O_2(g) \rightarrow 2SO_3(g)$

3 Which of the following half equations represents a reduction reaction?

  A $CuCl \rightarrow Cu^{2+} + Cl^- + e^-$
  B $N_2O_4 + 2H_2O \rightarrow 2NO_3^- + 4H^+ + 2e^-$
  C $VO^{2+} + 2H^+ + e^- \rightarrow V^{3+} + H_2O$
  D $MnO_4^{2-} \rightarrow MnO_4^- + e^-$

4 Consider the following reactions for four metals:

  $Q(s) + X(NO_3)_2(aq) \rightarrow Q(NO_3)_2(aq) + X(s)$ $Q(s) + Z(NO_3)_2(aq) \rightarrow Q(NO_3)_2(aq) + Z(s)$

  $Z(s) + X(NO_3)_2(aq) \rightarrow Z(NO_3)_2(aq) + X(s)$ $D(s) + Z(NO_3)_2(aq) \rightarrow D(NO_3)_2(aq) + Z(s)$

  From these data it can be deduced that:

  A X is more reactive than Q
  B Q is the most reactive metal
  C Z is a stronger reducing agent than X
  D D is a stronger reducing agent than Q

5 How many electrons are required when the following half equation is balanced using the smallest possible integers?

$$Br_2 + H_2O \rightarrow BrO_3^- + H^+ + e^-$$

    A 2   **B** 5   **C** 10   **D** 12

HL **6** Use the following standard electrode potentials to calculate the cell potential when an Fe^{2+}/Fe^{3+} half cell is connected to a Cl_2/Cl^- half cell:

$$Fe^{3+}(aq) + e^- \rightleftharpoons Fe^{2+}(aq) \qquad\qquad E^\ominus = +0.77\,V$$

$$Cl_2(aq) + 2e^- \rightleftharpoons 2Cl^-(aq) \qquad\qquad E^\ominus = +1.36\,V$$

    A $-0.18\,V$ **B** $+2.13\,V$ **C** $+0.59\,V$ **D** $+0.09\,V$

7 Consider the following standard electrode potentials:

$$Mn^{2+} + 2e^- \rightleftharpoons Mn \qquad E^\ominus = -1.18\,V \qquad\qquad Pb^{2+} + 2e^- \rightleftharpoons Pb \qquad E^\ominus = -0.13\,V$$

$$Co^{2+} + 2e^- \rightleftharpoons Co \qquad E^\ominus = -0.28\,V \qquad\qquad Pd^{2+} + 2e^- \rightleftharpoons Pd \qquad E^\ominus = +0.99\,V$$

From these data it can be deduced that:

    A Co is a stronger reducing agent than Mn

    B Pb^{2+} is a stronger oxidising agent than Pd^{2+}

    C Mn is a stronger reducing agent than Pd

    D Co^{2+} is a stronger reducing agent than Mn^{2+}

8 Use the following standard electrode potentials to decide which reaction will be spontaneous:

$$Cr^{3+} + e^- \rightleftharpoons Cr^{2+} \qquad\qquad E^\ominus = -0.41\,V$$

$$Cr^{3+} + 3e^- \rightleftharpoons Cr \qquad\qquad E^\ominus = -0.74\,V$$

$$Po^{2+} + 2e^- \rightleftharpoons Po \qquad\qquad E^\ominus = +0.65\,V$$

$$UO_2^+ + 4H^+ + e^- \rightleftharpoons U^{4+} + 2H_2O \qquad E^\ominus = +0.62\,V$$

$$ReO_4^- + 8H^+ + 7e^- \rightleftharpoons Re + 4H_2O \qquad E^\ominus = +0.36\,V$$

    A $UO_2^+ + 4H^+ + 2Po^{2+} \rightarrow U^{4+} + 2H_2O + 2Po$

    B $2Cr + 3Po^{2+} \rightarrow 2Cr^{3+} + 3Po$

    C $Re + 4H_2O + 7Cr^{3+} \rightarrow ReO_4^- + 8H^+ + 7Cr^{2+}$

    D $3U^{4+} + 6H_2O + Cr^{3+} \rightarrow Cr + 3UO_2^+ + 12H^+$

9 An experiment is carried out to electroplate a key with nickel. Which of the following is correct about the way the experiment is set up?

    A The cathode is made of nickel and the key is the anode.

    B The electrolyte is a solution of copper sulfate.

    C The key is the cathode and the electrolyte is a nickel sulfate solution.

    D The cathode is made of nickel and the electrolyte is a nickel sulfate solution.

HL **10** A copper sulfate solution is electrolysed for 30 minutes using platinum electrodes. 0.010 mol copper is deposited on one of the electrodes. Which of the following is correct?

     A   0.020 mol of oxygen is produced at the cathode

     B   0.010 mol of oxygen is produced at the anode

     C   0.010 mol of hydrogen is produced at the cathode

     D   0.0050 mol of oxygen is produced at the anode

11 a Define **oxidation** in terms of electrons. [1]

   b Consider the following, unbalanced equation for a redox reaction:

$$MnO_4^-(aq) + H^+(aq) + Fe^{2+}(aq) \rightarrow Mn^{2+}(aq) + Fe^{3+}(aq) + H_2O(l)$$

     i What is the oxidation number of Mn in MnO_4^-? [1]

     ii Identify the reducing agent in this reaction. [1]

     iii Balance the equation. [2]

12 a Define a **reducing agent** in terms of electrons. [1]

   b A series of experiments was carried out in order to work out a reactivity series for some metals. Different metals were added to solutions of salts and the following experimental data were obtained:

	Metal	Salt solution	Observations
I	zinc	copper(II) sulfate	brown deposit formed and the blue colour of the solution fades
II	zinc	lead(II) nitrate	grey crystals formed on the piece of zinc
III	copper	lead(II) nitrate	no reaction
IV	zinc	magnesium nitrate	no reaction

     i Write an ionic equation for the reaction that occurs in experiment **I**. [2]

     ii What do the results of experiment **III** indicate about the relative reactivity of copper and lead? [1]

     iii Arrange the metals in order of reactivity, stating clearly which is the most reactive and which the least. [1]

     iv Explain which of the four metals is the strongest reducing agent. [3]

     v Write an ionic equation for the reaction between magnesium and lead nitrate. [2]

   c A voltaic cell was set up with a piece of magnesium dipping into a solution of magnesium nitrate and a piece of zinc dipping into a solution of zinc nitrate.

     i Draw a labelled diagram of the voltaic cell. Label the anode in the cell and show the direction of electron flow in the external circuit. [3]

     ii Write an ionic equation for the reaction that occurs in the zinc half cell and classify this reaction as oxidation or reduction. [2]

   d When a chlorine solution is added to a solution containing bromide ions, a reaction occurs.

     i Write an ionic equation for this reaction. [2]

     ii Identify the oxidising agent in this reaction. [1]

13 Sodium metal can be obtained by the electrolysis of molten sodium chloride.

   a Explain why solid sodium chloride does not conduct electricity but molten sodium chloride does. [2]

   b State the name of the product at the anode in this process and write half equations for the reactions at each electrode, stating clearly which is which. [3]

14 Standard electrode potentials are measured relative to the standard hydrogen electrode.

   a Draw a labelled diagram showing the essential features of a standard hydrogen electrode. **[5]**

   b The diagram shows a voltaic cell:

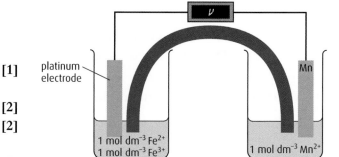

     i Use standard electrode potentials in the IBO Chemistry Data booklet to calculate the standard cell potential. **[1]**

     ii Write an equation, including state symbols, for the overall cell reaction. **[2]**

     iii Explain which electrode is the anode. **[2]**

     iv Show on the diagram the direction of electron flow in the external circuit. **[1]**

     v Explain the role of the salt bridge in this cell. **[2]**

15 Consider the following half equations and standard electrode potentials:

$$MnO_4^-(aq) + 8H^+(aq) + 5e^- \rightleftharpoons Mn^{2+}(aq) + 4H_2O(l) \qquad E^\ominus = +1.51\,V$$

$$Cl_2(g) + 2e^- \rightleftharpoons 2Cl^-(aq) \qquad E^\ominus = +1.36\,V$$

$$Cr_2O_7^{2-}(aq) + 14H^+(aq) + 6e^- \rightleftharpoons 2Cr^{3+}(aq) + 7H_2O(l) \qquad E^\ominus = +1.33\,V$$

$$Br_2(l) + 2e^- \rightleftharpoons 2Br^-(aq) \qquad E^\ominus = +1.09\,V$$

   a Use these equations to identify, giving a reason, the strongest oxidising agent. **[2]**

   b A solution of acidified potassium dichromate(VI) is added to a solution containing equal concentrations of bromide ions and chloride ions. Give the balanced equation for the reaction that occurs. **[3]**

   c State and explain the sign of $\Delta G^\ominus$ for the following reaction: **[2]**

$$2Cl^-(aq) + Br_2(l) \rightarrow Cl_2(g) + 2Br^-(aq)$$

   d Consider the unbalanced half equation:

$$\underset{\text{methanoic acid}}{HCOOH(aq)} + H^+(aq) + e^- \rightarrow \underset{\text{methanal}}{HCHO(aq)} + H_2O(l) \qquad E^\ominus = +0.06\,V$$

     i State the oxidation numbers of C in HCOOH and HCHO and use these to explain whether HCOOH is oxidised or reduced. **[3]**

     ii Balance the half equation. **[1]**

     iii Write a balanced equation for the spontaneous reaction that occurs when a solution containing MnO_4^- and H^+ is added to a solution containing methanal. **[2]**

     iv Explain why, when the two solutions in **iii** are mixed, a reaction may not occur. **[1]**

16 a A concentrated solution of sodium chloride is electrolysed using platinum electrodes. State the products formed at the anode and the cathode and write half equations for their formation. **[4]**

   b When a solution of copper sulfate is electrolysed using platinum electrodes, a gas is formed at one of the electrodes.

     i Identify the electrode at which the gas is formed and state an equation for its formation. **[2]**

     ii State two ways in which the electrolyte changes during this experiment. **[2]**

   c When a solution of copper sulfate is electrolysed using copper electrodes, no gas is evolved.

     i Write equations for the half equations occurring at the anode and cathode in this cell. **[2]**

     ii State and explain any changes in the appearance of the electrolyte during this experiment. **[2]**

Summary

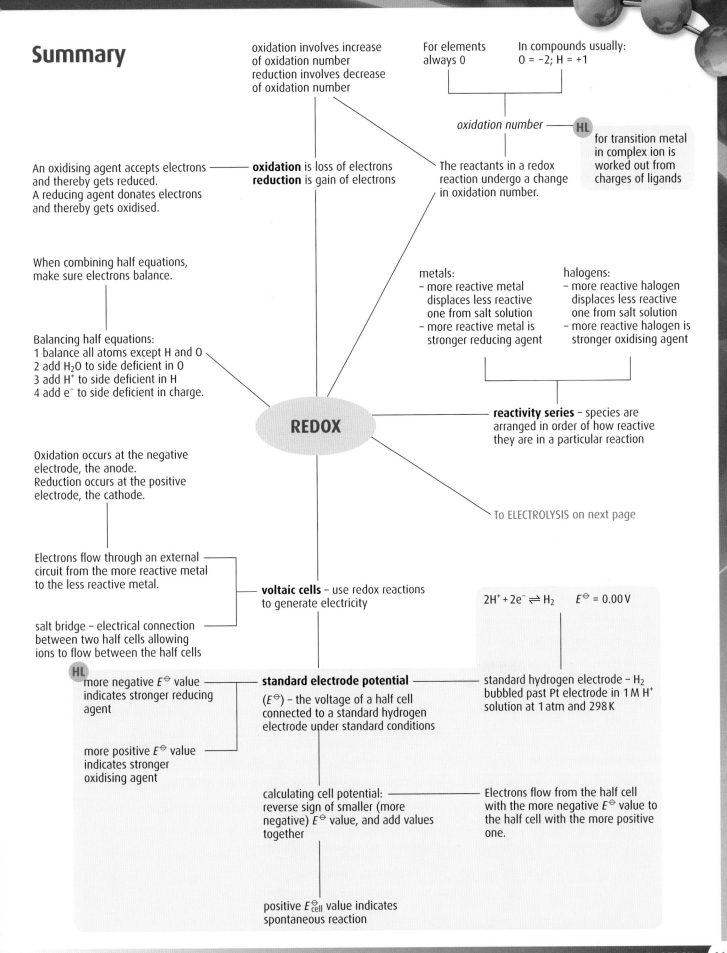

oxidation involves increase of oxidation number
reduction involves decrease of oxidation number

For elements always 0

In compounds usually: $O = -2$; $H = +1$

oxidation number — **HL** for transition metal in complex ion is worked out from charges of ligands

An oxidising agent accepts electrons and thereby gets reduced.
A reducing agent donates electrons and thereby gets oxidised.

oxidation is loss of electrons
reduction is gain of electrons

The reactants in a redox reaction undergo a change in oxidation number.

When combining half equations, make sure electrons balance.

Balancing half equations:
1 balance all atoms except H and O
2 add H_2O to side deficient in O
3 add H^+ to side deficient in H
4 add e^- to side deficient in charge.

metals:
– more reactive metal displaces less reactive one from salt solution
– more reactive metal is stronger reducing agent

halogens:
– more reactive halogen displaces less reactive one from salt solution
– more reactive halogen is stronger oxidising agent

REDOX

reactivity series – species are arranged in order of how reactive they are in a particular reaction

Oxidation occurs at the negative electrode, the anode.
Reduction occurs at the positive electrode, the cathode.

To ELECTROLYSIS on next page

Electrons flow through an external circuit from the more reactive metal to the less reactive metal.

voltaic cells – use redox reactions to generate electricity

$2H^+ + 2e^- \rightleftharpoons H_2$ $E^\ominus = 0.00\,V$

salt bridge – electrical connection between two half cells allowing ions to flow between the half cells

HL more negative $E^\ominus$ value indicates stronger reducing agent

standard electrode potential
($E^\ominus$) – the voltage of a half cell connected to a standard hydrogen electrode under standard conditions

standard hydrogen electrode – H_2 bubbled past Pt electrode in 1 M H^+ solution at 1 atm and 298 K

more positive $E^\ominus$ value indicates stronger oxidising agent

calculating cell potential: reverse sign of smaller (more negative) $E^\ominus$ value, and add values together

Electrons flow from the half cell with the more negative $E^\ominus$ value to the half cell with the more positive one.

positive $E^\ominus_{cell}$ value indicates spontaneous reaction

Summary – continued

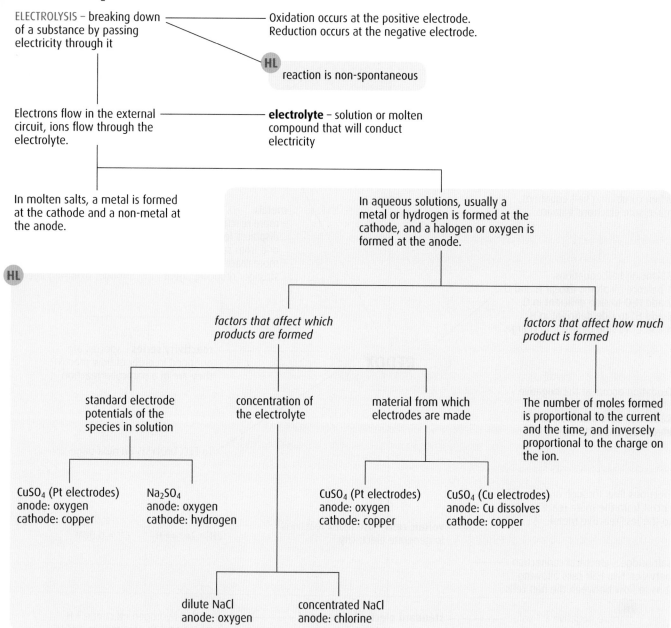

ELECTROLYSIS – breaking down of a substance by passing electricity through it

Oxidation occurs at the positive electrode.
Reduction occurs at the negative electrode.

HL reaction is non-spontaneous

Electrons flow in the external circuit, ions flow through the electrolyte.

electrolyte – solution or molten compound that will conduct electricity

In molten salts, a metal is formed at the cathode and a non-metal at the anode.

In aqueous solutions, usually a metal or hydrogen is formed at the cathode, and a halogen or oxygen is formed at the anode.

HL

factors that affect which products are formed

factors that affect how much product is formed

standard electrode potentials of the species in solution

concentration of the electrolyte

material from which electrodes are made

The number of moles formed is proportional to the current and the time, and inversely proportional to the charge on the ion.

$CuSO_4$ (Pt electrodes)
anode: oxygen
cathode: copper

Na_2SO_4
anode: oxygen
cathode: hydrogen

$CuSO_4$ (Pt electrodes)
anode: oxygen
cathode: copper

$CuSO_4$ (Cu electrodes)
anode: Cu dissolves
cathode: copper

dilute NaCl
anode: oxygen

concentrated NaCl
anode: chlorine

Organic chemistry 10

10.1 Homologous series

Introduction to organic chemistry

Organic chemistry is the study of carbon compounds, and specifically compounds containing a C–H bond. The chemistry of carbon is more extensive than that of any other element, and there are more compounds of carbon than of all other elements put together. There are so many carbon compounds because of the fact that the C atoms can join together to form chains and rings: a property called catenation. The source of many carbon compounds is crude oil (petroleum), and very many substances may be separated from this complex mixture by the process of fractional distillation. These molecules form the basis of organic synthesis reactions, in which ever-more complex molecules may be made and used as medicines, cosmetics, polymers, etc.

Alkanes

The alkanes are a family of hydrocarbons. The first few members are shown in Table **10.1** (page **422**). These compounds are all straight-chain alkanes, and the molecular formula of any of these alkanes can be represented by the general formula C_nH_{2n+2}. So, for instance, eicosane, the alkane that has 20 C atoms, would have $(20 \times 2) + 2$, i.e. 42, H atoms and the molecular formula $C_{20}H_{42}$.

Two types of structural formula are shown in Table **10.1**. The condensed structural formula is the simplest representation that shows how the atoms are joined together in a molecule. C_4H_{10} is not a structural formula, as it could represent either of these molecules:

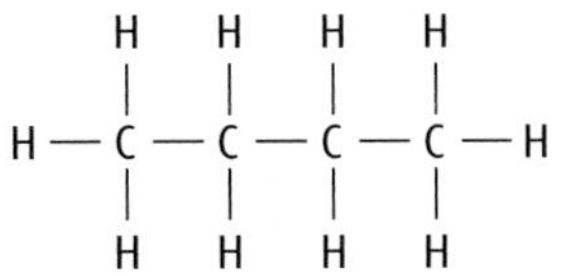

An alternative way of writing the condensed structural formula for butane would be $CH_3(CH_2)_2CH_3$.

The full structural formula, also called a displayed or graphic formula, shows all the atoms and bonds in the molecule. Although we draw the full structural formula with 90° bond angles, it must be remembered that, with four electron pairs around each C, the shape is tetrahedral around each C atom and butane should be more correctly drawn as shown in Figure **10.1**. This form is, however, significantly less convenient to draw.

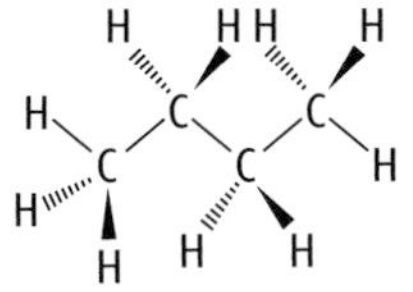

Molecules may also be represented by using skeletal formulas like the one shown in Figure **10.2**. Skeletal formulas are very convenient and widely used for drawing more complex molecules.

Learning objectives

- Understand what is meant by a **homologous series**
- Explain trends in boiling points within a homologous series
- Identify functional groups in molecules
- Explain how the functional group affects boiling point and solubility in water

Hydrocarbon: a compound containing **only** carbon and hydrogen.

Empirical formula: the simplest whole number **ratio** of the elements present in a compound.

Molecular formula: the total number of atoms of each element present in a molecule of the compound. (The molecular formula is a multiple of the empirical formula.)

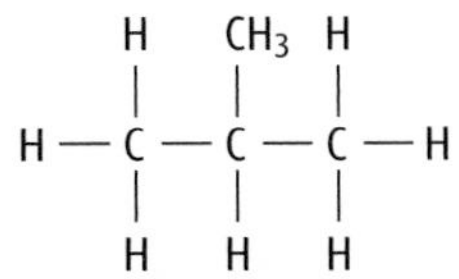

Figure 10.1 The full structural formula of butane, showing the correct tetrahedral arrangement around the C atoms.

Examiner's tip
Skeletal formulas must not be used in examinations.

Name	Molecular formula	Empirical formula	Structural formula	
			Condensed	Full
methane	CH_4	CH_4	CH_4	H | H—C—H | H
ethane	C_2H_6	CH_3	CH_3CH_3	H H | | H—C—C—H | | H H
propane	C_3H_8	C_3H_8	$CH_3CH_2CH_3$	H H H | | | H—C—C—C—H | | | H H H
butane	C_4H_{10}	C_2H_5	$CH_3CH_2CH_2CH_3$	H H H H | | | | H—C—C—C—C—H | | | | H H H H
pentane	C_5H_{12}	C_5H_{12}	$CH_3CH_2CH_2CH_2CH_3$	H H H H H | | | | | H—C—C—C—C—C—H | | | | | H H H H H
hexane	C_6H_{14}	C_3H_7	$CH_3CH_2CH_2CH_2CH_2CH_3$	H H H H H H | | | | | | H—C—C—C—C—C—C—H | | | | | | H H H H H H

Table 10.1 The first six straight-chain alkanes.

Figure 10.2 The skeletal formula for hexane.

Different ways of representing the structures of molecules are shown here. Why is sometimes one way preferred to another? What is the relationship between ease of use and sophistication? Which is probably the most accurate way of representing a molecule? Which is the most useful if we wish to draw out a reaction scheme?

Some other ways of representing the structure of butane are shown in these computer-generated images:

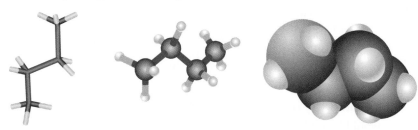

The third image shows a space-filling model.

Homologous series

The alkanes represent a homologous series.

A **homologous series** is a series of compounds with the same functional group, in which each member differs from the next by $-CH_2-$.

A functional group is the atom/group of atoms in a molecule that gives it its characteristic chemical properties. Although there is not really a functional group in alkanes, as only single C–C and C–H bonds are present, examples of functional groups in other homologous series are C=C in alkenes and –OH in alcohols.

The features of a homologous series are:

- they can usually be described by a general molecular formula, e.g. C_nH_{2n+2} for alkanes (non-cyclic) or C_nH_{2n} for alkenes
- members of the series show similar chemical properties
- members of the series show a gradation in physical properties such as boiling point

Other homologous series will be discussed in the appropriate sections below.

> Chemical properties: how a substance reacts.

Alcohols

An example of another homologous series is the alcohols. These all have the general molecular formula $C_nH_{2n+2}O$, which can also be written as $C_nH_{2n+1}OH$, showing the –OH (hydroxyl) functional group, which is what distinguishes an alcohol from other types of organic compound. The first four members of the series, in which the –OH group is on the first carbon, are shown in Figure **10.3**.

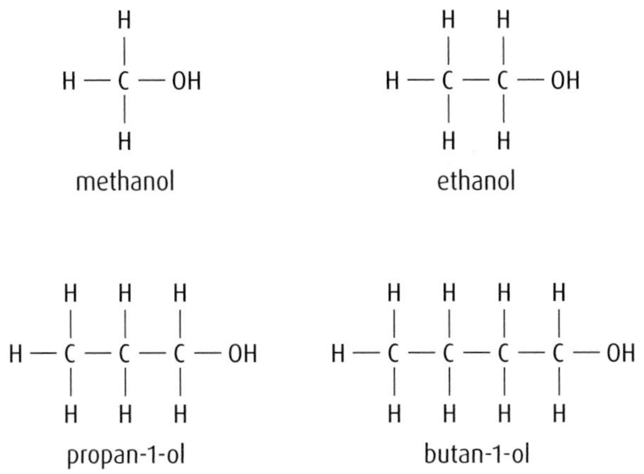

Figure 10.3 The first four members of the alcohol series.

It is important to note that Figure **10.3** does not show the **full** structural formulas as the O–H bonds are not shown. However, it is a structural formula that is often drawn to represent the molecule. A skeletal formula for butan-1-ol is shown in Figure **10.4**.

Figure 10.4 The skeletal formula for butan-1-ol.

Boiling point and homologous series

> As the number of carbon atoms in a molecule in a particular homologous series increases, the boiling point increases.

The boiling point of straight-chain alkanes increases when a methylene (–CH₂–) group is added, because the strength of the van der Waals' forces between molecules increases as the relative molecular mass of the alkane increases. A similar trend is seen in the boiling points of other homologous series.

Figure **10.5** compares the boiling points of alcohols (with the –OH group on the first carbon atom) with the boiling points of alkanes. It can be seen that both series show the same trend, in that the boiling point increases as the number of C atoms increases, but the alcohol with one C atom (M_r 32.05) has a higher boiling point than the alkane with five C atoms (M_r 72.17). It is important to realise that comparisons based on the relative molecular mass (and hence strength of van der Waals' forces) may be made within a particular homologous series but not between homologous series. The boiling points of the alcohols tend to be higher due to the presence of hydrogen bonding between alcohol molecules.

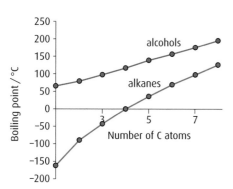

Figure 10.5 The boiling point of alkanes and alcohols.

Other homologous series

Table **10.2** shows various functional groups that you are likely to encounter during the course. The ones required for Higher Level only have been highlighted.

'R' may be used to stand for an alkyl group. Therefore, a general carboxylic acid may be represented as 'RCOOH' and an aldehyde as 'RCHO'.

Benzene and aromatic compounds

Benzene has the formula C_6H_6 and is usually represented by a skeletal formula showing a benzene ring.

Compounds that contain a benzene ring are called **aromatic**, whereas compounds without benzene rings are called **aliphatic**. When determining molecular formulas or condensed structural formulas for compounds containing benzene rings, it must be remembered that there is a C and, if there is nothing else attached, an H atom at each vertex. Therefore methyl benzene has the molecular formula C_7H_8:

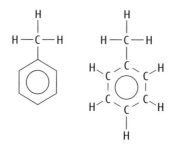

The condensed structural formula may be written as $C_6H_5CH_3$ or may be shown as a benzene ring with CH_3 attached.

A major use of benzene is to produce other chemicals such as ethylbenzene, which can be converted into styrene (phenylethene), from which polystyrene is made.

CH₃

Homologous series	Functional group	Functional group name	Example	General name	Name
alkane			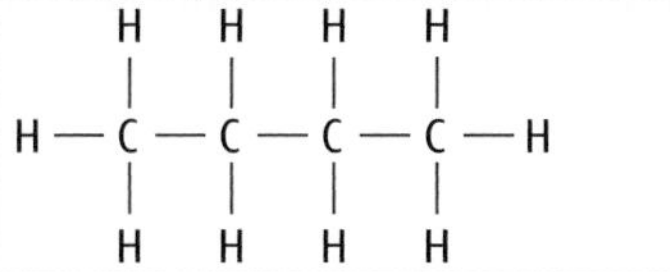	alkane	butane
alkene	C=C		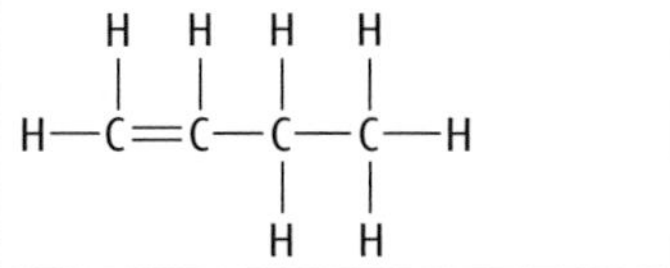	alk-x-**ene** (or x-alkene)	but-1-**ene** (or 1-butene)
alcohol	–OH	hydroxyl	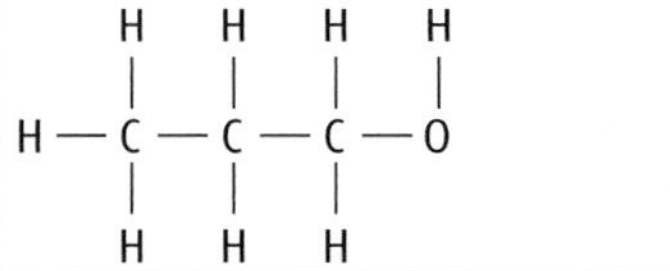	alkan-x-**ol** (or x-alkanol)	propan-1-**ol** (or 1-propanol)
aldehyde		carbonyl	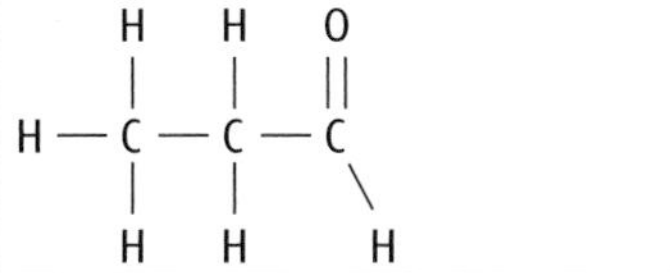	alkan**al**	propan**al**
ketone	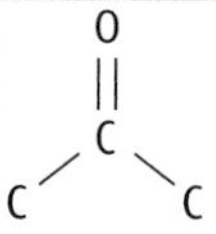		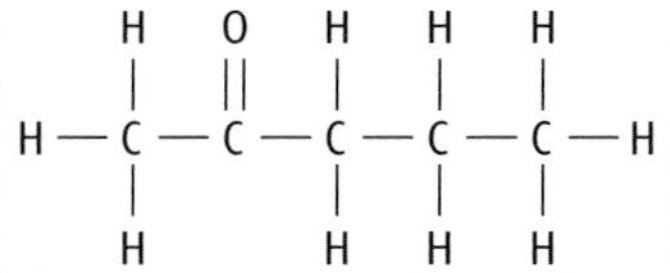	alkan-x-**one** (or x-alkanone)	pentan-2-**one** (or 2-pentanone)
carboxylic acid	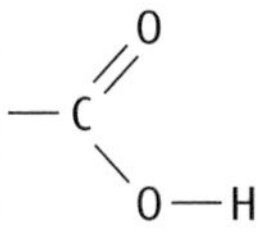	carboxyl	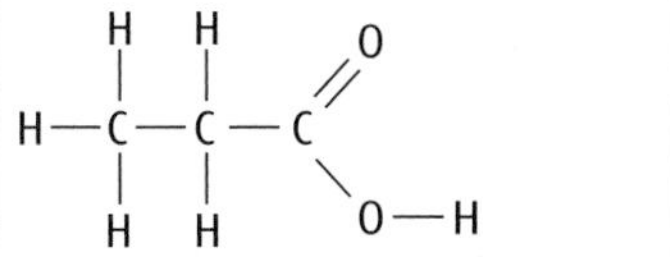	alkanoic acid	propanoic acid
halogeno-alkane	–X X=Cl/Br/I		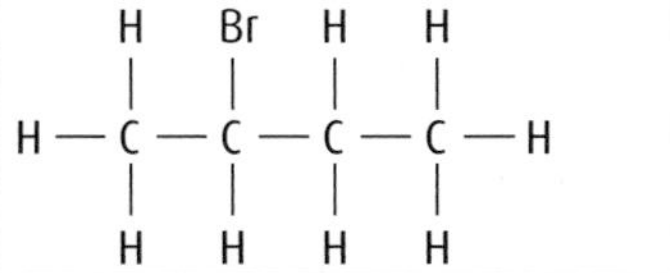	x-haloalkane	2-bromobutane
amine	–NH$_2$ –NHR –NR$_2$	amino	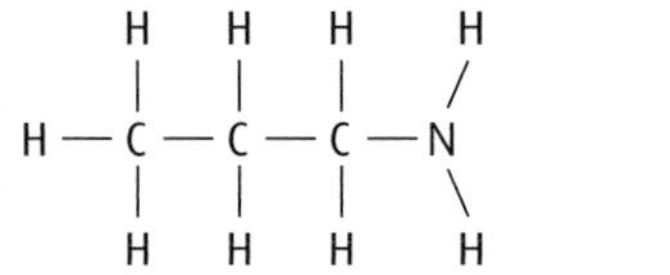	alkylamine or x-aminoalkane or alkan-x-amine (or x-alkanamine)	propylamine or 1-aminopropane or propan-1-amine (or 1-propanamine)
ester	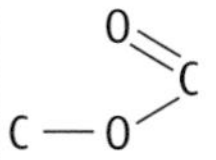		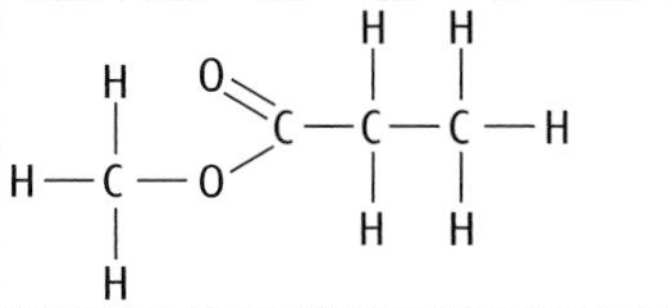	alkyl alkanoate	methyl propanoate
nitrile	–C≡N		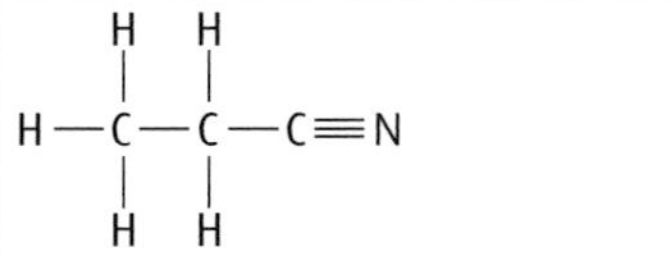	alkanenitrile (C of C≡N included in chain)	propanenitrile
amide	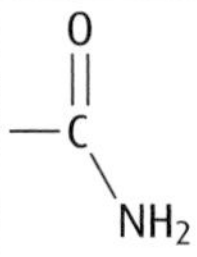		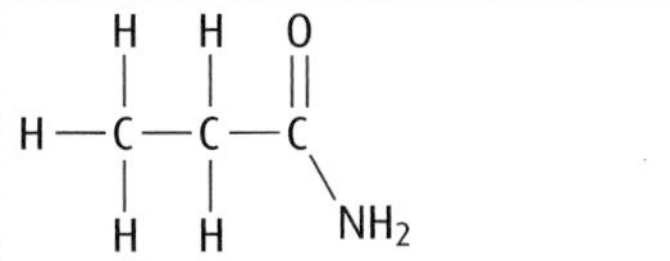	alkanamide	propanamide

Table 10.2 Functional groups that you are likely to encounter in the course.

Solubility in water and boiling point of different homologous series

The functional group present in a molecule will influence its physical as well as chemical properties. A summary of the physical properties of the various homologous series is given in Table **10.3**. The individual functional groups will be discussed in more detail below.

Homologous series	Polarity	Intermolecular forces	Boiling point	Solubility in water
alkane	non-polar	van der Waals'	low	insoluble
alkene	non-polar	van der Waals'	low	insoluble
alcohol	polar	hydrogen bonding	high	lower members soluble; hydrogen bonding to water
aldehydes/ketones	polar	dipole–dipole	higher than alkanes; lower than alcohols	lower members soluble; polar and water can hydrogen bond to them
carboxylic acid	polar	hydrogen bonding	high: higher than alcohols; more hydrogen bonding	lower members soluble; hydrogen bonding to water
halogenoalkane	polar	dipole–dipole	For same number of C atoms: iodo > bromo > chloro; van der Waals' forces stronger if M_r higher	insoluble

Table 10.3 The physical properties of some homologous series.

In general, solubility in water decreases as the hydrocarbon chain gets longer, owing to the non-polar nature of the hydrocarbon chain.

10.2 Isomers

There are various forms of isomerism. The simplest of these is structural isomerism.

The two structural isomers with the molecular formula C_4H_{10} are:

The second molecule has a branched chain.

Learning objectives

- Understand what is meant by structural isomerism
- Draw structural isomers for molecules with up to six C atoms

Structural isomers are two or more compounds that have the same molecular formula but different structural formulas, i.e. the atoms are joined together in a different way.

The structural isomers of C_5H_{12} are:

The second and third isomers could also have been drawn with the CH_3 group in condensed form instead of given in full.

It is important to note that the structures shown in Figure **10.6** are **not** separate isomers of C_5H_{12} but are identical to each other. In a molecule in which only C–C single bonds are present, there is fairly free rotation about the single bond; therefore, although we can show a molecule bent around into various conformations, if the atoms are joined together in the same way the molecules are not isomers.

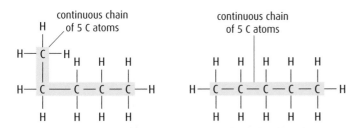

Figure 10.6 These two structures are drawn slightly differently, but careful examination reveals that all atoms are joined together in exactly the same way and that there is a continuous chain of five C atoms present in both structures.

Isomers of C_6H_{14} are shown in Table **10.4**.

Longest carbon chain in the molecule		
Chain of six C atoms	 H H H H H H | | | | | | H—C—C—C—C—C—C—H | | | | | | H H H H H H	
Chain of five C atoms	 H H CH₃ H H | | | | | H—C—C—C—C—C—H | | | | | H H H H H	 H H H CH₃ H | | | | | H—C—C—C—C—C—H | | | | | H H H H H
Chain of four C atoms	 H CH₃ H H | | | | H—C—C—C—C—H | | | | H CH₃ H H	 H CH₃ H H | | | | H—C—C—C—C—H | | | | H H CH₃ H

Table 10.4 Isomers of C_6H_{14}.

Note: in general, branched-chain isomers have lower boiling points than straight-chain isomers, as the branches prevent the main chains from getting as close together, and so van der Waals' forces are weaker between the molecules.

Some isomers of $C_5H_{12}O$

If we consider isomers that are alcohols, we can see that different isomers may be generated by just moving the OH group to different C atoms:

–OH attached to carbon 1	–OH attached to carbon 2	–OH attached to carbon 3

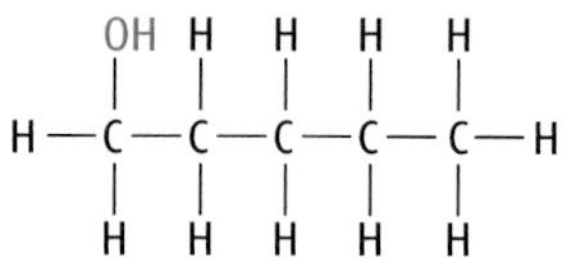 OH H H H H
  | | | | |
H—C—C—C—C—C—H
  | | | | |
  H H H H H
	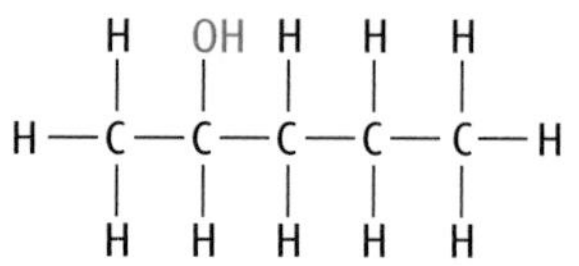 H OH H H H
	 | | | | |
	H—C—C—C—C—C—H
	 | | | | |
	 H H H H H
		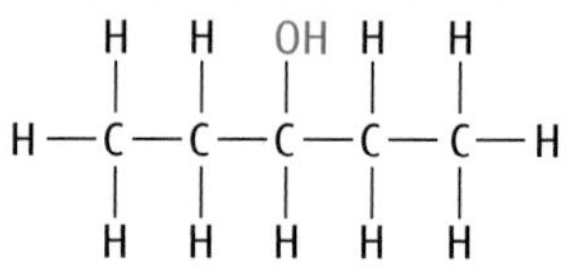 H H OH H H
		 | | | | |
		H—C—C—C—C—C—H
		 | | | | |
		 H H H H H

There are many more isomers of $C_5H_{12}O$ that are alcohols, and also some that are not alcohols. An isomer of $C_5H_{12}O$ is shown in Figure **10.7**.

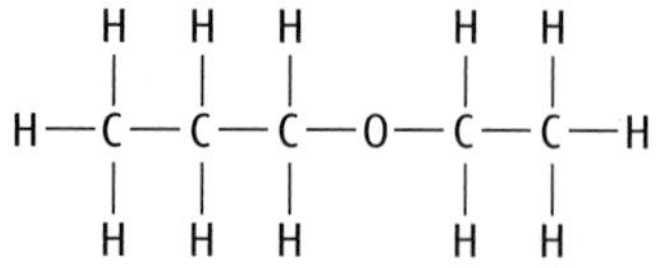

$$\text{H}-\overset{\overset{\displaystyle H}{|}}{\underset{\underset{\displaystyle H}{|}}{C}}-\overset{\overset{\displaystyle H}{|}}{\underset{\underset{\displaystyle H}{|}}{C}}-\overset{\overset{\displaystyle H}{|}}{\underset{\underset{\displaystyle H}{|}}{C}}-\text{O}-\overset{\overset{\displaystyle H}{|}}{\underset{\underset{\displaystyle H}{|}}{C}}-\overset{\overset{\displaystyle H}{|}}{\underset{\underset{\displaystyle H}{|}}{C}}-\text{H}$$

Figure 10.7 An isomer of $C_5H_{12}O$ that is not an alcohol. This is an ether and contains C–O–C as the functional group.

Self-test 1

Test yourself

1 What is the molecular formula of the alkane with 15 carbon atoms?

2 Give the molecular formula and empirical formula of each of the following:

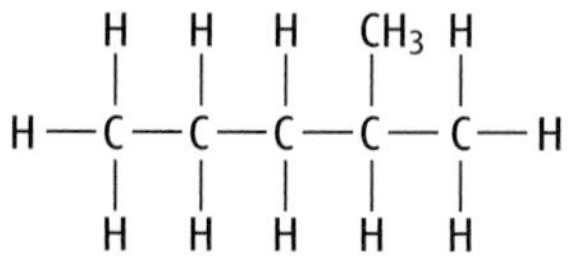 a	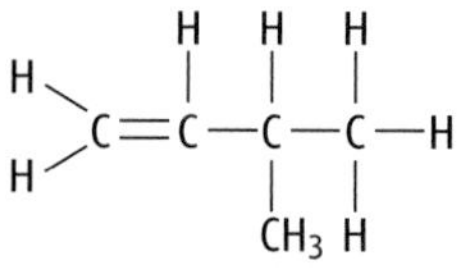 b	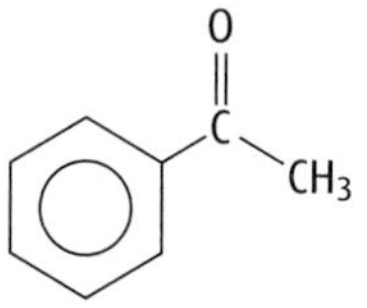 c	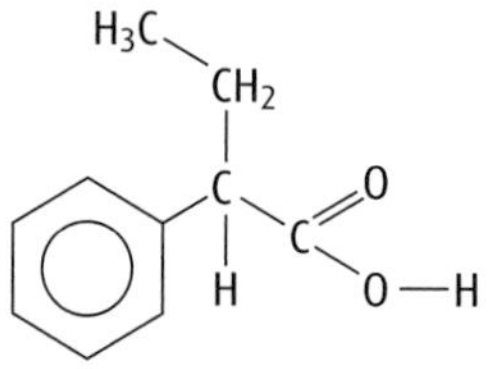 d
H H H CH₃ H | | | | | H—C—C—C—C—C—H | | | | | H H H H H	(structure: C=C–C–C with CH₃ groups)	(benzene ring with C=O and CH₃)	(benzene ring with H₃C, CH₂, C=O, O—H)

3 Identify the functional group(s) present in each of the following molecules.

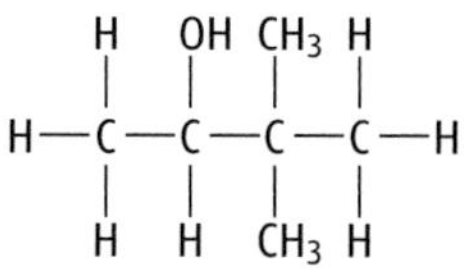 a	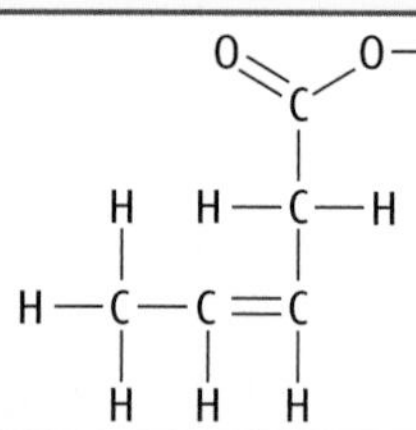 b	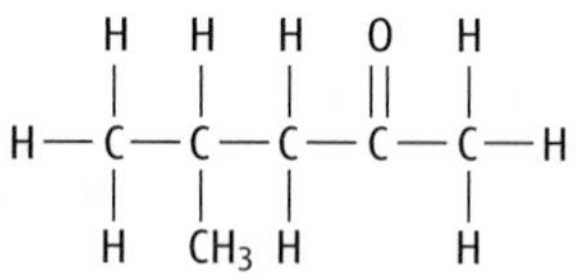 c	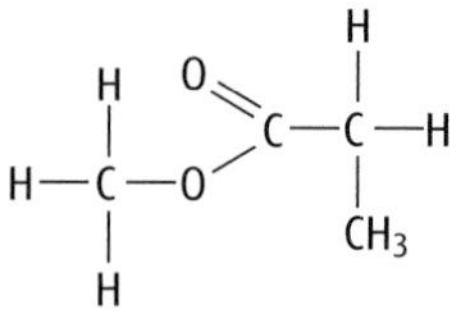 d
H OH CH₃ H | | | | H—C—C—C—C—H | | | | H H CH₃ H	(structure with O=C–O—H and C=C)	H H H O H | | | || | H—C—C—C—C—C—H | | | | H CH₃ H H	(structure with O=C–C–H, CH₃, O, C)

4 Draw all the isomers of $C_4H_{10}O$ that are alcohols.

10.3 Naming organic compounds

Naming alkanes

Organic molecules are named according to the International Union of Pure and Applied Chemistry (**IUPAC**) system. Although older, non-systematic names are still in use in some situations, molecules should, wherever possible, be named according to the following systematic set of rules:

1 find the longest **continuous carbon chain** in the molecule
2 use the prefix in Table **10.5** corresponding to the number of carbon atoms in the longest continuous carbon chain and the ending 'ane' to symbolise an alkane
3 look for substituent groups (alkyl groups) – the names for these are shown in Table **10.6**
4 number the positions of the substituent groups using the combination that includes the lowest individual numbers (not the sum)
5 use the prefixes shown in Table **10.7** to indicate the number of each substituent present
6 arrange the names of the substituent groups in alphabetical order (ignoring the prefix indicating number, i.e. di-, tri-, etc.)

Number of identical substituents	Prefix
2	di-
3	tri-
4	tetra-

Table 10.7 Prefixes corresponding to the number of identical substituents in an alkane.

Learning objectives

- Use IUPAC rules to name alkanes

C atoms	Prefix
1	meth-
2	eth-
3	prop-
4	but-
5	pent-
6	hex-

Table 10.5 Prefixes corresponding to the number of carbon atoms in the longest continuous carbon chain of an alkane.

$-CH_3$	methyl
$-C_2H_5$	ethyl
$-C_3H_7$	propyl

Table 10.6 The names for substituent groups in alkanes.

Examples

2-methylpentane

The longest continuous carbon chain consists of five C atoms, and this gives rise to the basic name of 'pentane'. A methyl group is present in the molecule, and this is on carbon number 2 if we start numbering from the right-hand carbon atom. If we had started numbering from the left-hand carbon atom, we would have a methyl group on carbon 4, which is a higher number than the 2 obtained if we number from the other side and therefore not used.

2,2-dimethylbutane

The longest continuous carbon chain is of four C atoms, and this gives rise to the butane part of the name. There are two methyl groups, so we use 'dimethyl'. As these methyl groups are both on carbon 2 (this time we count from the left-hand side to generate the lowest numbers) we have '2,2-dimethyl'. Both 2s are needed in the name.

Note: when naming molecules we use a comma between numbers and a dash between numbers and letters.

methyl group

longest continuous carbon chain

longest continuous carbon chain

methyl group

methyl group

3-methylhexane

The longest continuous carbon chain may not always be shown as a horizontal straight line of C atoms, as in this 3-methylhexane molecule:

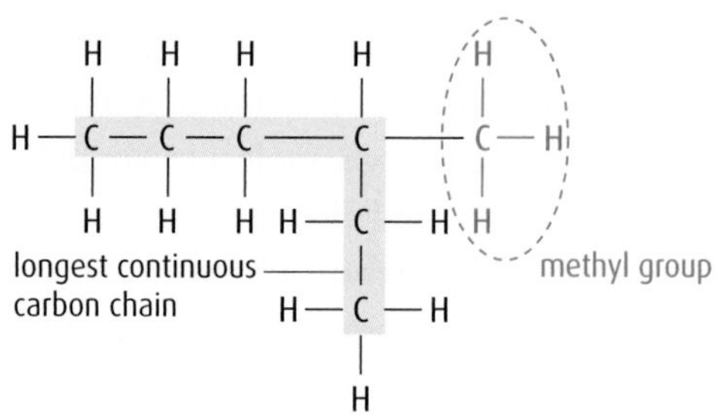

4-ethyl-2-methylhexane

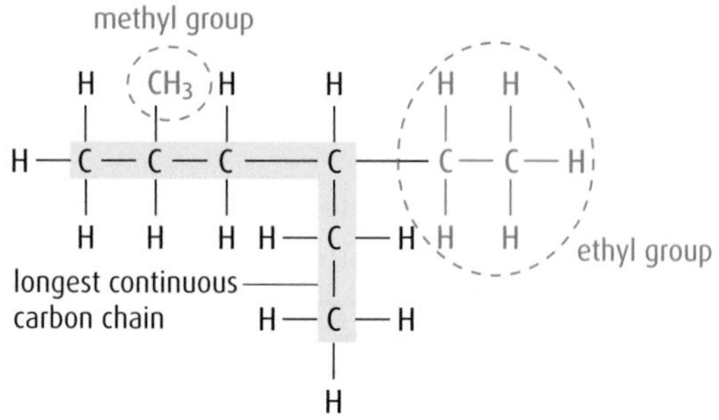

This combination of numbers gives the lowest number, as the alternative name would be 3-ethyl-5-methylhexane, and 2 is lower than 3. The substituent (alkyl) groups are arranged in alphabetical order.

2,6,6-trimethyloctane

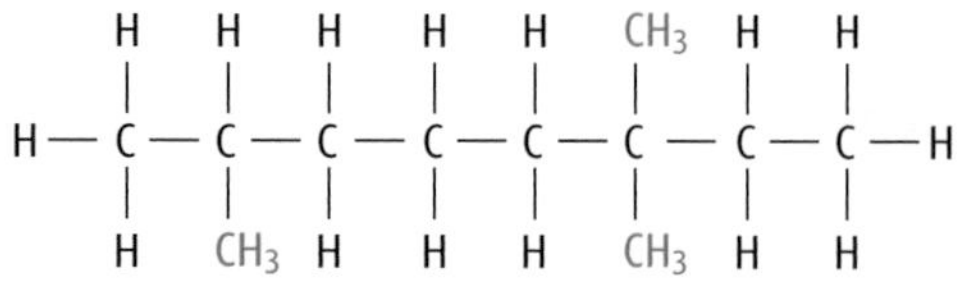

If we numbered the carbon atoms from the other direction, we would have obtained the name 3,3,7-trimethyloctane. Although the sum of the numbers in this name is lower, the lowest number here is higher than the lowest number in the accepted name, and so this name is not used.

3,3,4-trimethylhexane

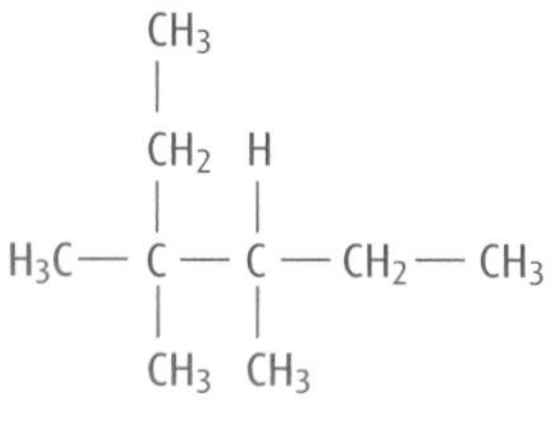

When the first number is the same when numbering from both directions, the second number, etc. is investigated and the name is chosen to give the lower number at the first position at which the names differ. Thus, this molecule could be named 3,3,4-trimethylhexane or 3,4,4-trimethylhexane, depending on whether we start the numbering from one side or the other. Both names start with 3 but they differ at the second digit, and so the name 3,3,4-trimethylhexane is chosen as it gives the lower number at the second position.

Examiner's tip
You should be required to name alkanes with a maximum of only six C atoms. The examples here are just for a bit of extra practice and to illustrate all the rules available.

Isomers of C₄H₁₀

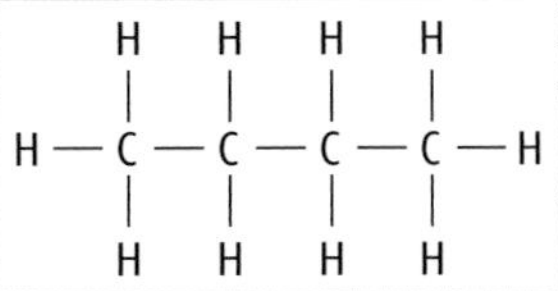	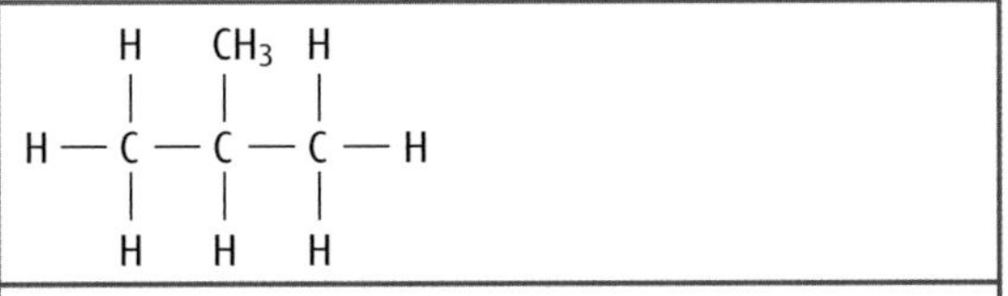
butane	2-methylpropane
	The 2 in this name is usually included, although the name would actually be unambiguous without it – there is only one possible structure for methylpropane. 1-methylpropane is butane!

Isomers of C₆H₁₄

Names of the isomers of C_6H_{14} are shown here, together with various condensed structural formulas. (The only full structural formula is that shown for hexane.)

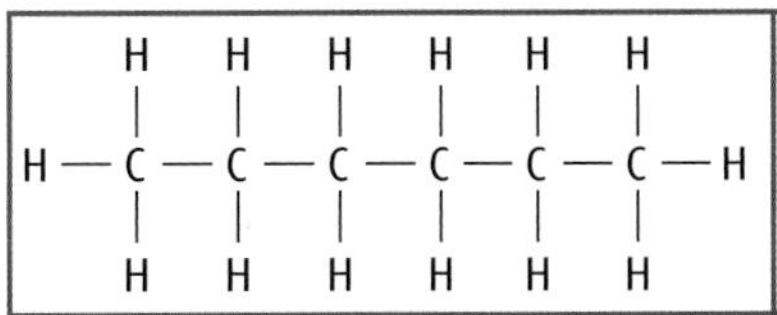	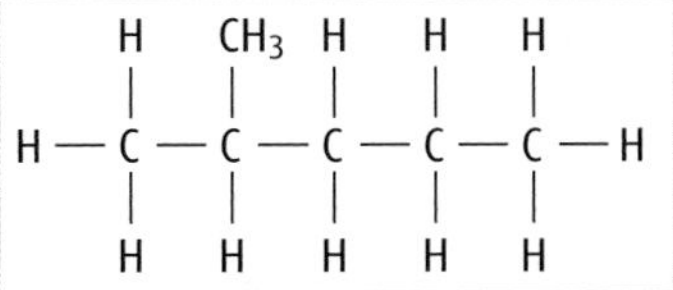	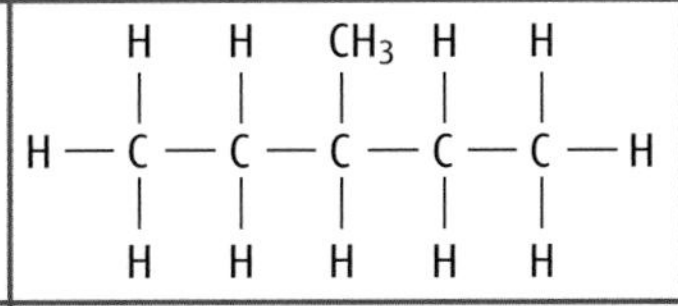
$CH_3CH_2CH_2CH_2CH_2CH_3$	$(CH_3)_2CHCH_2CH_2CH_3$	$CH_3CH_2CH(CH_3)CH_2CH_3$
hexane	2-methylpentane	3-methylpentane
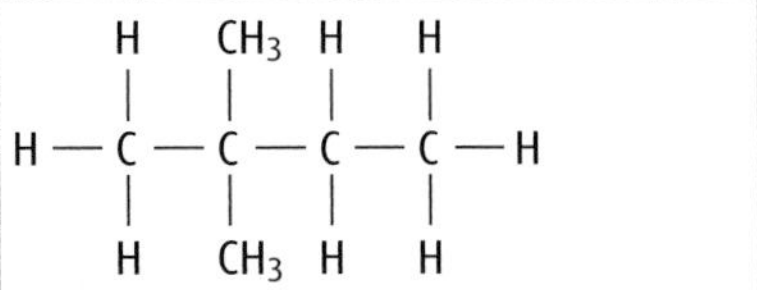	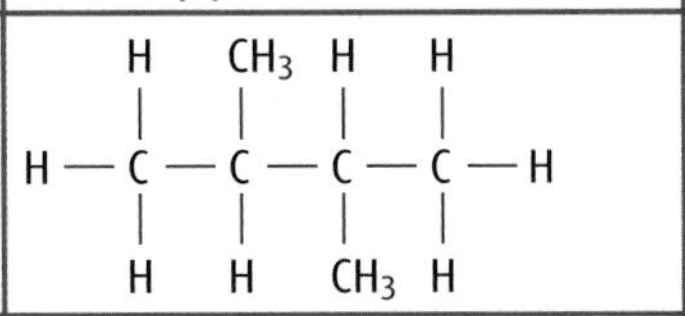	
$(CH_3)_3CCH_2CH_3$	$(CH_3)_2CHCH(CH_3)_2$	
$CH_3C(CH_3)_2CH_2CH_3$	$CH_3CH(CH_3)CH(CH_3)CH_3$	
2,2-dimethylbutane	2,3-dimethylbutane	

Chemists have agreed on a system for naming and classifying different molecules. Using various types of formula and this agreed system of names, chemists have their own language with which they can communicate with each other even when – in their everyday lives – they speak different languages.

How precise must the set of rules for this language be for chemists to make themselves understood? For instance, if you named pentane as '1-methylbutane' or 2-methylpentane as '4-methylpentane', would everyone still understand what you meant? What if you named 2,2-dimethylbutane as '2-dimethylbutane'?

Beyond school level, chemists often do not use systematic names when communicating with each other – why?

5 Name the following molecules:

CH₃ H │ │ H — C — C — H │ │ CH₃ CH₂ │ CH₃	CH₃ CH₃ │ │ H — C — C — CH₃ │ │ CH₃ CH₃	CH₃(CH₂)₂C(CH₃)₃	H H │ │ H — C — C — H │ │ H H — C — H H │ │ H — C — C — H │ │ H H — C — H │ H
a	**b**	**c**	**d**

6 Draw the following molecules:
   a 3-methylhexane
   b 2,2,3-trimethylpentane
   c 2,4-dimethylhexane

7 Give the correct name for each of the following:
   a 1,2-dimethylbutane
   b 1,2,3-trimethylpropane
   c 1-ethyl-2,2-dimethylpropane

Learning objectives

- Write equations for the complete and incomplete combustion of alkanes
- Explain why alkanes are not very reactive
- Write equations for the reactions of alkanes with halogens
- Explain the free radical substitution mechanism

Figure 10.8 The carbon compounds in crude oil can be used to make medicines, plastics (polymers) and lots of other extremely useful chemicals and products. Is crude oil too valuable to burn?

10.4 Alkanes

The alkanes are non-polar molecules with only van der Waals' forces between molecules. This means that they are volatile (evaporate easily), with the first four members being gases at room temperature. Due to their non-polar nature, they are also insoluble in water.

Reactions of alkanes

From a global perspective, the most important reaction of alkanes is combustion, as these molecules are the basis of fuels such as petrol and natural gas (Figure **10.8**). Complete combustion of hydrocarbons requires the presence of excess oxygen and produces carbon dioxide and water.
   Complete combustion of ethane:

$$2C_2H_6(g) + 7O_2(g) \rightarrow 4CO_2(g) + 6H_2O(l)$$

Complete combustion of butane:

$$2C_4H_{10}(g) + 13O_2(g) \rightarrow 8CO_2(g) + 10H_2O(l)$$

When there is a limited supply of oxygen, incomplete combustion occurs, which produces carbon monoxide and soot (C) as well as water.
   Incomplete combustion of ethane producing CO:

$$2C_2H_6(g) + 5O_2(g) \rightarrow 4CO(g) + 6H_2O(l)$$

Incomplete combustion of ethane producing soot:

$$2C_2H_6(g) + 3O_2(g) \rightarrow 4C(s) + 6H_2O(l)$$

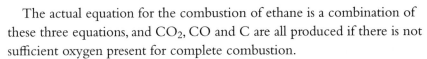

The actual equation for the combustion of ethane is a combination of these three equations, and CO_2, CO and C are all produced if there is not sufficient oxygen present for complete combustion.

Incomplete combustion is dirtier than complete combustion, producing a smoky flame and the toxic gas carbon monoxide (which binds to haemoglobin more strongly than oxygen does, so oxygen is prevented from being transported by the blood).

Many deaths occur each year through accidental carbon monoxide poisoning, which occurs as a result of poorly serviced or ventilated heating systems.

Unreactivity of alkanes

Apart from combustion alkanes are generally fairly unreactive. The reasons for this are:
- the high strength of the C–C and C–H bonds means that it is generally energetically unfavourable to break them in a reaction
- the C–C and C–H bonds are essentially non-polar, so unlikely to attract polar molecules or ions

Reaction of alkanes with halogens

Alkanes react with halogens in the presence of sunlight or UV light. There is no reaction in the dark at room temperature.

The equation for the reaction between methane and chlorine in the presence of UV light is:

$$CH_4 + Cl_2 \xrightarrow{UV} \underset{\text{chloromethane}}{CH_3Cl} + \underset{\text{hydrogen chloride}}{HCl}$$

Or that between ethane and bromine is:

$$C_2H_6 + Br_2 \xrightarrow{UV} \underset{\text{bromoethane}}{C_2H_5Br} + \underset{\text{hydrogen bromide}}{HBr}$$

Chloromethane is an important contributor to the destruction of the ozone layer. A significant source of chloromethane is from natural sources such as wood-rotting fungi.

If we look at this reaction in terms of full structural formulas, we can see what is happening more clearly:

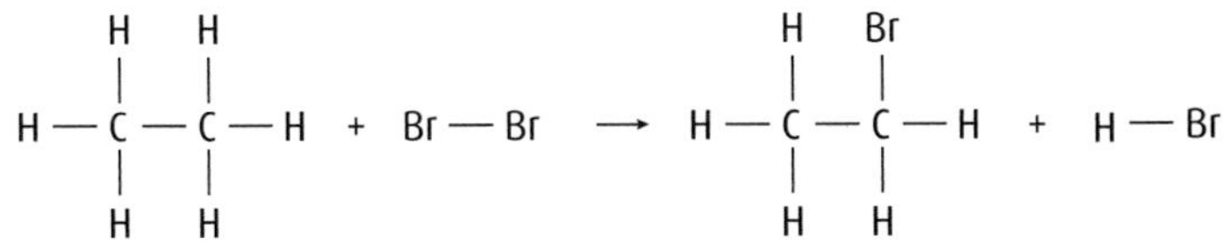

$$
\begin{array}{c}
\quad\ H\ \ H \\
\quad\ |\ \ \ | \\
H-C-C-H \\
\quad\ |\ \ \ | \\
\quad\ H\ \ H
\end{array}
+\ Br-Br\ \longrightarrow\
\begin{array}{c}
\quad\ H\ \ Br \\
\quad\ |\ \ \ | \\
H-C-C-H \\
\quad\ |\ \ \ | \\
\quad\ H\ \ H
\end{array}
+\ H-Br
$$

A substitution reaction is one in which one atom or group is replaced by another atom or group.

An H atom in ethane is replaced by a Br atom. This is, therefore, called a **substitution** reaction.

The reactions shown here all involve mono-substitution: that is, the replacement of one H atom in the molecule with a halogen atom. However, the reactions are difficult to control and a mixture of products, some of which involve multiple substitution, is formed.

$$CH_4 + Cl_2 \rightarrow CH_3Cl + HCl$$

$$CH_3Cl + Cl_2 \rightarrow \underset{\text{dichloromethane}}{CH_2Cl_2} + HCl$$

$$CH_2Cl_2 + Cl_2 \rightarrow \underset{\text{trichloromethane}}{CHCl_3} + HCl$$

$$CHCl_3 + Cl_2 \rightarrow \underset{\text{tetrachloromethane}}{CCl_4} + HCl$$

The mechanism for these reactions is **free radical substitution**.

A free radical substitution mechanism

Consider the reaction between methane and chlorine:

$$CH_4 + Cl_2 \rightarrow CH_3Cl + HCl$$

Initiation

The first stage of the reaction is the breaking apart of the chlorine molecule into two chlorine atoms:

$$Cl_2 \xrightarrow{\text{UV}} 2Cl\bullet$$

The energy required to do this is provided by the UV light. The Cl–Cl bond ($242\,\text{kJ}\,\text{mol}^{-1}$) is weaker than the C–H bond ($412\,\text{kJ}\,\text{mol}^{-1}$), and therefore it is the Cl–Cl bond that is broken.

The chlorine atoms produced have seven electrons, and thus an unpaired electron, in their outer shell. This is represented by the dot in the symbol. The chlorine atom is described as a **free radical**.

This step in the reaction mechanism involves an increase in the number of free radicals – it starts off the reaction and is called the **initiation** step.

This process is known as **homolytic fission**, because when the covalent bond, made up of two electrons, breaks, one electron goes back to each atom making up the original covalent bond (in this case to form two species that are the same: 'homo' = the same).

Propagation

The chlorine free radical is a very reactive species and when it collides with a methane molecule in the reaction mixture it will combine with a hydrogen atom to pair up its unpaired electron. The equation for this step is:

$$Cl\bullet + CH_4 \rightarrow \underset{\text{methyl free radical}}{\bullet CH_3} + HCl$$

A highly reactive methyl free radical is generated in this step, and this will react with a Cl_2 molecule to form a C–Cl bond.

$$\bullet CH_3 + Cl_2 \rightarrow CH_3Cl + Cl\bullet$$

The $Cl\bullet$ generated in this step can go on to react further with another methane molecule, so that the cycle of propagation steps starts again. This is an example of a **chain reaction**, as one initial event causes a large number of subsequent reactions – the reactive species is regenerated in each cycle of reactions.

All reactions require the presence of UV light.

$Cl \bullet \longleftarrow$ unpaired electron

Free radicals are species (atoms or groups of atoms) with an unpaired electron. Free radicals are very reactive because of this unpaired electron.

Animation 1

Animations 2 & 3

$Cl\bullet + CH_4 \longrightarrow \bullet CH_3 + HCl$
$\bullet CH_3 + Cl_2 \longrightarrow CH_3Cl + Cl\bullet$

$Cl\bullet + CH_4 \longrightarrow \bullet CH_3 + HCl$
$\bullet CH_3 + Cl_2 \longrightarrow CH_3Cl + Cl\bullet$

$Cl\bullet + CH_4 \longrightarrow \bullet CH_3 + HCl$
$\bullet CH_3 + Cl_2 \longrightarrow CH_3Cl + Cl\bullet$

The two steps detailed above are called propagation reactions – they involve no change in the overall number of free radicals present in the reaction mixture.

Termination

Animation 4

The free radicals are present in very low concentrations, so the chance of two colliding is very low. However, they do sometimes collide, and this brings the chain reaction to an end. There are several possible termination reactions:

$$Cl\bullet + Cl\bullet \rightarrow Cl_2$$

$$Cl\bullet + \bullet CH_3 \rightarrow CH_3Cl$$

$$H_3C\bullet + \bullet CH_3 \rightarrow C_2H_6$$

Each termination reaction involves a decrease in the number of free radicals. Overall the reaction mechanism can be written as:

$$Cl_2 \xrightarrow{UV} 2Cl\bullet$$ **Initiation**
$$Cl\bullet + CH_4 \rightarrow \bullet CH_3 + HCl$$ **Propagation**
$$\bullet CH_3 + Cl_2 \rightarrow CH_3Cl + Cl\bullet$$ **Propagation**
$$Cl\bullet + Cl\bullet \rightarrow Cl_2$$ **Termination**
$$Cl\bullet + \bullet CH_3 \rightarrow CH_3Cl$$ **Termination**
$$H_3C\bullet + \bullet CH_3 \rightarrow C_2H_6$$ **Termination**

Initiation: increase in the number of free radicals.
Propagation: no change in the number of free radicals.
Termination: decrease in the number of free radicals.

Formation of other products

Formation of multi-substituted products occurs when the chlorine free radical collides with a different molecule in the first propagation step:

$$Cl\bullet + CH_3Cl \rightarrow \bullet CH_2Cl + HCl$$ **Propagation**
$$\bullet CH_2Cl + Cl_2 \rightarrow \underset{\text{dichloromethane}}{CH_2Cl_2} + Cl\bullet$$ **Propagation**

$$Cl\bullet + CH_2Cl_2 \rightarrow \bullet CHCl_2 + HCl$$ **Propagation**
$$\bullet CHCl_2 + Cl_2 \rightarrow \underset{\text{trichloromethane}}{CHCl_3} + Cl\bullet$$ **Propagation**

$$Cl\bullet + CHCl_3 \rightarrow \bullet CCl_3 + HCl$$ **Propagation**
$$\bullet CCl_3 + Cl_2 \rightarrow \underset{\text{tetrachloromethane}}{CCl_4} + Cl\bullet$$ **Propagation**

Ethane and bromine

The mechanism for the reaction of ethane with bromine can be shown as:

$$Br_2 \xrightarrow{UV} 2Br\bullet$$ **Initiation**
$$Br\bullet + C_2H_6 \rightarrow \bullet CH_2CH_3 + HBr$$ **Propagation**
$$\bullet CH_2CH_3 + Br_2 \rightarrow CH_3CH_2Br + Br\bullet$$ **Propagation**
$$Br\bullet + Br\bullet \rightarrow Br_2$$ **Termination**
$$Br\bullet + \bullet CH_2CH_3 \rightarrow CH_3CH_2Br$$ **Termination**
$$\bullet CH_2CH_3 + \bullet CH_2CH_3 \rightarrow CH_3CH_2CH_2CH_3$$ **Termination**

Other alkanes

These reactions do not just occur with methane and ethane, and other alkanes will react in a similar way. For instance, when butane reacts with chlorine in the presence of UV light, there are two possible mono-chlorinated products:

There are, of course, many multi-substituted products as well.

The scientific method

In the tube on the left, some hexane has been added to some bromine water. The hexane is a colourless liquid that is immiscible (does not mix) with water and is less dense than water, so it floats on top. The tube on the right has been shaken and allowed to settle. One of the most important skills of a scientist is that of observation, and hopefully you are able to see some change has occurred and that the top layer is now orange. Let us now follow the scientific method as described by Karl Popper and try to explain what is going on here. The first stage is to make a hypothesis as to what we think may have happened.

Hypothesis: when hexane is shaken with bromine water, the two layers switch places so that the bromine water is now on the top.

This is a 'good' hypothesis, as it is one that can be tested by experiment in an attempt to falsify it.

Once we have a hypothesis we must consider ways of testing it experimentally.

Experiment: add water to the mixture and see which layer gets bigger.

The result of this experiment is that the bottom layer gets bigger, which suggests that this is the aqueous layer. We have thus disproved (falsified) our hypothesis, and it can be dismissed. We must now come up with other hypotheses, and each must be tested experimentally. If the hypothesis is falsified by the experiment, then we can dismiss it (assuming all the time that we have designed a suitable experiment in which all variables are controlled!), but what if we design an experiment to test a particular hypothesis and the experimental data support the hypothesis? Does this prove that the hypothesis is a true representation of what is happening? Unfortunately not! What if we design 100 different experiments and each one supports our hypothesis? Sorry, still not proved! What about a million, or ten million, experiments? The problem is that we cannot actually prove that something is true, we can only collect evidence to show that it is not not true (that is, not false)!

So, what would be a better hypothesis to try and explain the above observations?

Hypothesis 2: bromine is more soluble in hexane than in water, and when the mixture is shaken much more of the bromine dissolves in the hexane than in the water.

Can you think of an experiment that would allow you to test this hypothesis?

We could have made lots of other hypotheses to try and explain the observations.

Hypothesis 3: when bromine comes into contact with hexane, they react to form an orange substance, and this orange substance is less dense than water.

This hypothesis seem reasonable and would be classified by Popper as a good hypothesis, as it can be tested experimentally. How would you test this hypothesis experimentally?

What about other hypotheses?

Hypothesis 4: this happens as the result of magic.

Hypothesis 5: an invisible demon living between the layers makes the hexane become orange and the bromine water become colourless.

These hypotheses would be regarded as non-scientific, as they cannot be tested experimentally. The trouble with these hypotheses are that if someone says this happens as the result of magic you would be very hard pressed to prove that it didn't – you could suggest a more reasonable hypothesis (more reasonable to you and the rest of the scientific community), but could you really convince someone who believed that it happened as a result of magic that this is not the case?

Now we have another problem with science, in that there are an awful lot of possible hypotheses that could be put forward to explain this phenomenon – do they all require testing? Is this what scientists do all day: come up with new hypotheses and test them out?

How do we come up with hypotheses? Is this just random or do we you use our existing knowledge to limit the number of possible hypotheses. For instance, we know that bromine is a non-polar substance with van der Waals' forces between molecules and is therefore more likely to be soluble in other non-polar substances than in water. When we have come up with the hypothesis that the change in colour is due to differences in solubility and we have tested this experimentally, do we have to bother coming up with other ways of explaining it and testing these out? Most scientists would agree that this is probably going to be a waste of time and that they have better things to do.

However, if all the experimental data support our hypothesis, can we accept the hypothesis and stop wasting time trying to disprove it?

Most scientists would say yes, and this is Kuhn's view of science, in which scientists work within the accepted paradigm (a paradigm is a framework that allows us to make sense of the world) and solve problems and make advances. This is what Kuhn calls 'normal science'. For instance, scientists at the moment will use the atomic theory to explain the world around us and to develop new substances, medicines to cure diseases, etc. Chemists work within the accepted framework in which we talk in terms of atoms, covalent bonds, etc. to make new discoveries, and if they were constantly just thinking up new ways to test the existence of atoms then we almost certainly would not have many of the things that we take for granted in everyday life, such as common drugs, plastics, mobile phones, etc. Scientists work within a paradigm until the weight of evidence against it requires a paradigm shift (an example of a paradigm shift is the demise of **phlogiston theory** in the eighteenth century).

What if someone does an experiment in the future that throws our theory into doubt? Well, the first thing to do would be to check the experiment – our first instinct when we encounter something that goes against the dominant paradigm at any one time is to question the data and then repeat the experiment – the experiment should normally be repeated by independent groups of scientists. What if they all agree with the original experiment, which suggests that our theory is wrong? Will this mean that everyone will now change their opinion and look for a different explanation? Not necessarily – scientists are human!

This experiment also presents us with another problem – that of using language to communicate ideas. It is commonly stated that alkanes do not decolorise bromine water – when an alkane is shaken with bromine water, the bromine water remains orange (see page **443**). This is clearly not true, as the alkane has decolorised the bromine water – the aqueous layer is now fairly colourless. Why do we say this when it is not true? If you write down anything in the examination other than the bromine water is not decolorised by the alkane it will be marked incorrect. When we say that the alkane does not decolorise the bromine water do we actually mean something else: the bromine water does not react with the alkane?

Self-test 3

Test yourself

8 Write an equation for the complete combustion of pentane.

9 Write an equation for the incomplete combustion of propane, producing carbon monoxide.

10 Write an equation for the reaction of ethane with chlorine in the presence of UV light.

11 How many mono-chlorinated organic products are possible when chlorine reacts with each of the following molecules in the presence of UV light?
   a hexane
   b 2-methylpropane
   c 2,2-dimethylpropane

12 Write the mechanism for the reaction between chlorine and ethane in the presence of UV light.

Learning objectives

- Understand how to name alkenes
- Describe the addition reactions of alkenes
- Explain how to distinguish between alkanes and alkenes using bromine water
- Understand the polymerisation reactions of alkenes
- Describe the economic importance of reactions of alkenes

A functional group is an atom or group of atoms that gives an organic molecule its characteristic chemical properties.

10.5 Alkenes

Alkenes

Alkenes contain a C=C double bond. Another way of saying this is that the functional group present in alkenes is C=C.

The alkenes, like alkanes, are non-polar molecules with only van der Waals' forces between them. This means that they are volatile, with the first four members being gases at room temperature. Owing to their non-polar nature, they are also insoluble in water.

The first five members of an alkene homologous series are shown in Table **10.8**. The alkenes containing just one C=C all have the same empirical formula: CH_2.

The general formula of an alkene containing only one C=C is C_nH_{2n}. This has two fewer hydrogen atoms than the alkane with the same number of C atoms; in general, the number of C=C (or rings) present in a molecule can be determined by comparing the formula with that of the appropriate alkane. Every two H atoms fewer than the equivalent alkane indicates one double bond (or ring). For example, the alkene with the formula C_5H_8 has four H atoms fewer than the alkane with five C atoms (C_5H_{12}) and thus contains two C=C. The alkene with formula C_8H_{10} has

Name	Molecular formula	Empirical formula	Structural formula	
			Condensed	**Full**
ethene	C_2H_4	CH_2	CH_2CH_2	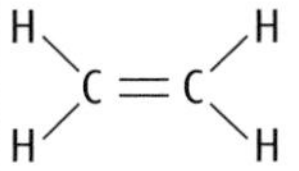
prop-1-ene	C_3H_6	CH_2	CH_2CHCH_3	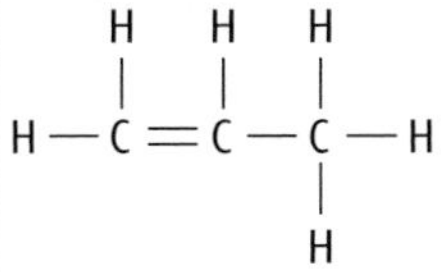
but-1-ene	C_4H_8	CH_2	$CH_2CHCH_2CH_3$	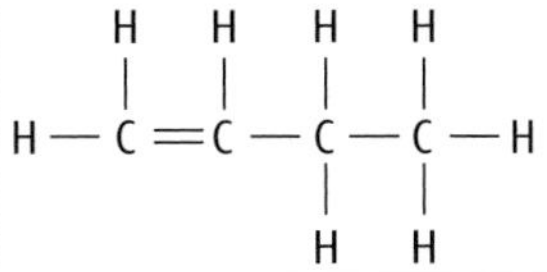
pent-1-ene	C_5H_{10}	CH_2	$CH_2CHCH_2CH_2CH_3$	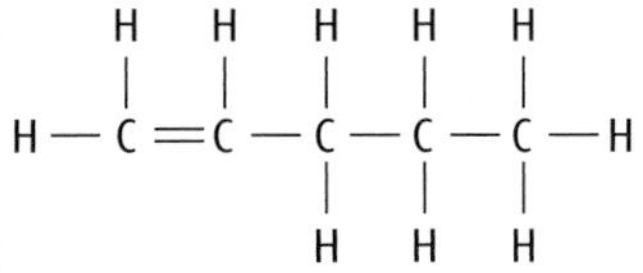
hex-1-ene	C_6H_{12}	CH_2	$CH_2CHCH_2CH_2CH_2CH_3$	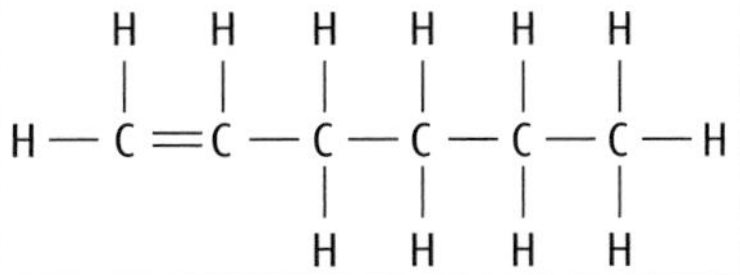

Table 10.8 The first five members of an alkene homologous series.

eight H atoms less than the equivalent alkane (C_8H_{18}), and therefore four C=C are suggested (it could also contain rings/triple bonds).

The condensed structural formula for alkenes such as prop-1-ene is often written as $H_2C=CHCH_3$.

Saturated and unsaturated compounds

Alkenes are described as **unsaturated** compounds, as they contain C=C (Figure **10.9**). Alkanes and other compounds not containing multiple bonds are described as **saturated**.

Alkynes, which contain a triple bond between two carbon atoms, are also unsaturated.

Naming alkenes

The names of alkenes are of the form **alk-*x*-ene** (*x*-alkene is also acceptable) The number, *x*, indicates the position of the double bond. If there is a double bond between carbon 1 and carbon 2, the lower number is taken to generate a '-1-ene'.

If there are alkyl groups present in the molecule, the numbering is chosen to give the double bond the lowest possible number.

The alkane may be thought of as being saturated with hydrogen – having the maximum number of H atoms for that many Cs – whereas the alkene does not have as many H atoms as possible and is therefore not saturated (it is unsaturated).

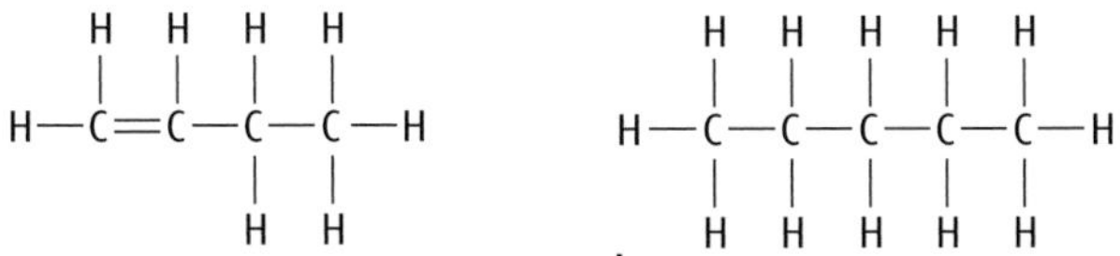

a   b

Figure 10.9 (a) Unsaturated; (b) saturated.

Examples

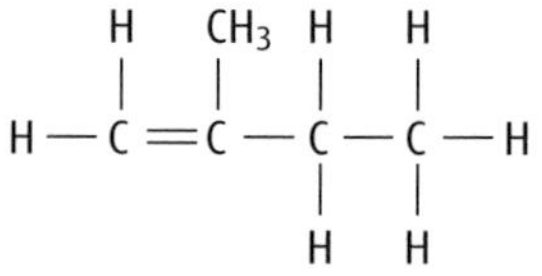

2-methylbut-1-ene

Four carbon atoms in the longest continuous carbon chain produces the stem 'but'; a double bond between carbon 1 and carbon 2 gives us '-1-ene'; the methyl group on carbon 2 produces '2-methyl'.

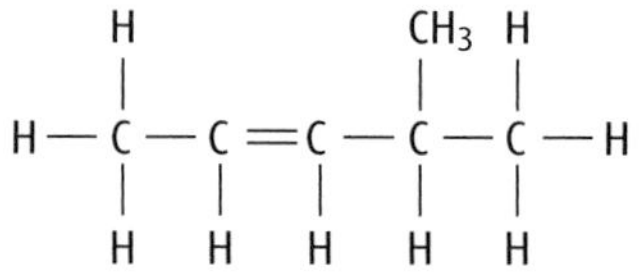

4-methylpent-2-ene

This could also have been named 2-methylpent-3-ene, but the lowest possible number is given to the double bond component; hence it is more correctly named 4-methylpent-2-ene.

The names of some isomers of C_6H_{12} are shown in Table **10.9**.

| 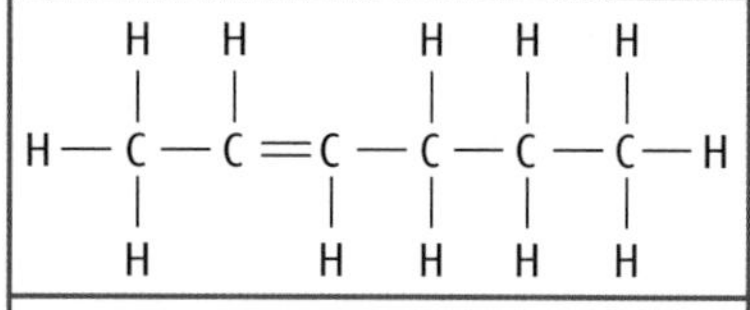 hex-2-ene | 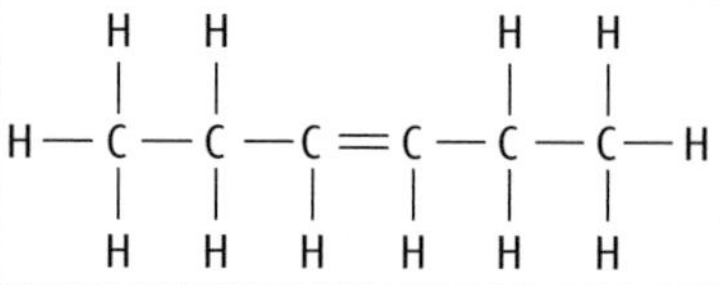 hex-3-ene | 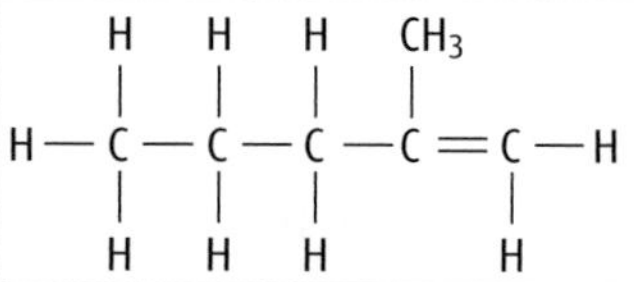 2-methylpent-1-ene |
| 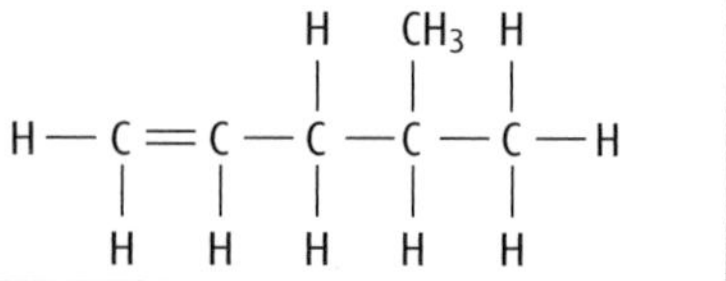 4-methylpent-1-ene | 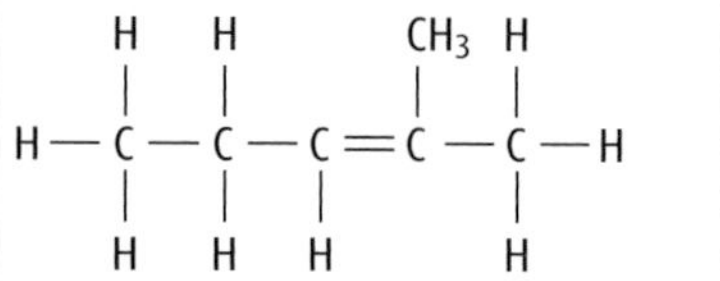 2-methylpent-2-ene | 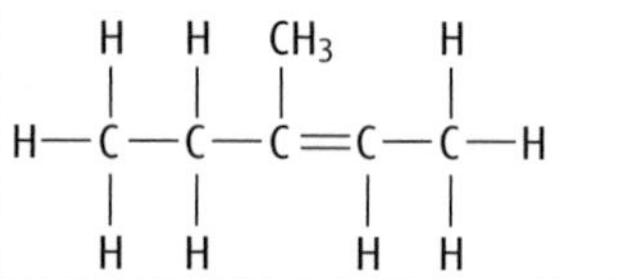 3-methylpent-2-ene |

Table 10.9 Some isomers of C_6H_{12}.

There are also structural isomers of alkenes that do not contain a double bond – these are cycloalkanes and will be discussed on page **490**.

When more than 1 C=C is present in a molecule, the name changes slightly (Figure **10.10**).

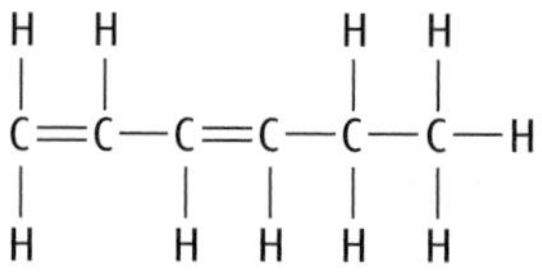

Figure 10.10 The names of two compounds containing more than one C=C. There is an extra 'a' on the stem: (**a**) hex**a**-1,3-diene; (**b**) hex**a**-1,3,5-triene.

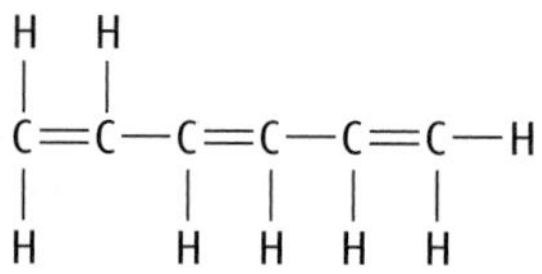

	C–C	C=C
Bond energy / kJ mol⁻¹	348	612

The difference between these two bond energies is $264\,kJ\,mol^{-1}$.

Reactions of alkenes

Alkenes are more reactive than alkanes. There are two reasons for this.

1. The double bond is less than twice the strength of a single bond. The reactions of alkenes usually involve the C=C bond breaking to form a C–C bond. The second component (π bond) of the C=C bond is weaker than a normal C–C single bond and is, therefore, more easily broken.
2. The double bond (four electrons) represents a region of high electron density, and therefore attracts electrophiles.

An electrophile is a reagent (a positively charged ion or the positive end of a dipole) that is attracted to regions of high electron density and accepts a pair of electrons to form a covalent bond.

Addition reactions

Alkenes undergo addition reactions. The basic general reaction is:

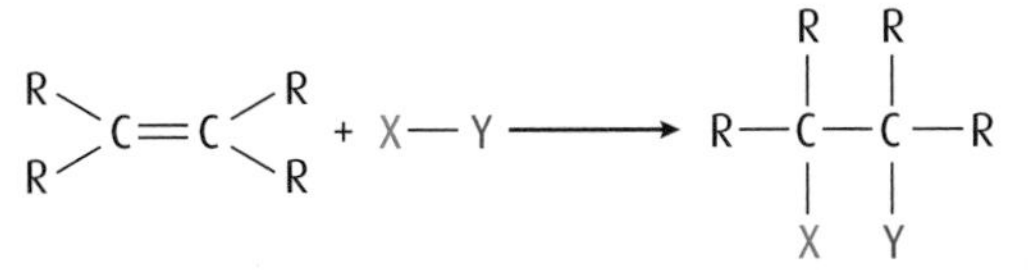

The molecule X–Y is added either side of the double bond, which breaks to a single bond.

> R stands for an alkyl group or H in this equation.

Alkenes and halogens

Alkenes react with halogens at room temperature.

1,2-dichloroethane

> The reaction with iodine is very slow at room temperature.

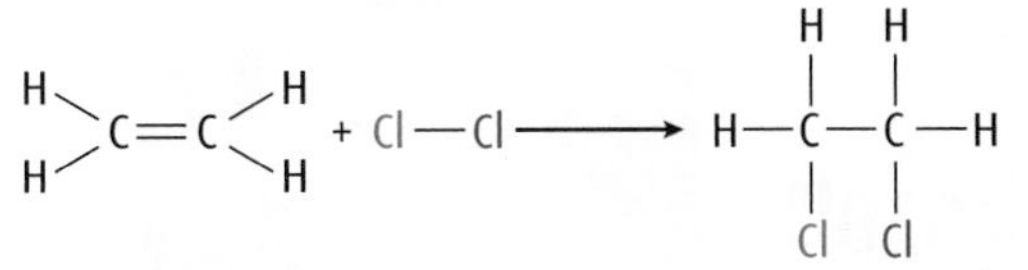

Alkenes and hydrogen

Alkenes react with hydrogen when heated in the presence of a catalyst, such as finely divided nickel, to form alkanes.

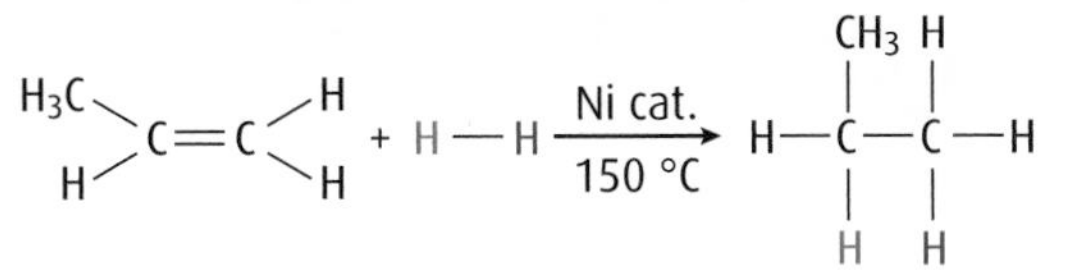

propane

> This reaction is called **hydrogenation**.

Alkenes and hydrogen halides

Alkenes can react with hydrogen halides such as HBr by bubbling the alkene through a concentrated solution of the hydrogen halide at 100 °C.

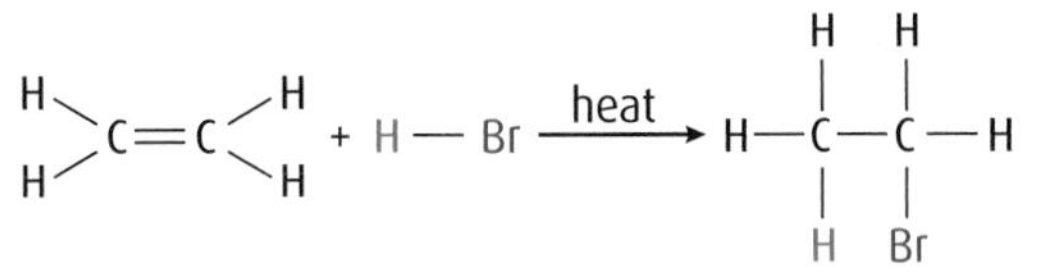

bromoethane

> The reaction with HI is also rapid, but that with HCl is very slow, and a catalyst (such as $AlCl_3$) is often used for that reaction.

Alkenes and water

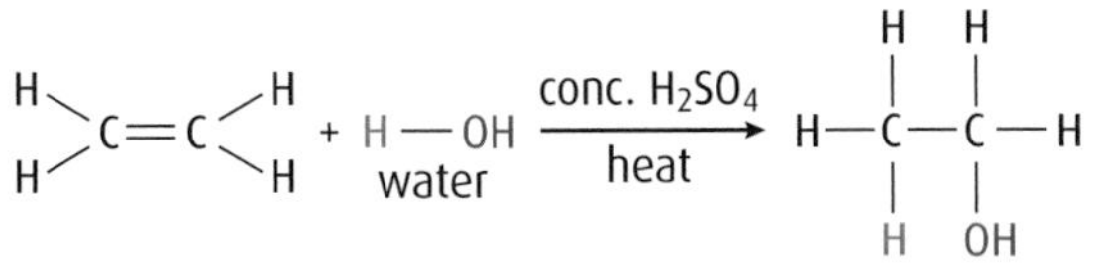

ethanol

> This process is called catalytic hydration and is used industrially for the production of ethanol, an important solvent. Industrially, the process is carried out by reacting ethene with steam at 300 °C and 60 atm pressure with an H_3PO_4 catalyst.

In the laboratory, this reaction may be carried out by passing ethene through concentrated sulfuric acid at room temperature, then warming the product with water.

Unsaturated fats (C=C present) from vegetable sources tend to be liquids at room temperature and are called oils. Saturated fats (no C=C) from animal sources are solids at room temperature.

Hydrogenation of alkenes is often used in the manufacture of margarine. A polyunsaturated oil contains many C=C (Figure **10.11**). The double bonds here are all shown as *cis* (groups either side of the C=C on the same side of the C=C). It is the presence of *cis* double bonds that give oils their low boiling point.

Margarine is made from vegetable oils (liquids), and partial hydrogenation may be carried out to convert some of the carbon–carbon double bonds into carbon–carbon single bonds. This increases the melting point of the margarine so that it is a solid at room temperature. The process, however, produces *trans*-fatty acids (where the groups either side of the C=C are on opposite sides of the carbon chain), which are believed to be bad for health. Partially hydrogenated vegetable oils have been banned in some countries.

Figure 10.11 The basic structure of a polyunsaturated fat.

The reactions described above may be regarded as applicable to all alkenes and, although the conditions may vary slightly, the basic reactions are the same. Thus, but-2-ene would react with HBr according to the equation:

$$H_3C{\scriptstyle\diagdown}\atop H{\scriptstyle\diagup}C{=}C{H\atop CH_3} + H{-}Br \xrightarrow{\text{HEAT}} H_3C{-}\underset{\underset{H}{|}}{\overset{\overset{H}{|}}{C}}{-}\underset{\underset{Br}{|}}{\overset{\overset{H}{|}}{C}}{-}CH_3$$

or pent-2-ene would react with chlorine:

$$H_3C{\scriptstyle\diagdown}\atop H{\scriptstyle\diagup}C{=}C{H\atop CH_2CH_3} + Cl{-}Cl \longrightarrow H_3C{-}\underset{\underset{Cl}{|}}{\overset{\overset{H}{|}}{C}}{-}\underset{\underset{Cl}{|}}{\overset{\overset{H}{|}}{C}}{-}CH_2CH_3$$

Examiner's tip

In this chapter we are learning about the reactions of functional groups, not individual molecules. The reactions here are of the C=C group, and it makes little difference what the rest of the molecule is like.

Distinguishing between alkanes and alkenes

Alkenes may be distinguished from alkanes by shaking them with bromine water. The bromine water, which is orange, is decolorised to colourless when shaken with an alkene, but there is no change in colour when it is shaken with an alkane (Figure **10.12**).

> Alkene: bromine water – orange to colourless
> Alkane: bromine water – no colour change

The reaction that occurs with an alkene is:

$$\underset{H}{\overset{H}{>}}C=C\underset{H}{\overset{H}{<}} + H_2O + Br_2 \longrightarrow H-\underset{Br}{\overset{H}{\underset{|}{C}}}-\underset{OH}{\overset{H}{\underset{|}{C}}}-H + HBr$$

To understand why the product of this reaction is not 1,2-dibromoethane, we have to consider the reaction mechanism. This is discussed in Option **G**.

Examiner's tip
The bromine becomes **colourless**, not clear. Clear and colourless are not the same thing. The orange bromine water was originally clear, as it was not cloudy and you could see through it!

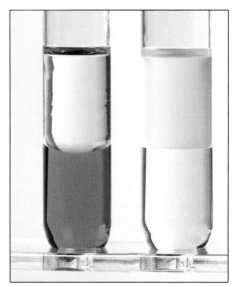

Figure 10.12 When shaken with an alkene, orange bromine water is decolorised.

Addition polymerisation

Alkenes undergo **addition** polymerisation, in which a large number of monomers are joined together into a polymer chain. The general equation for addition polymerisation is:

$$n\ \underset{R}{\overset{R}{>}}C=C\underset{R}{\overset{R}{<}} \longrightarrow \left[\overset{R}{\underset{R}{\overset{|}{\underset{|}{C}}}}-\overset{R}{\underset{R}{\overset{|}{\underset{|}{C}}}}\right]_n$$

monomer   polymer

It is important to realise from this reaction that it is only the C=C group that reacts when the polymerisation reaction occurs – all the other groups attached to the C=C are unaffected.

Poly(ethene)

In the production of low-density poly(ethene), the reaction takes place at high temperature and high pressure in the presence of a small amount of oxygen or an organic peroxide. High-density poly(ethene) is produced at a much lower temperature and lower pressure in the presence of a catalyst.

$$n\ \underset{H}{\overset{H}{>}}C=C\underset{H}{\overset{H}{<}} \xrightarrow[O_2/peroxide]{200°C\ 2000\ atm} \left[\overset{H}{\underset{H}{\overset{|}{\underset{|}{C}}}}-\overset{H}{\underset{H}{\overset{|}{\underset{|}{C}}}}\right]_n$$

ethene   poly(ethene)

Ethene is the monomer and poly(ethene) is the polymer. A section of the polymer chain is shown in Figure **10.13** (overleaf).

n represents a large number.

Addition polymers are named according to the monomer from which they were made.

$$-C-C-C-C-C-C-C-C-C-C-C-C-C-C-C-C-C-C-C-C-$$

(with H above and below each C)

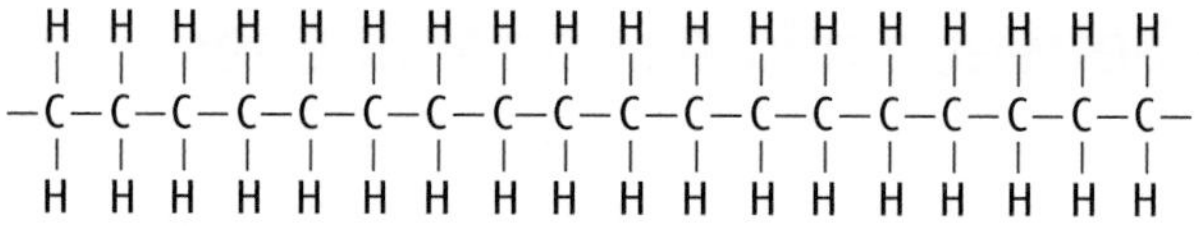

Figure 10.13 A section of the poly(ethene) polymer chain.

This is an example of addition polymerisation, because the monomers are simply added to each other without anything being lost.

PVC [poly(vinylchloride)]

This is more properly known as poly(chloroethene). It is made by the polymerisation of chloroethene monomers at moderate temperature and pressure in the presence of an organic peroxide:

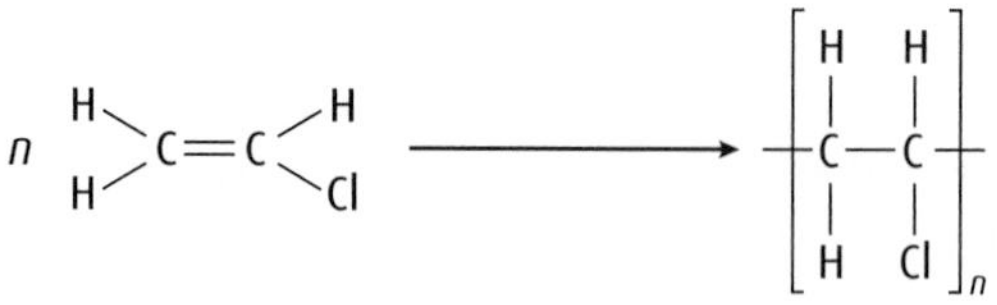

chloroethene → poly(chloroethene)

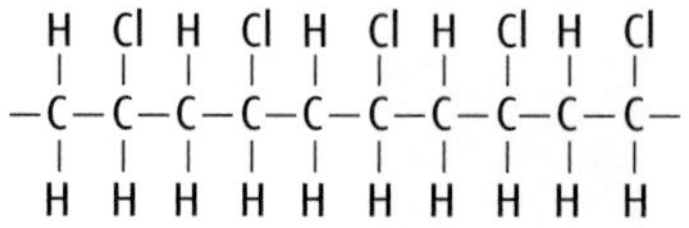

A section of a polymer chain of poly(chloroethene) is shown in Figure **10.14**.

Figure 10.14 A section of the poly(chloroethene) polymer chain.

Poly(propene)

It is important to remember that it is only the C=C group that reacts when the polymerisation reaction occurs – all the other groups attached to the C=C are unaffected. This can be seen if we look at the polymerisation of propene – the methyl group attached to the C=C does not become part of the main polymer chain but is just a side group on the chain.

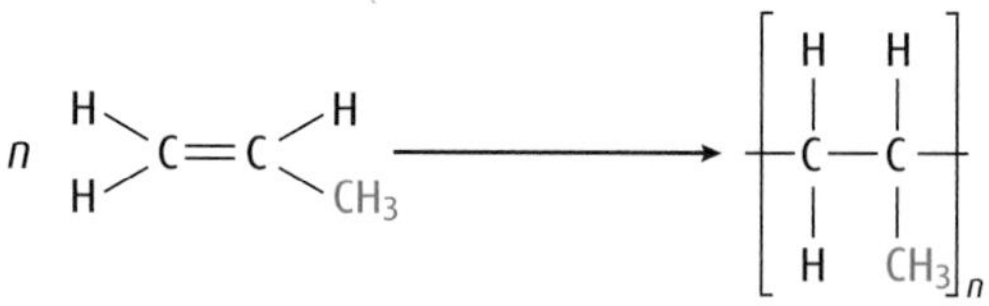

propene → poly(propene)

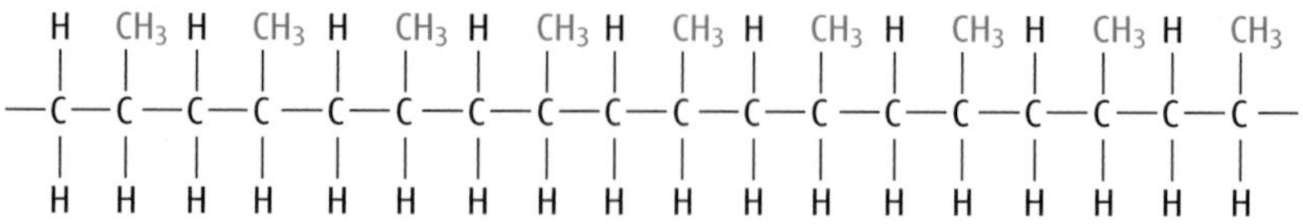

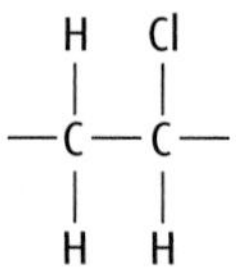

The **repeat unit** or **repeating unit** of a polymer is the basic unit from which the whole polymer chain can be made up. In each of the equations seen so far, this has been shown in brackets. The repeat unit for poly(chloroethene) is shown in Figure **10.15**.

Figure 10.15 The repeat unit for poly(chloroethene).

The repeat unit for a polymer may be obtained simply by taking any two **adjacent** carbon atoms in the main polymer chain:

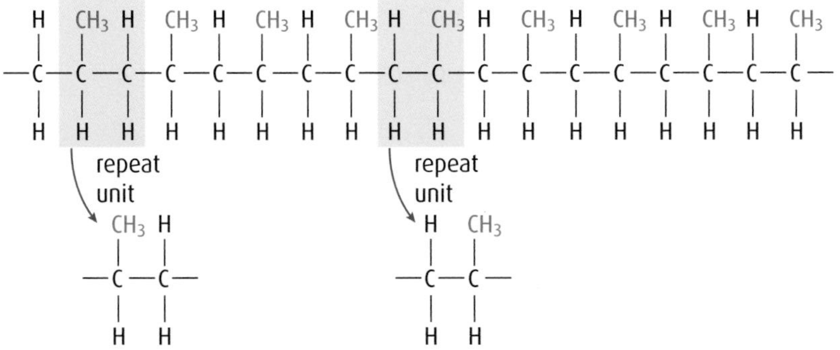

The monomer for a polymer can be derived by simply placing a double bond between the carbons of the repeat unit:

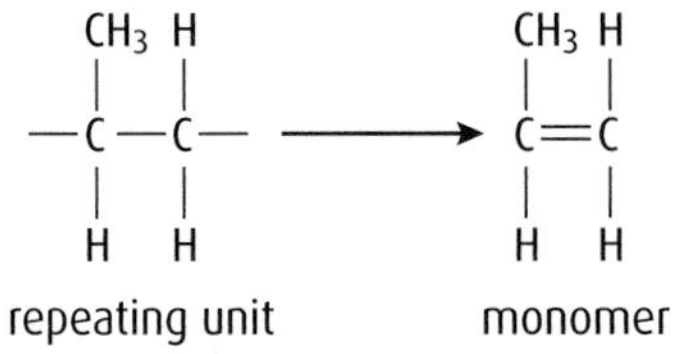

repeating unit → monomer

Economic importance of polymers

The polymers described here are more commonly known as plastics and find extensive uses in everyday life. Among other things, poly(ethene) is used for plastic bags, washing-up bowls and bottles, poly(chloroethene) is used for electrical insulation and window frames, and poly(propene) is used for car bumpers and carpet fibres.

These substances are produced in vast quantities by the petrochemical industry but do present a huge environmental problem, both from the point of view of using crude oil (petroleum), which is a limited natural resource, in their manufacture and due to problems with disposing of them after use, as they are non-biodegradable.

Self-test 4

Test yourself

13 Name the following compounds.

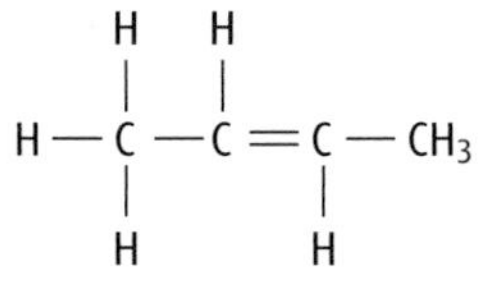 a	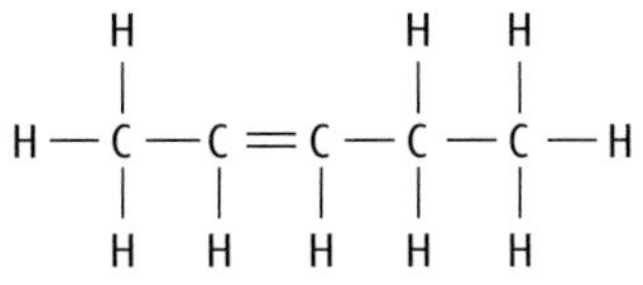 b	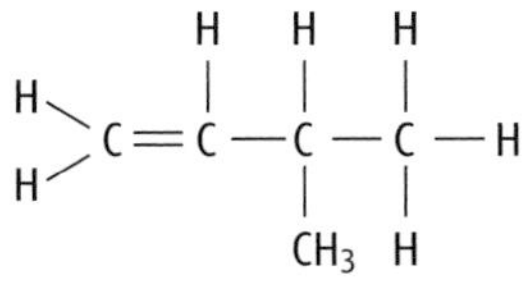 c	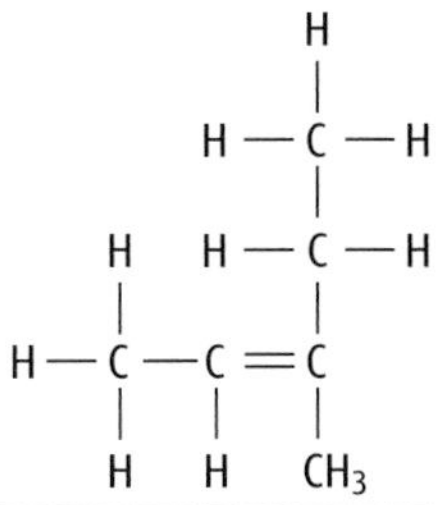 d

14 Draw out and name all the isomers of C_4H_8 that are alkenes.

15 Draw out the structures of the products of the following reactions (which occur under the appropriate conditions):

   a but-1-ene + hydrogen

   b hex-3-ene + hydrogen bromide

   c pent-2-ene + chlorine

   d but-2-ene + water

16 Write an equation for the formation of the following compounds from an appropriate alkene:

a

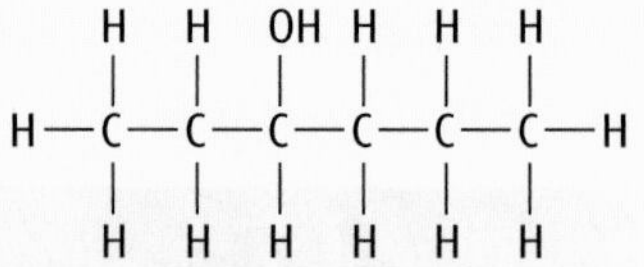

b

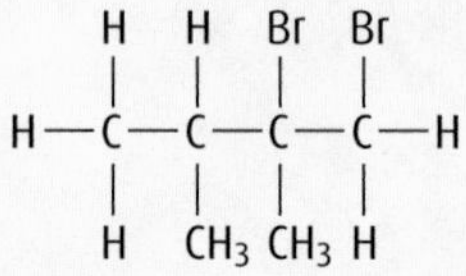

17 Draw two repeat units for the polymers formed from the following alkenes:

a

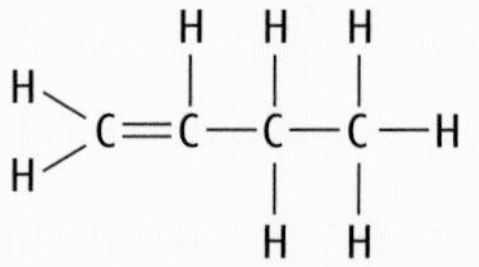

b

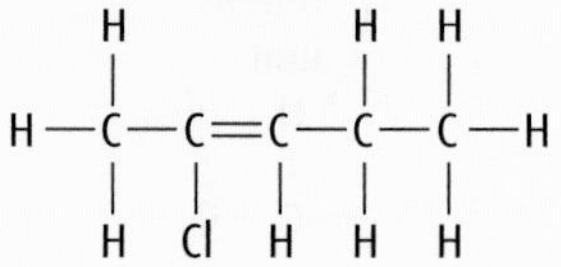

18 Draw the monomers for the following polymers:

a

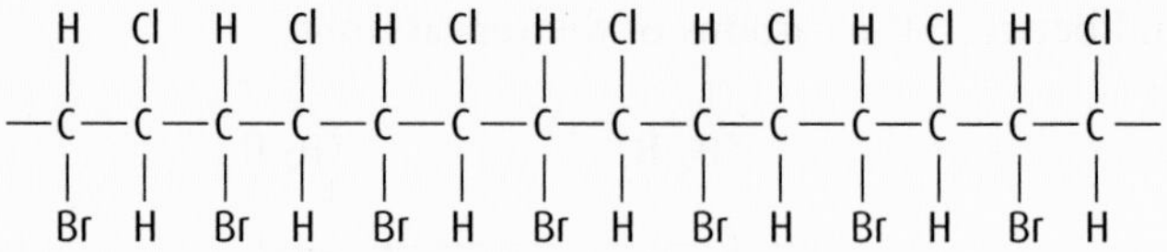

b

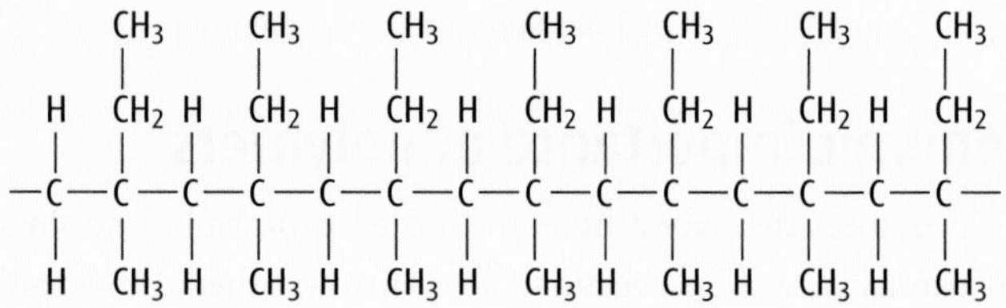

Learning objectives

- Write equations for the complete combustion of alcohols
- Classify alcohols as primary, secondary or tertiary
- Describe the oxidation reactions of alcohols
- Compare the boiling points of alcohols, carbonyl compounds and carboxylic acids
- Name aldehydes and ketones
- Name carboxylic acids

10.6 Compounds containing oxygen

Alcohols

The structures of the first six members of the alcohol homologous series are shown in Table **10.10**. These all have the general molecular formula $C_nH_{2n+2}O$, which can also be written as $C_nH_{2n+1}OH$. It can be seen from the first of these formulas that alcohols have the same number of hydrogen atoms as alkanes.

The functional group of alcohols is –OH. They have much higher boiling points than alkanes (see Figure **10.5** on page **424**) as a result of hydrogen bonding between molecules.

The lower members of the series are very soluble in water because of the hydrogen bonding. For example, ethanol is soluble in water in all proportions, and this is because the –OH group allows it to hydrogen bond to water. However, solubility decreases as the length of the hydrocarbon chain increases (see page **132**) so that pentan-1-ol and hexan-1-ol are only sparingly soluble in water.

Name	Molecular formula	Structural formula	
		Condensed	**Full**

methanol	CH_3OH	CH_3OH	H H
			   | |
			H—C—O
			   |
			   H

ethanol	C_2H_5OH	CH_3CH_2OH	H H H
			  | | |
			H—C—C—O
			  | |
			  H H

propan-1-ol	C_3H_7OH	$CH_3CH_2CH_2OH$	H H H H | | | | H—C—C—C—O | | | H H H
butan-1-ol	C_4H_9OH	$CH_3(CH_2)_2CH_2OH$	H H H H H | | | | | H—C—C—C—C—O | | | | H H H H
pentan-1-ol	$C_5H_{11}OH$	$CH_3(CH_2)_3CH_2OH$	H H H H H H | | | | | | H—C—C—C—C—C—O | | | | | H H H H H
hexan-1-ol	$C_6H_{13}OH$	$CH_3(CH_2)_4CH_2OH$	H H H H H H H | | | | | | | H—C—C—C—C—C—C—O | | | | | | H H H H H H

Table 10.10 The first six members of the alcohol homologous series.

Naming alcohols

Alcohols are named as **alkan–x–ol** (x-alkanol is also acceptable). The carbon atoms are numbered to given the lowest possible value for x.

The name changes slightly when more than one –OH group is present:

H   H   OH H
 \| \| \| \|
H—C—C—C—C— OH
 \| \| \| \|
 H   H   H   H

butane-1,2-diol

Examples

H OH H | | | H—C—C—C—H | | | H H H	propan-2-ol
OH H H H H H | | | | | | H—C—C—C—C—C—C—H | | | | | | H H H H CH$_3$ H	5-methylhexan-1-ol

H H OH H H | | | | | H—C—C—C—C—C—H | | | | | H H H CH$_3$ H	2-methylpentan-3-ol	

CH$_3$ OH H   H
  | | | |
H—C—C—C—C—CH$_3$
  | | | |
  H   H   H   CH$_3$
	5-methylhexan-3-ol	the numbering is chosen to give a lower number to the OH group rather than to the CH$_3$ group

Primary, secondary and tertiary alcohols

Alcohols (and other compounds) may be described as primary, secondary or tertiary, depending on the number of H atoms attached to the carbon with the −OH group on it. Ethanol is a primary alcohol, as it has two hydrogens attached to the C with the −OH attached. A primary alcohol thus contains the −CH$_2$OH group.

The symbol 1° is sometimes used for primary.

Another way of looking at this, which is almost entirely equivalent, is that the C with the −OH attached has one other C attached to it. **One** C attached = **primary**.

Methanol is also a primary alcohol, as it contains a −CH$_2$OH group.

Propan−2−ol is a secondary alcohol, as it has one H atom attached to the C with the −OH attached. A secondary alcohol contains the −CHOH group.

The symbol 2° is sometimes used for secondary.

In a **secondary** alcohol there are **two** carbon atoms attached to the C with the −OH attached.

2−methylpropan−2−ol is a tertiary alcohol, as there are no H atoms (or three C atoms) attached to the C with the −OH attached.

The symbol 3° is sometimes used for tertiary.

448

Reactions of alcohols

Combustion of alcohols

In a plentiful supply of oxygen, alcohols burn to produce carbon dioxide and water:

$$C_2H_5OH + 3O_2 \rightarrow 2CO_2 + 3H_2O$$

$$2C_3H_7OH + 9O_2 \rightarrow 6CO_2 + 8H_2O$$

Examiner's tip
When balancing these equations, don't forget the O in the alcohol!

Oxidation

Primary and secondary alcohols may be oxidised using an oxidising agent such as acidified potassium dichromate(VI) ($K_2Cr_2O_7/H^+$) or acidified potassium manganate(VII) ($KMnO_4/H^+$).

The potassium ions are not important here – the $Cr_2O_7^{2-}$ and MnO_4^- ions are the important parts.

Primary alcohols

Primary alcohols are oxidised first of all to an aldehyde (**partial oxidation**), and then the aldehyde is oxidised further to a carboxylic acid (**complete oxidation**).

$$\text{primary alcohol} \xrightarrow[\text{heat}]{Cr_2O_7^{2-}/H^+} \text{aldehyde} \xrightarrow[\text{heat}]{Cr_2O_7^{2-}/H^+} \text{carboxylic alcohol}$$

Aldehydes contain the

functional group.

For example:

Each individual reaction may be shown as a balanced equation:

$$CH_3CH_2OH + [O] \rightarrow CH_3CHO + H_2O$$

$$CH_3CHO + [O] \rightarrow CH_3COOH$$

$Cr_2O_7^{2-}$ is the oxidising agent and is therefore reduced during the reaction. $Cr_2O_7^{2-}$ is orange and is reduced to the green Cr^{3+}(aq) ion. The half equation for the reduction is:

$$Cr_2O_7^{2-} + 14H^+ + 6e^- \rightarrow 2Cr^{3+} + 7H_2O$$

Carboxylic acids have the

functional group.

[O] represents oxygen from the oxidising agent.

Colour change: orange → green

If the reaction mixture is heated under **reflux**, ethanoic acid is obtained as the main product and the aldehyde is not usually isolated. However, it is possible to set up the experiment so that the **aldehyde** is **distilled** off as soon as it is formed and before it can be oxidised further (Figure **10.16**, overleaf).

Aldehydes have a lower boiling point than alcohols, as they do not have an H attached directly to an O and therefore do not have hydrogen bonding between molecules.

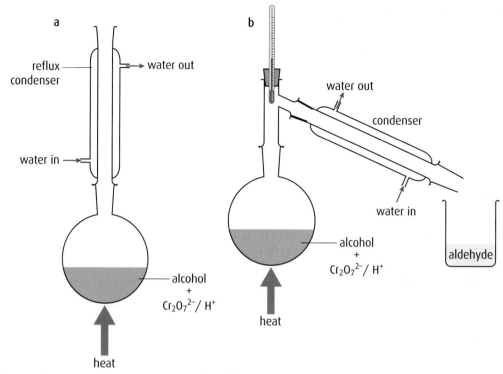

Figure 10.16 (a) Apparatus set up for reflux. Reflux produces the carboxylic acid – complete oxidation. **(b)** Apparatus set up for distillation. Distillation produces the aldehyde – partial oxidation.

Examiner's Tip

In organic chemistry, it is important to focus only on the changes to a particular functional group – the rest of the molecule (the carbon skeleton) should remain unchanged.

If we look at the reactions in terms of changes to the functional groups, it is easier to generalise the reaction to other molecules:

Thus, if we look at the reaction for another primary alcohol, we get:

2-methylpropan-1-ol   2-methylpropanal   2-methylpropanoic acid

The only change is to the group highlighted in red – the rest of the molecule is unchanged.

Here we are using inductive reasoning. We are making the assumption that, because all primary alcohols we have so far encountered can be oxidised by potassium dichromate(VI) to an aldehyde and then a carboxylic acid, then **all** primary alcohols will be oxidised in this way. Can we ever know this?

Secondary alcohols

Secondary alcohols are also oxidised by heating with acidified potassium dichromate(VI) (or acidified potassium manganate(VII)). They are oxidised to **ketones**, which cannot be oxidised any further.

$$\text{secondary alcohol} \xrightarrow[\text{heat}]{Cr_2O_7^{2-}/\,H^+} \text{ketone} \xrightarrow[\text{heat}]{Cr_2O_7^{2-}/\,H^+} \times$$

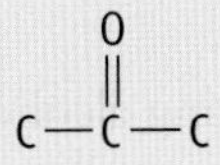

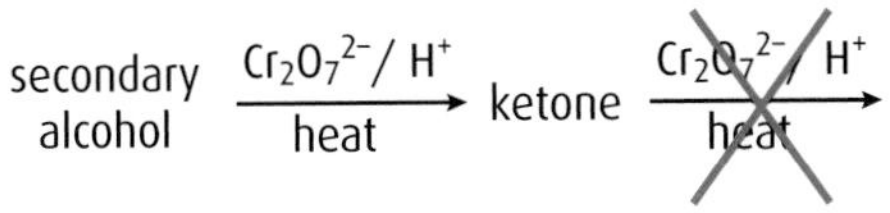

For example:

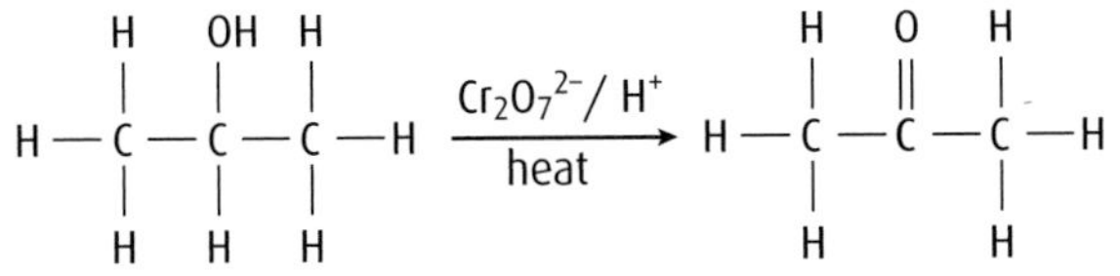

propan-2-ol → propanone

The balanced equation for the reaction is:

$$CH_3CH(OH)CH_3 + [O] \rightarrow (CH_3)_2CO + H_2O$$

In terms of change to the functional group, the reaction can be represented as:

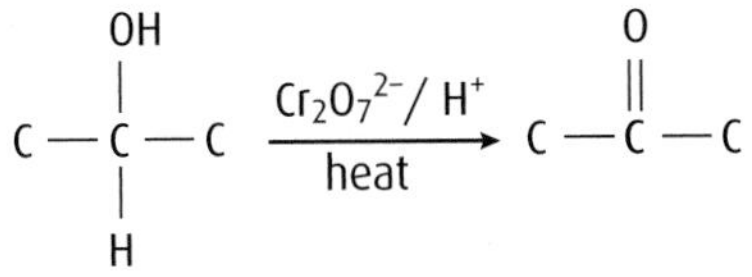

Thus, if we look at the reaction for another secondary alcohol we get:

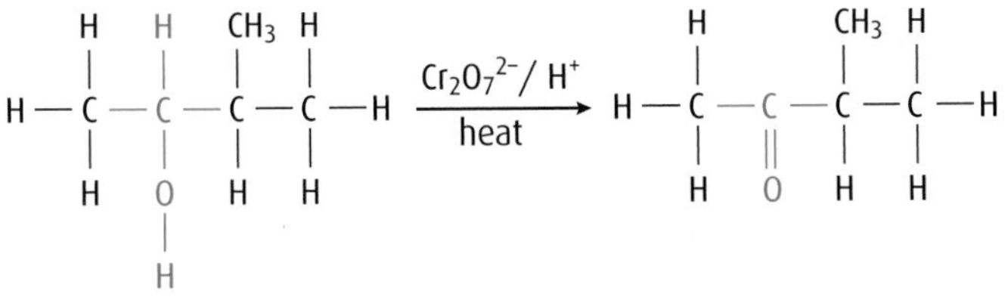

3-methylbutan-2-ol → 3-methylbutanone

Tertiary alcohols

Tertiary alcohols are resistant to oxidation.

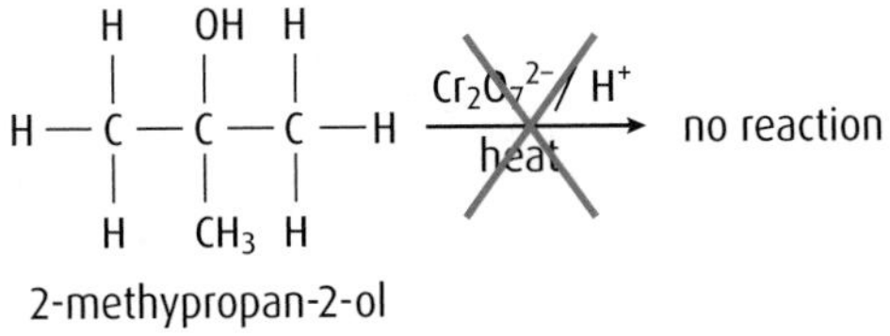

2-methypropan-2-ol

Ketones contain the

$$\underset{}{C}-\overset{\displaystyle O}{\underset{\displaystyle \|}{C}}-C$$

functional group.

[O] represents oxygen from the oxidising agent.

The only change is to the group highlighted in red – the rest of the molecule is unchanged.

Test yourself

19 Name the following alcohols and classify each as primary, secondary or tertiary:

a	b	c	d
OH H H | | | H—C—C—C—H | | | H H H	H H H OH H | | | | | H—C—C—C—C—C—H | | | | | H H H H H	H OH H H | | | | H—C—C—C—C—H | | | | H CH₃ H H	H CH₃ H OH | | | | H—C—C—C—C—H | | | | H CH₃ H H

20 For each of the alcohols in question **19**, give the structural formula of the product (if any) of complete oxidation when they are heated with acidified potassium dichromate(VI).

21 Write a balanced equation for the complete combustion of butan–1–ol.

22 Give the structure of the organic product formed when each of the following alcohols is heated with acidified potassium dichromate(VI) with the apparatus set up for distillation:

a 3-methylbutan–1–ol

b 2-methylpentan–3–ol

c 2,3-dimethylpentan–1–ol

Functional group	
$\overset{\displaystyle O}{\underset{\diagdown H}{\overset{\|\|}{C}}}$	$\underset{C}{\overset{\displaystyle O}{\underset{\diagdown C}{\overset{\|\|}{C}}}}$
aldehyde	ketone

Aldehydes and ketones

Aldehydes and ketones are also known as **carbonyl** compounds and contain the carbonyl (C=O) functional group.

Physical properties of aldehydes and ketones

The boiling points of alkanes, alcohols and aldehydes are compared in Figure **10.17**.

The boiling points of ketones are very similar to those of aldehydes of the same relative molecular mass. Aldehydes have higher boiling points than alkanes of similar relative molecular mass and lower boiling points than alcohols of similar relative molecular mass.

Aldehydes have higher boiling points than alkanes, as aldehydes are polar whereas alkanes are non-polar. Aldehydes are polar because of the presence of the very electronegative O atom.

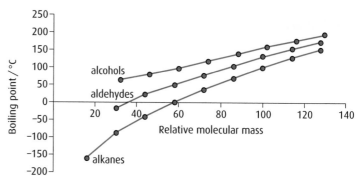

Figure 10.17 The boiling points of alkanes, aldehydes and alcohols.

The intermolecular forces between aldehyde molecules are stronger than those between alkane molecules of similar relative molecular mass because of the presence of dipole–dipole interactions between the aldehyde molecules but only van der Waals' forces between alkane molecules.

Alcohols are also polar molecules, but, because the O is joined directly to an H atom, they are also able to participate in hydrogen bonding. Hydrogen bonding is a stronger intermolecular force than dipole–dipole interactions.

Solubility

Lower members (methanal, ethanal, propanal, propanone, butanone) are soluble in water because of their polarity and also because they are able to hydrogen bond to water molecules.

> Note: aldehydes do not hydrogen bond to each other, but they are able to participate in hydrogen bonding with water.

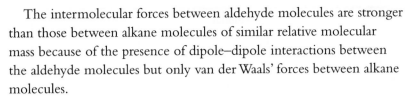

The solubility decreases as the hydrocarbon chain gets longer, because of the non-polar nature of the hydrocarbon chain.

Naming aldehydes and ketones

Aldehydes are named in the form alkan**al** and ket**one**s are named in the form alkan-x-**one** (x-alkanone is also acceptable). Examples of some names of aldehydes and ketones are given in Table **10.11** (page **454**).

The condensed structural formulas for aldehydes can be written using the $-CHO$ group, so ethanal can be written as CH_3CHO and butanal as $CH_3CH_2CH_2CHO$. The condensed structural formulas for ketones can be written using the $-CO$ group, so propanone can be written as CH_3COCH_3 or $(CH_3)_2CO$ and pentan-2-one as $CH_3COCH_2CH_2CH_3$.

> Formalin is a solution of methanal (formaldehyde). It is used to preserve biological specimens.

Reactions of aldehydes and ketones

Aldehydes can be oxidised by heating with acidified potassium dichromate(VI) to carboxylic acids, but ketones are resistant to oxidation.

$$\text{aldehyde} \xrightarrow[\text{heat}]{Cr_2O_7{}^{2-}/H+} \text{carboxylic acid}$$

(structure: methanal)	methanal		aldehydes
(structure: propanal)	propanal		
(structure: 4-methylpentanal)	4-methylpentanal	numbering starts from the aldehyde group	
(structure: propanone)	propanone		ketones
(structure: pentan-2-one)	pentan-2-one		
(structure: 4-methylpentan-2-one)	4-methylpentan-2-one	the ketone group is given the lower number	

Table 10.11 The names of some aldehydes and ketones.

Carboxylic acids

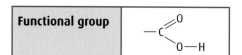

Functional group	(structure)

Physical properties of carboxylic acids

A comparison of the boiling points of aldehydes, alcohols and carboxylic acids is shown in Figure **10.18**.

Carboxylic acids have hydrogen bonding between molecules and therefore have higher boiling points than aldehydes of similar relative molecular mass. They also have higher boiling points than alcohols of the same relative molecular mass, as they have two O atoms per molecule

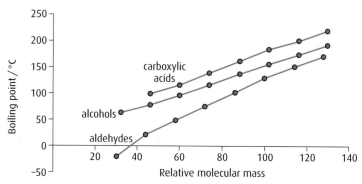

Figure 10.18 The boiling points of aldehydes, alcohols and carboxylic acids.

and therefore have **stronger hydrogen bonding than alcohols**, which have only one O atom per molecule. The hydrogen bonding between two carboxylic acid molecules is shown in Figure **10.19**.

Carboxylic acids with lower relative molecular mass are generally soluble in water, owing to the ability to hydrogen bond to water. However, the solubility decreases as the length of the hydrocarbon chain (non-polar) increases, so octanoic acid is essentially insoluble in water.

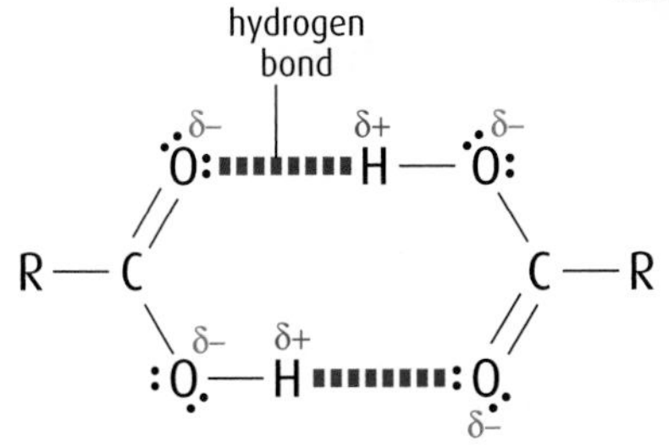

Naming carboxylic acids

Carboxylic acids are named in the form **alkanoic acid**.

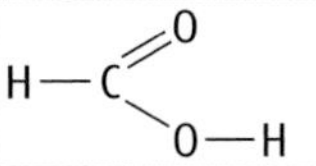

Figure 10.19 The hydrogen bonding between two carboxylic acid molecules.

H—C(=O)(O—H)	methanoic acid
H—C(H)(H)—C(=O)(O—H)	ethanoic acid
H—C(H)(H)—C(H)(H)—C(=O)(O—H)	propanoic acid
H—C(H)(H)—C(H)(H)—C(H)(H)—C(=O)(O—H)	butanoic acid

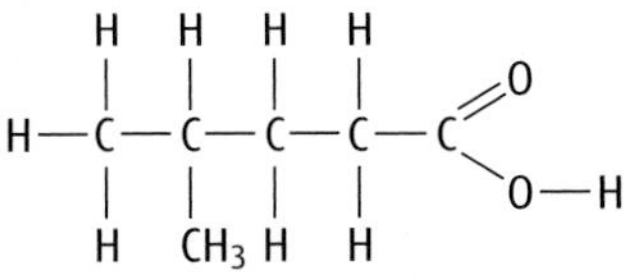 H—C(H)(H)—C(H)(CH₃)—C(H)(H)—C(=O)(O—H)	4-methylpentanoic acid	numbering starts from the carboxylic acid group
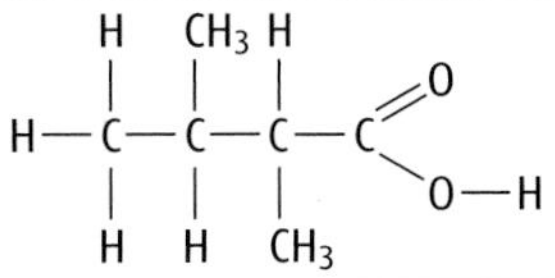 H—C(H)(H)—C(CH₃)(H)—C(H)(CH₃)—C(=O)(O—H)	2,3-dimethylbutanoic acid	
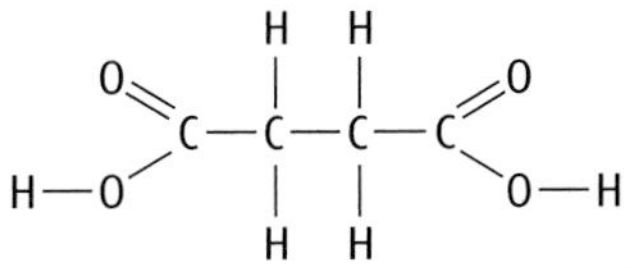 H—O—C(=O)—C(H)(H)—C(H)(H)—C(=O)(O—H)	butanedioic acid	

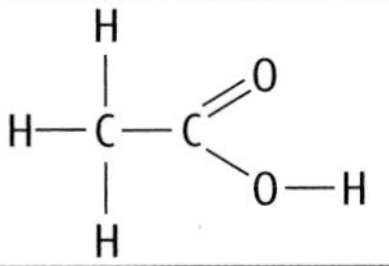

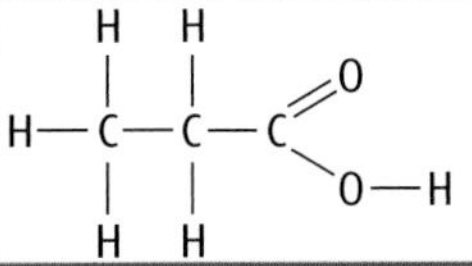

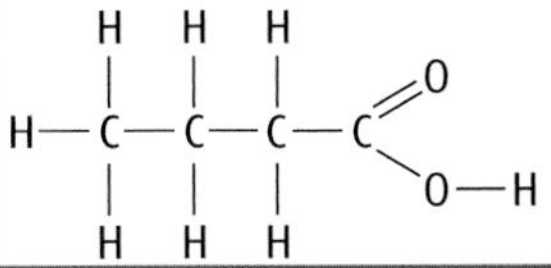

The condensed structural formulas for carboxylic acids can be written using the –COOH or –CO₂H groups, so ethanoic acid is often shown as CH_3COOH and butanoic acid as $CH_3CH_2CH_2COOH$.

Self-test 6

Test yourself

23 Name the following compounds:

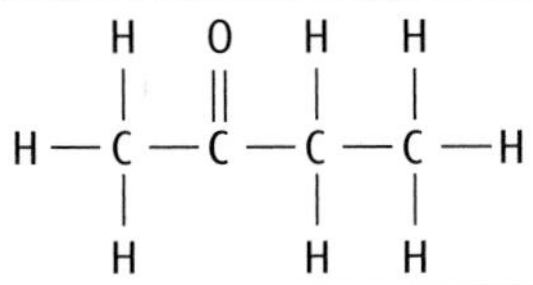 a	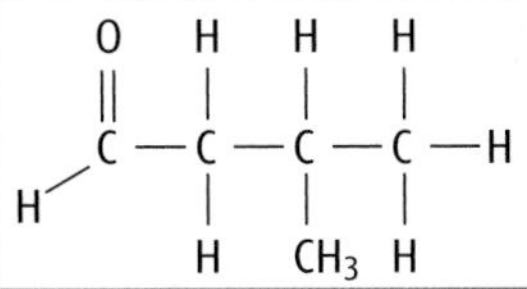 b	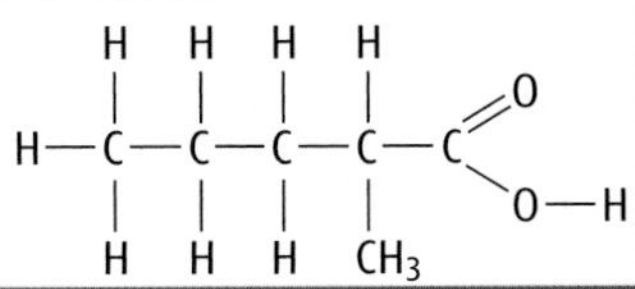 c	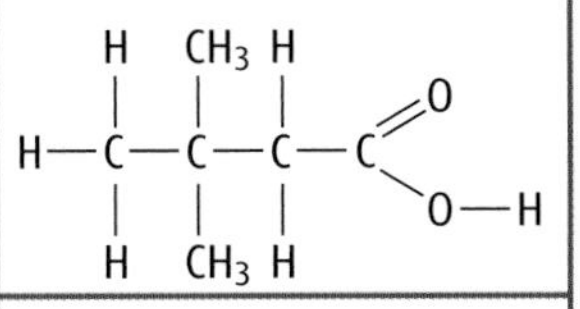 d
H—C(H)(H)—C(=O)—C(H)(H)—C(H)(H)—H	H—C(=O)—C(H)(H)—C(CH₃)(H)—C(H)(H)—H	H—C(H)(H)—C(H)(H)—C(H)(H)—C(H)(CH₃)—C(=O)(O—H)	H—C(H)(H)—C(CH₃)(H)—C(H)(CH₃)—C(=O)(O—H)

24 Draw the structures of each of the following molecules and give the full structural formula and name of the product formed (if any) when it is heated with acidified potassium dichromate(VI):

   a butanal   **b** 2-methylpentanal   **c** pentan-3-one

10.7 Halogenoalkanes

Learning objectives

- Describe the reaction of halogenoalkanes with aqueous sodium hydroxide
- Explain the S_N1 and S_N2 mechanisms

HL
- Explain the factors that affect the rate of nucleophilic substitution of halogenoalkanes
- Describe and explain (including mechanisms) the substitution reactions of halogenoalkanes with ammonia and potassium cyanide
- Understand that nitriles can be reduced to amines
- Understand how to name nitriles and amines
- Describe and explain (including the mechanism) the elimination reactions of halogenoalkanes

Halogenoalkanes

Halogenoalkanes contain a halogen atom as the functional group.

Boiling points

A comparison of the boiling points of halogenoalkanes with alkanes is not simple. If we compare them in terms of the number of carbon atoms in the chain, then the halogenoalkanes all have higher boiling points than alkanes with the same number of carbon atoms. The boiling points also increase from chloro- to bromo- to iodo- compounds (Table **10.12**).

No. carbon atoms	Boiling point /°C			
1	methane	chloromethane	bromomethane	iodomethane
	−162	−24	4	43
2	ethane	chloroethane	bromoethane	iodoethane
	−89	13	38	72

Table 10.12 A comparison of boiling points in halogenoalkanes and alkanes, according to number of carbon atoms.

This increase in boiling point is due mostly to the halogenoalkanes having a higher relative molecular mass and hence stronger van der Waals' forces. However, if we compare compounds of similar relative molecular mass (Table **10.13**), it can be seen that the bromo- and iodo- compounds have substantially lower boiling points than the alkanes of similar relative molecular mass. This can be attributed to the alkanes being longer–chain molecules, so that, in the liquid state, there is more surface area of the molecules in contact and therefore stronger intermolecular forces.

Compound	decane	undecane	1-chlorooctane	1-bromobutane	iodomethane
Formula	$C_{10}H_{22}$	$C_{11}H_{24}$	$C_8H_{17}Cl$	C_4H_9Br	CH_3I
M_r	142.32	156.35	148.68	137.03	141.94
Boiling point /°C	174	196	183	101	43

Table 10.13 A comparison of boiling points in halogenoalkanes and alkanes, according to relative molecular mass (M_r).

There is very little difference between the boiling points of the alkanes and chloroalkanes of similar relative molecular mass (Figure **10.20**). It might be expected that the chloroalkanes would have higher boiling points than the alkanes, as they are polar molecules whereas the alkanes are non-polar, but this is balanced out almost exactly by the fact that the alkanes have a longer chain and therefore the van der Waals' forces act over a greater area.

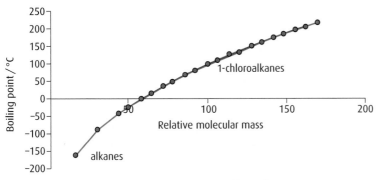

Figure 10.20 The boiling points of alkanes and 1-chloroalkanes.

Solubility

Although slightly more soluble than alkanes, halogenoalkanes are still only either sparingly soluble or insoluble in water. To all intents and purposes, they may be regarded as insoluble in water but soluble in organic solvents.

Naming halogenoalkanes

Halogenoalkanes are named according to the format **x–haloalkane**, where *x* indicates the position of the halogen atom in the chain. Examples of some names of simple halogenoalkanes are given in Table **10.14**.

Cl H H | | | H—C—C—C—H | | | H H H	H Br H H | | | | H—C—C—C—C—H | | | | H H H H	H Br Br H | | | | H—C—C—C—C—H | | | | H H H H
1-chloropropane	2-bromobutane	2,3-dibromobutane

Table 10.14 The names of some simple halogenalkanes.

Where more than one substituent is present on the chain, they are arranged in alphabetical order with the numbering system chosen to give the lowest possible number for any substituent. Where two or more substituents would have the same numbers when numbering from either side, the substituent that comes first in the alphabet (ignoring di-, tri-, etc.) is chosen to have the lowest position number.

3-bromo-2-chloropentane

The two possible names for this are 3–bromo–2–chloropentane and 3–bromo–4–chloropentane. The first name gives the lowest individual number (2), and so the name is **3–bromo–2–chloropentane**.

2-bromo-5-methylhexane

There are two substituents on the chain – a bromo group and a methyl group. The two possible names are 2-bromo-5-methylhexane and 5-bromo-2-methylhexane. Both names contain the same numbers, and so the name is chosen according to position in the alphabet. Bromo comes before methyl in the alphabet, and so the numbering is chosen to give the lower number to the bromo, which leads to the name **2-bromo-5-methylhexane**.

Some more examples of halogenoalkane names are given in Table **10.15**.

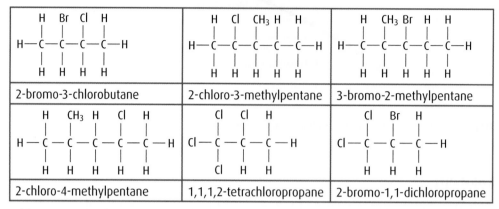

H Br Cl H ... 2-bromo-3-chlorobutane	H Cl CH₃ H H ... 2-chloro-3-methylpentane	H CH₃ Br H H ... 3-bromo-2-methylpentane
H CH₃ H Cl H ... 2-chloro-4-methylpentane	Cl Cl H ... 1,1,1,2-tetrachloropropane	Cl Br H ... 2-bromo-1,1-dichloropropane

Table 10.15 Examples of halogenoalkanes.

Primary, secondary and tertiary halogenoalkanes

As with alcohols, it is useful to classify halogenoalkanes as primary, secondary or tertiary (Table **10.16**).

structure	type	description
Cl H H / H—C—C—C—H	primary	the C attached to the Cl has one C atom attached
H Br H H / H—C—C—C—C—H	secondary	the C attached to the Br has two C atoms attached
H CH₃ H H H / H—C—C—C—C—C—H with Cl below	tertiary	the C attached to the Cl has three other C atoms attached

Table 10.16 Examples of primary, secondary and tertiary halogenalkanes.

Nucleophilic substitution reactions

Halogenoalkanes usually undergo **substitution** reactions; for example, when 1-bromopropane is heated with **aqueous** sodium hydroxide, the Br is replaced by an OH to form propan-1-ol:

Substitution reaction: one atom/group is replaced by another atom/group.

$$\text{1-bromopropane} \xrightarrow[\text{heat}]{\text{NaOH(aq)}} \text{propan-1-ol}$$

1-bromopropane   propan-1-ol

The balanced equation for this reaction is:

$$CH_3CH_2CH_2Br + NaOH \rightarrow CH_3CH_2CH_2OH + NaBr$$

or, as an ionic equation:

$$CH_3CH_2CH_2Br + OH^- \rightarrow CH_3CH_2CH_2OH + Br^-$$

The type of mechanism by which this reaction occurs is **nucleophilic substitution**: the halogenoalkane is attacked by a nucleophile and the nucleophile replaces the halogen atom.

The exact nature of the nucleophilic substitution reaction depends on which type (primary, secondary or tertiary) of halogenoalkane reacts.

Primary halogenoalkanes (S_N2 mechanism)

Consider the reaction of bromoethane with sodium hydroxide.

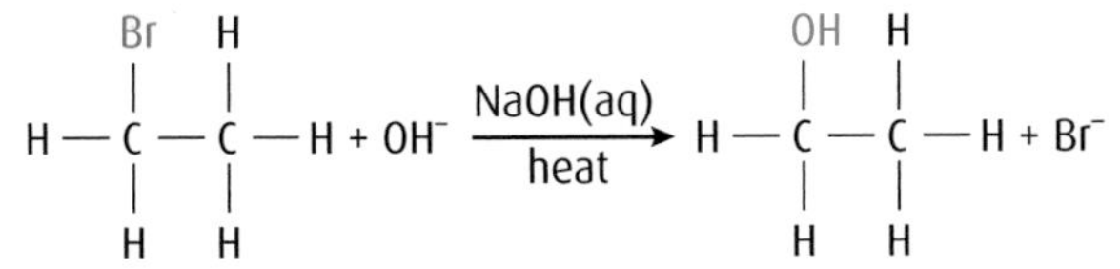

The initial part of the mechanism is the attack of the OH^- on the C attached to the Br. As the Br is more electronegative than the C, the C atom is slightly positive and the OH^- is attracted to it. The **OH^- is the nucleophile** and donates a lone pair of electrons to the C to form a (dative) covalent bond. The curly arrow shows the lone pair on OH^- becoming a bonding pair of electrons between the O and C. C can have a maximum of only eight electrons in its outer shell, and therefore as the C–O bond forms the C–Br bond must break.

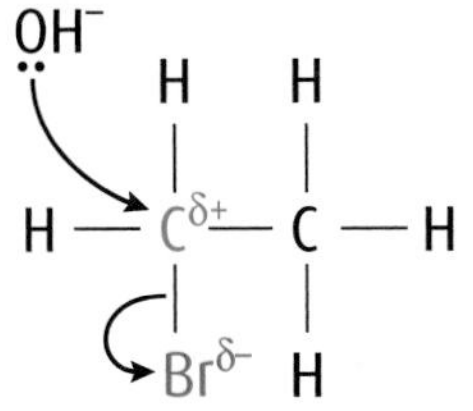

> The arrow from the lone pair of the OH^- to the $C^{\delta+}$ is called a **curly arrow** and is used when drawing out mechanisms in organic chemistry to represent the movement of **a pair of electrons**.

The curly arrow shown in red in Figure **10.21** indicates that the C–Br bond breaks. Both electrons from the C–Br bond go back to the bromine atom to form a bromide ion. This is called **heterolytic fission** – the bond breaks so that both electrons go to the same atom.

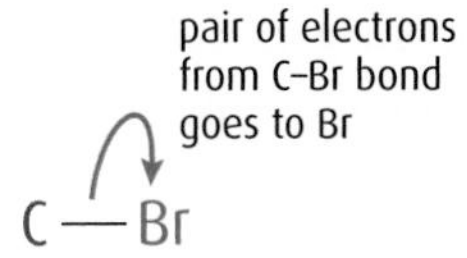

Part of the way through the process, the OH and Br are both partially joined to the C, and this is often shown in the mechanism. This is not an intermediate in the reaction but is the highest point on the reaction energy profile, which is often called the **transition state** or **activated complex**.

> This reaction is known as **hydrolysis**, as it essentially equivalent to breaking apart the molecule using water.

> A nucleophile is a molecule/ negatively charged ion, possessing a lone pair of electrons, which is attracted to a more positively charged region in a molecule (a region with lower electron density) and donates a lone pair of electrons to form a covalent bond.

Animation 5

Examiner's tip
The curly arrow must come from the O and not from the H of the OH^-.

pair of electrons from C–Br bond goes to Br

Figure 10.21 Heterolytic fission.

Animation 6

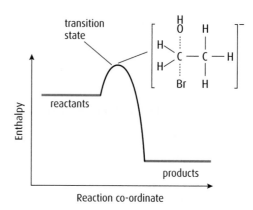

Overall then, we can draw the mechanism as:

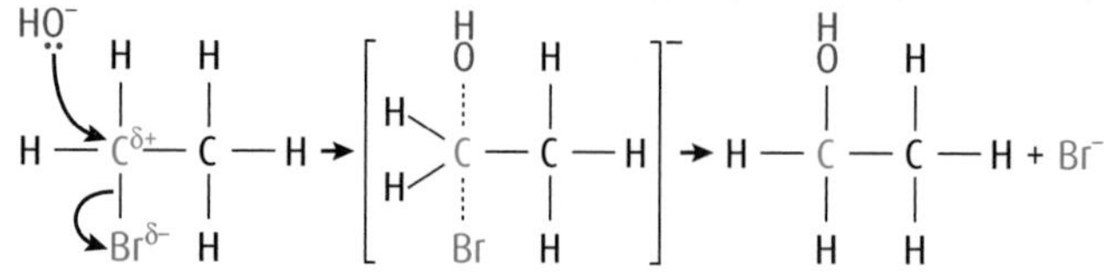

This is a single-step mechanism, and the formation of the transition state is just part of the way along this step. The mechanism could just as well be shown without this, as:

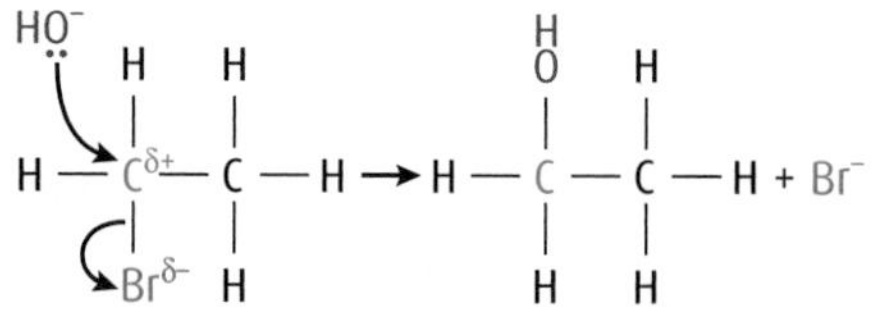

This mechanism is known as an S_N2 mechanism.

> S_N2 is the main mechanism for substitution in primary halogenoalkanes.

The rate-determining step is the slowest step in a reaction mechanism and, therefore, the step that governs the overall rate of reaction. The S_N2 mechanism occurs in a single step, so this must be the rate-determining step.

HL The rate equation for the above reaction is:

rate $= k[CH_3CH_2Br][OH^-]$

This means that, if the concentration of bromoethane or sodium hydroxide is doubled, the rate of reaction is doubled.

> Note: molecularity and order are not the same. Order is an experimentally determined quantity that relates concentrations of reactants to the rate. Molecularity refers to the number of molecules (or ions) that take part in a particular step (usually the rate-determining step) in a mechanism.

Extension

The OH^- approaches the $C^{\delta+}$ from the opposite side to the Br, and the reaction results in inversion of the tetrahedral configuration at the central C, like an umbrella turning inside out.

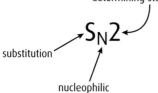

bimolecular - two molecules involved in a particular step, usually the rate-determining step.

substitution

nucleophilic

The 2 indicates the molecularity of the reaction.

Examiner's tip
The term **rate-determining step** is required only at Higher Level.

Tertiary halogenoalkanes

Consider the reaction of 2-bromo-2-methylpropane with sodium hydroxide. This occurs fairly rapidly at room temperature:

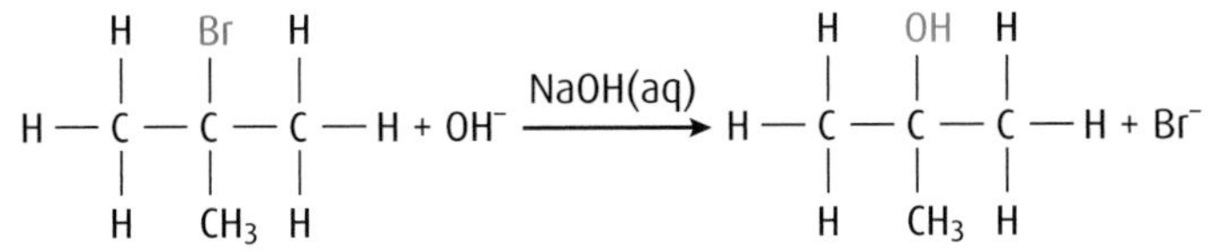

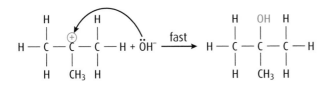

2-bromo-2-methylpropane   2-methylpropan-2-ol

Studies of the rate of this reaction determined that the rate of reaction does not seem to depend on the concentration of the sodium hydroxide. However, in the S_N2 mechanism studied above, the rate would be dependent on the concentration of NaOH. This reaction must, therefore, occur via a different mechanism. The proposed mechanism is:

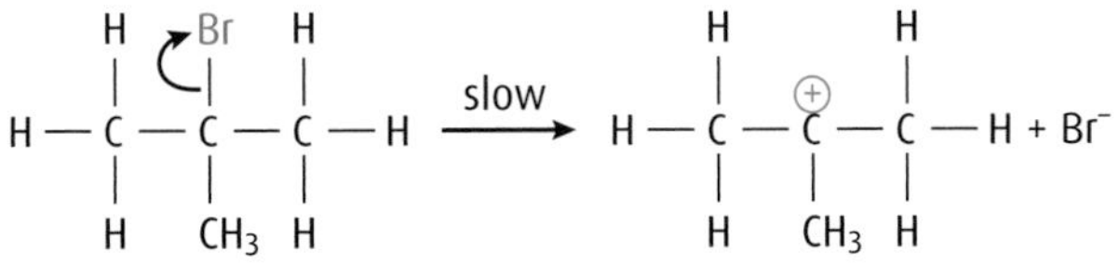

carbocation

This mechanism is described as S_N1, i.e. substitution nucleophilic unimolecular.

> In the first step, the C–Br bond breaks to form a positively charged carbocation. This is the rate-determining step in the mechanism.

Animation 7

For primary halogenoalkanes the dominant mechanism is S_N2, whereas for tertiary halogenoalkanes it is S_N1. Secondary halogenoalkanes undergo nucleophilic substitution via a mixture of mechanisms (i.e. both mechanisms); the more dominant mechanism will depend on the specific conditions of the reaction.

Extension

The carbocation formed is planar so that the OH⁻ can attack from either side. A racemic mixture would be formed if the original bromoalkane were optically active.

A useful rule for answering examination questions is:

> for the reaction of aqueous sodium hydroxide with halogenoalkanes, the S_N1 reactions of tertiary halogenoalkanes are faster than S_N2 reactions of primary halogenoalkanes

The reason for this is that the highly polar nature of the water from the aqueous sodium hydroxide is able to stabilise the carbocation formed in the S_N1 mechanism and favour its formation.

S_N1 being faster than S_N2 is indeed the case if the reaction is carried out by adding aqueous sodium hydroxide to the halogenoalkanes. However, owing to the fact that the S_N1 mechanism involves an increase in the number of ions present because of the formation of a carbocation in the rate-determining step, whereas S_N2 reactions do not, the rates of the two different mechanisms will be influenced very strongly by changing the polarity of the solvent. This rule is then only really applicable when a significant amount of water/very polar solvent or an aqueous reagent is used. The polar solvent stabilises the carbocation formed in the S_N1 mechanism (or more correctly, if we are considering rate, the transition state leading to the formation of the carbocation).

Self-test 7

Test yourself

25 Name the following molecules and classify each as primary, secondary or tertiary:

a	b	c	d
H H H Br H—C—C—C—C—H H H H H	H Br H H H—C—C—C—C—H H CH₃ H H	H Cl H H—C—C—C—H H H H	H H H I H—C—C—C—C—H H CH₃ H H

26 State whether each of the halogenoalkanes in question **25** reacts with NaOH(aq) via an S_N1 or an S_N2 mechanism.

27 Give the structural formula of the product formed when each of the molecules in question **25** reacts with NaOH(aq).

Standard Level continues on page 482

Weaker C–X bond = faster

Bond	Bond energy / kJ mol⁻¹
C–F	484
C–Cl	338
C–Br	276
C–I	238

Table 10.17 C–halogen bond energies.

The rate of an S_N1 reaction is not affected by changing the nucleophile, as the nucleophile attacks only **after** the rate-determining step.

HL ## The effect of the halogen on the rate of nucleophilic substitution

The rate of nucleophilic substitution of halogenoalkanes by the hydroxide ion is fastest with iodo- compounds, and the order of decreasing rate is:
R–I > R–Br > R–Cl > R–F.

Both S_N2 and S_N1 mechanisms involve C–X bond breaking in the rate-determining step. The C–I bond is easiest to break (Table **10.17**), so the reaction will be fastest for the iodoalkane. This factor dominates any effects due to electronegativity of the halogen atom (the C–X bond is least polar in iodoalkanes, so the C should attract a nucleophile least strongly).

Effect of the nucleophile on the rate of nucleophilic substitution

Mechanism	Rate equation	Effect of doubling [OH⁻]
S_N1	rate = $k[(CH_3)_3CBr]$	no effect, as OH⁻ not in the rate equation
S_N2	rate = $k[CH_3CH_2Br][OH^-]$	rate of reaction doubles, as it is first order with respect to OH⁻

S_N2 reactions will generally be faster with ions rather than neutral molecules, e.g. OH^- will react faster than H_2O, as the greater negative charge on the O in OH^- means it will be more strongly attracted to $C^{\delta+}$ in the halogenoalkane.

Why two different mechanisms?

Why is S_N2 more favourable for primary halogenoalkanes than for tertiary halogenoalkanes?

This is mainly because of **steric effects**. The methyl groups surrounding the central C in a tertiary halogenoalkane make it much more difficult for the nucleophile to get in to attack the central C (Figure **10.22**). This can also be seen if we look at the space-filling model of 2-bromo-2-methylpropane in Figure **10.23**.

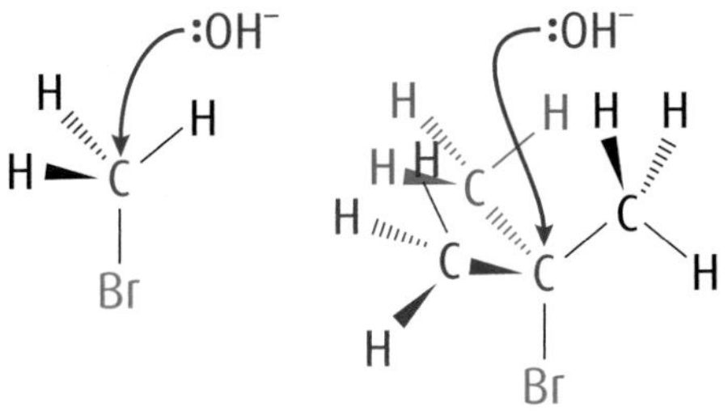

Figure 10.22 Attack of OH^- on a primary or a tertiary halogenoalkane.

Another way of explaining this is that, if the OH^- did get in to attack the C, there would be five large groups surrounding the central C in the transition state, which would make this very unstable. The activation energy would therefore be very high.

Thus the overall rate of reaction for S_N2 is: **Primary > Secondary > Tertiary**

Why is S_N1 more favourable for tertiary halogenoalkanes?

This is because of the stability of the intermediate carbocation. Methyl groups (and alkyl groups in general) have an electron-releasing effect (also called a positive inductive effect) so that they are able to stabilise a positively charged carbon atom to which they are bonded. The order of stability of carbocations is shown in Figure **10.24**.

This electron-releasing effect of methyl groups means that the charge is spread out most in the tertiary carbocation, as it has most methyl groups around the positively charged C. This stabilises the ion, making it more likely to be formed. Thus the overall rate of reaction for S_N1 is: **Tertiary > Secondary > Primary**

primary carbocation   secondary carbocation   tertiary carbocation

increasing stability of carbocation

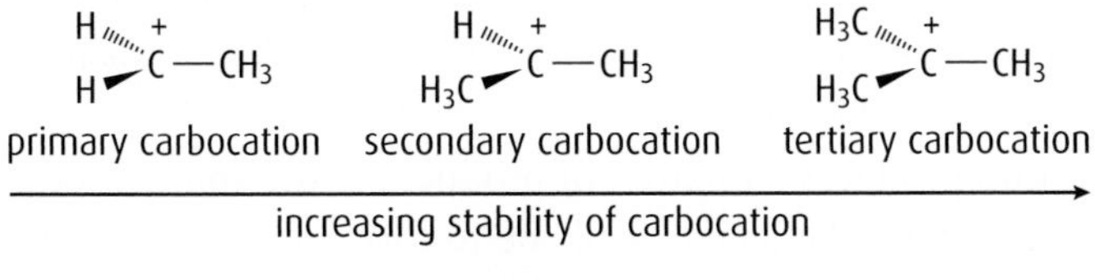

Figure 10.24 The order of stability of carbocations.

HL

OH^- is a better nucleophile than water.

Steric effects are to do with the size/bulkiness of groups.

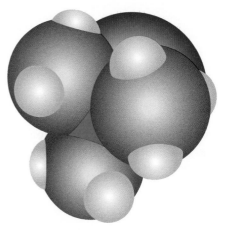

Figure 10.23 A space-filling model of 2-bromo-2-methylpropane. The nucleophile must attack the area highlighted in pink.

The more highly substituted the C the slower the rate of the S_N2 reaction.

The more highly substituted the C, the faster the rate of the S_N1 reaction.

Extension

The electron-releasing effect of alkyl groups can be understood in terms of donation of electron density from a σ-bond of the C attached to C^+ into the vacant p orbital on the C^+. This is called σ-conjugation, or hyperconjugation.

Overall, if we study both mechanisms, we get the overall rates of reaction for nucleophilic substitution by sodium hydroxide solution as:

Tertiary > Primary > Secondary

Other nucleophilic substitution reactions

Reaction of halogenoalkanes with ammonia:

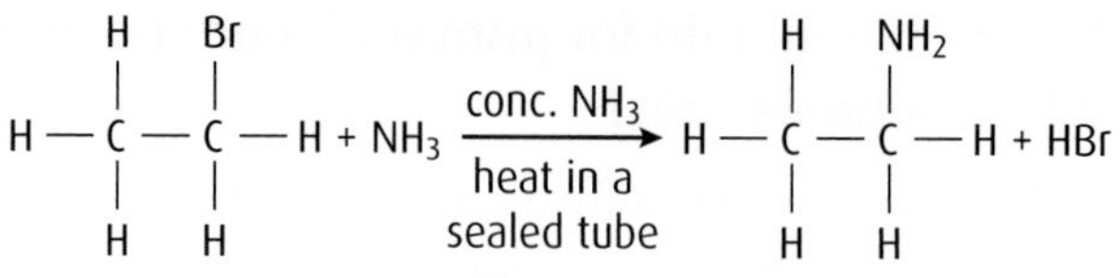

ethylamine

The product of the reaction is an amine, containing the $-NH_2$ group.

The mechanism for this reaction is:

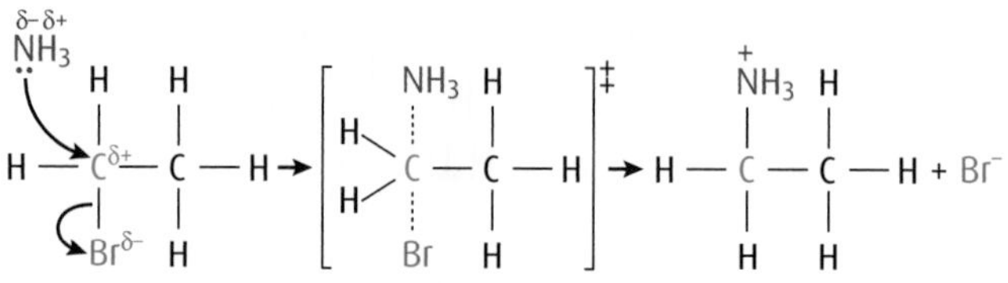

transition state

An H^+ ion is then removed from the NH_3^+ group by another molecule of ammonia:

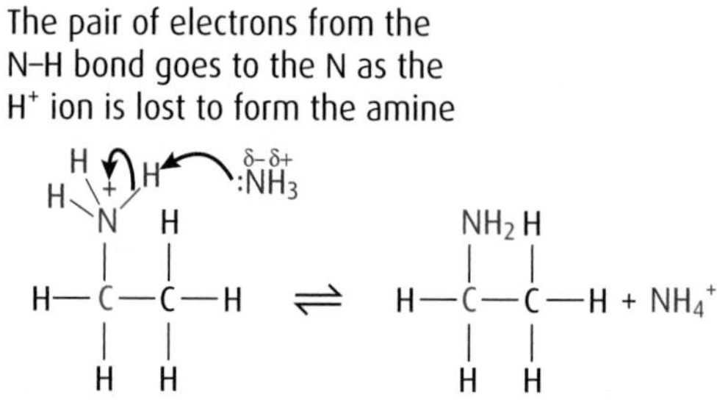

The pair of electrons from the N–H bond goes to the N as the H^+ ion is lost to form the amine

Ammonia is the nucleophile in the first step of the reaction. The nitrogen of the NH_3 is δ- and has a lone pair of electrons. It attacks the δ+ C of the halogenoalkane. The transition state is not charged, as it was formed when two neutral molecules reacted. In the product formed in the first step, a positive charge is present on the nitrogen atom, as it has formed a dative covalent bond to the C atom and has essentially given one electron to the C to enable it to form a covalent bond. Alternatively, this could also be considered from the point of view that nitrogen must have a positive charge when it forms four covalent bonds, as otherwise it will have more than eight electrons in its outer shell. The second step of the reaction is essentially just the loss of H^+ from the amine salt.

The reaction mechanism shown is for a primary halogenoalkane and is therefore an S_N2 mechanism.

This reaction produces a mixture of products, as the amine produced can react further with the halogenoalkane to form secondary and tertiary amines (and quaternary ammonium salts – $N(C_2H_5)_4^+Br^-$), for example:

This order is very dependent on solvent.

Amines are bases, and owing to the presence of the HBr, the salt of the amine ($CH_3CH_2NH_3^+Br^-$) will be formed, from which the amine can be generated by reaction with sodium hydroxide.

S_N2

The symbol ‡ indicates a transition state/activated complex.

diethylamine

Diethylamine is a secondary amine.

Naming amines

	Primary	Secondary	Tertiary
functional group	— NH$_2$	— N — H | R	— N — R | R

Where R is an alkyl group (or a benzene ring)

There are several systems commonly used to name amines, and the names using the various systems are given in Table **10.18**. It is best to just stick to one system and name amines accordingly.

Amines are strong-smelling substances (often said to smell like fish) and some of the trivial names for them reflect this. Cadaverine (1,5–diaminopentane) and putrescine (1,4–diaminobutane) are produced in rotting flesh.

Primary amines			
	methylamine	methanamine	aminomethane
	propylamine	propan-1-amine (the format 1-propanamine is also acceptable)	1-aminopropane
	1-methylpropylamine	butan-2-amine	2-aminobutane
	1,2-dimethylpropylamine	3-methylbutan-2-amine	2-amino-3-methylbutane
	4-methylpentylamine	4-methylpentan-1-amine	1-amino-4-methylpentane

Table 10.18 Systems for naming amines.

HL In the first method of naming, the amines are named taking the longest carbon chain with the amine group on the end. All other groups are then named as substituents on this chain. For instance, let us consider the following molecule:

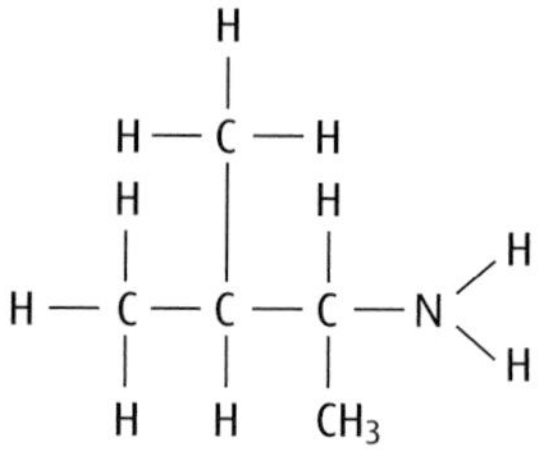

Although the longest continuous carbon chain in the molecule has four C atoms, the longest chain with the NH_2 at the end has three C atoms, and so the name is based on propylamine. The position of substituents (methyl groups in this case) are then numbered, starting numbering from the C bearing the N atom.

The second method for naming amines uses a system exactly equivalent to that for naming alcohols, except the suffix '-amine' is used instead of '-ol'.

The third method names the amine group as a substituent on the chain. The names of some secondary and tertiary amines are shown in Table **10.19**.

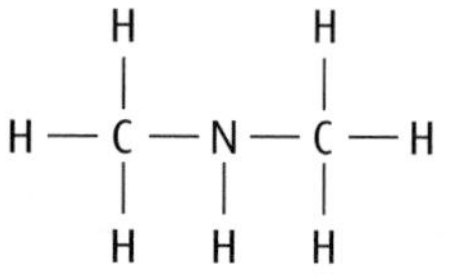	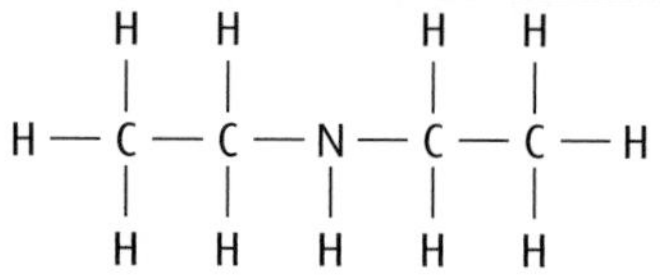	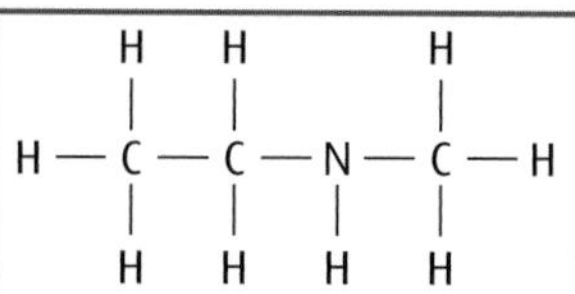	secondary
dimethylamine	diethylamine	ethylmethylamine	
N-methylmethanamine	N-ethylethanamine	N-methylethanamine	
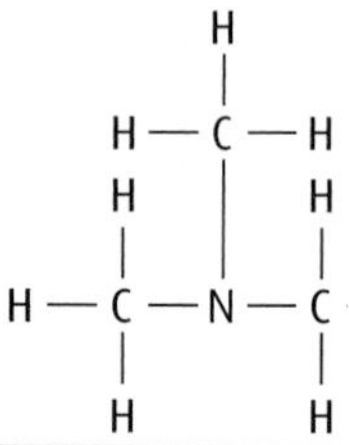	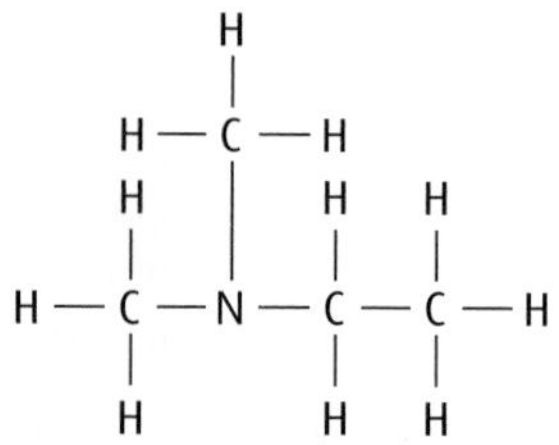	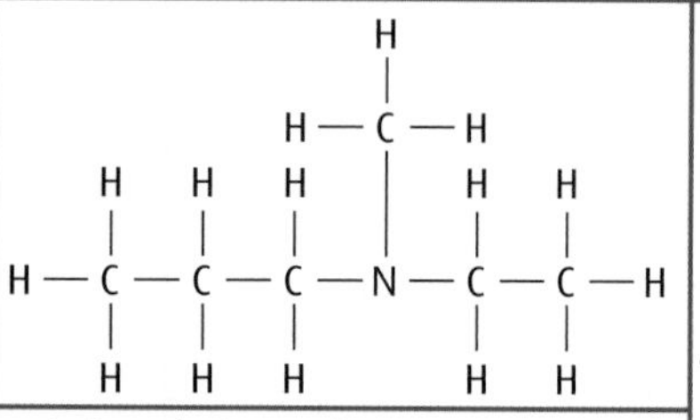	tertiary
trimethylamine	ethyldimethylamine	ethylmethylpropylamine	
N,N-dimethylmethanamine	N,N-dimethylethanamine	N-ethyl-N-methylpropan-1-amine	

Table 10.19 The names of some secondary and tertiary amines.

Amines with two NH_2 groups can be named as:

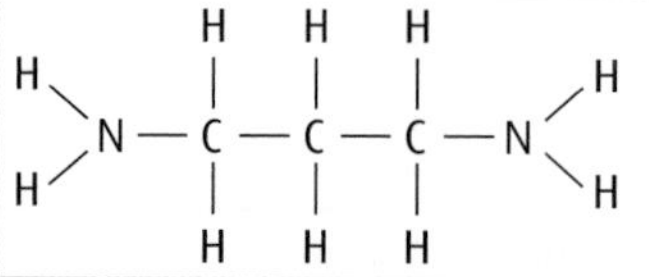	propane-1,3-diamine	1,3-diaminopropane
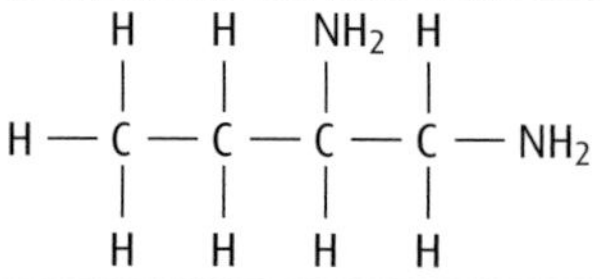	butane-1,2-diamine	1,2-diaminobutane

The condensed structural formulas for ethylamine (ethanamine) may be shown as $CH_3CH_2NH_2$ and that for dimethylamine (*N*-methylmethanamine) as $(CH_3)_2NH$. 1-methylpropylamine (butan-2-amine) may be written as $CH_3CH_2CH(CH_3)NH_2$ or $CH_3CH_2CH(NH_2)CH_3$.

Reaction of halogenoalkanes with the cyanide ion

If bromoethane dissolved in methanol is refluxed with aqueous KCN, a nitrile is formed:

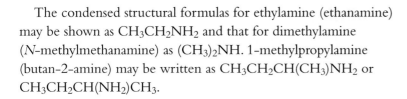
propanenitrile

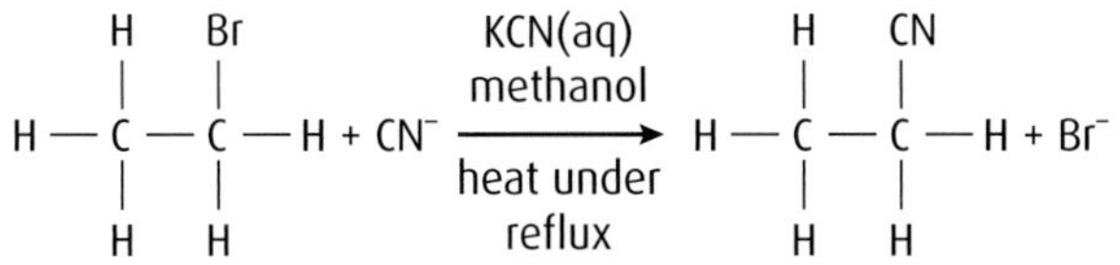

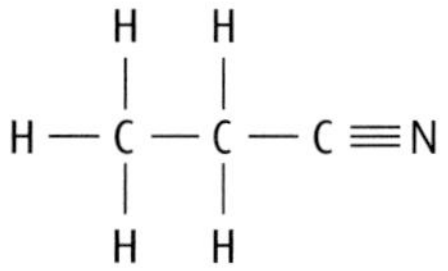

The nitrile contains the CN functional group with a triple bond between the C and the N. The longest continuous carbon chain in the molecule is now three C atoms, and so the name is **propane**nitrile.

This reaction is therefore useful as it provides a way of increasing the length of the carbon chain.

The mechanism for the reaction between the cyanide ion and bromoethane is the same as that for the reaction with the hydroxide ion:

transition state

S_N2

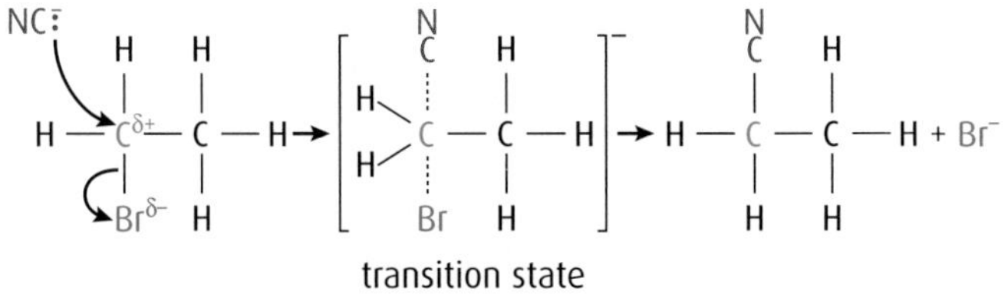

Nitriles may be reduced to amines

This is usually carried out in the laboratory using $LiAlH_4$ or sodium and ethanol, but industrially it may be carried out by using hydrogen gas and a nickel catalyst:

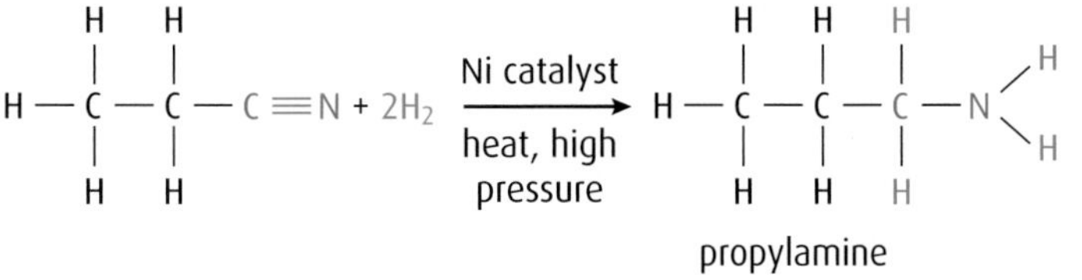

propylamine

Addition of hydrogen = reduction

Functional group	$-C{\equiv}N$

Naming nitriles

Nitriles are named in the form alkanenitrile. It is important to remember to include the C that is in the CN group as part of the carbon chain.

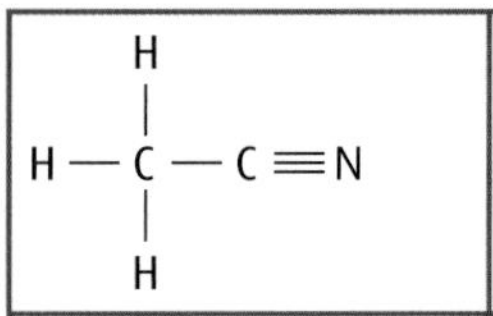	ethanenitrile
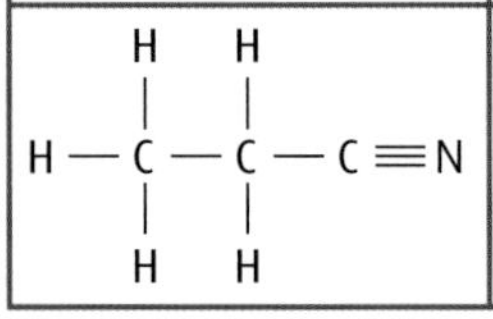	propanenitrile

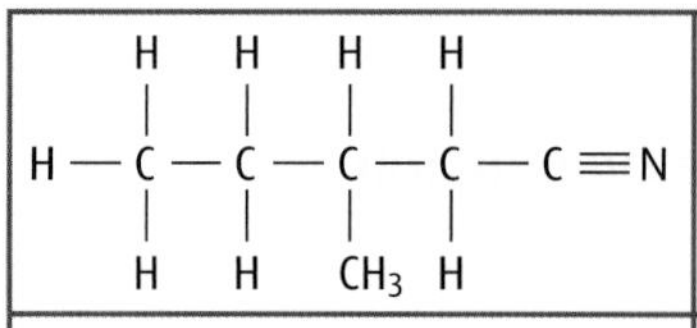	3-methylpentanenitrile	numbering starts from the C of the nitrile group
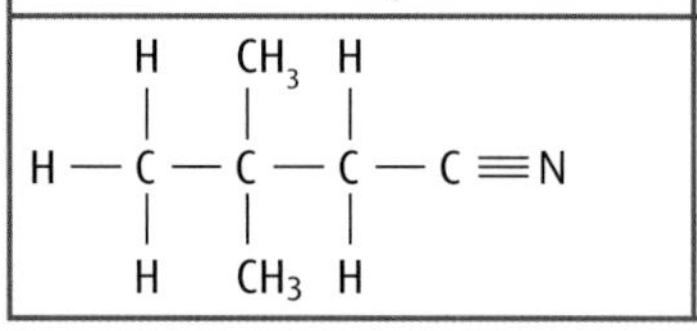	3,3-dimethylbutanenitrile	

In condensed structural formulas, the nitrile group is indicated as –CN, so propanenitrile may be written as CH_3CH_2CN.

Elimination reactions

As well as nucleophilic substitution reactions, halogenoalkanes can also undergo elimination reactions. For example:

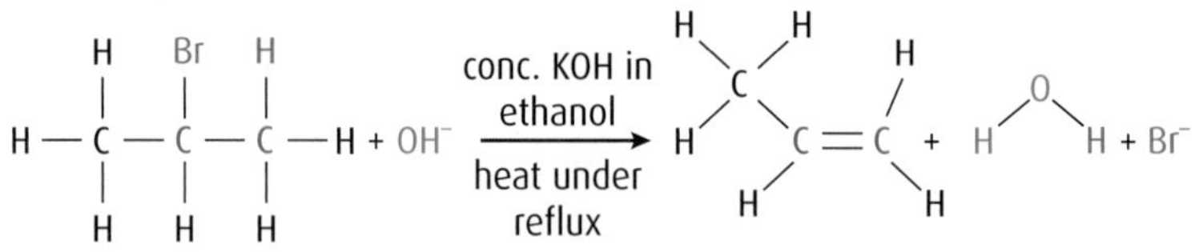

prop-1-ene

Conditions that favour substitution	Conditions that favour elimination
Lower temp.	Higher temp.
dilute NaOH/KOH	conc. NaOH/KOH
primary halogenoalkene	tertiary halogenoalkene

This is an elimination reaction, as HBr is removed from the molecule without anything else being added.

Nucleophilic substitution and elimination reactions occur simultaneously when potassium hydroxide is added to a halogenoalkane, and so the conditions must be selected to give the maximum percentage of elimination. This is achieved by using a **concentrated ethanolic solution of potassium hydroxide** (that is KOH dissolved in ethanol) and **high temperature**. A much higher percentage elimination also occurs when a secondary or a tertiary halogenoalkane is reacted with concentrated ethanolic KOH than when a primary halogenoalkane is used.

KOH dissolved in water → nucleophilic substitution
KOH dissolved in ethanol (or another alcohol) → elimination

It is important to note that the H and the Br are eliminated from **adjacent carbon atoms** and that the double bond forms between these C atoms, shown in green in the equation.

Another elimination reaction would be:

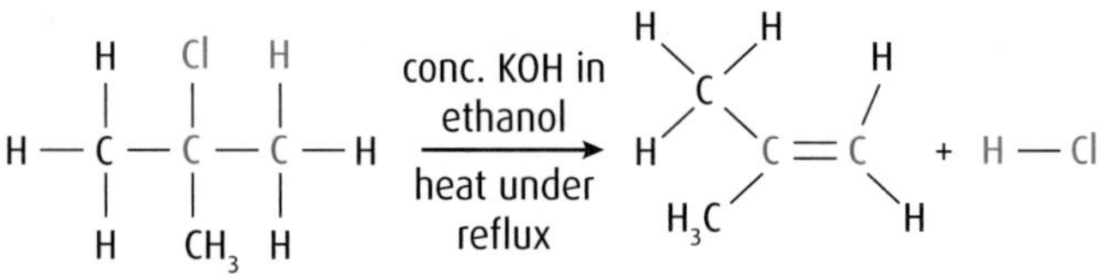

2-methylprop-1-ene

This is not shown as an equation with OH^- to show more clearly the elimination of HCl.

In the two reactions above, only one possible alkene could be formed. However, when H–Br is eliminated from 2–bromobutane, three isomeric products are formed:

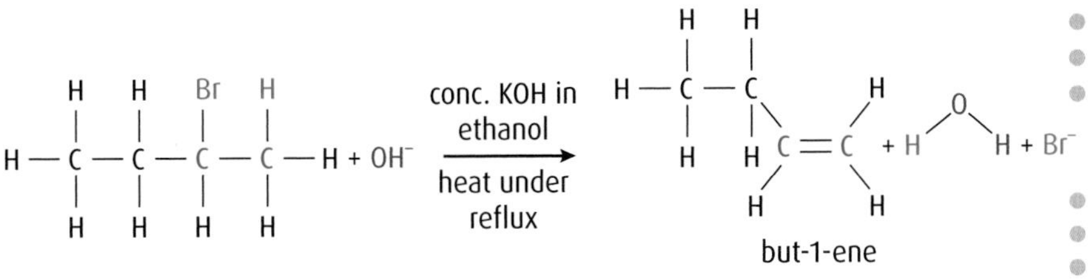

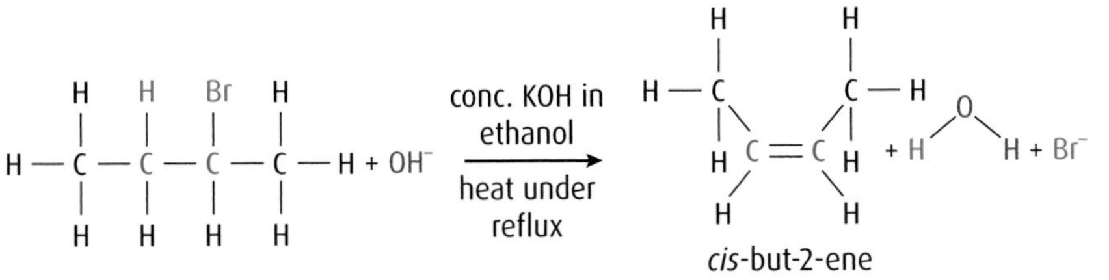

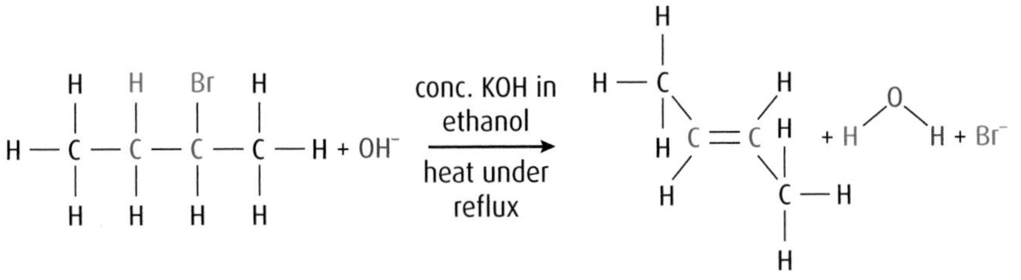

but-1-ene

cis-but-2-ene

See below for geometrical isomerism and an explanation of why the *cis* and *trans* forms are different.

trans-but-2-ene

As for nucleophilic substitution, there are two main mechanisms for an elimination reaction: these are E2 and E1 mechanisms.

The E2 mechanism

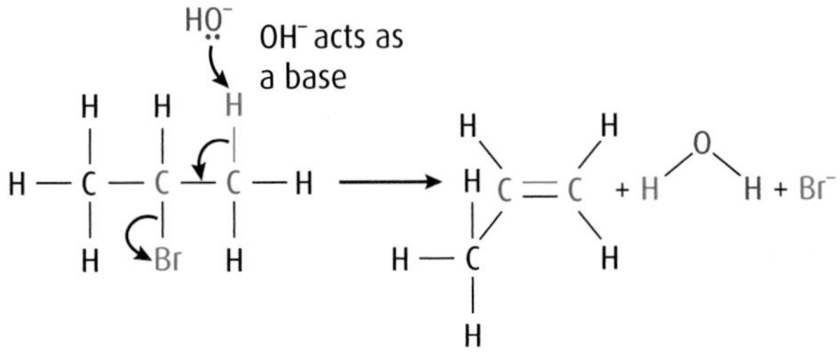

OH⁻ acts as a base

The OH⁻ acts as a base (rather than a nucleophile) and accepts H⁺. The pair of electrons from the C–H bond (shown in pink) goes to form the second component of the C=C. As the double bond forms, the C–Br bond must break so that the middle C does not have more than four pairs of electrons in its outer shell. The pair of electrons from the C–Br bond goes to the Br to form Br⁻.

When ethanol is used as the solvent, the ethoxide ion ($CH_3CH_2O^-$) will also be present. This is a stronger base than OH⁻, and the mechanism may be better represented with this acting as the base, instead of OH⁻. The products formed then would be the alkene, C_2H_5OH and Br⁻.

An E1 mechanism is also possible, and this involves formation of a carbocation:

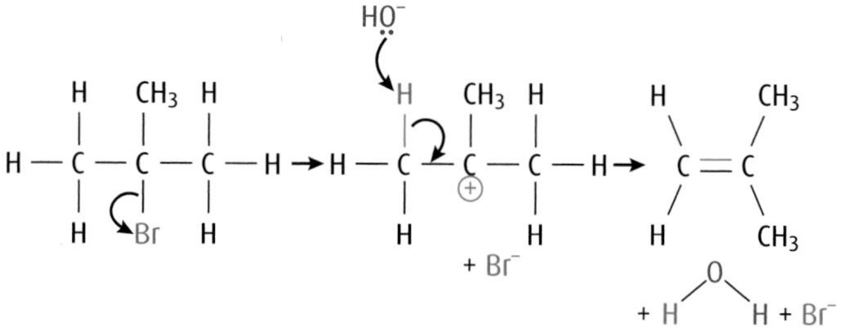

Self-tests 8 & 9

Test yourself

28 Name the following molecules:

a	b	c	d
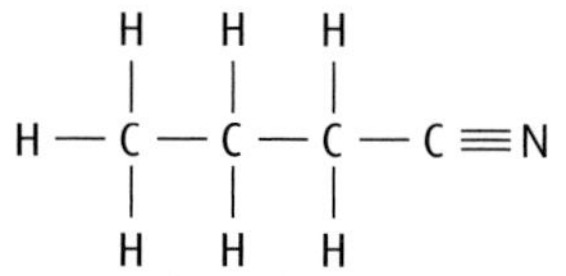 H—C—C—C—C≡N (with H's)	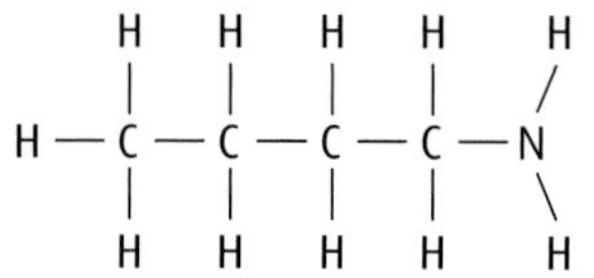 H—C—C—C—C—N (with H's)	$CH_3(CH_2)_4CN$	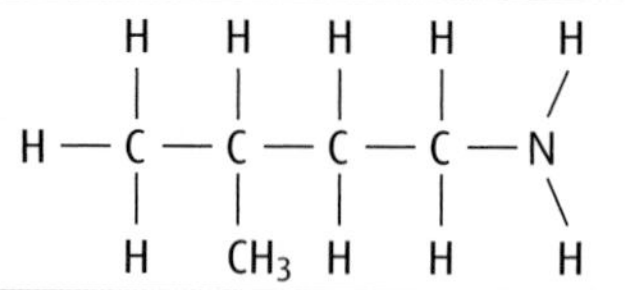 H—C—C—C—C—N (with H's and CH_3)

29 Draw out the structure of the organic products formed when the following halogenoalkanes react with ammonia under suitable conditions:

  a 1-bromobutane

  b 2-bromopropane

  c 3-bromo-2-methylpentane

30 Give the structures and names of the organic products formed when the following halogenoalkanes react with KCN under suitable conditions:

  a 1-chloropropane

  b 1-bromobutane

  c 2-bromobutane

31 Each of the products in question **30** is heated with hydrogen in the presence of a nickel catalyst. Draw out the structures of the products.

32 Each of the following halogenoalkanes is heated with a concentrated ethanolic solution of potassium hydroxide. Draw out the structures and give the names of all organic products formed.

  a 1-chloropropane

  b 1-bromopentane

  c 2-bromopentane

  d 2-chloro-3-methylbutane

10.8 Condensation reactions

Condensation reactions

Condensation reactions are reactions in which two molecules join together with the elimination of the elements of water. They are part of a more general class of reactions called addition–elimination reactions, in which molecules other than H_2O are eliminated.

Esterification

When an alcohol is heated with a carboxylic acid in the presence of a small amount of concentrated sulfuric acid as a catalyst, an ester is formed. For example:

$$\text{alcohol} + \text{carboxylic acid} \underset{\text{heat}}{\overset{\text{conc. } H_2SO_4}{\rightleftharpoons}} \text{ester} + \text{water}$$

$$\text{ethanol} + \text{ethanoic acid} \underset{\text{heat}}{\overset{\text{conc. } H_2SO_4}{\rightleftharpoons}} \text{ethyl ethanoate} + \text{water}$$

The alcohol and the carboxylic acid have been joined together and water has been eliminated (one H atom from the alcohol and –OH from the carboxylic acid molecule).

Learning objectives

- Describe the formation of esters
- Understand how to name esters
- Understand how polyesters may be formed in condensation polymerisation reactions
- Describe the formation of amides from amines and carboxylic acids
- Understand how to name amides
- Understand how polyamides may be formed in condensation polymerisation reactions
- Describe the economic importance of condensation reactions

Examiner's tip

The product formed when any alcohol and any carboxylic acid come together can be worked out simply by putting the alcohol and carboxylic acid together, so that the two O–H groups are next to each other, removing H from the OH of the alcohol and OH from the carboxylic acid and joining the O of the alcohol to the C=O of the carboxylic acid.

Other examples of esterification reactions are:

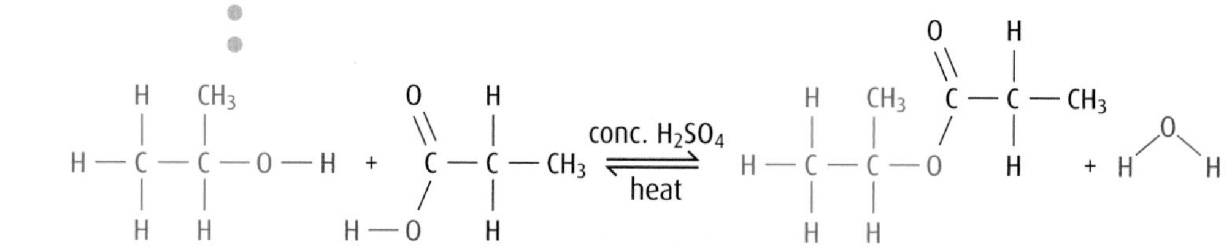

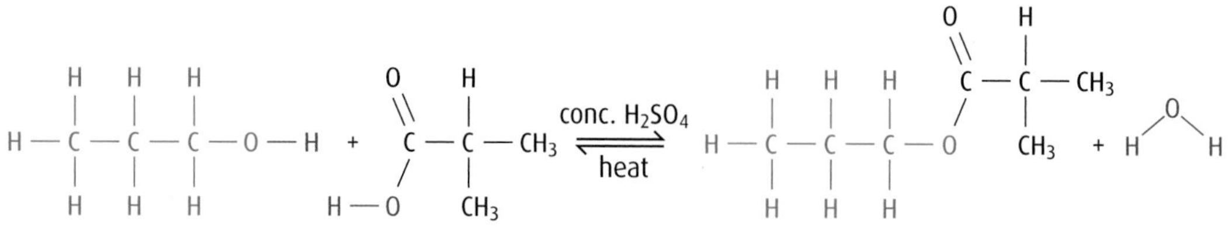

Naming esters

Esters are named according to the carboxylic acid from which they are derived.

methyl ethanoate

ethyl propanoate

Examiner's tip
You should only be required to name simple esters.

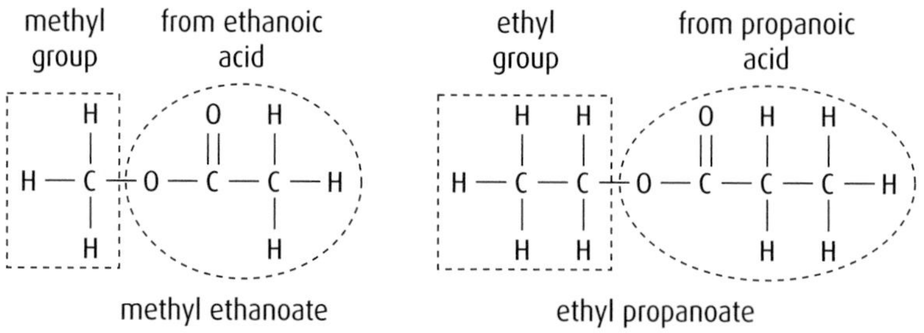

Examiner's tip
Esters are isomeric with carboxylic acids. Thus ethanoic acid and methyl methanoate are isomers, and propanoic acid, methyl ethanoate and ethyl methanoate are isomers.

The names of some other, more complicated, esters are shown in Table **10.20**.

When writing condensed structural formulas, the ester group can be represented as COOC, so ethyl ethanoate can be written as $CH_3COOCH_2CH_3$.

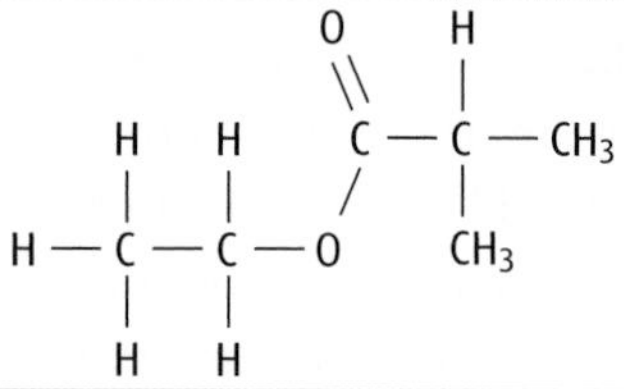	ethyl 2-methylpropanoate	numbering in the acid derivative starts from the C=O group
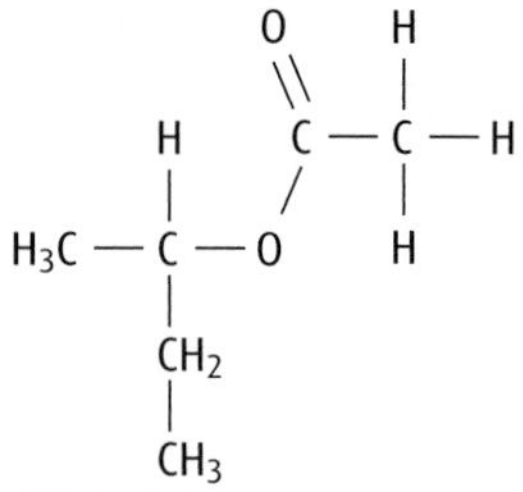	1-methylpropyl ethanoate	The longest carbon chain ending with the C attached to the O is taken. Thus, although there is a continuous carbon chain of 4 C atoms in the alkyl group, it does not have the C attached to the O at the end of the chain.

Table 10.20 Names of some esters.

Uses of esters

HL

Esters often have a sweet, fruity smell and are used as artificial flavours and odours (see Figure **10.25**). Other uses are as plasticisers (added to polymers to make them easier to process and reduce brittleness) and as solvents.

Fats and oils are esters of propane-1,2,3-triol (glycerol) and long-chain carboxylic acids (fatty acids).

Polyesters

Polyesters may be formed in a **condensation polymerisation** reaction when a dicarboxylic acid reacts with a dihydric alcohol (an alcohol with two –OH groups). It is the presence of two functional groups on each monomer that allows the production of a polymer chain, as an ester is formed on both sides of both monomers.

> Condensation polymerisation: a water molecule is eliminated each time two monomers are joined together.

The reaction scheme in Figure **10.26** shows a representation of the reaction of two dicarboxylic acid molecules with two dihydric alcohol molecules.

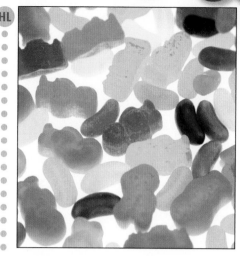

Figure 10.25 Esters are often used to flavour sweets.

> Two functional groups required on each monomer.

dicarboxylic acid dihydric alcohol dicarboxylic acid dihydric alcohol

condensation reaction

ester group

chain can continue

chain can continue

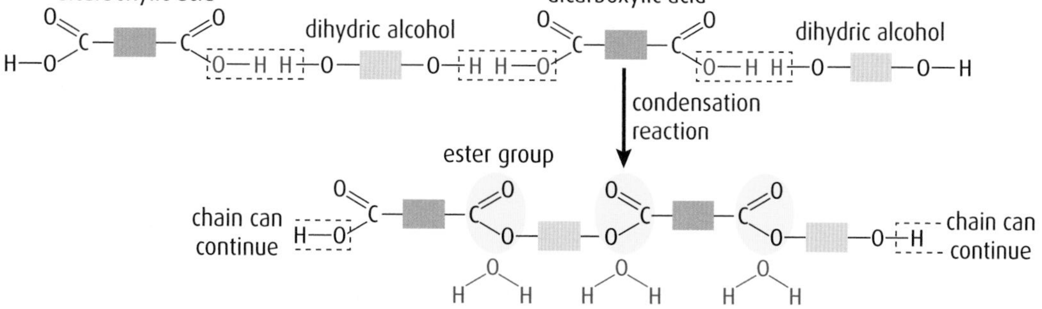

Figure 10.26 The dicarboxylic acid molecules and dihydric alcohol molecules combine together via condensation reactions to form the beginnings of a polymer chain.

The functional group joining the monomers together is the **ester** functional group, and so this is the beginning of a **polyester** chain. The chain can continue at both sides, as the two functional groups in the original monomers means that there will either be a free alcohol or carboxylic acid group on each end of the chain.

It can be seen from this reaction that when four monomer molecules join together, three water molecules are produced. The total number of water molecules is always one less than the total number of monomer molecules that join together.

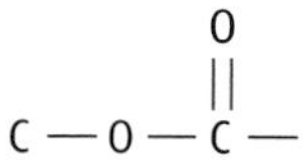

$$C - O - C -$$

ester functional group

Let us look at a specific example:

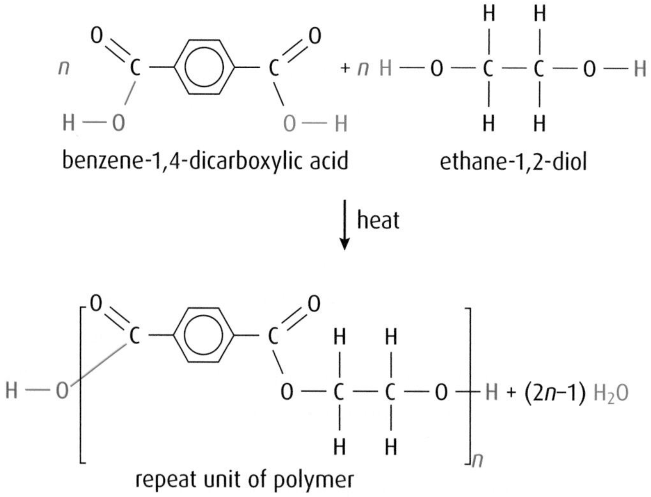

benzene-1,4-dicarboxylic acid   ethane-1,2-diol

heat

repeat unit of polymer

The polymer chain as a whole can be represented by the unit shown in brackets in the equation. This is called the **repeat unit** or **repeating unit** of the polymer. The whole polymer chain could be built up by just joining these units together:

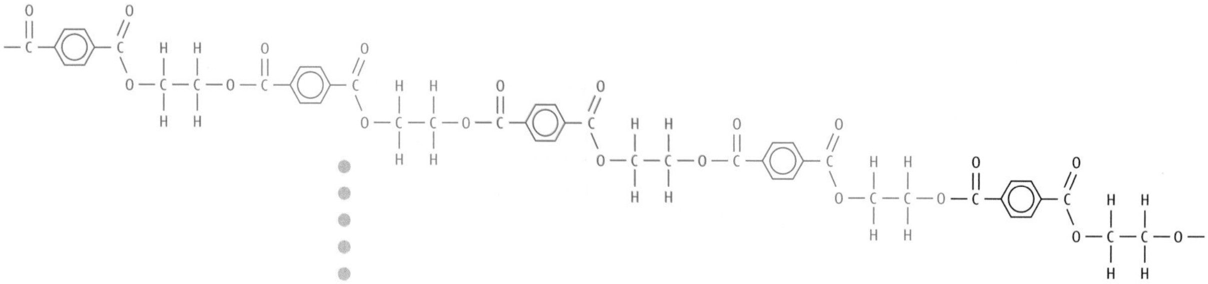

In general, the repeat unit for a condensation polymer may be generated as shown in Figure **10.27**.

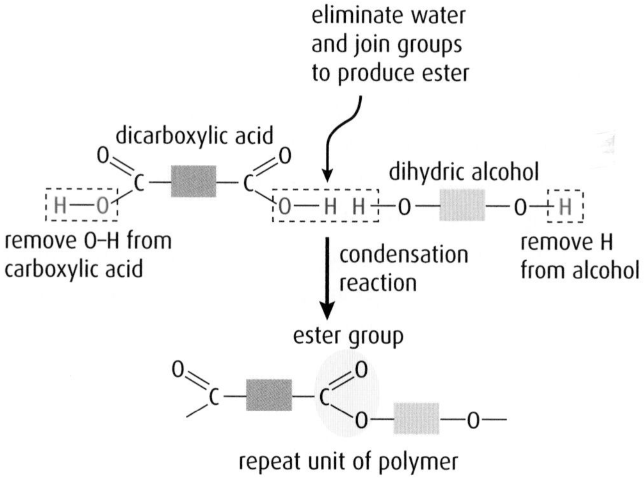

eliminate water
and join groups
to produce ester

dicarboxylic acid

dihydric alcohol

remove O–H from
carboxylic acid

condensation
reaction

remove H
from alcohol

ester group

repeat unit of polymer

Figure 10.27 Generation of the repeat unit for a condensation polymer.

Given a polymer chain, the repeat unit may be generated:

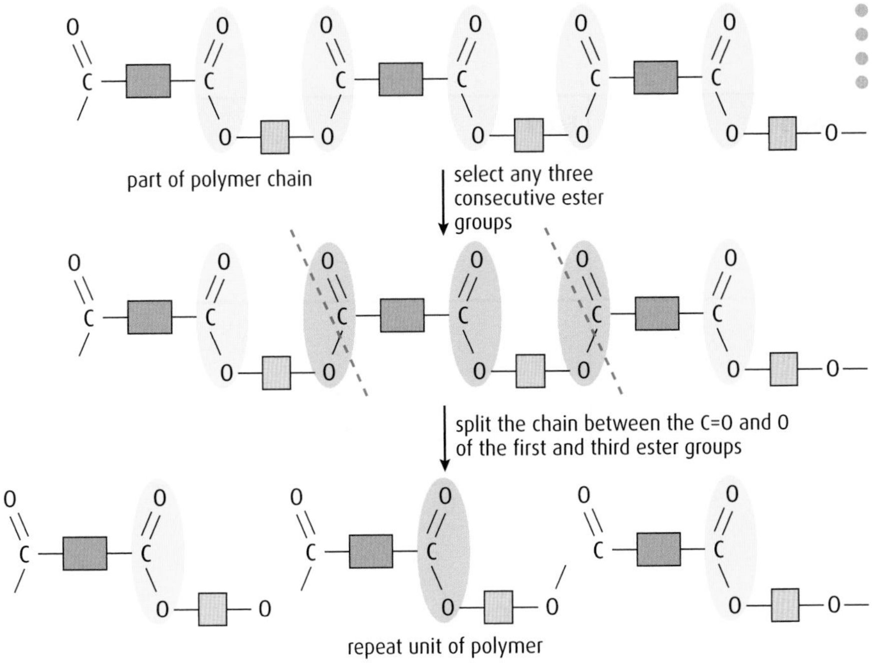

part of polymer chain

select any three consecutive ester groups

split the chain between the C=O and O of the first and third ester groups

repeat unit of polymer

To work out the monomers from a polymer chain the following procedure is followed:

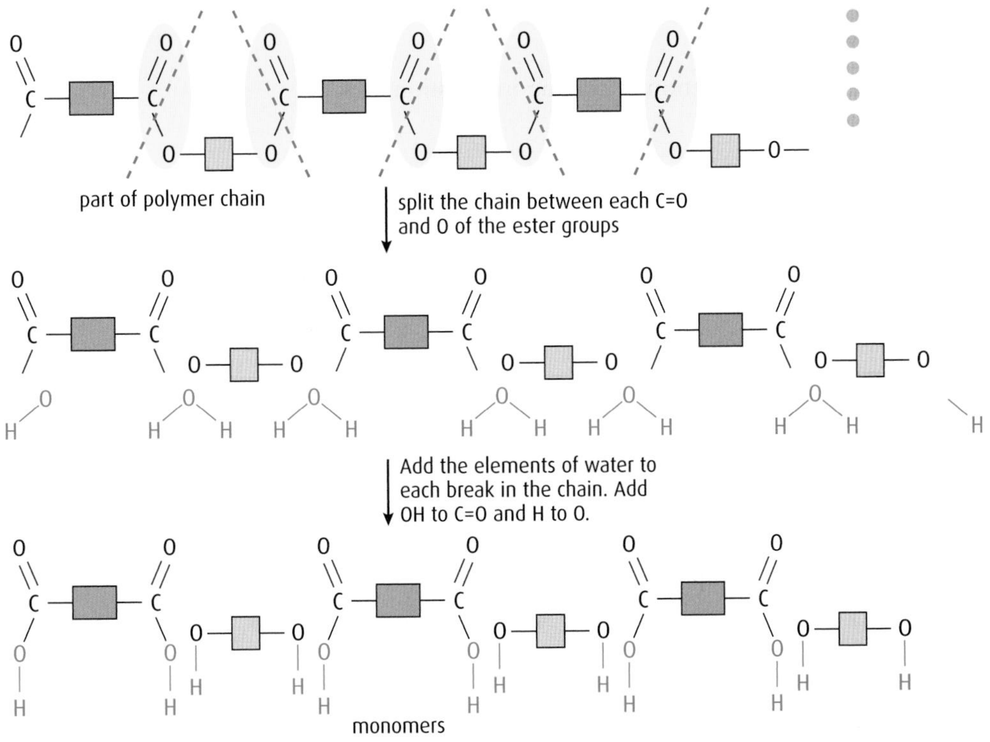

part of polymer chain

split the chain between each C=O and O of the ester groups

Add the elements of water to each break in the chain. Add OH to C=O and H to O.

monomers

33 Copy and complete the following table:

	Alcohol	Carboxylic acid	Ester
a	H—C—C—C—O (propan-1-ol structure with H's)	H—C(=O)—O—H	
b	CH₂OH group, H—C—C—C—H with CH₃	H—C—C—C—C(=O)—O—H with CH₃ groups	
c			H₃C—C(—O—)(CH₃)... C(=O)—C—CH₃ with H
d			ester structure with CH₃ groups and C—C—C—C—H chain

34 Name the ester formed in question **33a**.

35 Write a balanced chemical equation for the reaction occurring in question **33a**.

36 Name the following esters:

a	b	c
H—C—C—C—C—O—C(=O)—C—C—H (with H's)	H—C—C—C—O—C(=O)—H (with H's)	CH₃CH₂CH₂CH₂COOCH₂CH₂CH₃

37 Draw all the esters that are isomeric with the following carboxylic acids:
   a butanoic acid
   b pentanoic acid

38 Draw the repeat unit of the polymer formed when butane-1,4-diol reacts with propanedioic acid.

39 Draw two repeat units of the polymer formed when the following molecules react:

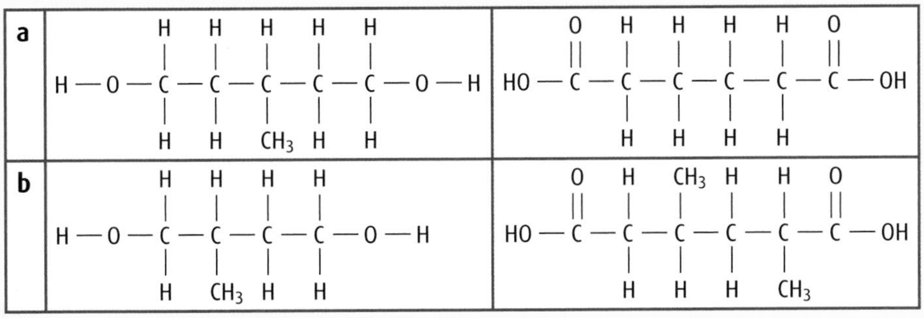

a	H—O—C—C—C—C—C—O—H with H, H, H, H, H top and H, H, CH₃, H, H bottom	HO—C—C—C—C—C—C—OH with O, H, H, H, H, O and H, H, H, H below
b	H—O—C—C—C—C—O—H with H, H, H, H top and H, CH₃, H, H bottom	HO—C—C—C—C—C—C—OH with O, H, CH₃, H, H, O and H, H, H, CH₃ below

40 From which monomers could the following polymers be formed?

a

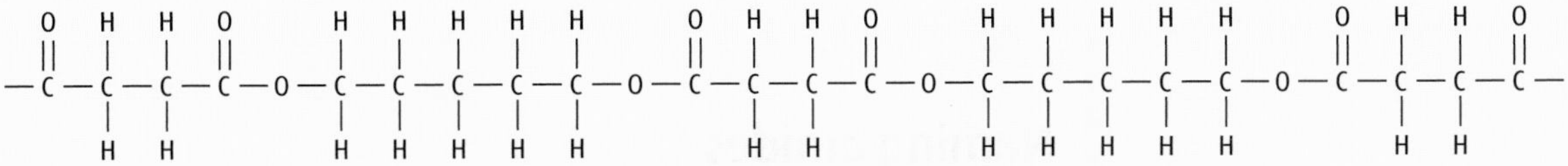

—C—C—C—C—O—C—C—C—C—C—O—C—C—C—C—O—C—C—C—C—C—O—C—C—C—C—

b

—C—C—C—C—C—C—C—O—C—C—C—C—C—O—C—C—C—C—C—C—C—O—C—C—C—C—C—O—

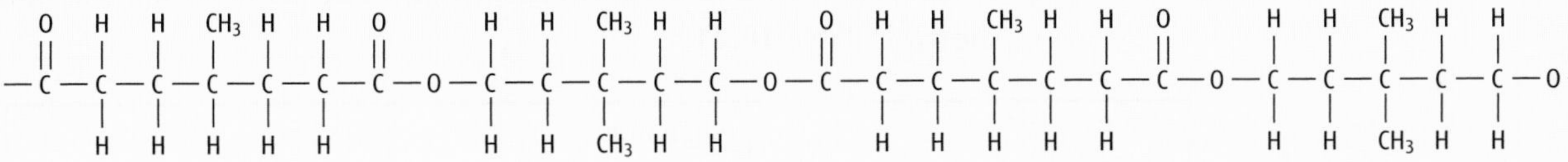

Amides

An amide may be formed when a carboxylic acid is heated with an amine. As an amine is a base and a carboxylic acid is an acid, the initial reaction is an acid–base reaction to form a salt. Upon strong heating, this is then converted slowly to an amide. Overall the general reaction is:

amine + carboxylic acid $\xrightarrow{\text{heat}}$ amide + water

For example:

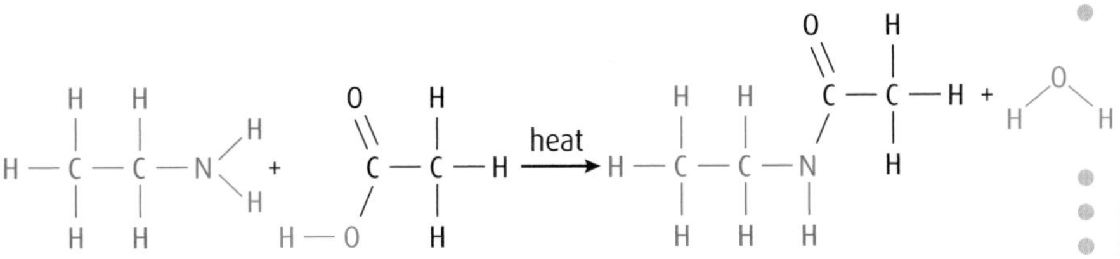

ethylamine + ethanoic acid $\xrightarrow{\text{heat}}$ an amide + water

This is a condensation reaction, as water is eliminated when the two molecules are added together. The reaction is equivalent to the esterification reaction shown previously.

Extension

This is not a very good method for making amides, and they are more usually prepared by reacting an acyl chloride or acid anhydride with an amine.

The amide functional group is:

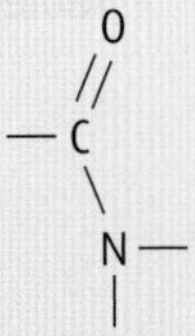

$$\begin{array}{c} O \\ \parallel \\ -C \\ \backslash \\ N- \\ \mid \end{array}$$

A nitrogen atom is joined directly to C=O.

More examples of reactions involving the formation of amides are:

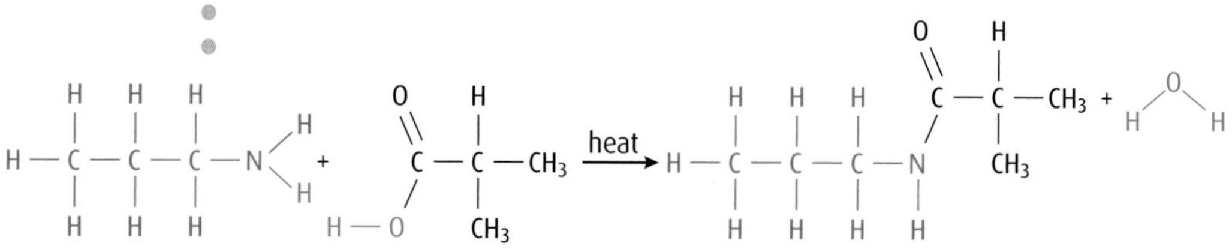

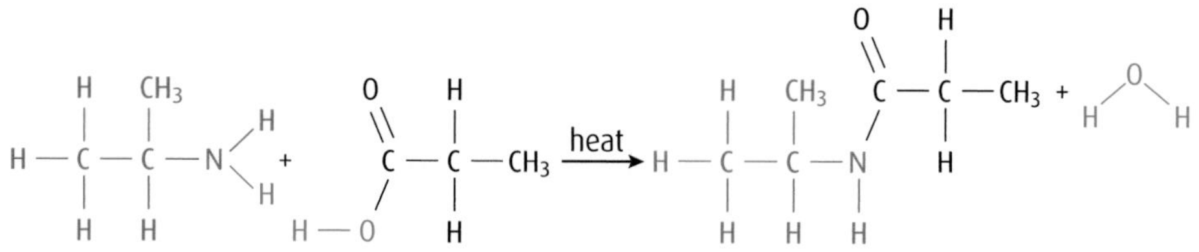

$$H_3C-CH_2-CH_2-NH_2 \;+\; \underset{\substack{| \\ H-O}}{\overset{O}{\underset{\|}{C}}}-\overset{H}{\underset{CH_3}{C}}-CH_3 \xrightarrow{\text{heat}} H_3C-CH_2-CH_2-N(CH_3)-C(=O)-CH(H)-CH_3 \;+\; H_2O$$

$$\text{(propylamine)} \;+\; \text{(acid)} \xrightarrow{\text{heat}} \text{(amide)} \;+\; H_2O$$

$$\text{(sec-butylamine)} \;+\; \text{(acid)} \xrightarrow{\text{heat}} \text{(amide)} \;+\; H_2O$$

Naming amides

Amides are named in the form alkanamide. The names of some amides are shown in Table **10.21**.

Structure	Name	Note	Class
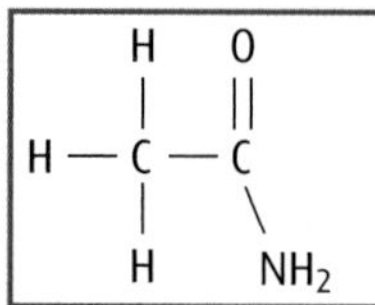 $H-\overset{H}{\underset{H}{C}}-\overset{O}{\underset{NH_2}{C}}$	ethanamide		primary
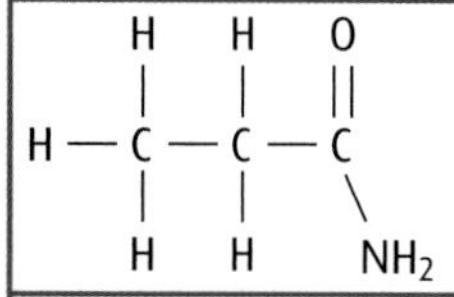 $H-\overset{H}{\underset{H}{C}}-\overset{H}{\underset{H}{C}}-\overset{O}{\underset{NH_2}{C}}$	propanamide		primary
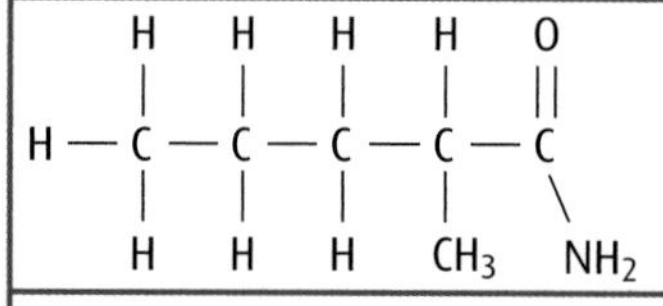 $H-\overset{H}{\underset{H}{C}}-\overset{H}{\underset{H}{C}}-\overset{H}{\underset{H}{C}}-\overset{H}{\underset{CH_3}{C}}-\overset{O}{\underset{NH_2}{C}}$	2-methylpentanamide	numbering starts from the C of the amide group	primary
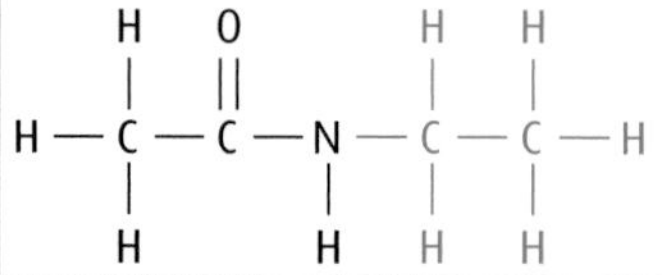 $H-\overset{H}{\underset{H}{C}}-\overset{O}{\underset{}{C}}-N-\overset{H}{\underset{H}{C}}-\overset{H}{\underset{H}{C}}-H$	N-ethylethanamide	the ethyl group is attached to the N of the amide	secondary
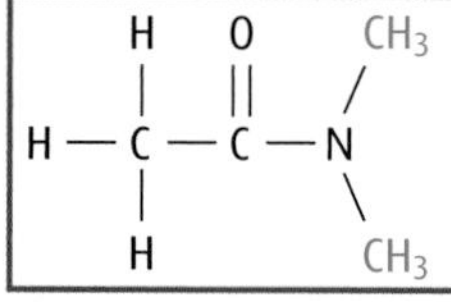 $H-\overset{H}{\underset{H}{C}}-\overset{O}{\underset{}{C}}-N\overset{CH_3}{\underset{CH_3}{<}}$	N,N-dimethylethanamide		tertiary

Table 10.21 The names of some amides.

As with the formation of polyesters, **two functional groups must be present on each monomer** to allow formation of a polymer.

Polyamides

Just as a dicarboxylic acid reacts with a dihydric alcohol to form a polyester, a dicarboxylic acid reacts with a diamine to form a polyamide. The type of polymerisation is condensation polymerisation, as a water molecule is eliminated each time two monomers are joined together.

478

A general scheme for the polymerisation reaction showing the formation of the repeat unit is shown in Figure **10.28**.

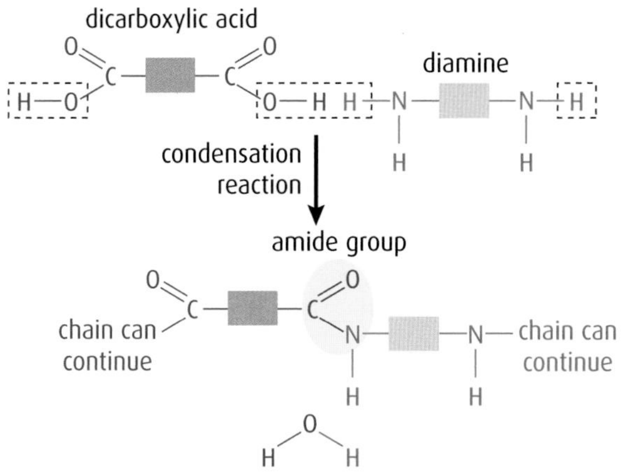

Figure 10.28 Generation of a repeat unit in a polymerisation reaction to form a polyamide.

An example of a reaction involving the formation of a polyamide is:

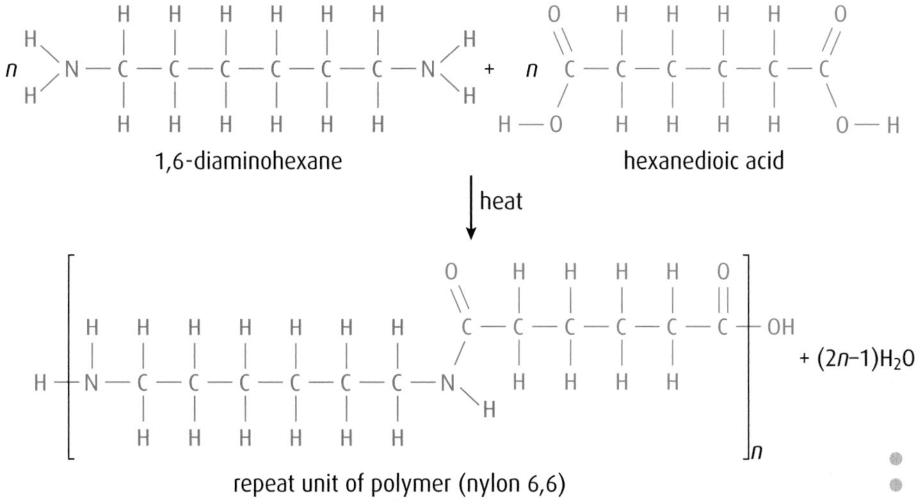

1,6-diaminohexane can also be called hexane-1,6-diamine.

The repeat units and monomers for polyamides may be worked out in basically the same way as described on pages **474** and **475** for polyesters.

This is not actually how this polymer is produced commercially.

HL A polyamide can also be formed by one monomer with two different functional groups reacting. For example:

6-aminohexanoic acid

$\downarrow$ heat

nylon 6

$+ (n-1)H_2O$

Part of the polymer chain is:

Figure 10.29 PET is used in the manufacture of plastic bottles for drinks and fibres for clothing. Increasingly more PET bottles are being recycled to reduce waste.

Figure 10.30 Nylon rope.

Economic importance of condensation reactions

The polyester formed from ethane-1,2-diol and benzene-1,4-dicarboxylic acid is commonly called poly(ethylene terephthalate), or PET (Figure **10.29**).

PET

The polyamide formed from 1,6-diaminohexane and hexanedioic acid is commonly called nylon 6,6 (or nylon 66). This is used for the manufacture of car parts, fibres for clothing and carpets, and rope (Figure **10.30**).

The '6,6' refers to the number of carbon atoms in each monomer.

The polyamide formed from 6-aminohexanoic acid is called nylon 6. This finds a major use as tyre cord.

Test yourself •••

41 Copy and complete the table:

Amine	Carboxylic acid	Amide
(structure)	(structure)	
(structure)	(structure)	
		(structure)
		(structure)

42 Name the following amides:

(structure)	(structure)	(structure)
a	**b**	**c**

43 Write an equation for the formation of a polymer from the monomers shown.

44 Give the structures of the monomers that could be used to produce the polymer shown:

Learning objectives

- Work out reaction pathways for the formation of organic compounds

10.9 Reaction pathways

Reaction pathways

We can use the reactions shown in Figure **10.31** to design syntheses for organic compounds. The important thing when working out the reaction scheme is to just concentrate on the functional groups in the molecules – the carbon skeleton should make very little difference to the products of the reactions. This means that 1-bromo-4-methylpentane and bromoethane react in basically the same way with aqueous sodium hydroxide to form alcohols.

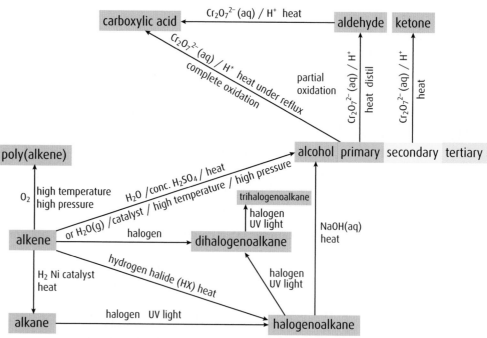

Figure 10.31 Reaction pathways required for Standard Level.

Worked example

Design a reaction pathway for the conversion of but-2-ene to butanone.

We will use Figure **10.31** to trace the pathway between an alkene and a ketone:

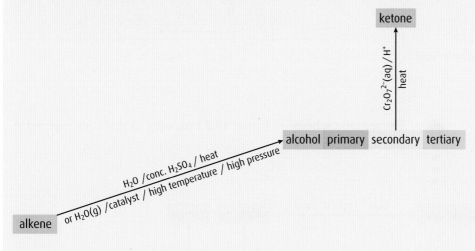

The reaction pathway is then:

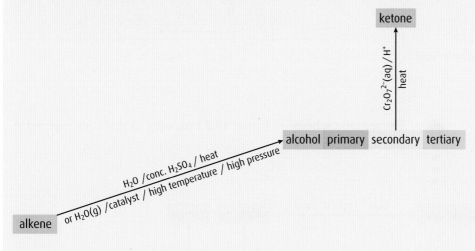

Benzene and aromatic compounds

As long as a particular functional group is **not attached directly to the benzene ring**, the reactions of compounds containing a benzene ring will be basically the same as the reactions encountered in other sections. Thus, we get the reaction scheme shown in Figure **10.32** (page **484**) for some reactions of ethylbenzene.

Figure 10.32 A reaction scheme for some reactions of ethylbenzene.

Test yourself

45 Draw out reaction pathways showing structural formulas and essential conditions for the following conversions:
 a ethane to ethanol
 b propene to propanone
 c 1-chloropropane to propanoic acid

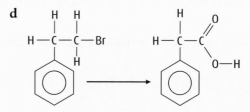

HL The reaction scheme in Figure **10.33** includes all reactions required at Higher Level.

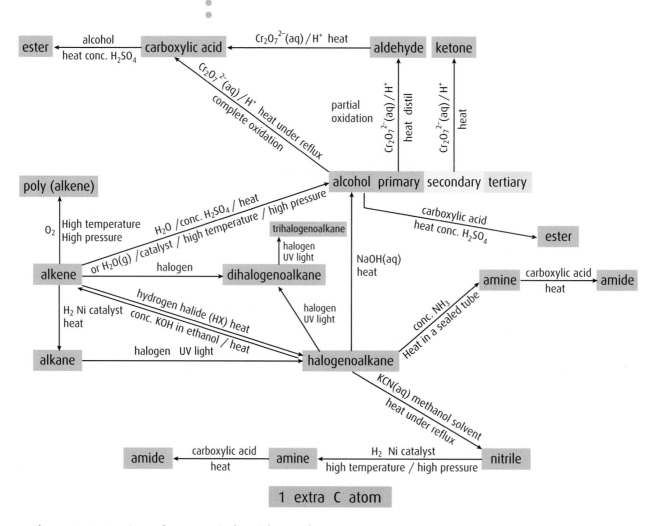

Figure 10.33 Reaction pathways required at Higher Level.

Worked examples

Design a reaction pathway for the conversion of ethene to ethylamine (ethanamine).

If we look at Figure **10.33**, we can trace the path from an alkene to an amine with the same number of C atoms:

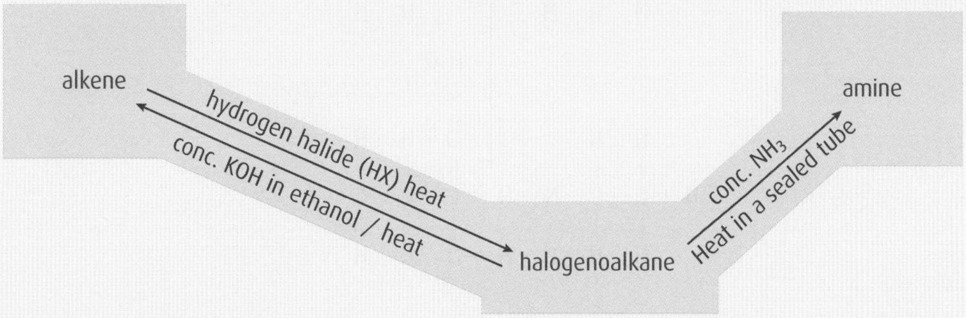

Thus the reaction pathway is:

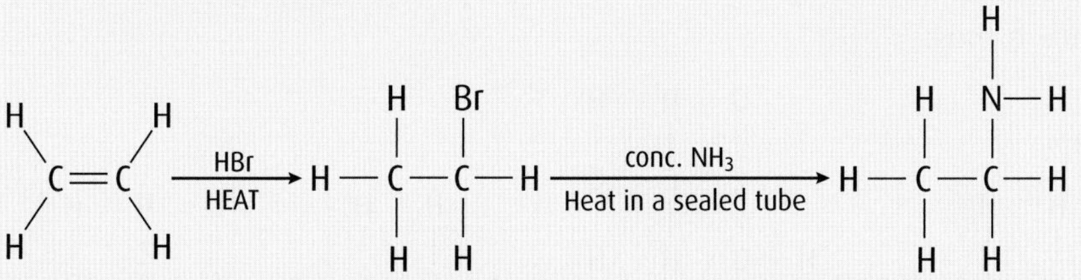

Design a reaction pathway for the conversion of 1-chloropropane to butylamine (butan-1-amine).

The first thing to notice here is that the final product has four carbon atoms, but our starting material has only three carbon atoms. The only method we have seen here for increasing the number of carbon atoms in a chain is via the cyanide ion (CN⁻). The reaction sequence is therefore halogenoalkane → nitrile → amine:

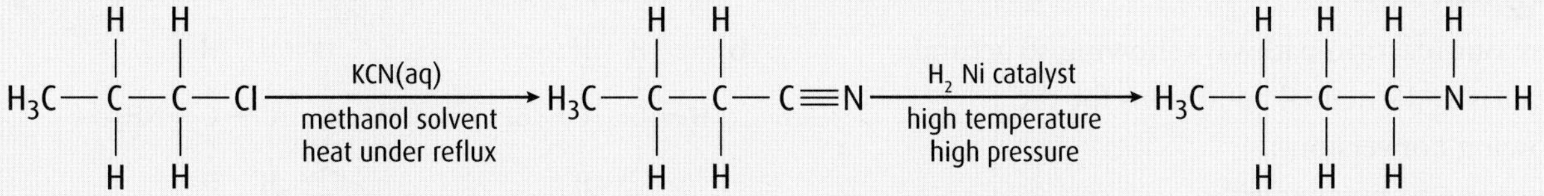

Design a reaction pathway for the conversion of bromoethane to *N*-ethylpropanamide.

The product is the amide as shown:

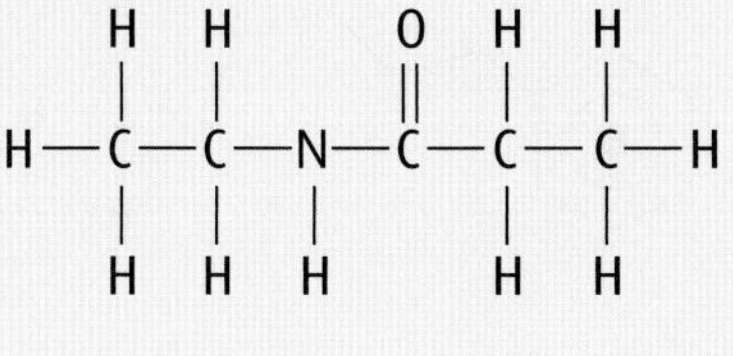

We can get some idea of how to make the amide by splitting it up into its components as shown in the sequence:

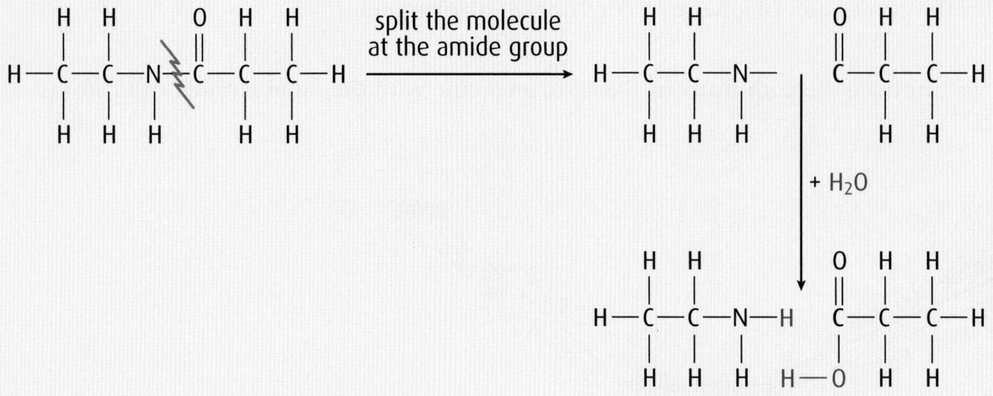

split the molecule at the amide group → + H₂O

It can be seen that the amide can be made from ethylamine (ethanamine), which can be made in one simple step from bromoethane. The ethylamine (ethanamine) so formed is then heated with propanoic acid to produce the required amide. The overall reaction sequence is thus:

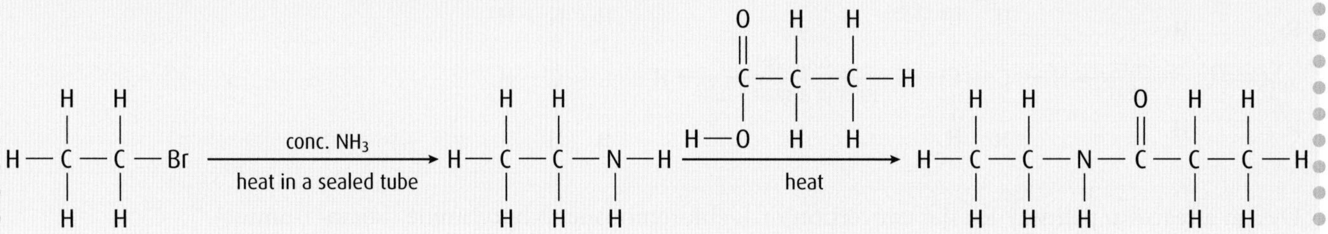

conc. NH₃, heat in a sealed tube → heat →

Self-test 14

Test yourself • • • • • • • • • • • • • •

46 Draw out reaction pathways showing structural formulas and essential conditions for the following conversions:
  a propane to butanenitrile
  b propan-1-ol to *N*-ethylpropanamide
  c 2-chlorobutane to 2-methylbutan-1-amine (1-amino-2-methylbutane)
  d ethene to ethyl ethanoate using ethene as the only organic starting material
  e 1-bromopropane to ethyl propanoate

47 Draw out reaction pathways showing full structural formulas and essential conditions for the following conversions:
  a

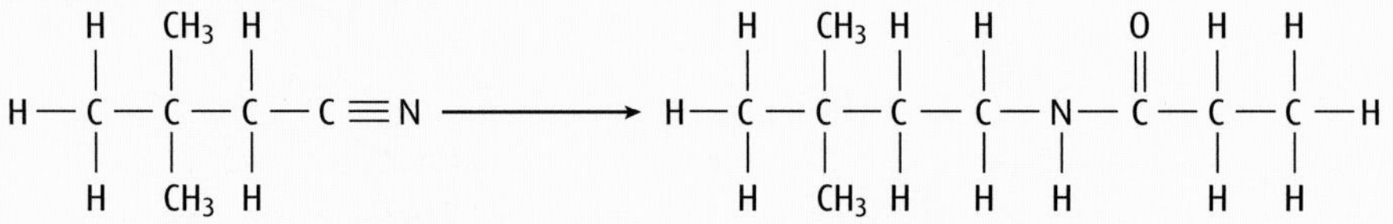

b

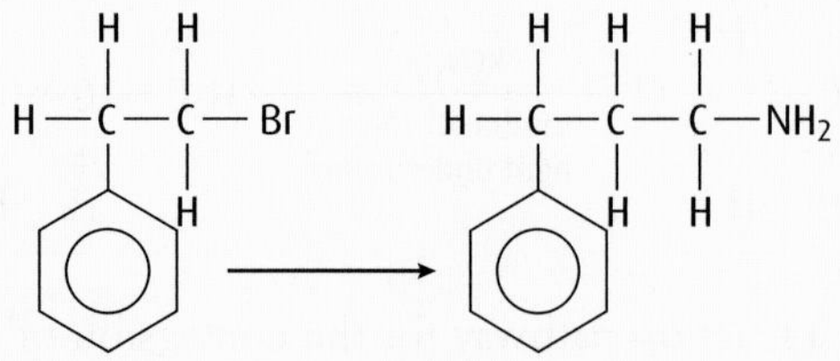

48 Design a reaction sequence for the conversion of molecule **A** into molecule **B**:

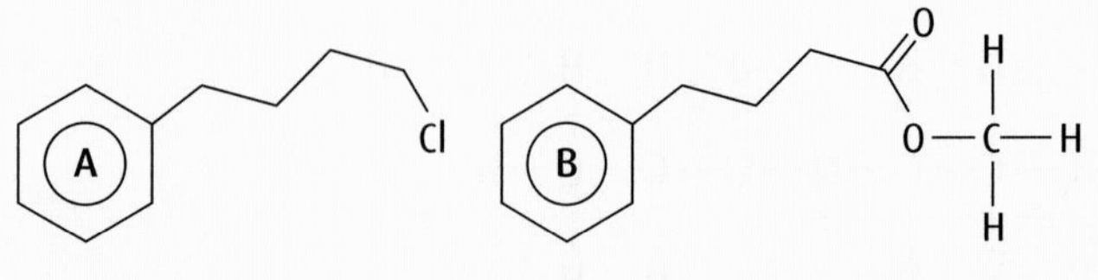

10.10 Stereoisomerism

Stereoisomerism

We have already met structural isomerism, in which molecules have the same molecular formula but the atoms are joined together differently. We will now consider stereoisomerism. Stereoisomers have the same structural formula (i.e. the atoms are joined together in the same way) but the atoms are arranged differently in space. One form of stereoisomerism is geometrical (*cis-* and *trans-*) isomerism, and another type is optical isomerism.

> Stereoisomers have the same structural formulas, but the atoms are arranged differently in space.

Geometrical isomerism

Geometrical isomerism occurs in alkenes and in cyclic (ring) compounds.

> Geometrical isomerism – compounds have the same structural formula, but groups are arranged differently in space about a double bond or a ring.

Before we can understand geometrical isomerism in alkenes, we must remind ourselves about the nature of the C=C double bond. A double bond consists of two components (Figure **10.34**).

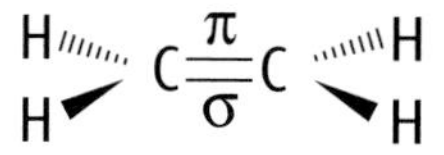

Fairly free rotation is possible about a C–C single bond, as the nature of the sigma bond does not restrict rotation. However, with C=C, the π component of the bond prevents the groups either side of it from rotating relative to each other (Figure **10.35**). The π bond would have to be broken to allow rotation to occur, and this takes a lot of energy.

The fact that rotation of groups about a double bond is restricted gives rise to a type of isomerism known as geometrical, or *cis-* and *trans-*isomerism. For example, two structures may be drawn for 1,2-dichloroethene:

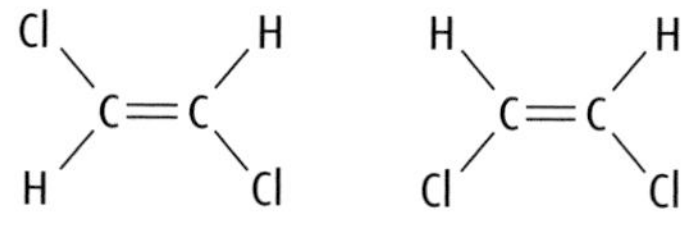

trans -1,2-dichloroethene   *cis* -1,2-dichloroethene

The chlorine atoms may either be arranged on the same side of the double bond, in which case the *cis* isomer is obtained, or they may be on opposite sides of the C=C, in which case we have the *trans* isomer. These cannot be easily interconverted because the π component of the C=C **restricts rotation of groups about the bond**.

Learning objectives

- Understand what is meant by stereoisomerism
- Understand how alkenes can exist as geometrical isomers
- Understand how cycloalkanes can exist as geometrical isomers
- Describe how geometrical isomers can have different physical and chemical properties
- Explain what is meant by optical isomerism
- Deduce whether a given molecule will exhibit optical isomerism
- Explain how optical isomers can be distinguished
- Describe the similarities and differences in the physical properties of enantiomers

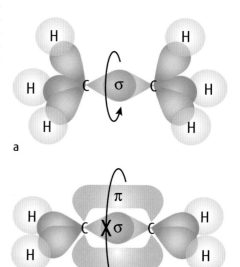

Figure 10.34 A double bond is composed of σ and π components.

Figure 10.35 (a) Free rotation of groups around a C–C bond; (b) restricted rotation of groups about a C=C bond.

cis: same side
trans: across

Extension

The *cis* and *trans* nomenclature for geometrical isomerism has limited value, and when there are four different groups around the C=C it provides no insight into the structure. In this case the isomers are labelled using the *E* and *Z* naming system.

HL

In order for a molecule to exhibit geometrical isomerism, there must be **two different groups** on **both sides** of the double bond. Thus geometrical isomers are possible for but-2-ene, but not for but-1-ene.

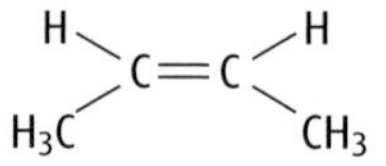
cis-but-2-ene

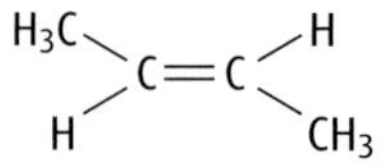
trans-but-2-ene

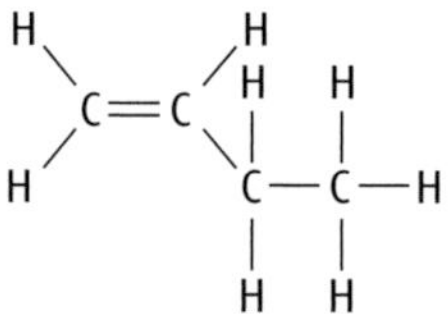
but-1-ene

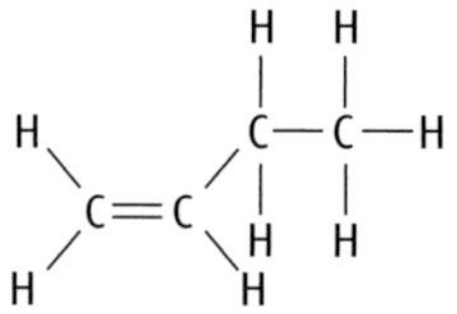
but-1-ene

The two molecules of but-1-ene shown here are **identical** – the second is simply the first turned upside down.

Other examples of molecules that do and do not exhibit geometrical isomerism are shown in Table **10.22**.

Compound	Geometrical isomers?	*cis*-isomer	*trans*-isomer
1-bromobut-1-ene	yes	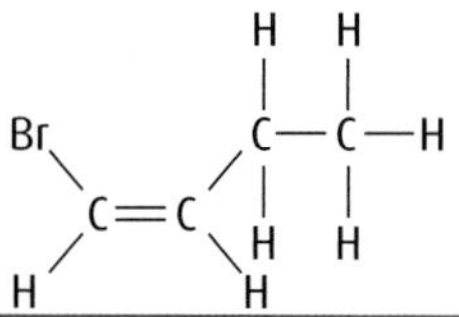	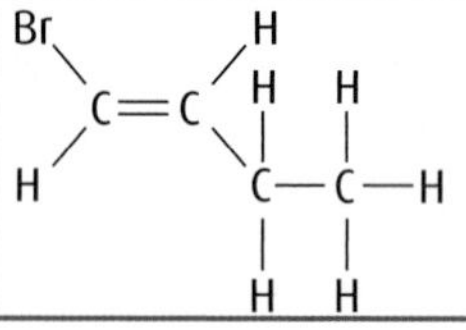
2-bromobut-1-ene	no	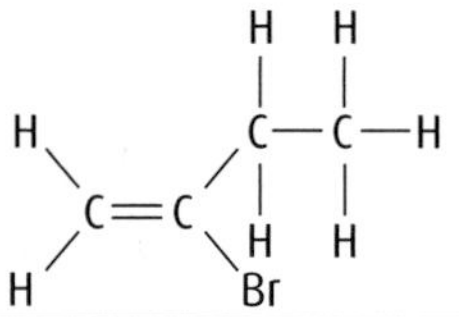	
3-methylpent-2-ene	yes	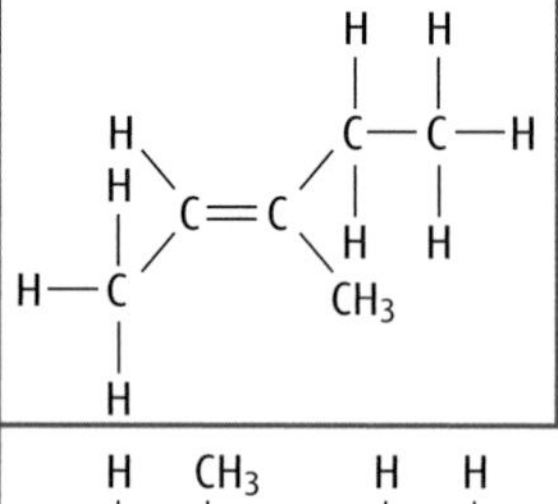	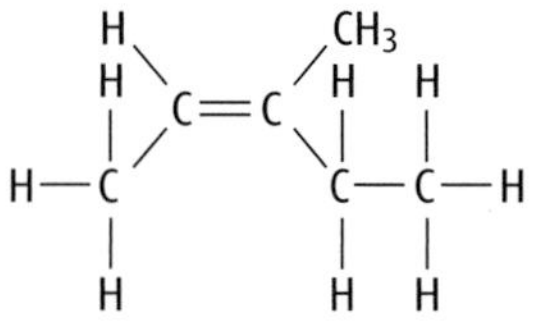
2-methylpent-2-ene	no	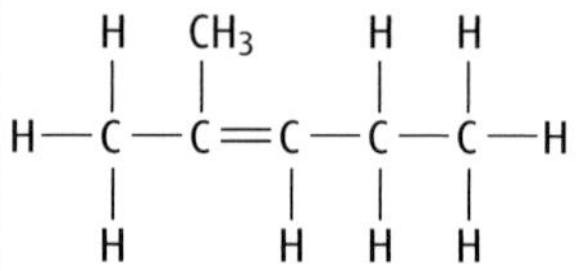	

Table 10.22 Examples of molecules that do and do not exhibit geometrical isomerism.

Physical and chemical properties of geometrical isomers

HL

1,2-dichloroethene

Physical properties, such as boiling point, of geometrical isomers are different. For instance:

	 cis-1,2-dichloroethene	trans-1,2-dichloroethene
M_r	96.94	96.94
Boiling point / °C	60.5	48.7

Cis-1,2-dichloroethene and *trans*-1,2-dichloroethene are geometrical isomers that differ only in the orientation of the Cl atoms about the C=C bond. The *cis* form is polar and the *trans* form is non-polar. The *trans* form is non-polar because the orientation of the Cl atoms about the double bond means that the dipoles cancel. There are thus permanent dipole–dipole interactions for the *cis* form but not for the *trans* form. Both molecules have the same relative molecular mass (and hence very similar van der Waals' forces), and therefore the difference between the boiling points is due to the permanent dipole–dipole interactions between molecules of the *cis* form.

cis-1,2-dichloroethene (polar)

trans-1,2-dichloroethene (non-polar)

But-2-ene-1,4-dioic acid

Consider the *cis* and *trans* forms of but–2-ene-1,4-dioic acid:

cis-but-2-ene-1,4-dioic acid (maleic acid)	trans-but-2-ene-1,4-dioic acid (fumaric acid)
melting point: 130 °C	melting point: 287 °C

The *cis* form has a lower melting point, because as well as intermolecular hydrogen bonding it is also able to participate in **intra**molecular hydrogen bonding. This means that some of the hydrogen bonding is within molecules and there is less hydrogen bonding between molecules. The *trans* form participates only in intermolecular hydrogen bonding, as the COOH groups are further away from each other; the intermolecular forces are therefore stronger in the *trans* form.

intramolecular hydrogen bond

ORGANIC CHEMISTRY 489

HL Geometrical isomers may also have different chemical properties

When the *cis* form of but-2-ene-1,4-dioic acid is heated at about 150 °C, it undergoes a cyclisation reaction to form an acid anhydride:

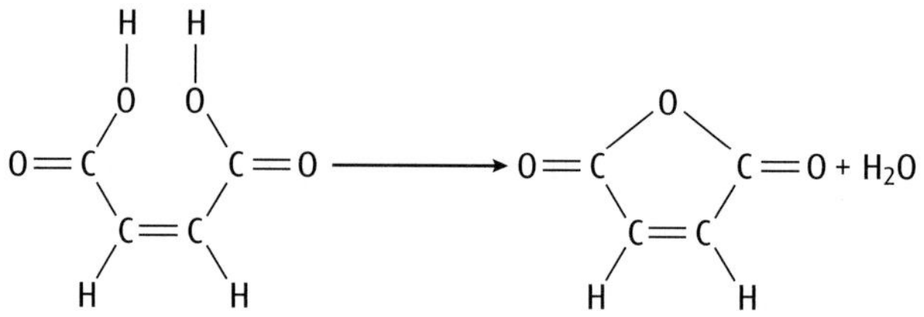

This is possible with the *cis* form, as the COOH groups are close together, but the *trans* form does not undergo this reaction, as the COOH groups are too far away.

Cycloalkanes

A cycloalkane is a ring (cyclic) compound just containing single C–C bonds. The simplest members of the homologous series are cyclopropane (C_3H_6) and cyclobutane (C_4H_8). Cycloalkanes are structural isomers of the corresponding alkene.

Two different ways of drawing these molecules are shown in Table **10.23**.

Table 10.23 Two ways of drawing cyclopropane and cyclobutane. Hydrogen atoms above the plane of the ring are shown in red and those below the plane of the ring are shown in blue.

Geometrical isomerism in substituted cycloalkanes

The ring structure prevents rotation of a group from the top of the ring to the bottom of the ring, and so geometrical isomers are possible in substituted cycloalkanes.

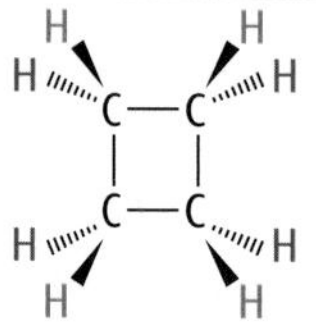

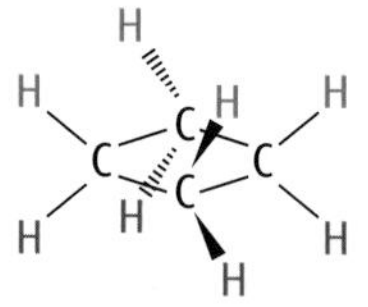

Extension

When the *trans* form is heated to a higher temperature, the same anhydride as with the *cis* form can indeed be formed. However, this reaction probably involves initial conversion of the *trans* form to the *cis* form of the acid.

A ring containing three atoms, such as in cyclopropane, is called a three-membered ring, whereas the ring in cyclobutane is a four-membered ring.

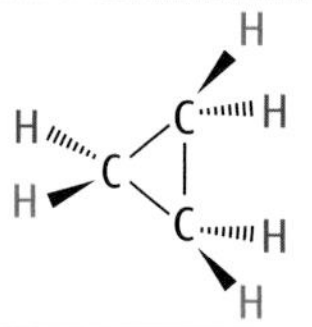

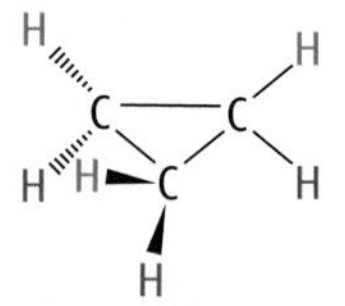

Extension

These belong to the general group of **cyclic** compounds: compounds that contain a ring of C or other atoms. If there is another atom, such as O or N, in the ring as well as C atoms, the compound is described as heterocyclic.

Groups can be rotated from the top to the bottom of the ring only if the ring is broken – this requires a lot of energy.

1,2-dimethylcyclobutane

The structures can be shown in two different ways:

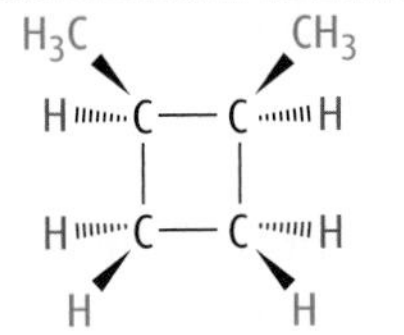

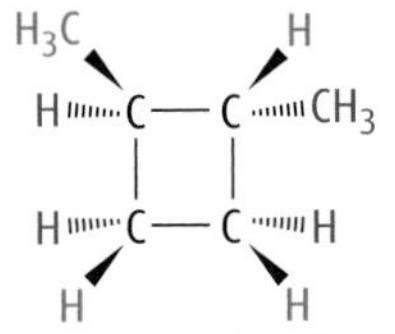

cis-1,2-dimethylcyclobutane	*trans*-1,2-dimethylcyclobutane
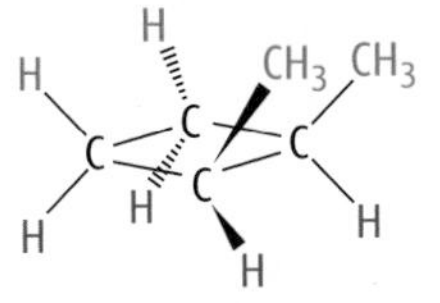	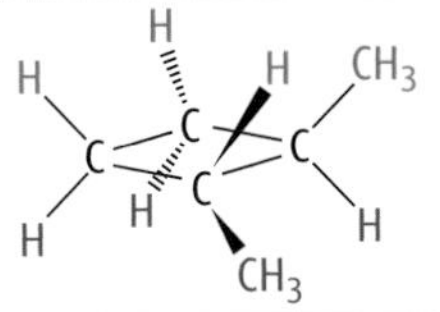

> The condition for a cycloalkane to exhibit geometrical isomerism is that at least two C atoms must have two different groups attached.

In the *cis* form the two methyl groups are on the **same side** of the ring and in the *trans* form they are on **opposite sides** of the ring.

Note:

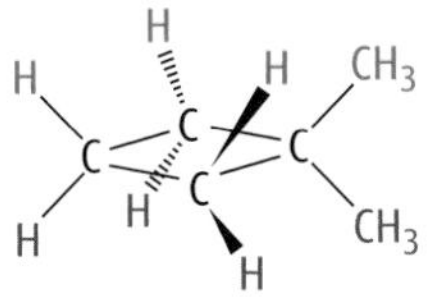

is not a geometrical isomer of 1,2-dimethylcyclobutane but a structural isomer. The atoms are joined together differently, with two methyl groups on the same C atom, and it has a different name: 1,1-dimethylcyclobutane. This molecule does not exhibit geometrical isomerism.

Self-test 15

Test yourself

49 Which of the following will exhibit geometrical isomerism? If the molecule exhibits geometrical isomerism, draw out the *cis* and *trans* forms.

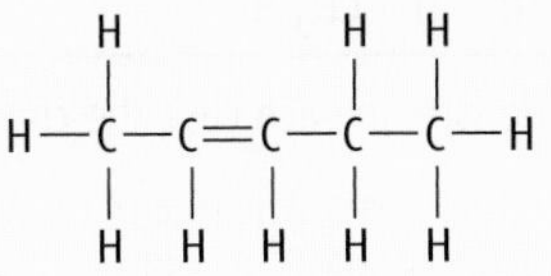

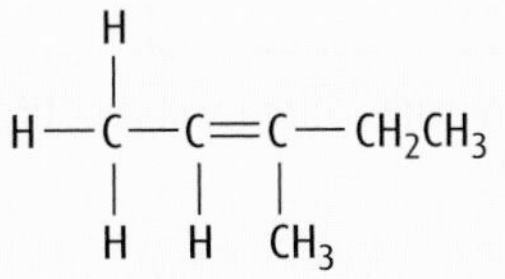

2,3-dimethylpent-2-ene   3,4-dimethylpent-2-ene

1,2,3-trimethylcyclopropane   1,3-dimethylcyclobutane

Optical isomerism

Optical isomerism is another type of stereoisomerism. The compound butan-2-ol exhibits optical isomerism. There are two forms of this compound, which are mirror images of each other.

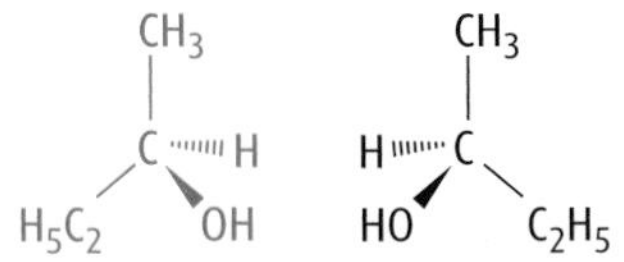

We say that the two isomers are **non-superimposable**.

The word 'chiral' is derived from the Greek word for hand – your hands are also non-superimposable mirror images of each other.

A carbon atom with four different atoms or groups attached is also sometimes called an **asymmetric** carbon atom.

Although these look identical, if we try to put one molecule on top of the other it can be seen that only two of the groups correspond with each other and the other two groups are distributed differently around the central C atom, therefore the molecules are not identical but isomers of each other.

In order to exhibit this property of optical isomerism – that is, that the mirror images are not superimposable – there must be **four different groups attached to a C atom**. Thus, if we look at butane, which has a maximum of three different groups attached to any one C atom, we can see that the mirror images are superimposable (Figure **10.36**).

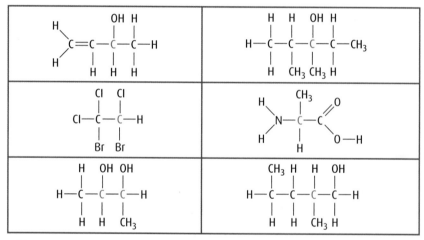

Figure 10.36 There is only one form of butane. These molecules are identical – butane does **not** have optical isomers.

A carbon atom with four different groups attached to it is called a **chiral centre**, and molecules that exhibit optical isomerism are often described as **chiral**.

Some molecules that exhibit optical isomerism are shown in Table **10.24**.

Table 10.24 Some molecules that exhibit optical isomerism. In each case the chiral centre is shown in red.

Some molecules that do **not** exhibit optical isomerism are shown in Table **10.25**.

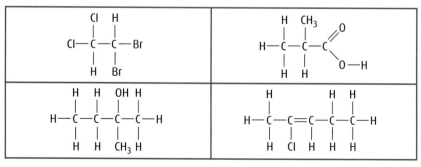

Table 10.25 Some molecules that do not exhibit optical isomerism.

In order to show the optical isomerism exhibited by compounds, the two optical isomers are usually drawn out in three dimensions, as shown in the diagrams in Table **10.26**. A solid wedge indicates a bond coming out of the plane of the paper and a dashed wedge is one that goes into the paper.

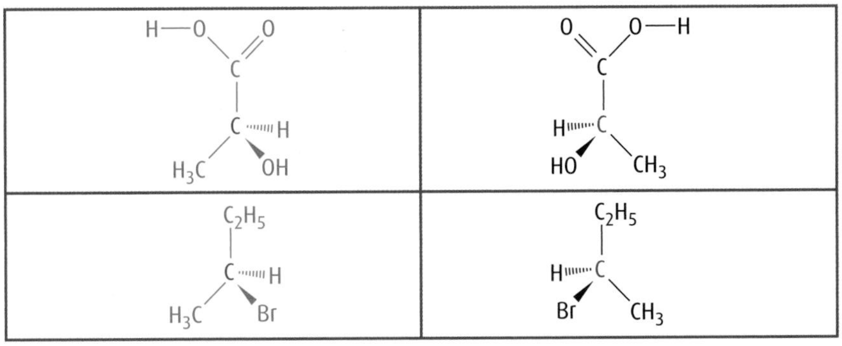

H—O O ⟍C⟋ C····H H₃C OH	O O—H ⟍C⟋ H····C HO CH₃
C₂H₅ C····H H₃C Br	C₂H₅ H····C Br CH₃

Table 10.26 The three-dimensional representation of optical isomers.

The individual optical isomers of a compound are called **enantiomers**. So, in the bottom row of Table **10.26**, the two enantiomers of 2-bromobutane are shown.

Optical isomerism and ring compounds

Optical isomerism may also occur with ring (cyclic) compounds. There are two chiral centres in *trans*-1,2-dichlorocyclopropane, each marked in red:

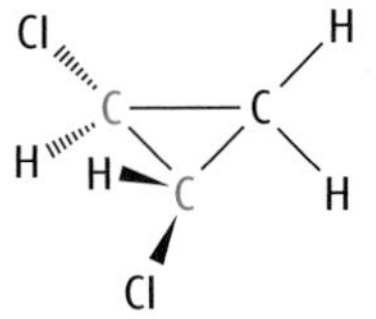

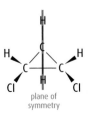

To determine whether a ring compound has optical isomers, it is necessary to look at whether the molecule has a plane of symmetry. If the molecule has a plane of symmetry, it will **not** have optical isomers.

The fact that the chiral centres in this molecule are indeed carbon atoms with four different groups attached can be seen by starting at the point shown and going around the ring in two different directions (Figure **10.37**). In addition to the H and Cl directly attached to the C, if we go clockwise around the ring, the group attached to the C is CHCl, but in the anticlockwise direction it is a CH_2 group.

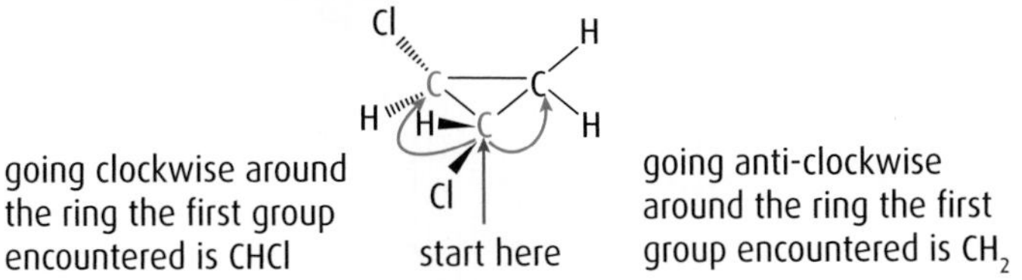

going clockwise around the ring the first group encountered is CHCl

start here

going anti-clockwise around the ring the first group encountered is CH_2

Figure 10.37 Checking that the chiral centres in a molecule are carbon atoms with four different groups attached.

cis-1,2-dichlorocyclopropane, however, has a plane of symmetry and therefore does not exhibit optical isomerism.

The fact that these carbon compounds exhibit optical isomerism allows us to reason that these molecules are tetrahedral. If they were square planar, optical isomers would not be possible (if you draw 2-bromobutane as a square planar structure you should be able to see that the mirror images are superimposable). This is an example of how reasoning can provide us with information about the microscopic world. Do we know, or believe, that these molecules are tetrahedral?

If a molecule has a **plane of symmetry** it will **not** exhibit optical isomerism.

cis-1,2-dichlorocyclopropane

plane of symmetry

Some ring compounds that do or do not have optical isomers are shown in Table **10.27**.

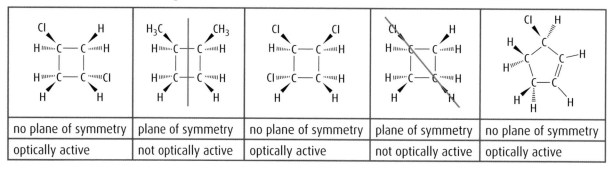

no plane of symmetry	plane of symmetry	no plane of symmetry	plane of symmetry	no plane of symmetry
optically active	not optically active	optically active	not optically active	optically active

Table 10.27 Some ring compounds with or without optical isomers.

Animation 8 **Optical isomers and plane-polarised light**

The two enantiomers of an optically active compound have the property that they rotate plane-polarised light in opposite directions. Or, more precisely, **they rotate the plane of polarisation of plane-polarised light in opposite directions**.

Normal, non-polarised, light vibrates in all planes (Figure **10.38**). If non-polarised light is passed through a polarising filter, plane-polarised light is produced (Figure **10.39**).

If plane-polarised light is passed through the two isomers of butan-2-ol, we find that one of the isomers rotates the plane of the plane-polarised light to the right (that is, clockwise), and the other isomer rotates the plane of the plane-polarised light to the left (that is, anticlockwise). The two enantiomers rotate the plane of the plane-polarised light by equal amounts.

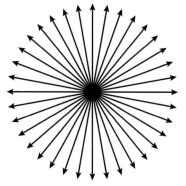

Figure 10.38 If we imagine being able to look at the vibrations in a beam of non-polarised light coming towards us, then it could be represented as shown here.

> Optical isomers rotate the plane of plane-polarised light in opposite directions.

Extension

There are various ways of labelling the two enantiomers. They may be labelled according to the direction in which they rotate plane-polarised light using +/− or d/l, or they may be labelled according to the absolute configuration (the arrangement of the groups around the chiral centre) using D/L or R/S. Systems for naming different enantiomers are discussed in Option **F**.

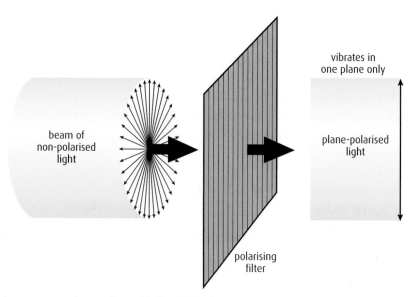

Figure 10.39 Plane-polarised light is light that vibrates in one plane only.

Using a polarimeter to determine the direction in which light is rotated

A simple polarimeter consists of a source of light, two polarising filters, a sample tube and a scale to measure the degree of rotation of the plane-polarised light (Figure **10.40**).

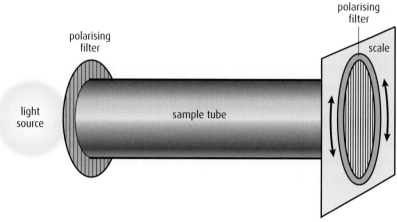

Figure 10.40 A simple polarimeter.

The solvent in which the test substance is to be dissolved is placed in the sample tube, and the second polarising filter is rotated until no light can be seen. At this point the polarising filters are exactly crossed. The solvent is then replaced by the sample dissolved in the solvent and the polarising filter rotated again until no light can be seen. The angle through which the light is rotated by the sample is the difference between the reading with and without the sample.

Racemic mixtures

An **equimolar** mixture of the two enantiomers of a chiral compound is called a **racemic** mixture. A racemic mixture has no effect on plane-polarised light, as the rotations of the two enantiomers cancel each other out.

As both enantiomers are equally stable, reactions that produce molecules containing a chiral carbon atom will usually produce a racemic mixture – the resulting reaction mixture will have no effect on plane-polarised light.

At a more advanced level, when attempting to make just one particular enantiomer of an optically active compound, either the synthetic route can be carefully designed to produce this isomer or the racemic mixture may be resolved into its various enantiomers.

Properties of enantiomers

Enantiomers have identical properties except when they interact with something else that is chiral.

HL **Extension**

Which absolute configuration corresponds to which direction the light is rotated may be calculated only by determining the absolute configuration using X-ray crystallography and the rotation of the light using a polarimeter. We cannot just look at a particular enantiomer's three-dimensional structure and say that it rotates plane-polarised light to the right or to the left.

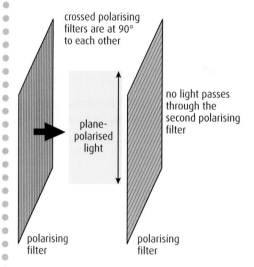

When the enantiomers of an optically active compound are reacted with **one** enantiomer of a different optically active compound in, for instance, an esterification reaction, the products of the reaction are not enantiomers of each other but are rather diastereomers of each other. Diastereomers have different properties and may be separated by normal methods.

Physical properties such as melting point, boiling point and solubility are identical in enantiomers. The only difference in physical properties is in the direction of rotation of the plane of plane-polarised light.

The chemical properties of enantiomers are identical for reactions with compounds that are not optically active. Enantiomers may, however, react differently with other optically active compounds.

Many biological compounds are optically active, and enzymes are often so specific that they are able to distinguish between different enantiomers, i.e. they will only catalyse the reactions of one enantiomer. For this to be possible, the active site, where the substrate binds to the enzyme, must be chiral, as only chiral molecules can distinguish between enantiomers. For this reason, enantiomers may also taste or smell different, as taste and smell receptors are chiral.

Self-test 16

Test yourself

50 Which of the following molecules exhibit optical isomerism? If a molecule exhibits optical isomerism, identify the chiral centre and draw three-dimensional diagrams showing the optical isomers.

a		b	
H H OH H ⎮ ⎮ ⎮ ⎮ H — C — C — C — C — OH ⎮ ⎮ ⎮ ⎮ H H H H		H H H H ⎮ ⎮ ⎮ ⎮ H — C — C — C — C — OH ⎮ ⎮ ⎮ ⎮ H H H H	
c		d	
H H H H ⎮ ⎮ ⎮ ⎮ HO — C — C — C — C — H ⎮ ⎮ ⎮ ⎮ H CH₃ H H		H H Cl H ⎮ ⎮ ⎮ ⎮ H — C — C — C — C — H ⎮ ⎮ ⎮ ⎮ H CH₃ H H	
e		f	
H ⎮ H — C — C = C — CH₂CH₃ ⎮ ⎮ ⎮ H H CH₃		H OH H ⎮ ⎮ ⎮ H — C — C = C — C — C — H ⎮ ⎮ ⎮ ⎮ ⎮ H H H H H	

51 Identify which of the following molecules is/are optically active:

$$H_3C, CH_3 \quad H\text{''''}C-C\text{''''}H \quad H\text{''''}C-C\text{''''}H \quad H$$

Exam-style questions

1 The functional groups present in the molecule shown are:

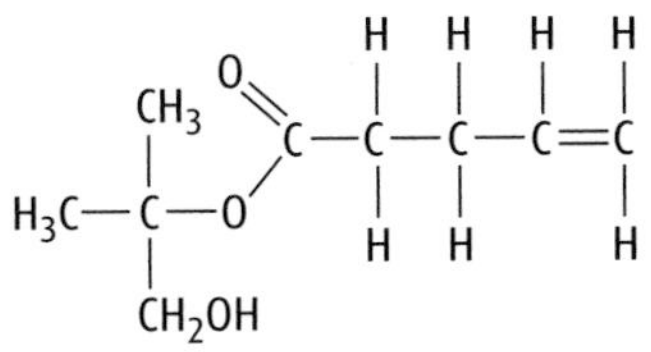

    A alcohol, ester, alkene
    B ketone, carboxylic acid, alkene
    C ester, aldehyde, alkene
    D alkene, ketone, alcohol

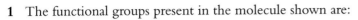

2 Which of the following is not a possible product when ethane reacts with chlorine in the presence of UV light?

    A HCl
    B CH_3CH_2Cl

    C H_2
    D $CH_3CH_2CH_2CH_3$

3 The product when but-2-ene reacts with bromine is:

    A $CH_3CHBrCH_2CH_3$
    B $CH_3CHBrCHBrCH_3$

    C $CH_3CBr_2CH_2CH_3$
    D $CH_3CHBrCH_2CH_2Br$

4 The condensed structural formulas of three alcohols are shown below:

    I $CH_3CH_2CH_2CH_2OH$
    II $CH_3CH_2CH(OH)CH_3$
    III $(CH_3)_3COH$

Which would be oxidised by heating with acidified potassium dichromate(VI)?

    A **I**, **II** and **III**
    B **I** only

    C **I** and **II** only
    D **III** only

5 The name of the molecule shown is:

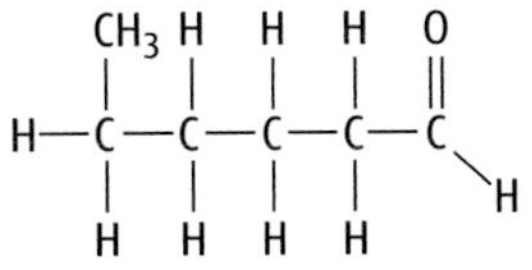

    A 5-methylpentanal
    B hexan-1-one
    C hexanal
    D 1-methylpentan-5-one

6 $CH_3CH_2CH_2CH_2Br$ reacts with sodium hydroxide. The name of the product formed and the type of reaction are:

	product	type of reaction
A	butanal	S_N1
B	butan-1-ol	S_N1
C	butan-2-ol	S_N2
D	butan-1-ol	S_N2

7 Which of the following substitution reactions is likely to occur most rapidly?

$$A \quad (CH_3)_3CBr + OH^- \rightarrow (CH_3)_3COH + Br^-$$
$$B \quad (CH_3)_3CCl + OH^- \rightarrow (CH_3)_3COH + Cl^-$$
$$C \quad CH_3(CH_2)_2CH_2Br + OH^- \rightarrow CH_3(CH_2)_2CH_2OH + Br^-$$
$$D \quad CH_3(CH_2)_2CH_2Cl + OH^- \rightarrow CH_3(CH_2)_2CH_2OH + Cl^-$$

8 Which of the following will exist as optical isomers?

    A 1-bromobutane
    B but-2-ene
    C pentan-2-ol
    D pentan-3-ol

9 The ester shown could be formed from the reaction between:

    A butanoic acid and propan-1-ol
    B propanoic acid and butan-2-ol
    C butanoic acid and propan-2-ol
    D butanoic acid and ethanol

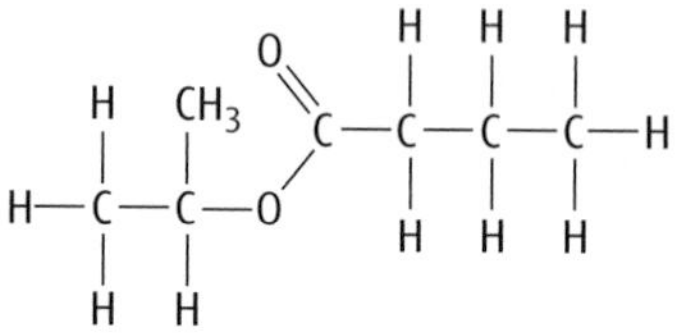

10 Consider the reaction sequence shown below.

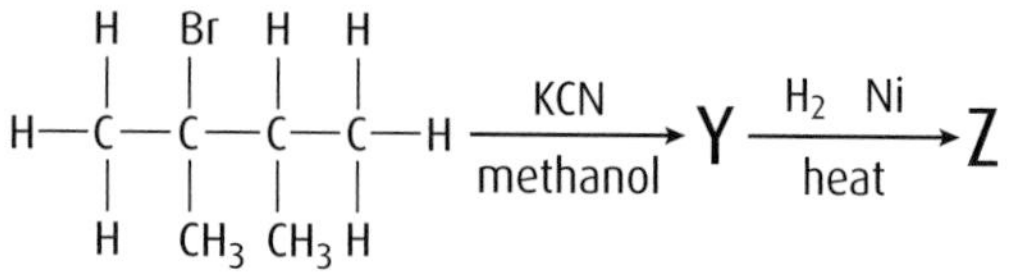

$$\text{(structure)} \xrightarrow[\text{methanol}]{\text{KCN}} Y \xrightarrow[\text{heat}]{H_2 \ Ni} Z$$

Y and **Z** are:

	Y	**Z**
A	amine	amide
B	nitrile	amine
C	nitrile	amide
D	amide	nitrile

11 Four of the structural isomers of $C_4H_{10}O$ are alcohols.

  a Draw the structures and give the names of these alcohols. **[4]**

  b Two of the alcohols can be oxidised to carboxylic acids. Give the name and formula of a suitable oxidising agent, the structures of the carboxylic acids formed and describe any colour change that occurs. **[6]**

  c Draw an isomer of $C_4H_{10}O$ that is not an alcohol. **[1]**

12 Ethane can react with chlorine in the presence of UV light to form chloroethane.

   a Write an equation for this reaction. **[1]**

   b **i** State the name of the mechanism by which this reaction occurs. **[1]**

      ii Use the mechanism of this reaction to explain the terms 'homolytic fission', 'free radical' and 'termination step'. **[4]**

   c Chloroethane reacts with aqueous sodium hydroxide.
      i Write an equation for the reaction that occurs. **[1]**
      ii Draw out the mechanism for this reaction. **[3]**

13 **a** Describe a chemical test that can be used to distinguish between butane and but-2-ene. **[3]**

   b Draw the structure of the compound formed when but-2-ene reacts with hydrogen bromide under appropriate conditions. **[1]**

   c But-2-ene can be converted to butanone in a two-step reaction sequence. Draw out the reaction sequence showing all structures and giving essential conditions. **[5]**

   d But-2-ene can undergo polymerisation under suitable conditions. Draw three repeat units of the polymer formed. **[2]**

HL **14** An organic compound has the percentage composition 48.6% C, 8.2% H, 43.2% O. The relative molecular mass of the compound is approximately 74.

   a Determine the empirical and molecular formulas of the compound. **[3]**

   b **i** Two of the isomers of this compound are esters. Draw out full structural formulas and name these compounds. **[4]**
      ii Write an equation for the formation of **one** of the esters from a carboxylic acid and an alcohol. **[2]**

   c A third isomer of this compound reacts with magnesium to form hydrogen gas. Draw the structure of this isomer and write an equation for the reaction with magnesium. **[3]**

15 This question is about 2-bromobutane.

   a 2-bromobutane exhibits optical isomerism. Explain what structural feature of 2-bromobutane allows it to exhibit optical isomerism and draw clear diagrams showing the optical isomers. **[3]**

   b **i** 2-bromobutane can react with ammonia via an S_N2 mechanism. Explain what is meant by the 'N' in S_N2. **[1]**
      ii Draw out the S_N2 mechanism for the reaction of 2-bromobutane with ammonia. **[3]**
      iii Explain whether you would expect 1-bromobutane or 2-bromobutane to react more or less slowly with ammonia via an S_N2 mechanism. **[2]**

   c When 2-bromobutane is heated with concentrated KOH dissolved in ethanol, three organic products are formed.
      i Draw out the structures of the organic products formed **[3]**
      ii Explain the types of isomerism shown by these compounds. **[3]**

16 The structure of a molecule, **X**, is shown below.

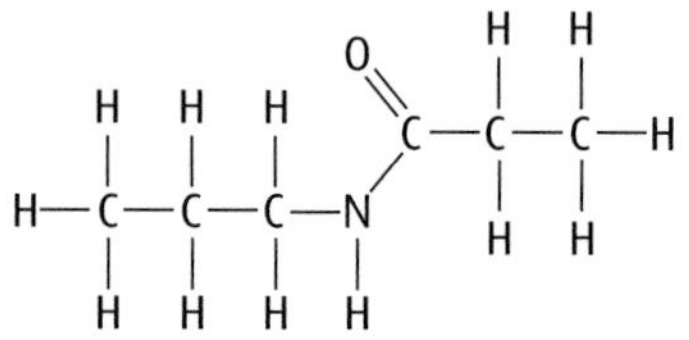

a State the name of the functional group in **X**. [1]

b **X** can be formed in a condensation reaction from two compounds, **P** and **Q**. Write a balanced equation, showing full structural formulas for the formation of **X** from **P** and **Q**. [3]

c **P** can be formed in a two-stage reaction pathway from bromoethane. State the name of **P** and draw out a reaction pathway for the formation of **P** from bromoethane showing the full structural formula of the intermediate compound and giving reagents and essential conditions. [4]

d Two repeat units for a polymer are shown below

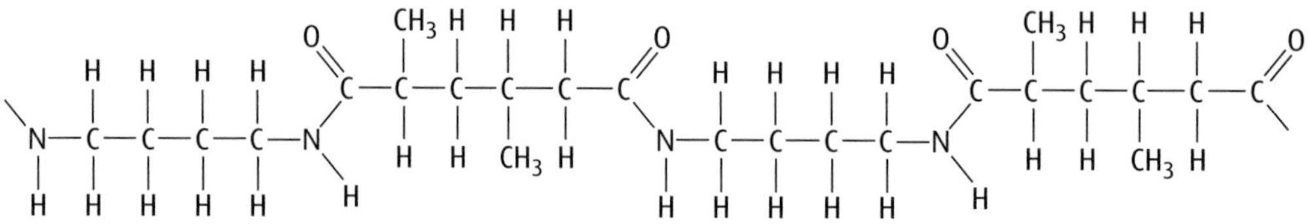

   i Name the type of polymerisation that has resulted in the formation of this polymer. [1]
  ii Draw the structures of the monomers from which this polymer could be formed. [2]

Summary

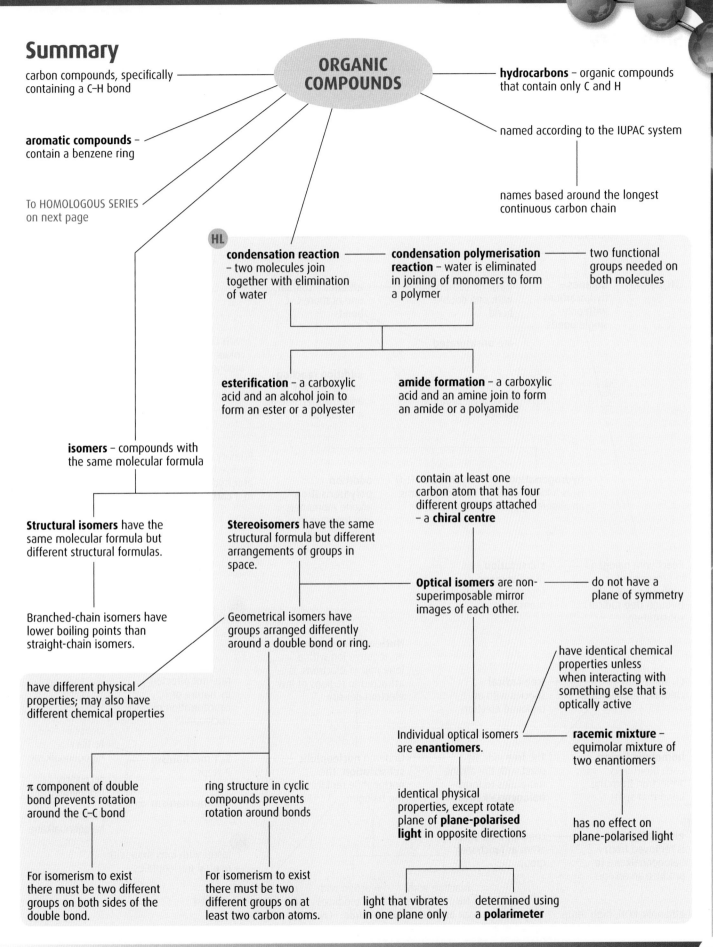

carbon compounds, specifically containing a C–H bond

ORGANIC COMPOUNDS

hydrocarbons – organic compounds that contain only C and H

named according to the IUPAC system

names based around the longest continuous carbon chain

aromatic compounds – contain a benzene ring

To HOMOLOGOUS SERIES on next page

HL

condensation reaction – two molecules join together with elimination of water

condensation polymerisation reaction – water is eliminated in joining of monomers to form a polymer

two functional groups needed on both molecules

esterification – a carboxylic acid and an alcohol join to form an ester or a polyester

amide formation – a carboxylic acid and an amine join to form an amide or a polyamide

isomers – compounds with the same molecular formula

contain at least one carbon atom that has four different groups attached – a **chiral centre**

Structural isomers have the same molecular formula but different structural formulas.

Stereoisomers have the same structural formula but different arrangements of groups in space.

Optical isomers are non-superimposable mirror images of each other.

do not have a plane of symmetry

Branched-chain isomers have lower boiling points than straight-chain isomers.

Geometrical isomers have groups arranged differently around a double bond or ring.

have identical chemical properties unless when interacting with something else that is optically active

have different physical properties; may also have different chemical properties

Individual optical isomers are **enantiomers**.

racemic mixture – equimolar mixture of two enantiomers

π component of double bond prevents rotation around the C–C bond

ring structure in cyclic compounds prevents rotation around bonds

identical physical properties, except rotate plane of **plane-polarised light** in opposite directions

has no effect on plane-polarised light

For isomerism to exist there must be two different groups on both sides of the double bond.

For isomerism to exist there must be two different groups on at least two carbon atoms.

light that vibrates in one plane only

determined using a **polarimeter**

Summary – continued

boiling point increases as chain length increases

members of a series have similar chemical properties

HOMOLOGOUS SERIES – series of compounds with the same functional group, in which each member differs from the next by a $-CH_2-$ group.

functional group – atom or group of atoms that gives an organic molecule its characteristic chemical properties

position

primary – group attached to carbon that is attached to **one** other carbon

secondary – group attached to carbon that is attached to **two** other carbons

tertiary – group attached to carbon that is attached to **three** other carbons

complete products: CO_2, H_2O

incomplete products: CO, C, H_2O

combustion

C_nH_{2n+2} — **alkanes** – hydrocarbons with only single bonds

C_nH_{2n} for compounds with one double bond — **alkenes** – contain one or more C=C bonds

are **unsaturated**

decolorise bromine water

addition reaction – molecule X–Y is added either side of a C=C bond

$C_nH_{2n+2}O$ — **alcohols** – contain a hydroxyl group: –OH

with $Cr_2O_7^{2-}/H^+$ colour change from orange to green — Primary and secondary alcohols can be oxidised using acidified $K_2Cr_2O_7$ or $KMnO_4$.

Primary alcohols are oxidised first to an **aldehyde** and then to a **carboxylic acid**.

Secondary alcohols are oxidised to a **ketone**.

hydrogenation – H_2 is added, forms an alkane

hydration – H_2O is added, forms an alcohol

addition polymerisation – alkene monomers join together in polymer chain

Aldehydes and ketones are **carbonyl compounds** – they contain a C=O group.

React with halogens in presence of sunlight or UV light through free radical substitution.

substitution – an atom or group is replaced by another atom or group

HL steric effects prevent S_N2 mechanism | more stable carbocation

rate not affected by nature or concentration of nucleophile

Nucleophile – molecule or negative ion with a lone pair of electrons. Is attracted to regions of low electron density.

Cl_2 splits into chlorine free radicals.

free radical – a species with an unpaired electron

homolytic fission – each atom gets 1 electron from the bond that splits

The free radicals react with the alkane molecules to form **halogenoalkanes**.

Undergo **nucleophilic substitution**. The nucleophile replaces the halogen.

S_N1 **mechanism** 2 steps

S_N2 **mechanism** 1 step

tertiary halogenoalkane

secondary halogenoalkane

primary halogenoalkane

HL faster with ions than with neutral nucleophiles

HL **elimination** – H–X is removed from a halogenoalkane to produce an alkene

contains a halogen atom as functional group

ethanolic KOH, high temp.

reaction with NH_3 produces an **amine**: $-NH_2$

reaction with CN^- produces a nitrile: –CN

reactions rate: R–I > R–Br > R–Cl > R–F

Measurement and data processing 11

11.1 Uncertainties in measurements

Measurements in science

Although in mathematics it is possible to have pure numbers and write down a number to any number of decimal places, in chemistry we are concerned with real quantities obtained by making measurements in a laboratory.

It is not possible to measure the actual, or true, value of a particular quantity. The true mass of a piece of magnesium could be 0.257 846 368 246 89 g, but we have no way of actually measuring that. The best we can ever get is an estimate. If we put the piece of magnesium on to an electronic balance that gives values to one decimal place, we might measure 0.3 g. If we had a balance that could measure to three decimal places, then we might get 0.258 g. Neither of these values is the true mass of the piece of magnesium ribbon.

Consider the following argument.
Experimental data can never provide a true value for a quantity. The knowledge we get from science is ultimately obtained from experimental data. The knowledge we obtain from science is never true.

Random uncertainties

We need to find the mass of a piece of magnesium ribbon 20 cm long. To do this we measured a piece of magnesium 20 cm long using a ruler on which the smallest division was 1 mm. The strip of magnesium ribbon was cut from the roll and weighed on an electronic balance that reads to two decimal places. The mass of the first strip of magnesium ribbon was 0.27 g. We then cut nine more strips in the same way from the same roll, and the results are shown in Table **11.1**.

The first thing we should notice is that not all the readings are the same. This is because of random uncertainties.

> **Random uncertainties are caused by the limitations of the measuring apparatus and other uncontrollable variables that are inevitable in any experiment.**

There are several sources of random uncertainty, even in this simple procedure. Firstly, there will be slight variations in the length of the strip of magnesium ribbon that we cut; secondly, the magnesium ribbon will not be of exactly uniform size throughout the roll; and, thirdly, when we measure the mass using the electronic balance, there could be variations due to air currents in the room, the heating effects of the current in the circuits, friction between various mechanical parts, etc.

Learning objectives

- Understand the difference between random uncertainties and systematic errors
- Understand the difference between precision and accuracy
- Understand how to quote values with uncertainties
- Understand the difference between significant figures and decimal places

Reading	Mass / g
1	0.27
2	0.28
3	0.28
4	0.27
5	0.27
6	0.27
7	0.26
8	0.28
9	0.28
10	0.27

Table 11.1 The results obtained from weighing ten strips of magnesium ribbon.

The effect of random uncertainties can be reduced by repeating the measurements more often.

The random uncertainties can never be completely eliminated.

The effects of random uncertainties should mean that the measurements taken will be distributed either side of the mean, i.e. fluctuations will be in both directions.

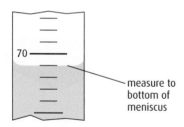

measure to bottom of meniscus

Note: this is only an estimate, so if you quoted this value as 69.0 ± 0.5 cm, this would not be incorrect.

We can give an indication of the size of the random uncertainty by quoting the measured value with an uncertainty. For instance, the mass of a piece of magnesium ribbon 20 cm long could be quoted as 0.27 ± 0.01 g, where '± 0.01 g' is the uncertainty in the measurement. That is, we are reasonably confident that the mass of a piece of magnesium ribbon 20 cm long is somewhere between 0.26 g and 0.28 g. If we kept cutting strips from this roll we would expect each mass to lie between 0.26 g and 0.28 g.

Taking more repeats gives a more reliable mean value. If we had just taken one measurement in the above example, we could have obtained 0.26 g, 0.27 g or 0.28 g as the value of the mass of the strip of magnesium. If, however, we take the reading 100 times and work out the mean value, we should get a value that more closely represents the true mean.

The effect of random uncertainties can also be minimised by careful design of an experiment. For instance, if you plan to carry out an experiment using 0.05 g magnesium and to measure the mass with a two decimal place balance then the uncertainty on the mass will be ± 0.01 g, which is 20% of the mass. If, however, you carry out the experiment instead with 0.20 g magnesium then the percentage uncertainty due to random error is reduced to 5%.

No matter to how many decimal places a piece of measuring apparatus is able to measure a quantity, there will always be an uncertainty in the value.

Estimating the random uncertainties associated with measuring apparatus

Analogue instruments

As a rule of thumb, the uncertainty on a measurement is half the smallest division to which you take a reading. This may be the division on the piece of apparatus used or it may be an estimate if the divisions are sufficiently far apart that you are able to estimate between them.

For instance, the smallest division on a 100 cm^3 measuring cylinder is 1 cm^3; however, the divisions are sufficiently far apart that we can probably estimate between these divisions to the nearest 0.5 cm^3. We can thus estimate that our actual value is greater than 68.75 and less than 69.25. The uncertainty is half the smallest division, i.e. 0.25 cm^3, or 0.3 cm^3 to one significant figure (uncertainties are usually only quoted to one significant figure). We can therefore quote the reading as 69.0 ± 0.3 cm^3, i.e. the volume of water is somewhere between 68.7 and 69.3 cm^3.

Digital instruments

On an electronic balance reading to two decimal places, the smallest division is 0.01 g, so the uncertainty associated with this is ± 0.005 g. Thus, if a particular reading is taken as 2.46 g, this means that the value is somewhere between 2.455 g and 2.465 g.

However, the balance will have been zeroed beforehand and this zero value also has an uncertainty associated with it. That is, when the reading on the balance is 0.00 g it indicates a value between -0.005 and 0.005 g. The largest possible value of the measured mass would be from -0.005 to

2.465 g, i.e. 2.47 g, and the smallest possible value is from 0.005 to 2.455 g, i.e. 2.45 g. The uncertainty on this measurement is thus ±0.01 g, and the measurement should be quoted as 2.46 ± 0.01 g.

Precision

> Precision relates to the reproducibility of results. If a series of readings is taken with high precision, it indicates that the repeated values are all very close together and close to the mean (average) value.

Consider the values in Table **11.2**. The results in the first column could be reported as $21.2 \pm 0.1 \, cm^3$, whereas the second column would yield $21.4 \pm 0.7 \, cm^3$. The larger uncertainty in the second set of readings indicates the greater spread of the values, i.e. lower precision.

Reading	Volume / cm³	Volume / cm³
1	21.2	21.0
2	21.3	21.9
3	21.1	22.1
4	21.3	21.2
5	21.1	20.7
6	21.2	21.5
mean value	21.2	21.4

Table 11.2 Measurements of the same quantity using two different pieces of apparatus: the first set of readings is more precise than the second set, as the values in the first set are much closer to each other and to the mean value.

If a single reading is taken, the uncertainty gives us an indication of the precision of the reading; for instance a temperature recorded as 21.33 ± 0.01 °C is more precise than 21.3 ± 0.1 °C. In the first case, repeat values of the quantity would be expected to mostly lie between 21.32 and 21.34 °C, whereas in the second (less precise) case, the values would be expected to lie between 21.2 and 21.4 °C.

Accuracy

> Accuracy refers to how close a measurement is to the actual value of a particular quantity.

In the example discussed before, if the true value of the temperature was 19.57 °C, although the value of 21.33 ± 0.01 °C is quite precise, it is not very accurate as it is not very close to the true value.

In this case, there appears to be some sort of **systematic error** with the procedure (for instance, perhaps the thermometer was not originally calibrated properly). In this case, repeating the readings will not improve the accuracy of the measurements, as all the values would be expected to be around 21.33 ± 0.01 °C.

In general, the uncertainty of a measurement made on a digital instrument should be quoted as ± the smallest division.

The uncertainties here are worked out from the range of the data, i.e. looking at how far the maximum and minimum values are from the mean.

It is not really correct to talk about the precision of a single reading, but the term is sometimes used. For a single reading, a more precise value is a value to more significant figures.

Extension

The standard deviation is often quoted to give an idea of the precision of a set of measurements. The larger the standard deviation, the less precise the measurements.

It is possible for a measurement to have great precision but to not be very accurate.

Systematic errors

A systematic error is an error introduced into an experiment by the apparatus or the procedure. Systematic errors result in a loss of accuracy, i.e. the measured value is further away from the true value.

Systematic errors are always in the same direction. For instance, you might measure the mass of some sodium chloride with a balance that has not been calibrated recently and the balance might always record a mass that is 1.00 g too much. The actual value of the mass is 23.25 g, but the balance reads 24.25 g. No matter how many times this reading is repeated, the mass will always be 1.00 g too large.

The above experiment could probably have been improved by using several different balances and taking an average of the values from all of them. (However, this is still no guarantee of greater accuracy, as each might have a systematic error associated with it!)

Consider an experiment carried out to measure the enthalpy change of neutralisation by reacting $50 \, cm^3$ of $0.10 \, mol \, dm^{-3}$ sodium hydroxide and $50 \, cm^3$ of $0.10 \, mol \, dm^{-3}$ hydrochloric acid in a beaker.

Systematic errors can be identified by comparison with accepted literature values. For instance, the above experiment might give a calculated heat of neutralisation of $-55.8 \pm 0.1 \, kJ \, mol^{-1}$. The ± 0.1 indicates the uncertainties due to random errors. The accepted literature value for this quantity is $-57.3 \, kJ \, mol^{-1}$. We can use the percentage error to compare the experimental value with the accepted literature value.

> The effect of a systematic error cannot be reduced by repeating the readings.

> |value| indicates the modulus of the value; i.e. ignore the overall sign

$$\text{percentage error} = \frac{|\text{experimental value} - \text{accepted value}|}{|\text{accepted value}|} \times 100$$

In this case, the percentage error $= \dfrac{|55.8 - 57.3|}{57.3} \times 100 = 2.6\%$

The percentage uncertainty due to random uncertainties:

$$\frac{0.1}{55.8} \times 100 = 0.2\%$$

> The percentage error is greater than any percentage random uncertainty. This suggests that the experiment involves some systematic errors.

Some of the systematic errors in this experiment could be:

- the beaker is not that well insulated so heat will escape: the measured temperature rise will be less than the actual value;
- the reaction does not occur instantaneously and the thermometer does not respond instantaneously and so the measured temperature rise will be less than the actual value;
- the concentration of the sodium hydroxide is less than $0.10 \, mol \, dm^{-3}$ and so the measured temperature rise will be less than the actual value.

These systematic errors can be reduced by changing the way the experiment is carried out, for instance by using an insulated container with a lid in which to do the reaction.

If your experiment involves finding a value for a quantity for which no literature value exists, it can be very difficult to spot systematic errors.

The difference between accuracy and precision

As we have seen, precision refers to the reproducibility of results (i.e. how close repeat readings are to each other and to the mean value), whereas accuracy refers to how close a value is to the true value of the measurement. The diference between accuracy and precision can be seen in Figure **11.1**.

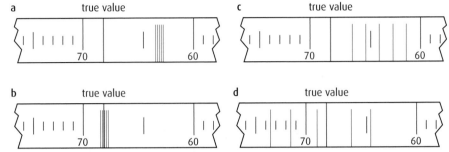

Figure 11.1a (**a**) A set of readings (shown in red) with high precision but poor accuracy; (**b**) a set of readings with high precision and high accuracy; (**c**) a set of readings with low precision and low accuracy; (**d**) a set of readings with low precision and high accuracy. In this last set, the accuracy is high, as the mean value is close to the true value. However, it is a poor set of data, and the high accuracy is probably more a case of luck than good experimental design!

Similarily, think about a tennis player serving the ball (Figure **11.2**). If they can hit nearly the same spot each time then they are serving with a great deal of precision. If this point is not in the service box, however, then their serve is not very accurate. In this case (and in the case of scientific experiments) precision without accuracy is useless – it doesn't win any points!

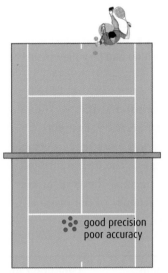

good precision
poor accuracy

Figure 11.2 Like a game of tennis, the goal of a scientific experiment is high precision and high accuracy.

Test yourself

1 The table shows data from five trials of two separate experiments. Which set of values is more precise?

Trial	Experiment	
	1	**2**
1	1.34	1.37
2	1.48	1.22
3	1.40	1.58
4	1.27	1.18
5	1.38	1.44

2 A series of experiments was carried out to determine the value for a particular quantity. The results are shown in the table. The literature value of this quantity is 47.0 J. Which experiment produced the most accurate value?

Experiment	Value / J
1	45.276
2	48
3	44.2
4	49.57

Quoting values with uncertainties

Consider a value of 1.735 ± 0.1 obtained from an experiment:

the uncertainty is in this decimal place, so no figures should be quoted beyond it. This quantity should then be quoted as 1.7 ± 0.1.

The uncertainty is usually quoted to one significant figure, and your measurement should be stated so that the uncertainty is in the last significant figure, i.e. no figures should be quoted after the uncertainty.

Measured value ± uncertainty	Value you should quote
151.3 ± 0.2	151.3 ± 0.2
157.47 ± 0.1	157.5 ± 0.1
0.06500 ± 0.0001	0.0650 ± 0.0001
363.2 ± 8	363 ± 8
363.2 ± 20	360 ± 20
363.2 ± 100	400 ± 100

Table 11.3 Measured values with uncertainties and how they should be quoted.

Examiner's tip

For internal assessment practical work it is acceptable to quote the uncertainty of the mean as the same as the uncertainty of the original data.

Reading	Volume / cm^3
1	21.0
2	21.9
3	22.1
4	21.2
5	20.7
6	21.5
Mean value	21.4

Table 11.4 The same quantity has been measured six times and the average taken.

23.14	4 significant figures	2 decimal places
0.012	2 significant figures	3 decimal places
1.012	4 significant figures	3 decimal places
100.35	5 significant figures	2 decimal places
0.0010050	5 significant figures	7 decimal places
50.0	3 significant figures	1 decimal place

Table 11.5 The difference between significant figures and decimal places.

Table **11.3** shows some more examples.

With 363.2 ± 8, the random uncertainties mean that the value is known only to within 8 either way – the 0.2 is thus meaningless. With 0.0650 ± 0.0001, the final zero is required, as the uncertainty is in the fourth decimal place. If the value were quoted as 0.065, this would imply that the value lies between 0.0645 and 0.0655 rather than between 0.0651 and 0.0649, and therefore there would be a loss of precision.

The uncertainty in a mean value

There are various more or less complicated ways of quoting the uncertainty in a mean (average) value. Consider the data give in Table **11.4**. One way of quoting the mean is as: $21.4 \pm 0.7 \, \text{cm}^3$. Here we are taking the uncertainty as the deviation of the maximum and minimum values from the mean. The largest value is $22.1 \, \text{cm}^3$, which is $0.7 \, \text{cm}^3$ greater than the mean value, and the smallest value is $20.7 \, \text{cm}^3$, which is $0.7 \, \text{cm}^3$ smaller than the mean value. However, if we have a large number of readings, quoting the uncertainty based on the range is probably pessimistic, as most of the values would be expected to lie closer to the mean than that.

A rough rule of thumb is to take the uncertainty of the mean to be two-thirds of the deviation from the mean. For example, with this set of data, the deviation from the menu is $\pm 0.7 \, \text{cm}^3$ and two-thirds of this is approximately $0.5 \, \text{cm}^3$, so we could quote our average value as $21.4 \pm 0.5 \, \text{cm}^3$ and be reasonably confident that, if we take any further measurements, most of them will lie between 20.9 and $21.9 \, \text{cm}^3$.

Significant figures and decimal places

When counting significant figures, we start counting from the left with the first non-zero digit. For example, 0.012 has two significant figures, as we do not count the first two zeros. 0.0010050 has five significant figures, as we do not count the first three zeroes but we must count any zeroes after the first non-zero digit and after a decimal point (Table **11.5**).

Problems come when numbers are quoted as 500, for example, as this could be one, two or three significant figures. This ambiguity is avoided by quoting the number in standard form. If it is quoted as 5.0×10^2, there are two significant figures, and if it is quoted as 5.00×10^2, there are three significant figures.

> The number could also be quoted with an uncertainty, e.g. 500 ± 1, so that it is clear that the value is known to three significant figures.

It is important to realise that 5 g, 5.0 g and 5.00 g are not the same: 5 g implies that the mass is between 4.5 and 5.5 g; 5.0 g implies that the mass is between 4.95 and 5.05 g; 5.00 g implies that the mass is between 4.995 and 5.005 g. A value of 5 g measured on a two decimal place electronic balance must be quoted as 5.00 g and not 5 g, otherwise there will be a loss of precision in your results.

Rounding to the appropriate number of significant figures

If a number is to be quoted to a certain number of significant figures, then we must look at the next figure after the last one that we wish to quote. If the next figure to the right is 5 or greater, the last significant figure should be rounded up, but if the next figure to the right is less than 5 the last significant figure stays the same. Some examples of rounding to the appropriate number of significant figures are shown in Table **11.6**.

Recurring decimals such as $0.\dot{3}$ should never be used in chemistry, as they imply infinite precision. A value should always be rounded to the appropriate number of significant figures, e.g. as 0.33 or 0.333.

Value	Number of significant figures	Rounded value
27.346	3	27.3
27.346	4	27.35
0.03674	2	0.037
0.03674	3	0.0367
0.399 967 2	3	0.400
0.399 967 2	4	0.4000
0.399 967 2	5	0.399 97

Table 11.6 Rounding to the appropriate number of significant figures.

Test yourself

3 Copy and complete the table:

Measured value ± uncertainty	Value you should quote
71.7 ± 0.2	
3.475 ± 0.01	
0.065 06 ± 0.001	
63.27 ± 5	
593.2 ± 30	
783.28 ± 100	

4 State the number of significant figures for each of the following numbers:

  a 2.78   **c** 0.003 480   **e** 80.00

  b 0.057   **d** 3.95×10^4

5 Round each of the following numbers to three significant figures:

  a 6.7863   **c** 0.004 999 31   **e** $1.783 39 \times 10^{-3}$

  b 0.000 079 835   **d** $8.245 7 \times 10^5$

11.2 Uncertainties in calculations

Significant figures and calculations

> When carrying out calculations, the general rule is that the final answer should be quoted to the number of significant figures of the piece of data with the fewest significant figures.

Example

Sulfuric acid is titrated against **25.00** cm^3 of **0.2000** $mol\,dm^{-3}$ sodium hydroxide solution. **23.20** cm^3 of sulfuric acid is required for neutralisation. Calculate the concentration of the sulfuric acid.

$$2NaOH(aq) + H_2SO_4(aq) \rightarrow Na_2SO_4(aq) + 2H_2O(l)$$

Learning objectives

- Quote the result of a calculation to the appropriate number of significant figures
- Understand what is meant by absolute uncertainties and percentage uncertainties
- Understand how to combine uncertainties in calculations

25.00 implies that the volume is somewhere between 24.995 and 25.005 cm^3.

$$\frac{c_1 V_1}{n_1} = \frac{c_2 V_2}{n_2}$$

All quantities are quoted to **four significant figures**.

volume of sodium hydroxide $= 25.00 \pm 0.005 \, cm^3$

concentration of sodium hydroxide $= 0.2000 \pm 0.00005 \, mol \, dm^{-3}$

volume of sulfuric acid $= 23.20 \pm 0.005 \, cm^3$

The equation for working out the concentration of the sulfuric acid is:

$$c = \frac{0.2000 \times 25.00}{23.20 \times 2} = 0.1077586 \, mol \, dm^{-3}$$

If maximum and minimum values are substituted into this equation:

$$\text{maximum concentration} = \frac{0.20005 \times 25.005}{23.195 \times 2} = 0.1078303 \, mol \, dm^{-3}$$

$$\text{minimum concentration} = \frac{0.19995 \times 24.995}{23.205 \times 2} = 0.1076869 \, mol \, dm^{-3}$$

The difference between these values occurs in the fourth significant figure, so they should be quoted to four significant figures as $0.1078 \, mol \, dm^{-3}$.

> If a calculation involves simply adding and/or subtracting numbers then the general rule is that the number of decimal places should be preserved.

For example:

$$22.3 - 14.8 = 7.5$$

Although the initial quantities are both to three significant figures, the final answer is quoted as 7.5, which is the same number of decimal places, rather than 7.50, which is the same number of significant figures.

Similarly:

$$89.3 + 76.6 = 165.9$$

Here the final answer is quoted to one decimal place, which is the same number of decimal places as the original data.

Rounding values in calculations

When carrying out multistage calculations, it is important to avoid rounding errors that could, after several stages, introduce large inaccuracies into the calculation. As a general rule, all numbers should be carried through in a calculation and rounding should only happen when an answer to a particular part of a question is required.

Note: these are only general rules of thumb, and in calculations involving measured quantities in the laboratory the absolute and percentage uncertainties should be considered to make sure that the data are quoted to the appropriate number of significant figures. This is considered below.

Absolute and percentage uncertainties

An uncertainty may be reported either as an absolute value, i.e.
1.23 ± 0.02 g, or as a percentage value, e.g. 1.23 g $\pm 2\%$.

The percentage uncertainty is worked out using the equation:

$$\text{percentage uncertainty} = \frac{\text{absolute uncertainty}}{\text{value}} \times 100$$

For example, for 0.257 ± 0.005 cm:

$$\text{percentage uncertainty} = \frac{0.005}{0.257} \times 100 = 2\%$$

The absolute uncertainty can be worked out from the percentage
uncertainty using the equation:

$$\text{absolute uncertainty} = \frac{\text{percentage uncertainty}}{100} \times \text{value}$$

For example, if the final value of a calculation is $0.518 \pm 1\%$:

$$\text{absolute uncertainty} = \frac{1}{100} \times 0.518 = 0.005$$

(to one significant figure). Therefore the final answer is 0.518 ± 0.005.

> The percentage uncertainty has
> no units.

Propagating uncertainties in calculations

Adding or subtracting

Worked example

Calculate the change in temperature from the following data:

	Value	Uncertainty
Maximum temperature / °C	57.58	±0.02
Initial temperature / °C	23.42	±0.02

> When quantities with uncertainties
> are added or subtracted, the **absolute**
> uncertainties are **added**.

change in temperature = maximum temperature − initial temperature

change in temperature = $57.58 - 23.42 = 34.16\,°C$

The uncertainty in the change in temperature is obtained by adding the uncertainty in the initial temperature to
the uncertainty in the maximum temperature:

uncertainty in change in temperature = $0.02 + 0.02 = 0.04\,°C$

Therefore the change in temperature is quoted as $34.16 \pm 0.04\,°C$.

That this is appropriate can be seen by considering maximum and minimum values of the temperature change.
Using the uncertainty we can see that the lowest value the initial temperature could have is:
$23.42 - 0.02 = 23.40\,°C$.

The highest maximum temperature is: $57.58 + 0.02 = 57.60\,°C$.

The largest value the temperature change could have is: $57.60 - 23.40 = 34.20\,°C$.

The highest value the initial temperature could have is: $23.42 + 0.02 = 23.44\,°C$.

The lowest maximum temperature is: $57.58 - 0.02 = 57.56\,°C$.

The smallest value the temperature change could have is: $57.56 - 23.44 = 34.12\,°C$.

The average of these two values is 34.16, and the range is from 34.12 to 34.20, so the temperature change should be quoted as $34.16 \pm 0.04\,°C$

Multiplying or dividing

Worked example

What is the absolute uncertainty when 2.57 ± 0.01 is multiplied by 3.456 ± 0.007 and to how many significant figures can the answer be quoted?

> When multiplying or dividing quantities with uncertainties, the **percentage** uncertainties should be added.

$2.57 \times 3.456 = 8.881\,92$

percentage uncertainties:

$$\frac{0.01}{2.57} \times 100 = 0.39\%$$
$$\frac{0.007}{3.456} \times 100 = 0.20\%$$

total percentage uncertainty $= 0.39 + 0.20 = 0.59\%$

To work out the absolute uncertainty of the final value, it is multiplied by its percentage uncertainty:

$$\text{absolute uncertainty} = \frac{0.59}{100} \times 8.88192 = 0.05$$

(to one significant figure). The absolute uncertainty is in the second decimal place, and therefore no figures should be quoted beyond that. The final answer should be quoted as 8.88 ± 0.05.

That this approach gives us valid answers can be justified by multiplying together the minimum values of the initial quantities and their maximum values:

minimum value $= 2.56 \times 3.449 = 8.83$

maximum value $= 2.58 \times 3.463 = 8.93$

The mean value of the final answer is 8.88, and the range is from 8.83 to 8.93, i.e. 8.88 ± 0.05.

> When multiplying or dividing a quantity with an uncertainty by a pure number, the absolute uncertainty is multiplied/divided by that number so that the **percentage uncertainty stays the same**.

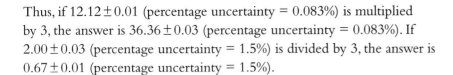

Thus, if 12.12 ± 0.01 (percentage uncertainty = 0.083%) is multiplied by 3, the answer is 36.36 ± 0.03 (percentage uncertainty = 0.083%). If 2.00 ± 0.03 (percentage uncertainty = 1.5%) is divided by 3, the answer is 0.67 ± 0.01 (percentage uncertainty = 1.5%).

> Sometimes the uncertainty in one quantity is so large relative to the uncertainties in other quantities that the uncertainty in the final value can be considered as arising just from this measurement.

Worked example

Weigh out accurately approximately 100 g of water in a polystyrene cup. Take the initial temperature of the water. Weigh out accurately approximately 6 g of potassium bromide. Add the potassium bromide to the water, stir rapidly until it has all dissolved and record the minimum temperature reached. Use the data below to work out the enthalpy change of solution to the appropriate number of significant figures.

mass of polystyrene cup / g	5.00 ± 0.01
mass of polystyrene cup + water / g	105.23 ± 0.01
initial temperature of water / °C	21.1 ± 0.1
minimum temperature of water / °C	19.0 ± 0.1
mass of weighing boat / g	0.50 ± 0.01
mass of weighing boat + potassium bromide / g	6.61 ± 0.01

The specific heat capacity of water $= 4.18 \, \mathrm{J\,g^{-1}\,^{\circ}C^{-1}}$.

mass of water $= (105.23 \pm 0.01) - (5.00 \pm 0.01) = 100.23 \pm 0.02 \, \mathrm{g}$

percentage uncertainty in mass of water $= \dfrac{0.02}{100.230} \times 100 = 0.02\%$

mass of KBr $= (6.61 \pm 0.01) - (0.50 \pm 0.01) = 6.11 \pm 0.02 \, \mathrm{g}$

percentage uncertainty in mass of KBr $= \dfrac{0.02}{6.11} \times 100 = 0.3\%$

change in temperature of water $= (21.1 \pm 0.1) - (19.0 \pm 0.1) = 2.1 \pm 0.2 \, ^{\circ}C$

percentage uncertainty in temperature change $= \dfrac{0.2}{2.1} \times 100 = 9.5\%$

The percentage uncertainty in the change in temperature is much larger than the other two uncertainties, and therefore we can assume that the uncertainty in the final value is also going to be about 9.5%.

heat taken in $= mc\Delta T = 100.23 \times 4.18 \times 2.1 = 879.82 \, \mathrm{J}$

no. moles of KCl $= \dfrac{6.11}{119.00} = 0.0513 \, \mathrm{mol}$

enthalpy change $= \dfrac{879.82}{0.0513} = 17150 \, \mathrm{J\,mol^{-1}} = 17.150 \, \mathrm{kJ\,mol^{-1}}$

We must now consider to how many significant figures the answer can be quoted. We will take the percentage uncertainty in the final answer as 9.5% and must work out 9.5% of 17.150.

$$\text{absolute uncertainty} = \frac{9.5}{100} \times 17.150 = 2 \text{ (to one significant figure).}$$

Therefore, the enthalpy change of solution should be quoted as $17 \pm 2\,\text{kJ mol}^{-1}$.

Working out the total percentage error as $(0.02 + 0.3 + 9.5)\%$ would have made no difference to the final value or uncertainty.

Self-test 1

Test yourself

6 Copy and complete the table:

0.345 ± 0.001	+	0.216 ± 0.002	=	
23.45 ± 0.03	–	15.23 ± 0.03	=	
0.0034 ± 0.0003	+	0.0127 ± 0.0003	=	
1.103 ± 0.004	–	0.823 ± 0.001	=	
1.10 ± 0.05	+	17.20 ± 0.05	=	

7 Copy and complete the table:

Value	Percentage uncertainty
27.2 ± 0.2	
0.576 ± 0.007	
4.46 ± 0.01	
$7.63 \times 10^{-5} \pm 4 \times 10^{-7}$	

8 a What is the absolute uncertainty when 2.13 ± 0.01 is multiplied by 4.328 ± 0.005? Give the final answer to the appropriate number of significant figures.

b What is the absolute uncertainty when 48.93 ± 0.02 is divided by 0.567 ± 0.003. Give the final answer to the appropriate number of significant figures.

9 Use the equation $E = mc\Delta T$ and the values in the table to calculate the energy released, to the appropriate number of significant figures, when a sample of a solution cools:

Mass of solution (m)	$43.27 \pm 0.01\,\text{g}$
Temperature change (ΔT)	22.8 ± 0.2
Specific heat capacity (c)	$4.2\,\text{J g}^{-1}\,^{\circ}\text{C}^{-1}$

11.3 Graphs

A graph is a very useful way to present the relationship between two quantities. Consider a graph of rate of reaction against concentration.

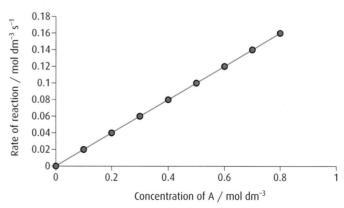

Figure 11.3 Rate of reaction against concentration for A → B.

Figure **11.3** shows a proportional (or directly proportional) relationship between the rate of reaction and the concentration. This can be seen, as the graph is a straight line passing through the origin.

If the concentration of A is doubled, the rate of reaction is doubled:

rate of reaction ∝ concentration

This graph has an equation of the form

$y = mx$

where m is the gradient (slope) of the line.

The graph in Figure **11.4** represents a linear (straight line) relationship. However the relationship between the two quantities here is **not** proportional, as the line does not pass through the origin. For this relationship, doubling the temperature will not cause the volume to be doubled. This graph has an equation of the form:

$y = mx + c$

Examiner's tip
Proportional and **directly proportional** mean the same thing.

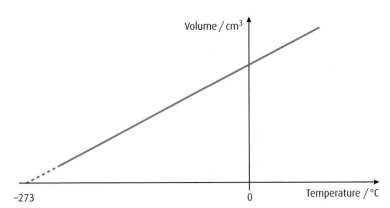

Figure 11.4 Volume versus temperature at constant pressure.

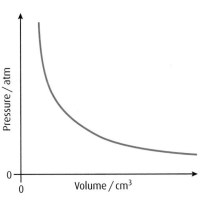

Figure 11.5 Pressure versus volume at constant temperature.

The relationship between volume and pressure, shown in Figure **11.5**, is an inversely proportional one:

$$\text{pressure} \propto \frac{1}{\text{volume}}$$

This means that doubling the volume causes the pressure to be halved, and vice versa.

That this is indeed an inversely proportional relationship can be confirmed by plotting pressure against $\frac{1}{\text{volume}}$. As pressure is proportional to $\frac{1}{\text{volume}}$, this graph should produce a straight line through the origin (Figure **11.6**).

The graph in Figure **11.7** (overleaf) shows that the rate of reaction increases as the concentration of A increases. The relationship between the two quantities is, however, not immediately obvious, other than that it is not a proportional relationship and that the rate of reaction more than doubles as the concentration of A doubles.

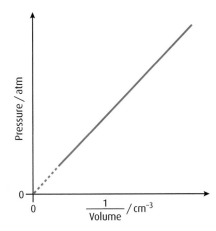

Figure 11.6 Pressure versus $\frac{1}{\text{volume}}$.

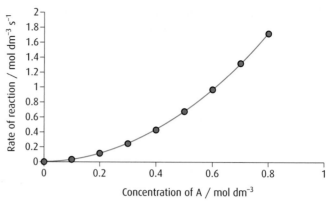

Figure 11.7 Rate of reaction against concentration of A.

Extension

This trial and error process can be laborious, and a shortcut is to plot log(rate of reaction) against log(concentration of A). In this case, a straight-line graph with gradient 2 will be obtained. The gradient indicates that the rate is proportional to the concentration of A to the power 2. This works for relationships of the form $y = x^n$. Either $\log_{10}$ or ln may be used.

We can, however, further analyse these data by trying out some relationships between the rate of reaction and concentration. If we try plotting the rate of reaction against (concentration of A)^2 (Figure **11.8**), we get a straight line through the origin.

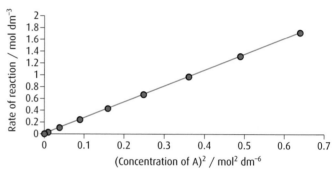

Figure 11.8 Rate of reaction against (concentration of A)^2.

The proportional relationship indicated by the straight line through the origin tells us that rate is proportional to (concentration of A)^2.

If this graph had not resulted in a straight line, we could have tried plotting rate against (concentration of A)^3, etc., until a proportional relationship was obtained.

Drawing graphs

There are several general rules for drawing graphs.

1 Make the graph as large as possible. Choose your scales and axes to retain the precision of your data as far as you can and to make the graph as easy as possible to interpret. A graph would usually be expected to fill most of a piece of graph paper. If the data are recorded as:

The independent variable is what has been changed in an experiment. The values of the independent variable are selected by the person carrying out the experiment.

Time / s	Temperature / °C
0	23.12
30	25.56
60	28.78
90	29.67
120	30.23

choosing a scale for the temperature where the smallest square is one unit would make it very difficult to plot 23.12 precisely. Ideally, if possible, one small square should represent one unit of the last significant figure of your data, i.e. 0.01 °C in this case. This may not be possible with the size of the piece of graph paper available, however!

2 The independent variable should be plotted along the horizontal (*x*) axis and the dependent variable should be plotted along the vertical (*y*) axis. For instance, consider how the rate of reaction between magnesium and hydrochloric acid is affected by changing the concentration of hydrochloric acid. You could conduct a series of experiments using different concentrations of hydrochloric acid and collecting the hydrogen given off every 30 seconds. The volume of hydrogen is the dependent variable, as it has been measured in the experiment, and the independent variable is the time, as its value has been set by the person carrying out the experiment. Thus a graph should be drawn with volume of hydrogen on the *y*-axis and time on the *x*-axis. Another graph could then also be drawn of the processed data; in this case, the rate of reaction would be plotted on the *y*-axis and the concentration of the acid on the *x*-axis.

3 Label the axes with the quantity and units. There are various conventions for laying out the units. One way that is commonly used is to have the quantity divided by the units, e.g. volume / cm^3 and pressure / 10^5 Pa. You could also put the units in brackets, e.g. volume (cm^3) and pressure (Pa).

4 Plot the points, which may be marked with a cross or as a dot with a circle around it.

5 Draw a line of best fit. This may be a straight line or a curve (Figure **11.9**) and should represent, as well as possible, the trend in the data. The points should be evenly distributed about the line. A line of best fit is very much a matter of judgement, and no two lines of best fit drawn by different people will be identical.

6 Give the graph a title describing what has been plotted.

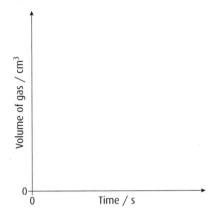

The dependent variable is what is measured in an experiment.

If the volume to be plotted is 23.0 cm^3, dividing by cm^3 gives the number 23.0, which will be plotted on the graph.

If the pressure to be plotted is 5.34×10^5 Pa, then dividing that by 10^5 Pa means that the number can be plotted on the graph as 5.34.

Do not join the points.

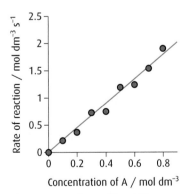

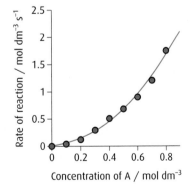

Figure 11.9 Lines of best fit.

The graphs shown here are for continuous data; that is, the quantities plotted can take any value. When discrete data are plotted a line of best fit should not be drawn, and points may be joined or the data could be plotted as a bar chart.

Deriving quantities from graphs

The gradient (slope) is one of the most important quantities that can be derived from a graph. The gradient gives us an idea how much one quantity (the dependent variable) is affected by another quantity (the independent variable). If the gradient is large, a small change in the independent variable has a large effect on the dependent variable. Sometimes the gradient can also have an important physical meaning, e.g. if a graph of the amount of a reactant or a product of a chemical reaction against time is plotted, the gradient represents the rate of the reaction.

Consider the graph of the volume of a fixed mass of gas against temperature shown in Figure **11.10**.

$$\text{gradient} = \frac{\text{change in } y}{\text{change in } x}$$

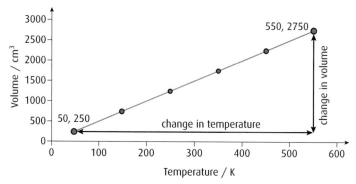

Figure 11.10 Volume versus temperature for a fixed mass of an ideal gas.

When determining the gradient from a straight-line graph, a triangle is drawn as shown in Figure **11.10**, and the change in the quantity on the vertical axis is divided by the change in the quantity on the horizontal axis. The triangle should be made as large as possible to minimise any uncertainties caused by reading from the graph.

$$\text{gradient} = \frac{\text{change in volume}}{\text{change in temperature}} = \frac{2750 - 250}{550 - 50} = 5$$

The units of the gradient are obtained by dividing the units of volume (y-axis) by the units of temperature (x-axis), i.e. cm^3/K or $cm^3\,K^{-1}$ in this case. Therefore the gradient (slope) of the line is $5\,cm^3\,K^{-1}$.

HL A common example of the use of the gradient to work out a particular physical quantity is in the determination of activation energy. A graph of the natural logarithm of the rate constant ($\ln k$) against the inverse of the temperature in kelvin ($1/T$) produces a straight-line graph (Figure **11.11**). The gradient of this graph is $-3010\,K$.

The relationship between $\ln k$ and $\frac{1}{T}$ is:

$$\ln k = \frac{-E_a}{R} \times \frac{1}{T} + \ln A$$

This can be compared to the equation of a straight line:

$$y = mx + c$$

$\ln k$ has no units and $1/(K^{-1})$ produces the units K.

$$\ln k = \frac{-E_a}{R} \times \frac{1}{T} + \ln A$$
$$y = m\,x + c$$

where y is $\ln k$ and x is $\frac{1}{T}$.

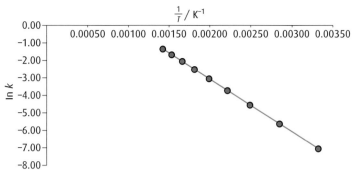

Figure 11.11 The label on the *y*-axis should more properly be ln (k/s^{-1}) (if the reaction is first order), showing that the natural log of the rate constant divided by its units is worked out to produce a pure number with no units.

The gradient of the line is equal to $\dfrac{-E_a}{R}$. Thus:

$$\dfrac{-E_a}{R} = -3010 \qquad \text{i.e. } E_a = 3010 \times R$$

i.e. $E_a = 3010 \times 8.31$ i.e. $E_a = 25\,000\,\mathrm{J\,mol^{-1}}$

i.e. the activation energy = $25\,\mathrm{kJ\,mol^{-1}}$.

The units of E_a are obtained as follows:

$$E_a = 3010 \times R$$

Substituting units into this equation:

$$E_a = \mathrm{K} \times \mathrm{J\,K^{-1}\,mol^{-1}}$$

K cancels with $\mathrm{K^{-1}}$, so the units of E_a are $\mathrm{J\,mol^{-1}}$, which can be converted to $\mathrm{kJ\,mol^{-1}}$.

Finding the gradient of a curve

A curved line has a constantly changing gradient, and therefore we can work out the gradient only at a particular point. This is done by drawing a tangent (straight line) to the curve at a particular point and working out the gradient of the tangent as normal.

In this graph the tangent is drawn at the initial point and the initial rate of reaction is the gradient of this tangent.

$$\text{gradient} = \dfrac{70 - 0}{32 - 0} = 2.2\,\mathrm{cm^3\,s^{-1}}$$

The initial rate of reaction is therefore $2.2\,\mathrm{cm^3\,s^{-1}}$.

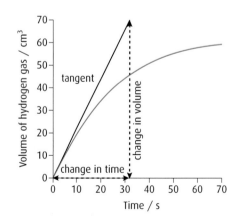

The tangent should be drawn as large as possible to minimise uncertainties caused by reading values off the graph.

1 Rosie carried out an experiment in which she measured a temperature change. Her data are shown in the table.

Initial temperature / °C	18.7 ± 0.5
Maximum temperature / °C	37.6 ± 0.5

The temperature change should be quoted as:

    A 18.9 ± 0.5 °C   **C** 18.9 ± 1.0 °C

    B 19 ± 1 °C   **D** 19.0 ± 1.0 °C

2 Jamal obtained the value $0.002\,560\,m^3$ from an experiment. The number of significant figures and decimal places is:

	Significant figures	Decimal places
A	4	6
B	6	4
C	6	6
D	3	6

3 Molly carried out an experiment to measure the enthalpy change of solution of a salt. In order to calculate a final value, the following calculation was carried out:

$$\frac{[(50 \pm 1) \times 4.2 \times (20 \pm 1)]}{1000 \times (0.10 \pm 0.01)}$$

Quantities without uncertainties can be assumed to be exact. How should the final value be quoted?

    A $-42 \pm 7\,kJ\,mol^{-1}$ **C** $-42.00 \pm 2.01\,kJ\,mol^{-1}$

    B $-42 \pm 2\,kJ\,mol^{-1}$ **D** $-42.1 \pm 7.1\,kJ\,mol^{-1}$

4 Which of the following would be a good method for reducing the random uncertainty in an experiment to measure the enthalpy change of neutralisation when $50\,cm^3$ of $0.50\,mol\,dm^{-3}$ sodium hydroxide reacts with $50\,cm^3$ of $0.50\,mol\,dm^{-3}$ hydrochloric acid?

    A insulate the reaction vessel with cotton wool

    B stir the mixture more rapidly

    C repeat the experiment

    D measure out the liquids using a $50\,cm^3$ measuring cylinder instead of a burette

5 The graph shows the results of a series of experiments to investigate how the rate of the reaction A → B varies with the concentration of A.

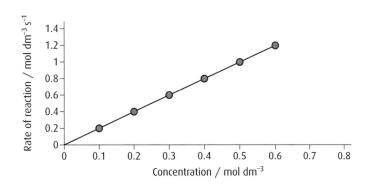

The gradient (slope) of this graph is

A $2.0\,\text{mol}\,\text{dm}^{-3}\,\text{s}^{-1}$ **C** $2.0\,\text{s}^{-1}$

B $0.5\,\text{s}$ **D** $0.5\,\text{mol}^{-1}\,\text{dm}^3$

6 Two separate experimental methods were used to determine the value of a particular experimental quantity. Each experiment was repeated five times. The values obtained from these experiments are shown in the table.

Experiment	1	2
Trial	Value	Value
1	49.7	50.6
2	53.2	51.2
3	51.5	51.1
4	52.3	50.8
5	49.2	51.0

The literature value for this quantity is 50.9.

a Explain which set of experimental values is more precise.   [2]

b Work out a mean value for each experiment and use this to explain which set of data is more accurate.   [3]

7 Lai Ping carried out an experiment to measure a certain quantity. The value she obtained was $56.1 \pm 0.5\,\text{kJ}$. The literature value for this quantity is $55.2\,\text{kJ}$.

a Calculate the percentage error for this experiment.   [1]

b The student maintained that any errors could be explained solely by random uncertainties. Is she correct? Explain.   [2]

8 Tyrone carried out an experiment to measure the rate of the reaction between magnesium and hydrochloric acid. He did this by recording the volume of hydrogen gas collected every 15 s. The student's data are shown in the table.

Time / s	Volume ± 1 / cm³
0	0
15	19
30	33
45	44
60	50
75	54
90	56
105	57
120	57

a Plot a graph of these data.   [3]

b Use your graph to determine the initial rate of reaction with units.   [3]

Summary

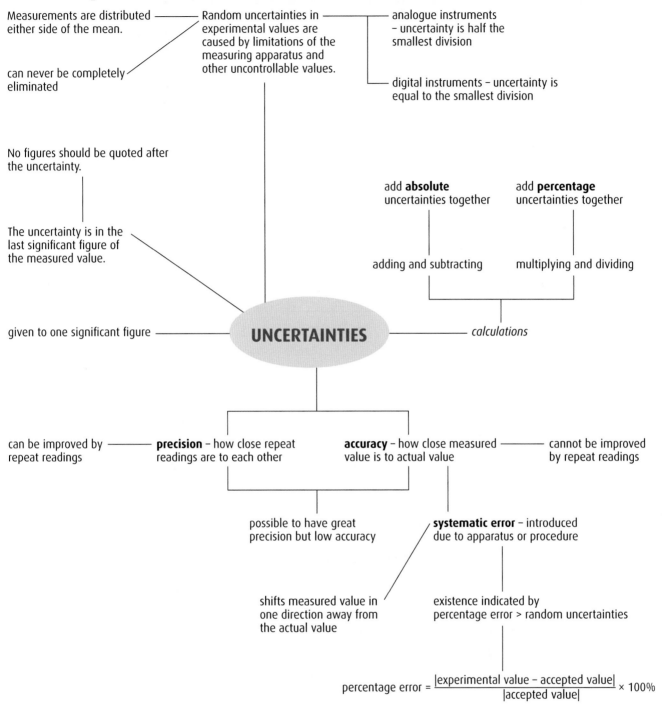

Measurements are distributed either side of the mean.

can never be completely eliminated

Random uncertainties in experimental values are caused by limitations of the measuring apparatus and other uncontrollable values.

analogue instruments – uncertainty is half the smallest division

digital instruments – uncertainty is equal to the smallest division

No figures should be quoted after the uncertainty.

The uncertainty is in the last significant figure of the measured value.

add **absolute** uncertainties together

add **percentage** uncertainties together

adding and subtracting

multiplying and dividing

given to one significant figure

UNCERTAINTIES

calculations

can be improved by repeat readings

precision – how close repeat readings are to each other

accuracy – how close measured value is to actual value

cannot be improved by repeat readings

possible to have great precision but low accuracy

systematic error – introduced due to apparatus or procedure

shifts measured value in one direction away from the actual value

existence indicated by percentage error > random uncertainties

$$\text{percentage error} = \frac{|\text{experimental value} - \text{accepted value}|}{|\text{accepted value}|} \times 100\%$$

Appendix: the periodic table

Key

| relative atomic mass |
| **atomic symbol** |
| name |
| atomic number |

| 1.01 |
| **H** |
| hydrogen |
| 1 |

Group

I	II	III	IV	V	VI	VII	0
							4.00 **He** helium 2
6.94 **Li** lithium 3	9.01 **Be** beryllium 4	10.81 **B** boron 5	12.01 **C** carbon 6	14.01 **N** nitrogen 7	16.00 **O** oxygen 8	19.00 **F** fluorine 9	20.18 **Ne** neon 10
22.99 **Na** sodium 11	24.31 **Mg** magnesium 12	26.98 **Al** aluminium 13	28.09 **Si** silicon 14	30.97 **P** phosphorus 15	32.06 **S** sulfur 16	35.45 **Cl** chlorine 17	39.95 **Ar** argon 18

Transition elements

39.10 **K** potassium 19	40.08 **Ca** calcium 20
85.47 **Rb** rubidium 37	87.62 **Sr** strontium 38
132.91 **Cs** caesium 55	137.34 **Ba** barium 56
(223) **Fr** francium 87	(226) **Ra** radium 88

44.96 **Sc** scandium 21	47.90 **Ti** titanium 22	50.94 **V** vanadium 23	52.00 **Cr** chromium 24	54.94 **Mn** manganese 25	55.85 **Fe** iron 26	58.93 **Co** cobalt 27	58.71 **Ni** nickel 28	63.55 **Cu** copper 29	65.37 **Zn** zinc 30
88.91 **Y** yttrium 39	91.22 **Zr** zirconium 40	92.91 **Nb** niobium 41	95.94 **Mo** molybdenum 42	98.91 **Tc** technetium 43	101.07 **Ru** ruthenium 44	102.91 **Rh** rhodium 45	106.42 **Pd** palladium 46	107.87 **Ag** silver 47	112.40 **Cd** cadmium 48
138.91 * **La** lanthanum 57	178.49 **Hf** hafnium 72	180.95 **Ta** tantalum 73	183.85 **W** tungsten 74	186.21 **Re** rhenium 75	190.21 **Os** osmium 76	192.22 **Ir** iridium 77	195.09 **Pt** platinum 78	196.97 **Au** gold 79	200.59 **Hg** mercury 80
(227) ** **Ac** actinium 89									

Group III–0 (lower rows):

III	IV	V	VI	VII	0
69.72 **Ga** gallium 31	72.59 **Ge** germanium 32	74.92 **As** arsenic 33	78.96 **Se** selenium 34	79.90 **Br** bromine 35	83.80 **Kr** krypton 36
114.82 **In** indium 49	118.69 **Sn** tin 50	121.75 **Sb** antimony 51	127.60 **Te** tellurium 52	126.90 **I** iodine 53	131.30 **Xe** xenon 54
204.37 **Tl** thallium 81	207.19 **Pb** lead 82	208.98 **Bi** bismuth 83	(210) **Po** polonium 84	(210) **At** astatine 85	(222) **Rn** radon 86

lanthanides *

140.12 **Ce** cerium 58	140.91 **Pr** praseodymium 59	144.24 **Nd** neodymium 60	146.92 **Pm** promethium 61	150.35 **Sm** samarium 62	151.96 **Eu** europium 63	157.25 **Gd** gadolinium 64	158.92 **Tb** terbium 65	162.50 **Dy** dysprosium 66	164.93 **Ho** holmium 67	167.26 **Er** erbium 68	168.93 **Tm** thulium 69	173.04 **Yb** ytterbium 70	174.97 **Lu** lutetium 71

actinides * *

232.04 **Th** thorium 90	231.04 **Pa** protactinium 91	238.03 **U** uranium 92	(237) **Np** neptunium 93	(244) **Pu** plutonium 94	(243) **Am** americium 95	(247) **Cm** curium 96	(247) **Bk** berkelium 97	(251) **Cf** californium 98	(254) **Es** einsteinium 99	(257) **Fm** fermium 100	(258) **Md** mendelevium 101	(259) **No** nobelium 102	(260) **Lr** lawrencium 103

Glossary

absolute scale of temperature Kelvin scale of temperature, which starts at absolute zero; $1\,^{\circ}\text{C}$ is the same as $1\,\text{K}$ and so $0\,^{\circ}\text{C}$ is equivalent to $273\,\text{K}$

absolute zero the temperature at which everything would be in its lowest energy state $0\,\text{K}$ or $-273\,^{\circ}\text{C}$

accuracy how close a measurement is to the actual value of a particular quantity

acid dissociation constant (K_a) in general, for the dissociation of acid HA: $\text{HA(aq)} \rightleftharpoons \text{H}^+\text{(aq)} + \text{A}^-\text{(aq)}$ the expression for the acid dissociation constant is:
$$K_a = \frac{[\text{A}^-\text{(aq)}][\text{H}^+\text{(aq)}]}{[\text{HA(aq)}]}$$
the higher the value of K_a, the stronger the acid

activation energy (E_a) the minimum energy that colliding species must have before collision results in a chemical reaction

addition polymerisation alkenes undergo addition polymerisation, in which a large number of monomers are joined together into a polymer chain; no other groups are lost in the process

addition reaction in organic chemistry, a reaction in which a molecule is added to a compound containing a multiple bond without the loss of any other groups

alkali a base that is dissolved in water

alkali metal the elements in group 1 of the periodic table

allotropes different forms of the same element; e.g. diamond, graphite and fullerene are allotropes of carbon

anode the electrode at which oxidation occurs

Arrhenius equation an equation showing the variation of the rate constant with temperature:
$$k = A\text{e}^{-E_a/RT}$$
'A' is the frequency factor or pre-exponential factor and contains information related to the frequency of collisions and the orientation of the collisions

atom the smallest part of an element that can still be recognised as the element; in the simplest picture of the atom, the electrons orbit around the central nucleus; the nucleus is made up of protons and neutrons (except for a hydrogen atom, which has no neutrons)

atomic number (Z) the number of protons in the nucleus of an atom

atomic radius half the internuclear distance between two atoms of the same element covalently bonded; atomic radius is usually called 'covalent radius' in more advanced work; it is also possible for an element to have a 'van der Waals' radius'

Aufbau principle the process of putting electrons into atoms to generate the electronic configuration

average bond enthalpy the average amount of energy required to break one mole of covalent bonds, in a gaseous molecule under standard conditions; 'average' refers to the fact that the bond enthalpy is different in different molecules, and therefore the value quoted is the average amount of energy to break a particular bond in a range of molecules; bond breaking requires energy (endothermic) ΔH +ve; bond making releases energy (exothermic) ΔH −ve

Avogadro's constant (L) $6.02 \times 10^{23}\,\text{mol}^{-1}$

Avogadro's law equal volumes of ideal gases measured at the same temperature and pressure contain the same number of molecules

base ionisation constant (K_b) consider the ionisation of a weak base, $\text{B(aq)} + \text{H}_2\text{O(l)} \rightleftharpoons \text{BH}^+\text{(aq)} + \text{OH}^-\text{(aq)}$:
$$K_b = \frac{[\text{BH}^+\text{(aq)}][\text{OH}^-\text{(aq)}]}{[\text{B(aq)}]}$$
the higher the value of K_b, the stronger the base

boiling point the boiling point of a liquid is the temperature at which the vapour pressure of the liquid equals the external pressure

Born–Haber cycle an enthalpy level diagram breaking down the formation of an ionic compound into a series of simpler steps

Brønsted–Lowry definition of acids and bases an acid is a proton (H^+) donor; a base/alkali is a proton (H^+) acceptor

buffer solution is one that resists changes in pH when small amounts of acid or alkali are added

catalyst a substance that increases the rate of a chemical reaction without itself being used up in the reaction; a catalyst acts by allowing the reaction to proceed by an alternative pathway of lower activation energy

cathode the electrode at which reduction occurs

chain reaction one initial event causes a large number of subsequent reactions – the reactive species is regenerated in each cycle of reactions

chemical properties how a substance behaves in chemical reactions

chiral centre a carbon atom with four different atoms or groups attached to it; sometimes called an asymmetric carbon atom

closed system no exchange of matter with the surroundings

collision theory a reaction can occur only when two particles collide in the correct orientation and with $E \geq E_a$

concentration amount of solute dissolved in a unit volume of solution; the volume that is usually taken is $1\,\text{dm}^3$ (1 litre); the amount of solute may be expressed in g or mol, so the units of concentration are $\text{g}\,\text{dm}^{-3}$ or $\text{mol}\,\text{dm}^{-3}$

condensation polymerisation a water molecule is eliminated each time two monomers are joined together to form a chain; two functional groups are required on each monomer

condensation reaction reaction in which two molecules join together with the elimination of the elements of water

conjugate acid–base pair   these differ by one proton (H^+); when an acid donates a proton it forms the conjugate base (CH_3COO^- is the conjugate base of CH_3COOH); when a base gains a proton it forms the conjugate acid (H_3O^+ is the conjugate acid of H_2O)

Contact process   an industrial process for the manufacture of sulfuric acid

continuous spectrum   a spectrum consisting of all frequencies/wavelengths of light

convergence limit   the point in a line emission spectrum where the lines merge to form a continuum; may be used to determine the ionisation energy

covalent bond   the electrostatic attraction between a shared pair of electrons and the nuclei of the atoms making up the bond

dative covalent bond   a type of covalent bond in which both electrons come from the same atom

degenerate   describes orbitals with the same energy

delocalisation   the sharing of a pair of electrons between three or more atoms

dipole moment   the product of one of the charges making up a dipole and the distance between the charges; non-polar molecules have a zero dipole moment

diprotic acid H_2SO_4 is a diprotic acid, as it can dissociate to form two protons per molecule:

$$H_2SO_4(aq) + H_2O(l) \rightarrow HSO_4^-(aq) + H_3O^+(aq)$$
$$HSO_4^-(aq) + H_2O(l) \rightleftharpoons SO_4^{2-}(aq) + H_3O^+(aq)$$

dynamic equilibrium   macroscopic properties are constant; rate of the forward reaction is equal to the rate of the reverse reaction

electrolysis   the breaking down of a substance (in molten state or solution) by the passage of electricity through it

electrolyte   a solution, or a molten compound, that will conduct electricity with decomposition at the electrodes as it does so; electrolytes contain ions that are free to move towards the electrodes

electronegativity   a measure of the attraction of an atom in a molecule for the electron pair in the covalent bond of which it is a part

electrophile   a reagent (a positively charged ion or the positive end of a dipole) that is attracted to regions of high electron density and accepts a pair of electrons to form a covalent bond

electroplating   the process of coating an object with a thin layer of a metal using electrolysis

electrostatic attraction   attraction between positive and negative charges

element   a substance containing just one type of atom (although see **isotopes**)

emission spectrum of an atom   electromagnetic radiation given out when an electron falls from a higher energy level to a lower one; only certain frequencies of electromagnetic radiation are emitted; each atom has a different emission spectrum

empirical formula   the simplest whole number ratio of the elements present in a compound

enantiomers   optical isomers

endothermic reaction   a chemical reaction in which heat is taken in from the surroundings – the reaction vessel gets colder; ΔH for an endothermic reaction is positive

end point of a titration   the point at which an indicator changes colour

enthalpy change (ΔH)   the heat energy exchanged with the surroundings at constant pressure

enthalpy change of hydration (ΔH_{hyd})   the enthalpy change when 1 mole of gaseous ions are surrounded by water molecules to form an 'infinitely dilute solution' under standard conditions:

$$Na^+(g) \xrightarrow[\text{excess } H_2O]{\Delta H_{hyd}} Na^+(aq)$$

this is an exothermic process

enthalpy change of neutralisation (ΔH_n)   the enthalpy change when 1 mole of H_2O molecules are formed when an acid (H^+) reacts with an alkali (OH^-) under standard conditions, i.e.:

$$H^+(aq) + OH^-(aq) \rightarrow H_2O(l)$$

the enthalpy change of neutralisation is always exothermic

enthalpy change of solution (ΔH_{sol})   the enthalpy change when 1 mole of solute is dissolved in excess solvent to form a solution of 'infinite dilution' under standard conditions, e.g.:

$$NH_4NO_3(s) \xrightarrow{\text{excess } H_2O} NH_4^+(aq) + NO_3^-(aq)$$

'infinite dilution' means that any further dilution of the solution produces no further enthalpy change, i.e. the solute particles are assumed not to interact with each other in the solution; the enthalpy change of solution may be exothermic or endothermic

entropy (S)   a measure of the randomness or disorder of a system; standard entropy ($S^\ominus$) is the entropy of a substance at 1 atm and 298 K; units are $J\,K^{-1}\,mol^{-1}$; $\Delta S^\ominus$ is the entropy change under standard conditions – a positive value indicates an increase in entropy, i.e. an increase in disorder

equivalence point of a titration   the point at which equivalent numbers of moles of acid and alkali have been added

exothermic reaction   a chemical reaction that results in the release of heat to the surroundings – the reaction vessel gets hotter; ΔH for an exothermic reaction is negative

first electron affinity   enthalpy change when one electron is added to each atom in one mole of gaseous atoms under standard conditions:

$$X(g) + e^- \rightarrow X^-(g)$$

the first electron affinity is exothermic for virtually all elements

free energy change (ΔG)   or Gibbs free energy change; ΔG is related to the entropy change of the Universe and can be defined using the equation:

$$\Delta G = \Delta H - T\Delta S$$

for a reaction to be spontaneous, ΔG for the reaction must be negative; $\Delta G^\ominus$ is the standard free energy change

free radical   a species (atom or groups of atoms) with an unpaired electron; free radicals are very reactive because of this unpaired electron

functional group   an atom or group of atoms that gives an organic molecule its characteristic chemical properties

geometrical isomers   compounds that have the same structural formula but with groups arranged differently in space about a double bond or a ring

giant structure   bonding extends fairly uniformly throughout the whole structure; there are no individual molecules

group   vertical column in the periodic table

Haber (Haber–Bosch) process   an industrial process for the manufacture of ammonia

halogens   the elements in group 7 of the periodic table

Hess's law   the enthalpy change accompanying a chemical reaction is independent of the pathway between the initial and final states

heterolytic fission   a covalent bond breaks so that both electrons go to the same atom

homologous series   a series of compounds with the same functional group, in which each member differs from the next by $-CH_2-$

homolytic fission   a covalent bond breaks such that one electron goes back to each atom making up the original covalent bond

Hund's rule   electrons fill orbitals of the same energy (degenerate orbitals) so as to give the maximum number of electrons with the same spins

hybridisation   the mixing of atomic orbitals when a compound forms to produce a new set of orbitals (the same number as originally), which are better arranged in space for covalent bonding

hydrocarbon   compound containing carbon and hydrogen only

hydrogenation   addition of hydrogen (H_2) to a compound containing multiple bonds

hydrogen bonding   an intermolecular force resulting from the interaction of a lone pair on a very electronegative atom (N/O/F) in one molecule with an H atom attached to N/O/F in another molecule; these forces may also occur intramolecularly

hydrolysis   a reaction in which a bond in a molecule is broken by reaction with water; most commonly hydrolysis reactions occur when a molecule is reacted with aqueous acid or aqueous alkali

ideal gas   a theoretical model that approximates the behaviour of real gases; it can be defined in terms of macroscopic properties (a gas that obeys the equation $PV = nRT$) or in terms of microscopic properties (the main assumptions that define an ideal gas on a microscopic scale are that the molecules are point masses – their volume is negligible compared with the volume of the container – and that there are no intermolecular forces except during a collision)

indicator   an acid–base indicator has different colours according to the pH of the solution; indicators are usually weak acids (HIn); they dissociate according to the equation:
$$HIn(aq) \rightleftharpoons H^+(aq) + In^-(aq)$$
Colour I   Colour II
the ionised (In^-) and un-ionised (HIn) forms must have different colours

initiation step   a step that starts off a chain reaction; it involves an increase in the number of free radicals

intermolecular forces   forces between molecules

intramolecular forces   forces within a molecule – usually covalent bonding

ion   a charged particle that is formed when an atom loses or gains electron(s); a positive ion is formed when an atom loses (an) electron(s) and a negative ion is formed when an atom gains (an) electron(s)

ionic bonding   the electrostatic attraction between oppositely charged ions

ionic product constant (K_w)   a modified equilibrium constant for the dissociation of water:
$$K_w = [H^+(aq)][OH^-(aq)]$$
K_w has a value of $1.0 \times 10^{-14} \, mol^2 \, dm^{-6}$ at $25\,°C$

ionisation energy   the minimum amount of energy required to remove an electron from a gaseous atom/the energy required to remove one electron from each atom in one mole of gaseous atoms under standard conditions

isoelectronic   describes species with the same number of electrons

isotopes   different atoms of the same element with different mass numbers, i.e. different numbers of neutrons in the nucleus

lattice enthalpy ($\Delta H^{\ominus}_{latt}$)   the enthalpy change when one mole of ionic compound is broken apart into its constituent gaseous ions under standard conditions, e.g. for NaCl:
$$NaCl(s) \rightarrow Na^+(g) + Cl^-(g) \qquad \Delta H_{latt} = +771 \, kJ \, mol^{-1}$$
lattice enthalpy can be defined in either direction, i.e. as the making or breaking of the lattice

lattice structure   regular 3D arrangement

Le Chatelier's principle   if a system at equilibrium is subjected to some change, the position of equilibrium will shift in order to minimise the effect of the change

Lewis definition of acids and bases   an **ac**id is an electron pair **ac**ceptor; a base is an electron pair donor

Lewis (electron dot) structure   diagrams showing all the valence (outer shell) electrons in a molecule (or ion)

ligands   negative ions or neutral molecules that use lone pairs of electrons to bond to a transition metal ion to form a complex ion; dative covalent bonds (coordinate links) are formed between the ligand and the transition metal ion

limiting reactant   the reactant that is used up first in a chemical reaction; when the number of moles of each species is divided by their coefficient in the stoichiometric equation, the limiting reagent is the one with the lowest number; all other reactants are in excess

line spectrum   the emission spectrum of an atom consists of a series of lines that get closer together at higher frequency; only certain frequencies/wavelengths of light are present

lone pair   a pair of electrons in the outer shell of an atom that is not involved in covalent bonding

mass number (A)   the number of protons + neutrons in the nucleus of an atom

Maxwell–Boltzmann distribution   a graph showing the distribution of molecular kinetic energies in a sample of gas at a particular temperature

metallic bonding   the electrostatic attraction between the positive ions in a metallic lattice and the delocalised electrons

molar volume   the volume occupied by 1 mole of a gas; the molar volume of an ideal gas at STP is $22.4 \, dm^3 \, mol^{-1}$

mole   the amount of substance that contains the same number of particles (atoms, ions, molecules, etc.) as there are carbon atoms in 12 g of carbon-12 (6.02×10^{23})

molecular formula   the total number of atoms of each element present in a molecule of the compound; the molecular formula is a multiple of the empirical formula

monomer   a molecule from which a polymer chain may be built up, e.g. ethene is the monomer for poly(ethene)

monoprotic acid   HCl is a monoprotic acid as it dissociates to form one proton per molecule

noble gases   the elements in group 0 of the periodic table; also sometimes called the 'inert gases'

nucleophile   a molecule/negatively charged ion, possessing a lone pair of electrons, which is attracted to a more positively charged region in a molecule (region with lower electron density) and donates a lone pair of electrons to form a covalent bond

nucleophilic substitution   e.g. a halogenoalkane is attacked by a nucleophile, and the nucleophile replaces the halogen atom

optical isomers   these have the same molecular and structural formula, but the individual optical isomers are non-superimposable mirror images of each other; optical isomers rotate the plane of plane-polarised light in opposite directions

orbital   a region of space in which there is a high probability of finding an electron; it represents a discrete energy level; there are s, p, d and f orbitals; any orbital can contain a maximum of two electrons

order of a reaction   the power of the concentration of a particular reactant in the experimentally determined rate equation

overall order of reaction   the sum of the powers of the concentration terms in the experimentally determined rate equation

oxidation state   a purely formal concept that regards all compounds as ionic and assigns charges to the components accordingly; it provides a guide to the distribution of electrons and relative charges on atoms in covalent compounds

oxidation   loss of electrons or increase in oxidation number

oxidising agent (oxidant)   oxidises other species and, in the process, is itself reduced; an oxidising agent takes electrons away from something

Pauli exclusion principle   two electrons in the same orbital must have opposite spins

percentage error $\dfrac{|\text{experimental value} - \text{accepted value}|}{|\text{accepted value}|} \times 100$

percentage uncertainty $\dfrac{\text{uncertainty}}{\text{measured value}} \times 100$

when multiplying or dividing quantities with uncertainties, the percentage uncertainties should be added to give the percentage uncertainty of the final value

period   horizontal row in the periodic table

pH   a measure of the concentration of H^+ ions in an aqueous solution; it can be defined as the negative logarithm to base 10 of the hydrogen ion concentration in aqueous solution: $pH = -\log_{10}[H^+(aq)]$

pH meter   an electronic device for measuring the pH of a solution

pH range of an indicator   the pH range over which intermediate colours for an indicator can be seen

physical properties   properties such as melting point, solubility and electrical conductivity, relating to the physical state of a substance and the physical changes it can undergo

pi (π) bond   bond formed by the sideways overlap of parallel p orbitals; the electron density in the pi bond lies above and below the internuclear axis

plane-polarised light   light that vibrates in one plane only; optical isomers rotate the plane of plane-polarised light in opposite directions

polar molecule   molecule in which one end is slightly positive relative to the other; whether a molecule is polar or not depends on the differences in electronegativity of the atoms and the shape of the molecule

precision   relates to the reproducibility of results; if a series of readings is taken with high precision, it indicates that the repeated values are all very close together and close to the mean (average) value

propagation step   a step in a free radical substitution reaction that involves production of products and no change in the number of free radicals

radioisotopes   radioactive isotopes

random uncertainty   uncertainty in a measurement due to the limitations of the measuring apparatus and other uncontrollable variables that are inevitable in any experiment; the effects of random uncertainties should mean that the measurements taken will be distributed either side of the mean, i.e. fluctuations will be in both directions; the effect of random uncertainties can be reduced by repeating the measurements more often, but random uncertainties can never be completely eliminated

rate constant (k) a constant of proportionality relating the concentrations in the experimentally determined rate expression to the rate of a chemical reaction; the rate constant is only a constant for a particular reaction at a particular temperature

rate expression an experimentally determined equation that relates the rate of reaction to the concentrations of substances in the reaction mixture, e.g.: rate = $k[A]^m[B]^n$

rate of reaction the speed at which reactants are used up or products are formed; or, more precisely, the change in concentration of reactants or products per unit time:

$$\text{average rate} = \frac{\text{change in concentration}}{\text{time}}$$

reducing agent (reductant) reduces other species and, in the process, is itself oxidised; a reducing agent gives electrons to something

reduction gain of electrons or decrease in oxidation number

relative atomic mass (A_r) the average mass of the naturally occurring isotopes of the element relative to the mass of $\frac{1}{12}$ of an atom of carbon-12

relative formula mass if a compound contains ions, the relative formula mass is the mass of the formula unit relative to the mass of $\frac{1}{12}$ of an atom of carbon-12

relative molecular mass (M_r) the mass of a molecule of a compound relative to the mass of $\frac{1}{12}$ of an atom of carbon-12; the M_r is the sum of the relative atomic masses for the individual atoms making up a molecule

repeat unit (repeating unit) of a polymer the basic unit from which the whole polymer chain can be made up

salt bridge completes the circuit by providing an electrical connection between two half cells, allowing ions to flow into or out of the half cells to balance out the charges in the half cells; the salt bridge contains a concentrated solution of an ionic salt such as KCl

saturated compounds carbon compounds containing only single bonds

second electron affinity enthalpy change for the process:
$$X^-(g) + e^- \rightarrow X^{2-}(g)$$
the second electron affinity is always endothermic

sigma (σ) bond bond formed by the axial (head-on) overlap of atomic orbitals; the electron distribution in a sigma bond lies mostly along the axis joining the two nuclei

S$_N$1 a unimolecular nucleophilic substitution reaction – only one species involved in the rate-determining step

S$_N$2 a bimolecular nucleophilic substitution reaction – two species involved in the rate-determining step

solute one substance that is dissolved in another

solution that which is formed when a solute dissolves in a solvent

solvent a substance that dissolves another substance (the solute); the solvent should be present in excess of the solute

specific heat capacity the energy required to raise the temperature of 1 g of substance by 1 K (1 °C) – units $J\,g^{-1}\,°C^{-1}$; it can also be defined in terms of 'unit mass' with different units

spontaneous reaction one that occurs without any outside influence, i.e. no input of energy

stability usually refers to the relative energies of reactants and products – if the products are at lower enthalpy (energy) than the reactants, then they are more stable; it is also possible to define kinetic stability

standard conditions a common set of conditions used to compare enthalpy changes; in this course they are taken as 1.01×10^5 Pa (1 atmosphere) for pressure, and 298 K (25 °C) for temperature

standard electrode potential the emf (voltage) of a half cell connected to a standard hydrogen electrode, measured under standard conditions; all solutions must be of concentration $1\,mol\,dm^{-3}$

standard enthalpy change of combustion ($\Delta H_c^\ominus$) the enthalpy change (heat given out) when 1 mole of a substance is completely burnt in oxygen under standard conditions (298 K and 1 atm pressure)

standard enthalpy change of formation ($\Delta H_f^\ominus$) the enthalpy change when 1 mole of the substance is formed from its elements in their standard states under standard conditions (298 K and 1 atm pressure); $\Delta H_f^\ominus$ for any element in its standard state is zero

standard enthalpy change of reaction ($\Delta H_r^\ominus$) the enthalpy change (heat given out or taken in) when molar amounts of reactants as shown in the stoichiometric equation react together under standard conditions to give products

standard enthalpy change of vaporisation ($\Delta H_{vap}^\ominus$) the energy needed to convert 1 mole of a liquid to vapour under standard conditions

standard free energy of formation ($\Delta G_f^\ominus$) is the free energy change for the formation of 1 mole of substance from its elements in their standard states and under standard conditions (1 atm and 298 K)

standard hydrogen electrode the standard half cell relative to which standard electrode potentials are measured

standard state the state in which a substance exists under standard conditions, e.g. for iodine it is $I_2(s)$ but for nitrogen it is $N_2(g)$; more precisely the standard state is the pure substance at 1 atm and a specified temperature (assume 298 K)

standard temperature and pressure (STP) 273 K, 1 atmosphere pressure

state symbols used to indicate the physical state of an element or compound; these may be either written as subscripts after the chemical formula or in normal type (aq) = aqueous (dissolved in water); (g) = gas; (l) = liquid; (s) = solid

stereoisomers molecules with the same molecular formula and structural formula but the atoms are arranged differently in space; geometrical isomers and optical isomers are stereoisomers

strong acid an acid such as HCl, H_2SO_4, HNO_3 that dissociates completely in aqueous solution:
$$HCl(aq) \rightarrow H^+(aq) + Cl^-(aq)$$
strong acids are also strong electrolytes

strong base a base that ionises completely in aqueous solution; strong bases are the group 1 hydroxides (LiOH, NaOH, etc.) and Ba(OH)$_2$; strong bases are also strong electrolytes

strong electrolyte a substance that dissolves in water with complete ionisation; e.g. NaCl separates completely into its ions when it dissolves in water; strong acids are strong electrolytes because they dissociate completely into ions

structural isomers two or more compounds that have the same molecular formula but different structural formulas, i.e. the atoms are joined together in a different way

subshell/sub-level a group of degenerate orbitals in an atom; a p subshell is made up of the p_x, p_y and p_z orbitals

substitution reaction a reaction in which one atom or group is replaced by another atom or group

systematic error an error introduced into an experiment due to the apparatus used or the procedure; systematic errors result in a loss of accuracy, i.e. the measured value being further away from the true value; systematic errors are always in the same direction; the effect of a systematic error cannot be reduced by repeating the readings

termination step the step that ends a chain reaction – involves a decrease in the number of free radicals

titration a technique that involves adding measured amounts of a solution (from a burette) to another solution to determine the amounts that react exactly with each other

transition elements the elements in the central part of the periodic table; there are various ways of defining a transition element; the definition used in the IB course is 'an element which forms at least one stable oxidation state (other than 0) with a partially filled d subshell'

transition state (activated complex) the highest energy species on the reaction pathway between reactants and products; the highest point on an energy level/enthalpy level diagram

unsaturated compounds carbon compounds containing multiple bonds; this term is often just applied to compounds containing C=C and C≡C, but it is more widely applicable and compounds containing, e.g., C=O are also unsaturated

valence shell electron pair repulsion (VSEPR) theory a technique for working out the shapes of molecules/ions; pairs of electrons in the valence (outer) shell of an atom repel each other and therefore take up positions in space to minimise these repulsions, i.e. to be as far apart in space as possible

van der Waals' forces intermolecular forces resulting from temporary (instantaneous) dipole-induced dipole interactions

vapour pressure the pressure exerted by a vapour in equilibrium with a liquid (or a solid); the vapour pressure depends only on the nature of the liquid and the temperature

volatility how readily a substance evaporates

water of crystallisation water that is present in definite proportions in the crystals of hydrated salts, e.g. $CuSO_4.5H_2O$. The water may or may not be directly bonded to the metal (in hydrated copper sulfate four water molecules are bonded to the copper ion and one is not)

weak acid an acid such as a carboxylic acid (ethanoic acid, propanoic acid, etc.) or carbonic acid (H_2CO_3) that dissociates partially in aqueous solution:
$$CH_3COOH(aq) \rightleftharpoons H^+(aq) + CH_3COO^-(aq)$$
weak acids are also weak electrolytes

weak base a base that ionises partially in aqueous solution, e.g. ammonia and amines:
$$NH_3(aq) + H_2O(l) \rightleftharpoons NH_4^+(aq) + OH^-(aq)$$
weak bases are also weak electrolytes

yield the amount of product obtained from a chemical reaction; theoretical yield is the maximum possible amount of product formed; actual yield is the actual amount of product formed in the reaction:
$$\text{percentage yield} = \frac{\text{actual yield}}{\text{theoretical yield}} \times 100$$

Index

Terms and conditions of use for the CD-ROM

This is a legal agreement between 'You' (which means the individual customer or the Educational Institution and its authorised users) and Cambridge University press ('the Licensor') for *Chemistry for the IB Diploma CD-ROM*. By placing this CD in the CD-ROM drive of your computer, You agree to the terms of this licence.

1 Limited licence

a You are purchasing only the right to use the CD-ROM and are acquiring no rights, express or implied, to it, other than those rights granted in this limited licence for not-for-profit educational use only.

b The Licensor grants You the licence to use one copy of this CD-ROM.

c You shall not: (**i**) copy or authorise copying of the CD-ROM, (**ii**) translate the CD-ROM, (**iii**) reverse-engineer, alter, adapt, disassemble or decompile the CD-ROM, (**iv**) transfer, sell, lease, lend, profit from, assign or otherwise convey all or any portion of the CD-ROM or (**v**) operate the CD-ROM from a mainframe system, except as provided in these terms and conditions.

d Permission is explicitly granted for use of the CD-ROM on a data projector, interactive whiteboard or other public display in the context of classroom teaching at a purchasing institution.

e If You are an Educational Institution, once a teacher ceases to be a member of the Educational Institution, all copies of the material on the CD-ROM stored on his/her personal computer must be destroyed and the CD-ROM returned to the Educational Institution.

f You are permitted to print reasonable copies of the printable resources on the CD-ROM. These must be used solely for use within the context of classroom teaching at a purchasing institution.

2 Copyright

a All original content is provided as part of the CD-ROM (including text, images and ancillary material) and is the copyright of the Licensor or has been licensed to the Licensor for use in the CD-ROM, protected by copyright and all other applicable intellectual-property laws and international treaties.

b You may not copy the CD-ROM except for making one copy of the CD-ROM solely for backup or archival purposes. You may not alter, remove or destroy any copyright notice or other material placed on or with this CD-ROM.

3 Liability and Indemnification

a The CD-ROM is supplied 'as is' with no express guarantee as to its suitability. To the extent permitted by applicable law, the Licensor is not liable for costs of procurement of substitute products, damages or losses of any kind whatsoever resulting from the use of this product, or errors or faults in the CD-ROM, and in every case the Licensor's liability shall be limited to the suggested list price or the amount actually paid by You for the product, whichever is lower.

b You accept that the Licensor is not responsible for the availability of any links within or outside the CD-ROM and that the Licensor is not responsible or liable for any content available from sources outside the CD-ROM to which such links are made.

c Where, through use of the original material, You infringe the copyright of the Licensor, You undertake to indemnify and keep indemnified the Licensor from and against any loss, cost, damage or expense (including without limitation damages paid to a third party and any reasonable legal costs) incurred by the Licensor as a result of such infringement.

4 Termination

Without prejudice to any other rights, the Licensor may terminate this licence if You fail to comply with the terms and conditions of the licence. In such an event, You must destroy all copies of the CD-ROM.

5 Governing law

This agreement is governed by the laws of England, without regard to its 'conflict of laws' provision, and each party irrevocably submits to the exclusive jurisdiction of the English courts. The parties disclaim the application of the United Nations Convention of the International Sale of Goods.